Five disputations of church-government, and worship

Richard Baxter

Ἀρχὴν ἐ̓ τέλος πάντων ποιεῖ θεόν. Gull. Jones.

FIVE
DISPUTATIONS
OF
Church-Government,
AND
WORSHIP.

I. *Whether it be Necessary or Profitable to the right Order or Peace of the Churches of England, that we Restore the extruded Episcopacy?* Neg.

II. *Assert.* *Those who Nullifie our present Ministry and Churches, which have not the Prelatical Ordination, and teach the People to do the like, do incur the guilt of grievous Sin.*

III. *An Episcopacy desirable for the Reformation, Preservation and Peace of the Churches.*

IV. *Whether a stinted Liturgie or Form of Worship be a desireable means for the Peace of these Churches?*

V. *Whether Humane Ceremonies be Necessary or Profitable to the Church?*

By *Richard Baxter.* Jones.

LONDON,
Printed by *R.W.* for *Nevil Simmons,* Bookseller in *Kederminster,* and are to be sold by him there, and by *Thomas Johnson* at the Golden Key in St. *Paul's* Church yard, 1659. At 4 s. d. bound. 4.0.

To his Highneſs

RICHARD.

Lord Protector

OF THE

Common-wealth of *England, Scotland* and *Ireland.*

SIR,

Heſe Papers are ambitious of accompany-
ing thoſe againſt Popery into your Highneſs preſence, for the tender of their ſervice, and that upon the ſame account.
The Controverſies here decided, are thoſe
that have had a hand in moſt of the great tranſactions
that of late years have here paſt; and that ſtill have a
hand in the differences that hinder our deſired peace. I

A   obſerve

obſerve that the Nation generally rejoyceth in your peaceable entrance upon the Government. And are affected with indignation, if they hear but any rumors that troubleſom perſons would diſturb their hopes. And many are perſwaded that you have been ſtrangely kept, from participating in any of our late bloody contentions, that God might make you an Healer of our breaches, and imploy you in that Temple-work, which *David* himſelf might not be honoured with, though *it was in his mind*, becauſe he had *ſhed blood abundantly, and made great wars*, 1 Chron. 22. 7, 8. I perceive alſo that ſome *ſettlement* of Church-affairs will be expected from you by the moſt. And therefore it concerneth all our welfare that you be well acquainted with the ſtate of thoſe differences, about which all will expect your judgement. For my own part I think not that matters are half ſo far out of order in the Churches, as moſt diſcontented men imagine: But yet I know there is much to be mended, wherein both God and moſt good men expect you ſhould contribute a conſiderable part. Some think there is no *ſettlement* in the Church, till *they* are in the ſaddle, and all their Brethren are become their ſervants, and do them obeyſance. And alas, we have thoſe that take it for no *ſettlement*, till they have the ſword in their own hands, or have engaged you to uſe it at their diſcretion, and may again fill the Priſons or other Lands, with their Brethren that are far better then themſelves: Thoſe I mean that in their writings ſo glory that their predeceſſors hang'd the Puritans, and lament that of late they were *but ſilenced*, as being a leſs effectuall means. Some would have no other *ſettlement* then we have, or elſe would have *Licentiouſneſs ſettled* by a Law, and have *unlimited Liberty* in Religion. Doubtleſs theſe are conſcious what it is that they have

need

need of : If Heathens, Infidels and Papifts be but excepted out of the Toleration, it difpleafeth them : And
we can eafily conjecture why. If we grant them all the
Liberty of their confciences (that is, of their mif-belief,
becaufe, alas, we cannot cure it) it fatisfieth them not,
unlefs they may have alfo Liberty of tongue and Practife. When I have heard and read the Reafonings of
fome of them againft the Immortality of the foul, and
the Chriftian Religion it felf, I have wondered why
they fhould take it for fuch a point of Liberty, to have
leave to draw others to their opinion, when they feem
to think that mens Happinefs or Mifery is no more
concerned in it. Thefe are the men that tell the world
that Magiftrates have nothing to do with Religion, but
only with our Peace and Bodily welfare, contrary to the
fulleft Teftimony of the Scriptures : Which is but to
perfwade men to efteem you as the dirt of the earth,
and to value the Miniftry above the Magiftracy, as much
as the Soul is better then the Body, and as Heaven is
better then this dunghill-world. And for this odious
doctrine, they have no ftronger reafon, then becaufe
that Heathen Princes are uncapable of deciding matters
about Religion. As if mens wilfull and wicked indif-
pofition would change the office, and difoblige both
them and thofe that are guilty of no fuch unfitnefs,
from the obligations laid upon them by the Lord :
They may as wifely fay that a fober Phyfitian is obliged to no more then a drunken one can perform ; or
that a *feeing* man may do no more then the *blind* can
do : Or that a Learned Prince may not meddle with
Learning, becaufe an unlearned Prince is unfit for it.
But any man that hath read *Bellarmine, Parfons, Greifer,*
or fuch like Jefuites, may know the Fathers of this doctrine : Nothing more familiar with them, then that

A 2

Princes

Princes have nothing to do but for our Bodies, and the Common Peace : but forsooth it is the Pope that must Rule all about our Souls. The *Libertines* know whose cause they plead. But verily men that regard the Interest of Christ and their salvation, would set light by Princes, if they believed them to be such terrestriall *animals* as Papists and *Libertines* would make them.

Some also there be, that would have a *settlement* upon too rigorous terms, though they would not have it executed with cruelty. Most men would fain have their *own opinions* prevail, and too many place too much of their Religion in censuring as Heterodox all that differ from them, and think it an evidence of their Godliness that they are Uncharitable ; and seeing many minds and waies, they think that punishment must heal them all : Not that they would be driven to their Brethren , but all their Brethren must be driven unto them.

In the midst of all these cross expectations , if you will consult with, and obey the Lord, I dare boldly tell you, it is past all doubt, that you must avoid extreams , and keep as tenderly the golden mean, in this point, as in any that concerns you. If you give Liberty to All that is called Religion, you will soon be judged of no Religion, and loved accordingly. If you so far close with any Party of them that walk in the faith of Christ, and the fear of God, as to deal rigorously with the rest, you will be hated by them as a Persecutor. And if men be oppressed in that which they value above their lives, it will tempt them to neglect their lives for their relief. If you joyn with no Church in the Lords Supper and other holy Communion, lest you seem to espouse the party that you joyn with, you will by most be judged to

be

be carnally wife, felf-feeking and irreligious, or one that is yet to feek for your Religion. If you *reftrain all* that are againft the *great undoubted Truths* of Chrift, from *infecting others*, and *own all* that hold the *Neceffary Truths in Godlinefs and Charity*, you will pleafe both God, and moft good men. And if you hold your perfonall Communion with thofe that are of your own judgement in leffer differences, this will not lofe you the affections of the godly (though of a few factious perfons it may) as long as you are a tender Father to them all, though you Communicate but with fome. The Godly Emperours that fuppreft the *Arrians* and many Herefies, maintained the *Novatians* in the Liberty of their Churches, and were beloved both by the *Novatians* and the *Orohodox*. But if you *could* be the happy inftrument of *taking away* the *Divifions* of the *Godly*, that there might be no fuch thing as *Parties* or *Separations* known among them (though diverfity of opinions there will be) (and if you *could* give all the Minifters of the Nation a pattern of fuch union of the tolerable diffenting parties in your own Paftors, with whom you fhall Communicate) this would be the way to lift you higheft in the Efteem and Love of all your people, and make them fee that you were appointed of God to be a Healer and Reftorer; and to glory in you, and blefs God for you as the inftrument of our chiefeft peace. And O what a precedent and preparative it would be, for the Healing of all the Proteftant Churches through the world! And certainly your Highnefs hath a fair opportunity for this happy work: You enter in a feafon when we are tired with contention, and fenfible of our lofs and danger, and tenderer then formerly of one another, and the moft angry parties are much affwaged, and there is not fo much reproach and bitter-

nefs

neſs among the Godly , as lately there hath been. A Spirit of Peace and Healing is lately riſen in the hearts of many thouſands in the Land, and Miniſters that differed ,do lovingly aſſociate, and moſt do feel the ſmart of our Diviſions , and are ſo prepared for a perfecter cloſure, that they wait but for ſome Leading hand. I am certain that there are Healing Principles before us, and a temperament is obvious to judicious charitable men, upon which we might accord. And, though ſome are too rough to lie in any building, yet moderate men are to be found of every party, that deſerveth your encouragement, whom you may uſe as a precedent to the reſt, and inſtruments to promote this work. It is you that have thoſe great advantages that can facilitate that which to others were impoſſible : and from you it is expected. In this Book, and one of Confirmation, which I lately publiſhed , I confidently affirm , is contained much of that Reforming, Reconciling Truth which muſt heal us if ever we be healed. And though the ſtudy of ſuch matters require much time, yet ſeeing God commandeth Princes that *the Book of his Law depart not out of their mouthes, but that they meditate in it day and night, that they may do according to it, Joſh.* 1. 8. I may ſuppoſe that they will be willing alſo to meditate on ſuch Books as help them to underſtand it. I ſhould have been as ready as another to cenſure ſuch an addreſs as this, as guilty of preſumptuous boldneſs, but that I conſider what is the work of my Calling, and what it is to be faithfull to the Eternall God , and am conſcious of fidelity to your Highneſs in my boldneſs , and know that theſe are neceſſary Truths , and that *to the Counſellors of Peace is joy, Prov.* 12. 20. and have no intereſt in this world that I regard ; in compariſon of the Churches happineſs. My earneſt Prayers for your Highneſs

Highneſs ſhall be , that your own ſoul being firſt ſubjected and devoted wholly unto God, you may Rule us
as one that is Ruled by him, and never know any Intereſt but his, and that which is ſubſervient to him , and
may eſcape that ſtumbling ſtone, on which the Princes
of the earth do commonly daſh themſelves in pieces ,
even by eſpouſing an Intereſt contrary to Chriſts, and
ſo growing jealous of his holy waies, and falling out
with them : and that God would endue your Highneſs
with that heavenly Wiſdom, that is firſt *Pure*, and then
Peaceable, Jam. 3. 17. and you may eſcape the flatter-
ing ſuggeſtions of the *Wiſdom of the fleſh*, and ſerious
Piety may be the firſt part of your *Policy*, that ſo the
Eternall God may be engaged in the Protection of your
Dominions and You: That you may alwaies remember, that you are Chriſts and your Peoples , and not
your Own : and that the diligent promoting of G O D-
L Y N E S S and C O N C O R D may be the ſtudy and reſolved work of your Life. This is the way ,
and only this, (let fleſh and blood ſay what it will) to
make you truly Great and Happy. God is the Center
and Common Intereſt of all his ſervants. Keep cloſe
to him, and they will all keep cloſe to you. There is no
other Common Intereſt, nor any thing that the Godly
do ſo highly value. If they ſee that it is indeed for God,
they can bear any thing, or do any thing; for they are
wholly devoted to him alone. The more of God appeareth on you, and the more you promote his Intereſt
in the world, the highlyer will you be advanced, and the
dearer will you be to all that Love him. And even with
the ungodly multitude, that Piety is honoured in Princes, that is deſpiſed in their neighbours ; and the hand
of God is plainly demonſtrated in their ſurviving Honour ; the names of Pious Princes being Great , when
the

the Greateſt leave a name that is vile, even in the mouthes of common worldly men, who are ready to keep a Holy-day for a Saint when he is dead, though they hate or will not imitate the living. Your Zeal for God will kindle in your ſubjects a Zeal for you. The more your Life and Government is Divine, the more Divine will you appear, and therefore the more Amiable and Honourable to the Good, and Reverend to the evil. Parliaments will Love and Honour you, and abhor the motions that tend to a diviſion, or your juſt diſpleaſure. Miniſters will heartily Pray for you, and Praiſe the Lord for his mercies by you, and teach all the people to Love, and Honour, and Obey you. The people will rejoyce in you; and you will be Loved or Feared of all: Such happineſs attendeth ſerious *Piety*, when impiety, ſelfiſhneſs, and neglect of Chriſt is the ſhame and ruine of Prince and People. I crave your Highneſs pardon of this boldneſs, and your favourable acceptance of the tendered ſervice of

> A faithfull ſubject to your Highneſs,
> as you are an Officer of the Uni-
> verſall King.

Richard Baxter.

A PREFACE to those of the Nobility, Gentry, and Commons of this Land, that adhere to PRELACY.

Honourable, Worshipful, and Beloved Country-men.

IT being much for your sakes that I have published the following Disputations, it behoveth me here to address my self to you, in a few preparatory words. What distance there hath long been, and still continueth between you and your Brethren (for so they are) is too much known to friends and foes, at home and abroad, and too much daily manifested by each side. Shall it still continue, or would you have it healed ? If it must continue, tell us how long, and tell us why: Would you have it go with us to Eternity? and will you not be reconciled, nor dwell with us in Heaven ? It is not in your Power to shut us out; And will you not be there, if we be there ? Or do you think there will be any Discord where Love is Perfected, and we are One in God? If you can be content to be saved with us, and believe that all of both Opinions, that truly love and fear the Lord, shall live there in dearest

(a)   *Love*

Love for ever ; how can you chuse, when you forethink of this, but **Love** *them now, that you must for ever Love ? and long to be reconciled to them, with whom you must there so harmoniously accord ? You know that Earth is our preparation for Heaven : and such as men would be there, they must begin to be here : As they must be Holy here, that ever will there see the Lord in Holiness ; so must they here be Loving and Peaceable, that ever will live in that perfect heavenly Love and Peace.   And why is it that the distance must be so great ? Are we not all the Children of one Father ? Have we not all the same God, the same Redeemer, the same Spirit in us ? (if we are Christians indeed,* Rom. 8. 9.) *Are we not in the same Baptismal Covenant with God ? Have we not the same holy Scripture for our Rule ? and are we not in the same universal Church, and of the same Religion ? some of you say,* No ; *to the grief of your friends, and the shame of your own understandings, and uncharitableness.   I beseech you bear it, if I touch the sore : For my work is* Healing ; *and therefore though it* Must *be touch't, it shall be as gently as the case will bear.   If I may judge by such as I have had any opportunity to know, I must say, that the distance on your part is continued in some by confused apprehensions of the case, and not distinguishing things that differ ; In some by discontents of mind, and too deep a sense of worldly losses, and the things that you take as injuries from others : In some by the advantage of a co-interest and consociation with those Divines that are of your way, and so by a* Willingness *to think them in the right, and those in the wrong that you take for adversaries : In some by a stiffness and stoutness of disposition, that cals it* Constancy *to hold your own, and* Manliness *not to stoop to others, and takes it as dishonourable to seek for Peace, even in Religion with your supposed adversaries ; or to yield to it, at least without much*

impor-

importunity : *With too many (miserable souls!) it is meer ungodliness, and enmity to that way of* Piety, *that in many that you differ from, appears : And in the best of you it is a Remissness of Charity, and want of Zeal for the Churches Peace, and the Love and Unity of Brethren.* To confute *the reasonings of all these sorts, would draw out this Preface to too great a length. The first sort my experience hath caused me to observe.* Oft have I faln into company with men that pour forth bitter odious words against *Presbyterie : and I ask them what that* Presbyterie *is that they speak of with so much abomination ? Is it the* Name *or the* Thing, *which they so abhor ? If the* Name, *is it not a term of Scripture used by the Holy Ghost ?* 1 Tim. 4. 14. *Are not the Pastors of the Church most frequently called the Presbyters, or Elders ?* Tit. 1. 5. Act. 14. 23. & 15. 2, 4, 6, 22, 23. 1 Tim. 5. 17. Act. 20. 17. James 5. 14. 1 Pet. 5. 1, &c. *It must needs then be the* Thing, *and not the* Name *which they abominate. And what is that* Thing ? *most of them cannot tell me. Some presently talk of the disuse of the Common Prayer ; as if that were a part of* Presbyterie, *and Government, and the form of worship were all one. Some presently run to* Scotland, *and talk of forcing men to Confession of sin, and of their secular enforcement of their Excommunications. But* 1. *If this be odious, why was it used by the Bishops ? Is it good in them, and bad in others ?* 2. *And why plead you for Discipline, and against Toleration, if you so loath the things you plead for ?* 3. *But will you not, when its known so openly, distinguish the Ministerial Power from the secular ? Its known by their Laws and constant Practice, that all the Power that was exercised by Violence, on Body or Estate, by the Assemblies, was derived from the Magistrate, whose Commisisoners also sate among them. And the Bishops in England were* ... *the* ... *&c.*

much as they. Its known that the Presbyterians commonly maintain in their Writings, that Pastors have no Coercive or Secular Power, but only the Keys of the Kingdom
of Heaven, to exercise on the Conscience, committed to
them by Christ. 4. And the writings and practice of those
in England, openly manifest it : and its them with whom
you have most to do. · Some tell me that Presbyterie is the
Government of the Church without Bishops : And is it only
the Negation of your Prelacy that is the odious thing ? Is
there nothing Positive odious in Presbyterie ? Thus our Belief is condemned by the Papists, even because we Believe
not so much as they ; when in the Positives of our Faith
there is nothing that they can blame. Some make it the
odious thing that they have Lay-Elders ; But 1. The Presbyterians account them not Lay, but Ecclesiasticks.
2. And what is the Odious harm that these men do
among them ? They are present, and Consent to the admonishing and censuring of offendors. And what great
harm doth that to the Church ? Is it because they do not
Preach ? No sure ; in that your Readers are much like
them. What work can you Name that these Elders are appointed to, that by your Confession is not to be done ? It is
not the Work then, that you blame, but that these men do
it. 3. But what is this to all that are in this point of your
mind, and think that unordained Elders wanting Power
to preach, or administer the Sacraments, are not Officers
in the Church of Gods appointment ? As far as I can understand, the greater part, if not three for one of the English Ministers that you stand at a distance from, are of this
mind, and so far against Lay-Elders as well as you ; of whom
I confess my self to be One. (and that Mr Vines was One,
I have shewed you in the End.) Surely then all we are none of
the odious Presbyterians in your eyes. Why then is there
such a distance ? And are Lay-Elders as bad as Lay-Chancellors ?

So also when some have been hotly condemning us as being against Bishops, I ask them what a Bishop is ? *and what sort of Bishops it is that they mean? And most of them are unable to give me a rational answer to either of the Questions ? But some that are wiser, though they know no more sorts of Bishops but one, yet they can say, that by a Bishop they mean an* Ecclesiastick Governour of Presbyters *and the people. And if so, then why do they vilifie Bishops under the name of Presbyters ? I have here shewed you that if this be all, then every Parish hath a Bishop where there is a Pastor that hath Chappels, and Curates under him: Or any two Ministers that will subject themselves to a third, do make a Bishop. You delude your selves and others, while you plead only in general for Bishops: We are all for Bishops as well as* you. *All the Question is, What sort of Bishops they must be ? Whether only* Episcopi gregis, *or also* Episcopi Episcoporum gregis ? *and if so, Whether they must be Bishops of single Churches, as our Parishes are , or a multitude of Churches, as Diocesses are ? And if the last were granted, Whether these be not properly Archbishops? In all other parts of the Controversie I find, that the followers of each party go much in the dark, and take much upon trust from the Teachers whom they value, and little understand the true state of our differences: So that it is more by that common providence, commonly called* Good luck, *that some of them are Protestants or Christians, then from any saving grace within them. Had* Papists *or* Mahometans *but as much interest in them, as the Bishops, it is like they would have been as much for them.*

As for those of you that know your own Opinions, and the Reasons of them, you must needs know that the Divines called Episcopal *in* England, *are of two sorts, that very much differ from one another: And therefore suppo...*

to be the followers of these differing Divines, I shall accordingly further speak to you as you are.

I. The Bishops of England, and their followers from the first Reformation, begun by King Edward the sixt, and revived by Queen Elizabeth, were found in Doctrine, adhering to the Augustinian Method, expressed now in the Articles and Homilies : They differed not in any considerable points from those whom they called Puritans : But it was in the form of Government, and Liturgy, and Ceremonies that the difference lay.

II. But of late years a new strain of Bishops were introduced, differing much from the old, & yet pretending to adhere to the Articles and Homilies, and to be Fathers of the same Church of England as the rest. I know of none before Bp. Mountague of their way, and but few that followed him, till many years after. And at the demolishing of the Prelacy, they were existent of both sorts. Would you know the difference ? If you have read the writings of Bp. Jewel, Pilkington, Alley, Parry, Babbington, Baily, Abbot, Carlton, Morton, Usher, Hall, Davenant, with such like on one side ; and the writings of the New Episcopal Divines that are now most followed, on the other side, I need not tell you the difference. And if you will not be at the labour to know it by their writings, its like that you will not believe it if I tell you. For if you will take all on trust, I must suspect that you will put your trust in them to whom you are addicted.

The New party of Episcopal Divines are also subdivided : some of them are (if their Defence of Grotius, and Grotius his own Profession may be believed) of Grotius his Religion, that is, Papists : Others of them, though they draw as neer the Grotians as Protestants may do, yet own not Popery it self. So that we have three notable parties of Episcopal Divines . . . . . 1. The old Orthodox Protestant

Protestant Bishops and their followers. 2. *The New Reconciling Protestant party.* 3. *The New Reconciling Papists, or* Grotians. *A brief taste of the difference I will give you.*

1. *The Old Episcopal party, as I said, in Doctrine agreed with the Non-conformist, and held that Doctrine that now we find in the Articles, and Homilies, and in the Synod of* Dort, *where* B^p Carlton, B^p Hall, B^p Davenant, *and three more Divines of this Nation were, and had a great hand in the framing of those Canons, and by consenting, did as much to make them obligatory to us in* England, *as commonly is done in General Councils by the Delegates of most Nations.*

But the New Episcopal Divines, both Protestants and Papists, do renounce the Synod of Dort, *and the Doctrine of our Articles and Homilies, so far as it is conform thereto, in the points of Predestination, Redemption, Free-will, Effectual Grace, Perseverance, and Assurance of Salvation : following that Doctrine which is commonly maintained by the Jesuites and* Arminians *in these points.*

2. *The Old Episcopal Divines did renounce the Pope as* Antichrist, *and thought it the duty of the Transmarine Churches to renounce him, and avoid communion with his Church, as leprous and unfit for their communion. But the New Episcopal Divines do not only hold that the Pope is not* Antichrist, *but one part of them (the Protestants) hold that he may be obeyed by the Transmarine Western Churches as the Patriarch of the West, and be taken by us all to be the* Principium unitatis *to the Catholick Church, and the Roman Determinations still may stand, except those of the last four hundred years, and those; if they obtrude them not on others. So* B^p Bramhall, *and many more : And* Mr Dow, *and others tell us that the Canon Law is still in force in* England, *except some that*

the Laws *of* the Land have cast out. And the Grotians teach, that the Church of Rome *is* the *Mistris of other Churches, and the Pope to stand as the Head of the Universal Church, and to Govern it according to the Canons and Decrees of Councils: and they receive the* Trent-Creed *and Council, and all other Councils which the Pope receives, excepting only against some School-points , and abuse of manners among the Papists, which their Canons and Decrees condemn.*

3. *The old Episcopal Divines did take Episcopacy to be better then Presbyterian Equality, but not necessary, to the Being of a Church, but to the Better being where it may be had. But the New Prelatical Divines, of both sorts, unchurch those Churches that are not Prelatical.*

4. *The Old Episcopal Divines thought that Ordination by Presbyters without Prelates was valid, and not to be done again, though irregular. But the New ones take it to be No Ordination, nor those so ordained to be any Ministers, but Lay-men.*

5. *And accordingly the Old Episcopal Divines did hold the Forrein Protestant Churches, of* France, Savoy, Holland, Geneva, Helvetia, *&c. that had no Prelates, as true Churches, and their Pastors as true Ministers of Christ, and highly valued and honoured them as Brethren. But the New sort do disown them all as no true Churches, though they acknowledge the Church of* Rome *to be a true Church, and their Ordination valid.*

6. *The Old Episcopal Divines thought it lawful to joyn in actual Communion with the Pastors and Churches that were not Prelatical. But the New ones separate from their communion, and teach the people to do so, supposing Sacramental administrations to be there performed by men that are no Ministers, and have no authority.*

7. *The Old Episcopal Divines thought it* not *meet to suspend,*

silence,

silence, imprison, or undo those Godly Divines that did not bow towards the Altar, or publish to their People Declarations or Instructions for Dancing on the Lords Day, or that did preach twice a day. But many of the New ones practically told us, that this was their judgement.

Of these differences I have given you some proof hereafter : and would do here in the express words of the Authors on both sides, were it not that I should be needlesly tedious, and that I should unnecessarily offend the particular Divines of the New party who are among us, by reciting their words. More of the differences I pass by.

I. *And now I would know of those of you that follow the Ancient Episcopal Divines, what hindereth you from a charitable, peaceable Communion with those Orthodox Ministers now in* England, *that some of you stand at a distance from ? Doctrinal differences (at least, requiring such a distance) you cannot pretend.* Bᵖ Hall *tels you in his Peace-maker (after cited) that there is none between you and the Forrein (Presbyterian) Churches. And as for the matter of Episcopacy, if you will insist upon the late* English *Frame as necessary, viz.* [*That there be but One Bishop over many hundred Churches, and that he have the sole power of Excommunication, and that he rule by a Lay-Chancellor, &c. and be a Lord, and seconded with a forcing-power, &c.*] *then you will forsake the Judgement of your Leaders: For they will tell you that some of these are but separable appurtenances, some of them corruptions and blemishes, and some not Necessary. What need we any more ado ? You see in the published Judgements of* Bᵖ Hall, Bᵖ Usher, Dʳ Holdsworth, Forbes, *and others, (after cited) that they would have all Presbyters to be Governors of the Churches, one of them having a stated Presidency or Moderatorship, and this will content them. And are we not then agreed ?* . . . . *ssident . . . of the Ministers in*

England

England *would be content to yield you this : But what if there be some that are not of your mind concerning the stated Presidency which you desire ? will you therefore uncharitably refuse communion with them ? so would not your Leaders!* In this *therefore you will forsake them, and forsake many holy Churches of Christ, and forsake charity, and Christ himself that teacheth you another lesson. Will it not content you that you have freedom your selves to do that which seemeth best in your own eyes, unless all others be of your opinion ?*

But perhaps you will say that you have not Liberty your selves to practise according to this your judgement. To which I answer, 1. *Your Brethren of the Ministery have not the power of the Sword, and therefore do neither deny you Liberty, nor can give it you: It is the Magistrates work. And will you separate from us for other mens doings ? For that you have no rational pretence. If you know of any that perswade Magistrates to restrain your Liberty, thats nothing to others : Censure none but those that you know to be guilty.* 2. *I never knew that you were deprived of the Liberty of exercising such an Episcopacy as the forementioned Bishops do desire. I do not believe you could be hindered; and we that are your neighbours never hear of it. I know not of either Law or Execution against you. If you think that the clause in the* Covenant, *or the Ordinance against Prelacy, or the late Advice that excepts Prelacy from Liberty, are any restraint to you, I think you are much mistaken. It is only the late frame of Prelacy as it stood by Law, exercised by Archbishops, Bishops, Deans, Chancellors, &c. and that by force upon dissenters, that is taken down. You have not Liberty to force any by corporal punishment to your obedience. But you have full Liberty (for ought that ever I heard) to exercise the meer Episcopacy desired by* Hall, Usher, *and such like, on all that are*

of your judgement, and will submit to it. That we may
hold constant Assemblies of Pastors we find by experience:
And in these Assemblies if you will choose one for
your stated President, who will hinder you? No one I am
confident; Tell us whoever suffered for so doing? or was
prohibited, or any way hindered from it by any force?
Nay more, if you will give this President a Negative vote, in
Ordination and Jurisdiction, who will hinder you? yea who
can? If twenty Ministers shall resolve that they will never
Ordain, or Excommunicate any without the consent (yea
or Command if you must have it so) of such a man whom
they take for their President, who can or will compell them
to the contrary? And all the People that are of your mind,
have Liberty to joyn themselves with such Pastors on such
terms, and submit themselves to you, if they will.

But you will say, that this is no setting up of Episcopacy,
while every one that is unwilling to obey us, may refuse it.
I answer, This is all that the Nature of Episcopacy requireth: And this is all that the Church saw practised (even
Rome it self) for above three hundred years after Christ.
And is not that now tolerable for your Communion with us,
which served then for the Communion of all the Churches
on earth? Is the Primitive pattern of purity and simplicity become so vile in your eyes, as to be inconsistent
with Christian Communion? Let not such principles
be heard from your mouths, or seen in your practises.
Whether the Magistrate ought to compell us all to be
of your mind or way, I will not now meddle with: but
if he will not, will you therefore separate from your Brethren? Or will you not exercise the Primitive Episcopacy
on Consenters, because you have not the sword to force Dissenters? And are you denied your Liberty, because you are
not backed by the Sword? This concerneth other mens Liberties, and not yours. You have in either

Episcopal Government, (though not of smiting others with the Magistrates Sword) and as much Liberty for ought I know as Presbyterians or Independents have (though not so much countenance) And how comes it to pass that the other modes of Government are commonly exercised upon meer Liberty, and yours is not ? Is it because you have no confidence in any Arm but flesh ? If your Episcopal Power be of Divine appointment, why may you not trust to a Divine assistance as well as others, that you think are not of God ? If it can do nothing without the Sword, let the Sword do all without it, and retain its proper honour. If it can do less on voluntary Subjects, then other ways of Church-government can do, say so, and confess it most infirm, and give place to them. But if yours have most Authority from Christ, and spiritual force upon the Conscience, exercise it, and let us see it by experience; or else expect not that any should believe you, or take you to be resolute servants of Christ, and true to your Ministry.

But perhaps you will say, that you cannot have Communion with us, because we are schismaticks : For so much BP. Usher himself doth seem to charge us with.] To which I answer, 1. BP. Usher chargeth none with Schism, but those that cast off Bishops to whom they had sworn obedience. But if I may judge of other Counties by this, there are so few of those that they can afford you no pretence of scruple against the Communion of our Assemblies. I know not (to my remembrance) of one Minister in this County liable to this charge : but most never swore to them, and the rest had no hand in their exclusion. 2. Whoever among us did either swear to, or disobey such Bishops as Bishop Usher there assureth us were the Bishops of the antient Churches ? If they set up another (intolerable) sort in stead of the Bishops which he himself requireth, judge whether it were a greater sin to swear to them, or to disobey them. 3. And
the

the schism which he mentioneth is not such in his own judgement as makes men uncaple of your Communion. This pretence therefore is frivolous.

Especially considering that most of us have no Prelates that so much as claim a Government over us. In this County since Bp Prideaux died (who was one of the ancient moderate sort) we know of none that ever made a pretence to the place. And are we schismaticks for not obeying a Bishop when we have none? And surely none can justly lay a claim to such a superiority, even according to the ancient Canons, unless he be first chosen by our selves, yea and the people, as a Reverend Bishop (I hope yet living) of the ancient sort hath told you, Morton Apolog. Cathol. Part. 1. cap. 85. p. 257. Bellarmine himself confessing that ut Clerus & populus Episcopum eligeret, hic modus fuit in usu tempore Chrysostomi, Ambrosii, Augustini, Leonis, Gregorii. Bellarm. l. 1. de Clericis cap. 9. And other of our Bishops say the same.

I conclude therefore that we are not only of one faith and Church with you, but differ so little in our opinions about lower things, that you can thence have no pretence for an alienation: And therefore with those of you that are godly and peaceable, I take it for granted that we are actually agreed. But if any will sacrifice the Churches Peace, their Charity, their souls to their parties, or passions and discontents, I leave them to God, and to the reading of other kind of Books, that tend to change an unrenewed mind.

II. And to those of you that follow the newer strain of Prelatical Divines, I shall adventure a few words, how small soever the probability is of their success. And 1. To those of you that are not departed from the Communion of all Protestants, nor gone with Grotius over to the Romanists. I beseech you, as before the Lord, proceed not in your bitterness, uncharitableness, or separation f...

*Brethren, nor your hindering the work of God in their mi-
nistration, till you are able to produce such solid grounds for
what you do, as you dare stand to at last, before the
Judgement-seat of Christ.* 1. *Some of you charge us with
no less then Heresie, as following* Aerius *in the rejecting of*
Bishops, *or equalizing Presbyters with them: and can you
hold communion with Hereticks?* I answer, 1. *All is not
heresie that every angry man hath called so, no not of the
venerable Ancients.* Do you indeed take your *Dignity and
preheminence to be an Article of our Faith? Why then was
it never in the Creed?* 2. Many among us are for Episcopacy, *that are not for your sort of Prelacy. It is that species that our Controversie is about.* 3. *I shall answer you
in the words of our Reverend* Morton *(a Prelate, though
not of the New strain)* Apolog. Cathol. Par. 1. cap. 33.
pag. 96, 97. *who answereth the Papists that use against
us the same objection* [Non de differentia omni, sed de
differentia *Ordinis,* seu Potestate Ordinandi (N B) quæ-
stio est instituenda. Adversar. Aerius hæreticus ordinis
differentiam negabat esse jure divino; idem Protestan-
tes: *Resp.* Quod idem forte sanctus *Hieronymus,* nec
aliud Patres alii asseverarunt: hoc scholæ vestræ Doctor primarius non ita pridem facile largiebatur: *Mich.
Medina,* lib. 1. de sac. orig. affirmat, non modo S. *Hiero-
nymum* idem in hoc cum Aerianis hæreticis sensisse, verum etiam *Ambrosium, Augustinum, Sedulium, Prima-
sium, Chrysostomum, Theodoretum, Oecumenium, Theophy-
lactum.* Bellarm. lib. 4. de Eccles. milit. c. 9. Ita, (inquit *Valent.* Jesuit. Tom. 4. disp. 9. qu. 1. punct. 2.) isti
viri alioqui sanctissimi & orthodoxi —— At (inquit id.
ibid.) non est tolerabilis hæc responsio. Probabo vero
hoc non modo ferendum, sed etiam omnibus aliis re-
sponsis præferendum esse. Advocatus. *Erasmus Annot.
in* 1 Tim. 4. [Antiquitas inter Præsbyterum & Episco-

pum

pum nihil intererat, ut testatur *Hieronymus* : Sed post propter schisma à multis delectus est Episcopus, & quotquot Presbyteri, totidem. erant Episcopi.] Tua, *Erasme*, apud Jesuitas sordet authoritas (*but not with you that I write to*) ———— Advocat. *Alphonsus à Castro* advers. hæres. tit. Episcop. [*Hieronymus* in ea opinione fuit, ut crederet Episcopum & Presbyterum ejusdem esse ordinis & authoritatis] Ecce etiam alterum : *Bellarm. lib.1. de Rom. Pontif. c.8.* [Videtur R E V E-R. A. *Hieronymus* in ea opinione fuisse.] An ille solus ? [*Anselmus* & *Sedulius* opinionem suam ad *Hieronymi* sententiam accommodarunt.] Quam eandem sententiam. *Medina* vester Patribus pariter omnibus tribuit ——— Quid ex. his, inquies ? ostendam ; si cognovissent Patres hanc in Aereo hæresin damnatam esse, tantum abest ut ei errori verbis suffragari viderentur ; ut potius in. contrarium errorem abriperentur : si non cognoverunt hanc opinionem in Aereo damnatam, cur vos eam hoc nomine in Protestantibus damnandam esse contenditis ? *Cassander lib. consult. art.* 14. [An Episcopatus inter Ordines Ecclesiasticos ponendus sit, inter Theologos & Canonistas non convenit : convenit autem inter O M N E S in Apostolorum ætate inter Episcopos & Presbyteros N U L L U M D I S-C R I M E N fuisse ; sed postmodum Schismatis evitandi Causa Episcopum Presbyteris fuisse præpositum, cui Chirotonia, id est Ordinandi potestas concessa est] *If you will not keep company with Reverend Morton, I pray you go not. beyond these Moderate Papists.*

2. *But you say, that at least we are Schismaticks, and you must not hold Communion with schism. And how are we proved Schismaticks ? Why,* [1. *Because we have cast off Bishops.* 2. *Because we now obey them not*]

have

have answered this already ; to which I add :] 1. Its a fine world, when men will separate themselves from the Churches of Christ to avoid schism, and they that are against separation, and offer Communion to the Separatists, must be taken to be the Schismaticks themselves. It is schism that we detest, and would draw you from, or else what need we say so much for Concord and Communion ? 2. I have told you already, that it is not one Minister of a Multitude in our Communion that did cast off the Prelates ; half of them did nothing to it, and the other half were Ordained since. 3. Nor can you truly say, that now they refuse obedience to Bishops, where there are none to obey, or none that command them. 4. Again I tell you, it is not Episcopacy, but only the sinful species of Prelacy, which the Parliament, and Assembly, and Covenanters did cast off. And what if you think this species best ? must all think so, or else be Schismaticks ? And why not all Schismaticks then that are against the Papacy, which is thought by others the best form ? I have here given you some Arguments to prove your Prelacy which was cast off, to be against the will of Christ, and the welfare of the Churches. And I shall not believe that its schism to be against sin and the Churches ruine. And I cannot but admire to read in your writings, that Discipline and Piety are pretended by you, as the things which you promote, and we destroy, when I am most certain that the destruction of Piety and Discipline are the very things by which you have so much offended your Brethren ; and we would heartily come as near you as we can, so that Piety and Discipline may not be destroyed. Had we not known that the able faithful Preachers whom you called Puritans (conformable and not conformable) that laboured in the word and doctrine, were fitter to promote piety then the ignorant, drunken, worldly Readers, and lazy Preachers, that once a day would

preach

preach against doing too much to be saved; and had we not known, that Piety was better promoted by Learning the will of God, and praying, and meditating on the Lords Day, then by dancing; and by cherishing men truly fearing God, then by scorning, imprisoning, persecuting and expelling them; we would never have been so much against your doings as we have been. But mens salvation is not so contemptible a thing, as to be given away to humour the proud, that cannot live in Communion with any, unless they may drive them to destruction. We will not sell mens souls to you at such rates, nor buy your Communion, nor stop the reproachful mouths of any by such horrid cruelties. We talk not now to you of matters that are known by hearsay only: we see which way promoteth Piety, and which destroyeth it: we see that most of the ungodly in the land, are the forwardest for your wayes. You may have almost all the Drunkards, Blasphemers, and Ignorant haters of godliness in the Country, to vote for you, and if they durst, again to fight for you at any time. I cannot be so humble as to say, I am blind, and see not what indeed I see, because another tells me, that his eyesight is better then mine, and that he seeth things to be other then I see them to be. I doubt not but there are some Pious persons among you: I censure you no further then experience constraineth me. But I know that the common sense of most that are serious in practical Christianity, is against your formal wayes of worship, and against the course that you have taken in this land; and the spirit of prophaneness complyeth with you, and doteth on you, in all places that ever I was acquainted in. Bear with plain truth: it is in a cause of everlasting consequence. There is somewhat in a gracious soul, like health in the body, that disposeth it to relish wholesom food, and perceive more difference between it, and meer air, or toyish kickshaws, then it can easily express. In abundance of

your

your most applauded *Preachers*, the things of *God* were spoken with so little life and seriousness, as if they had not been believed by the speaker, or came not from the heart; yea *Godliness* and *Diligence* for *Heaven*, was the thing that they ordinarily preached against under the name of preciseness, and being righteous overmuch. And the *Puritans* were the men that *Pulpits* rendered most odious to the people, and your *Preachers* exercised their wit and zeal against; while almost all their hearers through the *Land* did take a Puritan to be one that was seriously Religious. Many a place have I lived in, where there was not a man that ever spoke a word against *Bishops* or *Ceremonies*; but a few there were (alas, a few) that would sometime read a *Chapter* in the *Bible*, and pray with their *Families*, and speak of the life to come, and the way to it, and for this they were commonly called *Puritans*. If a man had but mildly askt a *swearer* why he swore, or a *drunkard* why he would be drunk, or had once named *Scripture*, or the life-to come, unless prophanely, the first word he should hear, was, [*O you are one of the holy Brethren! you would not drink or swear, but you will do worse in secret! It was never a good world since there was so much talk of Scripture and Religion: but the King and the Bishops will take an order with you, and all the Puritans and Precisians in the Land*] I profess upon my common sad experience, that this was the common language of the people that were ignorant and prophane in all parts of *England* that ever I came in (which were not a few;) and these were the men that they called *Puritans*, and on such accounts. And what could the *Prelates* and *Preachers* of the *Land* have done more to *mens* damnation, then to preach them into an hatred of *Puritanism*, when it was known by all that lived among them, that *Piety* was *Puritanism* in their account, and no man was so free from it,

as

as he that would scorn at the very name of Holiness, and drink and swear, as if he had defyed God. This is true, and England knows it : and if you will after this think that you have wiped your mouths clean, by saying as M͏ͬ Pierce, that by Puritans, he means none but [men of blood, sedition, violence, despisers of dominion, painted sepulchres, Protestants frightened out of their wits, &c.] the righteous God that loveth righteousness, and hath said, Be ye holy for I am holy, will make you know to your penitent or tormenting sorrow, that the thing which commonly was reputed Puritanism in England, was no such thing as you describe : And that its none of your wisdom to kick against the pricks, and play with the apple of Gods eye, and bring men to hate the members of Christ, and then tell them you meant the members of the Devil, and to thrust men into Hell in jest : I have heard before the King many a Sermon against Puritans, which I judged impious, but yet had this excuse, that much of the anditory partly understood, that it was not Piety as such, that was directly reviled : And so perhaps it might be in the Universities, and some few intelligent auditories : but so it was not among the common people through the Land. A Puritan with them was of the same signification as a serious Christian is with me. And if you bring the Land to an hatred of such as are called Christians, and then say that by Christians you meant none but mad men, seditious, bloody, &c. you shall answer in earnest for spitting in the face of Christ in jest; and that before him that will not take your jears or jingles, or adding reproach unto reproach for a sufficient excuse.

I know also that the casting out of the Ministers of your way, is much that offendeth you : concerning which I shall only say, that I meet with none, or very few that profess not their willingness that all men of your mind that truly fear God, and are able and diligent, should be kept in.

And

And if you be angry for the casting out of the ignorant,
insufficient, negligent or scandalous, there's no remedy.
But be ashamed to reproach us for casting out such from
the service of Christ, as Julian *the Apostate would have*
cast out from the Priesthood of his Idols: and let us crave
your leave to expect as much Devotion in the servants of
Christ, as he expected in his enemies. Vid. *Julian.* Oper.
pag. 549, 550, 551, *&c.* fragment. [Facessant itaque
procul à nobis illeberales joci, ac petulans omne collo-
quium ———— In his occupanda sunt studia, & cum
privatim, tum publice Diis sæpe supplicandum est ;
maxime quidem ter de die : sin minus, saltem diluculo
ac sub vesperam. Neque enim Sacerdotem decet, diem
ullum ac noctem sine sacrificio transigere. Est autem
ut initium diei diluculum, ita noctis vespera. Itaque
rationi consentaneum est, ut amborum intervallorum,
velut primitiæ quædam Diis consecrentur———.
Equidem sic statuo, sacerdotem oportere noctes atque
dies purum se ab omnibus & integrum servantem
————*p.555.* Non enim mediocriter adversus Deos
delinquimus cum sacras vestes ostentamus, & omnium
oculis tanquam mirum aliquid objicimus. Ex quo id
accidit, ut cum multi ad nos impuri homines accedant,
sacra illa Deorum symbola contaminentur. At vero
nos sacerdotali uti veste, nisi ut sacerdotibus dignum
est vitam instituamus, id ipsum noxas omnes crimi-
num, ac Deorum maxime contemptum in sese conti-
net. ——Ad obscæna illa theatrorum spectacula nullus
omnino sacerdos accedat ——neque cum histrione ullo
vel auriga, vel saltatore, sit amicitia conjunctus, ad
eorumve foras accedat.———Placeat eos ex omnibus
constitui qui in Civitatibus optimi sunt, & imprimis
quidem Dei, deinde vero hominum amantissimos quos-
que, sive pauperes sint, sive divites. ———*p.557.* Duo-
bus

bus hisce præditus sit ornamentis, Religione erga Deum, & in homines benignitate —— Et *Epist.* 49. *p* 203. [Sed velim omnes nostros sacerdotes omnino, qui Galatiam incolunt, vel minis impellas, vel ratione persuadeas, ut sint honesti ; vel sacerdotali ministerio abdices, si non una cum uxoribus, liberis, & famulis Diis colendis sedulo animos attendant —— Deinde sacerdotem quemque hortare ne accedat ad spectacula, neve in taberna bibat, neu' artem aliquam aut opificium turpe infameve exerceat. Et qui tibi in his rebus morem gerunt, eis honorem tribuito : qui autem resistunt expellito.] *Leg. & fragm. Epist.* 62. *We crave your leave to use the Presbyters as strictly as* Julian *did these Priests, and to expect as much piety and sobriety in them ; and that you will not condemn all those for Puritanism, that will not be worse then this Apostate Pagan.*

And for Discipline, could we have any from your Episcopacy worth the naming, we should be the more reconcilable to it : But it hath not been, nor it cannot be. Common drunkards that were for twenty or thirty years together drunk usually once or twice a week, and abundance as prophane in other kinds, were the stated members of this Parish Church where now I live, in the Bishops dayes ; and were safer from any trouble then the Puritans among them that would not imitate them. Let me here mind you of two of the following Arguments, which perswade us that your Prelacy is not of God, because it is destructive of Discipline.

1. *When Episcopacy was first known in the Church, every Presbyterie, or* Confessus Presbyterorum *had a Bishop ; and every Presbyter had right to be a member of some such Presbyterie. And seriously would you have all the Presbyters in a Diocess to be a Presbyterie, where your Bishop must preside for the ordinary Government of the*

Diocess

Diocess as one Church ? Are you strangers in England ?
Or do you not know what abundance we have that in one
Parish are every week scandalous, by drunkenness, cursing,
swearing, railing, or such like ? And can all the Pastors
travail so far to the Presbyterie so frequently without
neglecting their Pastoral work ? Or can all these people be
perswaded without the Magistrates sword to travail so
far to answer for their impiety ? Will they not tell us, we
have somewhat else to do ? Are we not like to make them
wait seven years and seven, before the most of them can
have a tolerable tryal, when so many hundred Parishes, of
which some one may have hundreds of obstinate scandalous
persons, must all go so far, and have but one Judicature ?

2. I beseech you give me leave but from Scripture, and
from Dr. Hammonds Paraphrase, to lay before you the
work of a Bishop, and then tell me whether one man, or ten,
or an hundred can do this work for one of our ordinary Diocess, any more then one man can build a City ?

1. A Bishop must be the publick Teacher of all the flock
which he is to Oversee. And can one man undertake this
for many score or hundred Churches ?

2. A Bishop must personally oversee and take care of
all the flock, as Ignatius speaks, enquiring of each one
by Name ; and can a Bishop know and personally instruct
so many hundred Parishes ? These two parts of his Office I
prove together : Act. 20. 20. [I taught you publickly,
and from house to house. 28. Take heed therefore to
your selves and to all the flock, over which the Holy
Ghost hath made you Overseers, to feed the Church
of God which he hath purchased with his own blood.
31. Therefore watch, and remember that by the space
of three years, I ceased not to warn every one night
and day with tears. See Dr. Hammond on the Text,
who tells you that it is spoke to Bishops.

1 Pet.

1 *Pet.*5.1,2,3. The Elders which are among you I exhort, who am also an Elder —— Feed the flock of God which is among you, taking the oversight thereof, not by constraint, but willingly, not for filthy lucre, but of a ready mind; neither as being Lords over Gods Heritage, but as ensamples to the flock] *See Dr.* Hammond *expounding it as spoken to Bishops,* q. d. [The Bishops of your several Churches I exhort —— take care of your several Churches, and govern them, not as secular Rulers by force (*N B*) but as Pastors do their sheep, by calling and going before them, that so they may follow of their own accord.]

Heb. 13. 7. Remember them that have the Rule over you, who have spoken unto you the word of God] *Dr.* Hammond *Paraphr.* [Set before your eyes the Bishops and Governors that have been in your Church, and preached the Gospel to you ——] *O all you Inhabitants of* Yorkshire, Lincolnshire, Norfolk, Suffolk, Essex, Middlesex, Kent, Worcestershire, &c. *how many of your Parishes did ever hear a Bishop preach the Gospel to them ?*

*Verf.*17. Obey them that have the Rule over you, and submit your selves, for they watch for your souls as they that must give account] *D. H.* [Obey those that are set to Rule you in your several Churches, the Bishops, whose whole care is spent among you; as being to give account of your proficiency in the Gospel.] *O dreadful account, for him that must give it for so many thousands whose faces he never saw; and whose names he never heard, much less did ever speak a word to them !*

1 *Tim.*5.17. Let the Elders that Rule well be counted worthy of double honour, especially they

who labour in the word and doctrine] *see Dr. H.* *expounding it of Bishops.*

1 *Thes.* 5. 12. And we beseech you Brethren to know them which labour among you, and are over you in the Lord, and admonish you, and to esteem them very highly in love for their works sake] *Dr. H.* [Pay all due respects to the Bishops of your several Churches———] *Tell us ye Parishes of* England, *what labours have Bishops bestowed among you ? or how many of you have they admonished ? and which of them are you hence obliged to honour for their works sake ? and is it them, or is it the Presbyters ? I mention none of this as blaming Bishops for negligence ; but as blaming them that will plead for, and undertake an impossible task ; and after all with an hardened forehead will defend it with violence and separation from dissenters, when so many ages have told the world to their faces, that the undertaken task was never done.*

3. *It is the work of Bishops to confirm the Baptized: and is now made peculiar to them.* D. H. [*on Heb.* 13. *a.* To teach, exhort, confirm, and impose hands, were all the Bishops office in that place] *And if so, then the examining all the persons in a Diocess, till they have just satisfaction that they are fit to be confirmed, and the actuall Confirmation of them all, will be a considerable task of it self.*

4. *It is the Bishops work to exercise Discipline in the Church, by admonishing the unruly and disorderly, and bearing the case when the Church is told of those that have continued impenitent, and openly to rebuke them, and to cast them out by Excommunication, if they remain impenitent and unreformed.* Dr. H. on *Tit.* 3. 10. [It is thy office and duty toward such an one, first to admonish him once or twice, and if that will not work upon
him

him or reduce him, then to set a mark upon him, to inflict the censures on him, and to appoint all men to break off familiar converse with him.] *And O what abundance of work is this in the several parts, even in one Parish, much more in a Diocess, see Dr. H. on Mat.* 18. 17, 18.

5. *It is the Bishops work to take the principal care of the poor, and their stock, or the contributions for them, which contributions were made at every Assembly. See Dr. H. on* 1 *Cor.* 12. 28. *e.* [The supream trust and charge was reserved to the Apostles and Bishops of the Church. So in the 41. Canon of the Apostles: A Bishop must have the care of the monies, so that by his Power all be dispensed to the poor by the Presbyters and Deacons; and we command that he have in his Power the goods of the Church. So *Justin Martyr Apol.* 2. That which is gathered is deposited with the Prefect or Bishop, and he helps, relieves the Orphans and Widdows, and becomes the Curator or Guardian to all absolutely (*N B*) that are in want. So *Ignatius* to *Polycarp*; After the Lord thou shalt be the Curator of the Widdows. And *Polycarp* himself speaking of the Elders or Bishops, They visit and take care of all that are sick, not neglecting the Widdow, the Orphan, or the poor.] *So Dr. H. read him further. Remember this, all you that are for our English Prelacy. See that the Bishop be at once in every Parish in his Diocess to receive the contributions. Or see that you put all into his hands and custody: see that he take care of all the poor, and widdows, and orphans, in all your Country, and that all their monies be disbursed by him, or his special appointment, and be the common Overseer of the poor for his Diocess. And when you and he have tryed this one seven years, come then and tell us, whether he will be*

(d)

any

any longer a Prelate, or you will any longer be for Prelacy. In the mean time judge in your Consciences by these passages of Antiquity cited by D. H. whether the antient Bishops had one Congregation, or many score or hundred to be their Pastoral charge?

6. Also it is a part of the Bishops work to visit the sick, and pray with them, and for them, Jam. 5. 14. Is any sick among you? let him call for the Elders of the Church, and let them pray over him] see Dr. H. that by Elders is meant the Bishops. e. [Because there is no Evidence whereby these (inferiour Presbyters) may appear to have been brought into the Church so early, and because Πρεσβύτεροι in the plural, doth no way conclude that there were more of these Elders then one in each particular Church (any more then that the sick man was bound to call for more then one) and because Πρεσβύτεροι Elders of the Church was both in the Scripture stile, and in the first writers the title of Bishops : and lastly, because the visiting of the sick is anciently mentioned as one branch of the Office of Bishops ; therefore it may very reasonably be resolved, that the Bishops of the Church, one in each particular Church, but many in the Universal, are here meant] so far Dr. H. Remember all you that are all for Prelacy, to send for the Bishop when you are sick, every person in the Diocess, according to this express command : And if he would do his work by a Deputy, remember, that in all that Diocess which was the Bishops charge in the Scripture-times, there was no Presbyter existent but himself, as is here confessed. So in the following words the same Learned Dr. further proveth from Antiquity, [that one part of the Bishops office is set down, that they are ἐπισκεπτόμενοι πάντας ἀσθενεῖς, those that visit all the sick] Let us have such Bishops as can and will do this, and our Controversie will soon be at an end about Episcopacy.   Were

Were it not that I have spoken of these things after-wards, and fear being tedious, I should have shewed, that 7. *Baptizing*, 8. *Congregating the Assemblies*, 9. *Administring the Lords Supper*, 10. *Guiding the Assembly in the whole publick worship*, 11. *Blessing the people at the dismission*, and 12. *Absolving the penitent; and more then all these were the works of the ancient Episcopal function. And now I leave it to the Conscience of any man that hath a grain of Conscience left him, whether one man be able, were he never so willing, to do any one of all these duties, much less to do all of them for many hundred Parishes? Can a Bishop teach them all, and Catechise and confer with all, and counsail, and comfort, and admonish all, and Govern all, and try all cases of every scandalous impenitent person of so many thousand, and Censure, and Absolve, and Confirm, and Try them for Confirmation, and receive all the Churches stock, and be the Overseer of all the poor, and take care of all the Orphans and Widdows, and visit, counsail, and pray with all the sick, and guide every Congregation in publick worship, and give the Sacrament to all, and pronounce the Blessing in every Assembly*, &c. *and this for a whole County or more? O wonderful, that ever this should become a Controversie among men, that vilifie others as unlearned and unwise in comparison of them? I must lay by respect to man so far, as plainly to profess, that I take these for such errors as must need proceed from want of Piety and Conscience, and practice of the duties that are pleaded for. If these men did not talk of Governing a Church, as those talk of Governing a Navy, an Army, or a Commonwealth, that never set their hand to the work, it is not possible sure, that they should thus err. O how many Bishops never tryed what it is to Govern the Church, or faithfully perform any one of all these works! I solemnly profess, that with*

the

the help of three more fellow Presbyters, and three or four Deacons, besides the greater help of abundance of Godly people here in their places, I am not able to do all this as it should be done, for this one Parish. And yet the greatest part of our trouble is taken off, by the refusal of the multitude of the ungodly to come under Discipline, or be members of our Pastoral charge. Sirs, these are not scholastick speculations! The everlasting Joy or Torment of our people lyeth upon the successful performance of these works (as we that are Christians verily believe) And therefore to Dispute, whether One man should do all this for a Diocess, is all one as to Dispute, whether it shall all be undone or no? and that is, whether we shall give up our Countries to the Devil or no? And shall the Prelatical Controversie come to this? You have no way to avoid it, but by Delegating your power to others, and casting your work upon them. But you confess that this was never done in Scripture-times, there being then no Subject Pesbyters to whom it might be committed. And by what authority then can you do it? Can Episcopacy be transferred by Deputation to another? This is long ago confuted by many writers, Popish and Protestant. Do the work by another, and you shall have your wages by another. And what is your Office, but your Authority and Obligation to do your work? He therefore that you commit this to is a Bishop. So that this is but to make us Deputy Bishops: And if so, let us call them Bishops.

I have read many of your writers of late, that say we have no Government, and saith one of them, the Presbyterian Government was never yet set up in any one Parish in England] These are strange things to be reported to English men. Perswade the world next that no man in England hath a nose on his face. Is it not known that the Presbyterian Government hath been exercised in London,

don, *in* Lancashire, *and in many Counties, these many years ? And what Government is it that you think we want ? The people are guided in the matters of God by their several Pastors. The Pastors live in Concord by Associations in many Countries. Both Pastors and People are Governed by the* Magistrate : *And what need we more ? Look into this County where I live, and you shall find a faithful, humble, laborious* Ministry, *Associated and walking in as great unity as ever I read of since the* Apostles daies. *No difference, no quarrels, but sweet and amicable Correspondency, and Communion, that I can hear of. Was there such a Ministry, or such love and concord, or such a godly people under them in the Prelates reign ? There was not : I lived where I do : and therefore I am able to say, there was not. Through the great mercy of God, where we had ten drunken Readers then, we have not one now : and where we had one able godly Preacher then, we have many now : and in my own charge, where there was one that then made any shew of the fear of God, I hope there is twenty now : And the Families that were wont to scorn at holiness, and live in open impiety, are now devoted to the worship and obedience of the* Lord. *This is our loss and misery in these times which you so lament.*

3. *But perhaps you will refuse Communion with us, because of our differences from you in doctrine about the Controversies called* Arminian. *But the fierceness of many of you hereabouts doth serve but to discover your ignorance and uncharitableness. The* Papists *that differ among themselves about these points, can yet hold Communion in one Church : and cannot you with us ? Will you be fiercer against us then the* Jesuites *against the* Dominicans *? Nay we go not neer so far as they. We cleave to* Augustine, *and the Synod of* Dort, *who own not Physical Predetermi-*

nation, and meddle not with Reprobation antecedent to foresight of sin, and who confess a sufficiency in Christs satisfaction for all. And yet must we have those impotent clamors, with which the writings of Mr. Pierce *and other such abound? Why then do you pretend to follow the Church of* England, *which Mr.* Hickman *hath shewed you plainly that you desert? Many of the highest meer* Arminians *are charitable peaceable men, that hate separation from their Dissenting Brethren.* Curcellaus *is one of the most eminent men living of that way. And how charitable and peaceable an Epistle hath he writ before* D. Blondels *book* de Papissa Joanna? *And I hear that Mr.* Hoard, *the Author of the Book called* Gods Love *to* mankind, *lives in peaceable Communion with the Neighbour Ministers in* Essex. *And I have had Letters from many of that way with whom I Correspond, full of Christian Love and Piety, and hatred of calumny and separations. But verily I must tell you, that when we find any of you in your writings and Sermons making it your work to vilifie the* Ministry, *and with the* Quakers *to make them odious to the people, and making your jeers, and railing, and uncharitableness the life of your Sermons, we cannot but suspect that you are Popish Emissaries, while we find you in their work, or else that you are Malignant Enemies, and of the serpentine brood, whose heads shall shortly be bruised by the Lord.*

4. *And if it be the disuse of your Common Prayer that you separate from us for, I would know of you, whether you would have denyed Communion with all that lived before it had a being. If this be your Religion, I may ask you, where was your Religion before* Luther? *before King* Edwards *daies? If you say in the Mass book (and what else can you say?) I ask you then, where was it before the Mass book had a being? Would you have denyed Commu-*

nion

*nion to the Apostles and all the Primitive Church for some
hundreds of years, that never used your Book of Common
Prayer? will you still make things indifferent, necessary?*

2. *One word to those of you that follow* Grotius: *I
have shewed that he professeth himself a Papist, even in
that Discussion which* Mr Pierce *so magnifieth as excellent. I hear Mr.* Thorndike *and others defend him: and
some think I injure him by calling him a Papist. Wonderful! what will not be a Controversie among learned men?
Are we faln among such that deny him to be a Papist,
that professeth expresly to be satisfied, if evil manners be
but corrected, (and school-opinions not imposed) which
are contrary to* Tradition *and all* Councils? *and that professeth to own the Creed and Council of* Trent, *and all the
Papish Councils whatsoever, and the Mistriship of* Rome,
*and the Catholick Mastership of the Pope governing the
Catholick Church according to these Councils? What is
a Papist if this be none? I refer you to my Evidence in
the Discovery of the* Grotian Religion, *and the first Chap.
of the second Part of my Catholick Key, replying to Mr.*
Pierce. *Confute it rationally if you can. I shall now only
desire you when you have read* Rivet, *to read a Book
called* Grotius Papizans, *and to hearken to the testimony
of an honest, learned Senator of* Paris, *that admired* Grotius, *and tells you what he is from his own mouth: and
that is,* Claud. Sarravius, *who saith in his Epistol. pag.*
52, 53. *ad* Gronov. [De ejus libro & libello postremis
interrogatus, respondit plane Milleterio Consona, Romanam fidem esse veram & sinceram, solosque Clericorum mores degeneres schismati dedisse locum; adferebatque plura in hanc sententiam. Quid dicam?
Merito quod falso olim *Paulo Agrippa* τὸ πολλά σε γράμματα
εἰς μανίαν περιτρέπει —— Deploro veris lachrymis tantam
jacturam] Here you have a credible witness, that from*
his

his own mouth reporteth it, that our Reformation was to Grotius *a schism, and nothing but the ill manners of the* Clergy *gave us the opportunity. And pag.* 190. *Epist. ad* Salmas. [Vis ergo me exerte dicere quid sentiam de postremo *Grotii* libro? & an omnia mihi in eo probentur? Rem rogas non magnam, nec adeo difficilem, quemque expedire promptum est. Tantum abest ut omnia probem, ut vix aliquid in eo reperiam, cui sine conditione calculum apponam meum. Verissime dixit ille qui primus dixit, *Grotium* Papizare. Vix tamen in isto scripto aliquid legi quod mirarer, quodve ἀπροσδόκη- τον occurreret. Nunquid enim omnes istiusmodi ejusdem authoris lucubrationes erga Papistarum errores perpetuam συγκατάβασιν & ῥύψιν, erga Jesuitas amorem, erga nos plus quam Vatinianum odium produnt & clamant: In Voto quod ejus nomen præferebat, an veritus est hæc προσμένως profiteri?]

Had none of you owned Grotius *his Popery, I would never have charged it on you. But when* Grotius *himself glorieth of his adherents in* England, *and so many of you plainly defend him, and profess your owning of those books, and those doctrines in which his Popery is contained, (if ever Popery were known in the world) I must then crave your pardon, if I think somewhat the worse of Popery, because they that hold it are ashamed of it. For I abhor that Religion which a man hath cause to be ashamed of, and will not save him from being a loser by it, that owneth it, and standeth to it to the last. And I think that man hath no Religion, who hath none which he will openly profess and stand to.*

I have at this time but these few requests to make to you, which I beseech you to answer without partiality. 1. *That you will seriously consider, whether it be truly* Catholick, *to unchurch us, and so many Churches of Christ as are of our mind, as your partakers do? Because Catholicism is your pretense, consider whether you be not further from it then most people in the world?*

.2. Because I conceive this Book is not suited to your great objections, I desire your perusal of another that comes out with it, called A Key for Catholicks, *especially the second Part, and if you cannot answer them, take heed how you continue Papists.*

3. While you hold us for no Ministers or Churches, or Capable of your Communion, it is in vain for us to hope for Communion with you: but we desire that you will consider of those terms of a more distant sort of Communion, which there I have propounded in the End of the first and second Part: and deny us not that much.

4. At least we beseech you, that while you are Papists, you will deal openly, and no worse with us then sober Papists that speak according to their Consciences use to do. Do not let it (as the Lord Falkland *speaks) be in the Power of so much* per annum *(nor of your factious interest) to keep you from professing your selves to be what you are; and do not make the Protestant name a meer cloak to secure you in the opposing of the Protestant Cause, and follow not the example of* Spalatensis, *and the Counsel of* Campian *and* Parsons, *in feigning a sort of Doctrinal Puritans, and railing at Protestants under that name. Deal with us but as sober Papists do, and we shall take it thankfully. How highly doth* Bodin *a Learned Papist extol the Presbyterian Discipline at* Genevah *from its effects, when among many of you it hath as odious titles as if it were some blasphemous damning thing. What sober Papist would talk as* Mr. Pierce *doth [* p. 30. *of the great abomination of the Presbyterian Directory,] and not be able to name one thing in it that is abominable. Is it a great abomination to exhort and direct men to preach, and pray, and* *praise God, &c ? If it be the Omission of his forms and Ceremonies, that is no Part of the book ; and if it be some Directions that are against them, they that revile the Common Prayer book, as most Papists have done, or they that count such Ceremonies and Forms* indifferent things, *as others have done, have little reason to account that so great an abomination that directeth men to omit them. What abominable thing is imposed by the Directory ? Tell us if you can. What excellent things doth* Thuanus *speak of the Presbyterians or Calvinists ? and how highly doth he extol the most of their Leaders or Teachers whom he mentioneth ? But to* Mr. Pierce ; *what a bloody perfidious sort of men are they, unfit to live in a Commonwealth ? And to* Grotius ; *the Protestants are not only of bad lives, but by the Power of their Doctrine they are such. I have shewed you in my* Key *for* Catholicks *how great the praises of* Calvin *are in the mouth of* Papir. Massonius, *and other sober Papists : and the same may be said of others of our Divines, who are mentioned by you with most calumniating odious words. Even* Maldonate *the* Jesuite, *when he is railing at the* Calvinists, *confesseth of them,* (in Matth. 7. 15.) *that* [Nothing was in their mouths but, the Lord, and our heavenly Father, and Christ, and Faith ; an Oath was not heard : nothing appeared in their deeds, but Almf-deeds, and Temperance, and Modesty] *Is this like your language of them ? Nay, if Satan had dictated to him, how could he have uttered more falshood and detestable calumniation then* Mr. Pierce *hath done,* p. 73. *when he saith* [were Hacket, Lancaster, Arthington *and others hanged for Nonconformity ? or was it nothing but Ceremonial which* Coppinger, *&c. designed against the lives of the whole privy Council, and against the person of the Queen ? were not* Cartwright, *and* Travers, *and* Wentworth, *and* Egerton,

Egerton, and other Presbyterian Ministers privy to the plot?] *The Lord will rebuke this slanderous tongue. Did ever* Cochlæus, *or* Bolseck *go beyond this man? How fully is it known that* Hacket *and his Companions were Grundletonians or Familists, just such as* James Nailor, *and the Quakers, (who are far nearer the Papists then the Puritans or Presbyterians) and that they madly came into* London, Coppinger *and* Arthington, *as his two Prophets, proclaiming* Hacket *to be* Jesus Christ; *and that for obstinate insisting on this Blasphemy,* Hacket *was hanged, and dyed blaspheming, and* Arthington *upon his Repentance published the whole Story of the beginning and progress of the business, as you may see it in the Book called* Arthingtons Seduction. *In which their madness, blasphemy, or any Treason of theirs or others, this man might as honestly have said, that* Augustine, *or* Luther, *or* Cranmer *had an hand, or were privy to the plot, as* Cartwright, Travers, *and such Presbyterian Ministers. What he hath read in* Bancroft, *I knew not, nor much regard, till* Bancroft *himself be better cleared of what he is by writers charged with, concerning* Ficlerus, Dolman, &c. *and while he was known to be the most violent persecutor of the Puritans. But I see as the Papists will take it for a currant truth, that* Luther *was fetcht away by the Devil, and that* Calvin *was stigmatized for Sodomy, and dyed blaspheming, &c. if they can but say, that one* Cochlæus *or* Bolseck *of their own hath spoke it; so such men among us dare tell the world the most odious falshoods of* Cartwright, Travers, *and the Presbyterian Ministers, if they can but say, that* Bancroft *said it before them. And now the rest may take it as unquestionable, when* Mr. Pierce *hath said it. Do these men believe that there is a day of Judgement? If they do, they wo be but lamentable* *[illegible] for it.*

(c 2)

that [Excommunicating Kings and killing them is the doctrine of the Presbyterians] *and much more of his writing is of the same kind. To this I have given him an Answer in my* Key for Catholicks, *where he shall see whether Papists or Protestants are for King-killing? Had you not gone so far beyond such moderate Papists as* Cassander, Hospitalius, Massonius, Bodin, Thuanus, &c. *in your enmity and bitterness against the Protestants, as clearly to contradict them, and to speak blood and venom, when they speak charitably, and honourably, we might have had more peaceable neighbours of you, though none of your Communion.*

And I suppose that those who separate from us, as having no true Ministry or Churches, would have all these Ministers that they take for none, to be silenced and cast out. I do not think you will deny this to be your desire, and your purpose, if ever you should have power? And if so, what men are you? and what a case would you bring this Nation in? To your Objections I have answered in this book, and said somewhat more to you in another Preface. And upon the whole matter am forced now to conclude, that it is an Enmity to holiness in unsanctified hearts that is the principal cause of our distance and divisions; and that the way to convince such men, as too many are that we deal with, is not Disputing, but praying to the Lord to change their hearts: And that if we could once perswade them but to the Love of God and Holiness, and to a serious practice of Christian Religion, and (if they be Bishops) to a faithful practice of those works of a Bishop which they confess are his duty, and to try Church-Government before they plead for what was never tryed by them, our Controversies would then be ended: they would never more plead for such a Prelacy that destroyeth Piety, and Discipline, nor never revile the Servants of the Lord:

nor never defire fo much to promote the work of Hell, as the cafting out all that they account no Minifters, and the cafting off of all that they account no Ordinances or valid Adminiftrations, would be. Farewel Difputing with fuch men, in order to their Conviction, and an healing peace.

Hoc non eft artis, fed pietatis opus.

POSTSCRIPT.

WHat the Publifher of Dr. *Stewards* Sermon doth mean by his *Commmend-ing it to my Confideration*, when there is not a word in it that I am concerned in more then he, I underftand not. If he thereby in-timate, that I charged Dr. *Steward* to be of *Grotius's* Religion, or any other that difowneth it, he egregioufly abufeth his Reader and himfelf. If he intend to argue that none of the Prelatical Party were *Grotians*, becaufe Dr. *Steward* was not: Let him prove his Confe-quence; I difprove it, 1. From the teftimony of *Grotius* himfelf. 2. From the mouths and books of thofe that have owned *Grotius* among us, even fince they were acquainted with his judgement, and have owned his *Vo-tum & Difcuffio* in particular. If his meaning be that ⌈ Dr. *Steward* was a *Grotian*, and yet no Papift : therefore *Grotians* are no Papifts ⌉ one branch of his antecedent is falfe : Either he was no *Grotian*, or he was a Papift. Again I profefs, that it is far from the defire of my foul, to raife fo much as the leaft fufpicion on any that own not the Doctrine and Defign of *Grotius*. Difclaim it, and we are fatiffied. Dr. *Heylin* was taken for as hot an antipuritan as moft in *England* : and yet (in a moderate Letter to me) he difclaimeth *Grotianifm* : which I mention, partly left any, by my naming him on another occafion in that Book, mifconceive me to have accufed him of this, and principally to difcourage the defenders of *Grotius*, when fuch men as Dr. *Heylin* and Dr. *Steward* are againft them.

The

The CONTENTS.

The Contents.

The Contents.

Objections

The Contents.

DISPUTATION 3.

The Contents.

DISPUTATION 4.

Whether a stinted Liturgy or Form of worship be a desirable means for the peace of these Churches?

Proposition.1. *A stinted Liturgy is in it self lawful,* p.359.

Prop.2. *A stinted Liturgy in some parts of publick holy service is ordinarily necessary,* p.365.

Prop.3. *In those parts of publick worship where a form is not of ordinary necessity, but only Lawful, yet may it not only be submitted to, but desired, when the peace of the Church doth accidentally require it,* p.367.

(f 2) Prop.4.

The Contents.

DISP.

The Contents.

DISPUTATION. 5.

The Contents.

ERRATA.

ERRATA.

PAge 10. l.4. r. *had not been by themselves.* p.24.l.23. for *Philetas,* r. *Alexander.* p. 30. l. *penult.* for *Perfect,* r. *President.* p.33.l.34,35.r.*the* 2000th. *or* 3000th. *person.* p.37.l.34. for *it,* r. *is.* p.41.l.9. r. *Presbyterie.* p.72. l. *ult.* for *that,* r. *the.* p.77.l.24. r. *occasioning.* p.78.l.16. r. *had in it.* p.81.l.1. blot out *any.* l.28. for *at all,* r. *all.* l.29. blot out *the.* p.87.l.17. for *had* r. *have.* Marg. l.5. r. καθισμον. p.88.l.17. for *Prelacy,* r. *Policarpe.* l.37. for *there that,* r. *that there.* p.89. l.2. r. ἐκχυθεν. p.93.l.3. r. *he was,* and l.34. for *ad,* r. *at.* p.94.l.29. r. *we well.* p.95. Marg.l.31. r. *Blondel,* and l. 33. for *yet,* r. *and.* p.96.l.9. r. *Churches.* p.97. l.5. for *Scholarum,* r. *Scotorum.* p.100. Marg.l.13. for *no,* r. *on.* p.104.l.8. for *I mean,* r. *I wave.* p.106.l.4. for *that,* r. *the.* Disp.2. Pref. p.117.l.16. for *pass,* r. *pase.* p.118.l.30. blot out *and.* p.121.l.14. r. *Bishop.* p.124. l.17. r. *Jansenius.* p.137.l.5. r. *Members.* p.139.l. 5. for *men,* r. *run.* p.157.l.3. & 4. r. *pleasure & Pastors,* & l.34. r. *and.* p.160.l.2. r. *will.* p.163.l.11. for *Proctors,* r. *Doctors.* p 166. l.14. r. *sin in the.* p.169.l.6. blot out *upon.* p.181.l.26. r. *owed.* p.182.l.11.r. *And yet.* p.182.l.ult. for *as,* r. *at.* p.184.l.3. for *Art.*11. r. *Act.*11. p.191.l.29. for *he,* r. *the,* & l.37. for *decase,* r. *depose.* p.194.l.29. for *and,* r. *&c.* p.199.l.13. for *Art.*11. r. *Act.*11. p.219.l.1. r. *Arrianus,* p.229.l.32. for *three and four,* r. *third & fourth.* p.241.l.22. for *name,* r. *main.* p.245.l.14. for *Davenant,* r. *Davenport.* p.253.l.18. blot out *do.* p.265.l.12. blot out *to.* p.277. l.2. r. *one & the.* & l.12. r. *works.* p.291.l.18. for *the,* r. *that.* p. 316.l.16. r. *as their.* p.317. l.33. for *Overseers,* r. *Others.* p.328.l.21. r. *Behmenists.* p.339.l.16. r. *had no other.* p.340.l.9. r. *the least.* p.367.l.9. r. *add to.* p.372.l.21. for *he,* r. *the.* p.409.l.34. r. *but what was.* p.420. l.16. r. *of the Will.* p.421.l.26. for *them,* r. *than,* p.430. l.28. r. *Law.*

An Advertisement to prevent mis-understanding.

MY exceeding scarcity of time, constraining me to write these Papers in much haste, and allowing me but a cursory perusal of them when written, and the like after the printing, for the collecting the Errata of the Press, I find by this hasty review, and by some observation of mens readiness to misunderstand me, that it is necessary to speak a little more about the following particulars, that I may be understood by such as are willing to understand me : and the mistakes of others I shall easily bear.

Sect. 1. Pag. 89. *There is somewhat that requireth correction of the pen, and somewhat that requireth explication. In translating that passage of* Ignatius, [Unus panis qui pro omnibus fractus est] *must be written next* [effusus est] *before* [& unus Calix.] *And for the following objection, though it was made by a discreet person, yet I know no ground for it : unless* Is. Vossius *his Edition leave out* [πάση τῇ ἐκκλησίᾳ] *(which I have not now at hand, but is likelyest) I know not of any* Greek *copy that leaves it out. Indeed Bishop* Ushers Latine *doth, and the Vulgar Latine leaves out the translation of the next words before it* [τοῖς ὅλοις διανειμάσθαι ἐν δυναστείον] *of which saith Bishop* Usher [Ex interpretatione hac excidisse videantur.] *And noting the corruption of the Vulgar Translation in this very place, I there premised to my Answer,*

that

that it might occasion a change in the Text : *that it hath done so* in many places, *I think is easie to prove ; but that it hath done so* here, *there is no probability, (if any* Greek *Copy be as is objected :) and the Reasons of my conjecture of the* possibility, *are so little for a probability, that as I express them not, so I think them not worth the expressing, but rather bid you take that as* non dictum. *Though of the general I find Bishop* Usher *himself saying, both of his* Latine *Version* [Ex eâ solâ integritati suæ restitui posse Ignatium . polliceri non ausim,] *and of the first* Greek *Edition* [Hanc reliqui sequuti sunt editores ; non ex Græco aliquo codice alio, sed partim ex ingenio, partim ex vetere Vulgato Latino Interprete, non paucis in locis eandem corrigentes] Epist.ad Lect. ante Annot. & pag. 26. Dissert.

Sect. 2. *I must intreat the Reader to observe that my drift in this writing is not so much to oppose any form of Government meerly as contrary to the Institution or Apostolical Rule, as to plead against that which I take to be destructive to the Ends of Government : Not that I desire not a careful adhering to the sacred Rule, but* 1. *Because I suppose that many circumstantials of Discipline undetermined in the Word are feigned by some to be substantial necessary things : and that many matters are indifferent that some lay the Peace if not the being of the Church upon.* 2. *Because I so far hate contention, that if any Government contrary to my Judgement were set up, that did not apparently in the nature of it wrong the Church, I would silently live under it in peace and quietness : and accordingly would be now loth to enter a quarrel with any Writers that differ from us in tolerable things : But if I know that their judgement reduced to practice is like to be the undoing of many souls, and to cast Discipline almost wholly out of the Church, I think it better to displease them,*

them, then let them undo the Church without contradiction. The best is, the serious Christians of this age have experience to help them to understand the case, and I suppose my Disputation to be unto them as if I Disputed before a man that is restored from want, or banishment or sickness, whether he should be reduced to the Condition from which he is restored?

Sect. 3. Some passages here will occasion the Question (as p. 5.) Whether and how far Church Government is jure Divino ?] But of this, in the main I am agreed with them that I dispute. To speak further, my own judgement is, 1. That the Spirit of God hath established all the Officers and worship-Ordinances of his Church; and that no new Church-office or Ordinance of worship (as to the substance) may be instituted by man; 2. But that there are many Circumstantials about the Exercise of those offices and Ordinances, that are not determined particularly by a Law, but are left to humane prudence to determine of, by the General directions of the Law. And so I suppose that Bishops and Presbyters are but one Office, of Gods institution; but in the exercise of this Office if one for order be made a Moderator or President of the rest, or by agreement (upon a disparity of parts or interest) do unequally divide their work between them, in the exercise, it is a thing that may be done, and is fit where the Edification of the Church requireth it, but not a thing that always must be done, nor is of it self a Duty, but a thing indifferent. The following Case therefore I hence resolve.

Sect. 4. Quest. [Whether the Order of subject Presbyters might lawfully be created by Bishops or any humane Power? and whether the Order of Bishops might lawfully be created for the avoiding of Schism by the consent of Presbyters? or Metropolitans by Bishops?]

Answ.

Answ. If you understand by the word [Order] *a distinct* Office, *none may create any of these but God. But if by* [Subject Presbyters] *be meant only men of the* same Office *with Bishops, that do for the Churches benefit subject themselves to the direction or Presidency of another, (upon some disparity in their gifts or the like) in the* exercise *of that Office, I suppose that this is a thing that by* Consent *may be lawfully done. And so I verily believe that betimes in the Church it was done, (of which anon.) So if by* [Bishops] *be meant no distinct* Office, *but one of the Presbyters chosen from among the rest, to exercise his Ministery in some eminency above the rest, by reason of his greater Gifts, or for Peace and Order, I doubt not but it is a thing that consent may do: (And accordingly the Canon Law defines a Bishop that he is* [Unus è Presbyteris, &c.] *So if by* [a Metropolitan] *be not meant* another Office, *but one in the* same Office, *by reason of the advantage of his Seat, chosen to some acts of Order for the common benefit, I doubt not but it may be done: but every such* Indifferent *thing, is not to be made* Necessary, *statedly and universally to the Church.*

Sect. 5. *When I do in these Papers plead that* the Order of Subject Presbyters *was not instituted in Scripture times, and consequently that it is not of Divine Institution, I mean as aforesaid, that as a distinct* Office, *or* Species *of Church ministers, as to the Power from God, it is not of Divine Institution, nor a lawful Institution of man; but that among men, in the* same Office, *some might Prudentially be chosen to an eminency of degree as to the* exercise; *and that according to the difference of their advantages there might be a disparity in the* use *of their authority and gifts, I think was done in Scripture times, and might have been after, if it had not then. And my judgement is, that ordinarily every particular Church*

(*such*

(*such as our Parish Churches are*)*had more Elders then* One, *but not such store of men of* eminent gifts *as that all these Elders could be* such. *But as if half a dozen of the most judicious persons of this Parish were Ordained to be Elders, of the same Office with my self, but because they are not equally fit for publick preaching, should most imploy themselves in the rest of the Oversight, consenting that the publick preaching lie most upon me, and that I be the Moderator of them for Order in Circumstantials: This I think was the true Episcopacy and Presbytery of the first times. From the mistake of which, two contrary Errors have arisen: The one of those that think* this Moderator *was of* another Office *in specie, having certain work assigned him by God, which is above the reach of the Office of Presbyters to perform; and that he had many fixed Churches for his charge. The other of them that think these* Elders *were such as are called now* Lay-elders, *that is,* Unordained men, *authorized to* Govern, *without* Authority *to* Preach, Baptize, *or* Administer the Lords Supper. *And so both the* Prelatical *on one side, and the Presbyterians and Independents on the other side, run out, and mistake the ancient form, and then contend against each other.* (*This was the substance of what I wrote to* Mr. Vines, *which his subjoyned Letter refers to, where he signifieth that his judgement was the same.*) *When* Paul *and* Barnabas *were together,* Paul *was the chief speaker, and yet* Barnabas *by the Idolaters called* Jupiter. *Nature teacheth us that men in the same Office should yet have the preheminence that's due to them by their* Age, *and* Parts, *and* Interests, &c. *and that* Order *should be kept among them, as in* Colledges *and all* Societies *is usual. The most* excellent *part of our work is publick preaching, but the most of it for quantity is the rest of the Oversight of the Church (in Instructing personally, admonishing, reproving, enquiring into the truth of accusa-*

C 3

·tions, comforting, visiting the sick, stabl·shing the weak, looking to the poor, absolving, answering doubts, excommunicating, and much more.) And therefore as there is a necessity (as the experienced know) of many Elders in a particular Church of any great number, so it is fit that most hands should be most imployed about the said works of Oversight, yet so·as that they may preach as need and occasion requireth (and administer Sacraments) and that the eminent Speakers be most employed in publick preaching, yet so as to do their part of the rest as occasion requireth: And so the former Elders that Rule well shall be worthy of double honour, but especially these that labour in the Word and Doctrine, by more ordinary publick preaching: And such kind of seldom-preaching Ministers as the former, were in the first times, and should be in most Churches yet that are numerous.

Sect. 6. When I speak in these Papers therefore of other mens Concessions that there were de facto in Scripture times, but One Bishop without any subject Presbyters to a particular Church, remember that I speak not my own judgement, but urge against them their own Concessions: And when I profess my Agreement with them, it is not in this, much less in all things, (for then I needed not dispute against them,)but it is in this much, that in Scripture times there was de facto, 1. No meer Bishop of many particular Churches (or stated worshipping Congregations,) 2. Nor any distinct Office or Order of Presbyters, that radically had no Power to Ordain, or Govern, or Confirm, &c. (which are the subject Presbyters I mean.)

Sect. 7. Specially remember that by [Bishops] in that dispute, I mean, according to the Modern use, one that is no Archbishop, and yet no meer Presbyter, but one supposed to be between both, that is, a Superior to meer Presbyters in Order or Office, and not only in degree or modification

cation of the exercise ; but below Archbishops (whether in Order or Degree :) These are they that I dispute against ; excluding Metropolitans, or Archbishops from the question, and that for many Reasons.

Sect. 8. If it were proved or granted that there were Archbishops in those times, of Divine Institution, it would no whit weaken my Arguments ; For it is only the lowest sort of Bishops that I dispute about : yea it confirmeth them. For if every combination of many particular Churches had an Archbishop, then the Governors of such Combinations were not meer Bishops, and then the meer Bishops were Parish Bishops, or Bishops of single Churches only : and that is it that I plead for, against Diocesan Bishops, that have many of these Churches (perhaps some hundreds) under one Bishop of the lowest rank, having only Presbyters under him of another Order.

Sect. 9. If any think that I should have answered all that is written for an Apostolical Institution of Metropolitans, or of Archbishops, or of the subject sort of Presbyters, or other points here toucht, I answer them, 1. In the former my work was not much concerned ; nor can any man prove me engaged to do all that he fancieth me concerned to do. 2. Few men love to be contradicted and confuted, and I have no reason to provoke them further then necessity requireth it. 3. I take not all that I read for an argument so considerable, as to need Replyes. If any value the Arguments that I took not to need an Answer, let them make their best of them : I have taken none of them out of their hands by robbing them of their Books ; if they think them valid, let them be so to them. Every Book that we write must not be in folio ; and if it were, we should leave some body unanswered still. I have not been a contemner or neglecter of the writings of the contrary-minded. But voluminously to tell the world of that I

think

think they abuse or are abused in, is unpleasing and un-
profitable.

Sect. 10. *And as to the* Jus Divinum *of limited Dio-*
cesses to the Apostles as Bishops, and of Archbishops,
Metropolitans, &c. I shall say but this : 1. *That I take*
not all for currant in matter of fact, that two, or three, or
twice so many say was done, when I have either cross te-
stimony, or valid Reasons of the improbability : I believe
such Historians but with a humane faith, and allow them
such a degree of that, as the probability of their report,
and credibility of the persons doth require. 2. *I take it*
for no proof that all that was done *in all the Churches,*
that I am told was done in some. 3. *I take the Law of*
Nature and Scripture to be the entire Divine Law, for the
Government of the Church and World. 4. *And therefore*
if any Father or Historian tell me, that this was delivered
by the Apostles as a Law to the Universal Church, which
is not contained in Scriptures, nor to be proved by them, I
will not believe them ; no more then I would have believed
Papias and all his Millenary followers, that pretended
Tradition from Saint John ; nor any more then I would
have believed the Asians or Romans that pretended dif-
ferent times for Easter, as a Tradition Apostolical bind-
ing the whole Church. 5. *If it were proved that de facto*
the Apostles did thus or thus dispose of a circumstance of
Government or Worship, which yet is undetermined in
Scripture, I take it not for a sufficient proof, that they
intended that Fact for an Universal Law, or that they
meant to bind all the Churches in all ages to do the like :
no more then Christ intended at the Institution of his
Supper to tie all ages to do it after Supper, in an upper
room, but with twelve, and sitting, &c. 6. *Yea if I had*
found a Direction or Command from the Apostles, as
Prudential determiners of a Circumstance pro tempore &
loco

loco only (*as of the kifs of love, hair, covering, eating things strangled, and blood, &c.*) I take it not for a proof that this is an univerfal ftanding Law. One or two of thefe exceptions wil fhake off the proofs that fome count ftrong, for the univerfal obligation of the Church to Diocefans or Metropolitans.

Sect. 11. *That the* Apoftles *had* Epifcopal Power (*I mean fuch in each Church where they came, as the fixed Bifhops had*) I doubt not. And becaufe they founded Churches according to the fuccefs of their labors, and fetled them, and if they could, again vifited them, therefore I blame not the Ancients for calling them the Bifhops of thofe Churches. But that each man of them was really a fixed Metropolitan, or Patriarch, or had his proper Diocefs, in which he was Governor in chief, and into which no other Apoftle might come as an equal Governor without his leave, this and fuch like is as well proved by filence as by all that I have read for it of Reafon, or Hiftory, that is, the Teftimonies of the Ancients. I find them fometime claiming a fpecial intereft in the Children that they have begotten by their Miniftry: But doubtlefs when Paul & Barnabas or Silas went together, fome might be converted by one, and fome by another within the fame Diocefs or City. If any man fhall convince me, that any great ftrefs doth lie upon this queftiõ, I fhal be willing to give him more of my reafons for what I fay.

Sect. 12. And as to them that confidently teach that the Apoftles fuited the Ecclefiaftical Government to the Politick, and that as by a Law, for the Church univerfally to obey: All the confutation at prefent that I will trouble them with, fhall be to tell them, that I never faw any thing like a proof of it, to my underftanding, among all the words that are brought to that purpofe: and to tell them, 1. That if Paul chofe Ephefus, Corinth, and other the moft populous places to preach in, it was but a prudential circumftantiating of his work, accord ṣ to that General Law of doing all to Edification: and not an obli-

gation

gation on all the Pastors or Preachers of the Gospel to do the same where the case is not the same. 2. And if Paul having converted many in these Cities do there plant Churches (and no other can be proved in Scripture times) it follows not that we may plant no Churches but in Cities. 3. And if the greatest Cities had then the most numerous Churches and the most eminent Pastors fitted to them, and therefore are named with some note of excellency above the rest, it followeth not that the rest about them were under them by subjection. 4. Yea if the Bishops of the chief Cities for order sake were to call Provincial Assemblies, and the meetings to be in their Cities, and they were to be the Presidents of the rest in Synods, with such like circumstantial difference, it followeth not that they were proper Governours of the rest, and the rest to obey them in the Government of their proper charges. Nor that they had power to place and displace them. 5. Much less will it prove that these Metropolitans taking the name of Diocesans, might put down all the Bishops of two hundred Churches under them, and set up none but Presbyters (in order distinct from Bishops) over the flocks, besides themselves; and so the Archbishops having extinguished all the first Order of Bishops of single Churches, to take the sole Government of so many Churches, even people as well as Presbyters into their own hands. 6. And I do not think that they can prove that the Apostles did institute as many sorts of Church-Government then, as there were of civil Policy in the world. All the world had not the Roman form of Government: Nor had lesser Cities the same dependence upon greater, in all other Countryes. 7. Was it in one degree of subordination of Officers only, or in all, that the Apostles suited the Ecclesiasticall Government to the Civil? If in One, how is it proved that they intended it in that one, and not in the rest? If in all, then we must
have.

have many degrees of *Officers*, more then yet we have: *Inferiors very many*, and *Superiors some of all conscience too high*: then we must have some to answer the *Correctors*, the *Consular Presidents*, and the *Vicars*, and *Lieutenants*, the *Pro-consuls* and *Prefects*, and the *Emperor himself*: Even one to be *Universal in the Empire* (thats yet some Limit to the *Pope*, and will hazzard the removing of the *Supremacy* to Constantinople, by the Rule that the *Apostles* are supposed to go by.) And great variety must there be in the several *Dioceses* of the Empire (which *Blondell* hath punctually described de primatu in Eccles. pag. 511. to 519. shewing the causes of the inequality of *Bishopricks* and *Churches*.) 8. According to this Opinion the form of *Church* must alter as oft as *Emperours* will change their *Policy*, or *Wars* shall change them: And upon every change of the *Priviledges* of a *City*, the *Churches Preheminence* must change, and so we shall be in a mutable frame: Which if *Basil* and *Anthymius* had understood, might have quicklier decided their controversie. Yea according to this opinion, *Princes* may quite take down *Metropolitans* at pleasure, by equalling the priviledges of their *Cities*. The best is then, that it is in the power of our *Civil Governours* to dissolve our obligation to *Metropolitans*, yea and to all *Bishops* too, if *Cities* must be their only residence, as I have shewed.

Sect. 13. As for them that pretend *humane Laws* for their form of *Government*, that is, the decrees of *General Councils*; I answer, 1. I disown and deny all *humane Laws* as obligatory to the *Church Universal*: It is the prerogative of *God*, yea the greatest point of the exercise of his Soveraignty to be the *Law-giver* to his *Universal Church*. There can be no *Universal Laws* without an *Universal Law-giver*: and there is no *Universal Law-giver* under *Christ* in the world. 2. And for *General Councils* Sin:

Scripture times at least) *there have beeen no such things nor any thing like them*, *unless the Roman Empire, yea a piece of it, be the whole world.* *I know therfore no humane Universal Laws, whether it be for forms of Government, Liturgies, Holy dayes, or any thing else.*

Sect. 14. *But the principal matter that tends to end our difference, is, the right understanding of the Nature of that Government that is properly Ecclesiastical:* *What is it that we must have Diocesans and Metropolitans to do?* (*besides what I have granted to Apostolical Bishops in the third Dispute?*) *Is it to Teach or Rule the people of the particular Churches?* *They cannot do it at so great distance, not knowing them nor conversing with them;* *at least so well as they that are on the place, as the ancient Bishops were.* *Is it to Rule the* Presbyters *only?* *Why then hath not every Church a Bishop to Rule the flock, but a Presbyter that is forbidden to Rule them* (*in all that which they call Jurisdiction themselves*)? *And how is it that Presbyters shall be Ruled by Diocesans, and the Diocesans by Provincials?* *not by* force: *For the Pastors have no coercive power by violence, or touching mens bodies or estates.* *Is it by* bare commanding? *Why what will that do on dissenters that disobey? shall they* depose *the Bishops or* Presbyters *that disobey them?* *But how?* *Not by any* force, *but* command, *or* exhortation, *or Excommunication.* *They can do no more that I know of.* *And what if they* excommunicate a Pastor! *Let the case be supposed as now it is among us:* *What if a Bishop with the few that adhere to him, excommunicated all the Pastors in the County that are not satisfied of the Divine Right of Diocesans, or of the lawfulness of all his imposed Ceremonies and Forms?* *The people will take it to be their duty* (*most generally where the Ministry hath been savingly effectual*) *to own their Pastors notwithstanding such an Excommunication, and the Pastors will take it to*

be

be their duty to go on with their work : and the excommunication will do no good (unless perhaps to make some Division,
and make both parties the scorn of the ungodly, or procure
the rabble to rail more bitterly at their Pastors, and hate
all their advice, be a desireable good.) And as when the Pope
excommunicated them, some Bishops again excommunicated
the Pope; so some of these Pastors its like would excommunicate their Metropolitans: And why a Bishop, or at least a Synod of Bishops may not cast a wicked Metropolitan out of
their communion, is past my understanding to conceive.

Synods are for Communion of Churches ; and if we had a
Monarchical; National Church in conformity to the Common-wealth, I know not how it would stand with the Law
of God, for the whole Nation to hold Communion with an
Heretical Primate. A Roman Synod deposed John the
thirteenth, and other Popes have been deposed by Councils.
I conclude therefore, that what ever power men claim, if
the Magistrate interpose not (which is extrinsick to the
Church-Government in question) it will work but on mens
Judgements, call it Deposing, Excommunicating, or
what you please: and this power no man can take from you.
but by hindring you to speak. You may now depose thus
and excommunicate whom you please, and when they have
sleighted it, or excommunicated you again, you will have
done. Nay I think you do excommunicate us already :
For you withdraw from our Communion, and draw many
with you, and so you exercise your power (I mean it of
that party that in the second Disputation I have to do with.)

Sect. 15. Much of my Opposition to the English Prelacy
dependeth on the supposition, that they took all the people, and not only the Presbyters for the objects
of their Government, or for their charge : And I find
some of the younger sort that are sprung up since their fall,
do doubt of this. But 1. all men in England that knew

but twenty year ago what belonged to these matters, are past doubt of it. And I have no mind to dispute against them that contradict the common knowledge of the Nation: as if they should doubt whether we had ever a King in England. 2. Read over the Canons, and the yearly Visitation Articles (which the Church-wardens ordinarily sware to present by, before they had ever read the Book, or heard what was in it) and then judge. 3. Their arguing for the sole Jurisdiction of Bishops, and that they only were properly Pastors, and that Presbyters had not the Key of Discipline, but of Doctrine, is some evidence. 4. It is known to the Nation, that the Pastors of the Parish Churches had no power by their Laws (or sufferance) to cast out any the most enormous sinner or Heretick from the Church, nor to bring them to open confession of their sin, nor to Absolve the penitent, but by Reading of their Sentence, and publishing what they sent from their Courts; and consequently could do nothing of all the means in order hereto: (For the means cannot be used where the end is known to be impossible.) All the obstinate scandalous persons, and scorners at a holy life, we must take as members of our Churches, having no power to cast them out. Indeed we had the same power as the Church-wardens, to put our names to their presentments. But a power of accusing to a Chancellors Court is not a Power of Governing; especially when Piety under the name of Preciseness and Puritanism, was so hated and persecuted, that to have accused a man for meer prophaness would have been so far from obtaining the end, as that it was like to have been the undoing of the accuser, except he had been out of the suspicion of Preciseness (as they called it) himself. But I need not dispute this with any but those that being bred in better times (though far from what we desire) are unacquainted with the case of their Predecessors.

Sect. 16. Object. But do you not contradict your
self,

ſelf, in ſaying the Paſtors were degraded or ſuſpended, as to the exerciſe of ſo great a part of their work, and yet ſay here, *& Pref.* to the Reformed Paſtor, that the Power of Diſcipline was given them?] *Anſw.* 1. *In their Ordination the Biſhops ſaid to them* [Receive the Holy Ghoſt: whoſe ſins thou doſt remit they are remitted ; whoſe ſins thou doſt retain they are detained.] *And in the Book of Ordination it was asked of them* [Whether they would give their faithful diligence always to adminiſter the Doctrine and Sacraments, and the Diſcipline of Chriſt as the Lord hath commanded, and as this Realm hath received the ſame according to the Commandements of God?] *And the Rubrick of the Common Prayer Book enableth the Curate to admoniſh open and notorious evil livers by whom the Congregation is offended, and thoſe that have wronged their neighbors, that they come not till they have openly declared that they have repented and amended*] *But* 1. *This doth but ſerve to leave them unexcuſable, that acknowledged Diſcipline to belong to the Office of a Presbyter, when yet he might not exerciſe it. The Biſhops in the Ordination of Presbyters enabled them to preach the Goſpel: And yet they were after that forbidden to preach till they had a Licenſe ; and it was put into the Viſitation Articles, to preſent thoſe Miniſters that preached without Licenſe. If they will deny us the exerciſe of the Power that they firſt confeſs belongeth to our Office, we are not anſwerable for their ſelf-contradictions.* 2. *By Diſcipline I ſuppoſe they mean but our Inſtruction, and our publiſhing their Orders for Penance, Excommunication, or Abſolution.* 3. They were the Judges of the ſenſe of the Laws, as far as the execution required : And the Univerſal Practice of England, with their writings, ſhewed us, to our coſt, their judgement. What good would it do us, if the Law is *the Concur-*

rent *Judgement and Practice* of the Governors *denyed it,* *and went against it.* 4. *He that had kept a man from the* *Sacrament, according to the plain words of the Rubrick,* *was to have been accountable for it at their Courts, and so* *likely (if he had been a man of serious piety, and not a per-* *secutor of Puritans) to have been undone by it, and was like* *to make so little of it, as to the Ends of Discipline (all men* *being compelled by the Presentments to receive the Sacra-* *ment) that I never knew one (to my best remembrance) in* 25 *years time that I lived under the Bishops, that was kept* *from the Sacrament, except a Puritan that scrupled to* *take it kneeling. And what was this to true Church Go-* *vernment ?*

Sect. 17. *Object.* But either they did it according to the established Law, or not: If they did, the
fault was in the Law, and not in them : If they did
transgress the Law, then the fault was in mens abuse,
and the Law and Order cannot be blamed. Answ. *A* *sad case to poor ignorant miserable souls, that they must be* *left in obstinacy, and deprived of Gods means of Refor-* *mation without Remedy, because either the Law or Judges* *must be excused. The Judges are the mouth of the Law to* *us : that is Law in the issue to us which they unanimously call* *Law. If the fault were in the Law, it was time it should be* *altered : if it was in the Bishops universally, it was time* *they should be altered. Let us but have a Remedy, and en-* *joy Gods Ordinances, which he that is the Churches Head* *and King hath appointed for our benefit, and we have* *done.*

Sect. 18. *Object.* But may not Bishops when they
Ordain, Delegate what measure of Ministerial Power
they please? and if you never received more, why
should you use it ?] Answ. *A poor relief to the forsaken* *Church : Deprive her of Government, and then tell us that*
we

we had no power! Is the Power *defirable to us, if the Ordinance were not defirable to the Church?* 2. *What Power have Bifhops, and whence did they receive it, to change the Office of Chrifts inflitution, or his Apoftles? If fo, they may turn the three Orders (which the Papifts themfelves fay the Pope cannot alter) into as many more. Then they may create an Office for Baptizing only, and another for the Lords Supper only, and another for praying only, and fo of the reft ; which is worfe then making Lay-elders, or then taking away the Cup in the Sacrament. Hath Chrift by his Spirit inflituted Church-offices, and are they now at the Bifhops. power to transform them?* 3. *If they had power to diftribute the work in the exercife, part to one, and part to another, yet they have no power to deprive the* particular *Churches of the whole or any part ;* but one or more *muft* do it, and the Office *muft be the fame, and the power exercifed to the edification, and not the confufion and corruption of the Church.*

Sect. 19. *Object.* But the Keys were given only to the Apoftles , and not to the feventy Difciples nor to Presbyters.] Anfw. 1. *If the feventy were only Difciples, and not Church-officers, the Ancients and the Englifh Bifhops have been much miftaken, that have fo much urged it, that Presbyters fucceed them as Bifhops do the Apoftles : But if they be Officers, then they have the Keys.* 2. *The Epifcopal Divines, even the Papifts, commonly confefs that part of the Keys are given to the Presbyters ; and Chrift gave them together.* 3. *Were they given only to Apoftles* for themfelves, *or to* convey to others *? If to themfelves only, then no one hath them now. If to convey to others, then either to Apoftles only as their Succeffors (but there's none fuch) or to Patriarchs or Primates , or Metropolitans, or Archbifhops only : (but none of this will pleafe the Bifhops) or to Bifhops only ; which I grant , taking L* ⁿⁱˢ *in the Scripture sense. And I desire to see it proved, that it was not a presumptuous Innovation in them whosoever they were, that after the days of the Apostles Ordained a new sort of Presbyters in the Church that should have no power of the Keys.* 4. *They that must* use *the Keys, must have* Power *to use them. But Parish Bishops must use them (as the nature and necessity of the work doth prove:) Therefore Parish Bishops must have the Power. If only one man in a Diocess of an hundred or two hundred Churches shall have the power of the Keys, we may know after all the talk of Discipline, what Discipline to expect.*

    Sect. 20. *Object.* Why blame you Lay-chancellors, Registers, Proctors, *&c.* when you set up Lay-elders? we are as well able to call Chancellors Ecclesiastical, as you can call Lay-elders so.] Answ. *I never pleaded for Lay-elders: If other men erre, will it justifie your error? But I must tell you, an unordained man in a single Parish, having power only to assist the Pastor in Government, is far unlike a Lay-Court to Govern all the Churches of a Diocess.*

    Sect. 21. *Object.* Do not your Arguments against Bishops for excluding Discipline, make as much for the casting out of Ministers, of whom you complain in your Reformed Pastor for neglect of Discipline?] Ans. 1. *The Nature of Prelacy as set up in* England, *where only one man had the Government of so many Churches, unavoidably excludeth it, if the best men were Bishops (till it be otherwise formed:) But the nature of a Parochial Episcopacy is fitted to promote it.* 2. *Those* Presbyters *that I blamed for neglecting the higher acts of Discipline, do yet keep away more prophane persons from the Lords Supper in some one Church, then ever I knew kept away in all places under the Prelates.* 3. *If Ministers sinfully neglect Discipline, yet as* Preachers *and* Guides, *in publick worship, &c. they are of unspeakable need and value to the Church: But few Bishops of* England
preached

preached ordinarily : And 4. *We are desirous that Bishops shall continue as* Preachers, *but not as Diocesan excluders of Parochial Church-Discipline.*

Sect. 22. *Object.* By pretending to agree with them that say there were no Presbyters in Scripture times, you would put down Presbyters, and then the Government of the Church will be such as you blame. Ans. *It is the thing I plead for, that every Church may have such Bishops as they had in the Apostles days, and not meer (new devised) Presbyters that are of another Office and Order.*

Sect. 23. *Object.* Bishops had Deacons to attend them in the Scripture times, though not Presbyters; therefore it follows not that Bishops had then but One Congregation. Answ. *Yes beyond doubt : For Deacons could not, and did not perform the Pastoral part in the whole publick worship of any stated Churches. They did not preach (as Deacons) and pray and praise God in the publick Assemblies, and administer the Sacraments : It's not affirmed by them that are against us : therefore there were no more Churches then Bishops.*

Sect. 24. *Object.* But what doth your Arguing make against the other Episcopal Divines that are not of the opinion that there were no meer Presbyters in Scripture times? *Answ.* 1. Other Arguments *here are as much against them, though* this *be not (if they maintain that sort of Episcopacy which I oppose.)* 2. *They also confess the smalness of Churches in Scripture times : (as I have shewed out of Bishop* Downam; *) and that is it that I plead for.*

Sect. 25. *Object.* But if you would have all reduced to the state that *de facto* the Church Government was in in Scripture times, you would have (as but one Church to a Bishop, so) but One Bishop to a Church; as D^r. *H. Dissert.* 4 *c.* 19, 20, 21, 22. hath proved copiously, that is,

(i)   that

that Scripture mentioneth no assistant Presbyters with the Bishop : and would that please you, that think a single Congregation should have a Presbyterie? You should rather as he teacheth you, *c.*2 1.*p.*2 37. be thankful to *Ignatius* , and acknowledge the dignity of your Office, *ab eo primario defensore astrui & propugnari.*] Answ. *As we make no doubt from plain Scripture to prove, (and have proved it) that single Churches had then many Presbyters (some of them at least :) So having the greatest part of Fathers and Episcopal Divines of our mind herein, (even* Epiphanius *himself) we need not be very solicitous about the point of Testimony or Authority.* 2. *We had rather of the two have but one Pastor to a Congregation, then one to a hundred or two hundred Congregations, having a Presbyter under him in each , authorized only to a part of the work.* 3. *Either the distinct Office of the Presbyters is of Divine Institution, to be continued in the Church, or not.* If not, *Bishops or some body it seems may put down the Office.* If it be, *then it seems all Gods Universal standing Laws (even for the species of Church Officers) are not contained in Scripture. And if not in Scripture, where then ? If in the Fathers,* 1. *How shall we know which are they, and worthy of that name and honor ?* 2. *And what shall we do to reconcile their contradictions ?* 3 *And what number of them must go to be the true witnesses of a Divine Law ?* 4. *And by what note may we know what points so to receive from them, and what not ?*

But if it be *from Councils that we must have the rest of the Laws of God (not contained in the Scripture.)* 1. *Is it from all or some only ? If from all, what a case are we in, as obliged to receive Contradictions and Heresies ? If from some only, which are they, and how known, and why* they *rather then the rest ? Why not the second of* Ephesus *as well as the first at* Constantinople. *But this I shall not now further prosecute,*

prosecute, unless I were dealing with the Papists (to whom I have said more of it, in another writing.)

4. Ignatius *his Presbyters were not men of another Office, nor yet set over many Churches that had all but one Bishop: But they were all in the same Churches with the Bishop, and of the same Office, only subject to his moderation or presidency for Unity and Order sake: and this we strive not against, if limited by the general Rules of Scripture.*

Sect. 26. *Object.* Those that you have to deal with say not, that [There were no Presbyters in the Apostles days, but only that in the Apostles writings, the word [Bishops] always signifies Bishops, and the word Elders either never or but rarely Presbyters. But it is possible for them to be in the time of those writings that are not mentioned in those writings; and the Apostles times were larger then their writings, as you are told *Vind. against the Lond. Minist. p. 106.*] *Ans.* 1. *The words I cited (from* Annot. in Act. 11.) *faithfully, which you may peruse: which say that* there is no evidence that in Scripture times any of the second Order were instituted.] *So that it is not* Scripture writings *only, but* Scripture times *that's spoken of. And* 2. *If there be no evidence of it, the Church cannot believe it or affirm it; for it judgeth not of unrevealed things; and therefore to us it is no Institution that hath no evidence.* 3. *The Apostles were all dead save* John *before the end of* Scripture times: *So that they must be instituted by* John *only: And* John *dyed the next year after* Scripture times, *as the chief Chronologers judge: For as he wrote his* Apocalypse *about the* 14th *year of* Domitian, *so his Gospel the year before* Trajan, *and dyed the next year, being after the commoner reckoning, An. D.* 98. *and some think more. And what likelihood, or proof at least, that* John *did institute them the year that he dyed? when the same men tell us of his excursion into* Asia *to plant*

Elder.

, *Elders* (*before that year, it's like.*) 4. *And if they were not in-stituted in Scripture time, then no testimony from Antiquity can prove them then instituted.* But indeed *if we* had *such testimony and nothing of it in the Scripture it self, we should take it as little to our purpose. For* 5. *doth Antiquity say that the Institution was* Divine, *of Universal obligation to the Church, or only that it was but a prudential limitation of the exercise of the same Office* (*the like I demand of other like Testimonies in case of Dioc[i]sses, Metropolitans, &c.*) *If only the* later, *it binds us not, but proveth only the* licet, *and not the* oportet *at least, as to all the Church. And then every Countrey that finds cause, may set up another kind of govern-ment :* But *if it be the* former *that is asserted as from anti-quity, then the Scripture containeth not all Gods Universal Laws ; Which who ever affirmeth, must go to Fathers or Councils instead of Scripture to day, and to the infallibility of the Pope, or a Prophetical Inspiration to morrow, and* next ——

Sect. 27. *Once more to them that yet will maintain that the Apostles modelled the Ecclesiastical form to the Civil, and that as a Law to the whole Church, we take it as their Concession, that then we ow no more obedience to the Archbi-shop of* Canterbury, *then to the Civil Magistrate of* Can-terbury, (*and especially* London *sure is exempted from his superiority.*) *And I yet know not that any Civil Magistrate of* Canterbury, *or* York, *or* London, *or* Worcester, *hath any government in this Countrie, except the Soveraign Rulers at* Westminster *be meant. And I hope our Itine-rant course of Judges, will prove the right* (*to the Objectors*) *of Itinerant Apostolical Overseers of the Churches, for settlement at least.*

Sect. 28. *Object.* But Parishes being not divided till long after the Apostles days, there might be then no ordinary Assemblies but in the City ; and yet the whole
Territory

Territory adjacent be the Diocess.] Answ. *Were there in the Territories persons enough to make many Assemblies, or only so few as might travel to, and joyn with the City Assembly? If the latter, it's it that I assert, as usual in the first age at least; If the former, then either all those in the Territories met for publick Worship and Communion, or not: If* not, *they sinned against the Law of God that obliged them thereto as well as Citizens: If* they did, *then they must have either Bishop or Presbyter with them, for the due performance of that worship.*

Sect. 29. *If any think all these stragling objections and advertisements here unseasonable, I render him this true account of them: This first Disputation was prepared only for our ordinarily Monthly Exercises here, and so written long ago, before the* London *Ministers Book, or the Answer to it, and the rest that have followed, and therefore could not take notice of much that hath since passed, and withal was not intended for publick view: But when I saw so many of the Gentry and Commonalty withdraw from the publick worship, and the ignorant and prophane had learnt to refel their Pastors Instructions, by calling him a Layman, and saw how the new separation threatned the perdition of multitudes of the people, & especially was awakened by the Calls of Ministers in other Countries that were far more troubled with them then we, I thought meet to prefix this to the Second Disputation, which was it that was desired of me: and therefore to take notice of those things so late.*

Sect. 30. *And the common experience tells you that it is not a few that go the way that lately was singular even among the Episcopal; to which I may add the Testimony in* Vindic. *against the* London Ministers, *p.* 104. [And though I might truly say that for those more minute considerations or conjectures, wherein this Doctor differs from some others ——— he hath the suffrages of

many

many of the Learnedst men of this Church at this day (*and as* far as he knows, of all that embrace the same cause with him) *&c.*————]

Sect. 31. *And this at least I may expect from the Reader, that if he think we argue weakly, he will confess that we argue not for worldly greatness, but go against our carnal interest. We contend against Bishopricks of the* English *mode, as desiring no such Wealth or Honour. Some of us have as good opportunities to have a part in that kind of Greatness if it were again introduced, as they: But I am not able alone for a Parish charge, and am loth to have more on my hands, and my accounts; which is I suppose the mind of my Brethren also.*

Sect. 32. *One more Advertisement I owe the Reader, that this being written so long since I was made confident by Bishop* Usher, de Primordiis Eccl. Brit. *that* Ireland *was the Ancient* Scotia *where* Palladius, &c. *planted the Gospel, which* pag. 97. *I have signified. But I should wrong* Scotland, *if I should not tell thee, that I have received such Arguments to the contrary since then, from the Right Honourable, and my highly valued friend, the Earl of* Lawderdail, *that I am forced to suspend my judgement in that point, till I have leisure better to study the point, being yet unable to answer the said arguments.*

Whether it be Neceſſary or Profitable to the right order or the Peace of the Churches of *England* that we reſtore the extruded Epiſcopacy ?

 N this Queſtion here are theſe three things ſuppoſed. 1. That there are yet particular Churches of Chriſt in *England* : and therefore thoſe that conclude that there hath been no Church among us ſince the Dioceſan Biſhops were laid by, are none of them that we are now diſputing with : and indeed we think ſo groſs a conceit unworthy of a Confutation.

2. It is ſuppoſed that both the right Order and the Peace of theſe Churches are matters highly to be valued. 3. And alſo that its our duty for the obtaining of it, to do that which is neceſſary or profitable thereto. But the doubt is, Whether the Epiſcopacy in queſtion be neceſſary or profitable thereto ?

For the deciſion whereof I ſhall briefly tell you my Judgement, in theſe propoſitions, whereof the two firſt are but preparatory.

Propoſition 1. *A Peace with the Divines of the Epiſcopal judgement,*

ment , *is much to be desired and earneſtly to be endeavoured.*

Prop. 2. *A certain Epiſcopacy may be yielded to, for the Peace (if not for the right order) of the Church.*

Prop. 3. *The Dioceſan Epiſcopacy which was lately in England, and is now laid by, may not lawfully be re-aſſumed or re-admitted, as a means for the right Order or Peace of the Church.*

1. For the firſt of theſe, I think it eaſie to prove that we ought to ſeek an Agreement in the Epiſcopal controverſie, with thoſe that differ from us in that point.

For, 1. They are brethren, of the ſame faith with us, whom we are bound to love and honour, and therefore to uſe all juſt means for peace with them. If we muſt as much *as in us lyeth, if poſſible, live peaceably with all men*, Rom. 12. 18. much more with *Brethren* of the ſame family and profeſſion.

2. They are very many ; and the far greateſt (though not the pureſt) part of the Church is of their mind : All the Greek Church, and the Ethiopian Church, and the Jacobites, Armenians, and all other parties without the verge of the Reformation from Popery here in the Weſt, that ever I read or heard of, are all of that way , beſides all the Romane Church : And, though I know that much ignorance , and imperfection, if not ſuperſtition and fouler errors may be juſtly charged on the Greek, Ethiopian, *&c.* Churches, as well as on *Rome* (though not Popery it ſelf) yet I think there is ſcarce a good Chriſtian that is not unwilling to caſt off ſo great a part of the Church of Chriſt, as theſe are Indeed, he that dares ſo far deſpiſe all the Churches of Chriſt on earth except theſe few that are happily reformed , as to think that it is no duty of ours, to ſeek unity and peace with them, by all juſt means, I think is no meet perſon for us to diſpute with. It is the hainous ſin of *Rome*, to deſpiſe and unchurch Greeks, Ethiopians, and all ſave themſelves, which I hope Proteſtants will never imitate, who have juſtly condemned them ſo deeply for it. Let the Donatiſts ſhut up the Church of Chriſt in *Africa*, and call the reſt *Cecilians* ; and let the Papiſts reduce it to the ſubſcribers to their *Trent* confeſſion, or to them only that believe in the Popes univerſal Headſhip and Government, and call all others Hereticks : yet will all true Catholicks imitate *Auguſtine* and the Councils that were called againſt the Donatiſts, who ſtill deſcribed the Catholike Church to be that *which*

was

was disperfed over the world, having begun at Jerufalem: and though to Gods praife we dare rejoycingly affirm, that the moft illuftrious and the foundeft part of it is in *Europe*, among the Reformed, yet dare we not fay that it is all or the greateft part here; Nay we confefs that we are but a fmall part of Chrifts Church. And therefore common fobriety may tell us, that the Peace of fo great a part of Chrifts Church as is in all the reft of the world, is highly to be valued, and fought with all our might, in righteoufnefs.

Moreover, even among the reformed Churches there are many for fome Epifcopacy or Superintendency: As the Church of *England* and *Ireland* was lately for Diocefan Epifcopacy: fo the Churches in *Denmark*, *Sweden*, *Saxonie*, and other parts of *Germany*, *Tranfilvania*, &c. are for a lower fort of Epifcopacy, called Superintendency among them.

3. And the quality of many of the Divines of that way, is fuch as befpeaks our greateft reverence to them, and fhould move us to thirft after Unity and Reconciliation with them. Many of them are men of eminent Learning and Godlinefs, and found in the faith.

I know that it is commonly objected, that they are generally ungodly men that are that way; and though fome of them are Learned men, yet they are all, or almoft all, of carelefs and carnal lives, or meerly formal and fuperftitious, and therefore their Communion is not much to be defired.

To which I anfwer. 1. The plain undenyable truth is that it was fo here with the moft of them in the Bifhops dayes, where ever I was acquainted: There were more Minifters in many places that would have fcorned, threatned or troubled a man for a godly diligent life, then that would lead him that way by a good example. We muft fpeak that truth that cannot be hid, whoever be difpleafed. To this day, too many of that way are carelefs and fcandalous. But then Confider withall, 2. That it is but too common for the common fort even of Minifters as well as people, to be carelefs and bad, what ever opinions they are of: Efpecially if the times do difcountenance practical Religioufnefs, the greater part are likely to follow the times, being that way alfo fo ftrongly enclined by nature. 3. Confider alfo that we have had, and have men of that Judgement that have been ex-

B cellent

cellent Instruments of the Churches good, and so eminent for Gods graces and gifts, that their names will be pretious whilest Christ hath in *England* a Reformed Church: were there in all *England* but one such man dissenting from us, as *Hooper, Farrar, Latimer, Cranmer, Ridley, Jewel, Abbot, Davenant, Usher, Hall, &c.* what sober Godly man would not be exceeding solicitous for a reconciliation? I am sure (besides the godliness of their lives, and painful preaching) One *Jewel*, One *Usher*, One *Davenant*, hath done so much against the Roman Usurpers, as they will never well claw it off them to the last.

Moreover who knoweth not that most of the Godly able Ministers of *England* since the Reformation, did judge Episcopacy some of them Lawful, and some of them most fit (for the Nonconformists were but-few :) and that even before this late trouble and war, the most, even almost all, of those that were of the late Assembly at *Westminster*, and most through the land, did subscribe and conform to Episcopal Government, as a thing not contrary to the word of God : so that it is evident that it is very consistent with a Godly life to judge Episcopacy lawful and fit; or else we should not have had so many hundred learned and godly men of that mind.

And I am not altogether unapt to believe, that many of them yet are so far reconcileable to it (moderated,) that if it were again established, they would submit to it as they did : For I hear but of few that have made any recantation of their former conformity; but contrarily have known divers of them profess a reconcilableness as aforesaid, as Mr. *Gataker* doth in one of his books express his own Judgement.

If I have proved this preparatory proposition (which I think needeth but little proof,) then have I also proved 1. That they have sinned much who have hitherto forborn the use of any means for Peace which was in their power. 2. And that we are bound our selves to desire and seek after a peace with such men : and that we cannot discharge a good conscience while we neglect such means as is within our reach, and fit for us to use.

The second Proposition is, that [*A Certain Episcopacy may be yielded to, for the peace; if not also for the right order of the Church*] In the declaration of my judgement concerning this,

this, I make no doubt but I shall displease both sides; the one for yielding so much; the other for yielding no more. But *jacta est alea*: I live not upon mens favour, nor the air of their applause; That truth which displeaseth at present, may tend to peace, and produce it at the last, when the angry humour is allayed, or at least, when the angry age is gone.

For the clearer determination of this and the main Question following, it is necessary that I here say 1. To open the nature of Church-Government in general: 2. To open the sence of the word [*Episcopacy*] and the several sorts of Bishops. And then 3. I shall tell you what sort of Episcopacy it is that I could yield to for the Churches peace.

1. I must confess I think that the greatest part of the controversie by far, is in this first question, of the nature of Ecclesiastical Government, strictly so called, which is only in the hands of Christs Ministers, Bishops or whomsoever, commonly called, Clergy men. And concerning this (having written my thoughts more largely elsewhere) I shall now lay down these few Propositions.

Prop. 1. *All this power Ecclesiastical is* Jure' divino, *given from God himself; and that either immediately, or by the mediation only of the Apostles.* I mean as to the determination *in specie,* what it shall be, and the constitution of that order and power in the Church, though perhaps some other causes, at least * *sine quibus non* may intervene for the reception of this power by an individual person. These therefore that plead only the Laws of the Land, or only Canons of former Bishops for their standing or authority, do say nothing that as to our controversie is regardable. What men do, they may undo, if there be reason for it, and if it depend on their authority, we must submit to their reason.

Prop. 2. *This Divine Constitution of the Species of Church-Power and Government, is to be found wholly in the written word of God, called the holy Scriptures.* This we are agreed on against the Papists, who would supply the supposed defects of Scripture by their unwritten Traditions, which they call the other part of Gods word. Church Canons and Laws of men may determine of some modes and circumstances for the better execution of the Laws of God, by the People whom they are over: but they cannot make new Church Ordinances or Governments, nor

* Of the difference between Election and Ordination; and that neither gives the *Jus* or Power, but Christ only. See Gro:ius de *Imperio Sum. Potest.c.* 10.*p.* 269, 270.

convey

convey a Power which God the fountain of Power did not ordain and convey : nor can they give what they themselves had not. The Church-office and Authority therefore that is not proved from the Holy Scripture, is to be taken as the fruit of humane arrogancy and presumption. Yet I deny not but that we may find much in Antiquity, in Fathers and Councils about matters of fact to help us to understand some Scriptures, and so to discern the matter of right.

Prop. 3. *The Scripture doth not Contradict, but suppose and confirm the light of Nature; nor doth it impose upon any man Natural impossibilities, nor constitute offices which cannot be executed, or which would destroy that end to which they are supposed to be Constituted.*

Prop. 4. *Ecclesiastical Authority comprehendeth not the power of the sword, nor any power of using violence to mens bodies, or laying mulcts or confiscations on their estates.* The Ecclesiastical Power which Christ ordained, was exercised for the first three hundred years without any touching of mens bodies or purses, before there were any Christian Princes.

Prop. 5. *Magistrates are not eo nomine obliged to punish men because they are Excommunicated* (whether upon every just Excommunication they should punish, I will not now dispute) but they are bound to know that their penalties be deserved, before they inflict them; and therefore must themselves take Cognisance of the Cause, and as rational agents, understand before they act; and not blindly follow the Judgements of the Bishops, as if they were but as Executioners where the Bishops are Judges.

Prop. 6. * *The Power of the highest Church-governours is but an Authority of Directing in the way to salvation:* It is but Directive : but then there is no room for the common Objection, that [*then it is no greater then any other man may perform;*] for it is one thing to Direct Occasionally from Charity, and another thing to Direct by Authority in a standing office, as purposely appointed hereunto. † The Power of Church-Governors is but

* I comprehend in the word *Directive* all that is after expressed in the following Propositions.

† *Quæ ante Imperatores Christianos in Synodis conscripta sunt ad ordinem aut ornatum facientia, Leges non vocantur sed Canones, habentq; aut solam Concilii vim, ut in his quæ singulos magis spectant quam universos, aut obligant per modum pacti volentes & nolentes etiam pauciores ex necessitate determinationis, ac proinde ex lege naturali, non ex humano aliquo Imperio.* Grotius de Imperio pag. 209, 210. Lege & cap. 9. per totum.

of

of the fame nature as is the Power of a Phyſitian over his Patiſ-
ents, or of a School-maſter over his Schollers, ſuppoſing he had
not the power of the rod or actual force, but ſuch a power as
the Profeſſors of Philoſophy or other ſciences had in their ſeveral ſchools upon the adult (nor all ſo great neither; becauſe
the Laws by which we muſt rule, are made to our hands, as to
the ſubſtantials) Hence therefore it is plain, that as we can bind
or force no man to believe us, or to underſtand the truth, and
to be Chriſtians, but by the power of demonſtrated Evidence,
and by the light which we let in (through Gods grace) into
their Conſciences, ſo neither can we cauſe any to execute our
ſentences againſt offenders further than by light we convince,
them that it is their duty : ſo that if all the Biſhops or Presbyteries in the land ſhould judge ſuch or ſuch an opinion to be hereſie, and ſhould Excommunicate thoſe that own it as hereticks,
in this caſe if the Church do believe as the Paſtors believe, they
will conſent and avoid the Excommunicate perſon; but if they
take it to be Gods truth which the Paſtors call hereſie, they will
not take themſelves bound by that ſentence to avoid him : nor
will the Offender himſelf any further be ſenſible of a penalty in
the ſentence, then he ſhall be convinced that he hath erred; and if
the Church avoid him, he will juſtifie himſelf, and judge that they
do it wrongfully, and will glory in his ſuffering : ſo that it is on
the Conſcience that Church Governors can work; and no otherwiſe on the outward man, but *mediante Conſcientiâ*.

Prop. 7. *The ground of this is partly becauſe no Church Go-*
vernors can bind any man contrary to Gods word : Clave errante, &
ita apparente, *if the people know that he erreth, they are not to obey*
him againſt God. Yet in the bare inconvenient determination of
ſome Circumſtantials, by which the duty is not deſtroyed, but
leſs conveniently performed, the people are bound to obey their
Governors, becauſe it is not againſt Gods determination, and
becauſe he erreth but in an undetermined point, of which God appointed him to be the orderly determiner. But if God have once
determined, no mans contrary determination can oblige; nor
yet if they go beyond the ſphere of their own work, and determine of an aliene ſubject, which God did never commit to their
determination : elſe a Miniſter, or Biſhop, might oblige every
Taylor how to cut his garment, and every Shoo-maker how to
cut

cut his fhoe, fo that they fhould fin if they did difobey, which is ridiculous to imagine : and if they go about to introduce new ftated Ordinances or Symbols in the Church which they have nothing to do with, or in any other work fhall affume to themfelves a power which God never gave them, it doth no more oblige then in the former cafe.

Prop. 8. Another reafon of the fixth Propofition, is, becaufe *The People have a Judgement of difcerning, whether the Governors do go according to Gods word or not* : elfe they fhould be led blindfold, and be obliged by God to go againft Gods word, whenfoever their Governors fhall go againft it. It is not bruits or Infants, but rational men that we muft rule.

Prop. 9. *The three things which Church-power doth confift in, are* (in conformity to the three parts of Chrifts own office) 1. *About matter of Faith,* 2. *About matter of Worfhip,* 3. *About matter of Practice in other cafes.*

1. Church-Governors about Doctrine or Matters of Faith, are the Peoples Teachers, but cannot *oblige* them to *Err,* or to believe any thing againft God, nor make that to be truth or error that is not fo before.

2. In matter of Worfhip, Church-guides are as Gods Priefts, and are to go before the people, and ftand between God and them, and prefent their prayers and prayfes to God, and adminifter his holy myfteries, and blefs them in his name.

3. The *Commanding* Power of Paftors is in two things : 1. In *Commanding* them in the name of Chrift to obey the Laws which he hath made them already. And this is the principal. 2. To give them *new Directions* of our *own,* which as is faid, 1. Muft not be againft Gods Directions. 2. Nor about any matter which is not the object of our own office, but is without the verge of it. 3. But it is only in the making of *under laws,* for the better execution of the laws of Chrift ; and thofe *under-laws* muft be only the *Determination of Circumftances* about Gods fervice which Scripture hath made *neceffary in genere,* but left to the Governors determination *in fpecie* ; and they are fuch as are al-erable in feveral ages, countries, &c. fo that it had been unfit for Chrift to have determined them in his word, becaufe his word is an *univerfal* Law for all ages and countries ; and thefe Circumftances will not bear an univerfal determination : elfe why could not Chrift

Chriſt have done it ? nay how is his Law perfect elſe that doth omit it ? For example, God hath commanded us to read the word, preach, hear, ſing, which muſt neceſſarily be done in ſome time, place, geſture, number of words, &c. But he hath not commanded us on what day of the week our Lecture ſhall be, or at what hour of the day, nor what Chapter I ſhall read, nor how many at once, nor what Text I ſhall preach on, nor what Pſalm I ſhall ſing, nor in what words I ſhall pray, whether impoſed by others, or not, whether with a book, or foreconceived form, or not ; nor whether I ſhall read with ſpectacles or without, or whether I ſhall diſcern how the time paſſeth by an hour-glaſs, or by the clock, or by conjecture without them. Theſe therefore and other ſuch like, muſt humane Prudence determine of. But with theſe Cautions.

1. Theſe are moſtly matters that require a various determination in ſeveral places according to the great variety of Circumſtances ; and therefore it is for the moſt part fitter for the particular Paſtor of that Church, who is upon the place, and ſeeth the caſe, to determine them *pro re nata,* * then for Synods, or diſtant Prelates, to do it by general Laws or Canons binding all.

2. Though upon a ſmall miſdetermination of ſuch a Circumſtance, the people muſt obey, yet if it be ſo groſly miſdetermined as to deſtroy the duty it ſelf Circumſtantiated, or to be notoriouſly againſt the end which it is pretended for, then they are not to obey it. As if a Paſtor would appoint the People to hear in the night only, or at ſuch unſeaſonable times that they cannot come, or in many the like caſes.

Note alſo that it is one thing to preſcribe theſe matters in a direct Regimental Reſpect, and that belongeth to *him upon the Place* ; and its another thing to preſcribe them for *common Union or Concord* among many Churches, and that belongs *to a Synod,* (of which anon.)

And it is moſt certain by ſad experience, that ſcarce any thing hath broken the unity and peace of the Church more, then unneceſſary determinations pretended to be for its unity and peace. Could men have been content to have made Gods Laws the center and touchſtone of the Churches Unity, all had been well : but when they muſt make Canons for this Veſture, and that Geſture, and the other Ceremony, and determine in what words

*That Synods are not abſolutely neceſſary (and he thinks not of Scripture Inſtitution but Natural direction) ſee *Grot. de Imperio Cap. 7. per totum.*

(all

all men shall pray, and how many words he shall say, or how long he shall be, and so make standing Laws upon mutable circumstances, and this without any necessity at all, but meerly to domineer, as if they had been themselves ordained and entrusted with Gods worship and mens souls; such sottish Presbyters, that know not how to speak or do any thing but as it is prescribed them, nor how to carry themselves soberly or reverendly without being obliged which way to bow, and when and how oft, with the like. Unneceffary things made Neceffary have destroyed the Churches Peace; and so blind are the Authors of it, that yet they will not fee their errour, though the cries, and groans, and blood of the Churches have proclaimed it so long. The Church Historie of these one thousand and three hundred years at least doth tell us that it is the Church Governours by their too much business and overdoing in such wayes, even by too bold and busie determinations about doctrines or Ceremonies, that have broken all in peices and caused that confusion, diffention and feemingly remediless divisions in the Church.

Prop. 10. *In cases which are beyond the present understanding of the people, they are bound as Learners, to submit to the judgement of their Guides*: If they fee no sufficient cause, either in the matter to cause them to suspect that their Teachers are mistaken, or in their Teachers to cause them to suspect them to be seducers, they owe them so much credit and respect as their Guides, as to believe them *fide-humana*, or to suppose that they are likelier to be in the right then themselves; and therefore in matters of Doctrine not to contradict them, but to submit to learn of them, till by learning they come to that ripeness of understanding, as to be capable of discerning the errors of their Guides, and so to contradict them groundedly, if indeed they err: so also in the order of variable Circumstantials about the service of God, though the people ought not to obey their Governours, if under that pretence they should command them things sinful; yet when they are not able to fee any certain evil in the thing commanded, nor so strong a probability of evil as should cause them to suspend obedience while they take better advice, in such a case it is their Duty to obey the guides of the Church. For they are certain that they are commanded *to obey them that*

rule

rule over them, *and watch for their souls, Heb.* 13. 17. but they are not certain that in such a case it is an evil that is prescribed by them, nor is it supposed to be much probable ; therefore a certain evil of disobedience must be avoided before an uncertain and improbable evil. This the very office of Church Governours doth plainly import.

Object. *Then if the Minister mistake, all the people that understand not the grounds of the matter, must err for company.* Answ. If by *Must,* you speak of their Duty, I deny the consequence : For their Duty is to be men of understanding, and to see the truth in its own evidence, and so not to err ; But if by *Must,* you only express a Necessity of Infirmity which they have sinfully contracted themselves, then I yield all : but I say, that it is a greater sin to disobey their guides, without known reason, and consequently never to obey them in any case beyond the present knowledge of the people, then it is to follow them *fide humana* in such mistakes as we have no sufficient means at present to discover. For the former will overthrow almost all Ministration and Church-government.

Obj. *Then it is no sin for an Ignorant man to Err with his Teacher for company.* Answ. I deny that Consequence : for it is his sin to be an Ignorant man : and consequently to have any Error. But supposing him already Ignorant by his own sinfulness, and that the Ministers of the Gospel come to heal it, we may well say that it is his greater sin to disbelieve and disobey them without apparent cause, then to mistake with them where he is not able to discern the mistake.

Prop. 11. *He that disobeyeth the Word of God in the mouth of a Minister or Church-governor, committeth a double sin, in comparison of him that disobeyeth the same word in the mouth of a private man : for bsides the sin which he first committeth, he breaketh also the fifth Commandment, and despiseth Christ in his Messenger :* As a man that shall refuse to worship God, to use his name reverently, &c. when a private man telleth him that it is his duty, doth sin by that refusal : but if he refuse it when his *own Father or Mother,* or *Minister command* him, he also breaks the fifth Commandment besides the rest. Ministerial Authority therefore doth aggravate the sins of persons that are disobedient.

Prop. 12. *Yet for all this, one private man that evinceth out*

of

of Scripture a sin or a duty contrary to the doctrine or commands of our Guides, must be regarded in that before them; and the evidence and divine verity which he bringeth must not be refused, because Church Governors are against it. Otherwise we should make Gods Officers to be greater then himself; and the Promulgators and Preachers of his Law, to have power to null or fruſtrate the known Law which they should proclaim, and that the means is to be preferred before the end, and when it destroyes the end, and so ceaſeth it self to be a means, which are things not to be imagined.

Prop. 13. *Yet is it a great sin for any men lightly and rashly to suspect their Teachers and Rulers, and much more Councils or the whole Church; and too easily to credit the singular opinions of any private man or dissenting Pastor.* But we should be very suspicious of the private man rather, and of the singular man; and therefore should search well, and see good reason for it before we credit them; though we may not refuse any truth which they shall bring.

Prop. 14. *The uses of Synods or Councils, is not directly to be superiour Governours of particular Pastors and Churches; but it is Directly* 1. *For the Information and Edification of the Pastors themselves by the collation of their reasons and mutual advice;* 2. *For the Union and Communion of the said Pastors, and of the particular Churches by them:* that they may agree in one, and go hand in hand to do Gods work; and so may avoid the crossing and hindering of each other, and one may not receive those to communion without satisfaction, who are excommunicated by others, and so that by this concord of Pastors they may be ſtrengthened to a more successfull performance of their duties.

But then, these *Direct* ends of *Synods* being presupposed, *Indirectly* they may truly be said to be for Government; Because God in general having commanded us to carry on his work as much as we can in Unity and Peace, and it being the proper work of Councils to agree upon wayes of Unity, it followeth that for Unity sake it becomes our duty to submit to their just Agreements; and so that the forming of such Agreements or Canons, is consequently or Indirectly a part of Government, though Directly it is but for Unity and Concord. Pastors *in Synods* have the same power over their *people* as they have *out:* and therefore what Canons they make juſtly for the Government of the *people,*

as

as *Pastors*, are *Directly* acts of Government: but as *Assembled Pastors*, and also as to the Canons by which they bind each other, they act but by consent or contract in order to concord and communion, and not by a superiour Ruling power. So that Synods as Synods are Directly only *Gratiâ Unitatis & Communionis*, and not *Gratia Regiminis*; but *Indirectly* and by *consequence* from the first use, they are *after a sort Regimental*.

To conclude this about the Nature of Church-Government, in the two former similitudes it is somewhat apparent: For Christ calls himself the Physitian that comes to heal diseased souls: and his Church is also a School, and his people are all Schollars or Disciples, and Ministers his Ushers or under-Schoolmasters. Now the Physitian may prescribe to his Patient the times, the quantities of taking Medicines, and what diet to use, and what exercise in order to his health; and also Physitians may make a Colledge, and frequently meet for mutual Edification, and Agree what Patients to meddle with, and what not, and that they will not receive those Patients that run from one to another to their own hurt, and that they will use none but such and such approved Medicaments, with divers the like circumstances. But yet no Physitian can either compell men to be their Patients; nor compell them (any otherwise then by perswasion) to take their Medicines, when they are their Patients; nor can they corporally punish them for any disobedience to their directions: But this they may do: they may tell them first that if they will not be ruled, they shall be without the Physitians help, and then their desease will certainly kill them, or endanger them; and if the Patient continue so disobedient as to frustrate the means of cure, the Physitian may give him over, and be his Physitian no more; and this is the Power of a Church Guide, and this is his way of punishing: Only he may further acquaint them with a Divine Commission, then a Physician can do to his Patient, (at least gradually) and so press obedience more effectually on their consciences.

So a Schoolmaster may make orders for the right circumstantiating of matters in his School (supposing one Grammer enjoyned by superiour Authority,) and he may order what Authors shall be read, and at what hours, and how much at a time, and dispose of the seats and orders of his Schoilars: but

C

he be a Teacher of the Adult, according to our cafe, he cannot corporally punifh thofe that either refufe to be his Schollars, or to learn of him or obey him ; but the utmoft that he can do is to put fome difgrace upon them while they abide in his School, and at laft to fhut them out. And then all the Schoolmafters in the Countrey may well agree upon one Method of Teaching, and that they will not receive thofe without fatisfaction into one School, who are for obftinacy and abufe caft out of another. But fuch Agreements or Meetings to that end do not make either one Phyfitian or Schoolmafter to be the Governour of the reft, or above another, nor yet to have the charge of all the Schollars or Patients of all the reft ; fo is it in the cafe of Eccclefiaftical Affemblies.

HAving faid this much concerning the Nature of Church-Power and Government, I come to the fecond thing promifed, which is to enumerate the feveral forts of Bifhops that are to fall under our confideration, that fo we may next confider, which of them are to be allowed of.

And here I fuppofe none will expect that I fhew them all thefe forts diftinctly exiftent ; it is enough that I manifeft them to be in themfelves truly different.

1. And firft the name [*Bifhop*] may be given to one, that is only *the Overfeer or Ruler of the People of one particular Church*, and not of any Church-rulers themfelves : That ruleth the flock, but not any Shepherds.

2. Thofe alfo may be called *Bifhops*, who only are *Joint Rulers with others of a particular Church, and Prefidents among the Elders of that one Church for Unity and order fake, without affuming any Government over thofe Elders.*

3. A third fort there are that are *Prefidents in fuch an Elderfhip, and withal do take a Negative voice in the Government, fo that nothing fhall be done without them in fuch affairs.*

4. A fourth fort are the *fole Paftors of fuch a particular Church that have many Minifters under them as their Curates*, who are properly to be Ruled by them alone ; fo that the Paftor is the fole Ruler of that Church, and the Curates do only teach and otherwife officiate in obedience to him : Which is the cafe of

divers

divers Minifters of great Parifhes, that keep one Curate at their
Parifh Church, and others at their Chappels. Yet its one thing
to be the fole Ruler of the Parifh, and another to Rule the reft of
the Elders.

5. A fifth fort of Bifhops are thofe that are *the fixed Prefidents of a Claffis of the Paftors of many particular Churches*;
who hold the title *durante vitá*, or *quàm diu bene fe gefferint*,
though they are in ufe only while the Claffis fitteth, and have
only a power of Moderating and ordering things, as the fore-
man of a Jury, or a double or cafting voice, as the Bayliff in
Elections in moft Corporations, or as the Prefident in fome Colledges; but no *Negative voice*, which maketh a Power equal
with all the reft.

6. A fixth fort are *the heads of fuch Claffes, having a Negative voice, fo that the reft can do nothing without them.*

7. A feventh fort are *the Prefidents of Provinces or Diocffes* Chau. Occum. p.
containing many Claffes, which have only a Moderating Power, but £.2. p.191.
no Negative voice.

8 An eighth fort are *the Bifhops of particular Cities with all the
Rural parts that are near it, containing many Churches; who affume the Power of Governing that Diocefs to themfelves alone without the Presbyters of the particular Churches*, either not ufing
them at all in matter of Government, or only confulting with
them in Affemblies, but giving them no determining votes.

9. A ninth fort is *a Diocefan Bifhop of fuch a City, who doth
not take upon him the Rule of the people of the Diocefs* (beyond
his own Congregation) *but only of the Paftors*; fuppofing that
the feveral Paftors or Presbyters have power to Rule the feveral
Congregations, but withall that they themfelves are to be ruled
by him.

10. A tenth fort are *fuch Bifhops as affume the Government of
thefe Diocefan Bifhops, which are commonly called Archbifhops*:
to which alfo we adjoyn Metropolitans, Primates, and Patriarchs, who affume the Power of Governing all below them : as
under the feventh rank I do alfo for brevity comprehend Metropolitans, Primates, and Patriarchs, who affume no Governing
Power over other Bifhops, but only the *primam fedem*, and the
moderating Power in Councils.

11. The eleventh fort are *unfixed general Paftors, called Am-
vulatory.*

bulatory, or *Itinerant*, that have a care of all the Churches, and are no further tyed to any particulars, then as the necessary defect of their natural capacity (seeing they cannot be in all places at once,) or else the dispatch of that work which they there meet with, before they go further, and some such occasion *doth require*: and being excluded out of no part of the Church, further then by consent for the common good, they shall exclude themselves; such, I mean, as the Apostles were.

12. The twelfth and last sort is *the* Judas *that goes under the name of St.* Peters *Successor, and* Christs *Vicar General, or the* Vice-Christ, *who claimeth a power of Governing the whole universal Church as its Head, having Infallible power of determining Controversies, and matters of Faith, and whose Office must enter the definition of the Catholick Church*, and those that separate from him are no Catholikes, or true Christians. This is he that beareth the bag, and maketh the twelfth sort.

---

3. **I** Come now in the third place to tell you, how many and which of these sorts of Episcopacy I think may be admitted for the Peace of the Church: And,

1. Of the first sort there is no Controversie among us : few will deny the *Jus Divinum* of *Presbyters, as having the Rule of the people of a particular Church*, and the sole Rule, supposing that there is no other Pastor over that Church but himself.

2. Of the second sort of Parish Bishops (who are *meer Presidents over the whole Eldership of that particular Church, and that continually, or fixedly.*) I think there is little question will be made by any, but they also will easily be admitted.

3. The third sort (*A Parochial Bishop, having a Negative voice in a Parish Eldership*) I should be content to admit for the Peace of the Church : but whether of it self it be desirable, I do not dispute : for if one Pastor even in a Parish may have a Negative voice among two or three Curates, it will follow that the thing it self is not unlawful, *viz.* for one Minister to have a Negative vote among many, and so among an hundred, if there be nothing else to forbid.

4. The fourth sort (for brevity) Comprehendeth two sorts.

1. *Such*

1. *Such Pastors of a single Congregation, which having diverse Curates under them who are Presbyters, do yet themselves take upon them the sole Government of the people and of their Curates.* I think this is intolerable, and indeed a Contradiction, or a Nulling of the Presbyters office : for it is essential to the Presbyter of any Church to be a Guide or Ruler of that Church : to put them out of all Rule therefore is to Null, or suspend the exercise of their office ; which cannot statedly be done without destroying it. But then 2. if we speak of the second sort, that is, *such Pastors of particular Churches, as have Curats who are Presbyters, and they govern their Curates, but take the Curates as true Governors of the flock,* these as I dare not simply defend, (for if it be lawful for one Pastor to Rule two or three in a Parish, then why not twenty or an hundred, if nothing else forbid ?) so I confess I should be ready to admit of them, if it might attain the Churches peace : for I see many godly Divines that are against Episcopacy, yet practice this ; and will have no Curates in their Parish, that will not be Ruled by them. And there is a certain Obedience which Juniors and men of weaker parts, do owe to their Seniors and men of far greater knowledge, though the Office be the same. And the Nature of the Government being not Compulsive and Coercive, but only upon the voluntary, whose judgements approve and their wills consent, its considerable how far even a Ruler of others may voluntarily consent and so oblige himself to be Ruled by another, that could not have any power to Rule him, without that consent of his own, and voluntary Condescension.

5. As for the fifth sort, that is, [*The standing President of a Classis, having no Negative voice*] I should easily consent to them for order and Peace : for they are no distinct Office, nor assume any Government over the Presbyters. And the Presbyterian Churches do commonly use a President or Moderator *pro tempore.* And doubtless if it be lawful for a Month, it may be lawful for a year, or twenty years, or *quam diu se bene gesserit :* and how many years had we one Moderator of our Assemblies of Divines at *Westminster* ? and might have had him so many years more if death had not cut him off ? And usually God doth not so change his gifts, but that the same man who is the fittest this month or year, is most likely also to be the fittest the next.

D   6. And

6. And for the sixth sort, *viz.* [*A Prefident of a Claffes having a Negative voice,*] I confefs I had rather be without him, and his power is not agreeable to my Judgement, as a thing inftituted by God, or fitteft in it felf. But yet I fhould give way to it for the Peace of the Church, and if it might heal that great breach that is between us, and the Epifcopal Brethren, and the many Churches that hold of that way ; but with thefe Cautions and Limitations. 1. That they fhall have no Negative in any thing that is already a duty or a fin : for an Angel from heaven cannot difpenfe with Gods Law. This I doubt not will be yielded. 2. That none be forced to acknowledge this Negative vote in them, but that they take it from thofe of the Presbyters that will freely give or acknowledge it. For its a known thing that all Church-power doth work only on the Confcience, and therefore only prevail by procuring Confent, and cannot compell. 3. Nor would I ever yield that any part of the Presbyters diffenting fhould be taken as Schifmaticks, and caft out of Communion, or that it fhould be made the matter of fuch a breach. This is it that hath broken the Church, that Bifhops have thruft their Rule on men whether they would or not, and have taken their Negative voice at leaft, if not their fole Jurisdiction, to be fo neceffary, as if there could be no Church without it, or no man were to be endured that did not acknowledge it ; but he that denyeth their difputable Power muft be excommunicated with them that blafpheme God himfelf. And as the Pope will have the acknowledgement of his Power to be infeparable from a member of the Catholike Church, and caft out all that deny it, fo fuch Bifhops take the acknowledgement of their Jurisdiction, to be as infeparable from a member of a particular Church, and confequently (as they fuppofe) of the univerfal : and fo to deny them fhall cut men off, as if they denyed Chrift. This favoureth not of the humility that Chrift taught his followers. 4. Nor would I have any forced to declare whether they only fubmit for Peace, or confent in approbation : nor whether they take the Bifhops Negative vote to be by Divine Inftitution, and fo Neceffary, or by the Presbyters voluntary confent & contract, as having power in feveral cafes to fufpend the exercife of their own juft authority, when the fufpenfion of it tendeth to a publike Good. No duty is at all times a duty. If a man be to be or-

dained

· dained by a Presbytery, it is not a flat duty to do it at that time when the Preſident is abſent, except in caſe of flat neceſſity ; why may not the reſt of the Presbyters then, if they ſee it conducible to the good of the Church [reſolve never to ordain (except in caſe of ſuch Neceſſity,) but when the Preſident is there, and is one therein ;] which is indeed to *permit* his *exerciſe* of a Negative vote, without profeſſing it to be his *right* by any Inſtitution ? It is lawful to ordain, when the Preſident is preſent ; it is lawful (out of caſes of Neceſſity) to forbear when he is abſent : according therefore to the Presbyterian principles, we *may* reſolve to give him *de facto* a Negative voice, that is, not to ordain without him, but in Neceſſity : and according to the Epiſcopal principles, we *muſt* thus do : for this point of Ordination is the chief thing they ſtand on. Now if this be all the difference, why ſhould not our *May be*, yield to their, *Muſt be*, if the Peace of the Church be found to lye upon it. But 5. I would have this Caution too, that the Magiſtrate ſhould not annex his ſword to the Biſhops cenſure, without very clear reaſon : but let him make the beſt of his pure ſpiritual Authority that he can : we ſhould have kept peace with Biſhops better, if they had not come armed, and if the Magiſtrates had not become their Executioners.

7. As to the ſeventh ſort, viz. [*A Preſident of a Province fixed, without any Negative voice*] I ſhould eaſily admit of him, not only for Peace, but as orderly and convenient, that there might be ſome one to give notice of all Aſſemblies, and the Decrees to each member, and for many other mattters of order : this is practiſed in the Province of *London pro tempore*, and in the other Presbyterian Churches. And as I ſaid before in the like caſe, I ſee not why it may not be lawful to have a Preſident *quam diu ſe bene geſſerit*, as well for a moneth, or a year, or ſeven years, as in our late Aſſembly two ſucceſsively were more, (as I remember) ſo that this kind of Dioceſan or Provincial Biſhop, I think may well be yielded to for the Churches Order and Peace.

8. As to the eighth ſort of Biſhops, viz. [*The Dioceſan who aſſumeth the ſole Government of many Pariſh Churches both Presbyters and People*] as ten, or twelve, or twenty or more, as they uſed to do, even a whole Dioceſs, I take them to be intolerable.

and

and deſtructive to the Peace and happineſs of the Church, and therefore not to be admitted under pretence of Order or Peace, if we can hinder them. But of theſe we muſt ſpeak more when we come to the main Queſtion.

9. As for the ninth ſort of Biſhops, viz. [*A Dioceſan Ruling all the Presbyters, but leaving the Presbyters to Rule the People*] and conſequently taking to himſelf the ſole or chief Power of Ordination, but leaving Cenſures and Abſolution to them, except in caſe of Appeal to himſelf; I muſt needs ſay that this ſort of Epiſcopacy is very ancient, and hath been for many ages of very common reception, through a great part of the Church; but I muſt alſo ſay that I can ſee as yet no Divine inſtitution of ſuch a Biſhop taken for a fixed limited officer, and not the ſame that we ſhall mention in the eleventh place. But how far mens voluntary ſubmiſſion to ſuch, and conſent to be ruled by them, may authorize them, I have no mind to diſpute. Only this I will ſay, that though I allow not in my judgement this ſort of Epiſcopacy, yet I think it incomparably more tolereable than the eighth ſort, which taketh the whole Government of the people from the Presbyters to themſelves; And if I lived in a place where this Government were eſtabliſhed, and managed for God, I would ſubmit thereto, and live peaceably under it and do nothing to the diſturbance, diſgrace or diſcouragement of it. My reaſons Ile not ſtay to produce.

10. As for the tenth ſort of Biſhops, viz. *Archbiſhops, Metropolitans, Primates and Patriarchs, having not only the moderation of Synods but alſo either the ſole Government of all the Clergy, and cheif Government of all the people, or a Negative voice in all,* I am much more in judgement againſt them, then the former, and ſo much the more againſt them, by how much the larger their Juriſdiction is, for reaſons which I ſhall anon have occaſion to produce.

11. As for the eleventh ſort of Biſhops, that is [*ſuch as ſucceed the Apoſtles in the office of Preaching and Governing, to wit as unlimited univerſal Officers*] it is a great doubt among many whether any ſuch ſhould be? For though it be certain that ſuch were, yet we are in doubt whether they have any ſucceſſors. For my own part, I confeſs my ſelf ſatisfied in this, that the Apoſtles have Succeſſors, though not in their extraordinary Immediate man-

ner

ner of Miſſion, nor in their extraordinary Gifts of the Spirit, yet
in all that part of their office which is of ſtanding Neceſſity to
the Church : And I am ſatisfied that their general Miniſtry, or
ambulatory preaching as unfixed officers, and their Government of the Church by Office (ſuch as they did then uſe) are
of ſtanding Neceſſity to the Church : And therefore that as ſuch
unfixed general Officers, the Apoſtles *de jure* have Succeſſors. And
this I have formerly proved to you in my *Theſes de Polit. Eccle-
ſiaſt.* briefly thus.

Argument 1. Chriſt promiſed when he inſtituted this General
Office to be with them to the end of the world : therefore it was
his will that it ſhould continue to the end of the world, (*Mat.*
28 20, 21.) It was to a Miniſtry that were ſent to *preach the
Goſpel to every Creature, or to all the world, and to Diſciple Nations,*
that this promiſe was expreſly made ; therefore ſuch a Miniſtry
is to be continued.

Argum. 2. The ſame work and Neceſſity ſtill continueth :
For, 1. There are ſtill moſt of the Nations on earth unconverted.
2. The Converted and Congregated to be Confirmed and Governed, therefore the Office continueth.

Argum. 3. We can fetch no Argument from the Apoſtles Example or from any Precept or Promiſe to them , to prove the
ſucceſſion of fixed Paſtors, which is ſtronger then this by which
we prove the ſucceſſion of General unfixed Officers : therefore either we muſt yield to this, or by the ſame reaſons as we
deny it, we muſt deny the Miniſtry too : Which is not to be
done.

Argum. 4. The Apoſtles had many Aſſociates in this General
Office in their own times : Therefore it was not proper to them,
nor to ceaſe with them. *Barnabas, Sylas, Timothy, Titus, Apollo,*
with multitudes more in thoſe times, were unfixed General Officers, that went up and down to convert the world, and ſtaid
only to order and confirm the new gathered Churches, and then
went further ; ſometimes returning to review, preſerve, and
ſtrengthen their converts.

Argum. 5. If we can prove that ſuch unfixed General officers

*h. de Cham.
Gram. font
l. 1. p. 60.*

*Apoſtoli vere
erant Presbyte-
rii atq̃ ita
ſeipſos vocant.
—— Nulla
tamen loco
aſcripta eorum
funſtio. Evan-
geliſta quoq̃
Presbyteri
erant, ſed nulli
loco alligati.
Sic & multo
poſt à Demetrio
Alexandriæ
Epiſcopo Pan-
tænus, ab
Athanaſio Fru-
mentius, ordi-
nati, miſſiq̃ ut
Evangelium
per Indiam
prædicarent,
quod hodie
quoq̃ fieri vi-
demus ; Atq̃
utinam dili-
gentius fieret.
☞ Grotius
de Impe-
rio. p. 271.
And of the
Can. Concil.
Calced. 6.
againſt or-
daining Pres-
byters ſine ti-
tulo, he ſaith ;
[Quum ut re-*

*Ete notat Balſamon, Ipſe Canon indicio eſt aliter fieri ſolitum : Etiam poſt Calced. Synod. Juſti-
nianus Periodentarum meminit quorum & in Laodicena aliiſq̃ vetecribus Synodis eſt mentio. o.
Ibid. :*

were.

were by Chrift fettled in his Church, and that by fuch the Churches were in any fort then to be governed, then our caufe is good, till the repeal or revocation of this office and order be proved. Let them therefore that affirm fuch a revocation prove it : for till then, we have proved enough, in proving that once it was inftituted. But they cannot prove that revocation, I think, nor yet any Ceffation, or that the inftitution was but *pro tempore.*

Argum 6. It is not a tolerable thing to charge God with fuch a fudden Mutation of his Law or Order of Church Government without very certain proof. If we find Chrift fetling one way of Church Government, in his own time, and prefently after, for the firft age, it is a moft improbable thing that he fhould take that down again, and fet up another kind of Government to continue ever after. This feems to charge Chrift with fo great mutability, that it is not to be done without very clear proof. But fuch proof is not produced.

I know it is eafily proved that the immediate Miffion, and extraordinary meafure of the Spirit , for Miracles, tnogues , Infallible delivery of the doctrine of Chrift are ceafed : But this is nothing to the general office of Preaching or Governing the Church, which is of ftanding ufe.

So that I am fatisfied of this , that the Apoftles as General Preachers and Governours have fucceffors. But then I muft confefs my felf not fully fatisfied, what Governing Power it was that the Apoftles had over the Paftors of the Church. I find that when *Saravia,* and after him, the Difputants in the Ifle of *Wight,* do infift on this Argument from the way of Church Government by the Apoftles, that their Antagonifts do prefently grant the Minor [*that The Government of the Church at firft was by men authorized to Rule the Presbyters and their Churches.*] but they deny the Major, that [*the Government which was then in the Church fhould continue till now,*] becaufe it was by Apoftles, whofe Office they think ceafeth. Whereas I muft confefs I am unavoidably forced to yield the Major, that we muft have the fame kind of Government that was at firft inftituted, unlefs we had better proof of a change : For the ftablifhment of particular Churches and Presbyters was no change of the Apoftles power, feeing they gave not away their power to the Presbyters

nor

nor ceafed to have the fame Apoftolical power which they had
before. Only the Apoftles extraordinary Miſſion, Gifts and Priviledges, I confefs are ceaſed. But then I conceive that the
Minor which is fo eafily granted, *viz.* [*that the Apoſtles had the
Government of the particular Presbyters*] will hold more diſpute,
at leaſt as to the nature and degree of their power : and were I
as fully fatisfied about the Minor as I am of the Major, I muſt
by this one Argument be forced to be for the *Jus Divinum* of
Epiſcopacy. What at prefent feems truth to me, I ſhall lay down
in theſe Propoſitions.

Prop. 1. It is certain that the Apoſtles were general unfixed
Officers of Chriſt, having the care of the whole world committed to them within the reach of their natural Capacity : and
that their bufinefs was to take that courfe in the particular management of their work, as is moſt conducible to the propaga-
tion of the faith through the whole world : and that in all places
where they came, they had the fame power over the Churches
gathered, as the fixed Paſtors of thoſe Churches have. This much
is paſt doubt.

Prop. 2. It is as certain that common prudence required them
to make a convenient diſtribution of the work, and not go all
one way, and leave other places that while without the Goſpel.
But fome to go one way, and fome another, as moſt conduced to
the converfion of all the world.

Prop. 3. It is certain that the Apoſtles were not armed with
the fword, nor had a compulfive coercive power by fecular force;
but that their Government was only forcible on the Confcience,
and therefore only on the Confcientious, fo far as they were
fuch ; unlefs as we may call mens actual exclufion by the Church
and their defertion and mifery the effect of Government.

Prop. 4. It is moſt certain that they who had the extraordinary priviledge of being eye-witneſſes of Chriſts Miracles and
Life, and ear-witneſſes of his Doctrine, and had the extraordinary power of working Miracles for a Confirmation of their
Doctrine, muſt needs have greater * *Authority in mens Confciences* then other men, upon that very account, if there were no
other. So that even their Gifts and Priviledges may be (and
doubtlefs were) one ground at leaſt of that higher degree of
Authority, which they had above others. For in fuch a Rational

* Authority
is, 1. Rational
and of meer
Intereſt upon
Confenters.
2 Imperial,
over Diſſen-
ters alfo.

nal perswasive Authority which worketh only on the Conscience, the case is much different from the secular power of Magistrates. For in the former, even Gifts may be a ground of a greater measure of Power, in binding mens minds. And here is the greatest part of the difficulty that riseth in our way, to hinder us from improving the example of the Apostles, in that it is so hard to discern how much of their power over other Presbyters or Bishops was from their supereminency of Office and Imperial Authority, and how much was meerly from the excellency of their Gifts and Priviledges.

Prop. 5. Its certain that the Magistrates did not then second the Apostles in the Government of the Church, but rather hinder them by persecution. The excommunicate were not punished therefore by the secular power, but rather men were enticed to forsake the Church for the saving of their lives : so that worldly prosperity attended those without, and adversity those within : which further shewes that the force of Apostolical Government was on the Conscience, and it was not corrupted by an aliene kind of force.

Prop. 6. Yet had the Apostles a power of Miraculous Castigation of the very bodies of the Offenders, at least sometimes : which *Peter* exercised upon *Ananias* and *Sapphyra*, and *Paul* upon *Elymas*, and some think upon *Hymenæus* and ~~*Philetus*~~ *Alexander*, and those other that were said to be delivered up to Satan : certainly *Paul* [*had in readiness to revenge all disobedience*] 2 Cor. 10.6. which its like extendeth somewhat farther than to meer censures. But its most certain that the Apostle used not this power of hurting mens bodies ordinarily, but sparingly as they did other Miracles ; perhaps not according to their own wills, but the Holy Ghosts. So that this did not corrupt their Government neither, and destroy the Spirituality of it. Yet this makes it somewhat more difficult to us to improve the Apostles example, because we know not how much of their power upon mens Consciences might be from such penal Miracles.

Prop. 7. The Apostles had power to Ordain and send others to the work of the Ministry. But this only by the consent of the ordained, and of the people (before they could be compleat fixed Pastors) for they forced not any to go, or any people to entertain them. And it seemeth they did not Ordain singly, but

many

many together, *Acts* 14.23. *Timothy* had *his Gift by the lay-ing on of* Pauls *hands and of the hands of the Presbyterie,* 1 Tim. 4.14. and 2 Tim 1.6.

Prop. 8. It feems that each Apoftle did exercife a Govern-ment over the Churches which were once planted : but this was principally in order to well fetling and confirming them.

Prop. 9 No one Apoftle did appropriate a Diocefs to himfelf, and fay, *Here I am fole Governor, or am chief Governor* ; nor did they or could they forbid any others to Govern in their Diocefs : though, as is faid, they did agree to diftribute their work to the publike advantage, and not to be all in one place at once : but yet fucceffively they might.

Prop. 10. Nay its certain that they were fo far from being the fole Bifhops of fuch or fuch a Diocefs, that they had ufually fome more unfixed general Officers with them. *Paul* and *Bar-nabas* went together at firft : and after the Divifion, *Barnabas* and *Mark,* *Paul* and *Silas,* and fometimes *Timothy,* and fome-time *Epaphroditus,* and fometime others went together after-ward. And others as well as *James* were ufually at *Jerufalem* : and all thefe had a general power where they came. And it cannot be proved that *James* was Ruler of *Peter, Paul* and the reft when they were at *Jerufalem,* nor that he had any higher power then they.

Prop. 11. Yet it feems that the feveral Apoftles did moft look after thofe fame Churches which themfelves had been the inftru-ments of gathering, and that fome addition of refpect was due to *thofe* that had been fpiritual Fathers to them, above the reft, 1 *Cor.*4.15.

Prop. 12. It was therefore by the *General* Commiffion of Apoftlefhip that they Governed particular Churches *pro tempore* while they were among or neer them, and not by any *fpecial* Commiffion or Office of being the Diocefan or Metropolitane of this or that place. 1. It was below them, and a diminution of their honor to be fo affixed, and take the charge of any par-ticular Churches. 2. We find not that ever they did it. 3 If they had, then all the diforders and ungovernednefs of thofe Churches would be imputable to them, and therefore they muft be ftill with them as fixed Bifhops are, feeing they cannot go-vern them at fuch a diftance as makes them uncapable. 4. W'en

* If one were not meant of Confirmation or giving the Holy Ghoft, and the other of Ordinati-on, which I rather incline to think.

E

Peter

Peter drew *Barnabas* and many more to diffimulation, and almoft to betray the liberties of the Gentiles, *Paul* doth not fay, *This is my Diocefs, and I mujt be the Ruler here*: nor doth *Peter* plead this againft him, when *Paul* and *Barnabas* fell out, whether *Mark* fhould be taken with them or not; neither of them did plead a Ruling Authority, nor fay, *This is my Diocefs, or I am the fuperior Ruler*, but they produced their reafons, and when they could not agree concerning the validity of each others reafons, they feparated and took their feveral companions and waies.

Prop 13. It was not only the Apoftles, but multitudes more that were fuch general unfixed Minifters: as the feventy, *Barnabas, Silas, Epaphroditus. Timothy* and many others. And all thefe alfo had a Power of Preaching and Ruling where they came.

Prop. 14. None of thefe General Officers did take away the Government from the fixed Presbyters of particular Churches; nor kept a Negative vote in their own hands, in matters of Government: for if no fixed Bifhop (or Presbyter) could excommunicate any member of his Church without an Apoftle, then almoft all Churches muft remain polluted and ungovernej, through the unavoidable abfence of thofe twelve or thirteen men.

The Apoftles therefore did admonifh Paftors to do their duties, and when themfelves were prefent had power to do the like, and to cenfure Paftors or people that offended: but they did not take on them the full Government of any Church, nor keep a Negative vote in the Government.

Prop. 15. It feems utterly untrue that Chrift did deliver the Keyes only to the twelve Apoftles as fuch, and fo only to their Succeffors, and not the feventy Difciples or any Presbyters. For 1. The feventy alfo were General unfixed Officers, and not like fixed Presbyters or Bifhops: and therefore having a larger Commiffion muft have equal power. 2. The Apoftles were not fingle Bifhops as now they are differenced from others: but they were fuch as had more extenfive Commiffions, then thofe now called Arch Bifhops or Patriarchs. If therefore the Keyes were given them as Apoftles, or General Officers, then they were never given to Bifhops. For Bifhops as fixed Bifhops of

this

this or that Diocefs are not Succeffors of the Apoftles, who were Genetal unfixed Officers. 3. It is granted commonly by Papifts and Proteftants, that Presbyters have the power of the Keyes, though many of them think that they are limited to exercife them under the Bifhops, and by their Direction and Confent, (of which many School-men have wrote at large) 4. The Key of Excommunication is but a Minifterial Authoritative Declaration, that fuch or fuch a known Offendor is to be avoided, and to charge the Church to avoid Communion with him, and him to avod or keep away from the Priviledges of the Church; and this a meer Presbyter may do : he may authoritatively Declare fuch a man to be one that is to be avoided , and charge the Church and him to do accordingly. The like I may fay of Abfolution : if they belong to every authorized Paftor, Preacher and Church guide, as fuch, then not to a Bifhop only, but to a Presbyter alfo. And that thefe Keyes belong to more then the Apoftles and their Succeffors, is plain, in that thefe are infufficient Naturally to ufe them to their Ends. An Apoftle in *Ant och* cannot look to the cenfuring of all perfons that are to be Cenfured at *Athens, Paris, London*, &c. fo that the moft of the work would be totally neglected, if only they and their fuppofed Succeffors had the doing of it. I conclude therefore that the Keyes belong not only to Apoftles and their Succeffors in that General Office, no nor only to Diocefan Bifhops : for then Presbyters could not fo much as exercife them with the Bifhops in Confiftory, which themfelves of late allow.

Prop. 16. The Apoftles were fallible in many matters of fact, and confequently in the Decifions that depended thereupon; as alfo in the Prudential determination of the time and feafon and other Cirumftances of known duties. And thence it was that *Paul* and *Barnabas* fo difagreed even to a parting, where one of them was certainly in the wrong. And hence *Peter* withdrew from the uncircumcifion, and mifled *Barnabas* and others into the fame diffimulation fo far that he was to be blamed and withftood, *Gal.*2.

Prop. 17. In fuch Cafes of mifleading, an Apoftle was not to be follownd : no more is any Church-Governor now : but it is lawful and needful to diffent and withftand them to the face, and to blame them when they are to be blamed, for the Churches safety, as *Paul* did by *Peter, Galatians* 2. 1.

Prop. 18. In this Case the Apostles that by Office were of equal Authority, yet were unequal when the Reasons and Evidence of Gods mind which they produced was unequal : so that a Presbyter or Bishop that produceth better Reasons, is to be obeyed before another that produceth less Reason, or that Erreth. And the Bishop of another Church that produceth better Evidence of Gods mind, is to be obeyed before the proper Bishop of that same Church that produceth weaker and worse Evidence. Yea a private man that produceth Gods Word is to be obeyed before Bishops and Councils that go against it, or without it (in that case, where the word bindeth us :) so that, in all cases where Scripture is to determine, he that bringeth the best Scripture proof, is the chief Ruler, that is, ought chiefly to prevail. Though in the determination of meer Circumstances of duty, which Scripture determineth not, but hath left to Church-Guides to determine *pro re nati*, it may be otherwise, so that the Apostles power in determining matters of faith, was not as Church Governors, but as men that could produce the surest Evidence.

Prop. 19. It is not easie to manifest, whether every Presbyter *in prima instantia* be not an Officer to the Church Universal, before he be affixed to a particular Church ; and whether he may not go up and down over the world to exercise that office, where ever he hath admittance. And if so , what then could an Apostle have done by vertue of his meer office, without the advantage of his extraordinary abilities , and priviledges, which the Presbyter may not do ? May an Apostle charge the people where he comes to avoid this or that seducer or heretick ? so may any Preacher that shall come among them, and that by authority. May an Apostle Excommunicate the very Pastor of the place, and deprive him ? why what is that but to perswade the people , and Authoritatively require them, to avoid and withdraw from such a Pastor, if the Cause be manifest ? And so may any Pastor or Preacher that comes among them. For if (as *Cyprian* saith) it chiefly belong to the people even of themselves to reject and withdraw from such a Pastor, then a Preacher may by Authority perswade and require them to do their own duty, Yet I shall acknowledge, that though both may do the

the same duty, and both by Authority, yet possibly not both by equal Authority, but an Apostle *Majore authoritate*, and so may lay a stronger obligation on men to the same duty ; but the rest I determine not, but leave to enquiry.

Prop. 20. In making Laws or Canons to bind the Church which are now laid down in Scripture, the Apostles acted as Apostles, that is, as men extraordinarily Commissioned, illuminated and enabled infallibly to deliver Gods *will* to the world. And therefore herein they have no Successors.

In Conclusion therefore seeing that matters of meer Order and Decency depending on Circumstances sometime rationally mutable, sometime yearly, daily, hourly mutable, are not to be determined *Universally* alike to all the Church, nor to all a Nation, nor by those that are at too great a distance, but by the present Pastor, who is to manage the work, and being intrusted therewith; is the fittest Judge of such variable Circumstances : and seeing for standing Ordinances that equally belong to all ages and places, Gods word is perfect and sufficient without the Bishops Canons ; and seeing that Scripture is a perfect Law of God, and Rule of Christian faith ; and seeing that in the expounding of the Scripture, they that bring the best Evidence will beget the most Knowledge, and they that produce the clearest Divine Testimony, will beget most effectually a Divine belief, and those that are known to be of far greatest abilities in learning, experience and grace, and consent with the most of the Church, will procure more effectually an humane belief, then a weak unlearned unexperienced Pastor of our own ; therefore the Jurisdiction of supereminent Bishops, Metropolitans, Primates and Patriarchs, will appear to be reduced into so narrow a room, and written in so small a character, that he hath need of very quick sight that can read it, and humble men may be easily drawn to think, that the Unity, Happiness, and Safety of the Church lyeth not in it, and that if it had been only for Christ and not their own Greatness, there had not been such Contention and Division made about it in the Church, as there hath been.

TO

TO draw some of this which I have said into a narrower room, I shall briefly tell you what I could heartily wish both Magistrates and Ministers would speedily accomplish for the order and Peace of the Church in these matters.

1. I could wish that they would choose out the ablest Godly men, and let them be appointed General Teachers, and Guides, to call the uncalled, and to order, confirm, and so take care of the Churches that are gathered: And if by the Magistrates consent and their own, they divide their Provinces, it will be but meet. These I would have to go up and down to the several Parishes in their Provinces, and to have no particular Parishes of their own, nor to take the fixed Pastors power from them, but to take care that it be by themselves well exercised: And I would have the Magistrate keep his sword in his own hand, and let these prevail with mens consciences as far as they can; and in that way, if they would exceed their bounds, and arrogate any unjust power to themselves, we shall dissent and deny it them, and stand upon our ground, and deal with them upon equal terms, and so need not to fear them. And I have cause to think that neither Presbyterians nor all the Independents will be against such General Officers (Successors of the old ones) as I here describe : Nor the Presbyterians : for in *Scotland* they appointed and used such in the beginning, of their Reformation when they made Visitors of the particular Churches, and assigned to each their limited Provinces, and so they were Commissioners, to cast out Ministers, put in others, and plant Kirks, and they had several Superintendents, all which is to be seen in the Doctrine and Discipline of the Kirk of *Scotland* (printed not long agoe again.) And the Itinerant Comm[missioners] in *Wales* that were set there to go about preaching and Reforming, doth shew that their Judgements were not against the Power.

2. I could wish that every Parish Church may have one Eldership (where they may be had) or some Elders and Deacons, with one Constant Fixed, Perfect for Order and Unity.

3. I

3. I could wish that Ordination and Constitutions for Unity and Communion may be done only in Synods, less or greater : and that of many Presbyteries there may consist a *Classis*, as commonly called, and of many of those a Province: And that the Classical meeting may be frequent, and that some one, the fittest man, may be standing President of that *Classis* during life, except he deserve removal.

4. I could wish also that the Provincial Assembly (to be held once a quarter or half year in each County) may have the most able, discreet, godly Minister chosen to be the standing President also during life, unless he deserve removal.

So that here are four several sorts of Bishops that for Peace and Order I could consent to : to wit, 1. A General unfixed Superintendent. 2. A fixed Parochial Bishop President of that particular Presbytery. 3. A Classical Bishop, President of that Classis. 4. A Provincial Bishop, President of the Provincial Assembly. But there is no necessity of these.

5. Of the degree of their Power I said enough before.   It is intolerable they should have a Negative vote in Excommunications and Absolutions and such Government of the people (except the Parochial Bishop) save only in case of appeals, and there I leave it to each mans consideration, though I had rather they had none : But whether they should be admitted a Negative in Ruling the Pastors, I determine not.   Only in case of Ordination, I would have all resolve to do nothing (except in a case of Necessity) but when the President is One: and stop there; which will permit him *de facto* the use of his *Negative*, and yet trouble no mans conscience to acknowledge *de jure* that it *Must* so be; for to that none should be forced.

This much I could willingly yield to for reconciliation and unity : And I doubt not but I shall be sufficiently reproached by some for yielding so far, and by others for yielding no further.

Essentiale fuit, quod ex Dei ordinatione perpetua; necesse fuit, est & erit ut Presbyterio quispiam & loco & dignitate primus actioni gubernandæ præsit, cum eo quod ipsi divinitus attributum est jure. Beza de Minist. Evang. Grad. cap. 23.

AND now at last after these (not needless) preparations, I come to the main Question it self, *Whether it be Necessary or Profitable for the right Order or Peace of the Churches, to restore the extruded Episcopacy*? And this I deny, and having said so much already for explication, shall presently give you the Reasons of my denyal; in which the rest of the necessary explication will be contained.

Argument 1. *That sort of Prelacy or other Government which destroyeth the End of Government, and is certainly inconsistent with the Necessary Government and discipline to be exercised in the Churches, is not to be restored, under pretence of the Churches Order or Peace* (nor can be consistent with its right Order and Peace.) *But such is the Episcopacy which was of late exercised in England, and is now laid by.* Therefore, *&c.*

The Major needs no proof; for few Christians I think, will deny it. If Episcopacy as lately here exercised, be the certain excluder of Government it self and Christs discipline, while it only retains the empty name, then doubtless it is not to be restored.

The Minor I prove thus. If there be a very Natural Impossibility that the late English Episcopacy though in the hands of the best men in the world , should Govern the Churches as Christ hath appointed , and as they should and may otherwise be Governed; then the foresaid inconsistency and destructiveness is apparent. But that there is such a Natural Impossibility for the late English Episcopacy to Govern the Church , thus I shall prove. 1. By shewing you what is undoubtedly necessary in Christs Government; 2. And then what was the late English Episcopacy; and then 3. The Impossibility will appear of it self when both these are opened and compared together without any more ado.

1. And 1. It is past controversie among us, that Church Governours should watch over each particular soul in their flock, and instruct the ignorant, admonish the faln, convince gainsayers, counterwork seducers among them, seek to reclaim the wandring, strengthen the weak, comfort the distressed, openly rebuke the open obstinate offendors, and if they repent not, to require the Church to avoid their Communion, and to take cognisance of their cause before they are cut off: as also to Absolve the penitent, yea to visit the sick (who are to send for the Elders of the Church :) and to pray with and for them, *&c.* yea and to go before them in the worship of God. These are the acts of Church Government that Christ hath appointed , and which each faithful Shepherd must use, and not Excommunication, and

other

other Cenſures and Abſolution alone.

2. But if they could prove that Church Government containeth only Cenſures and Abſolution, yet we ſhall eaſily prove it
Impoſſible for the late Engliſh Epiſcopacy to do that. For, 3. It
is known to our ſorrow that in moſt Pariſhes there are many
perſons, and in ſome greater Pariſhes very many, that have lived, common open ſwearers, or drunkards, and ſome whoremongers, common ſcorners of a godly life, and in many more of thoſe
offences, for which Scripture and the ancient Canons of the
Church do excommunicate men, and we are commanded with
ſuch no not to eat. And its too well known what numbers of
Hereticks and Seducers there are, that would draw men from
the faith, whom the Church-Governours muſt after the firſt and
ſecond admonition reject. 4. And then its known what a deal
of work is Neceſſary with any one of theſe, in hearing accuſations, examining Witneſſes, hearing the defendants, ſearching
into the whole cauſe, admoniſhing, waiting, re-admoniſhing,
&c. 5. And then its known of how great Neceſſity, and moment all theſe are to the honour of the Goſpel, the ſouls of the
offendors, to the Church, to the weak, to them without, &c. So
that if it be neglected, or unfaithfully mannaged, much miſchief
will enſue. Thus in part we ſee what the Government is.

Next let us ſee what the Engliſh Epiſcopacy is. And 1. For the
extent of it, a Dioceſs contained many ſcore or hundred Pariſhes,
and ſo many thouſands of ſuch ſouls to be thus Governed. Perhaps ſome Dioceſſes may have five hundred thouſand ſouls, and it
may be *London* Dioceſs nearer a million. And how many thouſand of theſe may fall under ſome of the forementioned acts of
Government, by our ſad experience we may conjecture.

2. Moreover the Biſhop reſideth, if not at *London* (as many of them did) yet in his own dwelling, many miles, perhaps
twenty or thirty from a great part of his Dioceſs, ſo that moſt
certainly he doth not ſo much as know by face, name, or report
the hundreth, perhaps the thouſandth, or perhaps the ~~ſecond~~ or 2000ᵗʰ
1000ᵗʰ ~~third thouſandth~~ perſon in his Dioceſs. Is it Poſſible then for
him to watch over them, or to underſtand the quality of the perſon and fact ? In Church Caſes the quality of the perſon is of ſo
much moment, that without ſome knowledge of it, the bare
knowledge of the fact ſometimes will not ſerve.

F

3. And

* I know Bishop *usher* in his papers to the King, doth say that by the Order of the Church of *England*, all Presbyters are charged (in the form of Ordering of Priests) to administer the Discipline of Christ : But the Bishops understood that only of their publishing their Censures. For no such Administration was known among us, or allowed: Nor would they suffer men to suspend them from the Sacrament, as the Rubrick in the Common Prayer Book requireth.

*3. And then it is known that the English Episcopacy denyeth to the Presbyters all power of Excommunication and Absolution, unless to pronounce it as from the Bishop when he hath past it : And they deny him also all power so much as of calling a sinner to open Repentance, which they called Imposing penance : and also they denied all power of denying the Lords Supper to any without the Bishops censure, except in a sudden case, and then they must prosecute it after at the Bishops Court; and there render the Reason of that suspension : So that the trouble, danger, labour, time would be so great that would be spent in it, that scarce one Minister of a hundred did venture on it once in seven and seven years, except only to deny the Sacrament to a man that would not kneel , and that they might do easily and safely.

4. And then Consider further , that if the Minister should be one of an hundred, and so diligent as to accuse and prosecute all the open scandalous offendors of his Parish, before the Bishops Court, that so he might procure that act of Government from them, which he may not perform himself, it would take up all his time, and perhaps all would not serve for half the work, considering how far he must ride, how frequently he must attend, &c. And then all the rest, or most of the Pastoral work must be neglected, to the danger of the whole Congregation.

5. It is a great penalty to an innocent man to travail so far to the trial of his Cause. But the special thing that I note is this, that it is Naturally Impossible, for the Bishop to hear, try and judge all these causes, yea or the fifth or hundredth of them, or in some places one of five hundred. Can one man hear so many hundred as in a day must be before him, if this discipline be faithfully executed ? By that time that he hath heard two or three Causes, and examined Witnesses , and fully debated all, the rest can have no hearing ; and thus unavoidably the work must be undone. It is as if you set a Schoolmaster to teach ten or twenty thousand Schollars? Must they not be needs untaught ? Or as if you set one Shepherd to look to two or three hundred several flocks of Sheep, that are every one of them three or four miles asunder, and some of them fourty miles from some of the rest. Is it any wonder then if many of them be lost ?

6. But

6. But what need we further witnefs then the fad experience of the Church of late ? Are we not fure that difcipline lay unexercifed, and our Congregations defiled, and Gods Laws and the old Canons were dead letters, while the Bifhops keep up the lame and empty name of Governours ? How many drunkards, fwearers, whoremongers, raylers, Extortioners, fcorners at a godly life did fwarm in almoft every Town and Parifh ? and they never heard of difcipline, except it were one Adulterer or fornicator once in feven years within twenty miles compafs (where I was acquainted) that ftood in a white fheet in the Chuch: We know that there was no fuch Matter as Church Government exercifed to any purpofe, but all left undone, unlefs it were to undoe a poor Difciplinarian (as they therefore fcornfully called them) that blamed them for neglect of Difcipline. For my part, the Lord my Judge knows, that I defire to make the matter rather better then it was, then worfe then it was ; and I folemnly profefs that for the Peace of the Church, I fhould fubmit to almoft any body that would but do the work that is to be done. Here is ftriving between the Epifcopal, Presbyterian and Independent, who it is that fhall Govern. I would make no great ftirr againft any of them all that would but do it effectually. Let it be done, and its not fo much matter by whom it is done, as it is to have it lie undone. But I can never be for that party that neither did the work, when they might, nor poffibly can do it. To be for them, is to confent that all fhould be undone; and that Drunkards and Railers and all wicked perfons fhall continue fo ftill, or continue members of our Churches in all their obftinacy : and that there fhall be nothing but the name of Government and Cenfure without the thing. Its hard making men of Confcience believe the contrary that have had the triall that we have had : If where good men were Bifhops thus it was, what hope of better by that way ? We cannot fhut our eyes againft fo great experience. And certainly thofe Learned men among us that think fo much Difcipline may ferve turn to all the Congregations in the whole Diocefs, as the Bifhop can perform or have a Negative Vote in, do too manifeftly fhew that they * are lefs friends to real godlinefs, and greater friends to fin,

* Its an eafie matter to preach or write a ftrict Leffon ; but they that would practically when they have done open a gap to licentioufnefs, and overthrow all Difcipline almoft, will hardly perfwade men that they mean as they

teach, or are themfelves fuch as they defcribe, or really would promote a holy life ; efpecially when Scorners at a godly life were favoured more then the practifers of it.

and

and care too little for the matter it self while they contend about
the manner or agent, then serious Christians should do. If men
once plainly shew themselves meer formalists , and would set up
a scarecrow, and pull down all true Discipline, by setting up
one man to do the work of five hundred , and making the exercise of it impossible , what serious Christian will ever take their
part ? Not I while I breath : Who can choose but see that such
do seek their dignity, and Lordships, and worldly Mammon
more then the Kingdom of Christ. I know they will be angry
with me for this language ; but so are most impenitent persons
with reproofs. I would advise all of them that survive to lay
to heart before the Lord , what they did in undertaking such
an impossible task , and leaving so many souls and Congregations without Christs remedy, and suffering the Churches to
be so foul, while they had the Beesom in their hands.

This being so manifest that it is impossible for an English Bishop to Govern as they undertook so many Congegations, I may
well next argue from the mischiefs that follow.

Argum. 2.   That Government which gratifieth the Devil
             and wicked men, is not to be restored under any
pretence of the Order or Peace of the Church : But such was the
English Episcopacy; therefore, &c.

The Major is unenyable, supposing that it do not this by an
avoidable accident, but by natural Necessity , as I have proved.
I confess some of the Men were so Learned and Good men, that
I think few men honour their names more then my self. But it
is the way of Government that I have spoke of.

And for the Minor, it is as plain from experience, and the argument before used. If it necessarily exclude the exercise of Christs
discipline from most Congregations, then doth it gratifie Satan :
But, &c.

And if it keep wicked obstinate sinners from the power of
discipline, then doth it gratifie sinners in their Sins, and consequently please Satan. But this it doth : therefore, &c.

Who knows not (for it cannot be denied) that the generality
of the rabble of ignorant persons, worldlings, drunkards, haters
of Godliness, &c. are very zealous for Episcopacy, whilest multitudes

tudes of truly conscientious people have been against it ? And who knows not that they both fetcht their chief Motives from experience ? The ungodly found that Bishops let them keep their sins, and troubled them not with this preciseness, but rather drove away the precise preachers and peop'e whom they abhorred. And the godly people that disliked Ep scopacy, did it principally on the same experience, observing that they befriended the wicked, at least by preserving them from the due rod of discipline ; but exercised their zeal against them that scrupled or questioned at least their own standing or assumed power, or the abuse of it. And then further,

---

Argum. 3. *That Government which unavoidably causeth separations and divisions in the Church, is not to be restored under any pretence of its Order and Peace ? But such is the English Episcopacy ? therefore ; &c.*

I know the clean contrary is strongly pretended, and they tell us that we may see how Episcopacy kept men in Unity, by the many Sects that since are risen. But let it be observed, 1. That these Sects were hatched in the separation which was caused by themselves. 2. That the increase hath been since there was no Government at all. 3. It was not Episcopacy, but the Magistrates Sword whose terror did attend it, that kept under heresies in that measure that they were : Had Episcopacy stood on its own legs, without the support of secular force, so that it might have workt only on the conscience, then you should have seen more Sects then now. Do you think that if Episcopacy were in *Scotland* in the Case as Presbytery is now, without the Sword to enforce it, that it would keep so much Unity in Religion as is there ? Its known in *France* and other places that Presbytery hath kept more Unity, and more kept out Heresies and Schisms, even without the Sword, then Episcopacy hath done with it. 4. But the thing that I speak of is undenyable, that it was the pollution of our Churches that caused the Separatists in the Bishops dayes to withdraw. This was their common cry against us, Your Churches bear with Drunkards, Whoremongers, Railers, open Scorners at Godliness, with whom the Scripture bids us not eat ; And we could not deny it : for the Bishops did keep

See my Preface to Mr. *Pierce* of *Grotius* Religion. Were Prelacy now tolerated only as Presbyterie and the Congregational way are, doth any man think it would cast or keep out Heresies ?

F 3

it fo, by keeping out all effectual Difcipline. Only we told them, that it was the Prelates fin, and not theirs that could not help it, and that a polluted Church might be a true Church. And fo the Difciplinarian Non-Conformifts were fain by many painful writings to fupprefs the fpirit of feparation, or elfe it had been like to have overwhelmed all; Mr. *John Paget*, Mr. *Bradfhaw*, Mr. *Arthur Hilderfham*, Mr. *John Ball*, Mr. *Brightman*, Mr. *Paul Bains*, Mr. *Dod*, Mr. *Parker*, Dr. *Ames*, and many other fuch, were fain to make it a great part of their bufinefs, to quench the fire of feparation, which even their perfecutors kindled by the exclufion of Difcipline. And yet the fenfe of the Churches uncleannefs was fo deep in mens minds, that it had bred fuch abundance of difcontended humors, that they eafily broke out, and turned into this diforderly fwarm which we have feen, as foon as the wars had but given them liberty.

And even to this day it is the uncleannefs of our Churches, (wherein I would the Paftors were wholly innocent) which maintaineth much of the feparation, among many fober godly men. For the Churches were left fo polluted by the Bifhops, that in moft places the Presbyters dare fcarce go roundly about the cure, unlefs they had the help of the fword, wherein yet for my part I think them deeply finful.

Argum. 4. THat Epifcopacy which degradeth all the Presbyters in the Diocefs, or caufeth them to fufpend the exercife of an Effential part of their Office, is not to be reftored under any pretence of right order, or peace. But fuch was the late Englifh Epifcopacy : therefore.

I confels this is the fecond inconvenience which followeth it, which I think utterly intolerable, where there is any pofsibility of a remedy. The Major I fuppofe will be granted. For though an Office may be unexercifed for a time on fome fpecial reafon, yet if it be ftatedly fufpended, and that fufpenfion eftablifhed by Law or Cuftom, during the life of the Minifter, this is plainly a deftroying or nulling of the Office it felf, and not to be endured.

And that it is not to be endured appeareth thus ; 1. Becaufe the Office of the Presbyter is of Divine Inftitution, and therefore
fore

fore not to be nulled by man. I never yet read or heard of any more but one Divine of any reputation who denyed that Presbyters as now called are appointed in the Scriptures, and I think, that one hath deſtroyed his cauſe by it, of which more anon. 2. Becauſe the Church cannot with any ſafety ſpare the Office of the Presbyters, becauſe they are many, perhaps many hundred to one Prelate : and if ſo many of Chriſts Officers be laid by, it is eaſie to ſee what loſs the vineyard and harveſt may ſuſtain.

The Minor I prove thus. That Epiſcopacy which taketh from the Presbyters the power of Church Government, and alloweth them only the power of preaching and adminiſtring Sacraments, and thoſe other parts of the work which they diſtinguiſh from Government, do thereby deſtroy the very Office of the Presbyters (and ſo degrade or ſuſpend them) But the late Engliſh Epiſcopacy taketh from the Presbyters the power of Church Governing ; &c. therefore.

The Antecedent is well known by thoſe that know their Canons, claim and conſtant practice in *England*, till the time of their excluſion. That the Conſequence is currant appeareth thus. Church-Government is as real and as eſſential a part of the Presbyters work and office as any other whatſoever. Therefore they that take this from him, do deſtroy his Office.

The Antecedent is proved thus : if thoſe Texts of Scripture which mention the Office of Presbyters, *Acts* 20. and 14.23. and many other places do ſpeak of Presbyters as now underſtood, and not of Prelates, then Ruling is as much eſſential to their office as Preaching. This is proved, 1. From the expreſs words of the ſeveral Texts, which make them Overſeers of the flock, *Acts* 20. 28. and to be over the people in the Lord, to whom they are to ſubmit, 1 *Theſ*. 5. 12, 13. and Rulers of them, whom they muſt obey, as well as Preachers to them, *Heb* 13. 7. 17. 24. 1 *Tim*. 3, 4, 5. 2. Its proved from common Conſent. For, 1. Thoſe that think theſe Texts ſpeak of Presbyters as now underſtood, do moſt commonly confeſs this ſenſe of the Text, *viz.* that it makes them Rulers ; only ſome of them add, that themſelves muſt be Ruled by the Biſhops. 2. He that denyeth theſe Texts to ſpeak of ſuch Presbyters, doth confeſs that thoſe of whom it doth ſpeak, are certainly Rulers of the Church.

And then I aſſume : But the general vote of almoſt all Expoſitors

Functiones in Ecclesiâ perpetuæ ſunt duæ ; Presbyterorum & Diaconorum : Presbyteros voco cum omni Eccleſiâ veteris, qui Ecceſiam paſcunt verbi prædicatione, Sacramentis & Clavibus ; quæ ſine Divino ſunt individua : (he meaneth inſeparable) ſo that its inſeparable from a Presbyter to have the Power of the Keyes. *Grot. de Imperio, pag.267 c.10.*

Paſtorum ergo eſt Ordinare Paſtores: neq́; id officium eis competit q̄ ta hujus aut illius Eccleſiæ Paſtores ſunt, ſed qui miniſtri Eccleſiæ Catholicæ. Grotius ibid. p.273.

Paſtores tales (ubi nulli ſunt Epiſcopi) etſi cum meris Presbyteris id Commune habent quod aliis non præſunt; habent tamen illud Epiſcopale, quod nemini Paſtori ſubſunt; atq̄; adeo dubium eſt, Epiſcopiſne, an meris Presbyteris rectius aunumerentur. Idem pag.320.

ſitors old and new, Epiſcopal and others from the Apoſtles daies till now, as far as we can know by their writings, did take theſe Texts, at leaſt many of them, to ſpeak of ſuch Presbyters: and I think the new expoſition of one man, is not to be taken against the Expoſition of the whole ſtream of Expoſitors in all ages, without better reaſon to evince them to have erred, then any I have yet ſeen produced. At leaſt, all the Epiſcopal Divines except that one man, and thoſe that now follow his new Expoſition, muſt yield to what I ſay, upon the authority of theſe Texts.

But if this Divine were in the right, and none of theſe Texts be ſpoken of Presbyters, yet I make good my Antecedent thus.

For 1. If Presbyters be of humane Inſtitution, then neither Preaching or Ruling is any Eſſential part of their Office by Divine Inſtitution; becauſe they have none ſuch: and therefore I may ſay one is as eſſential as the other : that is, neither is ſo. But yet of their humanly inſtituted Office, it is as eſſential a part ſtill : for if it be true, that there were no Presbyters in the Church till about *Ignatius* his daies, yet its certain that when they were inſtituted (whether by God or man) they were as truly made Rulers as Preachers. And therefore we find their *Ignatius* ſtill cal'ing on the people to obey the Presbyters as well as the Biſhops. And *Hierom* tells us, (*Epiſt. ad Evagr.*) how long the Presbyters governed the Churches *Communi Conſilio*, by Common Counſel or Conſent, and how themſelves at *Alexandria* choſe out one and made him their Biſhop : and *Cyprian* tells us enough of the Presbyters ruling in Council or Conſiſtory with the Biſhop in his time : ſo that he would do nothing without the Presbyters. Much more proof may eaſily be brought of this, but that I find it now acknowledged, and ſo it is needleſs. I will not go far, but only note a few Canons, eſpecially of the fourth Council of *Carthage*. Can.23. is, *Ut Epiſcopus nullius Cauſam audiit abſque præſentia Clericorum ſuorum; alioquin irrita erit ſententia Epiſcopi, niſi Clericorum præſentia confirmetur.*

Can.22. *Epiſcopus ſine Conſilio Clericorum ſuorum Clericos non ordinet ; ita ut Civium aſſenſum, & conniventiam, & teſtimonium quærat.*

Can. 29. *Epiſcopus ſi Clerico vel laico crimen impoſuerit, deducatur ad probationem in Synodum.*

Can.

Can. 32. Irrita erit donatio Episcoporum, vel venditio, vel com-
mutatio rei Ecclesiasticæ, absq; conniventia & subscriptione cleri-
corum.

   Can. 34. Ut Episcopus in quælibet loco sedens stare Presbyterum
non patiatur.

   Can. 35. Ut Episcopus in Ecclesia in confessu Presbyterorum
sublimior sedeat : Intra domum verò collegam se Presbyterorum
esse cognoscat.

   Can. 36. Presbyteri qui per diæceses Ecclesias regunt, non à qui-
buslibet, &c.

   Can. 37. Diaconus ita se Presbyteri ut Episcopi Ministrum
esse cognoscat.

Here you see that Bishops may not Ordain, hear any cause, accuse a Clergy man or Lay-man, not give, sell, or Change any Church goods, without the Presbyters : and that he is their Collegue , and must not let them stand if he sit, and that they Rule the Churches through the Diocesses, and that the Deacons are Servants as well to them as to the Bishop. *Aurelius* and *Augustine* were in this Council.

If they that think it uncertain whether Presbyters be mentioned in the New Testament, and that think they began about *Ignatius* his time, do mean that yet they were of Divine Apostolical Institution, then they strike in with the Papists in making the Scriptures to be but part of Gods word, and insufficient to reveal all Divine institutions about his Church-Government, and Worship, and so we must look for the rest in uncertain Tradition. Nay I know not of any Papist to my best remembrance that ever reckoned up the Office of Presbyters under their meer unwritten Traditions. *Communi Presbyterorum Concilio gubernabuntur,* saith *Hier.* See *Grotius ubi sup. p. 354, 355, 356, 357.* proving that Prelacy is not of Divine precept, and that of old many Cites had many Churches and Bishops in each: and that Presbyters , except ordination (as *Hier.*

If they say that they are of Ecclesiastical Episcopal Institution, not by inspired Apostles, but by Ordinary Bishops, then 1. They make all Presbyters to be *jure Episcopali,* and Bishops only and their Superiours to be *jure Divino,* as the Italians in the Council of *Trent* would have had all Bishops to depend upon the Pope : But in this they go far beyond them ; for the Italian

and *Chrysost.*) may do all that a Bishop ; and he addeth, *Quid obstat quo minus id ita interpretemur ut Presbyteri neminem potuerint ordinare contempto Episcopo ?*

   And pag. 359. He shews that where Bishops are not , Presbyters do rightly ordain. See the [illegible]

Papifts themfelves thought *Presbyterie jure Divino*. 2. Either
they may be changed by Bifhops who fet them up, or not : If
they may be taken down again by man, then the Church may
be ruined by man ; and fo the Bifhops will imitate the Pope ;
Either they will Reign, or Chrift fhall not Reign, if they can hinder it : Either they will lead the Church in their way , or Chrift
fhall have no Church : If man cannot take them down, then
1. It feems man did not Inftitute them ; for why may they not
alter their own inftitutions ? 2. And then it feems the Church
hath univerfal ftanding, unchangeable Inftitutions, Offices and
binding Laws of the Bifhops making : And if fo, are not the
Bifhops equal to the Apoftles in Law making, and Church Ordering ? and are not their Laws to us as the word of God , and
that word infufficient ? and every Bifhop would be to his Diocefs, and all to the whole Church , what the Pope would be to
the whole.

    3. Moreover , how do they prove that ever the Apoftles
gave power to the Bifhops to inftitute the order of Presbyter.e?
I know of no text of Scripture by which they can prove it And
for Tradition, we will not take every mans word that faith he
hath tradition for his conceits, but we require the proof. The
Papifts that are the pretended keepers of Tradition, do bring
forth none as meerly unwritten, but for their *ordines inferiores,*
and many of them, for Bifhops as diftinct from the Presbyters;
but not for Presbyters themfelves. And Scripture they can plead
none ; For if they mention fuch texts where *Paul* bids *Titus*
ordain Elders in every City, *&c.* they deny this to be meant of
Elders as now, but of Prelates whom *Titus* as the Primate or Metropolitane was to ordain: And if it be meant of Elders, then
they are found in Scripture, and of Divine Apoftolical Inftitution.

    4. If they were Inftituted by Bifhops after the Scripture was
written , was it by one Bifhop, or by many ? If by one, then
how came that one to have Authority to impofe a new Inftitution on the univerfal Church ?· If by many, either out of Council, or in ; if out of Council, it was by an accidental falling into
one mind and way, and then they are but as fingle men to the
Church : and therefore ftill we ask, how do they bind us ? If by
many in Council, 1. Then let them tell us what Council it was.

that Instituted Presbyterie, when and where gathered, and where we may find their Canons, that we may know our order, and what Authors mention that Council. 2. And what authority had that Council to bind all the Christian world, to all ages? If they say it bound but their own Churches, and that age; then it seems the Bishops of *England* might for all that have nulled the Order of Presbyters there. But O miserable *England* and miserable world, if Presbyters had done no more for it, then Prelates have done!

I conclude therefore that the English Prelacy either degraded the Presbyters, or else suspended totally an essential part of their office: for themselves called them *Rectors*, and in ordaining them said, [*Receive the Holy Ghost: Whose sins thou dost remit they are remitted, whose sins thou dost retain they are retained*] And therefore they delivered to them the Power of the Keyes of opening and shutting the Kingdom of Heaven; which themselves make to be the opening and shutting of the Church, and the Governing of the Church by Excommunication and Absolution: And therefore they are not fit men to ask the Presbyters; *By what authority they Rule the Church, by binding and loosing,* when themselves did expresly as much as in them lay, confer the Power on them: And we do no more then what they bid us do in our Ordination; Yea they thereby make it the very work of our office: For the same mouth, at the same time that bid us [*take authority to preach the word of God*] did also tell us that *whose sins we remit or retain they are remitted or retained:* and therefore if one be an Essential, or true integral part at least of our office, the other is so too. From all which it is evident, that if there were nothing against the English Prelacy, but only this that they thus suspend or degrade all the Presbyters in *England*, as to one half of their office, it is enough to prove that they should not be restored under any pretence whatsoever of Order or Unity.

Argum.

Argum. 5. THat Episcopacy which giveth the Government of the Church, and management of the Keys of Excommunication and Absolution into the hands of a few Lay-men, while they take them from the Presbyters, is not to be restored under any pretence of Unity or Peace: But such was the English Prelacy: therefore, &c.

The Major is plain: because it is not Lay-men that are to be Church Governours, as to Ecclesiastical Government: This is beyond Question with all save the Congregational, and they would not have two or three Lay men chosen, but the whole Congregation to manage this business.

The Minor is known by common experience, that it was the Chancelor in his Court, with his assistants and the Register, and such other meer Lay-men, that managed this work. If it be said, that they did it as the Bishops Agents and Substitutes, and therefore it was he that did it by them; I answer, 1. The Law put it in the Chancellors, and the Bishops could not hinder it. 2. If the Bishops may delegate others to do their work, then it seems Preaching and Ruling, Excommunicating and Absolving may as well be done by Lay-men as Clergy men: Then they may commission them also to administer the Sacraments: And so the Ministry is not necessary for any of these works, but only a Bishop to depute Lay-men to do them; which is false and confusive.

I have, it and can produce it under the Kings own hand and seal, wherein he forbids that any Church man or Priest in holy orders should be a Chancellor: And this was the occasion of all the corruptions, &c. They must for their own advantage and profit have instruments according'y: So the Registers, Proctors, Apparators, were *pessimum genus hominum*: G. *Goodman*, Bishop of *Gloc.* in the Preface to his Two Mysteries, &c.

Argum. 6. THat Episcopacy which necessarily overwhelmeth the souls of the Bishops with the most hainous guilt, of neglecting the many thousand souls whose charge they undertake, is not to be restored for Order or Peace (For men are not to be overwhelmed with such hainous sin on such pretences) But such is the English Prelacy: and that not accidentally, through the badness of the men only, but unavoidably through the greatness of their charge, and the Natural Impossibility of their undertaken work. How grievous a thing it is to have the blood of so many thousands charged on them, may soon appear. And that man that undertakes himself the Government of two or
three

three, or five hundred thousand souls that he never seeth or knoweth, nor can possibly so Govern, but must needs leave it undone (except the shadow of a Government which is committed to a Lay Chancellor,) doth willfully draw this fearful Guilt upon himself.

Argum. 7.   THat Episcopacy which is the product of Proud Ambition and Arrogancy, contrary to the express command of Christ, is not to be restored for Order or Peace. But such is the late English Prelacy: therefore, &c.

The Major is undoubted. The Minor is proved thus. Were it not for proud Ambition men would not strive to have the doing of more work then an hundred times as many are able to do, and the answering before God for as many souls: But the English Prelates did strive to have the work and account of many hundreds: therefore, &c.

The Minor is proved and known by experience. And the Major is proved thus. 1. From the common averseness that all men have to labour, excessive oppressing labour, and that spiritual too. 2. From the self-love that is naturally in all: No man can naturally and rationally desire that which would tire him, oppress him, and finally damn him, without great repentance, and the speciall mercy of God, unless by the power of some lust that draweth him to it. 3. And common prudence will teach men not to thrust themselves into impossible undertakings. If we see a man desirous to have the Rule of a whole County under the Prince, and that there should be no Justice of Peace, or other Magistrate to Rule there but he, though he know that he must answer it upon his life, if the County be not well Ruled, as to the punishing of all the known drunkards, swearers, adulterers &c. in the County; may not any man see that Ambition makes this man in a manner besides himself, or else he would never set so light by his own life, as certainly and willfully to cast it away, by undertaking a work which he knoweth many men are unable to perform: And Ambition it must needs be, because Honour and Preheminency is the bait and thing contended for, and there is nothing else to do it. And how expressly doth Christ forbid this to his ministers, saying, &c.

not be so : but he that will be the greatest shall be the servant of all] Luke 22.26. As the old Rimer hath it [*Christus dixit quodam loco ; Vos non sic, nec dixit joco: dixit suis ergo isti Cujus sunt ? non certè Christi*] Speaking of the Prelates. I own not the Censure, but I own Chrits prohibition. Certainly the Honour is but the appendix for the work sake, and the work is the first thing and the main of the office. And I would know whether they would strive thus for the work and the terrible account, without the honour and worldly gain. Nay do they not destroy the work, while they quarrel for the doing of it, for the honor sake ? If it were the Churches good and the work that they so much minded, they would contend that so many should have the doing of it as are necessary thereto, and not that none should do it but they. He that would turn all the labourers out of the Harvest saving himself, in all this County, that he may maintain his own priviledge, I should think doth not much mind the good of the owner, or the well doing of the work, or his own safety, if he were to answer for all upon his life.

Argum. 8. THat *Episcopacy which so far gratifieth lazy Mi i-sters as to ease them of the most painful, troublesom and hazardous part of their work, is not to be restored for order or unity : but such was the late English Prelacy : therefore, &c.*

The Major is undoubted. The Minor is before proved as to the work it self. And as to the quality and consequents, experience putteth it past all doubt, that the work of Government and Oversight, is incomparably more troublesom then the preaching of a Sermon, Baptizing, administring the Lords Supper, and praying with them. When we come to touch men by personal reproof, and make that publike, and that for disgraceful sins, and suspend or excommunicate them if they be obstinate, usually we do not only turn their hearts against us, but they rage against us, and could even be revenged on us with the cruellest revenge. We find that all the Preaching in the world doth not so much exasperate and enrage men, as this Discipline. I can Preach the most cutting and convincing truths, in as close a manner as I am able, to notorious wicked livers, and they will bear it patiently, and say it was a good Sermon, and some of them say

that

that they care not for hearing a man that will not tell them of their fins. And yet call them to an open confeffion of thefe fins in the Congregation, or proceed to cenfure them, and they will rage againft us as if we were their mortal enemies. The Bifhops let all thefe men (almoft) alone; and therefore never exafperated them : and fo now they rage the more againft us, and love the Bifhops the better, becaufe they were never fo troubled by them.

And here I cannot but note, how groundlefs that accufation is of fome Prelatical men againft the Confcionable adverfaries of their way, when they fay, the Presbyters would fain have the Reins of Government in their own hand : which may be true of the unconfcionable, that know not what it is that they undertake: but for others, it is all one as to fay, They would fain have all the trouble, hatred and danger to themfelves. Thefe Objecters fhew their own minds, and what it is that they look at moft themfelves : and therefore think others do fo : its dear bought honour that is purchafed at fuch rates of labour and danger. I here folemnly profefs for my own part, that if I know my heart, I am fo far from thinking it a defirable thing to Rule, much lefs to Rule a Diocefs, that if I might fo far gratifie my carnal defires, and were not under the bond of Gods Commands, and fo were it not for fear of finning and wronging mens fouls that are committed to my charge, I would give, if I had it, many thoufand pounds, that I might but Preach, Pray, Read, Baptize, administer the Lords Supper, though I did more then I do in them, and be wholly freed from the care and trouble of overfight and government of this one Congregation, which is further required. O how quiet would my mind be, were I but fure that God required none of this at my hands, nor would call me to any account for the neglect of it ! And that this is not my cafe only, but the common cafe to find Difcipline fo troublefom, is apparent in this ; that the whole body of the Nation (for the generality) have contended againft it thefe many years, and in almoft every Congregation in *England*, the greater part do either feparate from the Minifters, and forbear the Lords Supper, or fome way oppofe it and withdraw, that they may avoid it. And moft of the Minifters in *England*, even godly men, do much, if not altogether neglect it. So that fome through a Carnal indulging of

their

their own eafe and quiet, and to avoid mens ill will ; and fome through the great oppofitions of the people, or for one fuch caufe or other, do let all alone. In fo much, as even here in this County where we have affociated and engaged our felves to fome execution of Difcipline, this work goes on fo heavily as we fee, and need not mention further : when yet there is not a daies omifsion of Sermons and other Ordinances : fo that its apparent that its it which all lazie, carnal, man-pleafing Minifters may well comply with, as that which fuites their Carnal Interefts, to be free from the toil and care of Difcipline.

If you fay, why then do the Bifhops defire it, if flefh and blood be againft it ? I anfwer ; Experience and the impofsibility of performance tells us, that it is not the work, but the empty name and honour that they took up : and that indeed the flefh doth much more defire. Had they defired or been willing of the work, as they were of Lordfhips and Riches, they would not have done it.

Argum. 9. NO Epifcopacy, (at leaft which hath fo many evils as aforefaid attending it) which is not of Gods Inftitution, fhould be admitted into the Church. The late Englifh Prelacy, as to the difapproved properties before mentioned, is not of Gods Inftitution : therefore it is not to be admitted into the Church.

The Major is confeffed by all that plead for the *Jus Divinum* of Epifcopacy, or moft : and with the qualification, from the ill confequents, will be yielded by all.

The Minor I prove by parts : 1. That the exclufion of Prefbyters from Rule, and the putting the Government from them into a Lay-mans hand, with the reft before mentioned, are not of Divine Inftitution, is proved already, as much as needs. 2. If at the prefent we yield a fuperintendency or preheminence of one Paftor before others, yet the Controverfie remaineth, whether a Prelate fhould be only Parochial, that is, only the Prefident of the Elders of one particular Church, or at the utmoft of that with two or three, or a few neighbour fmall Parifhes which he may well overfee, without the neglect of the Difcipline. Now I know not how any man of that way can prove

out

out of Scripture, that a Bishop must have more then one Parish, much less more then three or four, or a few. For it is confest by them, for ought I know, that Scripture doth not determine how many Presbyters, or Churches a Bishop must have under him, (only *we* say he must have but one :) for the main thing that they labour to prove is, that a Bishop is above Presbyters as to Ordination and Jurisdiction : and so he may be if he be a Parish-Bishop : for a Parish-Church may have a Curate, and 2 or 3 Chappels with Curates at them, besides Deacons ; and according to the old course, perhaps many Presbyters more that did not publikely preach (though they wanted not authority) but oversee the flock. Now one man may have all that most of their Arguments require, if he be but the chief over this Parish Presbytery.

But perhaps they will say, that according to Scripture, every City only must have a Bishop, and therefore all the Country about must be his Diocess, though the number of Churches and Presbyters under him be not determined. To which I answer, that the word *Only*, is not in Scripture : no Text saith that it was *Only* in Cities that Churches or Bishops were to be seated. There is no prohibition of setling them in Villages.

It will be said, that *There is no example of any Bishop but in a City.* To which I answer. 1. Themselves ordinarily tell us in case of Sacrament gesture, and many other things, that examples do not alway bind affirmatively ; much less can they prove that they bind negatively ; I mean, not to do that which was not done. Can you prove in Scripture that there were any particular Churches or Assemblies for Sacraments and other worship in Villages ? If not, then is it lawful now to have any ? If not, then all our Parish Churches in the Country are unlawful. If yea, then why may we not have Bishops in the Countreys without Scripture example, as well as Churches ? for we shall prove that the reasons why there were none or few Bishops in the Country, was for want of Churches for them to oversee. The Gospel was not then preached, nor any Bishops placed in many Nations of the world : it doth not follow therefore that there must be none since. 2. The reason is evident why Churches and Bishops were first planted in Cities ; because there was the greatest Concourse of people : not that God loves a Citizen better then a

H   Countrey-

Countrey-man, or that he will have his Churches so limited to soil, or place, or scituation: it is the number of persons where-ever they live, that must be regarded, that the Church be not too great nor too small · but if there be the same number of people Cohabiting in the Countrey, as one of the Apostolical Churches did consist of, then there is the same reason to have a Church and Bishop in that Country Village, as was then for having one in a City. 3. Elders should be ordained in every Church, and therefore Bishops (for some of them say that these were Bishops) But Churches may be in Country Villages; therefore Elders and Bishops may be in Country-Villages. 4. I prove from Scripture that there were Bishops in Villages, or out of Cities, thus. Where there was a Church, there was a Bishop. But in a Village there was a Church; therefore. The Major I prove from *Act.*14.23. compared with 1 *Tim.*3. They ordained them Elders in every Church, or Church by Church: but these Elders are called Bishops in 1 *Tim.*3. (and by some of that way maintained to be such.)

For the Minor I prove it from *Rom.*16.1. where there is men-tion of the Church at *Cenchrea*: but *Cenchrea* was no City, but as *Grotius* speaks, *Portus Corinthiorum, ut Pireus Atheniensium,* viz. *ad sinum Saronicum: apparet ibi Ecclesiam fuisse Christiano-rum.* Grot. in Act. 18.18. *& in* Rom.16.1. *vide et* Downam, *Defens.* pag.105. who out of *Strabo* saith, it was the Port that served most properly for *Asia.* But Bishop *Downam* saith (ibid.) that *Cenchrea was a Parish subordinate to the Church of Corinth, having not a Bishop or Presbytery, but a Presbyter as-signed to it :* so before he saith, *by a Church,* he means *a Compa-ny of Christians having a Bishop and Presbytery.*] But if he will so define a Church as that the Prelate shall enter the Definition, then he may well prove that every Church had a Prelate. And so a Patriarch may be proved to be Necessary to every Church, if you will say, you mean only such congrega-tions as have a Patriarch. But it was denominated a Church, *Act.* 14.23. before they had Presbyters ordained to them, and so before fixed Bishops: when the Apostles had converted and congregated them, they were Churches. And the Text saith, that they ordained them Elders in every Church, or Church by Church; and therefore *Cenchrea* being a Church, must have such.

Elders

Elders ordained to it, according to the Apostles Rule. And that it was a Parish with one Presbyter subject to *Corinth*, is all unproved, and therefore to no purpose.

5. Yet I prove that the English Prelacy on their own grounds, is not *Jure Divino* in that it is against the word of God, according to their own interpretation; of which next.

Argum. 10. THat Episcopacy which is contrary to the word of God, or Apostolical Institution, according to *their own interpretation, is not to be restored. But such is the late English Episcopacy: therefore, &c.*

I prove the Minor (for the Major needeth none :) according to their own interpretation of *Tit.*1.5. and other Texts; Every City should have a Bishop, (and if it may be, a Presbytery.) (And so many Councils have determined, only when they grew greater, they except Cities that were too small : but so did not *Paul*) But the late Episcopacy of *England* is contrary to this : for one Bishop only is over many Cities. If therefore they will needs have Episcopacy, they should at least have had a Bishop in every City : and though we do not approve of confining them to Cities, yet this would be much better then as they were : for then 1. They would be nearer their charges, and within reach of them. 2. And they would have smaller charges, which they might be more capable of overseeing ; for there would be ten or twenty Bishops for one that be now.   If they say that except *Bath and Wells, Coventry and Lichfield*, or some few, they have but one City. I answer, its not so. For every Corporation or Burrough-Town is truly πόλις; and therefore should have a Bishop. Let them therefore either prove that a Market-Town, a Burrough, a Corporation, is not πόλις, or else let every one of these Towns and Burroughs have a Bishop, to govern that Town with the Neighbouring Villages by the consent and help of the Presbyters of these Villages, (according to their own grounds,) And if it were so, they would be no more then Classical Bishops at most.

Perhaps they'le say that, while we pretend to take down Bishops, we do but set up more, and would have many for one, *Object.* while we would have every Corporation or Parish to have a Bishop.   To which I answer, its true : but then it is not the same *Answ.* sort of Bishops which we would exclude and which we would

multiply : we would exclude those Bishops that would undertake
two or three hundred mens work themselves, and will rule a
whole Diocess alone (or by a Lay Chancellor) when every
conscionable man that hath faithfully tryed it, doth feel the
oversight of one Congregation to be so great a burden, that
it makes him groan and groan again. We would exclude those
Bishops that would exclude all others in a whole Diocess, that
they may do the work alone, and so leave it undone, while they
plead that it belongs to them to do it. If they will come into the
Lords Harvest, and exclude from the work of Government,
the Labourers of a whole County or two, we have reason to
contradict them. But this is not to bring in more such Bishops
as they that will shut out others, but to keep in the necessary labouring Bishops whom they would shut out. Nor do we shut
out them themselves as Labourers or Rulers, but as the excluders
of the Labourers or Rulers. If we have a Church to build that
requireth necessarily two hundred workmen, and some Pillars
in it to Erect, of many hundred tun weight, if one of the workmen would say, that it belongs to him to do it all himself, or at
least when the materials are brought to the place prepared, to
rear and order and place every stone and pillar in the building, I
would no otherwise exclude the vain pretender then by introducing necessary help that the work may be done ; and I should
think him a silly Caviller that would tell me, that while I exclude
him, I do but multiply such as he ; when his very fault consisted
in an hinderance of that necessary multiplication.

Object. 2.

I know that some will say, that we feign more work then is to
be done ; and we would have the sentence of Excommunication pass upon every light offence. I answer ; that its a thing

Answ.

that we abhor : we would have none Excommunicated but for
obstinacy in hainous sin ; when they will not hear the Church
after more private admonition. But there's much more of the
work of Government to be done on men that are not Excom-
municable, to bring them to Repentance, and open confession,
for manifestation of that Repentance to the satisfaction of the
Church : but what need we plead how great the work is which
every man may see before his eyes, and experience putteth beyond dispute ?

Furthermore that the English Episcopacy is dissonant from all
Scripture

Scripture Episcopacy, I prove thus. The Scripture knoweth but two sorts of Episcopacy : the one General, unfixed as to any Church or Country or Nation ; which was not called Episcopacy in the first times : the other fixed Overseers of determinate Churches appropriated to their special charge : these were called Bishops in those times : whereas the former were, some called Apostles, from their immediate mission and extraordinary Priviledges; or Evangelists, or Fellow-labourers and helpers of the Apostles, or by the like titles signifying their unlimited indeterminate charge. But our English Bishops are neither of these : therefore not any of Scripture appointment but different from them. 1. They are not of the Apostolical Order of General Ministers : for 1. Their principal work was Preaching to convert, and congregate, and then order Churches; but our Bishops seldom preached, for the most part. 2. They were not tyed to any particular Church more then other, save only as prudence directed them *pro tempore & re nata*, for the success of their work for the Church Universal ; nor were they excluded or restrained from any part of the world as being another mans Diocess ; save only as prudence might direct them for the common good; to distribute themselves *pro tempore.* This is apparent 1. by Chrifts Commission, who sendeth them into all the world, only by certain advantages and particular calls, fitting *Peter* more for the Circumcision, and *Paul* for the Uncircumcision, when yet both *Peter* and *Paul* and all the rest, did preach and look to both Circumcision and Uncircumcision. 2. By the History of their peregrinations and labours, which shew that they were not so fixed, whatever some writers may ungroundedly affirm. *Eusebius* (discrediting by fabulous mixtures the lighter sort of his Testimonies, and censured by some rejection by *Gelasius* and others) and some with him, do tell us of some such things, as some Apostles being fixed Bishops, but with no such proofs as should satisfie a man that weighs the contrary intimations of Scripture, and the discord of these reporters among themselves. Only it is certain, that nature it self would so restrain them that as they could be but in one place at once, so they could not be in perpetual motion : and prudence would keep them longest in those places where most work was to be done. And therefore *Pauls* three years abode at *Ephefus* and the neighbouring

bouring parts of *Asia*, did not make him the fixed Diocesan Bishop of *Ephefus*.

And what I fay of the Apostles, I fay alfo of many fuch Itinerant unfixed Minifters which were their helpers, as *Silas, Apollo, Barnabas, Titus, Timothy,* &c. For though *Timothy* be called by fome Antients the firft Bifhop of *Ephefus*, and *Titus* of *Crete*; yet it is apparent they were no fuch fixed Minifters, that undertook a Diocefs *durante vita* as their proper charge, which were then called Bifhops; but they were Itinerant helpers of the Apoftles in gathering, planting and firft ordering of Churches. And therefore *Titus* was left in a whole Nation or large Ifland, to place Bifhops or Elders in each City, and fet things in order, and this but till *Paul* come, and not to be himfelf their fixed Bifhop: and *Timothy* is proved by Scripture to have been unfetled and itinerant as a helper of *Paul*, after that he is by fome fuppofed to be fixed at *Ephefus*. I will not needlefly *actum agere*: let any man that is unfatisfied of this, read impartially Mr. *Prin* unbifhoping of *Timothy* and *Titus*, and note there the Itinerary of *Timothy* from Scripture Texts. If therefore our Bifhops would have been of the Apoftles and their General helpers race, they fhould have gone up and down to gather and plant Churches, and then go up and down to vifit thofe which they have planted; or if they live where all are Enchurched already, they fhould go up and down to preach to the ruder fort of them, and by the power of the word to fubdue men further to Chrift, and to fee that all Minifters where they come do their duty, reproving and admonifhing thofe that neglect it, but not forbidding them to do it, as a thing belonging only to them. And by Spiritual weapons and authority fhould they have driven Minifters to this duty, and not by meer fecular force (of which more anon.)

2. And as for the fixed Bifhops of Apoftolical Inftitution, our Englifh Prelacy are not like them. For the fixed Bifhops eftablifhed by the Apoftles were only Overfeers of one particular Church: But the Englifh Prelates were the Overfeers of many particular Churches. Therefore the Englifh Prelates were not the fame with the old Bifhops of the Apoftles inftitution.

The courfe that the Prelates take to elude this argument is by giving us a falfe definition of a particular Church. That we may not therefore have any unprofitable ftrife about words,

I

I shall signifie my own meaning. By a Particular Church I mean an Associated or combined company of Christians, for Communion in Publick Worship, and Furtherance of each other in the way to heaven, under the Guidance of Christs Church Officers, (one Elder or more;) such as are undivided, or Churches of the first order commonly called *Ecclesiæ Primæ*, as to existence, and which contain not divers Political Churches in them. A family I mean not: for thats not a Political Church, having no Pastor. An accidental company of Christians I mean not. For those are no Association, and so no Political Church: Nor do I mean a National, or Diocesane or Classical Church, or any the like; which are composed of many particular Churches of the first order, conjunct. It is not of Necessity that they alway or most usually meet in one Congregation: because its possible they may want a capacious convenient room, and its possible they may be under persecution, so that they may be forced to meet secretly in small companies; or there may be some aged weak people or children that cannot travail to the chief place of Meeting; and so may have some Chappels of ease, or smaller meeting. But still it must be a number neither so big, nor so small as to be uncapable of the ends of Association, which enter the definition; how ever weakness, age or other accidents may hinder some members from that full usefullness as to the main end, whith other members have. So that they which are so many, or live at such a distance as to be uncapable of the ends, are not such a Church, nor are capable of so being: For the number will alter the species. In a word, it cannot, I think, be proved that in the Primitive times, there was any one fixed Bishop that Governed and Oversaw any more then one such particular political Church, as was not composed of divers lesser political Churches: nor that their Churches which any fixed Bishop oversaw were more then could hold Communion in Worship in one publick place, for so many of them as could ordinarily bear at once (for all the families cannot usually come at once:) they were not greater then some of our Englsh Parishes are, nor usually the tenth part so great. I have been informed by the judicious inhabitants, that there are fourscore thousand in *Giles Cripple-gate* Parish in *London*: and about fifty thousand in *Stepney*, and fourty thousand in *Sepulchres*. There cannot any Church in Scripture be found

that

that was greater, nor neer so great as one of these Parishes. No
not the Church at *Jerusalem* it self of which so much is said : No
not if you admit all the number of moveable Converts and So-
journours to have been of that particular Church, which yet cannot be proved to have been so. I know Bishop *Downam* doth with
great indignation Dispute that Diocesses were before Parishes,
and that it was more then one Congregation that was contained in those Diocesses ; We will not contend about the name
Diocess and Parish , which by the Ancients were sometime
used promiscuously for the same thing : But as to the
thing signified by them, I say that what ever you call it, a Diocess, or a Parish, there were not near so many souls as in some
English Parishes ; nor take one with another , their Churches
commonly were no more Numerous then our Parishes, nor so
numerous. A Diocess then and a Parish were the same thing,
and both the same as our particular Churches now are ; that is,
the *Ecclesæ primæ*, or Socceties of Christians combined under
Church-Rulers, for holy Communion in Worship and Discipline.
And there were no otherwise many Congregations in one
Church, then as our Chapples of ease, or a few meeting in a
private house because of rainy weather, are many Congregations
in one Parish. The foresaid Learned and Godly, (though
angry) Bishop *Downame*, saith *Def. li. 2. cap. 1. page 6.* that [*Indeed at the very first Conversion of Cities, the whole Number of the
people converted, being some not much greater then the Number of the Presbyters placed among them, were able to make but a
small Congregation.*] Call that Church then a Diocess or a Parish,
I care not, so we come near an agreement, about the proportion of Members that the definition be not overthrown, and the
ends of it made impossible by the distance, number , and unac-
quaintedness of the members that cannot have any Church communion immediately one with another. If there be no communion, how is it a Church ? Nay or if there be no such communion as consists in mutual assistance and conjunction in Worship, and holding familiarity also in our conversation (which
the excommunicated are excluded from) And if a communion there be, it is either Immediate by the members themselves
Assembled, or else but Mediately by their Officers or Delegates.
If it be only by the latter Mediately , then it is not the *Ecclesia*

clesia prima, but orta: It is an *association of several Political Churches*: For that is the difference between the communion of a single particular Church, and many combined Churches, that as the first is a combination of persons and not of Churches, so the communion is held among the Members in common, whereas the other being a combination of Churches, the communion is maintained orderly by Officers and Delegates, joyning in Synods, and sent from the Congregations. If therefore it be an Immediate ordinary communion of members in Ecclesiastical affairs, *viz.* Worship and Discipline, that is the Particular Church that I intend, call it what you will else, and whether there may be any private meetings in it besides the main body, or not, as possibly through some accidents there may be; and yet at Sacrament and on the most solemne occasions, the same persons that were at Chappels or less meetings, may be with the chief Assembly.

But I shall proceed in the proof of this by the next Argument, which will serve for this and the main together.

Argum. 11. *That sort of Church Government may most safely be now practised which was used in the Scripture times, and thats less safe which was not then used. But the Government of many Elders and particular Churches by one Bishop (fixed, and taking that as his proper Diocess, such as the English Bishops were) was not used in Scripture times. Therefore it is not so safe to use it or restore it now.*

The Major is proved hence: 1. In that the Primitive Church which was in Scripture times, was of unquestionable Divine Institution, and so most pure. And it is certainly lawful to practice that Church-Government which alone was practised by all the Church in the Scripture times of the New Testament. 2. Because we have no certain Law or Direction but Scripture for the frame of Government as *jure Divino*. Scripture is Gods sufficient and perfect Law. If therefore there be no mention of the Practice of any such Episcopacy in Scripture, no nor any precept for the practice of it afterwards, then cannot we receive it as of Divine Institution. The Objections shall be answered when we have proved the Minor.

And for the Minor I shall at this time argue from the Concessions

I
tions

fions of the moft Learned and Reverend man that at this time hath deeply engaged himfelf in defence of Epifcopacy, who doth grant us all thefe things following. 1.That in Scripture times they were the fame perfons,and of the fame office that were called Bifhops and Presbyters. 2. That all the Presbyters mentioned in Scripture times, or then inftituted (as far as we can know, had a Power of Ordination.3.And alfo a Power of Ruling theChurch, Excommunicating and Abfolving. 4. That there was not then in being any Presbyter (fuch as the Bifhops would have in thefe times) who was under the Bifhop of a particular Church or Diocefs. His words are thefe [*And although this title of* Πρεσβυτεροι, *Elders, have been alfo extended to a fecond Order in the Church, and is now only in ufe for them, under the Name of Presbyters, yet in the Scripture times it belonged principally, if not alone to Bifhops; there being no Evidence, that any of that fecond order were then inftituted, though foon after, before the writing of Ignatius Epiftles there were fuch inftituted in all Churches.*] 5. It is yielded alfo by him that it is the office of thefe Presbyters or Bifhops to Teach frequently and diligently,to reduce Hereticks, to reprove, rebuke, Cenfure and abfolve, to vifit all the fick and pray with them, *&c.* And therefore it muft needs follow that their Diocefs muft be no larger then that they may faithfully perform all this to the Members of it: And if there be but one Bifhop to do it,I am moft certain then by experience that hisDiocefs muft be no bigger then this Parifh, nor perhaps half fo big.6.And it muft needs follow, that in Scripture times a Particular Church confifted not of feveral Churches affociated,nor of feveral Congregations ordinarily meeting in feveral places for Chriftian communion

quod pro conceffo fumitur (in una civitate non fuiffe plures Epifcopos) Quamvis enim in una Ecclefiâ aut Cœtu plures fimul Epifcopi nuaquam fuerint,nihil tamen obftare q sin in eidem civitate duo aliquando difterminati Cœtus fuerint,duobus Apoftolis ad fidem adducti,diverfis forfan diatectis & aliquando ritibus disjuncti, quibus duo itidem Epifcopi feorfim, & divifis ακ̔εσις præfiderent.

Et p. 211. §. 11. [*Ex his ratio conftat, quare fine Presbyterorum mentione interveniente, Epifcopis Diaconi immediate adjiciantur, quia fcilicet in fingulis Macedoniæ civitatibus, quamvis Epifcopus effet, nondum Presbyteri conftituti funt, Diaconis tantum πρὸς ὑπηρεσιαν ubiq; Epifcopis adjunctis.*

Mark well the ftating of the queftion by Dr. H. Differt. Epift.§. 30,31. The controverfie is not *Quibus demum nominibus cogniti fuerint Ecclefiarum Rectores, fed an ad unum in*

fingulari

ſingulari Ecclesiæ, an ad plures, potestas ista devenerit. Nos ad unum singularem Præfectum, quem ex famosiore Ecclesiæ usu Episcopum vulgò dicimus, potestatem istam in singulari Cœtu ex Christi & Apostolorum institutione nunquam non pertinuisse affirmamus.] You ſee here that it is but [*in ſingulari Ecclesiæ*] & [*in ſingulari Cœtu*] that he affirmeth an Epiſcopacy of Chriſts and the Apoſtles inſtitution. And ſuch Biſhops moſt Churches in *England* have already.

munion in the ſolemn Worſhip of God, but only of the Chriſtians of one ſuch Congregation with a ſingle Paſtor (though in that we dſſent, and ſuppoſe there were more Paſtors then one uſually, or often.) That this muſt be granted with the reſt is apparent.
1. The Reverend Author ſaith as Biſhop *Downam* before cited [*That when the Goſpel was firſt preached by the Apoſtles and but few Converted, they ordained in every City and region, no more but a Biſh p and one or more Deacons to attend him, there being at the preſent ſo ſmal ſtore out of which to take more, and ſo ſmall need of ordaining more, that this Biſhop is conſtituted more for the ſake of thoſe which ſhould after believe, then of thoſe which did already.*]
2. And its proved thus : If there were in Scripture times any more ordinary Worſhiping Aſſemblies on the Lords dayes then one under one Biſhop, then either they did Preach, Pray, Praiſe God, and adminiſter the Lords Supper in thoſe Aſſemblies, or they did not : If not, then 1. They were no ſuch Worſhipping Aſſemblies as we ſpeak of. 2. And they ſhould ſin againſt Chriſt who required it. 3. And differ from his Churches which ordinarily uſed it. But if they did thus, then either they had ſome Paſtor (Presbyter or Biſhop) to perform theſe holy actions between God and the people, or not : If not, then they ſuppoſe that Lay-men might do all this Miniſterial work, in Word, Sacraments, Prayer, and Praiſe in the name of the Aſſembly, &c. And if ſo, what then is proper to the Miniſtry? then farewell Biſhops and Presbyters too. If not, then either the Biſhop muſt be in two Aſſemblies at once performing the Holy Worſhip of God in their communion (but thats impoſſible :) or elſe he muſt have ſome aſſiſting Presbyters to do it ; But thats denyed : Therefore it muſt needs follow that the Church order, conſtitution and practiſed Government which was in Scripture times, was this ; that a ſingle Worſhipping Congregation was that particular Church which had a Presbyter or Biſhop (one or more) which watched over and ruled that only Congregation as his Dioceſs or

I 2 proper

proper charge, having no Government of any other Church (Congregation) or Elders. *De facto* this is plainly yielded.

Well : this much being yielded, and we having come so far to an agreement, about the actual Church Constitution and Government of the Scripture times, we desire to know some sufficient reason, why we in these times may not take up with tha Government and Church order which was practised in the Scripture times ? And the Reason that is brought against it is this ; Because it was the Apostles intention that this single Bishop who in Scripture times had but one Congregation, and Governed no Presbyters, should after Scripture times, have many settled Congregations, and their Presbyters under them, and should have the power of ordaining them, *&c.* To this I answer, 1. The Intentions of mens hearts aje secret till they are some way revealed. No man of this age doth know the Apostles hearts but by some sign : what then is the revelation that Proveth this Intention ? Either it must be some Word or Deed. For the first I cannot yet find any colour of proof which they bring from any word of the Apostles, where either they give power to this Presbyter or Bishop to Rule over many Presbyters and Congregations for the future : Nor yet where they do so much as foretell that so it shall be. As for those of *Paul* to *Timothy* and *Titus*, that they *rebuke not an Elder, and receive not accusation against them but under two or three Witnesses*, the Reverend Author affirmeth that those Elders were not Presbyters under such Bishops as we now speak of, but those Bishops themselves, whom *Timothy* and *Titus* might rebuke. And for meer facts without Scripture words, there is none that can prove this pretended Intention of the Apostles. First, there is no fact of the Apostles themselves or the Churches or Pastors in Scripture time to prove it. For *Subordinate Presbyters* are confessed not to be then *Instituted*, and so not *existent* : and *other* fact of theirs there can be none. And no fact *after* them can prove it. Yet this is the great Argument that most insist on , that the practice of the Church after Scripture times, doth prove that Intention of the Apostles which Scripture doth not (for ought is yet proved by them that I can find) at all express. But we deny that, and require proof of it. It is not bare saying so that will serve. Is it not possible for the succeeding Bishops to err and mistake the

Apostles·

Apostles Intentions ? If not, then are they Infallible as well as the Apostles, which is not true. They might sin in going from the Institution : And their sin will not prove that the Apostles intended it should be so *de jure*, because their followers did so *de facto*.

If they say that it is not likely that all the Churches should so suddenly be ignorant of the Apostles Intention, I answer, 1. We must not build our faith and practice on Conjectures. Such a saying as this is no proof of Apostolical intentions, to warrant us to swerve from the sole practised Government in Scripture times. 2. There is no great likelihood that I can discern that this first practised Government was altered by those that knew the Apostles, and upon supposition that these which are pretended were their intents. 3. If it were so, yet is it not impossible, nor very improbable, that through humane frailty they might be drawn to conjecture that that was the Apostles intents which seemed right in thier eyes, and suited their present judgements and interests. 4. Sure we are that the Scripture is the perfect Law and Rule to the Church for the Establishing of all necessary Offices and Ordinances : and therefore if there be no such intentions or Institutions of the Apostles mentioned in the Scripture, we may not set up universally such Offices and Ordinances, on any such supposed intents.

De facto we seem agreed, that the Apostles settled *One Pastor over one Congregation having no Presbyters under his Rule : and that there were no other in Scripture time :* but shortly after when Christians were multiplied, and the most of the Cities where the Churches were planted, were converted to the faith, together with the Country round about, then there were many Congregations, and many Pastors, and the Pastor of the first Church in the City did take all the other Churches and Pastors to be under his Government, calling them Presbyters only, and himself eminently or only the Bishop. Now the Question between us is, *Whether this was well done or not ? & Whether these Pastors should not rather have gathered Churches as free as their own? & Whether the Christians that were afterward converted should not have combined for holy Communion themselves in particular distinct Churches, and have had their own Pastors set over them, as the first Churches by the Apostles had ?* They that deny it, and Justifie

I ?   their

their fact, have nothing that we can see for it, but an ungrounded surmise, that it was the Apostles meaning that the first Bishops should so do : But we have the Apostles express Institution, and the Churches practise during Scripture times, for the other way. We doubt not but Christians in the beginning were thin, and that the Apostles therefore preached most, and planted Churches in Cities because they were the most populous places, where was most matter to work upon , and most disciples were there ; and that the Country round about did afford them here and there a family which joyned to the City Church : Much like as it is now among us with the Anabaptists and Separatists , who are famed to be so Numerous and potent through the Land , and yet I do not think that in all this County, there is so many in Number of either of these sects as the tenth part of the people of this one Parish ; nor perhaps as the twentieth part. Now if all the Anabaptists in *Worcestershire* , or at least that lived so neer as to be capable of Church communion , should be of Mr. *T's.* Congregation at *Bewdley* , or of a Church that met in the chief City, *Worcester*, yet doth not this intimate that all the space of ground in this County is appointed or intended for the future as Mr. *T's.* Diocess ; but if the successive Pastor should claim the whole County as his charge, if the whole were turned to that opinion , no doubt but they would much cross their founders mind. And (if the comparison may be tolerated) we see great reason to conceive that the Ancient Bishops did thus cross the Apostles minds.   When there were no more Christians in a City and the adjoyning parts, then half some of our Parishes, the Apostles planted fixed Governours called Bishops or Elders over these particlar Churches, which had constant communion in the worship of God : And when the Cities and Countreyes were converted to the faith, the frailty of ambition co-working thereto, these Bishops did claim all that space of ground for their Diocess where the members of their Church had lived before ; as if Churches were to be measured by the acres of Land, and not by the number of souls; whereas they should have done as the Bee-hives do , when they are ready to swarm, so that the old hive cannot contain them all, the swarm removes and seeks them another habitation, and makes them a New hive of their own. So when a Church grows big enough for two Churches, one part should

remove

remove to another meeting place, and they should become two Churches, and the later be of the same sort as the former, and as free, and not become subject to the former, as if men had right to be Rulers of others, because they were Converted before them, or because they dwell in a walled City, and others in the Villages. This Error therefore was no contrived or suddain thing, but crept on by degrees, as Countries were Converted and Churches enlarged; we are agreed therefore *de facto*, that it was otherwise in the Apostles daies, and that soon after, in some places, it came to that pass as the Prelates would have it (in some degree.) But whether the Apostles were willing of the change, is the Question between us; we deny it, and expect their better proof. And till they prove it, we must needs take it for our duty to imitate that Government which themselves confess was *only practised* in Scripture times; supposing this the safest way.

BUt yet, though the proof lye on their part, who affirm the Apostles to have had such Intentions, that Pastors of single Congregations should afterward become the Pastors of many, I shall *ex superabundanti* give them some Reasons for the Negative.

1. And first we are most certain that the *holyest Pastors of the Church, had so much Pride and Ambition, that might possibly make them guilty of such a mistake as tended to the increase of their own power and rule.* We find even the twelve Apostles contending in Christs own presence for the Primacy, till he is put sharply to rebuke them, and tell them the Necessity of humility, and teach them better the state of his Kingdom. *Paul* met with many that contended against him for a preheminence, and put him up on all those defences of the dignity of his Apostleship which we find him using. *Peter* found it necessary to warn the Pastors

Reason 1. Conqueritur jam olim Socrates Episcopatus quosdam suis temporibus extra sacerdotii sines egressos & in Tyrannidem esse delapsos: Conqueritur apud Eusebi- . . .

tam Hierax *lenitatis & mansuetudinis dignitatem in Tyrannidem transisse: conqueritur de Episcoporum ambitione* Nazianzenus; *& propterea si non Episcopatum, certe civitatum jus perpetuum in retinenda Episcopali dignitate mutatum velle.* He addeth yet more such, and concludeth, that Ecclesiastical Ambition never made such progress from the Apostles daies to those, as it hath done since to ours, almost incurably. *Grotius de imperio pag.* . . .

that they should not Lord it over Gods Heritage. And *John* did meet with a Lording *Diotrephes*, that loved to have the pre-heminence. While they lay under the Cross, the Bishops were aspiring, and usurping authority over one another; or else *Victor* of *Rome* had not presumed to Excommunicate the *Asian* Bi-shops for not conforming to his opinion: What abundance of un-wo thy contentions did the Bishops of the first ages fill the Churches with? and much about superiority, who should be greatest; what should be the priviledges of their several Seas · &c. Their pride no doubt was a great cause of their contention; and those contentions necessitated the interposition of Emperors to reconcile them that could not agree of them-selves. If the Emperors called a Council to that end even the Council it self would fall to pieces, and make all worse, if the Magistrate did not moderate them. Had not *Constantine* burnt the *Nicene* Schedules, and done much to maintain an Uni-on among them, the success of that Council might have been such as would have been no great encouragement to succeeding ages to seek for more. What bitter quarrels are there between the most eminent of all the Fathers and Bishops of the Church? between *Chrysostom* and *Epiphanius*; *Chrysostom* and *Theophilus Alexandrinus*; *Hierom* and *John* of *Jerusalem*; *Jerome* and *Ruffinus*; besides his quarrels with *Chrysostom* and *Augustine*. I open not the concealed nakedness of the Saints; but mention those publike doleful tragedies which made the Church an amazement to it self, and a scorn to the Heathens that lived about them; witness the well known censure of *Ammianus Marcellinus*: when so many people shall be murdered at once in contention for a Bishoprick as were at the choice of *Damasus*; ambition was too predominant. The mentioning of the conten-tions of those most excellent Bishops, and the first four general Councils, makes *Luther* break out into so many admiring excla-mations, in his Treatise *de Conciliis*, that ever such men should so ambitiously quarrel about toyes and trifles, and childish things, and that even to the disturbing of all the Churches, and setting the Christian world on a flame. Of the two Churches of *Rome* and *Constantinople* he saith, *Ita hæ duæ Ecclesiæ ambitiose rixata sunt, de re nihili, vanissimis & nugacissimis næniis, donec tandem utraque horribiliter vastata & deleta est.* pag. 175. This

caused

caused *Nazianzen* (who complaineth so much himself of the *odium* or displeasure of his fellow Bishops) to profess himself to be so affected, that he would avoid all Assemblies of Bishops, because he had never seen a good end of any Synod, and which did not rather increase the evils than remove them ; and his reason is not as *Bellarmine* feigneth, only because they were all *Arrians*; but because, The desire of contending, and of preheminency or principality, and their emulation, did overcome reason, (which *Luther* mentioning *ib. pag.* 225. wondereth that for these words he was not excommunicated as an arrant heretick) Who knoweth not, that knoweth any thing of Church history, how the Church hath been torn in pieces in all ages except the first, by the dissention of the Bishops, till the Pope drew part of them to unite in him ? And who knoweth not, that knoweth any thing of the present state of the Christian world, into how many fractions it is broken at this day, and almost all through the Division of these Guides? If therefore we shall imagine that the Pastors of the Church could not be tainted with so much ambition as to inlarge their own Diocesses, and gather the new Chuches under themselves, when they should have formed them into the same order and freedom as were the first, we shall shut our eyes against the most full experience of the Christian world : especially when the change was made by degrees.

2. The second Reason that perswadeth me to stick to the sole practised Government in Scripture times, and not to alter it upon pretended Intentions of the Apostles, is this : *Nothing that intimateth temerity or mutability, is to be charged upon the Holy Ghost but to institute one frame or species of Church-government for Scripture times, and to change it presently into another species to all succeeding ages, doth intimate temerity or mutability*; or at least, is so like it, that therefore without good proof it is not to be charged on the Holy Ghost. That they are two distinct *species* of Government is plain : one is the Government of a Particular Congregation, without any other Congregations or Elders under that Government : the other is the Governing of many Elders and Churches by one supereminent Prelate : and if these be not two differing sorts of Government, then let the Prelates confess that the Government which we would continue

Reason 2.

K   is

is of the same sort with theirs : for ours is of the first sort ; and if theirs be of the same, we are both agreed.

And that the Lord Jesus Christ should settle one kind of Government *de facto* during Scripture time, and change it for ever after, is most improbable : 1. Because it intimateth levity, or mutability in a Law-giver, so suddenly to change his Laws and form of Government ; either something that he is supposed not to have foreseen, or some imperfection is intimated as the cause. Or if they say, that it was the change of the state of the body Governed, *viz.* the Church : I answer, 2. There was no change of the state of the Church to necessitate a change of the kind of Officers and Government : for (as I shall shew anon) there was need of more Elders then one in Scripture times ; and the increase of the Church might require an increase of Officers for Number, but not for Kind. There was as much need of assisting Presbyters, as of Deacons. I may well conclude therefore, that he that will affirm a Change of the Government so suddenly, must be sure to prove it ; and the rather, because this is the Bishops own great and most considerable Argument on the other side, when they plead that the Apostles themselves were Rulers of Presbyters, therefore Rulers over Presbyters (and many Churches) should continue as Gods Ordinance : many on the other side answer them, (though so do not I) that this Ordinance was temporary, during the Apostles times, who had no Successors in Government : to which the Prelates reply, that its not imaginable that Christ should settle one sort of Church-Government for the first age, and another ever after, abolishing that first so soon : and that they who affirm this, must prove it. For my part, I am overcome by this Argument, to allow all that the Apostolical pattern can prove, laying aside that which depended on their extraordinary gifts and priviledges ; but then I see no reason but they should acknowledge the force of their own *Medium* ; and conclude its not imaginable that, if God settled fixed Bishops only over particular Congregations, without any such order as subject Presbyters, in the first age, he should change this, and set up subject Presbyters and many Churches under one man for ever after.

If they say, that this is not a change of the *species*, but a growing up of the Church from Infancy to Maturity : I answer,

It

It is a plain change of the *Species* of Government, when one
Congregation is turned into Many, and when a new order of
Officers, *viz.* subject Presbyters without power of Ordination
or Jurisdiction, is introduced, and the Bishops made Governours
of Pastors, that before were but Governours of the People,
this is plainly a new *Species*. Else I say again, let them not blame
us for being against the right *Species*.

3. The third Reason is this: *They that affirm a change* (not Reason 3.
of the Governours, but also) *of the very nature or kind of a particular Governed or Political Church, from what it was in Scripture times, do affirm a thing so improbable, as is not without very
clear proof to be credited. But such are they that affirm that Congregational Bishops were turned to Diocesan: therefore, &c.*

The Church that was the object of the Government of a fixed
Bishop in Scripture times, was, [*A competent Number of per-* A particular
sons in Covenant with Christ (*or of Christians*) *co-habiting, by* Church,
the appointment of Christ and their mutual expressed consent, united what.
(*or associated*) *under Christs Ministerial Teachers and Guides for
the right worshipping of God in publick and the Edification of the
Body in Knowledge and Holiness, and the maintaining of obedience
to Christ among them, for the strength, beauty and safety of the whole
and each part, and thereby the Pleasing and Glorifying God the Redeemer, and Creator,*] It would be too long, rather then difficult to stand to prove all the parts of this Definition, of the first
particular Political Church. That part which most concerneth
our present purpose, is the *Ends*, which in Relations must enter
the Definition: which in one word is, *The Communion of Saints
personally*, as Associated Churches consisting of many particular
Churches, are for the Communion of Saints by officers and Delegates. And therefore this communion of Saints is put in our
Creed, next to the Catholick Church, as the end of the combination. I shall have occasion to prove this by particular Texts
of Scripture anon. A Diocesan Church is not capable of these
Ends. What personal communion can they have that know not
nor see not one another? that live not together, nor worship
God together? There is no more personal communion of Saints
among most of the people of this Diocess, then is between us and
the inhabitans of *France* or *Germany*: for we know not so much
as the names or faces of each other, nor ever were together to

K 2

any holy ufes. So that to turn a Congregation into a Diocefan Church, is to change the very fubject of Government.

Obj. *This is meer independency, to make a single Congregati-on, the fubject of the Government.* Anfw. 1. I am not deterred from any truth by Names. I have formerly faid, that its my opi-nion that the truth about Church-Government, is parcelled out into the hands of each party, Epifcopal, Presbyterian, Indepen-dents, and Eraftian : And in this point in Queftion the Indepen-dents are moft right. Yet I do not affirm (nor I think they) that this one Congregation may not accidentally be neceffitated to meet in feveral places at once, either in cafe of perfecution, or the age and weaknefs of fome members, or the fmalnefs of the room : But I fay only that the Church fhould contain no more then can hold communion when they have opportunity of place and liberty; and fhould not have either feveral fettled So-cieties or Congregations, nor more in one fuch Society then may confift with the Ends. And that thefe Affemblies are bound to Affociate with other Affemblies, and hold communion with them by the mediation of their Officers ; this, as I make no doubt of, fo I think the Congregational will confefs. And whereas the common evafion is by diftinguifhing between a Worfhipping Church and a Governed Chuch , I defire them to give us any Scripture proof that a Worfhipping Church and a Governed Church were not all one, fuppofing that we fpeak of a fettled fociety or combination. I find no fuch diftinction of Churches in Scripture. A family I know may perform fome worfhip, and accordingly have fome Government : And an occafional meet-ing of Chriftians without any Minifter, may perform fome Wor-fhip without Government among them. But where was there ever a Society that ordinarily affembled for publick worfhip, fuch as was performed by the Churches on the Lords dayes, and held communion ordinarily in worfhip, and yet had not a Go-verning Paftor of their own? Without a Presbyter they could have no Sacraments and other publike Worfhip? And where was there ever a Presbyter that was not a Church Governour ? Certainly if fubject Presbyters were not till after Scripture times, nor any fettled Worfhipping Church without a Presbyter (un-lefs the people preached and adminiftred the Sacraments,) then there could be no Worfhipping Church that had not their own

proper

proper Governour , nor any such Governour (fixed) that had more Churches then one.

Reason 4. *The contrary opinion feigneth the Apoftles to have al-* *lotted to each Bifhop a fpace of ground for his Diocefs, and to have measured Churches by such fpaces, and not by the number of fouls:* But this is unproved, & abfurd. 1. Unproved, For there is no place in Scripture that giveth the Bifhop charge of all that fpace of ground, or of all the Chriftians that fhall be in that fpace during his time. Indeed they placed a Bifhop in each City, when there was but a Church in each City : But they never faid, there fhall be but one Church in a City, or but one Bifhop in a City ; much lefs in all the Country region. 2. And its abfurd : For its the number of fouls that a Church muft be measured by , and not a fpace of ground, (fo they do but co-habite :) For if in the fame fpace of Ground, there fhould be twenty or an hundred times as many Chriftians, it would make the number fo great as would be uncapable of perfonal communion , and of obtaining Church Ends. If a Schoolmafter have a School in the chief City or Town of this County , and there come as many from many miles com-pafs as one School can hold, and there be no more there : fo long all that fpace may belong to his School, not for the fpace fake, but the number of Schollars : For if there be afterward an hundred times as many in that fpace to be taught, they muft fet up more Schools, and it were no wife part in the old School-mafter to maintain that all that Country pertaineth to his School, becaufe that it was fo when there were fewer. So that to mea-fure out the matter of Churches by fpace of ground , and not by number of fouls, is plainly againft the Reafon of the Relation.

Reason 5. *The oppofed opinion doth imply that God more re-* *gardeth Cities then Country Villages , or that Churches are to be meafured according to the number and greatnefs of Cities rather then according to the number of fouls.* For they fuppofe that every City fhould have a Bifhop if there be but twenty, or four-ty, or an hundred Chriftians in it : but if there be five hundred Country Parifhes, that have fome of them many thoufand fouls in them , thefe fhall have no Bifhops of their own , but be all ruled by the Bifhop of the City. Now how unreafonable this is, methinks fhould not be hard to difcern. For , 1 What

City to God any more then a Village, that for it he should make so partial an institution ? Doth he regard *Rome* any more then *Eugubium*, or *Alexandria* more then *Tanis*, for their worldly splendor or priviledges ? No doubtless it is for the multitude of inhabitants. And if so, its manifest that an equal number of inhabitants elsewhere, should have the same kind of Government. 2. Is it probable that God would have twenty thousand or an hundred thousand people in a Diocess (and in some a Million) to have but one Church-Ruler, and yet would have every small congregation in a City to have one, though there be none else under him ? What proportion is there in this way of Government, that an hundred or fifty men shall have as many Governours as a Million ? as if ten thousand or an hundred thousand Schollars out of a City shall have no more Rulers, then an hundred in a City ; and all because one part are in a City, and the other not ? Or a Physitian shall have but an hundred Patients to look to in a City, and if there be a Million in that City and Country, he shall also upon pain of Gods everlasting wrath undertake the care of them all? Let them that strive for such a charge look to it; I profess I admire at them, what they think 1. Of the needs of mens souls : 2. Of the terrours of Gods wrath. 3. And of their own sufficiency for such a work ? Were it my case, if I know my own heart at all, I should fear that this were but to strive to damn thousands, and to be damned with them, by undertaking on that penalty to be their Physitian (under Christ) when I am sure I cannot look to the hundreth man of them, and I had rather strive to be a gally-slave to the Turks, or to be preferred to rid Chanels, or the basest office all my dayes.

Reason 6. *According to the opposed opinion, it is in the power of a King to make Bishops to be either Congregational or Diocesan, to make a Bishop to have a Million of souls or a whole Nation in charge, or to have but a few.* For if a King will but dissolve the Priviledge and title, and make that no City which was a City, though he diminish not the number of souls; and if he will do thus by all the Cities, save one in his dominion, then must there be but one Bishop in his dominion. And if he will but make every countrey Town, that hath four or five hundred or a thousand inhabitants to be incorporate, and honour it with the title and priviledge of a City, then shall they have a Bishop. Moreover, thus every Prince may *de jure* banish Episcopacy out of his

Reason 6.

his Dominions , without diminiſhing the number of Chriſtians , if he do but defranchiſe the Cities, and be of the mind
as I have heard ſome men have been , that Cities are againſt
the Princes intereſt , by ſtrengthening the people , and
advantaging them to rebellions. Alſo if there be any Indian Nations ſo barbarous as to have no Cities , though they
were converted, yet muſt they have no Biſhops : Alſo it would
be in the Princes power *de jure* to depoſe any of thoſe Biſhops
that the Apoſtles or their Succeſſors are ſuppoſed to ſet up :
For the *Roman* Emperour might have proclaimed *Antioch, Alexandria*, or any of the reſt to be no Cities, and then they muſt
have no longer have had any Biſhops. And what Biſhops ſhall
Antioch have at this day ?

Now how abſurd all this is , I need not manifeſt : that whole
Contreyes ſhall have no Government for want of Cities , that
Kings ſhall ſo alter Church Officers at their pleaſure when they
intend it not, meerly by altering the Civil Priviledges of their
people , that a King may make one Dioceſs to become an hundred, and an hundred become one, by ſuch means. And yet all this
doth undenyably follow , if the Law be that every City, and only
every City ſhall be a Biſhops Sea where there are Chriſtians to be
governed.

Reaſon 7. *There is no ſufficient Reaſon given, why ſubject Pref-* Reaſon 7.
*byters ſhould not have been ſet up in the Scripture times, as well as
after , if it had been the Apoſtles intent that ſuch ſhould be inſtituted.* The Neceſſity pretended, was no neceſſity, and the Non-
neceſſity is but pretended. Firſt it is pretended that there were
ſo few fit men that there was a Neceſſity of forbearance.
But this is not ſo : For, 1. The Church had larger gifts of the
Spirit then, then now, and therefore proportionable to the flocks
they might have had competent men, then as well as now. 2. They
had men enough to make Deacons of, even ſeven in a Church :
And who will believe then that they could find none to make
ſuch Elders of? Was not *Stephen* or *Philip* ſufficiently qualified
to have been a ſubject Elder ? 3. They had many that prophe-
ſied , and interpreted , and ſpake with tongues in one Aſſembly, as appears , 1 *Cor.* 14. And therefore its manifeſt
that there were enough to have made Ruled Elders : At leaſt
ſure the Church at *Corinth*, where there were ſo many th .

.d.

ſands, would have afforded them one ſuch, if it had been requiſite.

But ſecondly, its pretended not to have been Neceſſary, becauſe of the fewneſs of the people. But I anſwer, 1. The ſame
perſons ſay that in *Ignatius* his time all Churches had ſuch Preſ-
byters : And its manifeſt that many Churches in the Scripture
times, were more populous or large, then many or moſt beſide
them were in *Ignatius* time. 2. Did the numerous Church at *Jeruſalem* ordinarily meet on the Lords dayes for holy communion,
or not ? If they did, then it was but a Church of one Congregation (which is by moſt denyed) If not, then the ſeveral Aſſemblies muſt have ſeveral Presbyters (for ſeveral Biſhops they
will not hear of,) Doubtleſs they did not celebrate the holy communion of the Church and Ordinances of God, by meer Lay-
men alone. 3. What man that knows the burden of Paſtoral
Overſight, can ſay that ſuch Churches of thouſands, as *Jeruſalem,
Rome, Alexandria, &c.* had need of no more than one man, to
Teach them, and do all the Paſtoral work ? and ſo that aſſiſting
Ruled Presbyters were then needleſs ? If they were needleſs to
ſuch numerous Churches then ; let us even take them for needleſs ſtill, and ſet up no new orders which were not ſeen in Scripture times.

Reaſ. 8. *The Apoſtles left it not to the Biſhops whom they*
Reaſon 8. *eſtabliſhed to make new Church-offices and orders* quoad ſpeciem,
but only to ordain men to ſucceed others in the offices and orders
that themſelves had (by the inſpiration of the Holy Ghoſt) appointed,
or elſe Chriſt before them. A Biſhop might make a Biſhop or a Deacon perhaps, becauſe theſe were *quoad ſpeciem* made before, and
they were but to put others into the places before appointed.
But if there were no ſuch creature in Scripture times as a *ſubject Presbyter*, that had no power of Ordination and Juriſdiction,
then if the Biſhops afterward ſhould make ſuch, they muſt
make a new office, as well as a new officer. So that either this
new Presbyter is of the inſtitution of Chriſt by his Apoſtles, or of
Epiſcopal humane inſtitution. If the former, and yet not inſtitu-
tuted in Scripture times, then Scripture is not the ſufficient rule
and diſcoverer of Divine Inſtitutions and Church Ordinances :
and if we once forſake that Rule, we know not where to fix, but
muſt wander in the Romane uncertainty. If the latter, then we
muſt

must expect some better proof then hitherto we have seen, of the Episcopall (or any humane) power to make new Offices in the Church of Christ, and that of universal and standing necessity. Till then we shall think they ought to have made but such Presbyters as themselves.

Reason 9. *If there be not so much as the name of a Ruled Presbyter without power of Ordination, or Jurisdiction, in all the Scripture, much less then is there any description of his Office, or any Directions for his ordination, or the qualifications prerequisit in him, and the performance of his office when he is in it: And if there be no such Directory concerning Presbyters, then was it not the Apostles intent that ever any such should be ordained.* The reason of the consequence is, 1. Because the Scripture was written not only for that age then in being, but for the Church of all ages to the end of the world: And therefore it must be a sufficient directory for all. The second Epistle to *Timothy* was written but a little before *Pauls* death. Surely if the Churches in *Ignatius* daies were all in need of Presbyters under Bishops, *Paul* might well have seen some need in his time, or have foreseen the need that was so neer, and so have given directions for that office. 2. And the rather is this consequence firm, because *Paul in his Epistles to Timothy* and *Titus* doth give such full and punctual Directions concerning the other Church officers, not only the Bishops, but also the Deacons, describing their prerequisite qualifications, their office, and directing for their Ordination, and conversation: Yea he condescendeth to give such large Directions concerning Widows themselves, that were serviceable to the Church. Now is it probable that a perfect Directory written for the Church to the worlds End, & largely describing the qualifications and office of Deacons, which is the inferiour, would not give one word of direction concerning subject Presbyters without power of Ordination or Rule, if any such had been then intended for the Church? No nor once so much as name them? I dare not accuse *Pauls* Epistles written to that very purpose, and the whole Scripture, so much of insufficiency, as to think they wholly omit a necessary office, and so exactly mention the inferiour and commonly less necessary, as they do.

Reason 10. *The new Episcopal Divines do yield that all the texts*

texts in Timothy, Titus, *and the rest of the New Testament, that mentitn Gospel Bishops or Presbyters, do mean only such as have power of Ordination and Jurisdiction, without the concurrence of any superiour Bishop.* The common Inerpretation of the Fathers, and the old Episcopal Divines of all ages, of most or many of those texts, is, that they speak of the office of such as now are called *Presbyters.* Lay both together, and if one of them be not mistaken, they afford us this conclusion, that *the Presbyters that now are, have by these texts of Scripture, the power of Ordination and Jurisdiction without the concurrence of others.* And if so, then was it never the Apostles intent, to leave it to the Bishops to ordain a sort of Presbyters of another order, that should have no such power of Ordination or Jurisdiction, without the Bishops Negative.

Reason 11. We find in Church History that *it was first in some few great Cities* (especially *Rome* and *Alexandria*) *that a Bishop ruled many settled worshipping Congregations with their Presbyters; when no such thing at that time can be proved by other Churches:* therefore we may well conceive that it was no Ordinance of the Apostles, but was occasioned afterwards, by the multiplying of Christians in the same compass of ground where the old Church did inhabite; and the adjacent parts, together with the humane frailty of the Bishops, who gathered as many as they could under their own Government when they should have erected new Churches as free as their own.

Reason 12. *If the Description of the Bishops settled in the New Testament, and the work affixed to them, be such as cannot agree to our Diocesan Bishops but to the Pastor of a single Church, then was it never the mind of the Holy Ghost that those Bishops should degenerate afterwards into Diocesan Bishops: But the Antecedens is certain ? therefore so is the Consequent.*

I here still suppose with Learned Dr. *H Annot in Act.* 11. *& passim*, that the name Presbyter in Scripture signifieth a Bishop, there being no Evidence that in Scripture time any of that Second Order, (*viz.* subject Presbyters) were then instituted. Though I am far from thinking that there was but one of these Bishops in a Church at least as to many Churches. Now as we are agreed *de facto* that it was but a single Church that then was under a Bishop and not many such Churches (for that follows

unde-

undenyably upon the denying of the existence of subject Presbyters; seeing no such Churches can be, nor the worshipping Assemblies held without a Bishop or Presbyter;) so that it was the mind of the Apostles that it should so continue, is proved by the Desciption and work of those Scripture Bishops.

Argument 1. From *Acts* 20. 28, 29, 31. The Bishops instituted and fixed by the Holy Ghost were and are to *take heed to all the Flock over which the Holy Ghost hath made them overseers, to feed the Church of God, and to watch against Wolves, and to warn every one night and day*] But this cannot be done by Diocesan Bishops, nor any that have more then one Church: Therefore Diocesan Bishops are not the Bishops that the Holy Ghost hath so fixed and instituted, such as *Paul* describeth were to continue: and thats such as can do that work.

Argument 2. The Bishops that the Holy-Ghost settled and would have continue, (and had the Power of Ordination given them,) were such as were to be *Ordained in every City and every Church, Acts* 14. 23. *Tit.* 1. 3, 4, 5. See Dr *Hammonds Annotat.* But it is not Diocesan Bishops that are such (for they are over many Churches and Cities) therefore it is not Diocesan Bishops that were settled by the Holy Ghost, nor meant in those texts.

Ar. 3. The Bishops which were instituted by the Holy Ghost, and are meant in Scripture, were to *watch for their peoples souls as those that must give account, Ruling over them, and to be obeyed by all, and speaking to them the word of God, Heb.* 13. 7, 17, 34. But this cannot be done by a Bishop to a whole Diocess, (nor will they be willing of such an account if they be wise:)therefore it is not Diocesan Bishops that are meant in Scripture.

Argument 4. The Bishops settled for continuance in Scripture were such as all the people were *to know as labouring among them, and over them in the Lord, and admonishing them, and to esteem them very highly in love, for their work sake,* 1 *Thes.* 5. 12, 13. But this cannot be meant of our Diocesan Bishop, (whom the hundreth part of the flock shall never see, hear, nor be admonished by:) therefore it is not such that were settled for continuance in the Church.

Argument 5 The Bishops settled by the Holy Ghost, must by any that are *sick be sent for, to pray over them.* But this a Dio-

cesan

cefan Bifhop cannot do , to the hundreth or thoufandth perfon in fome places ; therefore it is not Diocefan Bifhops (but the Bifhops of a fingle Church that are capable of thefe works, that are meant by the Holy Ghoft, to continue in the Church, and confequently, to whom the power of Ordaining was committed. If any queftion whether the Texts alleadged do fpeak of fubject-Presbyters, or Bifhops, I refer them to the forefaid Reverend Doctor, with whom I am agreed, that there were no fubject-Prefbyters inftituted in Scripture times.

Reafon. 13.

See *Grotius de Imperio.p.351.* Proving that the Chriftian Church-Government was not fitted to that of the Temple , but that of the Synagogues, and endeavouring to prove Bifhops, he doth it thence, that they are fuch as the αρχι-συνάγωγοι. Let them then hold to fuch a Congregational Epifcopa-cy.

Reafon 13. *It was not one or two or all Churches for a year or two or more in their meer fieri or infancy before they were well formed, that confifted only of one fettled worfhipping Affembly and its guides ; but it was the formed and ftablifhed ftate of the particular Churches.*

To prove this I fhall briefly do thefe three things. 1. I fhall fhew it in refpect to the Jewifh Synagogues. 2. As to the Churches in the Apoftles dayes after many years growth ; even of every Church thats mentioned in the New Teftament, as a particular Political Church. 3. As to fome of the Churches after the Apoftles dayes, mentioned by the ancients.

1. It is apparent that the Jews Synagogues were particular Congregational Churches, having each one their feveral Rulers, and as many Learned men fuppofe, they had an Ecclefiaftical Judicature of Elders , belonging to each of them, where fit men could be found , and this diftinct from the Civil Judicature : Or as others think , they had a Sanhedrim which had power to judge in both Caufes, and one of thefe was in every City, that is, in Places of Cohabitation. For in every City of Ifrael which had one hundred and twenty families (or free perfons fay others) they placed the Sanhedrim of twenty three. And in every City which had not one hundred and twenty men in it, they fet the fmalleft Judicature of three Judges , fo be it there were but two wife men among them, fit to teach the Law and refolve doubts. See *Ainfworth on Numb.* 11. 16. *citing Talmud Bab. & Maimonides,* more at large. And doubtlefs many of our Country Villages, and almoft all our Parifhes have more then 120. and every Country Village may come in , in the leffer number below 120. which are to have three Elders : and that fay fome, was every place where were ten men. And that thefe were under the great Sanhedrim at *Jerufalem,* is nothing to the

the matter; For so we confess that such particular Churches as we mention, have some such General officers over them *de jure*, as the Apostolical men were in the Primitive Church; but not that any of these Synagogues were under other Synagogues; though one were in a great City, and the other but in a small Town: And that these Synagogues were of Divine institution, is plain in divers texts, particularly in *Lev.* 23. 1, 2, 3. where *a convocation of holiness, or a holy Convocation* is commanded to be on every Sabboth in all their dwellings, which most plainly could be neither the meeting at *Jerusalem* at the Temple, nor yet in single families: and therefore it is not to much purpose that many trouble themselves to conjecture when Synagogues began, and some imagine it was about the Captivity: For as their controversie can be but about the form of the meeting place, or the name, so its certain that some place there must be for such meetings; and that the meetings themselves were in the Law commanded by God: and that not to be tumultuary confused ungoverned Assemblies. If the scourging in the Synagogues prove not this power (which is much disputed,) *Mat.* 10. 17. *and* 23. 34. *Luke* 6. 22. *and* 12. 11. *and* 21. 12. *Acts* 22. 19. *and* 26 11. Yet at least, excluding men their Synagogue Communion, may *John* 9. 22, 34. *and* 12. 42. *and* 16. 2. But because this argument leads us into many Controversies about the Jewish customes, lest it obscure the truth by occasioning quarrels, I shall pass it by.

2. I find no particular Political Church in the New Testament, consisting of several Congregations, ordinarily meeting for communion in Gods Worship; (unless as the forementioned accidents might hinder the meeting of one Congregation in one place) nor having half so many members as some of our Parishes.

When there is mention made of a Country, as *Judea, Galile, Samaria, Galatia,* the word [Churches] in the plural number is used, *Gal.* 1. 2. *Acts* 15. 41. *and* 9. 31. 2 *Cor.* 8. 1. But they'l say, *These were only in Cities:* But further consider, there is express mention of the Church at *Cenchrea,* which was no City; and they that say that this was a Parish subject to *Corinth,* give us but their words for it, without any proof that ever I could see: and so they may as well determine the whole

L 3   cause

cause by bare affirmation, and prevent difputes. The Apoftle intimateth no fuch diftinction, *Rom.* 16. 1. 1 *Cor.* 11. 18,20,
22. 16. [*When ye come together in the Church , I hear that
there be divifions among you.* ——————— *When ye come together
therefore into one place , this is not to eat the Lords Supper.*]
——————— 16. *We have no fuch Cuftome, nor the Churches of God*]
Here the Church of *Corinth* is faid to *come together into one place:*
And for them that fay , This is *per partes* , and fo that *one place*
is *many* to the whole ; I anfwer, the Apoftle faith not to a part,
but to the *whole Church,* that they *come together in one place,* and
therefore the plain obvious fence muft ftand, till it be difproved.
And withall he calls the *Chriftian Affemblies* in the plural number [*Churches* :] for its plain that it is of *Affembly Cuftomes*
that he there fpeaks. So 1 *Cor.* 14. there is plainly expreffed that it
was a *particular Affembly* that was called *the Church,* and that
this Affembly had in many Prophets, Interpreters, & others that
might fpeak. *Verfe* 4. [*He that Prophefieth, Edifieth the Church*]
that is, *Only that Congregation that heard.* And *Verfe* 5. [*Except he interpret that the Church may receive Edifying*] And
Verfe 12. [*Seek that ye may excell to the Edifying of the Church.*]
Verfe 19. [*In the Church I had rather fpeak five words with my
underftanding , that I may teach others alfo.* ——] And *Verfe* 23.
[*If therefore the whole Church be come together into one place, and
all fpeak with tongues*———] One would think this is as plain
as can be fpoken to affure us that the *whole Churches* then were
fuch as might, and ufually did come together for holy communion into one place. So *Verfe* 28. [*If there be no Interpreter, let
him keep filence in the Church* :] And which is more, left you
think that this was fome one fmall Church that *Paul* fpeaks of,
he denominateth *all other particular Congregations,* even Ordered
Governed Congregations, [*Churches*] too. *Verfe* 33. *For God
is not the author of confufion but of peace, as in all the Churches of
the Saints.*] So that all the Congregations for Chriftian Worfhip,
are called, *All the Churches of the Saints.* And it feems all as well
as this, fo ftored with Prophets and gifted men that they need
not take up with one Bifhop only for want of matter to have
made fubject Elders of: And *Verfe* 34. [*Let your women keep
filence in the Church*] *for it is a fhame for a woman to fpeak
in the Church.*] So that fo many Affemblies, fo many Churches.
Object.

Obj. *But it seems there were among the* Corinthians *more then one Congregation by the plural* [Churches.] *Answ.* 1. Many particular seasons of Assembling, may be called many Assemblies or Churches, though the people be the same. 2. The Epistle was a Directory to other Churches, though first written to the Corinthians. 3. Those that say, it was to *Corinth*, and other City-Churches that *Paul* wrote, need no further answer: It seems then each City had but a Congregation, if that were so. 4 *Cenchrea* was a Church neer to *Corinth*, to whom *Paul* might well know his Epistle would be communicated: and more such there might be as well as that, and yet all be entire free Churches.

So in *Col.* 4. 16. [*And when this Epistle is read among you, cause that it be read also in the Church of the* Laodiceans, *and that ye likewise read the Epistle from* Laodicea] This Church was such as an Epistle might be read in, which doubtless was an Assembly. The whole matter seems plain in the case of the famous Church at *Antioch*, *Acts* 11. 26. *A whole year they assembled themselves with the Church, and taught much people*] Here is mention but of *One Assembly*, which is called *the Church*; where the people, it seems, were taught. And its plain that there were many Elders in this one Church; for *Acts* 13. 1. it said [*There were in the Church that was at* Antioch *certain Prophets and Teachers*] And five of them are named, who are said to Minister there *to the Lord*] And though I do not conclude that they were all the fixed Elders of that particular Church, yet while they were there they had no less power then if they had been such. In the third Epistle of *John*, where there is oft mention of that particular Church, it appeareth *Verse* 6. that it was such a Church as before which the Brethren and strangers could bear witness of *Gaius* Charity: And its most probable that was one Assembly; but utterly improbable that they travailed from Congregation to Congregation to hear this witness. And *Verf.* 9, 10. it was such a Church as *John* wrote an Epistle to, and which *Diotrephes* cast men out of: which is most likely to be a Congregation, which might at once hear that Epistle, and out of which *Diotrephes* might easilier reject strangers, and reject the Apostles letters, then out of many such Congregations, *Gal.* 1. 22. When *Paul* saith, he was *unknown by face to the Churches of Judea*, it is most likely that they were Churches which were
capable

capable of seeing and knowing his face not only by parts, but as Churches. And its likely those Churches that praised *Luke, and sent him with* Paul *as their chosen messenger,* were such as could *meet to choose him,* and not such as our Diocesses are, 1 *Cor.* 16. 1, 2. *Paul* gives order both to the Church of *Corinth,* and the Churches of *Galatia,* that upon the Lords day at the Assembly (as it is ordinarily expounded) they should give in their part for the relief of the Churches of *Judea.* So that it seems most likely that he makes [*Churches*] and such Assemblies to be all one, *Acts* 14. 23. *They ordained them Elders, Church by Church, or in every Church.* Here it is confessed by those we plead against, that Elders signifie not any subject Elders having no power of Ordination or Government: And to say that by *Elders* in each Church is meant only one Elder in each Church, is to forsake the letter of the text without any proved Necessity: We suppose it therefore safer to believe according to the first sence of the words, that it was *Elders in every Church,* that is, more then one in every Church that were ordained. And what sort of Churches these were, appears in the following verses, where even of the famous Church of *Antioch* its said, *Verse* 27. *when they were come, and had gathered the Church together, they rehearsed all that God had done by them* —— So that its plain that this Church was a Congregation to whom they might make such rehearsal. And *Chap.* 15. 3. Its said that *they were brought on their way by the Church:* And if it be not meant of all, but a part of the Church, yet it intimateth what is aforesaid.

To conclude, though many of these texts may be thought to speak doubtfully, yet consider 1. That some do most certainly declare that it was particular stated Assemblies that were then called Churches, even Governed Churches, having their Officers present. 2. That there is no certain proof of any one particular Political Church that consisted of *many such stated Assemblies.* 3. That therefore the Texts that will bear an exposition either way, must be expounded by the certain, and not by the uncertain texts; so that I may argue thus.

If in all the New Testament, the word [*Church*] *do often signifie stated worshipping single Assemblies, and often is used so as may admit that interpretation; and is never once used certainly to signifie many particular stated worshipping Assemblies ruled by*

one

one fixed Bishop, then we have any just cause to suppose that the particular Political Churches in Scripture times consisted but of one such stated Congregation. But the Antecedent is true, therefore so is the Consequent.

As for the New Episcopal Divines that say *There were no subject Presbyters in Scripture times:* I suppose according to their principles, they will grant me all this, as is aforesaid. And for *others,* the Instances that they bring to the contrary should be briefly considered. The great swaying Instance of all (which did sometime prevail with me to be my self of another mind) is the Numerous Church at *Jerusalem:* Of which its said that three thousand were converted at once, and five thousand at another time, and the word mightily grew and prevailed, and daily such were added to the Church as should be saved : to which some add the mention of the Miriades of believing Jews yet zealous of the Law, which the brethren mentioned to *Paul, Acts* 21. 20. And the instance of *Ephesus* and *Rome* come next. But I remember how largely this business is debated between the late Assembly at *Westminster* and the Dissenting Brethren, that I think it unmeet to interpose in it any further then to annex these few considerations following.

1. That all that is said on that side, doth not prove certainly that that one Church at *Jerusalem* was the eighth part so big as *Giles Cripple-gate Parish,* or the fifth part so big as *Stepney* or *Sepulchres,* nor neer so big as *Plimoth* or some other Country Parishes. 2. That it is past doubt that the magnitude of that Body of Believers then at *Jerusalem,* was partly accidental, and the members cannot all be proved settled cohabitants, nor that Church as in its first unordered Mass be proved to be the fittest pattern for imitation. 3. That Christ hath not punctually determined how many members shall be in a particular Church. 4. But the ends (being personal holy communion) are the Rule by which humane prudence must determine it. 5. That its fitter one Church instance give way to many in point of our imitation, then of many to that one, *cæteris paribus.* 6. That its known among us that give account of all. On which text Dr. *Jer. Taylor* in his late Book of Repentance, Pref. faith [I am sure we cannot give account of souls of which we have no Notice] And so presseth to personal conduct. Let them then be Bishops of no bigger a Diocess then they can take such personal notice and conduct of, left they par ... ...

Heb. 13. 17. proveth that Churches should be no bigger then that the Ruler may watch for all their souls as one that must

M   more

more then are proved to have been members of that Church, may hear one man preach at the same time. I have none of the loudest voices, and yet when I have preached to a Congregation judged by judicious men to be at least ten thousand, those farthest off said they could well hear (as I was certainly informed.) 7. That its certain by many passages historicall in Scripture that men did then speak to greater multitudes, and were heard at far greater distance then now they can orderly be : which I conjecture was because their voices were louder, as in most dryer bodies (which dryer Countreys have) is commonly seen, when moister bodies have ofter hoarser voices; and other reasons might concur. 8. That it is confessed or yielded that the Church at *Jerusalem* might all hear at once, though not all receive the Lords Supper together. And if so, then they were no more then might at once have personal communion in some holy Ordinances, and that the Teachers might at once make known their minds to. 9. And then the reason of receiving the Supper in several places seems to be but because they had not a room so fit to receive all in, as to hear in. And so we have now in many Parishes Assemblies subordinate to the chief Assembly : For divers families at once may meet at one house, and divers at another, for repetition, prayer or other duties ; and some may be at Chappels of ease that cannot come to the full assembly. 10. They that are for Presbyterial Churches of many Congregations, do not say, that *There must be many*, to make the first political Church, but only that, *There may be many* ? If then there be no Necessity of it, 1. Should it not be forborn when it appeareth to prudence most inconvenient (as frequently it will no doubt.) 2. And when it is Necessary for a peaceable Accommodation, because others think it a sin, should not a *May be* give place to a *Must not be*, in pacificatory consultations, *cæteris paribus* ? 11. It is granted also by them, that the Pastors of one Congregation have not a charge of Governing other neighbour Congregation in Consistory, (one rather then another, which they govern not, though perhaps as neer them) but by consent. And therefore as there is but a *licet*, not an *oportet*, of such consent pleaded for : so while *no such consent* is given, we have *no such charge* of Governing neighbour Congregations ; and none may force us to such consent. 12. And Lastly, that if a single Congregation
gregation

gregation with it own Officer, or Officers, be not a true particular Political Church; then our ordinary Parish assemblies are none; and where the Presbyterian Government is not set up (which is up but in few places of *England*) it would then follow that we have no true Political Churches left among us (& perhaps never had:) which I meet yet with few so uncharitable as to affirm, except the Papists and the Separatists and a few of the new sort of Episcopal Divines, who think we have no Churches for want of Bishops, (except where Bishops yet are retained and acknowleged.)

For my part I would not lay too great a stress upon any forms or modes which may be altered or diversified. *Let the Church have but such a Number of souls as may be consistent with the ends and so the essence of a particular Church, that they may hold personal holy communion, and then I will not quarrel about the name of one or two Congregations, nor whether they must needs all meet together for all ordinances, nor the like.* Yea I think *a full number* (so they be not so full or distant, as to be uncapable of that communion) are desireable, for the strength and beauty of the Church; and too smal Churches, if it may be, to be avoided. So that all the premises being considered, our difference appears to be but smal *in these matters* between the Congregational and Presbyterian way, among them that are moderate.

I shall not presume more particularly to enter into that debate, which hath been so far proceeded in already by such Reverend men, but shall return to the rest of the task before promised against the Diocesan Churches as the supposed subject of the Bishops Government.

As for Scripture times and the next succeeding together, I shall before I look into other testimonies, propound these two Arguments. 1. From the Bishops office, which was before mentioned. If the office of a Bishop in those times, was to do so much work as could not be done by him for a Church any greater than our Parishes, then were the Churches of those times no greater then our Parishes: But the Antecedent is true; therefore so is the consequent. The works are before mentioned, Preaching, Praying, administring the Lords Supper, visiting the sick, reducing hereticks, reproving, censuring, absolving: to which they quickly added too much more of their

own

own. The impossibility of a faithful performance of th's to more is so undenyable, that I cannot suppose any other answer but this that they might ordain Presbyters to assist them in the work, and so do mnch of it by others. But 1. I before desired to see it proved by what authority they might do this. 2. Their office and work are so inseparable that they cannot depute others to do their work (their proper work) without deputing them also to their office. For what is an office but the state of one *Obliged and Authorized* to do such or such a work? A Presbyter may not authorize another to preach as the Teacher of a Congregation, and to administer the Sacraments, without making him a Presbyter also: Nor can a Bishop authorize any to do the work of a Bishop in whole or by halves without making him a Presbyter or half a Bishop. And he is not authorized either to make new officers in the Church, or to do his work by deputies or substitutes.

2. I argue also from the Identity of that Church to which the Bishops and Deacons were appointed for ministration. It was not a Church of many stated Congregations, or any larger than our Parishes for number of souls that the Deacons were made Ministers to : therefore it was no other or bigger which the Bishops were set over. The consequence is good : because where ever Deacons are mentioned in Scripture or any Writer that I remember neer to Scripture times, they are still mentioned with the Bishops or Presbyters as Ministers to the same Church with them, as is apparent both in the seven chosen for the Church at *Jerusalem*, and in *Phil.* 1. 1, 2. and in the Direction of *Paul* to *Timothy* for ordaining them. And the Antecedent is proved from the nature of their work : For they being to attend on the tables at the Love feasts and the Lords Supper, and to look to the poor, they could not do this for any greater number of people then we mention ; Whether they had those feasts in one house or many at once, I determine not ; but for the number of people, it was as much as a Deacon could do at the utmost to attend a thousand people.

I shall proceed a little further towards the times next following ; and first I shall take in my way the confession of one or two learned men that are for Prelacy.

Grotius in his *Annotat.* on 1 *Tim.* 5. 17. saith [*Sed notandum est*

est in una Urbe magna sicut plures Synagogas, ita & plures fuisse Ecclesias, id est, conventus Christianorum. Et cuiq; Ecclesia fuisse suum præsidem, qui populum alloqueretur, & Presbyteros ordinaret. Alexandriæ tantum enim fuisse morem, ut unus esset in tota urbe præses qui ad docendum Presbyteros per urbem distribueret, docet nos Sozomenus 1.14. & Epiphanius, ubi de Ario agit, dicitq; Alexandriæ nunquam duos fuisse ἐπισκόπους voce ea sumpta κατ᾽ ἐξοχήν, ita ut significat jus illud quod habebat ὁ ἄρχων τῆς συναγωγῆς.] So that *Grotius* affirmeth that Bishops had not then so much as all the converted persons of a great City under their care, but the Churches and Assemblies were the same, and each Assembly had a Prelate, and in the great Cities there were many of these Churches and Prelates, and that only the City of *Alexandria* had the custom of having but one such Bishop in the whole City.

2. Those learned men also must grant this cause who maintain that *Peter* and *Paul* were both of them Bishops of *Rome* at once, there being two Churches, one of the Circumcision under *Peter*, the other of the uncircumcision under *Paul:* and that one of them had *Linus*, and the other *Cletus* for his Successor, and that this Church was first united under *Clemens*: and the like they say of two Churches also at *Antioch*, and elswhere. If this be so, then there is no Law of God that Bishops should be numbred by Cities, but more Bishops then one may be in one City, and were, even when Christians comparatively were a small part of them.

3. Also Mr. *Thorndike* and others affirm that it was then the custome for the Bishops and Presbyters to sit in a semicircle, and the Bishop highest in a Chair, and the Deacons to stand behind them: This he gathereth from the *Apost. Constitut.* *Ignatius, Dionysius Areop.* and the Jews Constitutions, (in his Apost. form *page* 71. and Right of the Church, &c. p. 93. 94. 95.) And if this were so, it seems that Bishops, Presbyters and Deacons were all the Officers of one such stated Congregation, and had not many such Congregations under them: For the Bishop could be but in one place at once, and therefore this could be the custome but of one Church in his Diocess, if he had many, whereas it is made the form of the ordinary Christian Assemblies.

The same learned man (Right of Church p. 65.) saith that

About

See the same thing proved at large by *Grotius de Imperio page* 355, 356, 357. Yet I think as *Blondell* that he mistook *Epiphanius de Alex. Eccl.*

[*About* Saint *Cyprians time, and not afore, he finds mention of fet-led Congregations in the Country*] By which it may be well conjectured what a small addition the Bishops had out of the Countreys to their City Churches, and how many Congregations they Governed in the Apostle dayes and after.

He affirmeth also that [*the power of the Keyes belongeth to the Presbyters, and that its convertible with the power of celebrating the Eucharist, and thats the Reason why it belongs to them,* page 98. ibid. and that [*the Power of the Keys, that is, the whole power of the Church whereof that power is the root and fourfe; is common to Bishops and Presbyters*] page 128 and that to this all sides agree, *page* 106. and that by *their Grant Deacons and others may preach, but not Rule or administer the Lords Supper:* fee page 118. 123. And he is far from being of their mind that think in Scripture times there was but one single Bishop without other Presbyters in a Diocesan Church: For he supposed many in a Congregation. *Page* 126 he faith [*You fee by St. Paul,* 1 Cor. 14. *that one Assembly whereof he speaks there, furnished with a great number of Prophets, whether Presbyters, or over and above them. In the Records of the Church, we find divers times a whole Bench of Presbyters presiding at one Assembly.*] And before he had shewed how they fate about the Bishop, and the congregation stood before them. And *page* 127. he faith that [*Clemens the Disciple of the Apostles, in his Epistle to the Corinthians to compose a difference among the Presbyters of that Church partly about the celebration of the Eucharist, adviseth them to agree and take their turns in it.*] I confefs I knnw not whence he hath this (doubtlefs not in the true approved Epistle of *Clement,*) but it shews in his judgement, 1. That there were then many Presbyters in the Church of *Corinth.* 2. And that that Church was but one Congregation, or not very many: Else what need the Presbyters take their turns, when they might have done it at once? 3. That the word *Presbyter* in *Clemens* signifieth not a Prelate. 4. And it seems this intimateth there was then no Bishop in *Corinth*: else no question but *Clemens* would have charged these disagreeing Presbyters to obey their Bishop, and used some of *Ignatius* language: 5. Nay if Bishops had been then known in the world, is it not likely that he would have charged them to get a Bishop if they had not, to Govern fuch a disagreeing Presbytery?

And

And page 129, 130, 131. he shews that [*the condemning of* Marcion *at* Rome, *and of* Noelus *at* Ephesus , *are exprefly faid by* Epiphanius, *Heref.* 42. *num.* 1. *& 2. Heref.* 57 *num.* 1. *to have been done and paffed by the Act of the Presbyters of thofe Churches* ———— *And which is of later date, the Excommunication of* Andronicus *in* Synefius 57. *Epift. I find reported to have paffed in the fame fort, and all this agreeable to the practice recorded in Scripture* alledging, 1. *Tim.* 5. 19. *Acts* 21. 18. citing *Cyprian Ep.* 46. and the *Apoft. Conftit.* and faith, *Blondell* in this might have fpared his exact diligence, it being granted, *&c.* Mr. *Thorndike* alfo tells us *pag.* 62. of the words of *Ninius* , that [in *Ireland* alone, Saint *Patrick* at the firft plantation of Chriftianity founded three hundred and threefcore and five Bifhopricks] And can any man believe that all thefe had Cities or more then one of our Parifh Churches , when all *Ireland* to this day hath not feven Cities ? and when all this was done at the firft plantation of the Gofpel ? I think we had this fort *of Epifcopacy.* Even fince the Refor-*have* mation there is reckoned in *Ireland* but four Arch-bifhops, nineteen Bifhops. What think you then were 365. Bifhops at the firft plantation of the Gofpel ?

To proceed to fome further Evidence. 1. Its manifeft in *Clemens Rom. Epift.* to the *Corinthians* there is mention of no more but two Orders, the one called fometime Bifhops, fometime Presters, the other Deacons, *page* 54, 55, 57. * and this he faith the Apoftles did *as knowing that contention would arife about the name of Epifcopacy,* and that they fo fetled the Minifterial Offices that *others fhould fucceed in them when fome were deceafed.* For my part I cannot fee the leaft reafon to be of their mind that think *Clemens* here doth fpeak only of Prelates or fupereminent Bifhops, (of which I refer the Reader to Mr. *Burtons* notes in his Englifh Tranflation of *Clemenr*) But fuppofe it were fo : If at that time the Churches had none but fingle Bifhops, it is plain then that they were but fingle Congregations : For no other Congregations having communion in their-then-ordinary, publike worfhip, could be managed without a Bifhop or Presby-

* Pag. 54, he faith [Κατα Χώρας ἐν και πόλεις κηρύσσοντες, καθίστανον τὰς ἀπαρχὰς, &c.] i. e. [Per regiones igitur & urbes praedicantes, conftituerunt primitias eorum, approbantes in Spiritu, Epifcopos & Diaconos eorum qui Credituri erant.]

I know that ταὶ χώρας is fuppofed by fome to refpect only the place of their preaching , and not of their fettling Bifhops : But the words according to the more obvious plain fenfe feem to extend it to both, and make no fuch difference at all

ter to do the work. But for them that fleight Mr. *Burtons* & other mens plain Reafons concerning the judgement of *Clem. Romanus*, and force his words to fpeak what they mean not, I defire them to obferve the judgement of *Grotius* whom they profefs fo much to value: who in his *Epiftol.* 162 *ad Bignon.* gives this as one Reafon to prove this Epiftle of *Clemens* genuine [*Quod nufquam meminit, exfortis illius Epifcoporum autoritatis, quæ Ecclefiæ confuetudine poft Marci mortem Alexandria, atq; eo exemplo alibi, introduci cepit, fed planè ut Paulus Apoftolus oftendit Ecclefias communi Presbyterorum qui iidem omnes & Epifcopi ipfi Pauloq; dicuntur, confilio fuiffe gubernatas. Nam quod* ἀρχιερέα, λευίτας, & λαϊκὸς *nominat, omnia ifta nomina non ad Ecclefiam fed ad Templum Hierof. pertinent : unde infert omnia recto ordine agenda, fi Judæis, tanto magis Chriftianis*] You fee that *Grotius* (then,) and *Clemens*, in his judgement, were againft Prelacy.

2. The very fame I fay of ~~Prelacie~~ *Polycarpe, Epift. ad Philip.* which mentioneth only two forts, Presbyters and Deacons.

3. And though *Ignatius* oft mention three, it feems to me that they were all but the Governours or Minifters of one Congregation, or of no more people then one of our Parifhes. In the *Epift. ad Smyrn.* he faith [ὅπου ἂν φανῇ ὁ ἐπίσκοπθ, ἐκεῖ τὸ πλῆθθ ἔσω, ὥσπερ ὅπου ὁ χριςὸς, πᾶσα ἡ ἐράνιθ ςρατιὰ παρίσνκεν. i. e. *Ubi Epifcopus præfens fuerit, illuc & plebs Congregetur, ficuti & ubi Chriftus eft omnis militia cœleftis adeft* as the common interpreter tranflateth it, [*ut vid. eft in Edit. Perionii & Ufherii,*] &c. [*Ubi comparuerit Epifcopus, ibi & Multitudo fit; quemadmodum ubi Chriftus, ibi omnis aftat exercitus cœleftis*] as *Hier. Vairlenius & Videlius* tranflate it: Or, [*Ubi utiq. apparet Epifcopus, illic multitudo fit; quemadmodum utiq, ubi eft Chriftus Jefus, illic Catholica Ecclefia*] as *Ufhers* old Tranflation. And by the Context it appeareth that this *plebs, or multitudo* is the Church which he ruleth, and not only one Congregation among many that are under him : For this doth without diftinction bind all the people one as well as another, to be where the Bifhop is or appeareth, *viz.* in the publick Affembly for Communion in Worfhip. It is plain therefore there that were not then many fuch Affemblies under him : otherwife all fave one muft have necefarily difobeyed this command.

And

(89)

And in the Epistle to the *Philadelphians* he hath [Μία γάρ
ἐστιν ἡ σάρξ τȣ κυρίȣ Ιησȣ , κ̀ ἓν αὐτȣ τὸ αἷμα τὸ ὑπὲρ ἡμῶν ἐκ-
χυθέν. Εἷς κ̀ ἄρτȣ τοῖς πᾶσιν ἐθρύφθη, κ̀ ἓν ποτήριον τοῖς ὅλοις
διενεμήθη, ἓν θυσιαστήριον πάσῃ τῇ ἐκκλησίᾳ, κ̀ εἷς ἐπίσκοπ©
ἅμα τῷ πρεσβυτερίῳ, κ̀ τοῖς διακόνοις τοῖς συνδȣλοις μȣ.
ιτε. [*Una enim est caro Domini nostri Jesu Christi, & unus illius sanguis qui pro nobis effusus est, & unus calix qui pro omnibus
nobis distributus est,* ~~unus panis qui omnibus fractus est~~ *unum altare omni Ecclesiæ, & unus Episcopus cum presbyterorum Collegio & Diaconis conservis meis.*]

Here it is manifest that the particular Church which in those
dayes was governed by a Bishop, Presbytery and Deacons, was
but one Congregation; for every such Church had but one
Altar.

Object. But some Greek Copies leave out πάσῃ τῇ ἐκκλησίᾳ.
Answ. 1. The corrupt vulgar translation might occasion the
change of the text, saith Bishop *Usher* (*Annot. in loc. page* 40.)
[*intermedia illa, ex interpretatione hâc excidisse videantur.*]
2. The old translation of Bishop *Usher* which leaves it out, yet
hath *Unum Altare & unus Episcopus, &c.* and the sence is the
same if the other words were out. 3. *Ignatius* hath the like in
other places, as we shall see anon; which forbiddeth such quarrels
here.

Object. But saith the Learned and Godly Bishop *Downame,*
(*Def. li. 2. cap. 6. page* 109) *the word Altar being expounded
for the Communion table, is not likely, and too much favoureth
of Popery: but by one Altar is meant Christ who sanctifieth all our
Sacrifices and Oblations and maketh them acceptable to God; as*
Ignatius *expoundeth himself in his Epistle to the Magnesians: All
as one run together into the Temple of God, unto one Jesus Christ as it
were unto one Altar.*]

To this I answer, that it is some confirmation to me, that
the words are so express, that so learned a man hath no more
to say by way of evasion. For doubtless this is too gross and
palpable to satisfie the judicious impartial reader. 1. That the
very text which he citeth of the Epistle to the *Magnesians*
doth make fully against him I shall shew anon. 2. That it is not
Christ that is meant here by the ἓν θυσιαστήριον, is evident. 1. In
that Christ his flesh and blood are before distinctly mentioned:

N

2. In that the word is put in order among the external Ordinances: 3. In that it is so usual with other ancient writers and *Ignatius* himself to use the word θυσιαστήριον in the sence as we now take it, that it will be plain violence to imagine that it is Christ that was meant by it. And for Popery, there is no such matter of danger, in using a word *Metaphorically*: Otherwise we must make the Ancients commonly to be friends to Popery; for they ordinarily call the Lords Table and the place where it stood θυσιαστήριον: I say *The Table and the Sacrarium: or place of its standing*: for this seems plainly the meaning of *Ignatius*: so saith Bishop *Usher Annot. in loc. ubi sup.* [*Altare apud Patres mensam Dominicam passim denotat apud* Ignatium *&* Polycarpum, *Sacrarium quoq;.*] So *H. Stephens Altarium Sacrarium.* See what Learned Mr. *Thorndike* himself in his *Right of the Church, &c. page* 116. saith to this purpose more largely; where concerning *Ignatius* his use of the same word to the Ephesians he saith [*Where it is manifest that the Church is called a Sanctuary or place of sacrificing*: Mr. *Mead* in his Discourse of the name Altar *page* 14. sheweth that *Ignatius* by θυσιαστήριον means the *Lords Table*, and takes *Videlius* his concession, as of a thing that could not be denyed. In the Epistle of *Ignatius* (or whoever else) to Polycarp Bishop of *Smyrna* he saith, *Crebrius celebrantur conventus Synodiq; Nominatim omnes inquire. Servos & ancillas ne fastidias* (as *Vairlenius* translateth) or (as Bishop *Ushers* old Translation) *Sæpe Congregationes fiant. Ex nomine omnes quære: Servos & ancillas ne despicias.* ————] Whether this were *Ignatius* or not, alls one to me, as long as I use it but historically to prove the matter of fact in those times. But surely no man should marvail if I hence gather that great *Polycarp* was Bishop but of one Congregation, when he must enquire or take notice of every one of his Congregation by name, even as much as servants and maids. I would every Parish Minister were so exactly acquainted with his flock!

Another passage there is in *Ignatius* to the same purpose, *Epist. ad Magnes.* [Πάντες ὡς εἷς, εἰς τὸν ναὸν θεῦ συντρέχατε, ὡς ἐπὶ ἓν θυσιαστήριον, ἐπὶ ἕνα Ἰησοῦν χριστὸν,] i. e. *Omnes adunati ad Templum Dei concurrite, sicut ad unum Altare; sicut ad unum Jesum Christum*, as the vulgar translation. Or as *Vairlenius*, [*Omnes velut unus quispiam in templum Dei concurrite, velut*

ad

ad unum Alnare ; ad unum Jefum Chriftum] So the old Latine in *Ufher* to the fame purpofe. And in the words beforegoing he bids them [*Come all to one place for prayer*] Here is no room for Bifhop *Downams* conceit, that its Chrift thats meant by θυσιασήριον : For they are plainly put as diftinct things : as if he fhould fay, *come all to one Altar, as to one Chrift.* i. e. becaufe *it is but one Chrift that is there to be partaked of.* All this doth fo evidently prove that in thofe dayes a Bifhop with his Presbytery and Deacons, had but one Congregation meeting at one Altar for Church Commnnion in the Eucharift, that it caufed Mr. *Mead* (in his *Difcourfe of Churches* pag. 48, 49, 50. *Cent.* 2.) to fay as followeth, having cited thefe words of *Ignatius* | *Loe here a Temple with an Altar in it, whether the Magnefians are exhorted to gather themfelves together to pray: To come together in one place, &c. For it is to be obferved that in thofe Primitive times they had but one Altar in a Church, as a Symbole, both that they worfhipped but one God through one Mediator Jefus Chrift, and alfo of the Unity the Church ought to have in it felf. Whence* Ignatius *not only here, but alfo in his Epiftle to the Philadelphians urgeth the unity of the Altar for a motive to the Congregation to agree together in one: For* unum Altare (faith he) omni Ecclefiæ, & unus Epifcopus cum Presbyterio & Diaconis confervis meis. *This cuftome of one Altar is ftill retained by the Greek Church: The contrary ufe is a transgreffion of the Latines, not only Symbolically implying, but really introducing a* πολυθεΐα, —— &c. *Nay more then this it fhould feem that in thofe firft times, before Diocefles were divided into thofe lefler and fubordinate Churches, we call now Parifhes, and Presbyters affigned to them, they had not only one Altar in one Church or* Dominicum, *but one Altar to a Church, taking Church for the company or Corporation of the faithfull, united under one Bifhop or Paftor, and that was in the City or place where the Bifhop had his See and Refidence, like as the Jews had but one Altar and Temple for the whole Nation united under one high Prieft. And yet as the Jews had their Synagogues, fo perhaps might they have more Oratories then one, though their Altar were but one; there namely where the Bifhop was.* Die folis *faith* Juftin Martyr, omnium qui vel in oppidis vel ruri degunt, in eundem locum conventus fit: *Namely as he there tells us, to celebrate, and participate the body*

Eucharift. Why was this, but becaufe they had not many places to celebrate in? and *unlefs this were fo, whence came it elfe, that a Schifmatical Bifhop* was faid conftituere or collocare aliud Altare? *and that a Bifhop and an Altar are made correlatives?* See S. Cyprian *Epift.* 40. 72, 73. *de unit. Ecclef.* And thus perhaps is Ignatius *to be underftood in that forequoted paffage of his* Εν θυσιαστήριον Unum Altare omni Ecclefiæ, & unus Epifcopus cum Presbyterio & Diaconis] So far Mr. *Mead.*

I hope upon the confent of fo admirable a Critick and learned man, it will not be fo much blame-worthy in me, if I fpeak fomewhat the more confidently this way; and fay, that I think that the main confufion and Tyranny that hath overfpread the Churches, hath been very much from the changing the Apoftolical frame of Churches, and fetting up many Altars and Congregations under one Bifhop in one (pretended particular) Church.

I had three or four paffages ready to cite out of *Ignatius*, but thefe are fo exprefs, that I apprehend the reft the lefs neceffary to be mentioned.

The next therefore that I fhall mention fhall be the forementioned words of *Juftin Martyr Apol.* 2, cited by Mr. *Mead*, and by others frequently to this purpofe: In which I obferve all thefe particulars full to the purpofe. 1. That they had but one Affembly each Lords day for Church communion for one Church. 2. That this was for reading and prayer and the Eucharift. 3. That the Prefident (who is commonly by thofe of the Epifcopal judgement faid to be here meant the Bifhop) did preach and give thanks and adminifter the fupper: fo that it was adminiftred but to one Congregation as under that Bifhop of that Church, for he could not be in two places at once. 4. That to the Abfent the Deacons carried their portion after the confecration: fo that they had not another Meeting and Congregation by themfelves for that end. This is all fo plain that I fhall think it needeth no Vindication. So that were there but thefe two Teftimonies, I fhould not marvail if Bifhop *Downam* had extended his confeffion a little further, when he acknowledgeth (*Def. li.* 2. *cap.* 6. *page* 104. that [*At the firft and namely in the time of the Apoftle* Paul, *the moft of the Churches fo foon after their Converfion, did not each of them exceed the proportion of a*

populous

populous Congregation,] (And then we are not out in so interpreting the words of *Paul* and other writers of the holy Scripture.) The next that I shall mention (whoever was or when ever he lived) is *Dionys. de Eccles. Hierarch. cap.* 4. where he tells us that the Præfect (who was the Bishop, if there were any) did Baptize those that were converted, and the Presbyters and Deacons did but assist him : And abundance of work he mentioneth which they had with all that they Baptized, and they called all the Congregation together who joyned in Prayers with the Bishop at the Baptism. All which shews that he was then the Bishop but of one particular Church, which ordinarily Assembled together for publick worship. For, 1. If he had many such Churches or Congregations under him, he could not be thus present to celebrate Baptism in them all. Nor would one only be mentioned as his charge. 2. Nor is it possible that one Bishop should with so long a way of Baptisme as is there described, be able to Baptize all the persons in a Diocess such as ours, or the twentieth part of them, much less in those times, when besides the Infants of Believers, the most eminent sort of Baptism, and greatest labour, was about the multitudes of Adult Converts, that by the Gospel were daily added to the Church.

Gregory Thaumaturgus was as by force made Bishop of *Neocesarea* : and yet his whole Diocess or City had but seventeen Christians in it at his entrance, though when he died he found upon enquiry but seventeen Pagans, so great a change was made by the Gospel and by Miracles : But by this Diocess of seventeen souls we may conjecture what the Churches were in those times (though we should allow others to be an hundred times as great, they would not be so great as the tenth part of many Parishes in *England*.) See the truth of this passage in *Greg. Nissen Oratio in Greg. Thaumatur.* twice over he recites it. And *Basil. Mag l. de Spir. Sanc. c.* 19. And *Roman. Breviar. Die* 15. *Novemb.* And the *Menolog Græc.* mentioned before *Greg. Neocesar.* works Printed at *Paris* 1622. But I shall return to some before *Gregory.*

The next that I shall cite is *Tertullian*, that well known place in his *Apolog. c.* 39. [*Corpus sumus de conscientia Religionis & Discipline unitate & spei fœdere. Coimus in cœtum & Congregationem ut ad Deum quasi manu facta precationibus ambiamus orantes.*

orantes. —— *Cogimur ad divinarum literarum Commemorationem* —— *Certè fidem sanctis vocibus pascimus, spem erigimus, fiduciam figimus, disciplinam praeceptorum nihilominus inculcationibus densamus: ibidem etiam exhortationes, Castigationes, & censura Divina: nam & judicatur magno cum pondere ut apud certos de Dei conspectu; summumq; futuri judicii praejudicium est siquis ita deliquerit, ut à communicatione Orationis, & conventus, & omnis sancti commercii relegetur. Praesident probati quiq, seniores, &c.*] If I be able to understand *Tertullian*, it is here plain that each Church consisted of one Congregation, which assembled for Worship, and Discipline at once or in one place, and this Church was it that had Presidents or Seniors to guide them both in Worship and by Discipline. So that if there were any more of these Assemblies in one particular Political Church, then there were more Bishops then one, or else others besides Bishops exercised this Discipline: But indeed its here plainly intimated that Bishops were then the Guides of Congregations (single,) and not of Diocesses consisting of many such.

I shall put *Tertullians* meaning out of doubt by another place, and that is, *de Corona Militis cap. 3.* [*Eucharistiae Sacramentum & in tempore victus, & omnibus mandatum à Domino, etiam antelucanis ritibus, nec de aliorum manuum praesidentium sumimus.*] And if they received this Sacrament of none but the Presidents, (and that every Lords day at least, as no doubt they did) then they could have no more Congregations in a Church then they had Presidents. And (though *Pamelius* say that by Presidents here is meant also Presbyters, yet) those that we now dispute against, understand it of the Prelates. And if they will not so do, then may we well interpret the foresaid passage Apol. to be meant of the same sort of Presidents. and then you may soon see what Bishops were in *Tertullians* dayes. For we have no reason to think that they are not the same sort of Officers which he cal'eth Presidents, and of whom he there saith, *Praesident probati Seniores.*

So in the foregoing words in *Tertullian*, ibid its said [*Aquam adituri ibidem, sed & aliquando prius in Ecclesia sub Antistitis manu contestamur nos renunciare Diabolo, & Pompa & angelis ejus*] Where it seems that there were no more thus initiated then the *Antistes* himself did first thus engage in the Congregation; And I believe they take this *Antistes* for a Bishop.

. And

And here by the way let this argument be noted. Seeing its past doubt that the first sence of the word ἐκκλησία is the *Cœtus* or holy Assembly it self, why should the *Meeting place* be so often called also *Ecclesia* in those times, in the *borrowed sence*, but only in Relation to the People there assembled? and its plain that it was but one Congregation and not many that assembled in that place: and therefore it was from that one that the Place is called *Ecclesia*. That it is oft so called, besides this place of *Tertullian* (which seems so to use the word) I refer you to Mr. *Meads* exercitation of Temples, who proves it distinctly in the several Centuries. That saying of *Theophilus Antiochenus ad Antolychum* seems to intimate the whole that I intend [*sic Deus dedit mundo qui peccatorum tempestatibus & Naufragiis jactatur, Synagogas, quas Ecclesias Sanctas Nominamus in quibus veritatis doctrina fervet, ad quas confugiunt veritatis studiosi, quotquot salvari, Deiq; judicium & iram evitare volunt.* So that the Churches of those times which were as *Noahs* Ark, and where safety was to be found for the soul, were Synagogues or Assemblies. So *Tertul. de Idololatr c.* 7. *pag.* (*mihi*) 171. *Tota die ad hanc partem zelus fidei peroravit, ingenuū Christianum ab Idolis in Ecclesiam venire, de adversaria officina in domum Dei venire.*] See more places of *Tertullian* cited by *Pamelius* on this place *num.* 29. *page* 177. specially see that *de virg. Veland. cap.* 13. *p.* 224

* *Clemens Alexandrinus* hath divers passages to the purpose

* Very many passages in *Cyprian* do intimate that then the Dioceses were small, perhaps having yet but *unum Altare*: As when he saith that [*à primordio Episcopatus mei statuerim nihil sine consilio vestro & sine consensu plebis meæ, privata sententia gerere,* &c. And

[*Prohibeantur offerre, acturi apud nos, & apud confessores ipsos, & apud plebem universam causam suam*] And [*Hæc singulorum tractanda sit & limanda plenius ratio, non tantum cum colegis meis, sed & cum plebe ipsa universa*] And [*Vix plebi persuadeo, immo extorqueo, ut tales patiantur admitti, & justior factus est fraternitatis dolor, ex eo quod unus atq; alius obnitente plebe & contradicente, mea tamen facilitate suscepti, pejores extiterunt —*] How the *universa plebs* of many Congregations or a Diocess like ours, should be consulted and hear and do any thing to admission or exclusion from Communion, and be advised with by *Cyprian* in all such affairs, is not easie to conceive. See his *Epist.* 3. 6. 10. 13, 14, 26, 31, 27, 28, 33, 40. &c.

Peruse all the citations of *Blondell de jure Plebis in Regim. Ecclef.* and see whether they intimate not the smalness of their Dioceses. (Though I believe they prove no such thing as proper Government in the people.) And peruse all the Authors cited by him there to prove that *de Ecclesia Math.* 18. refers to the Congregation of Pastors and people together; and it will much confirm the point in hand. I shall not recite any of them, because you may there find them in the end of *Grotius de Imperio Sum. Potest.*

now

now in hand. *Stromat. li.* 7. in the beginning, he mentioneth the Church and its officers, which he divideth only into two forts, *Presbyters and Deacons.* But I will name no more particular perfons, but come to fome intimations of the point before us from cuftomes or Practices of the Church and the Canons of Councils.

And it feems to me that the dividing of Parifhes fo long after (or of Titles as they are called) doth plainly tell us that about thofe times it was that particular Polcical Church did firft contain many ftated Congregations. And though it be uncertain when this began (Mr. *Thorndike* as we heard before, conjectureth, about *Cyprians* dayes) yet we know that it was long after the Apoftles, and that it was ftrange to lefs populous places long after it was introduced at *Rome* and *Alexandria*, where the number of Chriftians, & too much ambition of the Bifhop, occafioned the multiplication of Congregations under him, and fo he became a Bifhop of many Churches (named as one) who formely was Bifhop but of a fingle Church. For if there had been enough, one hundred or fifty or twenty or ten years before, to have made many Parifhes or ftated Affemblies for communion in worfhip, then no doubt but the light of Nature would have directed them to have made fome ftated divifions before; For they muft needs know that God was not the God of Confufion but of order in all the Churches: And they had the fame reafons before as after: And perfecution could not be the hindrance any more at firft then at laft: For it was under perfecuting Emperours when Parifhes or Titles were diftinguifhed, and fo it might, notwithftanding perfecutions have been done as well at firft as at laft, if there had been the fame reafon. it feems therefore very plain to me that it was the increafe of Converts that caufed this divifion of Titles, and that in planting of Churches by the Apoftles, and during their time, and much after, the Churches confifted of no more then our Parifhes, who being moft inhabitants of the Cities had their meetings there for full communion, though they might have other fubordinate meetings as we have now in mens houfes for Repeating Sermons and Prayer.

And as Mr. *Thorndike* out of *Ninius* tells us of 365. Bifhopricks in *Ireland* planted by *Patrick*, fo other Authors tell us us that *Patrick* was the first Bishop there; or as others and more credible, *Palladius* the first, and *Patrick* next : and yet the Scots in *Ireland* had Churches before *Palladius* his dayes, (as Bishop *Usher* sheweth *de Primordiis Ecclef. Britan.*798, 799, 800, &c.) *Johannes Major de gestis Scotorum li.* 2. *cap.* 2. *prioribus illis temporibus per Sacerdotes & Monachos, sine Episcopis Scotos in fide eruditos fuisse affirmat. Et ita sane ante Majorem scripsit* Johannes Fordonus *Scotichron. li.* 3. *cap.* 8. [*Ante* Palladii *adventum habebant Scoti fidei Doctores ac Sacramentorum Ministratores Presbyteros solummodo vel Monachos, ritum sequentes Ecclesiæ Primitivæ* (N. B.) Of which saith Usher [*Quod postremum ab iis accepisse videtur qui dixerunt* (*ut* Johan. Semeca *in Glossa Decreti dist.* 93. *ca. Legimus*) [*quod in Prima Primitiva Ecclesia commune erat officium Episcoporum & Sacerdotum: & Nomina erant communia, & officium commune ; sed in secunda primitiva cæperunt distigui & nomina & officia.*]So that it seems that some Churches they had before ; but *Palladius* and *Patrick* came into *Ireland,* as *Augustine* into *England,* and abundantly increased them, and settled withall the Roman Mode ; So that it seemed like a new Plantation of Religion and Churches there. Yet it seems that the Bishops setled by *Patrick* (save that himself an Archbishop was like our Bishops) were but such as were there before under the name of Presbyters, saith *Fordon,* after the rite or fashion of the Primitive Church.

And saith *Usher ibid. p.* 800. [Hector Boethius *fuisse dicit* Palladium *primum omnium qui Sacrum inter Scotos egere Magistratum à summo Pontifice Episcopum creatum : quum antea Populi suffragiis ex Monachis & Caldeis pontifices assumerentur.* Boeth. *Scotorum Histor. lib.* 7. *fol.* 128. *b.*

And he adds the saying of *Balæus,* (*Scriptor. Britanic. centur.* 14. *cap.* 6.) [*A Cælestino illum missum ait* Johannes Balæus, *ut Sacerdotalem ordinem, inter Scotos Romano ritu institueret. Habebant* (inquit) *antea Scoti suos Episcopos ac Ministros, ex verbi Divini Ministerio plebium suffragiis electos, prout Asianorum more fieri apud Britannos videbant : Sed hæc Romanis, ut magis ceremoniosis atque Asianorum osoribus, non placebant*] By these passages it is easie to conjecture whether they were Bishops of a County, or Bishops of a Parish that were there in those daies. For my part I heartily wish that *Ireland* had three hundred sixty

five

five good Bishops and Churches at this day, even when the whole Nation profess themselves to be Christians, (which then they did not.)

To this purpose runs the 14. *Canon Concilii Agath.* (and if it were so then, much more long before) [*Siquis etiam extra Parochias in quibus legitimus est ordinariusq; conventus oratorium habere voluerit reliquis festivitatibus, ut ibi Missam audiat, propter fatigationem familiæ, justa ordinatione permittimus. Pascha vero, Natali Domini, Epiphania, Ascensione domini, Pentecoste, & Natali Sancti* Johannis Baptistæ*, & siqui maxime dies in festivitatibus habentur, non nisi in Civitatibus, aut Parochiis audiant*] Here it appeareth that there was but one *legitimus ordinariusq; conventus* in a Parish ; though they tolerated an Oratory or Chappell of ease. And that a Parish here is taken for a Diocess, or such a Church as had proper to it self a Bishop and Presbyterie, as it is probable from the ordinary use of the word by *Eusebius* and other antients in that sence, so also from what is further said in the following Canons of this Council : And so the word Parish here may be expository of the word *City*, or else denote a Rural Bishoprick. For Can. 30. saith [*Benedictionem super plebem in Ecclesiâ fundere aut panitentem in Ecclesia benedicere presbytero penitus non licebit.*] And if a Presbyter may not bless the people or the penitent , (when the blessing of the people was part of the work in every Solemn Assembly for Church communion) then it is manifest that a Bishop must be present in every such Assembly to do that part which the Presbyter might not do : and consequently there were no more such Assemblies then there were Bishops. And to prove this more fully mark the very next Canon of that Council, *viz.* the 31. [*Missas die dominico secularibus totas audire speciali ordine præcipimus, ita ut ante benedictionem Sacerdotis egredi populus non præsumat. Quod si fecerint, ab Episcopo publicè confundatur*] So that its plain that on every Lords day all the people (for here is no distinction or limitation) were to be present in the publick worship to the end, and the Bishop to pronounce the blessing (whoever preached) and openly to rebuke any that should go out before it. From whence it is evident that all such Church Assemblies for communion every Lords day were to have a Bishop present with them to do part of the work : and therefore there

were

were no more such Assemblies then there were Bishops.

In the 38. Canon of the same Council we find this written [*Cives qui superiorum solennitatum, id est, Pasch & Natalis Domini, vel Pentecostes festivatibus cum Episcopis interesse neglexerint, quum in Civitatibus commnionis vel benedictionis accipienda causa positos se nosse debeant, triennio communione priventur Ecclesi.*] So that it seems there were no more Church-members in a City then could congregate on the festival daies for Communion and the Bishops Blessing : therefore there were not many such Congregations : when every one was to be three years excommunicate that did not Assemble where the Bishop was.

Moreover all those Canons of several Councils that forbid the Presbyters to confirm by Chrysm, and make it the Bishops work, do shew that the Diocess were but small when the Bishop himself could do that besides all his other work.

In the Canons called the Apostles, *cap.* 5. it is ordained thus [*Omnium aliorum primiti Episcopo & Presbyteris domum mittuntur, non super Altare. Manifestum est autem quod Episcopus & Presbyteri inter Diaconos & reliquos clericos eas dividunt.*] By which it appeareth that there was but one Altar in a Church to which belonged the Bishop, Presbyterie, and Deacons, who lived all as it were on that Altar.

And Can. 32. runs thus [*Si quis Presbyter contemnens Episcopum suum, seorsim collegerit, & Altare aliud erexerit, nihil habens quo rebrehendat Episcopum in causa pietatis & justitia, deponatur quasi principatus amator existens —— Hc autem post unam & secundam & tertiam Episcopi obsecrationem fieri conveniat.*] Which shews that there was then but one Convention and one Altar to which one Bishop and Presbyters did belong : So that no other Assembly or Altar was to be set up apart from the Bishop by any Presbyter that had nothing against the Bishop in point of Godliness or Justice.

And I believe if Bishops had a whole Diocesse of two hundred or three hundred or a thousand Presbyters to maintain, they would be loth to stand to the fifty eighth Canon which makes them Murderers if they supply not their Clergies wants : But let that Canon pass as spurious.

And long after when *Concilium Vasense* doth grant leave to the Presbyters to preach, and Deacons to read Homilies in Country

Parishes

Parishes as well as Cities, it shews that such Parishes were but new and imperfect Assemblies.

In the Council of *Laodicea* the 56. Canon is [*Non oportet Presbyteros ante ingressum Episcopi ingredi Ecclesiam, & sedere in tribunalibus, sed cum Episcopo ingredi: nisi forte aut agrotet Episcopus, aut in peregrinationis commodo eum abisse constiterit.*] By which it seems that there was but one Assemby in which the Bishop and Presbyters sate together: Otherwise the Presbyters might have gone into all the rest of the Churches without the Bishop at any time, and not only in case of his sickness or peregrination.

The fifth Canon of the Council of *Antioch* is the same with that of *Can. Apost.* before cited, that no *Presbyter or Deacon contemning his own Bishop, shall withdraw from the Church and gather an Assembly apart, and set up an Altar.* By which still it appears that to withdraw from that *Assembly*, was to withdraw from the Church, and that *one Bishop* had but *one Altar and Assembly* for Church Communion.

So *Cencil. Carthag.* 4. *Can.* 35. which order the sitting of the Presbyters and Bishop together in the Church: And many decrees that lay it on the Bishop to look to the Church lands and goods, and distribute to the poor the Churches Alms, do shew that their Diocesses were but small, or else they had not been sufficient for this.

All the premises laid together me thinks afford me this conclusion, that the Apostolical particular Political Churches were such as consisted of one only Worshipping Congregation (a Congregation capable of personal communion in publick worship) and their Overseers; and that by little they departed from this form, each Bishop enlarging his Diocess, till he that was made at first the Bishop but of one Church, became the Bishop of many, and so set up a new frame of Government, by setting up a new kind of particular Churches. And thus was the primitive Government corrupted, while men measured their charge by the circuit of Ground, thinking they might retain the old compass when they had multiplied converts; and therefore should have multiplyed Churches and Bishops. *

To all this I add these observations: 1. That the very *Nature of Church Government* tels us that a Governour must be *present*

*And it seems the Churches were not so large as some imagine, even at the sixth General Council at *Trul.* in *Constantinop.* when Canon 78. it was ordered that only the fifth day of the week the Baptized were to say over their Belief to the Bishop or the Presbyters: And it was not such Diocesses as ours that this work could be thus done for.

upon the place, and see to the execution: For God hath made *us the Laws* already, and *Synods* must in way of *Union determine* of the most advantagious *circumstances* for the performing of the duties which God imposeth: And particular Bishops are to guide their particular Congregations in Gods Worship, and in order thereto; Their guidance is but a subservient means to that worship: And therefore they must Rule the Church as a Captain doth his Company in fight, or a Physitian his Patient, or a Schoolmaster his School, by his own presence, and not at many miles distance by a Surrogate.

2. The doctrine which makes the first particular Political Church to consist of many stated Worshipping Churches like our Parishes, doth set on the saddle, if not also hold the stirrup for a Diocesan Bishop to get up, to head those prepared bodies.

3. Seeing the Presbyterians do confess that it is not *Necessary* (but lawful) for a particular Political Church to consist of many Worshipping Churches, and say, *It may consist only of one:* Common Reason and experience will then direct us to conclude that *its best-ordinarily take up with that one:* seeing people that know one another, and live within the reach of each other for common converse, and ordinarily meet and join in the same publick Worship, are most capable of the ends of Church Policy, and a Pastor capable of guiding such, better then other Parishes that he knows not.

4. He that makes the Pastor of one Parish the Ruler of the rest adjoining, doth lay upon him much more duty then sitting in a Presbyterie to vote in censures. For those censures are a small part of Church Government, comparatively (else most Congregations in *England* have little or no Government; for they have little or none of these Censures.) Yea indeed true Church Guidance or Government contains a great part, if not most of the Pastoral work, which a man would be loth to undertake over too many distant unknown Congregations: Though he may well undertake in Synods to promote Unity, and to do the best he can for the whole Church of Christ. If therefore those of the Congregational way, were as neer us in other things, as in this before insisted on, (especially if they would renounce* that great mistake of the Peoples having the Power of the Keys or Government: and take up for them with a *Judicium Discretionis.*

* As many of them do in sence, when they hold it in terms, of which see what I have said in the Preface to the *Reformed Pastor;* And even in this while they confess that Pastors are Rulers and the People must obey, according to the express words of the text, *Heb.* 13. 17. 1 *Tim.* 5. 17. 1 *Thes.* 5. 12; &c. They grant us what we plead for.

and

and juft liberty) we need not ftand at fo great a diftance.

And laftly, If Minifters of the Gofpel would tenderly weigh the greatnefs of their work and charge, and the dreadfulnefs of their account, the worth of fouls, the power and prevalency of fin, the rage of all the Churches enemies, and the multitudes of them, they would fooner tremble to think of the difficulties in Governing or guiding one Congregation in the way to heaven, than grafp at more, and think themfelves able to be the guides of many, and draw fuch a heavy burden on themfelves, and prepare for fuch a reckoning. Left they be offended with my words, I will fay the like in the words of *Chryfoftom* (or whoever elfe was the Author of the Imperfect work) on *Matth* 20. *Hom.* 35. *pag.* (*mihi*) 901. [*Si hac ergo ita fe habent , fecularem quidem primatum defiderare, etfi ratio non eft, vel caufa eft : quia etfi juftum non eft , vel utile eft. Primatum autem Ecclefiafticum concupifcere , neq; ratio eft , neq; caufa : quia neq; juftum eft , neq; utile. Quis exim fapiens ultro fe fubjicere feftinat fervituti, labori, dolori, & quod majus eft, periculo tali ut det rationem pro omni Ecclefia, apud juftum judicem ? nifi forte qui non credit Judicium Dei, nec timet, uti abutens primatu fuo Ecclefiaftico feculariter, convertat eum in Secularem. Sed ne forte qui talis eft in appetendo primatum, profectum pietatis pie pratendat, dico, Nunquid qui in ordine prior eft, jam & meritis eft melior?*] And of the Minifterial honours he faith (*ibid.*) *Deniq, ipfi honores in Chrifto in prima quidem facie videntur honores, revera autem non funt honores diverfi, fed funt diverfa Minifteria: ut puta honor oculi videtur, quia illuminat Corpus: Sed ipfe honor illuminandi non eft ei honor fed Minifterium ejus.* ——]

So much to prove the Propofition, that the late Englifh Epifcopacy is not to be reftored, under any pretence of Order or Peace.

Wherein I have purpofely forborn the mention of its Abufes, and doleful confequents, becaufe they may fuppofe that Abufe to be feparable from the thing.

Consequents of that which is already Proved.

TO save the debating of many great Controversies that break the peace and destroy or diminish the Charity of many, I may abbreviate the work, by giving you some of the true sequels of what hath been sufficiently proved.

Conf. I. The taking down of the English Episcopacy was *Conf.* I. (as to the thing) so far from being evil, and deserving the Accusations that some lay upon it; that it was a matter of Necessity to the Reformation and well being of the Churches of Christ in these Nations. It was no worse a work in it self considered, then the curing of a grievous disease is to the sick, and the supply of the necessities of the poor in their indigence. What guilt lieth upon that man, that would have all the sick to perish, for fear of injuring one Physitian, that had undertaken the sole care of all the County? or that would have all the County to have but one Schoolmaster: Or an hundred Ships to have but one Pilot, and consequently to perish: How much greater is their guilt, that would have had the forementioned Episcopacy continued, to the hazzard of many thousand souls, and the abasement and ejection of holy Discipline, the pollution of the Churches, and the hardening of the wicked, and the dishonour of God? I mention not this to provoke any to dishonour them, but to provoke the persons themselves to Repentance. And I intreat them to consider, how sad a thing it is, that without any great inducement, they should draw such a mountain of guilt upon their souls. The Bishops had the temptation of Honour and Riches: but what honour or gain have you to seduce you, to choose a share with other men in their sin and punishment?

I meddle not here with the *Manner* of demolishing Episcopacy, but with the *Matter*: because I would not mix other Controversies with this. But I am confident those men that usually own the late Episcopacy, and revile them that demolisht it, shall one way or other feel ere long, that they have owned a very unprofitable cause, and such as they shall wish they had let alone, and that it made not for their honour to be so much enemies

to

to the welfare of the Church, as the enemies of the abolition of that Prelacy will appear to be.

Conf. 2.   *Conf.* I I. The matter of that clause in the National Covenant, which concerneth the abolition of this Prelacy before mentioned, was so far from deserving the Reproaches and Accusations that are bestowed on it by some, that it was just and necessary to the well being of the Church.

wave   In this also I purposely ~~mean~~ the Civil controversie about the authority of imposing, taking, or prosecuting the Covenant, and speak only of the *Matter* of it : (to avoid the losing of the truth by digressions, and new controversies) They that by reproaching this clause in the Covenant, do own the Prelacy which the Covenant disowneth, might shew more love to the Church and their own souls, by pleading for sickness, and nakedness, and famine, and by passionate reproaches of all that are against these , then by such owning and pleading for a far greater evil.

Conf. 3.   *Conf.* I I I. Those of the English Ministry , that are against the old Episcopacy, and are glad that the Church is rid of it, are not therefore guilty of Schism, nor of sinfull disobedience to their spiritual superiours.

If any of them did *swear obedience* to the Prelates (a tyrannicall imposition that God never required, nor the Primitive Church never used) thats nothing to our present case, which is not about the keeping of oaths, but the obeying or rejecting the Prelacy in it self considered. It is not schismatical to depart from an usurpation that God disowneth, and the Church is endangered and so much wronged by, and to seek to pull up the Roots of Schism; which have bred and fed it in the Churches so long.

Conf. 4.   *Conf.* I V. Those that still justifie the ejected Prelacy, and desire the restauration of it, as they needlesly choose the guilt of the Churches desolations, so are they not to be taken for men that go about to heal our breaches , but rather for such as would widen and continue them , by restoring the main cause.

Conf. 5.   *Conf.* V. If we had had such an Episcopacy as Bishop *Hall* and Bishop *Usher* did propound as satisfactory, (and such men to manage it,) Episcopacy and Peace might have dwelt

together

together in *England* to this day : It is not the the Name of a Bishop that hath been the matter of our trouble, but the exorbitant *Species* introducing unavoidably the many mischiefs which we have seen and felt.

Conf. V I. Ordination by the ejected Prelacy, *in specie*, is not of necessity to the being or well being of a Presbyter or Deacon.   If the *Species* of Prelacy it self be proved contrary to the word of God, and the welfare of the Church, then the Ordination that is by this *Species* of Prelacy, cannot be necessary or as such desirable. *Conf.* 6.

Conf. V I I. A Parochial or Congregational Pastor, having assistant Presbyters and Deacons, either existent or in expectance, was the Bishop that was in the dayes of *Ignatius, Justin, Tertullian*, and that Dr. *Hammond* describeth as meant in many Scriptures, and existent in those dayes.   I speak not now to the question about Archbishops. *Conf.* 7.

Conf. V I I I. The Ordination that is now performed by these Parochial Bishops (especially in an assembly, guided by their Moderator) is, beyond all just exception, Valid, as being by such Bishops as the Apostles planted in the Churches, and neerer the way of the Primitive Church, then the Ordination by the ejected *Species* of Prelates is. *Conf.* 8.

Conf. I X. As the Presbyters of the Church of *Alexandria* did themselves make one their Bishop, whom they chose from among themselves, and set him in a higher degree (as if Deacons make an Archdeacon, or Souldiers choose one and make him their Commander, saith *Hierom ad Evagr.*) so may the Presbyters of a Parochial Church now.   And as the later Canons require that a Bishop be ordained or consecrated by three Bishops, so may three of these (Primitive) Parochial Bishops, ordain or consecrate now another of their degree.   And according to the Canons themselves, no man can justly say that this is invalid, for want of the Consecration by Archbishops, or of such as we here oppose. *Conf.* 9.

Conf. X. Those that perswade the People that the Ordination of those in *England* and other Churches is null that is not by such as the English Prelates were, and that perswade the people to take them for no Presbyters or Pastors, that are not ordained *Conf.* 10.

P

dained by such Prelates, and do make an actual separation from
our Churches and Ministers, and perswade others to the like, upon this ground, and because the Ministers have disowned the
English Prelacy, and withal confess the Church of *Rome* to be
a true Church, and their ordination and Priesthood to be just or
true, are uncharitable, and dangerously Schismatical (though
under pretence of decrying Schism,) and many wayes injurious to the Church and to the souls of men and to themselves.
This will not please; but that I not only speak it but further manifest it, is become Necessary to the right Information of others.

FINIS.

The Second
DISPUTATION:

VINDICATING

The Proteſtant Churches
and MINISTERS that have not
Prelatical Ordination, from the
Reproaches of thoſe Dividers that
would nullifie them.

WRITTEN

Upon the ſad complaints of many
Godly Miniſters in ſeveral parts of the
Nation, whoſe Hearers are turning Sepa-
ratiſts.

By *Rich. Baxter.*

LONDON,

Printed by *Robert White*, for *Nevil Simmons* Book-
ſeller in *Kederminſter.* 1658.

The Preface.

Christian Reader,

IF thou be but for the interest of Christianity, more than of a party, and a Cordial friend to the Churches Peace, though thou be never so much resolved for Episcopacy, I doubt not but thou and I shall be one, if not in each Opinin, yet in our Religion, and in Brotherly affection, and in the very bent of our labours and our lives: And I doubt not but thou wilt approve of the scope and substance of this following Disputation, what imperfections soever may appear in the Manner of it. For surely there is that of God within thee, that will hardly suffer thee to believe, that while Rome is taken for a true Church, the Reformed that have no Prelates must be none: that their Pastors are meer Lay-men, their Ordination being Null: and consequently their administrations in Sacraments, &c. Null and of no Validity. The Love that is in thee to all believers, and especially to the Societies of the Saints, and the honour and interest of Christ, will keep thee from this, or strive against it, as nature doth against poyson or destructive diseases. If thou art not a meer Opinionist in Religion, but one that hast been illuminated by the spirit of Christ, and felt his love shed abroad in thy heart, and hast ever had experience of spiritual communion with Christ and his Church, in his holy Ordinances, I dare then venture my cause upon thy judgement: Go

P 3

among

The Preface.

among those that unchurch our Churches, and degrade our Ministers, and perswade all people to fly from them as a plague; and try their doctrine, their spirits, their publick worship, their private devotion, and their whole conversation; and when thou hast done, come into our Assemblies, and spare not, if thou be impartial, to observe our imperfections: judge of our Order and Discipline and Worship, together with our Doctrine and our lives: and when thou hast done un-church us if thou darest, and if thou canst. We justifie not our selves or our wayes from blemishes: but if thou be but heartily a friend to the Bridegroom, offer us then if thou darest a bill of divorce, or rob him if thou darest of so considerable a portion of his inheritance. Surely if thou be his friend, thou canst hardly find in thy heart to deliver up so much of his Kingdom to his Enemy, and to set the name of the Devil on his doors, and say, This is the house of Satan and not of Christ. If thou have received but what I have done (though, alas too little) in those Societies, and tasted in those Ordinances but that which I have tasted, thou wouldst abhor to reproach them, and cut them off from the portion of the Lord.

Remember it is not Episcopacy nor the old conformity that I am here opposing. (My judgement of those Causes I have given in the foregoing and following disputation:) But it is only the New Prelatical Recusants or Separatists, that draw their followers from our Churches as no Churches and our Ordinances of Worship as none, or worse then none, and call them into private houses, as the meetest places for their acceptable worship. Who would have thought that ever that generation should have come to this, that so lately hated the name of separation, and called those private meetings, Conventicles, which were held but in due subordination to Church meetings, and not in opposition to them, as theirs are! Who would have thought that those that seemed to disown

Recusancy

Recufancy, and perfecuted Separatifts, fhould have come to this? Yea that thofe that under Catholick pretences can fo far extend their charity to the Papifts, have yet fo little for none of the meaneft of their Brethren, and for fo many Reformed Proteftant Churches? Yea that they fhould prefume even to cenfure us out of the Catholick Church and confequently out of heaven it felf. I have after here given thee an inftance in one, Dr. Hide, who brandeth the very front of his Book with thefe Schifmatical uncharitable ftigmata. The fenflefs Queres of one Dr. Swadling, and others run in the fame channel, or fink. If thefe men be Chriftians indeed, me thinks they fhould underftand, that as great (that I fay not greater) blemifhes, may be found on all the reft of the Churches, as thofe for which the Reformed are by them unchurched: and confequently they will deliver up All to Satan; and Chrift muft be depofed: And how much doth this come fhort of Infidelity? At leaft me thinks their hearts fhould tremble leaft they hear at laft, [In not loving the e you loved not me: in defpifing and reproaching thefe; you defpifed and reproached me.]

And yet thefe men are the greateft pretenders next the Romanifts, to Catholicifme, Unity, and Peace! Strange Catholicks that cut off fo great and excellent a part of the Catholick Church! And a fad kind of Unity and Peace which all muft be banifhed from, that cannot unite in their Prelacy, though the Epifcopacy which I plead for in the next Difputation they can own. The fumm of their offer, is, that if all the Minifters not Ordained by Prelates, will confefs themfelves to be meer Lay-men and no Minifters of Chrift, and will be Ordained again by them, and if the Churches will confefs themfelves No Churches, and receive the effence of Churches from them, and the Sacrament and Church-Affemblies to be Null, invalid, or unlawfull till managed only by Prelatical Minifters; then they will have Peace and communion

nion

nion with us, and not till then. And indeed must we buy your Communion so deer? As the Anabaptists do by us in the point of Baptism, so do these Recusants in the point of Ordination? You must be Baptized saith one party, for your Infant Baptism was none. You must be Ordained saith the other sort, for your Ordination by Presbyters was none. The upshot is, We must be all of their Opinions and parties, before we can have their Communion, or to be reputed by them the Ministers and Churches of Christ. And on such kind of terms as these, we may have Unity with any Sect.

If really we be not as hearty friends to Order and Discipline in the Church as they, we shall give them leave to take it for our shame, and glory in it as their honour. But the question is not, whether we must have Church-Order: but whether it must be theirs, and none but theirs? Nor whether we must have Discipline, but whether it must be only theirs? Nay, with me, I must profess, the question is, on the other side whether we must needs have a Name and shew of Discipline thats next to none, or else be no Churches or no Ministers of Christ? The main reason that turneth my heart against the English Prelacy is because it did destroy Church Discipline, and almost destroy the Church for want of it, or by the abuse of it, and because it is (as then exercised) inconsistent with true Discipline. The question is not, whether we must have Bishops and Episcopal Ordination. We all yield to that without contradiction. But the doubt is about their Species of Episcopacy, Whether we must needs have Ordination by a Bishop that is the sole Governeur over an hundred, or two hundred, or very many particular Churches? or whether the Bishops of single Churches may not suffice, at least as to the Being of our office? I plead not my own cause, but the Churches; For I was ordained long ago by a Bishop of their own with Presbyters. But I do not therefore take my self to be disengaged from Christianity or Catholicism,

and

and bound to lay by the Love which I owe to all Chrifts members, or to deny the Communion of the Churches, which is
both my Duty, and I am fure an unvaluable Mercy. And I
muft fay, that I have feen more of the Ancient Difcipline exercifed of late, without a Prelate, in fome Parifh Church
in England, than ever I faw or heard of exercifed by the
Bifhops in a thoufand fuch Churches all my dayes. And it
is not Names that are Effential to the Church, nor that will
fatisfie our expectations.

We are for Bifhops in every Church; And for Order fake,
we would have one to be the chief. We diflike thofe that difobey them in lawful things, as well as you. But let them
have a flock that is capable of their perfonal Government,
and then we fhall be ready to rebuke all thofe that feparate
from them, when we can fay as Cyprian (Epift. 69. ad
Pupian.) [Omnis Ecclefiæ populus collectus eft, &
adunatus, in individua concordia fibi junctus. Soli illi
foris remanferint, qui etfi intus effent, ejiciendi fuerant
——Qui cum Epifcopo non eft, in Ecclefia non eft (that
is, in that particular Church.) Cyprian had a people that
could all meet together to confult or confent at leaft about the
Communion or Excommunication of the members. Epift.
55. Cornel. he tells Cornelius how hard the people were to
admit the lapfed or fcandalous upon their return if the mani-
feftation of repentance were not full. The Church with
whom the perfon had Communion, was then it that had a Bifhop, and was no greater then to be capable of the Cogni-
zance of his caufe, and of receiving fatisfaction by his perfonal penitence.

Brethren ! (for fo I will prefume to call you, whether you
will or not) Some experience hath perfwaded me, that if
we had honeftly and faithfully joyned in the practice of fo
much of Difcipline, as all our principles require, it would
have helped us to that experimental knowledge (by the blef-

Q

fing

fing of God) which would have brought us nearer even in our Principles, then our idle Difputations, feparated from practice will ever do. As Auguftine faith of the difputes de causa mali (Lib. de utilitat. Credendi, cap. 18.) Dum nimis quærunt unde fit malum, nihil reperiunt nifi malum] fo I may fay of thefe difputes, while we thus difpute about the caufes of diforder and divifion, we find nothing but diforder and divifion.

It is eafie to conjecture of the ends and hearts of thofe that cry down Piety as precifenefs, while they cry up their feveral wayes of order : it feems they would have ordered impiety : and their order muft be a means to keep down holinefs, which all juft order fhould promote. Thofe men that can fall in with the moft notoriously ungodly, and favour and flatter them for the ftrengthening of their intereft, do tell us what Difcipline we may expect from them. If they tell us that our Churches alfo are corrupted, and all are not truly or eminently godly, we can fay to them as Auguftine, (lib. de utilitat. Credend. cap. 17.) [Pauci hoc faciunt, pauciores bene prudenterq; faciunt : fed populi probant, populi audiunt, populi favent] yea we can fay much more.

But for thofe that go further, and clap the prophaneft railers on the back, and hifs them on to hifs at thofe that differ from them, and are glad to hear the rabble revile our Miniftry and our Churches, in taking part with their Prelacy and Liturgy, they tell us lowder what unity and order they defire, and what a mercy of God it is, that fuch as they have not their will : and though among themfelves the flanders and reproaches of fuch men may go for credible or be accepted as conducing to their ends ; yet in the conclufion fuch witneffes will bring no credit to their caufe, nor with juft men much difcredit ours ; at leaft it will not diminifh our reputation with God, nor abate his

love,

love, nor hinder his acceptance, and then we have enough.
Saith (Cyprian Epift. 69. ad Pupian) Quasi apud lapfos
& prophanos, & extra Ecclesiam politos, de quorum
pectoribus excefferit Spiritus Sanctus, effe aliquid pof-
fit nifi mens prava, & fallax lingua, & odia venenata,
& sacrilega mendacia, quibus qui credit, cum illis necesse eft inveniatur, cum judicii dies venerit.] *That is*
[*As if with the fcandalous and prophane, and those that*
are without the Church, from whose brefts the holy Spirit is
departed, there could be any thing but a naughty mind, and
a deceitful tongue, and venemous hatred, and facrilegious
lies ; and those that beleeve them muft needs be found with
them when the day of judgement comes.]

   Me thinks rather the hatred, and railing of the un-
godly should intimate to you that our Minifiry is of God!
why elfe do all the moft obftinately wicked maligne us as
their enemies, though we never did them wrong ? why feek
they our deftruction, and are glad of any Learned men that
will encourage them in their malignity, and to ftrike in with
any party that are againft us ; when all the harm we wifh
or do them, is to pray for them, and perfwade them, and do
our beft to fave them from damnation ! As Cyprian (ubi
fup.) *faid to* Pupian [ut etiam qui non credebant Deo
Epifcopum conftituenti, vel Diabolo crederent Epifcopum profcribenti] *fo fay I* [*They that will not believe*
Gods teftimony of our Miniftry, let them believe the De-
vils teftimony, as the confeffion of an enemy, that by the
mouths of the wicked revileth us as Minifters, and perfecu-
teth us for doing our Mafters work.

   Another reproach is commonly laid upon our Miniftry
by those that vilifie them in order to their ends, viz. that
they are boyes, and raw and unlearned, and manage the work
of God fo coursely as tends to bring it into contempt.   I
would there were no ground for this accufation at all : but

The Preface.

I must needs say, 1. *That no men are more unmeet then you to be the accusers. Have you so corrupted the Ministry with the insufficient and ungodly, that we are necessitated to supply their places with men that are too young; and now do you reproach us, because we imperfectly mend your crimes? yea because we work not impossibilities? It is the desire of our souls, that no able useful man may be laid by, however differing in smaller matters, or controversies of policy? But we cannot create men, nor infuse learning into them; but when God hath qualified them, we gladly use them; the best that can be had are chosen; and what can be done more? And I hope you will acknowledge, that godly and tolerably able young men are fitter then impious, ignorant Readers.*

We excuse no mans weakness: but to speak out the truth, too many of the adversaries of our Ministry accuse our weakness with greater weakness; when they are unable or undisposed themselves to manage the work of God with any of that gravity, and seriousness as the unspeakable weight of the business doth require, they think to get the reputation of learned able men, by an empty childish, trifling kind of preaching; patching together some shreds of sentences, and offering us their Centons with as much ostentation, as if it were an uniform, judicious work. And then they fall a jeering at plain and serious Preachers, as if they were some ignorant bawling fellows, that were nothing but a voice, and had nothing to produce but fervent nonsence. Brethren, will you bear with us a little, while we modestly excuse our simplicity which you contemn. We will not say, that we can speak wisedom to the wise, nor make ostentation of our Oratory; but we must tell you that we Believe what we speak, and somewhat feel it; and therefore we endeavour so to speak what we believe and feel, that others also may believe and feel as. If a man speak smilingly, or not affectionately of very great affecting things, the hearers

use.

use to say, You are but in jeaſt ; *and they believe him not, becauſe he ſpeaks as one that doth not believe himſelf. It is not wit but* Levity *and ſtupidity that we renounce. As* Seneca *ſaith, we refuſe not an eloquent* Phyſitian *: but it is not eloquence, but Healing that we need : the eaſing of our pains, and ſaving of our lives, and not the clawing of our ears. We dare not ſpeak lightly or triflingly of Heaven or Hell. We more condemn our ſelves when we find within us but a dull apprehenſion of thoſe exceeding great eternal things, then we do for want of neat expreſſions. A vain curioſity in attire, doth ſhew that ſubſtantial worth is wanting. We moſt abhor the preaching of falſe doctrine : and next,* that manner of preaching Truth *that cauſeth an airy levity in the hearers ; and when the* manner *ſeemeth to contradict the* matter. *One taſte or ſight of Heaven or Hell would put you into another paſs your ſelves. Truly Brethren (though I am one my ſelf, that have the leaſt advantages to vie with you in that wherein you glory. yet) there are many among them whom you thus deſpiſe, that have wits inclined to as much unrulineſs and luxuriancy as yours : but being ballanced with the ſenſe of everlaſting things, and ſeaſoned with the Light and Life of Chriſt, they are as careful to keep under and rule their wit. as others are diligent to feed its wantonneſs, and make oſtentation of it to the world. It will ſhortly appear but ingenious folly which was not animated and regulated by Chriſt. The wiſedom of the world is fooliſhneſs with God : and the fooliſhneſs of God is wiſer then men,* 1 Cor. 1 .25. &c. *We find the moſt experienced Learned Divines betake themſelves to the plaineſt ſtile ; and much more addicted to the ancient ſimplicity, then green, inflated, empty brains. When we diſpleaſe both our ſelves, and our queaſie. coye and aery auditors by the homelyneſs of our ſtyle, we uſually hear more of the ſucceſs. of thoſe ſermons, then of thoſe wherein by a*

Q 3.

wordy

The Preface.

wordy Curiosity, we procure from the aery more applause. Saith Augustine (de Catechiz. rudib cap. 2.) [Nam & mihi semper prope sermo meus displicet — sic & tu eo ipso quod ad te sæpius adducuitur baptizandi —— debes intelligere non ita displicere aliis sermonem tuum ut displicet tibi : nec infructuosum te debes putare, quod ea quæ cernis non explicas ita ut cupis ; quando forte ut cupis nec cernere valeas] *Our business is to teach the ignorant, to convert the impenitent, and to edifie and confirm the weak ; and therefore if repetitions, and homely expressions, with all the seriousness we can use, be found the fittest means to attain these ends, we shall study them and not decline them, though some dislike them.* Augustine de doctrin. Christ. lib. 4. cap. 12. Qui ergo dicit cum docere vult, quamdiu non intelligitur, nondum se existimet dixisse quod vult ei quem vult docere: quia etsi dixit quod ipse intelligit, nondum ille (illi) dixisse putandus est, a quo intellectus non est: si vero intellectus est, quocunque modo dixerit, dixit.]

I confess when I heard a through-paced preacher in the Prelates reign, experience taught me presently to expect three great infirmities in him, viz. stumbling, spotling, and tiring: stumbling either in doctrine, conversation, or both; especially in a stony way: spotling even the clearest of his Brethren, and that both in the Pulpit, and behind their backs. For most of the wounds we have from such are in our back parts, though we never fled. They can most effectually confute us when we do not hear them. As one of them that I knew, divided his Text into one part, and so do many of them their Disputations : they are best at Disputing alone, when there is none to contradict them. They are better gun-men then sword-men : Eminus fortissimi; cominus—more valiant a far off than neer at
hand:

hand: and making more use of powder then of bullet; the noise exceeding the execution: and being nearest themselves, it is a wonder that their Consciences start not at the report. It is the reward of these pugnacious souls, to be cryed up as victorious, and to have their triumph attended by their like: and it is enough to prove them victors that they can but crow and erect the crist. And if they are soon tired we must not wonder; for they preach at too high rates to hold out long. Junkets are not for full meals; and feasting must not be all the year. When they preacht but seldom, they justified it by telling us, that one of their sermons was worth ten of theirs that preach d so often: and half a crown was as good as five six pences.

For my part, I do not undervalue their wit, nor envy them the honour of it: but I would fain have things Divine to be Divinely handled; and the weightiest matters to be spoken off in the most serious weighty manner. And I would not have a school boy when he hath said a Declamation, to think that he is more learned then Scotus or Ockam, because he hath a smoother style: nor to think that he hath done a gallanter piece of work, then he that hath read a Lecture in Metaphysicks. I am much inclined to honour their parts; I value the wit of a Comedian, when I value not the employment of it. I have often heard a Rustical Justice call a fidler a Rogue, that cal'ed himself a Musician; and perhaps he puts him in the stocks, that thinks he deserves a Princes ear: when I have thought of their Art, and forgotten the abuse, I have been apt to pitty their case. I could be well content that so great an Artist as Nero perish not: let him live as an Artist, but not as an Emperour. I honour and love the learning and industry of the Jesuits: let them be encouraged as Learned, but not as Jesuits. Let them all be used in that which they are good for. But a Comical wit is not enough to make a Minister of

the

the Gospel of salvation. Counters can jingle as well as gold. If such must be Bishops, let them be Diocesans, (so they be kept without a sword) for when they have an hundred Churches, they will trouble them but seldom, with their preaching : and that may be endured for a day that cannot for a year.

If you think I have turned my excuse of a plain and serious Ministry into a recrimination, or seemed guilty of what I blame, consider of what and to whom I speak.

I am far from a contempt of learning, or encourageing ignorant insufficient men, or justifying any ridiculous unseemly deportment, or any rash, irrational expressions, in the work of God. And I earnestly intreat the servants of the Lord to take heed of such temerity and miscarriages, and remember what a work they have in hand, and how much dependeth on the success, and that the eyes of God and men are on them, and that it is no light matter to an honest heart, that Christ and his cause should be dishonoured by our weaknesses, and our labours should hereby be frustrated, and sinners hardned in their impiety. But yet I must say, that many that are but low in Learning, have greater abilities (by grace and use) to manage the great essentials of Christianity, and set home a necessary truth upon the heart, and deal with ignorant dead-hearted sinners, then many very Learned men did ever attain to. And I confess I could wish for the service of the Church, that some such (now private) less-learned men, in great Congregations were yoaked with some Learned men that are less fit for lively rouzing application; that they might Lovingly go together, the one confessing his defect in Learning, and the other his defect in application, and the unlearned depending for guidance from the more Learned, in cases of difficulty, where his abilities fall short; that so they might be both as one able Minister, communicating the honour of their several abilities to each

other

other to supply and cover each others defects. **But if such a thing should be attempted (though agreeably to the Churches practice for many hundred years after Christ)** *what an outcry should we have from the men now in hand, against Mechanicks and unlearned men! and how many would reproach their work that cannot mend it! I have been long on this subject: I will end it with this story.*

Gregory Nysen *tells us in his relation of the Life of* Gregory Thaumaturgus, *that this holy man then Bishop of* Neocæsarea, *was so famous by his miracles* **and** *successes that the Neighbour Countreys sent to him, to preach and plant Churches among them.* Among others Comana *a neighbour City sent to him, to come and plant a Church and Bishops among them. When he had stayed a while, and preached and prepared them, and the time was come that he was to design them a chief Pastor (or Bishop.) the* Magistrates *and principal men of the City were very busie in enquiring anxiously and curiously, who was of most eminent rank and splendour, excelling the rest, that he might be chosen to the office and dignity of being their Bishop.* For Gregory *himself had all these Ornaments, and therefore they thought their Pastor must have them too. But when it came to choice they were all to pieces, some for one and some for another: so that Gregory looked to heaven for Directions, what to do. When they were thus taken up with proposing men of splendor and eminency,* Gregory *(remembring* Samuels *anointing David,) exhorted them to look also among the meanest: for possibly there might be found among them some of better qualifications of mind: Whereupon some of them signified, that they took it as a contumelie and scorn, that all the chief men for eloquence, dignity and splendor should be refused, and that Mechanicks and tradesmen that labour for their living should be thought fitter for so great an office. And saith one of them to him in derision, If you will pass*

X

by

by all these that are chosen out of the best of the Citizens, and go to the scum and basest of the people for a Pastor for us: its best for you even to make Alexander *the Collier a Priest, and lets all agree to choose him. The good man hearing these scornful words, it struck into his mind to know who that* Alexander *the Collier was? Whereupon they brought him presently with laughter, and set him in the midst of them collowed and half-naked, and ragged and sordid, and thus stood* Alexander *among them. But* Gregory *suspected somewhat better by him, then they that laught at him; and thereupon taking him out of the company, and examining his life, he found that he was a Philosophick man, that being of a very comely person, and loth it should be any occasion of incontinency, and also renouncing the vanities of the world, had addicted himself to the life of a Collier, that his person and worth might be hid from men, and his mind be kept in an humble frame. Whereupon* Gregory *appointeth some to take away* Alexander, *and wash him and cloath him with his Pastoral attire, and bring him into the Assembly as soon as they had done. In the mean time* Gregory *goes to the Assembly, and fals a preaching to them of the nature of the Pastoral office, and the holiness of life required thereto, entertaining them with such speeches, till* Alexander *was brought, and comely adorned in* Gregories *garments was set before them. Whereupon they all fell a gazing and wondering at* Alexander: *and* Gregory *fals a preaching to them again of the deceitfulness of judging by outward appearances, about the inward worth of the soul, and that* Satan *had obscured* Alexander, *lest he should subvert his kingdom. To be short, he ordaineth* Alexander *their Bishop (a Pastor of a single Church.) And when they desired to hear him preach, he shewed that* Gregory *was not deceived in him. His sermon was sententious and full of understanding: but because he had no flowers of Oratory, or exactness and cu-*

riosity

rofity of words, one that was a curious hearer derided him, who it is said was by a vision brought to repent of it. And thus despised Alexander the Collier was made Bishop (or Pastor) of Comana, when the great ones were rejected: and afterward proved a Champion for Christ, to whom he passed in Martyrdome through the flames. I have recited this for their sakes that deride the gifts of God in men whom they account unlearned: but not to encourage any to thrust themselves on so great a work without Ordination and due qualifications.

Object. But it is Ordination it self that is wanting to the Pastors of the Reformed Churches, and therefore they are no Pastors, &c. *Answ. The contrary is manifested in this ensuing Disputation. This separating Principle is it that I here purposely contend against. For it is cast in to divide and to destroy: And to quench such granado's and fire-works of the Devil, is a necessary work for them that will preserve a Churches Peace.* I read in Thuanus of a Bishop in France *that turning Protestant, took his Popish consecration for insufficient, and was again elect, and ordained by the Protestant Ministers, without a Prelate, to be a Prelate. But that Presbyters Ordained by a Presbytery of Protestants should be reordained by a Prelate; and that as necessary to the being of their office, is strange doctrine to all the Protestant Churches. It was rejected commonly by the English Bishops,* even by A. B. Bancroft *himself.* Saith Firmilian (inter Epist. Cypriani) [Omnis potestas & gratia in Ecclesia constituta est, ubi præsident Majores natu, qui & baptizandi, & Manus imponendi & ordinandi possident potestatem] *i. e.* All Power and Grace is placed in the Church where Elders do preside, who possess the power of Baptizing, Imposing hands, and Ordaining.]

I know it will be said that Firmilian *speak of Bishops on-*

R 2

ly. *But* I *believe* not that he *spoke of such Bishops only as we have in question, or that he did not plainly speak of Presbyters as such.* For he *speaks of the plenitude of Power and Grace in the Church: and therefore intended more then what was proper to a Prelate.* 2. He *mentioneth Elders,* Majores natu, *in general without distinction. And* 3. *His* præsident *is plainly related to the Church(as the* ubi *shews:)it being the People and not the Elders over whom these Elders are said to preside.* And 4. Baptizing *is first instanced, which was known to be commonly the work of Presbyters, and never appropriated to the Prelate. So that the same persons that did Baptize, even the Elders of the Church, according to* Firmilian, *did then possess the power of laying on hands and of ordaining. But these things are more fully discussed in what followeth. And if any either adversary or friend would see the Reformed Churches Ministry and Ordination more fully vindicated,* I *refer them to* Voetius *against* Jasenius Desperata causa Papatus: *which if I had read before I had written this Disputation, I think I should have spared my labour.*

Reader, *if others are too busie to mislead thee,* I *may suppose thee unwilling to be misled, especially in a matter of so great concernment:* 'For saith Blessed Agustine, Multos invenimus qui mentiri velint, qui autem falli neminem: de Doctrin. Christ. l. 1. cap. 36.) *And therefore as thou lovest* Christ, *his Church, and Gospel, and the souls of others and thine own, take heed how thou venturest in following a sect of angry men, to unchurch so great and excellent a part of the Catholick Church, and to vilifie and depose so great a number of able faithfull Ministers of* Christ, *as those that had not Prelatical Ordination.*

And if you are Gentlemen, or unlearned men, that for want of long and diligent studying of these matters, are uncapable of judging of them, and therefore take all on the Authority of those whose Learning and parts you most esteem, I
beseech

*befeech you before you venture your fouls on it any further,
procure a fatisfactory anfwer to thefe Queftions.*

1. *Whether the Reformed Churches that have no Prelates,
have not abounded with as learned men as any one of thofe
that you admire of a contrary judgement?*

2. *If you are tempted to fufpect men of partiality, whether
they that plead for Lorfhip, honour and preferment, or they
that plead againft it, and put it from them, are more to be
fufpected,* cæteris paribus?

3. *If you will needs fufpect the* Proteftant Minifters *of
partiality: what ground of fufpicion have you of them that
were no* Minifters? *fuch as the two* Scaligers, *whofe learning made them the admiration of the Chriftian world, even
to* Papifts *as well as Proteftants: and yet were cordial
friends to thofe Reformed Churches which thefe men deny
and draw men to difown. Such alfo as* Salmafius, *that hath
purpofely wrote about the fubject: with abundance more.*

4. *If thefe are not to be trufted, why fhould not Bifhops
themfelves be trufted? were not Bifhop* Ufher, Andrews,
Davenant, Hall, *and others of their mind, as learned pious
men as any whofe Authority you can urge againft them?*

5. *If all this be nothing, I befeech you get a modeft refoluti-
on of this doubt at leaft: whether the concurrent judgement of
all the Proteftant Churches in Chriftendom, even of the Englifh Bifhops with the reft, fhould not be of more authority with
any fober Proteftant, then the Contrary judgement of thofe
few that are of late rifen up for the caufe that you are by them
folicited to own. It is a known Truth that the generality of
the Bifhops themfelves and all the Proteftant Churches in the
world, have owned them as true Minifters that were ordained by Presbyteries, without Prelates: and have owned them as
true Churches that were guided by thefe Minifters, and have
taken them for valid adminiftrations that were performed
by them. And are your few Recufants that would draw you*

to separation of greater Learning, authorty and regard, then all the Protestants in the world besides? I beseech you if you will needs take things upon trust, consider this, and trust accordingly. Though I must say it is pitty that any truely Catholick Christian should not have better grounds than these, and be able himself in so palpable a case to perceive his duty.

For my own part, my conscience witnesseth that I have not written the following Disputation out of a desire to quarrel with any man, but am drawn to it, to my great displeasure, by the present danger and necessity of the Churches, and by compassion to the souls that are turned from the publick Ordinances, and engaged in the separation, and also of the Churches that are divided and troubled by these means. The sad complaints of many of my Brethren from several parts have moved my heart to this undertaking. Through Gods Mercy, I have peace at home: but I may not therefore be insensible of the divisions and calamities abroad. I shall adjoin here one of the Letters that invited me, and no more; because in that one you may see the scope and tenour of the rest, and that I rush not on this displeasing work, without a Call, nor before there is a cause. The passages that intimate an over-valuing of my self, you may charitably impute to the Authors juniority and humility, with some mistake through distance and disacquaintance.

One of the Letters that invited me to this task.

Reverend

Reverend Sir,

Understanding by the Preface to the Reader before your Gildas Salvianus, that you intend a second part, wherein you promise to speak of the way how to discern the true Church and Ministry, I make bold to present you with the desire of some Godly Ministers: viz. that if you see it convenient, you would do some thing towards the vindication of the present Churches and Ministers from the aspersions of the new Prelatical party in England. It is a principle much made of by many of the Gentry and others, that we are but Schismatical branches broken off from the true body; and this by faithfull tradition is spread amongst them: the learning of some rigid Prelatical Schollars is very prevalent with them to make them thus account of us. With these men we must be all unchurched for casting off Diocesan Episcopacy: though we be sound in the faith, and would spend our selves to save souls, and the main substance of our Ordination (at least) cannot be found fault with; yet because we had not a Bishop to lay his hands on us, we are not sent from God. Of what consequence this opinion may prove, if it spread without being checked, an ordinary apprehension may perceive. I can guess something from what I observe from those of this leaven already, that our most serious pains will be little regarded, if our people take this infection; when we would awaken them, we cannot, because they take it that we have no power to teach them. It must not be men of mean parts that must undertake more fully to wipe off this reproach: for the learned adversaries are tall Cedars in knowledge in comparison of many of us: and if men of parts do not grapple with them herein, they will easily carry the vote in many mens judgements; for they judge that the greater Schollars by far certainly have the better in the contest. Sir, we beseech you that you would improve your acquaintance in Antiquity for our help in this case. Not that we would engage you in wrangling with particular men by name, who will not want words: but however you would evidence it that our Ordination by Presbyters is not void, and of no effect I have this reason ready to give for this request: for (besides what I had formerly heard) I was lately with some of those not of the meanest influence, who urged Episcopacy as of absolute necessity, affirming that this order the Church of God ever observed: and that it was doubtless of Apostolical institution, being a thing of Catholick tradition, and that's the best standard to interpret Scripture by. What then are we arrived at, that have forsaken the whole Church herein? Though I am little versed in the Ancients, yet I tell them we acknowledge that soon after the Apostles times the name Bishop came up as distinct from the Presbyters; but then I call for their proof that the Primitive Bishops had the power of jurisdiction over Presbyters, or that to him only ordination was appropriated. I tell them also that we have certain evidence that in some Churches these Bishops were made by

Presbyters

Presbyters, so was the custom in Alexandria: and when did ever the Church judge them to be no Bishops or Ministers? And also of Tertullians Præsident probati quiq; Seniores, and of Cyprians Salvo inter Collegas pacis & concordiæ vinculo: and that doubtless if Cyprian be to be believed, the Church was then ruled by the joint consent of its Pastors, of whom one was indeed the President or Moderator, who yet called himself compresbyter, and the Presbyters fratres (not filios as it was of late.) This answer I have had from some of them, that the Church in those times was much under the cloud, being persecuted; and had not that liberty to settle Diocesan Episcopacy in that Glory, which the Apostolical institution aimed at, and that the Church was then what it could be, and not what it would be. Do you judge of its weight. For my part, I am most stumbled at the reading of Ignatius (whom Dr. H. so strenuously defends) and cannot tell how to evade that Testimony in the behalf of Episcopacy, if it be indeed the testimony of the true Ignatius. But methinks his phrase is much unlike either that of Clemens, or of Cyprian in this case. Its great pity that Dr. Bloudel wants his eyes, and so we are hindred of enjoying of more of his labours in this point. His Notion of the πρωτοχειροτονηθεις is a very pretty one, and it were well if we had fuller evidence added to that which he hath endeavoured after in his Preface, to his Apology for Hierom.

Or if your judgement about the power of every single Pastor were fully improved, it would conduce much to the clearing of these controversies. I could methinks be glad of the practice of those proposals which Bishop Usher hath made in a late printed sheet: But these angry Brethren who now oppose us are of a higher strain.

But I run out too far and forget whom I am writing to. Truly I am deeply sensible, what mischief those seeds which are as yet but thin-sown (as I may say) may grow up to in time: I know not how it is with you; but with us, I fear ten for one at least would be easily drawn to such an opinion of us, if the temptation were but somewhat stronger; multitudes observing how civil transactions have run in a round, begin also to think we shall also arive at our old Church-customs again: now if these Episcopal mens judgement should but be dispersed more abroad, how easily would it make these people think that we have deluded them all this while? and so will not regard us! Alas! what a sad thought is it if I should study and preach and pray for mens souls, and yet be rejected as one that had no charge of them as a Minister, laid on me for God! We thank you for what you said in your Christian Concord; and intreat you would enlarge further on this Subject, as you see convenient: That the striplings in the Ministry may be furnished with arguments against our adversaries from such able hands as yours are.

I have done; only I shall desire your pardon for my interrupting you in your other business; and if I shall hereafter crave your assistance and direction in some cases, I pray you excuse me if uncivil, and vouchsafe to let me hear from you: for I am about to settle where the charge is great. The Lord continue you amongst us, that you may be further an instrument of good. I rest,

Jan. 8.
1657.

Your Affectionate friend and weak
Brother M. E.

Assert.

Affert. *Those who nullifie our present Ministry and Churches, which have not the Prelatical Ordination, and teach the people to do the like, do incur the guilt of grievous sin.*

CHAP. I.

Sect. 1. FOR the making good this Assertion, 1. I shall prove that they groundlesly deny our Ministry and Churches ; and 2. I shall shew the greatness of their sin.

In preparation to the first I must 1. Take some notice of the true Nature of the Ministerial function: and 2. Of the Nature and Reasons of Ordination.

Sect. 2. We are agreed (*ore tenus* at least) that the *Power and Honour* of the Ministry is for the *work*, and the *work* for

S   the

the *Ends*, which are the revelation of the Gospel, the application or conveyance of the benefits to men, the right worshiping of God, and right Governing of his Church, to the saving of our selves and our people, and the Glorifying and Pleasing God.

Sect. 3. So that [*A Minister of the Gospel is an Officer of Jesus Christ, set apart (or separated) to preach the Gospel and thereby to convert men to Christianity, and by Baptism to receive Disciples into his Church, to congregate Disciples, and to be the Teachers, Overseers, and Governours of the particular Churches, and to go before them in publick worship and administer to them the special Ordinances of Christ, according to the word of God; that in the Communion of Saints, the members may be edified, preserved, and be fruitful and obedient to Christ; and the Societies well ordered, beautified and strengthened; and both Ministers and People saved; and the Sanctifier, Redeemer and the Father Glorified and Pleased in his People now and for ever*]

Sect. 4. In this Definition of a Minister, 1. It is supposed that he be competently qualified for these works : For if the *Matter* be not so far *Disposed* as to be capable of the *Form*, it will not be *informed* thereby. There are some Qualifications necessary to the being of the Ministry, some but to the *well being*. Its the first that I now speak of.

Sect. 5. Before I name them, lest you misapply what is said, I shall first desire you to observe this very necessary distinction : Its one thing to ask, *who is to take himself for a called and true Minister; and to do the work, as expecting Acceptance and Reward from God* : and its another thing to ask, *whom are the people (or Churches) to take for a true Minister, and to submit to as expecting the Acceptance and blessing of God in that submission from his administrations.* Or its one thing to have *a Call* which will *before God justifie his Ministration* and another thing to have *a Call* which will *before God justifie the Peoples submission*, and will justifie *in foro Ecclesiæ*, both him and them. And so its one thing to be a Minister whom God and Conscience will justifie and own, as to *Himself* : and another thing to be a Minister to the *Church*, whom they must own, and God will own and bless *only* as to *their* good.

See pag. 173.

In the first sence, none but truely sanctified men can be Ministers

nifters; but in the latter an unfanctified man may be a Minifter. As there is a difference among Members between the *Vifi-*
ble and *Myftical*, (of which I have fpoken elfewhere. *) So is
there between *Paftors.* Some have a Title that *in foro Ecclefiæ*
or *Ecclefia judice* will hold good , that have none that is good
in foro Dei : In one word . the Church is bound to take many a
man as *a true Minifter to them*, and receive the Ordinances from
him in faith, and expectation of a Bleffing upon promife; who
yet before God is a finful invader, an ufurper of the Miniftry, and
fhall be condemned for it.

 As in worldly Poffeffions, many a man hath a good Title, before men, and at the bar of man, fo that no man may difturb his
Poffeffion, nor take it from him, without the guilt of theft,
when yet he may have no good Right at the bar of God to juftifie him in his retention. So it is here.

 Sect. 6. It is too common a cafe in Civil Governments (the
ignorance of which occafioneth many to be difobedient.) A man
that invadeth the Soveraignty without a Title, may be no King
as to himfelf, before God, and yet may be truly a King as to the
People. That is, He ftands guilty before God of Ufurpation,
and (till he Repent, and get a better Title) fhall be anfwerable
for all his adminiftrations as unwarrantable : And yet, when he
hath fettled himfelf in Poffeffion of the Place, and exercife of the
Soveraignty, he may be under an obligation to do juftice to the
people, and defend them, and the people may be under an obligation to obey him and honour him, and to receive the fruits of his
Government as a bleffing. Mens Title in Confcience and before
God (for Magiftracy and Miniftry) themfelves are moft to look
after, and to juftifie; and its often crakt and naught, when their Title *in foro humano* may be good; or when the people are bound to
obey them. And thofe mifcarriages or ufurpations of Magiftrates
or Minifters which forfeit Gods Acceptance and Bleffing to themfelves , do not forfeit the bleffing of Chrifts Ordinances and
their adminiftrations to the Church : For it is the guilty and not
the Innocent that muft bear the lofs. A Sacrament may be as
effectual , and owned by God , for my benefit, when it is from
the hand of a man that fhall be condemned for adminiftring it,
as when it is from the hand of a Saint that hath a better
call ; fuppofing ftill that I be innocent of his ufurpation or error.

      This

* Difpute of
Right to
Sacraments.

This neceſſary diſtinction premiſed, I ſay, that *ſpecial Grace* is neceſſiry to that Call of a Miniſter that muſt be warrantable and juſtifyable to himſelf before God ; but it is not neceſſary to that call that's juſtifyable before the Church, and is neceſſiry to our ſubmiſſion and to the bleſſing of the Ordinances and their Validity to our good.

Sect. 7. But yet here are ſome Qualifications *eſſentially* neceſ-ſary, to Diſpoſe the man to be Receptive of the Miniſtry, *coram Eccleſia* (though ſaving grace be not.) As 1. It is of Neceſſi-ty that he be a *Chriſtian by Profeſſion* ; and ſo that he Profeſs that faith, repentance, love, obedience, which is ſaving. For the Miniſter in queſtion is only *A Chriſtian Miniſter*: and therefore he muſt be a Chriſtian, *& aliquid amplius* by profeſſion.

2. It is therefore Neceſſary that he Profeſs and ſeem to Under-ſtand and Believe all the Articles of the faith, that are eſſential to Chriſtianity, and do not heretically deny any one of theſe (what ever he do by inferiour Articles.)

3. He muſt be one that is able to preach the Goſpel : that is, in ſome competent manner, to make known the Eſſentials of Chriſtianity : or elſe he cannot be a Miniſter at all.

4. He muſt be one that underſtandeth the Eſſentials of Baptiſm, and is able to adminiſter it (Though the actual adminiſtration be not alway neceſſary.)

5. He muſt underſtand the Eſſentials of a particular Church, and profeſs to allow of ſuch Churches as Gods Ordinance, or elſe he cannot be the Paſtor of them.

6. He muſt Profeſs to Value and Love the Saints, and their communion : Or elſe he cannot be a Miniſter for the communion of Saints.

7. He muſt Profeſs and ſeem to underſtand, believe, and ap-prove of all the Ordinances of Chriſt which are of Neceſſity to Church-communion.

8. And he muſt be tolerably able to diſpenſe and adminſ-ſter thoſe Ordinances : Or elſe he is not capable of the office.

9. He muſt Profeſs and ſeem to make the Law of God his Rule in theſe adminiſtration.

10. And alſo to deſire the ſaving of mens ſouls, and the well-fare of the Church, and Glory and Pleaſing of God. If he have not beforehand all theſe Qualifications, he is not capable of the
Miniſtry,

Miniftry, nor can any Ordination make him a true Minifter.

Sect.8. If you demand my proof, it is from the common principles that 1. The *form cannot be received but into a difposed capable
matter* : but fuch are no difpofed capable matter : therefore ,
&c. ———— 2. *The office is for the work* . and therefore
prefuppofeth a Capacity and ability for the work. The office
containeth 1. *An Obligation to the Duty*: But no man can be
obliged to do that which is Naturally Impoffible to him (though
a Moral Impoffibility may ftand with an obligation to duty, and
a Natural only as founded in the Moral) 2. It containeth *an
Authority or Power to do the work* : But fuch *Power* (which is
but a *Right of excercifing Naturall Abilities*) doth prefuppofe
the Abilities to be exercifed : *Natural Power*, is prefuppofed to
Civil Authority.   3. It is *Effential* to fuch *Relations* that they
be *for their Ends* : And therefore where there is an apparent incapacity *for the end*, there is as apparent an incapacity of the Relation. But enough of this.

Sect. 9. 2. A Minifter is [*an officer of Chrift*,] and therefore receiveth his Authority from him, and can have none but
what he thus recieves. And therefore 1. He hath no Soveraignty
or Lordfhip over the Church, for that is the perogative of Chrift.
2. He hath no degree of underived Power, and therefore muft
prove his Power, and produce his Commiffion before he can expect the Church to acknowledge it.   3. He hath no Power to
work againft Chrift, or to deftroy the fouls of men, or to do
evil : (Though he hath a Power by which occafionally he may
be advantaged to evil, yet hath he no Authority to do it :) For
Chrift giveth no man power to fin , nor to do any thing againft
himfelf.   4. He deriveth not his authority *from man* (though.
by man , as an inftrument, or occafion, he may) The People
give him not his Power : The Magiftrate gives it not : The Ordainers (Bifhops or Presbyters) give it not, any further then
(as I fhall fhew anon) by fignifying the will of Chrift that indeed giveth it, and by invefting men in it by folemn delivery.
The Choofers may nominate the perfon that fhall receive it ; and
the Magiftrate may encourage him to accept it ; and the Ordainers may Approve him and Inveft him in it : but it is Chrift
only that gives the Power as from himfelf.   As in Marriage, the

perfons

persons consent, and the Magistrate alloweth it as Valid at his bar ; and the Minister blesseth them and declareth Gods consent : But yet the Power that the Husband hath over the wife is only from God as the conferring cause; and all that the rest do is but to prepare and dispose the person to Receive it ; save only that consequently, the consent of God is declared by the Minister. Of which more anon, when we speak of Ordination.

Sect. 10. 3. A Minister is a man [*separated*, or *set a part*] to the work of the Gospel. For he is to make a calling of it, and not to do it on the by. Common men may do somewhat that Ministers do, even in preaching the Gospel : but they are not [*separated* or *set apart to it, and so entrusted with it*, nor *make a Calling or Course of employment of it.*] Ministers therefore are *Holy persons* in an *eminent* sort, because they have a twofold Sanctification. 1. They are as all other Christians sanctified to God by Christ through the spirit , which so devoteth them to him, and brings them so neer him, and calls them to such holy honourable service, that the whole Church is called a Royall Priesthood, a Holy Nation, *&c.* to offer spiritual sacrifice to God. And Christ hath made them Kings and Priests to God. But 2. They are moreover devoted and sanctified to God, (not only by this separation from the world, but) by a separation from the rest of the Church to stand neerer to God, and be employed in his most eminent service ! I mention not mans Ordination in the Definition, because it is not essential to the Ministry, nor of Absolute Necessity to its being (of which anon.) But that they be set apart by the will of Christ and sanctified to him, is of Necessity.

Sect 11. 4. These Ministers have a double subject to work upon, or object about which their Ministry is Employed. The first is [*The world, as that matter out of which a Church is to be raised*] The second is, *Believers called out of the world*] These Believers are, [*Either Only Converted*, and *not invested in a Church state*; or such as are *both Converted and Invested* :] These later are either [such as are not yet gathered into a particular Church, or such as are.] For all these are the objects of our office.

Sect. 12. 5. Accordingly the first part of the Ministerial office is to *Preach the Gospel to unbelievers and ungodly ones for their Conversion.* This therefore is not, as some have imagined,

Rom. 1.1.2,

1 Pet. 2.5.9.
Rom. 1. 6.

.ned, a common work, any more then preaching to the Church: Occasionally *ex Charitate*, only another man may do it. But *ex Officio*, as a work that we are separated and set a part to and entrusted with, so only Ministers may do it. No man hath the *Power* of Office; but he that hath the *Duty or Obligation*, to make it the trade or business of his life, to preach the Gospel (though bodily matters may come in on the by.)

Sect. 13. 6. Hence it appears that a man is in order of *Nature a Preacher of the Gospel in General*, before he be the *Pastor of a particular flock*: though in time they often go together: that is, when a man is ordained to such a particular flock.

Sect. 14. 7. And hence it follows that a man may be ordained *sine Titulo* or without a particular charge, where the Converting preparatory work is first to be done.

Sect. 15. 8. And hence it appeareth that a Minister is first in order related to the unbelieving world, as the object of his first work, before he be related to the Church existent: either Catholick or particular: And that he is under Christ first a Spiritual Father, to beget children unto God, from the unbelieving world, and then a Governour of them. If others have already converted them to our hands, and saved us that part of our work, yet that overthroweth not the order of the parts and works of our office, though it hinder the execution of the first part (it being done to our hands by others in that office.)

Sect. 16. 9. The second part of the Ministers work is about Believers meerly converted, together with their Children, whom they yet have power to Dedicate to God: And that is to Invest them in the Rights of a Christian, by Baptism in solemn Covenanting with God the Father, Son and Holy Spirit. And these are the next Material objects of our Office.

Many of the Ancients (*Tertullian* by name, and the Council of *Eliberis*) thought that in case of Necessity, a Lay-man (though not a Woman) may Baptize: If that be granted, yet must not men therefore pretend a Necessity where there is none. But I am satisfied 1. That Baptism by a private man, is not *eo nomine* a Nullity, nor to be done again: 2. And yet that it is not only a part of the Ministers work to Baptize and approve them that are to be Baptized, *ex officio*, but that it is one of the greatest and highest actions of his office: Even an eminent exercise ercife of the Keyes of the Kingdom , letting men into the Church of Chrift: it being a principal part of their Truft and power to judge who is meet to be admitted to the Priviledges and fellowfhip of the Saints.

Sect. 17. 10. The third part of the Minifters work is about the Baptized, that are only entred into the univerfal Church (for many fuch there are,) or elfe the unbaptized that are Difcipled, where the former work and this are done at once : And that is , *to congregate the Difciples into particular Churches for Holy Communion in Gods Worfhip, &c.* They muft do part of this themfelves in Execution. But he leads them the way, by Teaching them their duty, and provoking them to it, and directing them in the execution , and oft-times offering himfelf or another to be their Teacher, and Leading them in the Execution. So that it belongeth to his office to gather a Church, or a member to a Church.

Sect. 18. 11. Hence is the doubt refolved, *Whether the Paftor, or Church be firft in order of time or Nature?* I anfwer : The Minifter as a Minifter to Convert and Baptize and gather Churches , is before a Church gathered in order of Nature and of time. But the Paftor of that particalar Church as fuch, and the Church it felf whofe Paftor he is, are as other Relations, together and at once ; as Father and Son, Husband and Wife, *&c.* As nature firft makes the Nobler parts, as the Heart and Brain and Liver ; and then by them as inftruments formeth the reft ; And as the Philofopher or Schoolmafter openeth his School, and takes in Schollars ; and as the Captain hath firft his Commiffion to gather Soldiers : But when the Bodies are formed, then when the Captain or Schoolmafter dieth, another is chofen in his ftead; So is it in this cafe of Paftors.

Sect. 19. 12. Hence alfo is the great controverfie eafily determined, *Whether a particular Church or the univerfal be firft in order, and be the Ecclefia Prima:* To which I anfwer 1. The Queftion is not *de ordine dignitatis,* nor which is finally the Minifters chief End : For fo it is paft controverfie that the Univerfal Church is firft. 2. As *to order of exiftence,* the univerfal Church is confidered either as confifting of Chriftians as Chriftians, convetted and Baptized : or further as confifting of Regular Ordered Affemblies, or particular Churches. (For all Chriftians

are

are not members of particular Churches: and they that are, are yet confiderable diftinctly, as meer Chriftians and as Church-members (of particular Churches) And fo its clear, that men are Chriftians in order of Nature, and frequently of time; before they are members of particular Churches: and therefore in this refpect the univerfal Church (that is, in its effence) is before a particular Church. But yet there muft be *One* particular Church, before there can be *many.* And the *Individual* Churches are before the *Affociation* or *Connection* of thefe individuals. And therefore though in its *effence* and the exiftence of that effence the univerfal Church be before a particular Church (that is, men are Chriftians before they are particular Church-members;) yet in its *Order,* and the exiftence of that *Order,* it cannot be faid fo: nor yet can it fitly be faid that thus the *Particular* is before the *univerfall.* For the firft particular Church and the univerfal Church were all one (when the Gofpel extended as yet no further) And it was *fimul & femel* an ordered *univerfal* and *particular Church:* (but yet not *quà univerfal*) But now, all the *Univerfal Church* is not *Ordered at all* into particular Churches: and therefore *all the Church univerfal* cannot be brought thus into the Queftion. But for all thofe parts of the univerfal Church that are thus *Congregate* (which *fhould* be *all* that have opportunity) they are confiderable, either as *diftinct Congregations independent;* and fo they are *all in order of nature together* (fuppofing them exiftent:) Or elfe as *Connexed and Affociated for Communion of Churches,* or otherwife related to each other: And thus *many Churches* are *after the Individuals,* & the *fingle Church* is the *Ecclefia prima* as to all *Church forms of Order;* and *Affociations* are but *Ecclefia orta,* arifing from a combination or relation or Communion of many of thefe.

Sect. 20. The fourth part of the Minifterial work is about *particular Churches Congregate,* as we are Paftors of them. And in this they fubferve Chrift in all the parts of his office.

1. Under his *Prophetical* office, they are to *Teach the Churches to obferve all things whatfoever he hath commanded them:* & deliver & open to them that Holy doctrine which they have received from the Apoftles that fealed it by Miracles, and delivered it to the Church. And as in Chrifts name to perfwade and exhort men to duty, opening to them the benefit, and the danger of *rg* &

Mat. 28 20.
Heb. 2.3.4.
2 Cor. 5.
19,20.

L   under

Jam 5.14.
Acts 2.41, 42.
& 4.35.
1 Cor.11.23.
Acts 20. 7.
1 Cor.10.16.
Acts 20. 28.
2 Cor. 5.11.
1 Tim.5.17,
20,22,24.
2 Cor.2.10.
Mat.18.18.

2. Under Chrifts Prieftly office they are to ftand between God and the People, and to enquire of God for them, and fpeak to God on their behalf and in their name, and to receive their Publick Oblations to God, and to offer np the facrifice of Praife and Thanksgiving on their behalf, and to celebrate the Commemoration of the facrifice of Chrift upon the Crofs ; and in his name to deliever his Body and Blood, and Sealed Covenant, and benefits to the Church.

3. Under his Kingly office (a Paternal Kingdom) they are to Proclaim his Laws, and Command obedience in his Name, and to Rule or Govern all the flock, as Overfeers of it, and to reprove, admonifh, cenfure and caft out the obftinately impenitent, and confirm the weak, and approve of Profeffions and Confeffions of Penitents, and to Abfolve them, by delivering them pardon of their fin, in the name of Chrift.

Sect. 21. 14. This work muft be done for the ends mentioned in the Definition. To his *own Safety, Comfort, and Reward,* it is neceffary that thofe Ends be *fincerely intended.* For the comfort and Satisfaction of the Church and the validity of the Ordinances (Sacraments efpecially) to their fpiritual benefit, it is neceffary that thefe ends be *profeffed to be intended by him*; and that they be *really intended by themfelves.*

Sect. 22. 15. By this the Popifh cafe may be refolved, *whether the Intention of the Prieft be neceffary to the Validity and fuccefs of Sacraments ?* The *reality* of the Priefts *Intention* is not neceffary to the Validity of them to the people : For then no ordinance performed by an hypocrite were Valid ; nor could any man know when they are Valid and when not. But that they may be fuch adminiftrations, as *he* may comfortably anfwer for to God, his *fincere Intention* is Neceffary. And that they be fuch as the People are bound to fubmit to, it is neceffary that he *profefs a fincere Intention* : For if he purpofely Baptize a man ludicroufly in profeffed jeft or fcorn, or not with a feeming intent of true Baptizing, it is to be taken as a Nullity and the thing to be done again. And that the ordinances may be bleffed and effectual to the *Receiver upon Promife* from God, it is neceffary that the *Receiver* have a *true intent* of receiving them to the ends that God hath appointed them. Thus and no further is *Intention* neceffary to the validity of the Ordinance and to the fuccefs.

The

The particular ends I shall not further speak of, as having been longer already then I intended on the Definition.

Sect. 23. But the principal thing that I would desire you to observe, in order to the decision of our controversie, hence, is that the Ministry is first considerable as a *Work* and *Service*, and that the *Power* is but a *Power to be a servant to all*, and to *do the work.* And therefore that the first Question is, *Whether the great burden and labour of Ministerial service may be laid on any man without Ordination by such as our English Prelates?* Or whether all men are discharged from this labour and service on whom such Prelates do not Impose it? If Magistrates, Presbyters and People conspire to call an able man to the work and service of the Lord, whether he be justified for refusing it, what ever the Church suffer by it, meerly because the Prelates called him not?

Sect. 24. Though the forementioned works do all belong to the Office of the Ministry, yet there must be *Opportunity* and a *particular Call* to the *exercise* of them, before a man is actually obliged to perform the several acts. And therefore it was not without sence and reason that in Ordination the Bishop said to the Ordained, [*Take thou authority to Read or to preach the word of God, when thou shalt be thereunto lawfully called*] Not that another *call of Authority* is necessary to *state* them in the office, or to oblige them to the Duty in *General*: But we must in the invitation of people, or their consent to hear us, or other such advantagious accidents, prudently discern when and where we have a Call to speak and exercise any act of our Ministry. Even as a Licensed Physitian must have a particular Call by his Patients before he exercise his skill. This call to a particular act, is nothing else but an intimation or signification of the will of God, that *hic & nunc* we should perform such a work: which is done by Providence causing a concurrence of such inviting Circumstances that may perswade a prudent man that it is seasonable.

Sect. 25. A man that is in general thus obliged by his office to do all the forementioned works of the Ministry, (that is, when he hath a particular call to each) may yet in particular never be obliged to some of these works, but may be called to spend his

life

life in some other part of the Ministry, and yet be a compleat. Minister, and have the obligation and Power to all, upon suppofition of a particular Call ; and not be guilty of negligence in omitting those other parts. One man man may live only among Infidels, and uncalled ones, and fo be obliged only to Preach the Gospell to them in order to Converfion, and may die before he fees any ready to be baptized : Another may be taken up in Preaching and Baptizing , and Congregating the Converted, and never be called to Pastoral Rule of a particular Church. Another may live in a Congregated Church where there is no ufe for the Difcipling·Converting·Preaching of the Gofpel, and fo may have nothing to do but to Overfee that particular Church and Guide them in holy Worfhip And in the fame Church if one Minifters parts are more for Publick preaching , and anothers more for Private inftruction, and acts of Guidance and Worfhip ; if one be beft in expounding, and another in lively application ; they may lawfully and fitly divide the work between them : and it fhall not be imputed to them for unfaithfulnfs and negligence that one forbeareth what the other doth. For we have our guifts to the Churches edification : Thus Paul faith he was not fent to *Baptize, but to Preach the Gofpel* : Not that it was not in his Commiffion, and a. work of his office : but *quoad exercitium* he had feldome a *fecond particular Call to exercife* it, being taken up with that Preaching of the Gofpel, and fettling and confirming Churches which to him was a greater work.

Sect. 26. This Miniftry before defcribed (whether you call it *Epifcopatum , Sacerdotium, Presbyteratum*, or what elfe is fit) is but one and the fame Order (for Deacons are not the Minifters defined by us :) It is not diftinguifhed into various *Species* : Even the Patrons of Prelacy, yea the Schoolmen and other Papifts themfelves, do ordinarily confefs, that a Prelate and Presbyter differ not *Ordine*, but only *Gradu*. So that it is not another office that they *afcribe* to Prelates, but only a more eminent Degree in the fame Office. And therefore they themfelves affirm, that in *Officio* the Power of Ordination is in both alike (the office being the fame.) But that for the honour of the Degree of Prelacy, for the unity of the Church, Presbyters are hindered from the Exercife of that Ordination, which yet is in their Power and Office.

Sect.

Sect. 27. As far as Ordination is a part of the Ministerial Work it is comprised in the forementioned acts, [*of Congregating, Teaching, Ruling, &c.*] and therefore is not left out of the Definition, as it is a duty of the office: though it be not expess'd among the Efficient causes, for the reason above mentioned: and because I am now more distinctly to treat of it by it self, and to give you further reasons hereof in the explication of the Nature and Ends of this Ordination.

CHAP. II.

Of the Nature and Ends of Ordination.

Sect. 1.  THat we may know how far the Ordination in question is necessary to the Ministry, and whether the want of it prove a Nullity, we must first enquire what goes to the laying of the Foundation of this Relation, and how many things concur in the efficiency, and among the rest, what it is that the Ordainers have to do as their proper part; and what are the reasons of their Power and Work.

Sect. 2. As all that deserve the name of men, are agreed that there is no Power in the world but from God the Absolute Soveraign, and first Cause of Power: so all that deserve the name of Christians are agreed that there is no Church Power but what is from Christ the head and Soveraign King of the Church.

Sect. 3. As the will of God is the Cause of all things: And no thing but the Signification of it is necessary to the conveying of meer Rights: So in the making a man a Minister of the Gopel, there needeth no other principal efficient caufe then the *Will* of Jefus Chrift ; nor any other Inftrumental Efficient , but what is of ufe to the *fignifying of his will*: So that it is but in the nature of *figns* that they are Neceffary. No more therefore is of *Abfolute Neceffity*, but what is fo neceffary to *fignifie* his will. If Chrifts will may be fignified without Ordination, a man may be a Minifter without it : (Though in other refpects he may be culpable in his entrance, by croffing the will of Chrift concerning his duty in the manner of his proceedings.)

Sect. 4. There is confiderable in the Miniftry, 1. *Beneficium.* 2. *Officium*. 1. The Gofpel, pardon, falvation-Ordinances are thofe *great Benefits* to the fons of men, which the Miniftery is to be a means of conveying to them : And is it felf a Benefit as it is the means of thefe Benefits. In this refpect the *Miniftry* is a *Gift* of Chrift to the Church, and his *Donation* is the neceffary act for their Miniftration. But of this gift the Church is the fubject. *He giveth Paftors to his Church*. 2. But in conjunction with the Churches Mercies, the Minifter himfelf alfo partakes of mercy : It is a double Benefit to him to be both receptive with them of the bleffing of the Gofpel, and to be inftrumentall for them in the conveyance , and to be fo much exercifed in fo fweet and honourable, though flefh-difpleafing and endangering work. As in giving Alms, the giver is the double receiver ; and in all works for God , the greateft Duties are the greateft Benefits; fo is it here. And thus the making of a Minifter is a Donation or act of bounty to himfelf. Chrift giveth *to us* the Office of the Miniftry, as he giveth *us* in that office to the Church. As a Commanders place in an Army is a place of Truft and Honour and Reward, and fo the matter of a gift , though the work be to fight and venture life.

Sect. 5. The Duty of the Minifter is caufed by an Obligation ; and that is the part of a Precept of Chrift : And thus Chrifts command to us to do his work doth make Minifters.

Sect. 6. From the work which the Minifters are to perform, and the command of Obedience laid upon the people, arifeth their duty, in fubmiffion to him, and Reception of his Minifterial work ; And in Relation to them that are to obey him, his office is a fuperiour Teaching Ruling Power, and fo is to be caufed by Commiffion from Chrift, as the fountain of Power that is to command both Paftor and People. Sect

Sect. 7. So that the Ministry consisting of *Duty, Benefit, and Power,* (or Authority,)it is caused by *Preceptive Obligation,* by *Liberal Donation,* and by *Commission.* But the last is but compounded of the two first, or a result from them. The *Command* of God to *Paul,* e. g. to preach and do the other works of the Ministry, doth of it self give him Authority to do them. And Gods command to the People to hear and submit, doth concur to make it a Power as to them. And the Nature and ends of the work commanded are such as prove it a Benefit to the Church ; and consequentially to the Minister himself. So that all is comprehended in the very imposition of the Duty : By commanding us to preach the word , we are Authorized to do it, and by Doing it we are a Benefit to the Church, by bringing them the Gospel and its Benefits.

Sect. 8. Our Principal work therefore is to find out, on whom Christ *imposeth* the *Duties* of Church Ministration : And by what signs of his will, the person himself and the Church may be assured that it is the Will of Christ; that this man shall undertake the doing of these works.

Sect 9. And therefore let us more distinctly enquire, 1. What is to be signified in order to a Ministers Call; and 2. How Christ doth signifie his will about the several parts ; and so we shall see what is left for Ordination to do, when we see what is already done, or undone.

Sect. 10. 1. It must be determined or signified that A Ministry there must be. 2. And what their Work and Power shall be. 3. And what the Peoples Relation and duty toward them shall be. 4. What men shall be Ministers, and how qualified. 5. And how it shall be discerned by themselves and others which are the men that Christ intends.

Sect. 11. Now let us consider 1. What Christ hath done already in Scripture, 2. And what he doth by Providence, towards the determination of these things. And 1. In the Scripture he hath already determined of these things, or signified that it is his Will, 1. That there be a standing Ministry in the Church, to the end of the world : 2. That their work shall be to preach the Gospel, Baptize, Congregate Churches, Govern them, administer the Eucharist, *&c.* as afore mentioned. 3. He hath left them Rules or Canons for the directing them (in all things of constant

universal

universal necessity) in the performance of these works. 4. He hath described the persons whom he will have thus employed, both by the Qualifications necessary to their Being, and to the *Well-being* of their Ministration. 5. He hath made it the Duty of such qualified persons to desire the work, and to seek it in case of need to the Church. 6. He hath made it the Duty of the people to desire such Pastors, and to seek for such and choose them or consent to the choice. 7. He hath made it the Duty of the present Overseers of the Church to *Call* such to the work, and *Approve* them, and *Invest* them in the office (which three acts are called Ordination, but specially the last.) 8. He hath made it the Duty of Magistrates to encourage and protect them, and in some cases to command them to the work, and set them in the office by their Authority. All these particulars are determined of already in the Laws of Christ, and none of them left to the power of men.

Sect. 12. The ordainers therefore have nothing to do to judge 1. Whether the Gospel shall be preached or no, whether Churches shall be Congregate or no, whether they shall be taught or governed or no? and Sacraments administred or no? 2. Nor whether there shall be a Ministry or no Ministry? 3. Nor how far (as to the Matter of their work and power) their office shall extend, and of what Species it shall be? 4. Nor whether the Scripture shall be their constant universal Canon? 5. Nor whether such qualified persons as God hath described, are only to be admitted, or not. 6. Nor whether it shall be the duty of such qualified persons to seek the office? or the Duty of the People to seek and choose such, or of Pastors to ordain such? or of Magistrates to promote such and put them on? None of this is the Ordainers work.

Sect. 13. If therefore any man on what pretence soever, shall either determine that the Gospel shall not be preached, nor the Disciples Baptized, the Baptized Congregated, the Congregations governed, the Sacraments administred, &c. or that there shall be no Ministers to do those works; or if any man Determine that which will infer any of these; or if he pretend to a Power of suspending or excluding them, by his Non-approbation, or not-authorizing them; he is no more to be obeyed and regarded in any of this Usurpation, then I were if I should make a

Law,

Law, that no King shall reign but by my nomination, approbation or Coronation. And if any man under pretence of Ordaining, do set up a man that wants the Qualifications which Christ hath made necessary to the *Being* of the Ministry, his Ordination is Null, as being without Power, and against that Will of Christ that only can give Power. And so of the rest of the particulars forementioned : Where the Law hath already determined, they have nothing to do but obey it. And though the miscarriages of a man in his own calling do not alwaies nullifie his acts, yet all that he doth quite out of the line of his Office are Nullities.

Sect. 14. We see then that all that the Law hath left to the Ordainer is but this : In General, to Discern and judge of the person that is Qualified according to the Description of the Law; and particularly to *call* him out to the work, if he need excitement, and to *Try and Approve* him, before he be admitted, and to *Invest him*, or solemnize his admittance, at his entry. So that the sum of all is, but to find out the qualified person, because he is not named by the Law.

Sect. 15. And even in this the Ordainers are not the only Discerners, or Judges; but the person himself, the People and the Magistrates, have all the forementioned parts in the work. And God himself goes before them all, and by providence frequently points them out the man whom they are bound to choose, Ordain, accept and submit unto : and that by these particular acts.

Sect. 16. 1. As God doth plainly describe the persons in the word, so he doth Qualifie them accordingly by his Guifts : and that of three sorts : Even, his special, Graces (necessary so far as was before mentioned) Ministerial Abilities of Knowledge and utterance, and a desire after the work, for its ends. 2. God useth to qualifie so small a number thus, compared with his Churches Necessities, that whether they should be Ministers (in general) or not, is seldom matter of controversie to prudent men, or at least a doubt that's more easie to decide. 3. God useth by Providence to give some one man, by advantage of parts, acquaintance, opportunity, interest, *&c.* a special fitness for one place and people above other men, and so to facilitate the decision. 4. God useth to stir up the hearts of the Church to choose or consent to the person thus qualified. 5 And he useth to stir up desires or consent in the man . . . . to be the . . . .

u   of

of that particular flock. 6. And he useth oft times to procure him Liberty , if not some call from the Magistrate. 7. And also to remove impediments in his way. 8. And to assist ordainers in discerning the qualifications of the person , when the work comes to their hands. All this God doth providentially.

Sect. 17. By this much it appeareth, that the Ordainers do not give the power as from themselves to others ; nor doth it pass through their hands. They are but the occasions, and the Instruments of Inauguration or solemn possession, when their interposition is due. It is the standing Act of Christ in his Law that giveth the Power immediately, I say immediately , as without any mediate receiving and conveying cause , that is directly efficient of the Power it self, though not so Immediately as to exclude all Preparations, and perfecting Instruments, accidentall causes & other means. As in case of Marriage, it is the womans consent that is of Necessity to the designation of the Person that shall be her husband. But it is not her Consent that properly giveth him the power of an husband over her. For that is done by God himself, in that Law by which he constituteth the husband to be head of the wife , and determineth *in specie* of his power, which one determination immediately conferreth the power on all individual persons, when once they are chosen and named : so that the Elector of the person doth but prepare and dispose him to receive the power, and not give it. He doth but open the door and let men in to the Ministry, & not give it. Its one thing to bring the person to the Pool that healeth, that he may be the man that first shall enter : and its another thing to heal him : Its one thing to Judge of the person that shall receive the Power immediately from God, and another thing to give it him our selves.

Sect. 18. Its thus in the case of Magistrates Power, in which mens interest hath ever been more discernable to the world and beyond controversie then in the power of Ministers. Though here there be a certain specification that dependeth on the will of man, yet the Power it self is immediately from God, and men do but choose the person that shall receive it, and present him to God, and solemnly inaugurate him. And for my part, I think I shall never consent to any side that will needs give more to men (whether Presbyters, Prelates, or people) in making a Minister, then in making a King. All power is of God; the powers that be are ordained of God.

Sect.

Sect. 19. If any doubt of this (as I perceive by many writings, they do) I shall, to spare the labour of a Digression, refer them to the copious unanswerable labours of abundance of Protestants that have written in *England* for the Royal Power: But instead of more, let them but read *Spalatensis*, and *Saravia* and *Bilson*, and rest satisfied, or confute them before they expect any more from me.

Sect. 20. As in the making of Bayliffs for our Corporations, either the people, or the Burgesses, have the power of choosing, and the Steward or Recorder hath the power of swearing him, and performing the Ceremonies: and yet none of these confer the power, but only design the person, who receives the power from the Prince alone, by the Charter of the Cities or Towns, as his Instrument: so is it in the ordaining of Ministers. The People may choose, and the Pastors may invest, but its God only by the Gospel Charter that confers the power from himself.

Sect. 21. Hence it is plain that the Argument is vain thats commonly used by the Prelates, from *Nemo dat quod non habet*. For it falsly supposeth that the Ordainers are the givers of Power (the master-error in their frame.) Christ hath it, and Christ giveth it. Men give it not, though some of them have it: For they have it only *to use* and not *to give*. When the People choose a King, they give him not the Power, but God giveth it to the man whom the people choose. When our Corporations choose their Bayliff, the choosers give him not the Power; for they had it not themselves; but they determine of the man that immediately from the Princes Charter shall receive it: Nor doth the Recorder or Steward give it Primarily, but only *Instrumentaliter & perfective* by a Ceremonial inauguration. So the People give not Pastors the Power: Nor the Ordainers, but only complementally.

Sect. 22. From what is aforesaid also it appeareth, that the work of the Ministry is founded first in the Law of nature it self, which upon supposition of mans misery and his recovery by Christ, and the Promise and means appointed for application, requireth every man that hath Ability and Opportunity, to do his best in the Order appointed him by God , to save mens souls by proclaiming the Gospel, and using Gods appointed means , for the great and blessed Ends that are before us.

U 2   Sect.

Sect. 23. Hence it also appeareth that Gods first command (partly in Nature and partly in the Gospel) is that [*The work shall be done, the Gospel shall be preached, Churches gathered and governed, Sacraments administred:*] and that the Precept *de ordine* is but secundary and subservient to this. And if at any time, alterations should make Ordination impossible, it will not follow that the duty Ordered ceaseth to be duty, or the precept to oblige.

Sect. 24. The Scriptures name not the man that shall be a Pastor, yet when it hath described him it commandeth the Described person duely to seek admittance, and commandeth the People, ordainers and Magistrates to [*Choose and Appoint these men to the Ministerial work.*] Now these Precepts contain in each of them two distinct determinations of Christ. The first is [*that such men be Ministers.*] The second is [*that they offer themselves to the office, and that they be Accepted and Ordained.*] For the first is implyed in the latter. If the Soveraign Power make a Law, that there shall be Physicians licensed by a Colledge of Physitians to Practice in this Common-wealth] and describe the persons that shall be licensed ; This plainly first concludeth that such persons shall be Physitians, and but secondarily *de ordine* that thus they shall be licensed : so that if the Colledge should License a company of utterly insufficient men, and murderers that seek mens death, or should refuse to License the persons qualified according to Law, they may themselves be punished, and the qualified persons may act as Authorized by that Law, which bindeth *quoad materiam*, and is by the Colledge (and not by them) frustrate *quoad ordinem.* So is it in this case in hand.

Sect. 25. Hence it appeareth that [Ordination is one means conjunct with divers others, for the Designation of right Qualified persons, described in the Law of Christ) for the reception and exercise of the Ministerial office. And that the ends of it are 1. To take care that the office fail not : and therefore to call out fit men to accept it, if modesty or impediments hinder them from offering themselves, or the people from nominating them. 2. To Judge in all ordinary cases of the fitness of persons to the office, and whether they are such as Scripture describeth and calls out. 3. And to solemnize their Admittance, by such an investiture, as when Possession of a House is given by a Ministerial tradition of a Key; or Possession of Land by Ministerial delivery of a twig and a turf, or as a Souldier is listed, a King Crowned, Marriage Solemnized, after consent and Title, in order to a more solemn obligation, and plenary possession; such is our Ordination.

Sect. 26. Hence it appeareth that as the Ordainers are not appointed to Judge whether the Church shall have Ordinances and Ministers, or not (no more then to judge whether we shall have a Christ and heaven, or not:) but who shall be the man; so it is not to the Being of the Ministry simply, and in all Cases that Ordination is necessary, but to the safe being and order of admittance, that the Church be not damnified by intruders.

Sect. 27. Ordination therefore is Gods orderly and ordinary means of a Regular admittance; and to be sought and used where it may be had (as the solemnizing of Marriage.) And it is a sin to neglect it wilfully, and so it is usually necessary *necessitate Præcepti, & Necessitate medii ad ordinem & bene esse.* But it is not of absolute Necessity *Necessitate medii ad esse Ministerii,* or to the Validity or Success of our office and Ministrations to the Church; nor in cases of necessity, when it cannot be had, is it necessary *necessitate præcepti* neither. This is the plain truth.

Sect. 28. There are great and weighty Reasons of Christs committing Ordination to Pastors. 1. Because they are most Able to judge of mens fitness, when the People may be ignorant of it. 2. Because they are men doubly Devoted to the Church and work of God themselves, and therefore may be supposed (regularly) to have the greatest care and most impartial respect to the Church and cause of God 3. And they must (regularly) be supposed to be men of greatest piety and holiness (or else they are not well chosen.) 4. And they being fewer, are fitter to keep Unity, when the people are usually divided in their choice. 5. And if every man should enter the Ministry of himself that will judge himself fit, and can but get a people to accept him, most certainly the worst would be oft forwardest to (before they are sent,) and for want of humility would think themselves fittest (the common case of the Proud and Ignorant) and the People would be too commonly poisoned by heretical smooth-tongue'd men; or more commonly would please and undo themselves by choosing them interest in them, by friends or acquaintance, and them that will most please and humour them, and instead of being their Teachers and Rulers, would be taught and ruled by them, and do as they would have them.   Order is of great moment to preserve the very being of the Societies ordered, and to attain their well-being.   God is not the God of Confusion but of Order, which in all the Churches must be maintained: No man therefore should neglect Ordination without necessity: And these that so neglect it, should be disowned by the Churches, unless they shew sufficient cause.

CHAP. III.

Ordination is not of *Necessity* to the being of the Ministry.

Sect. 1. Aving shewed what the Ministry is, and what Ordination is, and how the work is imposed on us, and the Power conferred, I may now come up to the point undertaken, to shew the sin of them that Nullifie all our Ministers calling and administrations, except of such as are ordained by the English Prelates. And for the fuller performance of this task, I shall do it in these parts. 1. I shall shew that Ordination it self by man is not of Necessity to the being of a Minister. 2. I shall shew that much less is an uninterrupted succession of Regular Ordination (such as either Scripture or Church Canons count valid) of Necessity to the being of Church or Ministry. 3. I shall shew, that much less is an Ordination by such as our *English* Bishops ne.

necessary to the Being of the Ministry. 4. I shall shew that yet much less is an Ordination by such Bishops *rebus sic stantibus*, as now things go, of necessity to the being of the Ministry. 5. I shall shew that without all these pretences of necessity for a Presbyterian Ordination, the present way of Ordination by this & other Reformed Churches is agreeable to the Holy Scripture, and the custome of the Ancient Church, and the *postulata* of our chief opposers. 6. I shall then shew the greatness of their sin that would Nullifie our Ministry and administrations. 7. And yet I shall shew the greatness of their sin that oppose or wilfully neglect Ordination. 8. And lastly I shall return to my former subject, and shew yet how far I could wish the Episcopal Brethren accommodated, and propound somewhat for a Peace.

Sect. 2. I shall be much briefer on all these, then evidence would invite me to be, because I apprehend the most of them to be of no great necessity to our cause, we having enough without them, and lest men should think that we need such *Mediums* more then we do; and because of my exceeding scarcity of time which forceth me to do all hastily.

And for the first that [*Humane Ordination is not of Absolute Necessity to the Being of the Ministry*] I argue as followeth. *Arg.* 1. If the Necessity of Ordination may cease (as to single persons) and the Necessity of Ministration continue (or if the obligations to each are thus separable) then is not Ordination of Necessity to the Being of the Ministry. But the Antecedent is true : which I shall prove by parts (for the consequence is past all doubt, nor will any I suppose deny it.)

Of this *Vocius* hath written at large *de desperata causa Papatus*, to which I refer the Reader.

Sect. 3. That the obligation to be Ordained may cease to some persons, I prove by instances in certain cases. And 1. In case of a mans distance from any that should Ordain him. As if one or many Christians were cast upon the Coasts of any Indian Heathen or Mahometan Nation, as many have been. There is no ordination Possible : and therefore not necessary or due. And to return for it to the Christian part of the world, may be as impossible : and if not, yet unlawfull by reason of delay.

Sect. 4. And 2. In case of the great Necessity of the People that cannot bear the absence of such as are able to teach them so long as while he travaileth many hundred or thousand miles for Ordination

dination ; As *Basil* in another case writes to the Bishops of the West, that if one of them (the Eastern Bishops) should but leave their Churches for a very small time, much more for a journey into the West, they must give up their Churches to the Wolves to be undone before they return ; And this case is ordinary abroad.

Sect. 5. And 3. That in case by Civil wars or enmity among Princes, men be unable to travail from one of their Countries into the other for an Ordination (which else ofttimes cannot be had) so the Turks and Persians, and the Indian Mogol, and the Tartarians and many other Princes, by such wars may make such passage an impossible thing : Nor is it like they would suffer their subjects to go into the enemies country.

Sect. 6. And 4. in case that Princes (Infidels or others) should persecute Ordination to the Death : I do not find that it were a Duty to be ordained, if it would cost all men that seek it their lives , and so made them uncapable of the Ends of Ordination : (For the dead preach not) If we were all forbid to preach on pain of death, I know we should not forbear, unless our places were so supplied, that mens souls were not apparently endangered by our omission. But he that may preach without Ordination, can scarce prove it a duty to seek Ordination when it would cost him his life. Or if he will plead it in Paper, he would soon be satisfied in tryal.

Sect. 7. And 5. In case that the Generality of Bishops within our reach turn Hereticks , (as in many parts of the East in the Arrian revolt, when scarce seven Bishops remained Orthodox) Or in case of a National Apostacie, as in the Kingdomes of *Nubia*, *Tenduc*, and many more that by the conquest of Infidels have revolted.

Sect. 8. And 6. Ordination is no duty in case that Bishops confederate to impose any unlawfull oaths or other Conditions on all that they will ordain. As the Oath of the Roman Prelates containing divers falshoods and unlawful passages doth make all Roman Ordination utterly impious and unlawfull to be received; and therefore not necessary.

Sect. 9. And 7. In case that Bishops themselves (whom those that we now speak to do suppose to have the whole Power of Ordination) should either have a design to corrupt the Church,

and

and ordain only the unworthy , and keep out such as the Necessities of the Church requireth, or set up a destructive faction, or by negligence or any other cause should refuse to ordain such as should be ordained; In all these cases Ordination is impossible to them.

Sect. 10. And 8. In case that death cut off all the Bishops within our reach, or that the remnant be by sickness, or banishment or imprisonment hindered, or by danger affrighted to deny Ordination, or by any such means become in accessible, Ordination must here fail.

Sect. 11. And 9. In case that Bishops through contention are unknown, as *Bellarmine* confesseth it hath been at *Rome*, that the wisest could not tell which was Pope : Especially if withall both parties seem to be such as are not to be submitted to, Ordination fails.

Sect. 12. And 10. In case of Prophetical immediate calls from God, which many had of old, and God hath not bound himself from the like again, though none have reason to expect it, and none should rashly presume of it : In all these ten cases Ordination faileth.

Sect 13. And that it doth so, needs no proof: the Instances prove it themselves. Briefly 1. *Nemo tenetur ad impossibile* : But in many of these cases Ordination is Impossible : therefore, *&c.*

Sect. 14. And 2. *Nemo tenetur ad inhonestum* : No man is bound to sin : For *Turpe est impossibile* in Law. But in many of these cases or all, is plainly sin : therefore *&c.*

Sect. 20. And 3 *Cessante fine cessat obligatio.* The means are for the end : But in many, if not all these cases, *Cessat finis, & ratio medii* : therefore *cessat obligatio,*

Sect. 21. And 4. *Cessante materia cessat obligatio.* But here *aliquando cessat materia* : As in case of the Apostacy, death, banishment, concealment of Bishops, therefore, *&c.* ——

Sect. 22. And now I am next to prove that when the *Obligation to Ordination* ceaseth, yet the *Obligation to Ministerial Offices* ceaseth not, but such must be done.

And 1. I prove it hence, because the obligations of the common Law of Nature cease not upon the cessation of a point of Order : But if the Ministerial works should cease, the Obligati-

X   ons

ons of the Law of Nature must cease.——— Here I have two points to prove. 1. That the Law of Nature (supposing the work of Redemption already wrought, and the Gospel and Ordinances established) obligeth men that are able and have Opportunity to do the work of Ministers . 2. And that this Law is not ceased when Ordination ceaseth.

Sect 23. The Law of Nature prohibits cruelty, and requireth Charity, and to shew mercy to men in greatest Necessities according to our ability : But to suspend the exercise of the Ministerial office, were the greatest cruelty , where there is Ability and opportunity to exercise it: and to exercise it is the greatest work of Mercy in all the World.   Nature teacheth us to *do good to all men while we have time, and to save them with fear, pulling them out of the fire, and to love our neighbours as our selves* ; and therefore to see a man, yea a town and Country and many Countries, lie in sin and in a state of misery, under the Wrath and Curse of God, so that they will certainly be damned if they die in that condition, and yet to be silent, and not Preach the Gospel to them, nor call them home to the state of life, this is the greatest cruelty in the world, except the tempting and driving them to hell.   To let the precious things of the Gospel lie by unrevealed, even Christ and pardon and holiness, and eternal life and the communion of Saints, and all the Church Ordinances, and withal to suffer the Devil to go away with all these souls, and Christ to lose the honour that his grace might have by their conversion, certainly this in it self considered is incomparably more cruelty to men, then to cut their throats, or knock them on the head, as such and as great an injury to God as by omission can be done. I need not plead this argument with a man that hath not much unmand himself, much less with a Christian. For the one is taught of God by nature, to save men out of a lesser fire then Hell, and a lesser pain then everlasting torment , to the utmost of his power : And the other is taught of God to love his brother and his neighbour as himself.   If the Love of God dwell not in him that seeth his brother in corporal need, and shutteth up the bowels of his compassions from him ; how then doth the love of God dwell in him, that seeth his brother in a state of damnation, Cursed by the Law, an enemy to God, and within a step of everlasting death and desperation, and yet refuseth to

afford

afford him the help that he hath at hand, and all because he is not ordained ?

Sect. 24. Let this be considered of, as in any lower case. If a man see another fall down in the streets, sha'l he refuse to take him up, because he is no Physician ? If the Country be infected with the Plague, and you have a Soveraign medicine that will certainly cure it with all that will be ruled, will you let them all perish, rather then apply it to them, because you are not a Physician, and that when the Physitians are not to be had ? If you see the poor naked, may no one make them cloaths but a Taylor? If you see the enemy at the Walls, will you not give the City warning, because you are not a Watch-man, or on the Guard ? If a Commander die in fight, any man that is next may take his place in case of Necessity. Will you see the field lost for a point of Order, because you will not do the work of a Commander ? A hundred such cases may be put, in which its plain, that the substance of the work in which men can do a great and necessary good, is of the Law of Nature, though the regulating of them in point of order is oft from Positive Laws: but the Cessation of the obligation of the Positives about Order, doth not disoblige us from the common Law of Nature: For then it should allow us to lay by humanity.

Fit autem missio aut per Deum mediate &c. aut per Deum mediante superiorum authoritate, &c. Fit rursus nonnunquam & ipsa necessitatis lege; quando non aliter posset fidei seu morum veritas inviolata servari; ubi verum est illud, Pasce fame morientem : si non Pavisti, Occidisti. Voetius.

Sect. 25. To this some may say, that [*Its true we may preach in such cases, but not as Ministers, but as private men : and we may baptize as private men in Necessity : but we may do nothing that is proper to the Ministry*] To this I answer. God hath not made the Consecration of the Bread and Wine in the Eucharist, nor yet the Governing of the Church, the only proper acts of the Ministry. To preach the word as a constant service, to which we are separated, or wholly give up our selves, and to baptize ordinarily, and to congregate the Disciples, and to Teach and Lead them in Gods worship, are all as proper to the Ministry as the other. And these are works that mens eternal happiness lieth on. If you would have an able gifted Christian in *China, Tartary, Indostan,* or such places, (supposing he have opportunity) to speak but occasionally as private men, and not to speak to Assemblies, and wholly give up himself to the work, and gather Churches, and set afoot all Church Ordinances among them, you would have him unnaturally cruell to mens souls. And if you would have him give up himself to these works, and yet not

be

be a Minister, you speak contradictions. For whats the office of a Minister, but [*a state of Obligation and power to exercise the Ministerial acts?*] As its nothing else to be a Physitian, supposing abilites, but to be obliged and impowred to do the work of a Physitian] The works of the Ministry are of Necessity to the salvation of mens souls ; Though here and there one may be saved without them by privater means, yet thats nothing to all the rest : It is the salvation of Towns and Contreyes that we speak of. I count him not a man, that had rather they were all damned, then saved by an unordained man.

Sect. 26. The End of Ordination ceaseth not, when Ordination faileth: the Ministerial works and the benefits to be thereby conveyed, are the Ends of Ordination : therefore they cease not. This is so plain that I perceive not that it needs explication or proof.

Sect. 27. Nature and Scripture teach us, that Ceremonies give place to the substance, and matters of meer Order give place to the Duty ordered ; and that Moral Natural duties cease not when meer Positives cease : But such is the case before us. Ordination is the ordering of the work : If that fail, and the work cannot be rightly Ordered , it follows not that it must be cast off, or forborn. On this account Christ justified his Disciples for plucking ears of Corn on the Sabbath day. Necessity put an end to the Duty of Sabbath keeping ; but the duty of preserving their lives continued. On this account he justifieth his own healing on the Sabbath day ; sending them to study the great rule [*Go learn what this meaneth, I will have Mercy and not Sacrifice :*] So here, he will have Mercy to souls and Countreyes, rather then Ordination : On this account he saith, that [*The Priests in the Temple break the Sabbath and are blameless*] and he tells them [*what David did when he was hungry, and they that were with him, how he eat the shewbread, which (out of Necessity) was not lawfull for him to eat, but only for the Priests.*] and yet he sinned not therein.

Sect. 28. Moreover, the Church it self is not to cease upon the ceasing of Ordination, nor to hang upon the will of Prelates. Christ hath not put it in the power of Prelates, to deny him a Church in any countries of the world. For he hath first determined that particular Churches shall be (and that determination.

nation ceaseth not,) and but secondly that they shall have
Pastors thus ordained : He is not to lose his Churches at the
pleasures of an envious or negligent man : But so it would be
if Pastors must cease when Ordination ceaseth : For though
without Pastors there may be communities of Christians, which
are parts of the universal Church, yet there can be no Organized
Political Churches. For 1. Such Churches consist essentially of
the *Directing or Ruling Part*, and the *Ruled Part*) (as a Re-
publick doth.) 2. Such Churches are Christian Associations for
Communion in such Church Ordinances which without a Pastor
cannot (ordinarily at least) be administred : And therefore
without a Pastor the Society is not capable of the *End*, and therefore not of the form or name ; (though it be a Church in the
fore-granted sense.) Nay indeed, if any should upon necessity
do the Ministerial work to the Church, and say he did it as a Private man, it were indeed but to become a Minister *pro tempore*,
under the name of a private man. If *Paul* had not his Power to
destruction but to Edification, neither have Prelates : And therefore the Acts are null by which they would destroy the Church.
Their Power of Ordering it (such as they have) occasionally enableth them to disorder it (that is, If they miss in their own
work, we may submit 1) but they have no authority to destroy
it, or do any thing that plainly conduceth thereunto.

Sect. 29. The ceasing of Ordination in any place, will not either disoblige the people from Gods publick Worship, Word,
Prayer, Praise, Sacraments ; Neither will it destroy their Right
to the Ordinances of God in Church communion. But this it
should do, if it should exclude a Ministry ; therefore, *&c.* — The
Major is proved, 1. In that the Precept for such Publick worship,
is before the precept for the right ordering of it. He that commandeth the Order, supposeth the thing ordered. 2. The precept
for publick worship, is much in the Law of Nature, and therefore
indispensable : and it is about the great and Necessary duties that
the honour of God and saving of men, and preservation of the
Church lieth on : it is a standing Law to be observed till the
coming of Christ. And the Rights of the Church in the excellent Benefits of Publick Ordinances and Church order, is better
founded then to depend on the Will of ungodly Prelates. If
Prince and Parliament fail, and all the Governours turn enemies.

X 3

to a Common wealth, it hath the means of Prefervation of it felf from ruine left in its own hands; or if the Common-wealth be deftroyed, the Community hath the Power of felf prefervation, and of forming a Common-wealth again to that end. The life and being of States, fpecially of mens eternal happinefs, is not to hang upon fo flender a peg as the corrupt will of a few Superiours, and the mutable modes and circumftances of Government; nor a Neceffary End to be wholly laid upon an uncertain and oft unneceffary means. The children lofe not their Right to Food and Rayment, nor are to be fuffered to famifh, when ever the Steward falls out with them, or falls afleep, or lofeth the Keyes. Another fervant fhould rather break open the doors, and more thanks he fhall have of the Father of the family, then if he had let them perifh, for fear of tranfgreffing the bounds of his calling. If inceft (that capital diforder in procreation) were no inceft, no crime, but a duty, to the Sons and daughters of *Adam* in cafe of Neceffity (becaufe Order is for the End and thing ordered) then much more is a difordered prefervation of the Church and faving of fouls and ferving of God, a duty, and indeed at that time, no diforder at all.

Sect. 30. 7. Moreover, if the failing of Ordination, fhould deprive the world of the preaching of the word, or the Churches of the great and neceffary benefits of Church Ordinances and Communion, then one man (yea thoufands) fhould fuffer (and that in the greateft matters) for the fin and wilfulnefs of others, and muft lie down under fuch fuffering, left he fhould diforderly redrefs it. But the confequent is againft all Juftice and Reafon: Therefore the Antecedent is fo to.

Sect. 31. In a word, it is fo horrid a conclufion, againft Nature, and the Gofpel, and Chriftian fence, that the honour of God, the fruits of Redemption, the being of the Church, the falvation or comfort of mens fouls, muft all be at the Prelates mercy, that a confiderate Chriftian cannot (when he is himfelf) believe it: that it fhould be in the power of heretical, malicious, or idle Prelates to deny God his honour, and Chrift the fruit of all his fufferings, and Saints their Comforts, and finners their falvation, and this when the remedie is before us, and that it is the will of God that all thefe evils fhould be chofen before the evil of an unordained Miniftry; this is an utterly incredible thing.

Sect.

Sect. 32. Argument 2. Another Argument may be this : If there may be all things essential to the Ministry without humane Ordination, then this Ordination is not of Necessity to its Essence; But the Antecedent is true ; therefore so is the consequent. That there be a people qualified to receive a Pastor, and persons qualified to be made Pastors, and that God hath already determined in his Law that Pastors there shall be, and how they shall be qualified is past all dispute ; So that nothing remains to be done by man (Ordainers, Magistrates or People) but to determine who is the man that Christ describeth in his Law, and would have to be the Pastors of such a flock, or a Minister of the Gospel, and then to solemnize his entrance by an Investiture. And now I shall prove that a man may be a Minister without the Ordainers part in these.

Sect. 33: If the will of Christ may be known without Ordination, that *this* man should be the Pastor of such a People, or a Minister of the Gospel, then may a man be a Minister without Ordination. But the will of Christ may be known, *&c. ergo.* ———

Sect. 34. Nothing needs proof but the Antecedent (For it is but the signification of the will of Christ that conferreth the Power, and imposeth the Duty ;) And that his will is sometime signified concerning the individual person without Ordination, is apparent hence : 1. The Description of such as Christ would have to preach the Gospel, is very plain in his holy Canons (in the Scripture.) 2. His Gifts are frequently so eminent in several persons, as may remove all just occasion of doubting, both from the persons themselves and others. 3. Their suitableness to a People by interest, acquaintance, *&c.* may be as notable. 4. The Peoples common and strong affection to them, and theirs to the People, may be added to all these. 5. There may be no Competitor at all ; or none regardable or comparable. and so no controversie. 6. The Necessities of the People may be so great and visible, that he and they may see that they are in danger of being undone, and the Church in danger of a very great loss or *hurt*, if he deny to be their Pastor. 7. The Magistrate also may call and command him to the work: 8. The People and he may consent and they may unanimously choose him, and he Accept their choice. And in all these the will of Christ is easily discerned, that this is the person whom he would have to undertake the Ministry.

Sect.

Sect. 35. For 1. Where there are so many evident signs of his Will, and Characters agreeing to the description in the Law, there the will of Christ may be discerned, and it may be known that this is the described person. But these are here supposed (or enough of these:) And indeed it is no very strange thing for all or almost all these to concur, where there are persons of excellent qualifications.

Sect. 36. And 2. Where there is no Controversie, or room for a Controversie, the determination may be made without a Judge: (The Principal reason and use of Ordainers is, that there may be standing Judges of the fitness of men, to prevent the hurt of the Church by the withdrawing of the Worthy, and the intrusion of the unworthy:) But here is no Controversie, or place for Controversie: therefore, &c.——

Sect. 37. But I suppose some will say that [*Though the Approbation of the Ordainers be not alwaies of Necessity: because the person may be easily known without them; yet their Investing the person with the Power is of Necessity, because without that he is but a person fit for the Office, but cannot receive it till some authorized persons shall deliver it*] Because the great mistake is involved in this objection, I shall answer it fully.

Sect. 38. The Law it self is it that directly gives the Power, and Imposeth the Duty, when the person is once determined of that falls under it: There needs no more but the signification of the Will of Christ, to confer the Power or Benefit, or impose the Duty. As an act of Oblivion pardoneth all the described persons; and an Act that imposeth any burden or office upon every man of such or such an estate or parts, doth immediately by it self oblige the persons; though some Judges or others may be appointed to call out the persons, and see to the execution (who do not thereby impose the duty) so is it in this case. Gods Law can Authorize and oblige without an Ordainer sometimes.

Sect. 39. The Investiture performed in Ordination by man, is not the first Obligation or Collation of the Power, but only the solemnization of what was done before. And therefore though it be *necessitate præcepti* a duty, and ordinarily necessary to Church Order and preservation, yet is it not necessary to the Being of the Ministerial Office or Power.

Sect

Sect. 40. And this will be made apparent, 1. From the common nature of all such subsequential Investitures and inaugurations, which are necessary to full possession and exercise of Power sometimes, but not to the first being of it, nor to the exercise neither in cases of Necessity, when the Investiture cannot conveniently be had.

Sect. 41. Ordination (as to the Investing act) is no otherwise necessary to the Ministry, then Coronation to a King, or listing to a Souldiour, or solemn investiture and taking his Oath to a Judge, or other Magistrate, &c. But these are only the solemn entrance upon Possession and exercise of Power, supposing a sufficient Title antecedent; and in cases of Necessity, may be unnecessary themselves; and therefore so is it here as a like case.

Sect. 42. 2. If want of Investiture in cases of Necessity, will not excuse the determinate person from the burden of the Ministerial work, then will it not prove him destitute of the Ministerial Authority: (For every man hath Authority to do his Duty, in that he is obliged to it;) But the Antecedent is plain; If once I know by certain signs, that I am a man that Christ requireth to be imployed in his work, I durst not totally forbear it, in a case of such exceeding moment, for want of the regular admittance, when it cannot be had; while I know that the work is the End, and the Ordination is but the means; and the means may promote the end, but must not be pleaded against the End, nor to destroy it, it being indeed no Means, when it is against the end. Ordination is for the Ministry, and the Ministerial Office for the Work, and the Work for Gods honour and mens salvation: And therefore God must be served, and men must be saved, and the Ministry to those ends must be used, whether there be Ordination to be had or not.—Necessity may be laid upon us, without Ordination, and then woe to us if we preach not the Gospel. The Law can make Duty without an Ordainer.

Sect. 43. If this were not so, a lazy person that is Able for the Ministry, might by pleasing or bribing the Ordainers, be exempted from abundance of duty, and escape the danger of Guilt and Judgement upon his Omission. And truly the burden is so great to flesh and blood, if men be faithful in their Ou-

Y   nce

fice, the labour fo unceffant, the people fo unconftant, ungrate-
ful and difcouraging, the worldly honours and riches fo tempting
which may be had in a fecular life, with the ftudy and coft that
fits men for the Miniftry, and the enemies of our work and us
are fo many and malicious, and times of perfecution fo frequent
and unwelcome, that if it were but in the Prelates power to
exempt all men at their pleafure, from all the trouble and
care and danger and fufferings of the Miniftery, they would
have abundance of Solicitors and Suitors for a difpenfation?
efpecially where the Love of God and his Church were not
very ftrong to prevail againft temptations (for this would free
them from all fear.)

Sect. 44. 3. If a man and woman may be truly busband
and Wife without a folemn Marriage, then a Minifter and
People may be truly conjoined in their Relations and Church-
State without his folemn Ordination.   For thefe are very neer
of a Nature.   A private Contract between themfelves may truly make them Husband and Wife: and then the ftanding Law
of God conveyeth to the man his Power, and obligeth him and
the woman to their duties, without any Inftrumental inveftiture: And yet if there be opportunity it is not lawful for any to
live together in this relation, without the invefticure of Solemn
Matrimony, for Order fake, and to prevent the fornication and
baftardy, that could not be avoided if Marriage be not Ordinarily publick.   Juft fo it is a very great fin to neglect Ordination
ordinarily, and where it may be had, and tendeth to the baftardy of the Miniftry, and of Churches, and foon would moft be
illegitimate if that courfe were taken.   And yet if Paftor and
People go together without Ordination, upon private Contract, in cafe of Neceffity, it is lawful: And if there be no Neceffity, it is finful, but yet doth not Null the Baptifm, and other
Minifterial adminiftrations of any fuch perfon, to the Church of
Chrift, or the upright members.

Sect 45. 4. If a man may be a *true Chriftian without Baptfm*,
and have Chrift and pardon and Juftification and eternal life
without it; then may a man be a true Minifter without Ordination.   For no man can reafonably plead that Ordination is
more neceffary to a Minifter then Baptifm to a Chriftian. Even
the Papifts that make a Sacrament of it, and afcribe to it an in-
delible

delible Character, muſt needs ſet it ſomewhat lower then Baptiſm. Baptizing is commonly called our Chriſtening, as that in
ſome ſort makes us Chriſtians. And yet for all that the true
uſe of Baptiſm is but to ſolemnize the Marriage between Chriſt
and us, and to Inveſt and inaugurate them in a ſtate of Chriſtianity ſolemnly, that were indeed Chriſtians before. And the
Papiſts themſelves confeſs that when a man firſt repenteth and
believeth (with a faith *formata Charitate*) he is pardoned, and
in a State of Salvation before Baptiſm, and ſhall be ſaved
upon the meer *Votum Baptiſmi*, if in caſe of Neceſſity he die
without it (Though the partial Doctors will damn the infants
for want of Baptiſm, that never refuſed it, when they ſave the
parents that have but the deſire.) No doubt but *Conſtantine*,
and many other, that upon miſtake deferred their Baptiſm,
were nevertheleſs Chriſtians; and judged ſo by the Church both
then and now. And yet to neglect it wilfully were no ſmal ſin.
So if in our caſe, men want Ordination, they may be really Miniſters, and their Miniſtrations Valid; but it is their very
great ſin, if their wilfull neglect be the cauſe that they are not
Ordained.

Sect. 46. As Baptiſm is the open badge of a Chriſtian, ſo
Ordination is the open badge of a Miniſter: and therefore
though a man may be a Chriſtian before God without Baptiſm,
yet Ordinarily he is not a Chriſtian before the Church without
Baptiſm, till he have by ſome equivalent Profeſſion given them
ſatisfaction: And therefore if I knew men to be utterly unbaptized, I would not at firſt have Communion with them as Chriſtians. But if they could manifeſt to me that Neceſſity forbad
them, or if it were any miſtake and ſcruple of their conſciences
that hindered them from the outward Ordinance, and they had
without that Ordinance made as publick and bold a profeſſion
of Chriſtianity, and ſatisfactorily declared themſelves to be
Chriſtians by other means, I would then own them as
Chriſtians, though with a diſowning and reprehenſion of
their error; Even ſo would I do by a Miniſter: I would not
own him as a Miniſter unordained, unleſs he either ſhewed a
Neceſſity that was the Cauſe, or elſe (if it were his weakneſs
and miſtake) did manifeſt by his abilities and fidelity and the
conſent and acceptance of the Church, that he were truly cal-

led

led : And if he did so, I would own him, though with a difowning and reproof of his miftake, and omiffion of fo great a
duty.

Sect. 47. 5. There is not a word of God to be found that
makes Ordination of abfolute Neceffity to the being of the Miniftry : therefore it is not fo to be efteemed. The examples of
Scripture fhew it to the regular way, and therefore Ordinarily
a duty : but they fhew not that there is no other way.

Sect. 48. Object. *It is fufficient that no other way is revealed;
and therefore till you find another in Scripture, this muft be taken
for the only way.* Anfw. 1. Scripture is the Rule of our Right
performance of all duties : We cannot imagine that in the Rule
there fhould be the leaft defect ; and therefore no precept
or imitable pattern of fin in the fmalleft matter is there
to be found. And yet it followeth not that every fin doth
Nullifie a Cailing, becaufe there is no Scripture warrant for that
fin. All that will follow is, that no other way is innocent or
warrantable : and that only when Neceffity doth not warrant
it. 2. I have fhewed already that there are other wayes warranted in fome cafes in the Scripture : And I fhall fhew anon
that as great omiffions nullifie not the office.

Sect. 49. Object. *But how fha'l they preach un'lefs they be fent?*
faith *Paul, Rom.* 10. Anfw. But the queftion is, Whether no
man be fent that have not humane Ordination? The text doth
not affirm this. Let that be Gods Ordinary way : but yet it
followeth not there is no other. If God fend them however,
they may preach ; as *Edefius, Frumentius, Origen,* and others
did of old.

Sect. 50. Argument 3. He that hath the Talents of Minifterial Abilities, is bound to improve them to the fervice of his
Mafter and beft advantage of the Church : But fuch are
many that cannot have Ordination : *ergo* ——— Concerning
the Major, note that I fay not that every man that is able is
bound to be a Minifter, much lefs to enter upon the facred function without Ordination : For 1. Some men that have Abilities may want liberty and opportunity to exercife them. 2. Others
that have Minifterial Abilities, may alfo have Abilities for Magiftracy, Phyfick, Law, &c. and may live in a Country where
the exercife of the later is more Neceffary and ufeful to the

good

good of men, and the service of God, then the exercise of the
Ministry would be. For these men to be Ministers, that either
want opportunity, or may do God greater service other waies,
is not to improve their Talents to their Masters chiefest service:
But still the general obligation holds, to improve our Talents to
the best advantage, and do good to as many as we can, and
work while it is day. And therefore 1. Such a man is bound
(if he be not otherwise called out first) to offer his service to
the Church and seek Ordination: And if he cannot have it upon just seeking, in case of Necessity, he is to exercise his Talents
without it: lest he be used as the wicked slothful servant, that
hid his Talent, *Mat. 25.*

Sect. 51: If this were not so, it would follow that the
Gifts of God must be in vain, and the Church suffer the loss
of them at the pleasure of Ordainers: and that the fixed
universal Law that so severely bindeth all men, as good
Stewards to improve their Masters stock (their Time, abilities, interest, opportunities) might be dispensed with at
the Pleasure of Ordainers. And that God hath bound us to
seek in vain, for Admittance to the exercise of the Talents
that he hath endowed us with: and that even in the Necessities of the Church. Which are not things to be granted.

Sect. 52. Object *By this doctrine you will induce disorder
into the Church, if all that are able must be Ministers when
they are denyed Ordination: For then they will be the Judges
of their own Abilities, and every brain-sick proud Opinionist,
will think that there is a Necessity of his Preaching; and so
we shall have confusion, and Ordination will be made contemptible
by Pretences of Necessity!*

Sect. 53. *Answ.1.* God will not have the Necessities of
mens souls neglected, nor allow us to let men go quietly
to damnation, nor have his Churches ruined, for fear of occasioning the disorders of other men. Its better that men be
disorderly saved, then orderly damned: and that the Church be
disorderly preserved, then orderly destroyed! God will not
allow us to suffer every Thief and Murderer to rob or kill our
neighbours, for fear lest by defending them, we occasion men
to neglect the thing that. nor will he allow us to

perish in their sicknefs, if we can help them, for fear of en-
couraging the ignorant to turn Phyfitians. 2. There is no
part of Gods fervice that can be ufed, without occafion of
fin to the perverfe: Chrift himfelf is the fall as well as the ri-
fing of many; and is a ftumbling ftone and Rock of offence:
and yet not for that to be denyed. There is no juft and rea-
fonable caufe of mens abufe in the doctrine which I here exprefs. 3. *True Necefsity* will excufe and Juftifie the unordained before God for exercifing their Abilities to his fervice. But
pretended counterfeit necefsity will not Juftifie any; And the
final judgement is at hand, when all things fhall be fet ftrait, and
true Necefsity and counterfeit fhall be difcerned. 4. Until
that day, things will be in fome diforder in this world, becaufe there is fin the world, which is the diforder. But our
Remedies are thefe, 1. To teach men their duties truly, and
not to lead them into one evill to prevent another, much lefs to
a mifchief deftructive to mens fouls, to prevent diforder.
2. The Magiftrate hath the fword of juftice in his hand, to reftrain falfe pretenders of Necefsity; and in order thereto, it
is he, and not the pretender that fhall be judge. And 3. The
Churches have the Power of cafting the pretenders (if the
cafe deferve it) out of their communion; and in order thereto, it is not he but they that will be Judges. And other remedies we have none till the laft day.

Sect. 54. Queft. *But what would you have men do that
think there is a Necefsity of their labours, and that they have
Miniftcrial abilities? Anfw.* 1. I would have them lay by pride
and felfifhnefs, and pafs judgement on their own Abilities in
Humility and felf-denyal. If their Corruptions are fo ftrong
that they cannot (that is, they will not) do this, thats long of
themfelves. 2. They muft not pretend a Necefsity where is
none. 3. They muft offer themfelves to the Tryal of the Paftors of the Church that beft know them. 4. If in the judgement of the godly able Paftors that know them, they are
unfit, and there is no need of them, they muft acquiefce in
their judgement. For able Godly men are not like to deftroy the Church or envy help to the fouls of men. 5. If
they have caufe to fufpect the Paftors of Corruption, and falfe
judgement, let them go to the other Paftors that are faithfull.

2.3 4.
2.6,7.8.

full. 6. If all about us were corrupt, and their judgements not to be rested in , and the persons are assured of their Ability for the Ministry , let them consider the State of the Church where they are : And if they are sure (on Consultation with the wisest men) that there is a Necessity, and their endeavours in the Ministry are like to prevent any notable hurt, without a greater hurt, let them use them without Ordination , if they cannot have it. But if they find that the Churches are so competently supplied without them, that there is no Necessity, or none which they can supply without doing more hurt by offence and disorder then good by their labours, let them forbear at home, and go into some other Countries where there is greater need (if they are fit there for the work.) if not, let them sit still.

Sect. 55. Argument 4. If unordained men may Baptize in case of Necessity, then may they do other Ministerial works in case of Necessity : But the Antecedent is the opinon of those that we now dispute against. And the Consequence is grounded on a Parity of Reason:No man can shew more for appropriating the Eucharist, then Baptisme to the Minister.

CHAP.

CHAP. IV.

An uninterrupted Succession of Regular Ordination, is not Necessary.

Sect. 1.

Of this I desire the Reader, to peruse what is written by *Voetius de desperata CausaPapatus, l.2.Sect.2.c. 21.& passim.*

HAving proved the Non-necessity of Ordination it self to the *Being* of the Ministry, and *Validity* of their administrations,I may be the shorter in most of the rest, because they are sufficiently proved in this. If Ordination it self be not of the Necessity which the adversaries do assert, then the *Regularity* of Ordination cannot be of more Necessity then Ordination it-self: Much less an *uninterrupted Succession* of such Regular Ordination : Yet this also is asserted by most that we have now to do with.

Sect. 2. By *Regular Ordination*,I mean in the sence of the adversaries themselves, such as the Canons of the Church pronounce not Null,and such as by the Canons was done by such as had Authority to do it: in special, by true Bishops (even in their own sence.)

Sect. 3. And if the uninterrupted succession be not Necessary, then neither is such Ordination at this present Necessary to the being of the Ministry : For if any of our predecessors might be Ministers without it, others in the like case may be so too. For we live under the same Law, and the Office is the same thing now as it was then.

Sect. 4. Argument 1. If uninterrupted Regular Ordination of all our predecessors be Necessary to the Being of the Ministry,

ſtry, then no man can know that he is truly a Miniſter of Chriſt. But the Conſequent is falſe, and intolerable; therefore ſo is the Antecedent.

Sect. 5. The truth of the Minor is apparent thus. 1. If we could not be ſure that we are true Miniſters, then no man could with comfort ſeek the Miniſtry, nor enter into upon it. For who can have encouragement to enter a calling when he knows not whether indeed he enter upon it or not? and whether he engage not himſelf in a courſe of ſin, and be not guilty as *Uzza* of medling with the Ark unlawfully? eſpecially in ſo great and tender a caſe where God is ſo exceeding jealous.

Sect. 6. And 2. who can go on in the Calling of the Miniſtry, and comfortably do the work, and bear the burden, that cannot know through all his life, or in any adminiſtration, whether he be a Miniſter or a Uſurper? What a damp muſt it caſt upon our ſpirits. in Prayer, Praiſe, adminiſtration of the Euchariſt and all publick worſhip, (which ſhould be performed with the greateſt alacrity and delight) when we remember that we are uncertain whether God have ſent us, or whether we are uſurpers, that muſt one day hear, [*Who ſent you? Whence had you your Power? and who required this at your hands?*

Sect. 7. And the Conſequence of the Major (that we are all uncertain of our Call and office, both Papiſts and Proteſtants) is moſt clear (in caſe of the Neceſſity of ſuch ſucceſsive Ordination) For 1. No man ever did, to this day demonſtrate ſuch a ſucceſſion, for the Proof of his Miniſtry. Nor can all our importunity prevail with Papiſts (Italians or French) to give us ſuch a proof. 2. It is a thing impoſſible for any man now alive, to prove the Regular Ordination of all his Predeceſſors, to the Apoſtles daies, yea or any Ordination at all. How can you tell that he that ordained you did not counterfeit himſelf to be Ordained? Or at leaſt that he was not ordained by an unordained man? or that his Predeceſſors were not ſo? It is a meer impoſſibility for us to know any ſuch thing; we have no Evidence to prove it.

Sect. 8. Object. *But it is probable though not certain: for the Church proceede by ſuch Rules, of so great weight, that there is no probability that they would suffer any to go for Pastors or Bishops that are unordained, in so great a case.*

Answ. 1. All this is *no certainty* : and therefore no proof : and no satisfaction to the mind of a Minister, in the forementioned doubts. 2. Yea we have so great reason to be suspicious in the case that we cannot conclude that we have so mnch as a probabily.

Sect. 9. For, 1. We know that there is so much selfishnef and corruption in man as is like enough to draw them to deceit. Ordainers may be bribed to consecrate or ordain the uncapable, and the Ordained or Consecrated may be tempted to seek it in their incapacity ; and many may be drawn to pretend that they were Ordained or Consecrated when it was no such matter. And so there is not so much as a Probability.

Sect. 10. 2. And we know that there were so many heresies abroad, and still have been, and so much faction and Schism in the Church : that we cannot be sure that these might not interrupt the succession, or that they drew not our predecessors to counterfeit a Consecration or Ordination when they had none, or none that was regular.

Sect. 11. 3. And we know our selves that the thing hath been too usual. When I was young, I lived in a village that had but about twenty houses. And among these there were five, that went out into the Ministry. One was an Old Reader whose Original we could not reach. Another was his son, whose self-Ordination was much suspected : The other three had Letters of Orders, two of them suspected to be drawn up and forged by him, and one that was suspected to Ordain himself. One of them, or two at laſt were proved to have counterfeit Orders, when they had continued many years in the Ministry. So that this is no rare thing.

Sect. 12. Among so many temptations that in so many ages since the Apoſtles dayes, have befallen so many men, as our predecessors in the Ministry, or the Bishops predecessors have been, it were a wonder if all of them should scape the snare : So that we have reason to take it for a thing improbable, that the succession hath not been interrupted.

Sect. 13. And we know that in several ages of the Church the

Prelates

Prelates and Priests have been so vile, that in reason we could expect no better from men so vicious, then forgery and abuse, he that reads what *Gildas* and others say of the Brittish, and what even *Baronius*, much more *Espencæus, Cornelius Mus.* and others say of the Romanists ; yea he that knows but what state the Bishops and Priests have been in and yet continue in, in our own dayes, will never think it an improbable thing that some of our predecessors should be guilty either of Simony or other vice that made them uncapable, or should be meer usurpers under the name of Bishops and Ministers of Chrift.

Sect. 14. Argument 2. If uninterrupted Regular Ordination of all our Predecessors be Necessary to the Being of the Ministry, then can no Bishop or Pastors whatsoever comfortably Ordain : For who dare lay his hand on the head of another, and pretend to deliver him authority, in the name of Chrift, that hath no assurance (nor probability neither) that he hath any Commission from Chrift to do it ? But the Consequent will be disowned by those that dispute against us ? therefore so should the Antecedent be also.

Sect. 15. Argument 3. If there be a Necessity of an uninterrupted succession of true Regular Ordination, then no man can know of the Church that he is a member of, or of any other Church on earth, that it is a true Church. (By a Church I mean not a Community, but a Society : not a company of private Chriftians living together as Chriftian neighbours, but a Politick Church consisting of Pastor and people associated for the use of publick Ordinances and Communion therein:) But the consequent is false ; —— &c.

Sect. 16. The Major, or consequence is certain : For no man can know that the Church is a true Political Organized Church, that knows not that the Pastor of it is a true Minister of Chrift. Because the Pastor is an Essential constitutive part of the Church in this acceptation. And I have proved already that the truth of the Ministry cannot be known upon the Opponents terms. And for the Minor, I think almost all Church members will grant it me. For though they are ready enough to accuse others, yet they all take their own Churches for true, and will be offended with any that question or deny it.

Sect. 17. Argument 4. If there be a Necessity of an unin-

terrupted

errupted succession of true Ordination, then cannot the Church or any Christian in it, know whether they have any true Ministerial administrations, whether in Sacraments or other Ordinances. For he that cannot know that he hath a Minister, cannot know that he hath the administration of a Minister) But the consequent is untrue, and against the comfort of all Christians, and the honour of Christ, and is indeed the very doctrine of the *Infidels and Papists*, that call themselves *Seekers* among us.

Sect. 18. Argument 5. If the Churches and each member of them are bound to submit to the Ministry of their Pastors without knowing that they are regularly ordained, or that they have an uninterrupted succession of such Ordination, then are they *quoad Ecclesiam*, true Pastors to them, and their administrations valid, though without Ordination or such a succession. But the Antecedent is true, and granted by all that now we have to deal with. Though they will not grant a *known* unordained man is to be taken for a Minister, or one whose succession had a known intercision; Yet they will grant that if the Nullity be unknown, it freeth not the people from the obligation to their Pastors.

Sect. 19. *Bellarmine* (*lib* 3. *de Ecclef.c.* 10.) was so stalled with these difficulties that he leaves it as a thing that we cannot be resolved of; that our Pastors have indeed [*Potestatem Ordinis & Jurisdictionis*] that is, that they are *true Pastors*. And he saith that [*Non habemus certitudinem nisi Moralem, quod illi sint vere Episcopi.*] But when he should prove it to us that there is a *Moral Certainty*, he leaves us to seek and gives us not so much as a ground to conjecture at any probability.

Sect. 20. But he saith that we may know that [*some Pastors at least are true*: or else God had forsaken his Church.] A. sw. But what the better are we for this, if we know not, *which they are that* are the true Pastors, nor cannot possibly come to know it?

Sect. 21. But he saith that [*Quod Christi locum tenent, & quod debemus illi obedientiam*] may be *known*: and thereupon he saith that [*Certe sumus certitudine infallibili quod isti quos videmus sint veri Episcopi & Pastores nostri: Nam ad hoc non requiritur, nec fides nec Character Ordinis, nec legitima Electio, sed solum ut*

ka-

habeantur pro talibus ab Ecclesia.] From all this you may note 1. That they are *veri Episcopi & Pastores nostri*, that were never ordained, if they are but reputed such by the Church, 2. That we may know this by *infallible Certainty*, 3. And that we owe them obedience as such. So that as to the Church they are true Pastors without Ordination, and consequenly to the Church a succession is unnecessary.

Sect. 22. Yet of such Usurpers he saith [*Eos quidem non esse in se veros Episcopos, tamen donec pro talibus habentur ab Ecclesia, deberi illis obedientiam, cum conscientia etiam erronea obliget.*] So that they are not *veri Episcopi in se*: and yet they are *veri Episcopi & Pastores nostri*, if *Bellarmine* say true; And the words have some truth in them, understood according to the distinction which I before gave, *Chap. 1. Sect. 5, 6.* He *p. 130.* hath no such Call as will save himself from the penalty of usurpation (if he knowingly be an usurper) but he hath such a Call as shall oblige the Church to obey him as their Bishop or Pastor.

Sect. 23 But his reason (*Cum conscientia etiam erronea obliget*] is a deceit; and neither the only, nor the chief reason, nor any reason. Not the *only* nor *chief* reason; because the obligation ariseth from God, and that is the greatest. Not *any* reason; 1. Because indeed it is *not an Erroneous* Conscience, that tells many people that their usurping Bishops or Pastors are to be obeyed as true Ministers; For as it is terminated on the Pastors act or state, it is no act of Conscience at all; and therefore no error of conscience. For conscience is the knowledge of our own affairs. And as it is terminated on our own Duty of obeying them, it is not *Erroneous*, but right; For it is the will of God, that for order sake we obey both Magistrates and Pastors that are setled in Possession, if they rule us according to the Laws of Christ; at least, if we do not know the Nullity of their call. 2. And its false that an *Erroneous Conscience bindeth*, that is, *makes us a Duty*; For at the same instant it *is it self a sin* and we are bound to depose it, and change it, and renounce the error. It doth but intangle a man in a Necessity of sinning till it be laid by. But it is God only that can make our duty, and cause such an obligation.

Sect. 24. From the adversaries Concessions then an uninter-

rupted

rupted fucceffion, or prefent true Ordination is not of Neceffity to the being of the Miniftry, Church or Ordinances *quoad*
Ecclefiam : for the Church is bound to obey the ufurpers, and
that as long as they are taken for true Paftors. Which is as much
as moft Churches will defire in the cafe.

Sect. 25. And the confequence is eafily proved : For where
God obligeth his Churches to the obedience of Paftors (though
ufurpers) and to the ufe of Ordinances and their Miniftration,
there will he blefs the Miniftry and thofe Ordinances (to the
innocents, that are not guilty of his ufurpation) and that obey
God herein. And confequently the Ordinances fhall not be
Nullities to them. God would never fet his fervants upon the
ufe of a means which is but a Nullity ; nor will he command
them to a duty, which he will blaft to them when he hath
done without their fault. Its none of the Churches fault
that the Bifhop or Paftor is an ufurper, while they cannot
know it, and that any of his Predeceffors were ufurpers
fince the Apoftles dayes. And therefore where God impo-
feth duty on the Church and prefcribeth means, (as Baptifm,
Prayer, the Lords Supper, Church-Government, &c.)
it is certain that he will not blaft it, but blefs it to the obedient, nor punifh the Church fo for the fecret fin of I know
not who, committed I know not where nor when, perhaps a
thoufand years ago.

Sect. 26. Argument 6. As other actions of ufurpers are not
Nullities to the innocent Church, fo neither is their Ordina-
nation : and confequently, thofe that are Ordained by ufurpers,
may be true Minifters. If their Baptizing, Preaching, Praifes,
Confecration and adminiftration of the Eucharift, binding and
loofing, be not Nullities, it follows undenyably on the fame
account, that their Ordinations are not Nullities : and confequently, that they are true Minifters whom they ordain; and
fucceffion of a more regular Ordination is not of Neceffity, to
the Miniftry, Church or Ordinances.

Sect. 27 Argument 7. If fuch uninterrupted fucceffion be
not Neceffary to be *Known*, then is it not Neceffary to the
Being of the Miniftry or Validity of Ordinances adminiftred;
But fuch a fucceffion is not Neceffary to be *known* : therefore ——————The Confequence of the Major is plain, becaufe

caufe the Being or Nullity of Office and adminiftrations, had never been treated off by God to men, nor had it been revealed, or a thing regardable, but that we may know it: Nor doth it otherwife attain its ends. And that it is not neceffary to be known, I further prove.

Sect. 28. If this fucceffion muft be known, then either to the Paftor, or to the Church, or both: but none of thefe: therefore —— 1. If it muft be known only to the Paftor, then it is not Neceffary as to the Church. And yet it is not Neceffary to be known to the Paftor himfelf neither. For (as is fhewed) its impoffible for him to know it, fo much as by a Moral Certainty. His Predeceffors and their Ordinations were ftrange to him. 2. Not to the Church. For it is not poffible for them to know it: Nor likely that they fhould know as much as the true Ordination of their prefent Paftor according to the Prelatical way, when it is done fo far out of their fight.

Sect. 29. If the forefaid uninterrupted fucceffion be neceffary to the being of our Miniftry, or Churches or Ordinances, then is it incumbent on all that will prove the truth of their Miniftry, Churches or Ordinances, to prove the faid fucceffion. But that is not true; for then none (as is aforefaid) could prove any of them. Either it is meet that we be able to Prove the truth of our Miniftry, Churches and adminiftrations, or not. If not, then why do the adverfaries call us to it? If yea: then no man among the Churches in *Europe* (on their grounds) hath any proof; and therefore muft not pretend to the Miniftry, Churches or Ordinances, but we muft all turn Seekers to day, and Infidels to morrow, by this device.

Sect. 30. Argument 8. The Miniftry of the Priefts and Levites before the incarnation of Chrift, and in his time, was not Null, though they wanted as much or more then fuch a fucceffion of right Ordination: therefore it is fo ftill with the Gofpel Miniftry. The Antecedent I fhall more fully manifeft neerer to the end: Only now obferve, that when *Abiathar* was put out by *Solomon*; and when fuch as were not of the line or Genealogie of the Priefts, were put as polluted perfons from the Priefthood (*Neh.* 7. 64, 65. and 13. 29, 30. *Ezra* 2. 62)
yet

yet were not any of their adminiſtrations taken to have been Null.

Sect. 31. Argument 9. If the Miniſtration or Governing acts of *Uſurping Princes* may be Valid, and there need no proof of an uninterrupted ſucceſsion to prove the validity, then is it ſo alſo in the Miniſtry : But the Antecedent is certain; therefore, *&c.* The Validity of the conſequence from the parity of Reaſon I ſhall manifeſt anon.

Sect. 32. Argument 10. If an uninterrupted Succeſsion of Canonical or true Ordination be Neceſſary to the Being of the Church, Miniſtry and Ordinances, then *Rome* and *England* have loſt their Miniſtry, Churches, and Ordinances. But the Conſequent will be denyed by the adverſaries; therefore ſo alſo muſt the Antecedent, if they regard their ſtanding.

Sect. 33. Though this be the Argument that I have the greateſt advantage to preſs the adverſary with, yet becauſe I have made it good already in two or three other writings (in my Key for Catholicks, and my Safe Religion, and Chriſtian Concord) I ſhall ſay but little of it now. But briefly this may ſuffice: 1. For the Church of *Rome*, if either Hereſie, Infidelity, Sodomie, Adultery, Murder, Simony, violent intruſion, ignorance, impiety, want of due election, or of due conſecration, or plurality of Popes at once, can prove an interruption of their ſucceſsion, I have ſhewed them already where its proved ; But if none of theſe prove it, we are ſafe our ſelves.

Sect. 34 But *Grotius* (*in Diſcuſ. Apolog. Rivet.*) pleads for them, that if *any interciſion have been made at* Rome, *it hath been made up from other Churches.*] *Anſw.* 1. That is not proved, but nakedly affirmed. 2. Nor will it ſerve the Papiſts turn, that muſt have all Churches hold from *Rome* and her ſucceſsion, and *Rome* from none, nor to be patcht up from their ſucceſsion. 3. *De facto* the contrary is certain : For 1. Thoſe other held their Miniſtry as from the univerſal Headſhip of the Pope ; and therefore had themſelves their interruptions in the former interruptions of *Rome* (as being but her members :) and therefore were not capable themſelves of repairing of her breaches, 2. The ſucceſſ-ſrs of the illegitimate Popes (ſuch as *depoſed Eugenius, &c.*) and men as bad as they, have continued the ſucceſsion : And the ſuccceſſors were conſecrated by power received from the illegitimate g:timate Popes, were the only persons that were the repairers of the breach. And yet the Pope will hardly yield that he receiveth his power from any of these. 3. There have been greater defects in the succession then this of Consecration, even of due Election, Capacity, yea of an office it self which Christ will own. The Vicechristship of the Pope is no office of Christs planting.

Sect. 35. And 2 For the English Prelates, as they are unable to prove their uninterrupted succession, so the interruption is proved, in that they derived and held their Power from the Vicechrist of *Rome*, and that *qua talis*, for so many ages. This was their own profession: and all that they did was as his Ministers by his Authority, which was none.

Sect. 36. Object. *But this nulled not the true Authority which they received from the Pope or Prelates as Prelates.* *Answ.* The Pope was uncapable of giving them Authority (and whether the Prelates as such were so too, we shall enquire anon.) And though I grant that (where the person was fit)there was yet a Ministry Valid to the Church(and perhaps to themselves in the main)yet that is because Canonical Ordination is not of Necessity to the Being of the Ministry; (but by other means they might be then Ministers, though this corruption was conjunct, that they received their Power imaginarily from *Rome*) But that the said Canonical succession was interrupted, by this Papal tenure, and many a delinquency, is nevertheless sure, and sufficient to inforce the Argument as to them that now are our adversaries. But so much shall suffice for the Non-necessity of this succession of a true and Regular Ordination.

A a   CHAP.

CHAP. V.

Ordination by such as the English Prelates, not Necessary to the Being of the Ministry.

Sect. 1.  Have made this work unnecessary by the two former Chapters : For if *no Ordination* be of Necessity to the Being of the Ministry, nor an uninterrupted Succession Necessary , then doubtless an Ordination by these Prelates *in Specie* is not Necessary at present, or as to succession. But yet *ex abundati* I add.

Sect. 2. Argument 1. *Ad hominem,* I may well argue from the Concession of the English Prelates themselves and their most zealous adherents ; And their judgements were 1. That such a succession as aforesaid of right Ordination was not of Necessity ; And for this they that write against the Papists, do commonly and confidently dispute.

Sect. 3. And 2. They maintained that the Protestant Churches that had no Bishops were true Churches, and their Ministers true Ministers, and so of their administrations. This was so common with them that I do not think a dissenting vote can be found, from the first Reformation, till about the preparations for the Spanish match or little before.

Sect. 4. I have in my *Christian Concord* cited at large the words of many, and the places of the writings of more, as 1. Dr. *Field,*

2. Bishop

2. Bishop *Downam*; 3. Bishop *Jewel*, 4. *Saravia*, 5. Bishop *Alley*, 6. Bishop *Pilkinton*, 7. Bishop *Bridges*, 8. Bishop *Bilson*, 9. *Alexander Nowel*, 10. *Grotius* (their friend then) 11, Mr. *Chysenhal*, 12. The Lord *Digby*, 13. Bishop *Davenant*, 14. Bishop *Prideaux*, 15. Bishop *Andrews*, 16. *Chillingworth*, 17. (To which I now add) Bishop *Bromhall* (of Schism) 18. Dr. *Fern*, 19. Dr. *Steward* (in his answer to *Fountains* letter (these of the later, or present sort) 20. And Bishop *Usher* (whose judgement of it is lately published by Dr. *Bernard* at his own desire) 21. And Mr. *Mason* (in a Book of of purpose for justification of the Reformed Churches) hath largely pleaded this cause. 22. And Dr. *Bernard* saith that Dr. *Overall* was judged not only to consent to that Book, but to have a hand in it. 23. And no wonder when even *Bancroft* himself (the violentest of all the enemies of them called *Puritans* in those times) is said by *Spotswood* (there recited by Dr. *Bernard*) to be of the same mind, and to give it as his judgement, that the Scotch Ministers (then to be Consecrated Bishops) were not to be reordained, because the Ordination of Presbyters was valid.

Sect. 5. These Novel Prelatical persons then, that so far dissent from the whole stream of the Ancient Bishops and their adherents, have little reason to expect that we should regard their judgement above the judgement of the English Clergy, and the judgement of all the Reformed Churches. If they can give us such Reasons as should conquer our modestie, and perswade us to condemn the judgement of the Prelates and Clergy of *England*, & all other Churches of the Protestants, and adhere to a few new men of yesterday, that dare scarcely open the face of their own opinions: we shall bow to their Reasons when we discern them: But they must not expect that their Authority shall so far prevail.

Sect. 6. And indeed I think the most of this cause is carried on in the dark: What Books have they written to prove our Ordination Null? and by what Scripture Reasons do they prove it? The task lieth on them to prove this Nullity, if they would be Regarded in their reproaches of the Churches of Christ. And they are not of such excessive Modesty, and backwardness to divulge their accusations, but sure we might by this time have expected more then one volume from them, to have proved us, No Minifters and Churchess if they could have done it. And till they do it; their whiſperings are not to be credited

Sect. 7. Argument 2. If that ſort of Prelacy that was exerciſed in *England* was not neceſſary it ſelf, yea if it were ſinfull, and tended to the ſubverſion or exceeding hurt of the Churches; then is there no Neceſſity of Ordination by ſuch a Prelacy. But the Antecedent is true : therefore ſo is the conſequent. The Antecedent hath been proved at large in the foregoing Diſputation. Such a Prelacy as conſiſteth in the undertaking of an impoſſible task, even for one man to be the only Governour of all the ſouls in many hundred Pariſhes, exerciſing it alſo by Lay men , and in the needful parts, not exerciſing it all all ; a Prelacy not choſen by the Presbyters whom they Govern ; yea ſuſpending or degrading the Presbyters of all thoſe Churches, as to the governing part of their office, and guilty of the reſt of the evils before mentioned , is not only it ſelf unneceſſary; but ſinful, and a diſeaſe of the Church which all good men ſhould do the beſt they can to cure. And therefore the effects of this diſeaſe can be no more Neceſſary to our Miniſtry, then the burning of a feaver, or ſwelling of a Tympany, is neceſſary to the body.

Sect. 8. No Biſhops are Neceſſary but ſuch as were in Scripture times : But there were none ſuch as the late Engliſh Biſhops in Scripture times : Therefore the Engliſh Biſhops are not neceſſary. He that denyeth the Major, muſt go further in denying the ſufficiency of Scripture, then I find the Papiſts ordinarily to do: For they will be loth to affirm that any office is of Neceſſity to the Being of the Church or of Presbyters, that is not to be found in Scripture, or that was not then in Being : Therefore ſo far we are ſecure.

Sect. 9. And for the Minor, I prove it thus. If the Engliſh Biſhops were neither ſuch as the unfixed General Miniſters, nor ſuch as the fixed Biſhops of particular Churches, then were they not ſuch as were in Scripture times. But they were neither ſuch as the unfixed General Miniſters, nor ſuch as the fixed Biſhops of particular Churches : therefore, &c.

Sect. 10. Beſides theſe two ſorts of Miniſters, there are no more in the New Teſtament. (And theſe are diverſified but by the exerciſe of their office, ſo far as they were ordinary Miniſters fters to continue.) The unfixed Ministers (whether Apostles, Evangelists or Prophets) were such as had no special charge of any one Church as their Diocess, but were to do their best for the Church in general, and follow the direction and call of the Holy Ghost for the exercising of their Ministry. But its known to all that our Engsish Bishops were not such. They were no ambulatory itinerant Preachers: they went not about to plant Churches, and confirm and direct such as they had planted: but were fixed to a City, and had every one their Diocess, which was their proper charge (but Oh how they discharged their undertaking!)

Sect. 11. Object. *The Apostles might agree among them selves to divide their Provinces, and did accordingly,* James *being* Bishop *of* Jerusalem, Peter *of* Rome, &c. Answ. No doubt but common reason would teach them when they were sent to preach the Gospel to all the world , to disperse themselves, and not be preaching all in a place, to the disadvantage of their work: But 1. Its one thing to travail several ways, and so divide themselves as itinerants ; and another thing to divide the Churches among them, as their several Diocesses to which they should be fixed : Which they never did , for ought is proved. 2. And its one thing prudently to disperse . themselves for their labour , and another thing to claim a special power. over a Circuit or Diocess as their charge , excluding a like charge and power of others. So far as any man, Apostle or other, was the Father of souls by their conversion, they ow ed him a special honour and love , which the Apostles themselves did sometimes claim : But this was nothing to a peculiar Diocess or Province. For in the same City (as *Jerusalem*) some might be converted by one Apostle, and some by another. And if a Presbyter convert them, I think the adversaries will not therefore make them his Diocess, not give him there an Episcopal Power, much less above Apostles in that place. Nor was this the Rule that Diocesses could be bounded by, as now they are taken.

Sect. 12. Nor do we find in Scripture the least intimation that the Apostles were fixed Diocesan Bishops , but much to the contrary. 1. In that it was not consistent with the General charge, and work that Christ had laid upon them to go into all the world, and preach the Gospel to

every

every creature : How would this ſtand with fixing in a peculiar Dioceſs ?

Sect. 13. And 2. We find them anſwering their Commiſſion in their practice, going abroad and preaching and planting Churches, and ſometimes viſiting them in their paſſage, but not ſetling on them as their Dioceſſes ; but going further, if they had opportunity, to do the like for other places. Yea they planted Biſhops in the ſeveral Cities and Churches which they had gathered to Chriſt. Though *Paul* ſtaid three years at *Epheſus* and other adjacent parts of *Aſia*, yet did not all that abode prove it his peculiar Dioceſs : (And yet its hard to find again ſo long an abode of *Paul* or any Apoſtle in one place.)Elders that were Biſhops we find at *Epheſus*, *Acts* 20.and ſome ſay *Timothy* was their Biſhop, and ſome ſay *John* the Apoſtle was their Biſhop : but its clear that it was no peculiar Dioceſs of *Paul*.

Sect. 14. And 3. We ſtill find that there were more then one of theſe general itinerant Miniſters in a Place, or at leaſt that no one excluded others from having equal power with him in his Province, where ever he came. *Barnabas*, *Silas*, *Titus*, *Timotheus*, *Epaphroditus*, and many more were fellow-labourers with *Paul* in the ſame Dioceſs or Province, and not as fixed Biſhops or Presbyters under him, but as General Miniſters as well as he. We never read that he ſaid to any of the falſe Apoſtles that ſought his contempt [This is my Dioceſs, what have you to do to play the Biſhop in another mans Dioceſs ?] Much leſs did he ever plead ſuch a Power, againſt *Peter*, *Barnabas* or any Apoſtolical Miniſter : Nor that *James* pleaded any ſuch prerogative at *Jeruſalem*.

Sect. 15. And therefore though we reverence *Euſebius* and other Ancients, that tell us of ſome Apoſtles Dioceſſes, we take them not as infallible reporters, and have reaſon in theſe points partly to deny them credit from the word of God. The Churches that were planted by any Apoſtle, or where an Apoſtle was longeſt reſident, were like enough to reckon the *ſeries* of their Paſtors from him : For the founder of a Church is a Paſtor of it, though not a fixed Paſtor, taking it as his peculiar charge, but delivering it into the hands of ſuch : And in this ſence we have great reaſon to underſtand the Catalogues of the Antients and

and their affirmations that Apostles were Bishops of the Churches.   For Pastors they were: but so that they had no peculiar Diocess, but still went on to planting and gathering and confirming Churches: Whereas the Bishops that were setled by them
(and are said to succeed them)had their single Churches which
were their peculiar charge; They had but one such charge or
Church, when the Apostles that lead in the Catalogues had ma ny;
& yet none so as to be limited to them. And why have we not the
Diocess of *Paul* and *John*, and *Mathew* and *Thomas*, and the rest
of the twelve, mentioned, as well of *Peter* and *James*? Or if *Paul*
had any, it seems he was compartner with *Peter* in the same City
(contrary to the Canons that requireth that there be but one
Bishop in a City.)

Sect. 16. Its clear then that the English Bishops were not
such Apostolical unfixed Bishops as the Itinerants of the first age
were. And yet if they were, I shall shew in the next Argument
that its nothing to their advantage; because Archbishops are
nothing to our question.   And that they were not such as the
fixed Bishops of Scripture times, I am next to prove.

Sect. 17. The fixed Bishops in the Scripture times had but a
single Congregation, or particular Church for their Pastoral
Charge: But our English Bishops had many (if not many
hundred) such Churches for their charge : therefore our English
Bishops were not of the same sort with those in Scripture. The
Major I have proved in the former Disputation.   The Minor needs no proof, as being known to all that know *England*.

Sect. 18. And 2. The fixed Bishops in the Scripture times had
no Presbyters, at least, of other particular Churches under
them, (They Governed not any Presbyters that had other
associated Congregations for publick Worship.)   But the English Bishops had the Presbyters of other Churches under them
(perhaps of hundreds :)   therefore they are not such as the
Scripture Bishops were.   There is much difference between a
Governour of People, and a Governour of Pastors; *Episcopus
gregis, & Episcopus Episcoporum*, is not all one. None of us saith,
Cyprian in Concil. Carthagin. calleth himself, or takes himself
to be *Episcopum Episcoporum*.   No fixed Bishops in Scripture
times were the Pastors of Pastors, at least, of other Churches.

Sect.

Sect. 19. This I suppose I may take as granted *de facto* from the Reverend Divine whom I have cited in the foregoing Disputation, that saith (*Annotat. in Act.* 11.) that [*Although this Title of* Πρεσβύτεροι *Elders, have been also extended to a second order in the Church; and now is only in use for them, under the name of Presbyters; yet in the Scripture-times it belonged principally, if not alone to Bishops; there being no Evidence that any of that second Order were then instituted; though soon after, before the writing of Ignatius Epistles, there were such instituted in all Churches*] So that he granteth that *de facto* there were then *no Presbyters but Bishops,* and that they were *not instituted:* and therefore Bishops had no such Presbyters to Govern; nor any Churches but a single Congregation: For one Bishop could guide but one Congation at once in publick worship; and there could be no Worshipping Congregations (in the sence that now we speak of) without some Presbyter to guide them in performance of the worship.

Sect. 20. So saith the same Learned man, *Dissertat. 4. de Episcop.* page 208, 209. [*in quibus plures absq; dubio Episcopi fuere, nulliq; adhuc quos hodie dicimus Presbyteri*] And therefore he also concludeth that the Churches were then Governed by Bishops assisted by Deacons without Presbyters, instancing in the case of the Church of *Jerusalem, Act.* 6. and alledging the words of *Clem. Roman.* Κατα χώρας η πόλεις Κηρύσσοντες καθίσανον τας απαρχας αυτων, εις επισκοπους η διακόνες, &c.. (How *Grotius* was confident that *Clemens* was against their Episcopacy, I shewed before) To the same purpose he citeth the words of *Clemens Alexandrinus in Euseb.* of *John* the Apostle; concluding [*Ex his ratio constat quare sine Presbyterorum mentione interveniente, Episcopis Diaconi immediate adjiciantur, quia scilicet in singulis Macedoniæ civitatibus, quamvis Episcopus esset, nondum Presbyteri constituti sunt; Diaconis tantum* προς υπηρεσίαν *ubiq, Episcopis adjunctis*] *Dissertat.* 4 *cap.* 10. *Sect.* 19, 20, 21. So also *cap.* 11. *Sect.* 2. *& alibi passim.*

Sect. 21. Object. *But though* de facto *there were no Bishops ruling Presbyters then, nor ruling any more then a single Worshipping Church, yet it was the Intention of the Apostles that they should afterwards enlarge their Diocess, and take the care of many Churches, and that they should ordain that sort of subject Presbyters that were not instituted in Scripture-times.* Answ. Do you prove

the

the secret Intention of the Apostles to be for such a Mutation, an I then we shall be satisfied in that. But till then it is enough to us that we have the same Government that *de facto* was set up by the Apostles, and exercised in Scripture times. And that its granted us that the office was not then instituted which we deny: For it is the office of such subject Presbyters having no Power of Ordination that we deny.

Sect. 22. Object. *But though in Scripture times there were no Bishops over many Churches and Presbyters, yet there were Archbishops that were over many.* Answ. Because this objection contains their strength, I shall answer it the more fully. And 1. If there were no subject Presbyters in those times, then Archbishops could rule none. But there were none such, as is granted: therefore, &c. And what proof is there of Archbishops then?

Sect. 23. Their first proof is from the Apostles: But they will never prove that they were fixed Bishops or Archbishops. I have proved the contrary before. But such an itinerant Episcopacy as the Apostles had (laying by their extraordinaries) for my part I think should be continued to the world and to the Church (of which after.)

Another of their proofs is from *Timothy* and *Titus*, who, thy say, were Archbishops. But there is full evidence that *Timothy* and *Titus* were not fixed Bishops or Archbishops, but Itinerant Evangelists, that did as the Apostles did, even plant and settle Churches, and then go further, and do the like. See and consider but the proofs of this *in Prins* unbishoping of *Timothy* and *Titus*. Such Planters and Itinerants were *pro tempore* the Bishops of every Church where they came, (yet so as another might the next week be Bishop of the same Church, and another the next week after him, yea three or four or more at once, as they should come into the place) And therefore many Churches as well as *Ephesus* and *Creet* its like might have begun their Catalogue with *Timothy* and *Titus*: and many a one besides *Rome* might have begun their Catalogue with *Peter* and *Paul*.

Sect. 24. Another of their proofs is of the Angels of the seven Churches which they say were Archbishops. But how do they prove it? Because those Churches or some of them were plant-

B b   ed

ed in chief Cities, and therefore the Bishops were Metropolitans. But how prove they the consequence? By their strong imagination and affirmation. The Orders of the Empire had not then such connection and proportion, and correspondency with the Orders of the Church. Let them give us any Valid proof that the Bishop of a Metropolis had then (in Scripture times) the Bishops of other Cities under him, as the Governor of them, and we shall thank them for such unexpected light. But presumption must not go for proofs. They were much later times that afforded occasion for such contentions as that of *Basil* and *Anthymius*, (Whether the bounds of their Episcopal Jurisdiction should change as the Emperours changed the State of the Provinces?) Let them prove that these *Asian* Angels had the Bishops of other Churches, and the Churches themselves under their jurisdiction, and then they have done something.

Sect. 25 . But if there were any preheminence of Metropolitans neer these times, it cannot be proved to be any more then an honorary Primacy : to be *Episcopus prima sedis*, but not a Governour of the rest. How else could *Cyprian* truly say (even so long after) as is before alledged, that none of them was a Bishop of Bishops, nor imposed on others, but all were left free to their own consciences, as being accountable only to God?

Sect. 26. Yea the Reverend Author above mentioned shews (*Dissertat. de Episcop.* 4. *cap.* 10. *Sect.* 9, 10, *& alibi*) that there were in those times more Bishops then one in a City, though not in *una Ecclesia aut Cœn.* And the like hath *Grotius* oft. So that a City had oft then more Churches then one, and those Churches had their several Bishops : and neither of these Bishops was the Governour of the *other*, or his Congregation: much less of the remoter Churches and Bishops of other Cities. And this they think to have been the case of *Peter* and *Paul* at *Rome*, yea and of their immediate successors there. And so in other places (*Lege Dissert.* 5. *c*, 1.)

Sect. 27. When the great *Gregory Thaumaturgus* was made Bishop of *Neocæsarea*, he had but *seventeen Christians* in his City; and when he had increased them by extraordinary successes, yet we find not that he had so much as a Presbyter under him. And if he had, its not likely that *Musonius*, his first and chief entertainer, would have been made but his Deacon, and be the only

man

man to accompany him and comfort him in his retirement in the persecution, and that no Presbyter should be mentioned : which shews that Bishops then were such as they were in Scripture-times (at least in most places) and had not many Churches with their Presbyters subject to them, as Diocesan Bishops have. And when *Comana*, a small place not far off him, received the faith, *Gregory* Ordained *Alexander* (the Colliar) their Bishop, over another single Congregation, and did not keep them under his own Pastoral charge and Government : *Vid. Greg. Nysen in vita Thaumat.*)

Sect. 28. But because that our Diocesan Bishops are such as the Archbishops that first assumed the Government of many Churches, and because we shall hardly drive many from their presumption, that *Timothy* and *Titus* were Archbishops (besides the Apostles,) I shall now let that supposition stand; and make it my next Argument that,

(Argument 3.) Ordination by Archbishops is not necessary to the Being of Ministers or Churches. Our English Bishops were indeed Archbishops : therefore Ordination by them is not Necessary ———] It is not the Name, but the office that is pleaded Necessary.

Arg. 3.

Sect. 29. And for the Major, I think it will not be denyed. All that I have to do with, Protestants and Papists, do grant the Validity of Ordination by Bishops. And for the Minor, it is easily proved. The Bishops that are the Governours of many Churches and their Bishops, are Archbishops. The Bishops of *England* were the Governours of many Churches with their Bishops : therefore they were Archbishops. The Major will be granted. And for the Minor I prove it by parts : 1. That they were (by undertaking) the Governours of many Churches. 2. And of many Bishops.

Sect. 30. He that is the Governour over many *Congregations of Christians associated for the publick Worship of God and holy communion and Edification, under their Proper Pastors*, is the Governour of many Churches. But such were our English Bishops : therefore, &c. That such Societies as are here defined are true Churches, is a truth so clear, that no enemy of the Churches is is able to gainsay with any shew of Scripture or reason, they being such Churches as are described in the Scriptures. And 2. That our Ministers were true Pastors, if any will deny, (as the Papists

and

and Separatifts do) I fhall have occafion to fay more to them anon.

Sect. 31. Argument 4. If Ordination by fuch as the Englifh Bifhops be of Neceffity to the Miniftry and Churches, then were there no true Miniftry and Churches in the Scripture times, nor in many years after: But the confequent is falfe; therefore fo is the Antecedent. The reafon of the Confequence is becaufe there were no fuch Bifhops in thofe times; and this is already proved, they being neither the Itinerant Apoftolical fort of Bifhops, nor the fixed Paftors of particular Churches; befides which there were no other.

Sect. 32. Argument 5. If Ordination by fuch as the Englifh Prelates be Neceffary to the Being of the Miniftry and Churches, then none of the Proteftants that have not fuch Prelates (which is almoft all) are true Churches or have true Minifters: But the Confequent is falfe: therefore fo is the Antecedent. Of this I fhall fay more anon.

Sect. 33. If none of the Proteftants Churches that have not fuch Bifhops are true Churches, and have not a true Miniftry, then neither *Roman*, *Greek*, *Armenian*, *Æthiopian*, &c. or almoft any through the world are true Churches: For they are defective in fome greater matters, and chargeable with greater errors then thefe. But the Confequent is falfe; therefore fo is the Antecedent. He that denyeth all thefe to be true Churches, denyeth the Catholick Church: And he that denyeth the Catholick Church, is next to the denying of Chrift.

Sect. 34. Having thus proved that there is no neceffity of Ordination by fuch as the Englifh Prelates, I have withall proved that men are not therefore ever the lefs Minifters, becaufe they have not *their* Ordination, nor our Churches or Ordinances ever the more to be difowned.

Sect. 35. Yet where there is no other Ordination to be had, it may be a duty to fubmit to theirs: Not as they are *Epifcopi exortes* (as even *Grotius* calls them) or of this *fpecies*, but as they are Paftors of the Church, notwithftanding fuch fuperfluities and ufurpations.

Sect. 36. It is not the duty therefore, but the fin, of any man that was Ordained by fuch Prelates to a lawful office, to difclaim and renounce that Ordination (as fome do.) For it is not every irregularity,

irregularity that nullifieth it : There may be many modal circumstantials , or accidental miscarriages that may not Null the
the substance of the Ordination it self.

Sect. 37. Yet it must be concluded, that we may not be wilfully
guilty of any sin in the modes or accidents : But that may be a sin
in the Ordainer, which the Ordained may not be guilty of, as doing nothing that signifieth an approbation of it, but perhaps disowning it.

Sect. 38. If we have been guilty of submitting to a corrupt ordination, as to the accidents, we must disown and repent of the
sinfull mode and accidents , though not of the Ordination
it self in substance. As we must bewail the errours and infirmities
of our preaching, prayer, and other holy duties , without renouncing the duty it self, which is of God, and to be owned.

Sect. 39. As to the Question of some, *Whether a man may be
twice Ordained, in case he suspect his first Ordination* : I answer,
1. You must distinguish between a General Ordination to the
office of the Ministry , and a special Ordination to a particular
Church. (As the licensing of a Physitian ; and the setling him
over a City or Hospital) The first may be done but once, in case
it be truely done : but the second may be done as oft as we remove to particular Churches : Though yet both may be done at
once, at our first Ordination ; they are still two things ; Even as
Baptizing a man into Member-ship of the universal Church, and
taking him into a particular Church. Its not like that the separation and Imposition of hands on *Paul* and *Barnabas*, *Act.* 13.
2,3. was to their first Apostleship.

Sect. 40. If a man have weighty reasons to doubt of his first
Ordination, his safest way is to renew it, as is usuall in Baptim,
with a [*Si non Baptizatus es Baptizo te*] If thou be not Ordained, I Ordain thee. This can have no danger in such a case.

CHAP.

CHAP. VI.

Ordination at this time, by English Prelates especially, is unnecessary.

Sect. 1.  Esides what is said against the Necessity of such Prelatical Ordination in it self, I conceive that more may be said against it as things now stand from several accidental reasons, which make it not only unnecessary but sinful, to the most.

Sect. 2. As 1. The Obligation that was upon us from the Law of the Land, is taken off (which with the Prelates themselves is no small argument when it was for them) So that we are no further now obliged, then they can prove us so from Scripture Evidence ; and how little that is, I have shewed before. The English Prelacy is taken down by the Law of the Land : we are left at Liberty from humane Obligations at least.

Sect. 3. If any man say, that *it is an unlawful power that hath made those Laws by which Prelatical Government is taken down.* I answer, 1. It is such a Power as they obey themselves, and therefore they may permit others to obey it. They hold their estates and lives under it, and are protected and ruled by it; and profess submission and obedience, for the generality of them. And when another *Species* of Government was up, that commanded men to take an engagement, to be true to the Government as established without a King and House of Lords, when our Consciences refused that Engagement as unlawful, the generality

of

of the contrary minded took it (even all that I was acquainted with, that were put upon it) So that I may take it for granted that they judge the power which they obey themselves, to be obeyed by others.

Sect. 4. And 2. I would be glad to hear from them any regardable proof that those that Governed when *Paul* wrote the 13th Chapter to the *Romans* had any better Title to their Government; Let them review their own late writings on that subject, and they may have arguments enough that are Valid *ad hominem* at least.

Sect. 5. The Laws of the Land do make the Acts even of an Usurper Valid while he is in possession, and make it treason to them that do against him that which is treason if it were against a lawfull Prince: and therefore if we granted them what they here affirm, it would be no advantage to their cause. Subjects must look at the present Governours with peaceable subjection: For if they be left to try their Princes titles, and suspend obedience upon their single opinions, you know what will follow.

Sect. 6. And 3. It will be hard to prove that many a Prince that hath ruled in *England*, had a better Title: Its known that many of their Titles were naught; And yet their Lawes are Valid still, or were so to Posterity. And how can they convey a better title to their Heirs then they had themselves? If you say that the Consent of the People gave them a better, I must return that if that will serve, the people in Parliaments (more then one) and in their real subjection, have consented to this. But this is a subject that requireth much more to be said of it, or nothing at all: and therefore I shall take up here, with this little which the present cause makes necessary.

Sect. 7. And I may add a further Reason; that we are not only disobliged by the Laws from former Prelacy, but we are obliged against it. The Rulers have deposed and forbidden it, And in lawful things it is a duty to obey our Governours. And that the demolishing of the Prelacy, is a lawful thing (in it self considered : For I meddle not with the manner at this time.) I have said enough before to prove. It hath been usual for Princes to depose bad Priests, and heretical or contentious Bishops, and to correct disorders, and restrain usurpations of Prelates among themselves. And if any such thing be now done

by

by our prefent Governours, I know not any thing of that neceffity in the Englifh *Species* of Prelacy, as will warrant us to
d fobey them.

Sect. 8. And it is a thing that is inconfiftent with the Peace
and Unity of thefe Churches : Which is another reafon.
For 1. We have feen the ill effects of it (which I am not willing
to open to the worft) 2. And the multitude of the moft confcientious people are againft it. 3. And the generality of the moft
confcionable faithful Minifters are againft it ; So that it could not
be reftored, without the apparent ruine of thefe Churches.
4. And a Learned Reverend Affembly of Divines, chofen out of
the feveral Counties by a Parliament, were againft it. 5. And
many Parliaments have been againft it. 5. And the generality
of their adherents in the two Nations, that then lived in their
Power , have taken a Solemn Covenant againft it. Not
againft all Epifcopacy, but againft the Englifh fort of Prelacie. So that it cannot be reftored, without incomparably
much more hurt , then the continuance of it would have done
good, and without fetting all thefe Churches on a flame : So
far is it now from being a likely means of Unity or Peace among
us.

Sect. 9. And if yet they plead the obligation of the ancient
Laws (which is moft infifted on by many) I muft by
way of juft excufe , remember them of one thing, which its
like they do not forget : that if thofe Laws are ftill in force to
oblige us to feek Ordination from the Prelates, and to Authorize the Prelates to Ordain, notwithftanding the Laws of
later Powers that have repealed them, then it muft needs follow that thofe later Powers are taken for no Powers: and confequently that the fame Laws do oblige the Prelates to put the
Oath of Allegiance and Supremacy, as to fome other Power, upon the Ordained before they lay hands upon them, and oblige
the Ordained to take thofe Oaths, as well as to be fo Ordained. For if they be yet of force in one, they are of
force in both. And fo no man can be Ordained by you
without being guilty of that which the prefent Lawes make
Treafon, and forfeiting his life : which I know nothing in the
caufe that requireth him to do.

Sect. 10. And I think I may conclude that it is your own
judge-

judgement, that men fhould rather forbear your Ordination, then hazard their lives, or violate the prefent Laws, becaufe when a Declaration or Order came forth not long ago, prohibiting men of your perfwafion that had been fequeftred to Preach or Adminifter Sacraments, the generality of you prefently obeyed it, and fome wrote for the forbearance that they practifed. And if an Ordained man fhould obey the prefent power, by forbearing to preach and adminifter Sacraments, or may forbear thefe to efcape a temporal danger; much more may men do fo about your fort of Ordination.

Sect. 11. Moreover 4. We fhall be guilty of a fixed Schifm among the Reformed Church s, and of making the healing of our breaches impoffible, if by our compliance we own your dividing Principle, that [No other are true Minifters or Churches but fuch as have your Manner of Ordination] For by this Rule all the Minifters in thefe and other Proteftant Nations muft be degraded, or taken for no Minifters, and all the Churches for no true Churches (though perhaps they may be confeffed Chriftian Communities,) Nor the Ordinances and adminiftrations true. And do you think thefe are likely terms for Peace ? Will they ever be yielded to by fo many Churches ? Or is it a defirable thing ? Should *Rome* be fo much gratified ? And our Churches ruined ? and the fouls of millions caft away, and facrificed to your opinions, or Peace ? While your Prelacy pretended to no more, but to be the *beft fort* of Government, and your Church to be the *beft* of Churches, we could fubmit to you in all things that were not flatly finful : But when you will be the *only* Churches, and unchurch all others, even the moft flourifhing Churches for knowledge and holinefs, and when you muft be the only Minifters, and others muft be none, unlefs they will be Ordained by you; this is enough to put a fober man to a ftand, whether he fhall not be guilty of notorious fchifm, by complying with fo fchifmatical a principle, if he fubject himfelf voluntarily to a Prelacy that hath fuch principles and pretences, and to an Ordination that is adminiftred on thefe grounds and terms. This was not the ground, nor thefe the principles of the former Englifh Prelates : and therefore we were more capable of fubjection to

C c

them

them or Communion with them. We could have lived in their Communion and in the Communion of the rest of the Protestant Churches that have no Prelacy. But if by innovation, you have made such a change, as that we must separate from all the Reformed Churches and Ministers that have not your kind of Ordination, if we will be your subjects or be Ordained by you according to your grounds, its time for us to look about us, that we escape that separation and schism, that you would lead us into and engage us in by your way of Ordination.

Sect. 12. Among your selves there are many that affirm that if the Pope would have been content with his old Patriarchal Power, and *principium unitatis*, or primacy of Order, and wave his last four hundred years determinations, or at least not obtrude them on other Churches (as Bishop *Bromhall* speaks) they could have held communion with him, that now cannot; If *Rome* would have been content to be a Member of the Catholick Church, though pretendedly the noblest, they could have owned it: But when it will be The Catholick Church, and separate it self from all the rest, unchurching all that are not subject to them, and united in their Government, they then drive us further from Communion with them. Imitate them not in any degree in this Notorious schism and separation. Be contented to be Ministers and Churches; and tell not Christ, he hath none but you, and such as you; and tell not Satan, that the Kingdom of Christ is thus cut short, to the honour or rejoycing of his adversary.

Sect. 13. It was not so ridiculous as sad to me, to read in Mr. *T. Ps. Self-revenger* against Mr. *Barlee*, pag. 37. and Ordination called a [" *Notorious Comœ Tragedie, equally* " *sad and ridiculous, which he and others lately acted in Dain-* " *try Church, intituled by the Actors, An Ordination of Mini-* " *sters, but by many of the Spectators, An Ordination of Lay-* " *Preachers to be Lay-preachers still, and (without repentance)* " *for ever uncapable of the Priesthood, by being Ordained by such* " *Priests as were uncapable of Ordaining.*] Thus Mr. *P.*

Sect. 14. And it seems he was of the same judgement, (whoever he was) that would have abused Bishop *Usher*, by giving out that he told him, that [*as for* Holland, *he question-*

ed

ed if there was a Church among them, or not, or words fully to that Purpose] Againſt which abuſe of the Dr. the Biſhop was fain to vindicate himſelf. See *page* 124, 125. Of his Poſthumous Judgement.

Sect. 15. Moreover, 5. We know not of almoſt any Biſhops in *England*, by whom men may be Ordained. Four or five Reverend Learned men of that degree are commonly ſaid to ſurvive among us (whom we much honour and value for their worth) But as theſe are ſo diſtant, and their reſidence to the moſt unknown, ſo the reſt (if there be any) are known to very few at all, that I can hear of: Its famed that many Biſhops there are ; but we know it not to be true, nor know not who they be: and therefore it cannot well be expected, that their Ordination ſhould be ſought. If they reveal not themſelves and their Authority, and do not ſo much as once command or claim obedience from the generality of Miniſters, how can they expect to be obeyed? If they plead the danger of perſecution, I anſwer, 1. What Perſecution do they ſuffer that *are* known (above others of their way?) 2. If that will excuſe them (when we never heard of any that ſuffered the loſs of a penny for being known to be a Biſhop, ſince the Wars were ended) then it ſeems, they take the Being of the Miniſtry and Churches to be but of ſmall moment, that are not worthy their hazzard in a manifeſtation of their power : And if this excuſe them from appearing, it muſt needs in reaſon excuſe others from knowing them, obeying them, and ſubmitting to them.

Sect. 16. And when they ſhall declare themſelves to be our Biſhops, they muſt in all reaſon expect that the proof of it as well as the naked affirmation, be deſired by us. For we muſt not take every man for a Biſhop that ſaith he is ſo. They muſt ſhew us according to the Canons that the Clergy of the Dioceſs lawfully Elected them, and Biſhops Conſecrated them ; which are tranſactions that we are ſtrangers to. If they take the ſecret Election of ſix or ſeven or very few in a Dioceſs, to be currant, becauſe the reſt are ſuppoſed to be uncapable by Schiſm ; 1. Then they ſhew themſelves ſo exceedingly unjuſt as to be unmeet for Government, if they will upon their ſecret preſump...

cut off or cenfure fo many parts of the Clergy , without ever accufing them, or calling them to fpeak for themfelves , or hearing their Defence. 2. And if upon fuch prefumptuous Cenfures you make your felves Bifhops befides the Canons, you cannot expect obedience from thofe that you thus feparate from, and cenfure unheard.

Sect. 17. Its known that the Englifh Bifhops (as *Grotius* himfelf affirmeth) were chofen by the King according to the cuftom here , the Chapter being fhadows in the bufinefs : And if the King may make Bifhops, he may make Presbyters ; and then Ordination is unneceffary. But if you fay that the Confecrators make them Bifhops , and not the Kings Election, then *Rome* had many Bifhops at once , when ever three or four Popes were confecrated at once (which marrs all fucceffion thence dirived,) and then if fome Bifhops confecrate one, and fome another, both are true Bifhops of one Diocefs, and many Paftors may be thus Ordained to one Church.

Sect. 18. And it concerneth us before we become their fubjects , to have fome credible Evidence that they are fo Orthodox, as to be capable of the place. And the rather becaufe that fome that are fufpected to be Bifhops (how truly I know not) have given caufe of fome fufpicion : Either by writing againft Original fin , or by owning *Grotius*'s Religion , (which what it was I have fhewed elfewhere ,) or by unchurching the Proteftant Churches , and Nullifying their Miniftry that have not their kind of Ordination, while they take the Roman Ordination to be Valid, and their Church and Miniftry to be true, with other fuch like.

Sect. 19. And 6. If we fhould now, when better may be had, fubject our felves to the Ordination and Government of the abolifhed Prelacy, we fhould choofe a more corrupt way of adminiftration , and prefer it to a more warrantable way: (That this way is corrupt, is proved in the former Difputation. That a way more warrantable may be had, I fhall prove anon.) Though fubmiffion to a faulty way in fome cafes of Neceffity is excufable , yet when we have our choice, the cafe is altered.

Sect. 20. And a tender Confcience hath very great reafon to fear left by fuch voluntary fubjection , they fhould incur moreover this double guilt : 1. Of all the hurt that this corrupt

fort

fort of Epifcopacy did, before the abolition. 2. And of all the hurt that it might do again if it were introduced : which is neither fmall, nor uncertain : He that hath feen the fruits that it brought forth but for a few years before the abolition, and weighs the arguments brought againft it, methinks fhould fear to be the reftorer of it.

Sect. 21. If any man (as Mr. *Thorndike* and others do) fhall write for a more regular fort of Epifcopacy, its one thing to find a *tolerable Bifhop in his Book*, and another thing to find him exiftent in *England* : For we know not of any New fort of Regulated Epifcopacy planted : and therefore muft fuppofe that it is the Old fort that is in being. Let them bring their Moderate forms into exiftence, and then its like that many may be more inclined to fubmit to their Ordination : but their moderate principles having not yet made us any Moderate Epifcopacy, I fee not how we fhould be ever the more obliged for them to fubmit to the Old : but rather are the more juftified in difowning it, when their own reformed modell is againft it.

CHAP.

CHAP. VII.

The Ordination used now in England and in other Protestant Churches, is Valid, and agreeable to Scripture and the Practice of the Ancient Church.

Sect. 1. Aving already proved that the late English Bishops Ordination is not of necessity; it is satisfactory without any more ado, to them that would nullifie our Ministry and Churches that have not their Ordination. But because we may meet with other adversaries, and because in a case of so much weight, we should walk in the clearest light that we can attain, for the satisfaction of our own Consciences, I shall further prove the Validity of our Ordination, and the truth of our Call, and Ministry, and Churches.

Whether many alwaies Ordained, or sometime one only, Calvin and after him Daniel Colonius (lib. 4. Disp. 2. ex Calvin Institut. l. 4. c. 3. Sect. 16.) thought uncertain because of 2 Tim. 1. 6, &c. Read their words.

Sect. 2. Argument 1. The Ordination is Valid which is performed by such Bishops as were instituted and existent in Scripture times. But our Ordination (used in *England* and other reformed Churches) is performed by such Bishops as were instituted and existent in Scripture times: therefore such Ordination is Valid.

The Major will not be denyed (being understood with a supposition of such requires that are not now in controversie:)

For

For those that we have to deal with do grant, that such Bishops as are mentioned, *Acts* 20. 1 *Tim.* 3. *Tit.* 1. *Phil.* 1. 1. and in other passages of Scripture, had the power of Ordination, and that it belonged not only to the Apostles and Evangelists, and (such as they call) Archbishops ; but that the fixed Bishops of particular Churches had it.

Sect. 3. The Minor I prove thus (that our Ordination is by Scripture Bishops.) The Scripture Bishops were the Pastors of Particular Churches, having no Presbyters subject to them. Most of our Ordainers are such Pastors : therefore most of our Ordainers are Scripture Bishops.

Sect 4. The Major is asserted at large by the foresaid Reverend Dr. *H.H.* *Annot. in Act.* 11.6. p. 407. Where he shews that [*Although this title of Πρεσβύτεροι Elders have been also extended to a second Order in the Church, & is now only in use for them, under the name of Presbyters, yet in the Scripture times, it belonged principally if not only to Bishops, there being no evidence that any of that second order were then instituted——*] So that the Scripture Bishops were the Pastors of single Churches having no Presbyters under them ; for there were no inferiour Presbyters (that had not the Power of Ordination) instituted in those times. This therefore may be taken as a granted truth.

Sect. 5. And that our Ordainers are such, is commonly known: 1. They are *Pastors* : (it is but few of the Prelates that denyed this :) They are * *Rectors* of the People , and have the Pastoral charge of souls. 2. They are Pastors of *Particular Churches.* 3. They have (for the most part at least) no subject or inferiour Presbyters under them : therefore they are Scripture Bishops.

* Mr. *T. P.* calls himself Rector of *Brington.*

Sect. 6. Object. *The difference lyeth in another point : The Scripture Bishops had the Power of Ordination : Your Pastors have not the Power of Ordination : therefore they are not the same.* *Answ.* That is the thing in Question. I am proving that they have the power of Ordination, thus : In Scripture times *all* single Pastors of single Churches had the Power of Ordination, there being no other instituted : But our Ordainers are the single Pastors of single Churches , (and of Christs institution :) therefore they have the Power of Ordination. If the Pastors now are denyed to be such as were instituted in Scripture times,

T. L. t

1. Let them shew who did institute them, and by what authority. 2. The sole Pastors of particular Churches were institu ed in Scripture times: But such are ours in question, therefore, &c.

Sect. 7. There is no sort of Pastors lawfull in the Church but what were instituted in Scripture times: But the sort of Pastors now in question are lawfull in the Church: therefore they were instituted in Scripture times: The Minor will be granted us of all those that were Ordained by Prelates: They would not Ordain men to an office which they thought unlawful. The Major is proved thus: No sort of Pastors are lawful in the Church but such of whom we may have sufficient evidence that they were instituted by Christ or his Apostles: But we can have sufficient evidence of none but such as were instituted in Scripture times, that they were instituted by Christ or his Apostles: therefore no other sort is lawfull. The Major is proved in that none but Christ and such as he committed it to, have power to institute new Holy Offices for Worship in the Church; But Christ hath committed this to none but Apostles (if to them,) therefore, &c. Whether Apostles themselves did make any such new Office, I will not now dispute; but if they did, 1. It was by that special Authority which no man since the planting of the Churches by them can lay claim to, or prove that they have. 2. And it was by that extraordinary guidance and inspiration of the Holy Ghost, which none can manifest to have been since that time communicated.

Sect. 8. Moreover, if there were a Power of instituting new Offices in the Church since Scripture times, it was either in a Pope, in Councils, or in single Pastors. But it was in none of these: not in a Pope; for there was no such Creature of long time after, much less with this authority: Not in a Council: For 1. None such was used: 2. None such is proved. 3. Else they should have it still. Not in every Bishop, as will be easily granted.

Sect. 9. If such a Power of instituting New Church-Offices were after Scripture times in the Church, then it is ceased since, or continueth still; Not ceased since. For 1. The Powers or officers then left continue still; therefore their authority continueth still. 2. There is no proof that any such temporary power was given to any since Scripture times. Nor doth any such continue still; Otherwise men might still make us more New Offices, and so we should not know when we have done, nor

should

should we need to look into Scripture for Chrifts will, but to the will of men.

Sect. 10. Argument 2. No men fince Scripture times had power to change the Inftitutions of Chrift and the Apoftles, by taking down the fort of Paftors by them eftablifhed; and fetting up another fort in their ftead. But if there be lawful Paftors of particular Churches that have not power of Ordination, then men had power to make fuch a change. For the fort of Paftors then inftituted were fuch as had but one Church, and were themfelves perfonally to guide that Church in actual Worfhip, and had the power of Ordination, and there was no fubject Presbyters, nor no fingle Paftors that had not the Power of Ordination: All fingle Paftors of particular Churches had that Power then: But all, or almoft all fuch fingle Paftors of particular Churches are by the Diffenters fuppofed to be without that Power now: Therefore it is by them fuppofed that Chrifts form of Church Government and fort of Officers are changed, and confequently that men had power to change them, for they fuppofe it lawfully done.

Sect. 11. Argument 3. The Paftors of City Churches may ordain (efpecially the fole or chief Paftors:) Many of our prefent Ordainers are the Paftors of City Churches (and the fole or chief Paftors in fome Places:) therefore they may Ordain. The Major is proved from the doctrine of the Diffenters, which is, that every City Church fhould have a Bifhop, and that every Bifhop is the chief (and fometimes only) Paftor of a City Church. If they fay that yet every Paftor (though the fole Paftor)of a City Church is not a Bifhop: I anfwer, that then they will infer the fame power of changing Scripture Inftitutions, which I mentioned, and difproved before. Let them prove fuch a Power if they can.

Sect. 12. The Minor is undenyable, and feen *de facto*, that many of our Ordainers are fuch Paftors of City Churches, and that of two forts: fome of fuch Cities as have both the Name and Nature of Cities: And fome of fuch Cities as have truly the nature, but in our Englifh cuftom of fpeech have not the name: fuch as are all Corporations, in the feveral Market Towns of England.

Sect. 13. Argument 4. Thofe Paftors that have Presbyters

D d   under

under them, have power of Ordination : But very many English Pastors at this day have Presbyters under them : therefore
they have Power of Ordination : By Presbyters I mean not men
of another office, but gradually inferiour in the same office. The
Major is proved *ad hominem* from the Concessions of the Dissenters : For (though I rarely meet in their disputations for Bishops, with any Definition of a Bishop, yet) This is it that they
most commonly give us as the Essential difference of a Bishop,
that he is one that is *over Presbyters*. Yea this agreeth with their
higher sort of Bishops that they say were in the Church in *Ignatius* daies, when subject Presbyters were instituted : and therefore those Pastors may ordain that are of that higher sort of
Bishops.

Sect. 14. The Minor is notorious : Many of our Pastors in
Market Towns and other large Parishes have a curate with them,
in the same Congregation, and one or two or more Curates at
several Chappels of ease, that are in the Parish. And these are
under them 1. *De facto*, being chosen and brought in by them,
Ruled by them, and paid by them and removed by them. 2. *De
jure*, the Bishops and Laws of the Land allowed this.

Sect. 15. Argument 5. The stated or fixed President of a Presbyterie may Ordain (with his fellow Presbyters) But many of
our Parish Pastors are the fixed Presidents of Presbyteries : therefore they may ordain, The Major I take for granted by all that
stand to the Ordinary descriptions of a Bishop : For the stated
President of a Presbyterie, is not only a Bishop, in the judgement
of *Forbes*, Bishop *Hall*, Bishop *Usher* and such other, but is indeed the Primitive Bishop in their judgement; and such a Bishop in whom they would *rest satisfied*, and do propose such
for the Churches Peace.

Sect. 16. And the Minor is notorious : For 1. In the most of
our ordered Churches there is a Presbyterie of Ruling Ecclesiastick Elders. 2. In many there are divers preaching Presbyters
(which may satisfie them that are against meer ruling Elders)
as I shewed before. And if these be not inferiour to the chief
Pastor in Ecclesiastical Degree, yet they are his Compresbyters,
and he is (in all Parishes that I know where Curates or Assistants are) their *stated President* or *Moderator*, so that we have in
all such Congregations (according to the doctrine of the Bishops
them-

themselves) not only such Bishops as were in the Apostles days when there was no subject Presbyters, but also such Bishops as were in *Ignatius* daies, when the fixed President or Bishop had many Presbyters, to whom he was the President or Moderator.

Sect. 17. Yea if you will make his Negative voice *Essential* to a Bishop (which Moderate Episcopal men deny) yet commonly this agreeth to such Parish Bishops as have Curates under them : For in the Presbyterie they have ordinarily a Negative Voice.

Sect. 18. Yea where there are no such Presbyteries with a President, it is yet enough to prove him a Bishop, that he hath *Deacons* under him, or but one Deacon : saith Dr. *H. H. Annotat. in Act. 11: b.* [*When the Gospel was first preached by the Apostles, and but few converted, they ordained in every City and Region, no more but a Bishop, and one or more Deacons to attend him, there being at the present so small store out of which to take more, and so small need of Ordaining more* ——]

Sect. 19. Argument 6. The Moderator or President of many Pastors of particular Churches assembled, may Ordain, and his Ordination is Valid. But such a Moderator or President is ordinarily or frequently One in our Ordinations : therefore they are Valid. The Major is granted by many of the Dissenters, and all their principles, I think, do infer it : For such a one is a Bishop, not only of the Apostolical institution : Nor only such as was in *Ignatius* days, but such an Archbishop as next afterward sprung up. When it is not only one Church and its Presbyters that are under him, but the Presbyters (or Bishops) of many Churches that he is Moderator or President of, methinks those that are for the highest Prelacy, should not deny the Validity of his Ordination.

Sect. 20. But two things will be here objected : The one is, that *he was not consecrated to this Presidency or Moderatorship, by Bishops.* To which I answer, 1. That Consecration is not of Necessity to such a Bishop according to the principles of Episcopal Divines; it being no new Office or Order that they are exalted to, but a new Degree; Ordination (which was received when they were made Presbyters) may suffice, and is not to be iterated. 2. The Election of the Presbyters served (as *Hierom* testifyeth) in the Church of *Alexandria* : therefore it may

serve

serve now: (of which more anon.) 3. He is chosen by true Bishops, as is shewed.

Sect. 21. The other Objection is, that *our Presidents are but pro tempore, and therefore are not Bishops.* To which I answer, 1. That in some Places they are for a long time, and in some for an uncertain time. Dr. *Twiss* was Moderator of the Synod at *Westminster,* for many years together, even *durante vita* ; and Mr. *Herle* after him was long Moderator: The *London* Province hath a President for many moneths ; even from one Assembly to another. 2. I never yet met with an Episcopal Divine, that maintained that it was essential to a Bishop, to be such *durante vita* : I am sure it is not commonly asserted. If a man be made the Bishop of such or such a Diocess, for one and twenty years, or for seven years, it will be said to be irregular ; but I know none of them that have averred it to be so great an Error as nullifieth his Power and administrations. And if it may stand with the Being of Episcopacy to be limited to seven years, then also to be limited to seven moneths, or seven weeks, or days : Especially when (as usually with us) they fix no time at the first Election, but leave it to the liberty of the next Assembly to continue or to end his power. Let them prove that affirm it, that duration for life is essentiall to a Bishop.

Sect. 22. Argument. 7. Where all these forementioned qualifications of the Ordainer do concur, (*viz.* 1. That he be the Pastor of a particular Church, and the chief Pastor of it, and the Pastor of a City Church, and have Deacons and Presbyters under him, and be the fixed President of a Presbyterie, and the Moderator or President of a larger Presbyterie of the Pastors of many Churches,) there (according to the principles, even of the rigider sort of Dissenters) the Ordination is valid : But all these forementioned qualifications do frequently concur to some of our present Ordainers in *England :* therefore even according to the more rigid Dissenters, their Ordination is Valid : The premises are so plain that they need no confirmation.

Sect. 23. Argument 8. Ordination by a Presbyterie is Valid. But in *England* and other Reformed Churches we have Ordination by a Presbyterie : therefore our Ordination is Valid. The Major is proved from 1 *Tim.* 4. 14. [*Neglect not the gift that is in thee which was given thee by Prophecy, with the laying on of the hands of the Presbyterie.*

Presbyterie. Also from *Act.* 13.1,2,3. They were the Prophets and Teachers of the Church of *Antioch* that imposed hands on *Barnabas* and *Saul*, (whether it were for their first Ordination to the Office, or only for a particular Mission , I now dispute not.) The Church of *Antioch* had not many Prelates, if any: but they had many Prophets and Teachers, and these and none but these are mentioned as the Ordainers. As for them that say these were the Bishops of many Churches of *Syria*, when the Text saith they all belonged to this Church of *Antioch*, they may by such presumptuous contradictions of Scripture say much, but prove little.

Sect. 24. As for them that grant us, that there were no subject Presbyters instituted in Scripture-times, and so expound the Presbyterie here to be only Apostles and Bishops of the higher order, I have shewed already, that they yield us the Cause: though I must add, that we can own no new sort of Presbyterie, not instituted by Christ or his Apostles. But for them that think that Prelates with subject Presbyters were existent in those times, they commonly expound this Text of Ordination by such subject Presbyters, with others of a Superior rank or degree, together : Now, as to our use, it is sufficient, that hence we prove that a Presbyterie may ordain : and that undeniably a Presbyterie consisted of Presbyters, and so that Presbyters may ordain. This is commonly granted us, from this Text. That which is said against us by them that grant it, is, that Presbyters did Ordain, but not alone, but with the Bishops.

Sect. 25. But, 1. if this were proved, its nothing against us : for if Presbyters with Bishops have power to Ordain, then it is not a work that is without the reach of their Office , but that which belongeth to them : and therefore if they could prove it irregular for them to Ordain without a Bishop, yet would they not prove it Null. Otherwise they might prove it Null, if a Bishop Ordain without a Presbyterie, because according to this Objection they must concur. 2. But indeed, they prove not that any above Presbyters did concur in *Timothies* Ordination, whatever probability they may shew for it. And till they prove it, we must hold so much as is proved and granted.

Sect. 26. As for 2 *Tim.* 1.6. it is no certain proof of it. It may be Imposition of hands in Confirmation, or for the first giving of the Holy Ghost after Baptism (ordinarily used by the Apostles) that is there spoken of : which also seemeth probable, by the Apostles annexing it to *Timothies* Faith, in which he succeeded his Mother and Grandmother ; and to the following effects of [*the Spirit of Power, and of Love, and of a sound mind,*] which are the fruits of Confirming Grace : admonishing him, that he *be not ashamed of the Testimony of our Lord* ; which is also the fruit of Confirmation. However the probability go, they can give us no certainty, that *Paul* or any Apostle had an hand in the Ordination here spoken of : when the Text faith that it was [*with the laying on of the hands of the Presbyterie*] we must judge of the office by the name : and therefore 1. we are sure that there were Presbyters. 2. And if there were also any of an higher rank, the Phrase encourageth us to believe, that it was *as Presbyters,* that they imposed hands in Ordination.

Sect. 27. Argument 9. If Bishops and Presbyters (as commonly distinguished) do differ only *Gradu, non Ordine,* in Degree and not in Order, (that is , as being not of a distinct office, but of a more honourable Degree in the same office) then is the Ordination of Presbyters valid, though without a Bishop (of that higher Degree) But the Antecedent is true : therefore so is the Consequent. The Antecedent is maintained by abundance of the Papists themselves ; much more by Protestants. The reason of the Consequence is, because *ad ordinem pertinet ordinare.* Being of the same office, they may do the same work. This Argument Bishop *Usher* gave me to prove that the Ordination of meer Presbyters without a Prelate is valid, when I askt him his Judgement of it.

Sect. 28. Argument 10. If the Prelates and the Laws they went by did allow and require meer Presbyters to Ordain, then must they grant us that they have the Power of Ordination : But the Antecedent is true, as is well known in the Laws, and common Practice of the Prelates in Ordaining : divers Presbyters laid on hands together with the Bishop : and it was not the Bishop but his Chaplain commonly that examined and approved : usually the Bishop came forth, and laid his hands on men that he never saw before, or spoke to, but took them as he found them presented to him by his Chaplain : so that Presbyters Ordained

as

as well as he, and therefore had power to Ordain.

Sect. 29. If it be Objected that *they had no power to Ordain without a Bishop*; I answer, 1. Nor a Bishop *quoad exercitium*, without them, according to our Laws and Customs, at least usually. 2. Ordaining *with a Bishop* proveth them to be *Ordainers*; and that it is a work that belongeth to the order or office of a Presbyter: or else he might not do it at all, any more then Deacons, or Chancellors, *&c.* may. And if it be but the work of a Presbyters office, it is not a *Nullity*, if Presbyters do it without a Prelate, if you could prove it an irregularity.

Sect. 30. Argument 11. If the Ordination of the *English Prelates be valid*, then much more is the Ordination of Presbyters, (as in *England* and other Reformed Churches is in use.) But the Ordination of English Prelates is valid, (I am sure in the judgement of them that we dispute against:) therefore so is the Ordination of English Presbyters much more.

Sect. 31. The reason of the Consequence is; because the English Prelates are more unlike the Bishops that were fixed by Apostolical Institution or Ordination, then the English Presbyters are, as I have shewed at large in the former Disputation: the Scripture Bishops were the single Pastors of single Churches, personally guiding them in the worship of God, and governing them in presence, and teaching them by their own mouths, visiting their sick, administring Sacraments, *&c.* And such are the English Presbyters: But such are not the late English Prelates that were the Governors of an hundred Churches, and did not personally teach them, guide them in worship, govern them in presence, and deliver them the Sacraments; but were absent from them all save one Congregation. These were unliker to the Scripture fixed Bishops, described by Dr. *H. H.* then our Presbyters are: therefore if they may derive from them a Power of Ordination, or from the Law that instituted them; then Presbyters may do so much more.

Sect. 32. Argument 12. If the Ordination of Papist Bishops be valid, much more is the Ordination of English Presbyters so: but the Antecedent is true, in the judgement of those against whom we dispute: therefore the Consequent must be granted by them on that supposition.

Sect. 33. The reason of the Consequence is, because the Popish

Bishops

Bishops are more unlike to the Scripture Bishops, and more uncapable of ordaining, then the Presbyters of the Reformed Churches are. For 1. The Papist Prelates profess to receive their Power from a Vice-christ, at least *quoad exercitium, & media conferendi*, which Protestant Presbyters do not. 2. The Papist Bishops profess themselves Pastors of a new Catholick Church, which is headed by the Papacy as an essential part; and which Christ will not own (as such:) But so do not the Protestant Presbyters. 3. The Papist Prelates Ordain men to the false Office of turning Bread into the Body of Christ by the way of Transubstantiation, in their Consecration, and offering it as a Sacrifice for the quick and dead, and delivering this as the very Body of Christ, and not Bread to the Communicants, and perswading them that it is such, and holding and carrying it to be Worshipped by them with Divine Worship, and the like : But the Protestant Presbyters are Ordained , and do Ordain others, to that true Office of a Presbyter or Pastor, or Bishop which Christ hath instituted. 4. The Papist Prelates have abundance of false doctrines, and practices in Worship, which the Protestant Presbyters have not. 5. And they have no more to shew for a Power of Ordination, then our Presbyters have : so that these, with many the like considerations , will prove, that if the Papists Ordination be Valid, that of the Protestant Churches by Presbyters is so much more. And doubtless, they that plead for a succession from the Papist Prelates, do hold their Ordination Valid.

Sect. 34. Argument 13. If the Protestant Churches that have no Prelates be true Churches (in a Political sense,) and the Ordinances among them valid, and to be owned and received, then are the Pastors of those Churches true Pastors, though they have no Ordination but by Presbyters. But the Antecedent is true : therefore so is the Consequent. The reason of the Consequence is clear, and granted by them that we have now to do with : Because the Pastors are essential to the Church as Political, and the said Ordinances of Publike worship, (as the Lords Supper,) and Government, cannot be allowable without them, nor such as the people should submit to or receive. This therefore we may take as granted.

Sect. 35. And for the Minor, that the Protestant Churches are

are true Churches that have no Prelates. 1. There are so few of them that have Prelates, that he that will unchurch all the rest, I suppose (when he playes his game above board) would take it for an injury, to be accounted a Protestant himself. 2. If the Churches of the West called Papists, and the Churches of *Africa, Asia,* and *America,* be true Churches of Christ, and have true administrations, then (much more confidently may we affirm that) the Protestants are so too. But the Antecedent is maintained by those that we now dispute against, (excepting the Papists, who yet maintain it as of their own Church) therefore, &c.

Sect. 36. The reason of the Consequence is, because the Papists, *Greeks, Armenians, Georgians, Syrians, Ægyptians, Abasines, &c.* have much more to be said against them then we have : And if the lesser (or supposed) imperfection of the Protestant Churches do unchurch them, (for wanting Prelates,) then the many great, and real defects of the other Churches will unchurch them much more. Especially this holds as to the Church of *Rome,* which yet is taken by the Dissenters to be a true Church, and by some of them, at least, denyed to be the seat of Antichrist. Their Vicechrist and usurping head, and all the Ministry that hold by him, afford us other kind of Arguments against their Church, then want of Prelates can afford them or others against our Churches.

Sect. 37. And if any will deny the Antecedent so far as to unchurch all the Churches in the world, that are more defective then the Protestants, he will blot out of his Creed the Article of the Catholick Church, and being a Seeker or next one to day, is like to be an Infidel ere long, as I shall further shew, when I speak of the sinfulness of such.

Sect. 38. Argument 14. If the Administrations of a Usurping Presbyter to an innocent people are Valid (and not Nullities,) then the Ordination of an Usurping Ordainer to an Innocent expectant, is Valid ; (and consequently the Ordination of Presbyters is Valid, if they were Usurpers, as they are unjustly said to be.) But the administrations of usurping Presbyters to an Innocent people are Valid : therefore, &c.

Sect. 39. The Antecedent is granted by *Bellarmine* himself (in the place before cited) who saith that no more is required to oblige the people to obey him, and submit, then that he be re-

Ee　　　　　　　　puted

puted a Paſtor : And all muſt ſay ſo, 1. That will not rob the
Innocent of the Benefit of Gods Ordinances, becauſe of an uſurpers fault. 2. And that will not leave the people, almoſt commonly, in an utter uncertainty, whom they ſhould take for a Paſtor and obey; and when the Ordinances are Valid for their good.

Sect. 40. The Conſequence is made good by the Parity of
Reaſon that is in the two caſes. If uſurpation cauſe not a Nullity, invalidity or unprofitableneſs in one caſe, to the innocent
receiver, no nor make it his ſin to receive, no more will it in the
other : For there is no Reaſon for any ſuch difference. Nay if
it be a duty to ſubmit to an unknown uſurper, in ſeveral caſes,
in receiving the Sacraments, hearing, praying, &c. ſo is it a
duty in ſuch caſes to receive Ordination.

Sect. 41. Object. *But the uſurping Presbyter doth nothing
but what belongeth to the office of a Presbyter : but the uſurping
Ordainer doth that which belongs not to the office of a Presbyter:
and therefore his action is a Nullity, as being* extra proprium
forum.

Sect. 42. *Anſw.* 1. It is proved before to belong to the office of a Presbyter to Ordain : 2. But ſuppoſe it were not; yet
the objection is vain : becauſe it is the office of *a Biſhop* that the
Ordaining Presbyter doth pretend to, and which you imagine that
he doth uſurp. *They ſay that ſubject Presbyters (quoad ordinem vel Officium)* are no creatures of Gods appointment ; and
therefore they renounce that Office ; and claim that office which
you call Epiſcopacy, and hath the Power of Ordination. The
quarrel between us is not about meer Biſhops (ſuch as Dr. *H. H.*
deſcribeth as aforeſaid) Theſe are not denyed: but the Pariſh Miniſters profeſs themſelves ſuch Biſhops: But it is about the other
ſort of Presbyters, ſubject to Biſhops, that the quarrel is : For
they ſay, that the Church ſhould have none ſuch, and Dr. *H. H.*
ſaith *there is no Evidence that any ſuch were inſtituted in Scripture times.* Now as a pretended Presbyters adminiſtrations
are Valid to the innocent receiver of the Sacrament, ſo a pretended Biſhops adminiſtration in Ordination is as Valid to the
innocent, *cæteris paribus.*

Sect. 43. Argument 15. They that have the *Keyes of the Kingdom of Heaven,* have the power of Ordination : But Parochiall Paſtors called Presbyters have the Keyes of the Kingdom of
Heaven:

Heaven: therefore they have the power of Ordination.

Sect. 44. The Minor is granted commonly by Papists and Protestants, as to *some* of the Keyes, but it is by many denyed as to other. They say that every Pastor hath the Key of doctrine and of Order, but not the Key of Jurisdiction. But 1. Christ gave the Keyes of the Kingdom of Heaven together and never divided them. Therefore they are not to be divided. He did not give one Key to one, and another to another, but all to the same men: And what God hath joyned together, let no man put asunder. 2. The Apostles in delivering these Keyes to others, are never found to have separated them. For Subject Presbyters *were not instituted in Scripture-times*: Therefore *all* that were then Ordained Presbyters had *all the Keyes* together, and so that of *Jurisdiction* (as it is called) with the rest. 3. That Presbyters had the Key of Order, will prove that they may Ordain, as is aforesaid. 4. But that English Presbyters had the Key of *Jurisdiction* is proved, 1. In that they were with the Bishops to Ordain by Imposition of hands. 2. In that they were by the Book of Ordination charged to administer *Discipline*: though this was disused, and the Prelates frustrated their power.

Sect. 45. I shall recite the words of Reverend *Usher* for the proof of this, Reduction of Episcopacy, &c. [*By Order of the Church of* England *all Presbyters are charged (in the Book of Ordination) to administer the Doctrine of Sacraments and the Discipline of Christ, as the Lord hath commanded, and, as this Realm hath received the same; and that they might the better understand what the Lord hath commanded therein, the exhortation of St. Paul to the Elders of the Church of* Ephesus *is appointed to to be read unto them at the time of their Ordination*, Take heed unto your selves and to all the flock, among whom the Holy Ghost hath made you Overseers, to Rule the Congregation of God which he hath purchased with his blood. *Of the many Elders who thus in common ruled the* **Church of** Ephesus, *there was one President, whom our Saviour in his*

sed & cum plebe ipsa universa: How big was the Diocess then, and how much the Bishop ruled alone, may be hence conjectured; and whether Presbyters had any hand in ruling.

Why doth *Ignatius* and *Tertullian* command them to be subject to the Presbyters as to the Apostles of Christ, if they had not the Key of Government?

Cyprian Ep: 28. p.64. *ad Clerum & Gaio.* —— *Desiderastis ut de Philumeno & Fortunato hypodiaconis, & Favorino acolutho scribam, cui rei non potui me solum judicem dare, cum multi adhuc de clero absentes sint, nec locum suum vel serio repetendum putaverint, & hec singulorum tractandi sit, & limanda plenius ratio; non tantum cum collegis meis*

r. e. 2   ep ile

Epistle unto this Church in a peculiar manner stileth the Angel of the Church of Ephesus. And Ignatius in another Epistle written about twelve years after unto the same Church, calleth the Bishop thereof. Betwixt the Bishop and the Presbyterie of that Church, what an harmonious consent there was in the ordering of the Church Government; the same Ignatius doth fully there declare, by the Presbyterie with St. Paul, understanding the Community of the rest of the Presbyters or Elders who then had a hand not only in the delivery of the Doctrine and Sacraments, but also in the Administration of the Discipline of Christ: For further proof of which we have that known Testimony of Tertullian in his General Apology for Christians: In the Church are used exhortations, chastisements and divine censure, for judgement is given with great advice as among those who are certain they are in the sight of God; and it is the chiefest foreshewing of the Judgement which is to come, if any man have so offended that he be banished from the Community of Prayer, and of the Assembly, and of all holy fellowship. The Presidents that bear rule therein are certain approved Elders, who have obtained this honour not by Reward, but by good report, who were no other (as he himself intimates) elsewhere, but those from whose hands they used to receive the Sacrament of the Eucharist.

For with the Bishop who was the chief President, (and therefore stiled by the same Tertullian in another place, summus Sacerdos for distinction sake) the rest of the dispensers of the Word and Sacraments joyned in the common Government of the Church; and therefore where in matters of Ecclesiastical judicature, Cornelius Bishop of Rome used the recieved form of gathering together the Presbyterie, of what persons that did consist, Cyprian sufficiently declareth, when he wisheth him to read his Letters to the flourishing Clergy which there did preside or rule with him. The presence of the Clergy being thought so requisite in matters of Episcopal audience, that in the fourth Council of Carthage it was concluded, That the Bishop might hear no mans cause without the presence of the Clergy; and that otherwise the Bishops sentence should be void, unless it were confirmed by the presence of the Clergy: which

which we find also to be inserted into the Canons of Egbert, who was Archbishop of York in the Saxon times, and afterwards into the body of the Canon Law it self.

True it is that in our Church this kind of Presbyterial Government hath been long disused, yet seeing it still professeth that every Pastor hath a right to rule the Church (from whence the name of Rector also was given at first unto him) and to administer the Discipline of Christ, as well as to dispence the Doctrine and Sacraments, and the restraint of the exercise of that right proceedeth only from the custom now received in this Realm ; no man can doubt but by another Law of the Land, this hinderance may be well removed)

Sect. 46. And indeed the stream of Antiquity, and the Authors that are principally rested on for Episcopacy, are full against them that deny the Government of the people to the Presbyters; And it is the principal mischief of the English Prelacy, thus to *degrade* (or *quoad exercitium* to suspend at least) all the Presbyters from their office : Not as it is a denying them any part of their honour (thats not to be much regarded ;) but as it is a discharging them of their work and burden, and consequently leaving the Churches ungoverned. And for the Government of Presbyters themselves, in *Cyprians* dayes the Bishop did not, could not, Ordain, or censure any Presbyter without his Clergy, and Councils have decreed that so it should be. Yea and the *plebs universa* also was consulted with by *Cyprian.*

Sect. 47. And now I come to the Major of my Arrgument, which I prove thus. Either Ordination is an act of the exercise of the power of the Keyes, or of some other power : But of no other power : therefore of the Keyes. If it be the exercise of any other power, it is either of a secular power, or an Ecclesiastick : but neither of these, therefore of no other. Not of another Ecclesiastick power : for there is no Ecclesiastical power, (at least which Ordination can be pretended to belong to) but the power of the Keyes ; not of a *secular* power; for that belongeth not to Ministers, nor is it here pretended.

Sect. 48. And I think it will appear that the power of Baptizing, and judging who shall be taken for Christians, and who not, and the power of administring the Eucharist and Eucharistical actions in the Church, is as great as this of Ordination,

especially

especially suppofing that a Presbyterie muft concur in this , and a fingle Pesbyter may do the other. And therefore the one being granted them, the other cannot be denyed.

Sect. 49. Argument 16. If the adminiftrations of the Priefts and Teachers in Chrifts dayes among the Jews was Valid to the people, then the Ordination of our Presbyteries, and the adminiftrations of our Presbyters fo ordained are Valid to the people and receivers now : But the Antecedent is true : therefore fo is the Confequent. This Argument is managed fo frequently and copiously by our Minifters heretofore againft the Separatifts, that I fhall need to fay but little of it.

Sect. 50. The Antecedent is proved eafily from Scripture. *Acts* 13. 27. & 15. 21. fhew that *Mofes* and the Prophets were read in the Synagogues every Sabbath day, and *Luke* 16. 29. fheu s. that it was the peoples duty to hear them , *Mat.* 23. 1, 2, 3. *Then fpake Jefus to the Multitude and to his Difciples, faying, The Scribes and the Pharifes fit in* Mofes *feat : all therefore whatfoever they bid you obferve, that obferve and do : but de not ye after their works : for they fay and do not.*] *Mat.* 8. 4. *Mark* 1. 44. *Luke* 16. 29. *But go thy way, fhew thy felf to the Prieft, and offer for thy cleanfing thofe things which* Mofes *commanded, &c.* So that it was the peoples duty to hear, and fubmit to the Teachers and the Priefts.

Sect. 51. The reafon of the Confequence is, becaufe thefe Priefts and Teachers had not fo good a Call as our Presbyters, to their Office, but were lyable to far more exceptions. The Priefts were not of the line that God had by his Law appointed to fucceed in the Priefthood : the fucceffion had long failed, as to the juft title of the Succeffors. The Priefthood was bought for money of the Civil Powers : and inftead of being the Prieft for life, he was oft changed every year : chofen by a Pagan Prince, and by him difplaced : and moft think there were two at once. The Scribes and Pharifes had abominably corrupted the Law by their traditions and falfe expofitions ; and their Calling was much more defective then ours : fo that if they muft pafs yet for Minifters of God, and their adminiftrations be valid, then fo muft Presbyters and their adminiftrations be efteemed much more. I know we need not this odious comparifon of our Miniftry with the Priefts or Pharifes, but to fhew the adverfaries

faries the odioufnefs of their accufations, and grofsnefs of their inferences.

Sect. 52. Argument 17. If Presbyters may make a Bifhop, then they may make a Presbyter. But they may make a Bifhop: therefore they may make (or ordain) a Presbyter. The Confequence of the Major is proved thus. 1. They that may confer the *higher* Degree, may confer the *lower* : the place of a Bifhop is fuppofed the higher Degree, and the place of a Presbyter the lower. 2. The Bifhops themfelves require more power in or to the Confecration of a Bifhop, then to the Ordination of a Minifter, called a Presbyter. The later may be done, according to their Canons, by one Bifhop (with affifting Presbyters,) but the former muft have three Bifhops at the leaft.

Sect. 53. To this it is commonly anfwered, that *Precife* the Ordination of a Presbyter, is a greater work then the making of a Bifhop; and therefore the Major is denyed. To which I reply. 1. I fpeak not of a *Greater* work ; becaufe the word *greater* is ambiguous, and may fignifie the greater change in regard of the *Terminus a quo*, which is not it that I intend. But the addition of an *higher* degree of power, may require more power to the effecting it, then the giving of the Lower degree, though the lower be *precife* the greater change : for the higher is the greater change as to the *terminus ad quem*; and as Epifcopacy comprehendeth or fuppofeth Presbyterie, fo the power of making a Bifhop comprehendeth or fuppofeth the power of Ordaining Presbyters. It may be *precife*, (or *cum precifione*, as the Schoolmen fpeak) it may be a greater work to make a beggar to be the chief Prince next to the King in a Kingdom : and yet *fine precifione* and in regard of the *terminus ad quem* it is a greater work to make him afterward a King ; and doubtlefs the addition of this Power requireth the Greater power to effect it.

Sect. 54. Otherwife , if the Diffenters will ftand to their anfwer, we fhall from their own grounds infallibly overthrow their caufe thus. It is a greater work to Baptize then to Ordain or Confirm : therefore he that may Baptize, may Ordain and Confirm. Juft as making a Presbyter is *cum precifione* , and in refpect to the *terminus a quo*, a greater work then Confecrating or making a Bifhop ; fo Baptizing is *cum precifione* and in refpect to the *terminus a quo*, a far greater work then Ordina⸌,

the

the one making a Christian, and the other a Minister of a Christian. See *Aquil. in Scotel. in 4. sent. d. 7. q. 2. pag.* 816. of Confirmation.

Sect. 55. It is only the Minor therefore that will hold dispute, which I prove from the well known words of *Hierom* to *Evagrius* (which Bishop *Usher* told me he alleadged to King *Charls* at the *Isle* of *Wight* to this end, when he was asked by him for an instance of Presbyters Ordaining) [*Quod autem postea unus electus est, qui cæteris præponeretur, in schismatis remedium factum est, ne unusquisque ad se trahens Christi Ecclesiam rumperet. Nam & Alexandria à Marco Evangelista usque ad Heraclam & Dionysium, Episcopos, Presbyteri semper unum ex se electum, in excelsiori gradu collocatum, Episcopum nominabant: quomodo si exercitus Imperatorem faciat: aut Diaconi eligant de se, quem industrium noverint, & Archidiaconum vocent.*] Presbyters then made the first Bishops at *Alexandria*.

Sect. 56. To this it is answered, *that it was only Election of Bishops that Hierom ascribeth to the Alexandrian Presbyters, and not Ordination of them; for that Was done by some other Bishops: and that it is Ordination that makes a man a Bishop.*

Sect. 57. To this I reply: 1. *Hierom* here undertakes to tell us, how Bishops were made at *Alexandria*; but maketh not the least mention of other Ordination or Consecration, then these words express as done by the Presbyters: And therefore till they prove it, we must take the affirmation of another Ordination to be but the groundless presumption of the Assertors. 2. *Hierom* doth purposely bring this as an argument, to prove the identity first, and the neerness afterward, of Bishops and Presbyters, that [*Presbyters made Bishops:*] which would have been no argument, if it was not Presbyters but Prelates that made them, and if the Presbyters only chose them; for, 3. The people may choose a Bishop, as well as the Presbyters, and ordinarily did it: and yet this proveth not that the people were neer the Bishop in degree; that which the people themselves may do, and frequently did, is not the only thing that *Hierom* here ascribeth to the Presbyters: but such is the Election of a Bishop: therefore, &c. 4. It is the Original or first making of Prelates at *Alexandria* that *Hierom* here speaks of; which he shews was from the Presbyters consent. This appeareth plainly in his words

words (though some can make the plainest words to signifie what they would have them) For 1. He begins with a [*Presbyteris, id est Episcopis,*] and 2. proceedeth from many scripture passages, to prove them in scripture times the same : and that not only *quoad nomen,* but *officium* ; for 3. When he had done with the Testimonies of Saint *John* in his two Epistles, he immediately addeth [*Quod autem postea unus electus est, qui cæteris præponeretur &c.*] where note, both that [*unus qui cæteris præponeretur*] is more then the bare name ; and also that [*Postea*] referreth to the date of *Johns* Epistles, and therefore he plainly averreth, that it was after *Johns* Epistles, that [*one was chosen to be before the rest.*] 5. And to the Answer I further reply, that here is all that was done, and all that was needfull to be done, ascribed to the Presbyters : For 1. They elected one. 2. They did *in excelsiori gradu electum collocare,* place him in an higher degree, and 3. *Episcopum nominabant* : they named him the Bishop (by way of excellency.) And if Election and placing him in the Degree, and giving him peculiarly the name, be not Ordination, then Ordination is but some Ceremony ; for these contain the substance. 6. And *Hierom* expresly resembleth this action of the Presbyters to an Armies making an Emperour or General ; as if he had said, As the Army makes an Emperour (*Imperatorem faciat*) so Presbyters made the Bishop : but the Army so made the Emperour, that they left it not to another power to make him (and to them only.) So that it is both [Making a Bishop] that is here ascribed to the Presbyters, and [*such a making*] as leaveth him not unmade, to the making of another. 7. And he resembleth it to the making of an Arch-deacon, supposing that the Deacons do 1. Elect. 2. Judge of the person (*quem industrium noverint.*) 3. And give him the name (*& Archi-diaconum vocent.*) 8. And he affirmeth this to be (*semper*) the constant custom of the Alexandrian Presbyters, till the dayes of *Heraclas* and *Dionysius* : intimating that then the custom changed : but what custom was then changed ? Not the Election of a Bishop by the Presbyters, (with the people) for that continued long after : and therefore it must be the *Constitution,* which afterward was done by Neighbour Bishops in *Consecration,* but till then by the *Election, Collocation, and nomination* of the Presbyters of that City-Church.

Alphonsus à Castro doth maintain that *Hierons* opinion was indeed the same that from his plain and frequent expressions we averr it to be, and rebuketh them that pretend the contrary.

Hector Boethius (before cited) saith (*Scot. Histor. l. 7. fol. 128. b.*) that *Ante Palladium Populi suffragis ex Monachis & Culdæis pontifices assumerentur.* No Bishop then ordained them but Presbyters.

And *Balæus* (*Centur. 14. 6.*) saith [*Habebant antea Scoti suos Episcopos ac Ministros ex verbi Divini Ministerio plebium suffragiis electios, prout Asianorum more fieri apud Britannos videbatur.*

Ff   9. Having

9. Having shewed thus, that Bishops and Presbyters were the same, and in the beginning called them by the same name, he affirms that [*Omnes Apostolorum successores sunt*] that is, *All these Bishops.* 10. And he plainly affirms that the *difference is made by Riches and Poverty: He is the greater that is the richer, and he is the inferiour that is the poorer.* [*Potentia divitiarum & paupertatis humilitas, vel sublimiorem, vel inferiorem Episcopum facit.*] Let any impartial Reader peruse the Epistle it self, and consider of these ten passages, and then believe if he can, either that *Hierom* did imply that other Bishops made these Alexandrian Bishops, and not the Presbyters, or that these Presbyters altered but the name, and gave not the Bishop his new degree, or that this was not a thing that was now *de novo in remedium, schismatis* contrived or performed by them. There is evidence enough against these conceits.

Sect. 58. And further, for them that think it was but the name that was now changed, I would ask them these few Questions, (supposing them to be of their mind, that tell us that Inferiour Presbyters were not instituted in Scripture times, and that it was only Prelates that are called Bishops and Presbyters in Scripture.) 1. Is it not strange, that when *after* Scripture-times, a New Office was made, it should not have a new Name also ; but should have the same name with the old superiour office ? 2. And is it not strange that both names of the superior Office, (Bishop and Presbyter) should be commonly given to the new inferior Office, at the first ? 3. And strange that the Church must afterward be put to change the names, and retrench or recall the name of a Bishop from the new sort of Presbyters, and confine it to the old, leaving (as old) the name of a Presbyter to the new inferior Office. 4. And if in Scripture-times (in the dayes when *John* wrote his Epistles and Revelation) the names of Bishop and Presbyter were both appropriated to Prelates, there being no Inferiour Presbyters then instituted ; and yet from *Mark* the Evangelist, the Alexandrian Presbyters brought back the name of a Bishop to the Prelates, retaining the name *Presbyter* themselves, *Quæro How long time was there after the Institution of Inferiour Presbyters, till the regulating of their names, from the dayes of* Mark ? About thirty four years backward. *Mark* dyed in the eighth year of *Nero*, and the

Presbyters

Presbyters made *Afianus* Bishop after his death, who continued twenty two years, even from the eighth of *Nero*, to the fourth
of *Domitian*, as *Eusebius in Histor. Eccles. l. 2. cap. 23. & lib. 3.
cap. 12. & in Chronic. & Hieronym. in Catalog. & ex illis* Usher
Annal. Vol. 2. ad an. Dom. 67. pag. 677. And *Helvicus* and others
are neer the same time. And saith *Helvicus, John* wrote the
Revelations about the fourteenth year of *Domitian*, and wrote
his Gospel about the first year of his Successor *Nerva*. So that
Mark dyed about thirty six years (or thirty four at least) before *John* wrote his Gospel ; so that here you have your choice,
whether you will believe, that subject Presbyters did regulate
the names of themselves and Bishops, and did elect (or make)
Bishops thirty six years before they were instituted themselves ;
or whether you will believe, that yet at the death of *Mark*
there were no inferior Presbyters at *Alexandria*, and so no superior Bishops, for all this that *Hierom* doth report.

Sect. 59 As for the Episcopal Divines that dissent from the
Principle of the forecited Learned Author (who saith that there
is no evidence that any of the second sort of Presbyters were
instituted in Scripture times) I need not deal with them in this
Disputation : for all of them that ever I yet met with, do grant
the validity of Presbyters Ordination, and the truth of the Reformed Churches and their Ministry, and Ordinances : otherwise
it were easie enough to vindicate all these from them also, if they
denyed them.

Sect. 60. Argument 18. *Ad hominem.* If the late English
Prelates had a lawful call to their Prelacy, then much more have
Ministers Ordained by Presbyters a lawfull call to their Ministry.
But the Prelates say that they had a lawfull Call to their Prelacy :
therefore, *&c.* The reason of the Consequence (which only will
be denyed) is, 1. Because the Presbyters are Ordained to an
Office that is of Christs Institution ; but the Prelates are Consecrated to an Office that is not of Christs Institution, but against
it, and against the light of Nature (in taking on them the impossible Government of an hundred or many hundred
Churches) as was shewed in the former Disputation. 2. Because the Prelates hold an uninterrupted Succession of Legitimate Ordination necessary to the Being of their Prelacie (I
mean, such as now we dispute against, hold this) but so do not
the

the Presbyters. The said diffenting Prelates are still upon their *Nemo dat quod non habet*; which therefore we may urge upon them. And 1: They cannot prove an uninterrupted Succession themfelves, on whom it is incumbent, according to their principles, if they will prove their Call. 2. We can prove that they are the fucceffors of fuch as claimed all their Power from the Roman Vicechrift, and profeffed to receive it from him, and hold it of him as the Catholick Head, and fo that their Ordination comes from a feat that hath had many interruptions, and fo had no power of Ordination, by their Rule: For when the fucceffion was fo oft and long interrupted, *Nemo dat quod non habet*: and therefore all that followed muft be ufurpers and no Popes: and thofe that received their Offices from them muft be no Officers: But the Presbyters that Ordain will give a better proof of their Call then this.

Sect.61. Argument 19.Where the Office is of Gods Inftitution, and the perfons are endued with Minifterial abilicities, and are Orderly and duly defigned and feparated to the Office of the facred Miniftry, there are true Minifters, and Valid adminiftrations. But all thefe are found in the Reformed Churches that have Ordination without Prelates: therefore, &c. The Major is undenyable, as containing a fufficient enumeration of all things neceffary to the Being of the Miniftry.

Sect. 62. The Minor is proved by parts. 1. That the *Office of a Presbyter* is of divine inftitution, is confeffed by moft: And I fuppofe thofe that deny it to be of Scripture infti:ution, will yet have it to be Divine: But if they deny that, yet it fufficeth us, that it is the fame officer that they call a Bifhop, and we a Presbyter; that is, the chief Paftor of a particular Church.

Sect. 63. 2. And that the perfons are *duly er competenly qualified* for the Miniftry, nothing but Ignorance, Faction and Malice, that ever I heard of, do deny. (Suppofing the humane frailties, that make us all infufficient gradually for thefe things) The Ignorant that know not what the Minifterial qualifications are, do judge as carnal intereft leadeth them. The Factious rail at all that be not of their mind. *Grotius* thought the opinions of the Calvinifts made them unfit materials for the Catholick Edifice that by his Pacification he was about to frame. So do moft other Sects, reject thofe as unworthy that fuit not with

their

their minds. And malice (whether animated by Herefie, Prophanefs or Carnal interest) will eafily find faults, and unweariedly flander and reproach: But befides fuch I meet with none that dare deny the competent abilities of thefe Minifters

Sect. 64. And 3. That the perfons are *Orderly and duly feparated to the work of the Miniftry* is thus proved. Where there is a feparation to the Miniftry by *mutual Confent* of the *perfon* and the *flock*, and by the *Magiftrates authority*, and by the *Approbation* and *Inveftiture* of the *fitteft Ecclefiaftical officers that are to be had*, there is an orderly and due feparation to the Miniftry; But all this is to be found in the Ordination ufed in *England* and other Reformed Churches, without Prelates: therefore &c. This proves not only the Validity of their Ordination, but the full Regularity.

Sect. 65. *God himfelf* (as hath been fhewed) doth by his Law appoint the *Office* of the Miniftry, impofing the duty upon the perfon that fhall be called, and giving him his power, by that Law. And then there is nothing to be done, but to *determine of the perfon* that is to receive this power and folemnly to put him in *Poffeffion* by *Inveftiture*. Now the principal part of the former work is done alfo by God himfelf: by his Qualifying the perfon with his eminent Gifts, and giving him opportunities and advantages for the Work. So that the people and Odainers have no more to do, but to find out the man that God hath thus qualified, and to elect, approve and inveft him; and ufually he is eafily found out, as a candle in the night. So that the two great acts by which God maketh Minifters, is his Inftituting Law that makes the office, and his Spiritual and Naturall Endowments given to the perfon; which the Church is but to find out, and call into ufe and exercife. And therefore we may ftill truly fay, that the Holy Ghoft maketh Paftors or Overfeers of the Church, as well as formerly he did (*Act.* 20.28.) becaufe he giveth them their Gifts, though not fuch Miraculous Gifts as fome then had; By his common Gifts of Knowledge and Utterance, and his fpecial Gifts of Grace, it is the fpirit that ftill makes Minifters, and ftill Chrift giveth Paftors to the Church.

Sect. 66. It is therefore to be noted that, *Eph.* 4.6,7,8,11. the way of Chrifts *giving officers* to his Church is faid to be by [*giving Gifts to men*] and the diverfity of *Offices* is founded in the

di-

diversity of the *Measure of Grace*, (or these Gifts) [*To every one of us is given Grace according to the measure of the gift of Christ. Therefore he saith, Ascending on high he led captivity captive, and gave Gifts to men* (ἔδωκε δόματα)—— *And he gave some Apostles, some Prophets, some Evangelists, and some Pastors and Teachers*] So that *giving Gifts*, and *giving Apostles, Prophets, &c.* are here made the same work of God : Not that the Trial and Approbation of these gifts is hereby made unnecessary, but that this is Gods principal act by which he giveth Pastors and Teachers to the Church, and by which the Officers are distinguished. For the Church is to discern and submit to those that are thus gifted ; and to *follow the Spirit*, and not either *contradict* or *lead* him. When God hath thus *gifted* men, the main work is done, for making them Ministers (if withall he give them *opportunities* and *advantages* for the work) and it is the Churches *Duty* to *Own* and *Approve* these *Gifts* of God, and to do their parts to introduce the person : And if the Ordainers refuse this, in case of *Necessity*, the gifted person is bound to improve his Gifts without them. I say [*in case of Necessity*] using the best Order that is left.

Sect. 67. This being premised, I come to the Argument (§. 64.) And the Major is undenyable, because there are all things enumerated, that are Necessary to the determination of the person qualified, that is to receive the power from Christ.

Sect. 68. And the Minor I prove by parts, 1. That our Ministry have usually the peoples consent, is a known case that needs no proof : 2. So is it that they have the Magistrates allowance, and his Authority appointing Approvers for their Introduction, and allowing Ordination and commanding Ministerial Works.

Sect. 69. And doubtless the Magistrate himself hath so much Authority in Ecclesiastical affairs, that if he command a qualified person to preach the Gospel, and command the people to receive him, I see not how either of them can be allowed to disobey him : (Though yet the party ought also to have recourse to Pastors for Ordination, and people for consent, where it may be done.) And *Grotius* commendeth the saying of *Musculus*, that would have no Minister question his Call, that being qualified, hath the Christian Magistrates Commission. And though
this

this affertion need fome limitations, yet it is apparent that Magiftrates power is great about the Offices of the Church. For Solomon put out Abiathar from the Priefthood, and put Zadeck in his place, 1 Kings 2. 27, 35. David and the Captains of the hoft feparated to Gods fervice thofe of the fons of Afaph and of Heman and of Jeduthun who fhould Prophefie with Harps, &c. 1 Chron 16. 4. And fo did Solomon, 2 Chron. 8. 14, 15. They were for the fervice of the houfe of God, according to the Kings Order, 1 Chron. 25. 1, 6. And methinks thofe men fhould acknowledge this, that were wont to ftile the King [In all caufes, and over all perfons the fupream Head and Governour]

Sect. 70 But 3. We have moreover in the Ordination of the Reformed Churches, The approbation and folemn Inveftiture of the fitteft Ecclefiaftical Officers that are to be had. And no more is requifite to an orderly Admiffion. There being nothing for man to do, but to determine of the qualified perfon, and prefent him to God to receive the power and obligation from his Law ; it is eafie to difcern, that where all thefe concur (the Peoples Election or Confent, the Magiftrates Authority, the determination of fit Ecclefiaftical Officers, and the qualification and confent of the perfon himfelf,) there needs no more to the defignation of the man. Nor hath God tyed the effence of the Church or Miniftry, to a certain formality, or to the intereft or will of Prelates : nor can any more ad ordinem be required, but that a qualified perfon do enter, by the beft and moft Orderly way that is open to him in thofe times and places where he is. And that we have the fitteft Approvers and Ordainers, I prove.

Sect. 71. If the moft of the Proteftant Churches have no other Ecclefiaftical Officers to Ordain but Presbyters, then is it the moft fit and orderly way to enter into the Miniftry in thofe Churches by their Ordination, and thofe Presbyters are the fitteft that are there to Ordain. But the Antecedent is a known truth. If any in denyal of the Confequence fay, that the Churches fhould rather be without Minifters then have Ordination by fuch, they are confuted by what is faid before.

Sect. 72. And if you fay, that they fhould have Bifhops, and it is their own fault that they have not ; I anfwer, fuppofe that were a granted truth, it can reach but to fome that have the

Rule: It is not the fault of every Congregation, or expectant of the Ministry : It is not in their power to alter Laws and forms of Government: and therefore they are bound to enter by the fittest way that is open to them.

Sect. 73. Moreover, even in *England*; the Presbyteries are fitter for Ordination then the present Bishops : (as to the Nation in general) therefore the Ordination by Presbyteries is done by the fittest Ecclesiastical officers, and is the most regular and desireable Ordination.

Sect. 74. I prove the Antecedent by comparing the Ordination of the Presbyteries and the present Prelates.   1. I have before shewed that the English Prelacy is more unlike the Primitive Episcopacy, then our Parochial Presbytery or Episcopacy is ;   and therefore hath less reason to appropriate to themselves the Power of Ordaining.   2. The Ordaining Presbyters are Many, and known persons ; and the Prelates few, and to the most (and except three or four, to almost all that I am acquainted with) unknown.   3. The Presbyters Ordain Openly where all may be satisfied of the impartiality and Order of their proceedings : But the Prelates Ordain in Private, where the same satisfaction is not given to the Church.   4. Hereupon it is easie for any vagrant to counterfeit the Prelates secret Orders, and say he was Ordained by them, when it is no such matter ; and who can disprove him ? But the publick Ordination of Presbyters is not so easily pretended by such as have it not, and the pretence is easily discovered.   5. The Prelates for ought I hear, are very few, and therefore few can have access to them for Ordination: But Presbyteries are in most countreyes. 6. The Prelates, as far as I can learn, Ordain Ministers without the peoples consent over whom they are placed, and without giving them any notice of it before hand, that they may put in their exceptions if they dissent: But the Presbyters ordinarily require the consent of the people ; or at least will hear the reasons of their dissent.   7. The Presbyteries Ordain with the Magistrates allowance, and the Prelates without and against them.   Those therefore that are Ordained by Prelates usually, stand on that foundation alone, and want the consent of People and Magistrates ; when those that are Ordained by Presbyteries have all.   8. Ordination by Prelates is now pleaded for on Schismatical grounds, and in submitting

mitting to it, with many of them, we must seem to consent to their Principles (that all other Ordination is Null, and the Churches are no true Churches that are without it.) But Presbyteries Ordain not on such dividing terms. 9. We hear not of neer so much care in the Prelates Ordinations in these or former times, as the Presbyteries; I could give some instances even of late of the great difference, which I will not offend them with expressing. 10. Most of them that we hear of, Ordain out of their own Diocesses, which is against the ancient Canons of the Church. 11. Some of them by their Doctrines and their Nullifying all the Reformed Churches and Ministry that have no Prelates, do shew us that if they had their will, they would yet make more lamentable destructive work in the Church then the hottest persecutors of their late predecessors did. For it is plain that they would have all the Ministers disowned or cast out, that are not for the Prelacy. And what a case then would this land (and others) be in ?(Of which more anon.)So that we have reason to fear that these are destroyers, and not faithful Pastors. I speak not of all, but only of the guilty : For again I say, we very much Reverence such Learned, Worthy men as Bishop *Morton*, Bishop *Brownrigg*, and some others yet surviving are. 12. The Ordination by Prelates, as things now stand, endangereth mens liberty in the exercise of the Ministry, by some things in the Manner which I shall not mention. Review the rest that I said before in *Cap.* 5. and 6. and then judge, Whether he that in these dayes is Ordained by a Learned Grave Presbytery (and perhaps where a City Pastor is Moderator or President, and many of the Ordainers are the fixed Presidents or Bishops of a Parochial Church, having a Presbytery where they preside,) I say, Whether such be not separated to the Ministry in the most orderly way that is now to be found existent ? and come not in at the door that God would have them to enter at.

Sect. 75. It is strange that those men (among the Papists) that allow of the *Cardinals* choosing a Pope, and exercising so much Government as they do over all the Christian world, and all this under the name of *Presbyters of Rome*, should yet be against Ordination by such Presbyters as are indeed Parochial Bishops, and accuse it to be a Nullity. I see not how these things cohere.

Sect.

Sect. 76. But yet many Papists are more moderate in this then those at home that we now deal with. That *Erafmus, Richardus Armachanus, Gui'el. Durantes*, and many more of them, were on our fide in this point, is commonly known, and manifested by abundance of our writers, fome of them Bishops, and fome Episcopal Divines themfelves.

Sect. 77. And divers of their Schoolmen do maintain that the [*Ordo Epifcopalis non differt à Caracthere Sacerdotali, nifi ficut forma intenfa a fe ipfa remiffa*] as *Soncinas* relateth (in 4. *Sent. d. 25.*) the fentence of *Paludanus*, which *Voetius* recites.

And the fame *Soncinas*, and *Voetius* after him do cite *Aureolus*, proving that *Gradus Epifcopalis & Sacerdotum non funt diftinctae poteftates*, &c. *Quia Sacerdos authoritate Papae poteft Sacerdotem inftituere. Ergo non differunt poteftas Epifcopalis & Sacerdotis, nifi ficut poteftas impedita & non impedita : quae tamen eft eadem. Antecedens probatur, quia omnis virtus activa, non impedita, poteft transfundere feipfam*] To the fame purpofe *Cufanus* and many more.

Sect. 78. Hence it is that Presbyters have of old had a place in Councils, yea and a fuffrage too : and the Council of *Bafil* did decide and practife it : which is allowed by many of the Papifts. And hence it is that divers of the Papifts do make Epifcopal preheminency to be but of *Ecclefiaftical* Inftitution.

Sect. 79. That the *Chorepifcopi* did ordain, and their Ordination was Valid, though they were not accounted B.fhops (any otherwife then our Parochial Bifhops are) is a thing that hath been fpoken of fo oft, and by fo many, even Bifhops themfelves, that I fhall pafs it by.

Sect. 80. And faith *Voetius*, even among the Papifts, the *Abbots* and fuch regular Prelates that are no Bifhops, and the *Chapter of Canons* may Ordain ; yea and exercife other acts of Jurifdiction, as excommunicating, *&c.* It is not therefore proper to the Bifhops.

Sect 81. It is therefore as *Hierom* fpeaks of *Confirmation* by a Bifhop only, *in honorem Sacerdotii*, a matter of Ecclefiaftical inftitution for Order, and not of Divine inftitution that Presbyters without Prelates fhould not Ordain : As *Leo* firft Bifhop of *Rome* faith (*Epiftol. 86. ad Epifcop. Gall. & German.*) there are *Quaedam Sacerdotibus Prohibita per Canones Ecclefiafticos, at Consecratio Presbyterorum & Diaconorum.*] It is the Canons that forbid Presbyters to Ordain, and not the Scriptures that never knew *a Presbyter without the power to Ordain.*

Sect 82. Were there no Ordainers to do that office, or none but such as would oblige us to sin, it were Gods regular way to enter by the Peoples choice and the Magistrates authority without them, this being in such case the open door: therefore it is more evidently Gods Regular way, when we have both these and the best Ministerial Ordination besides, that is on good terms to be had. I do not only here plead that such a Ministry is not Null (as I did before) but that the entrance in such a case is not sinfull.

Sect. 83. There being nothing left to men herein, but the due designation of the person (before the reception of his power from God) the Peoples Election it self may serve for that designation, where Ministerial Approbation is not to be had. But the ordinary course, where Necessity doth not prohibit us, is that all three concur, *viz.* The Consent of the people, because we cannot Teach and Rule them against their wills : 2 The Approbation of the Ministry, because they are best able to judge of mens abilities. 3 The Allowance of the Magistrate, for the orderly and advantagious exercise of our office. But the first is of the greatest necessity of the three.

Sect. 84. That the people have power of Election, when just authority (Civil or Ecclesiastical) doth not suspend it or limit it, is so easily proved that it is commonly confessed. Its well known that for many hundred years the people had in most or many Churches the Choice of their Bishops or Pastors, or joyned with the Presbyterie and Ordainers in the choice. *Blondellus, Voetius* and many more have sufficiently proved this and other parts of the peoples interest, by unanswerable evidence.

Sect. 85. *Cyprian* saith that this is by *Divine Ordination. Epist.* 68. (edit *Goulartii*) p. 201. [*Propter quod plebs obsequens præceptis Dominicis, & Deum metuens. à peccatore præposito separare se debet, nec se ad Sacrilegi Sacerdotis sacrificia miscere, quando ipsa maxime habeat potestatem vel eligendi dignos Sacerdotes, vel indignos recusandi : Quod & ipsum videmus de Divin.* S. r

Cyrian Epist. 11. Plebi-Contra Episcopatum meum, immo contra suffragium vestrum & Dei judicium &c.

sub omnium * *oculis deligatur, & dignus atq; idoneus publico judicio ac testimonio comprobetur* ———— *Coram omni Synagoga jubet Deus constitui Sacerdotem, id est, instruit & ostendit Ordinationes Sacerdotales non nisi sub populi assistentis conscientia fieri oportere, ut plebe præsente vel detegantur malorum crimina, vel bonorum merita prædicentur: & sit Ordinatio justa & legitima, quæ omnium suffragio & judicio fuerit examinata. Quod postea secundum Divina Magisteria observatur in Actis Apostolorum quando de Ordinando in locum* Judæ *Episcopo* Petrus *ad plebem loquitur, surrexit inquit* Petrus *in medio discentium; fuit autem turba in uno: Nec hoc in Episcoporum tantum & Sacerdotum, sed in Diaconorum Ordinationibus observasse Apostolos animadvertimus, de quo & ipso in Actis eorum scriptum est: Et convocaverunt, inquit illi duodecim totam plebem discipulorum* ———— *Quod utiqve idcirco tam diligenter & caute convocata plebe tota gerebatur, ne quis ad altaris Ministerium, vel ad Sacerdotalem locum indignus obreperet. Ordinari enim nonnunquam indignos non secundum Dei voluntatem, sed secundum humanam præsumptionem, & hæc Deo displicere, quæ non veniant ex legitima & justa Ordinatione, Deus ipse manifestat per Osee Prophetam dicens, sibi ipsi constituerunt Regem, & non per me. Propter quod diligenter de traditione Divina & Apostolica observatione observandum est & tenendum, quod apud nos quoq, & fere Provincias universas tenetur, ut ad Ordinationes rite celebrandas, ad eam plebem cui præpositus ordinatur, Episcopi ejusdem provinciæ proximi quiq; conveniant, & Episcopus deligatur plebe præsente, quæ singulorum vitam plenissime novit, & uniuscujusq; actam de ejus conversatione perspexit.* † *Quod & apud vos factum videmus in Sabini collega nostri ordinatione, ut de universæ fraternitatis suffragio & de Episcoporum qui in præsentia convenerant, quiq; de eo ad vos literas fecerant judicio, Episcopatus ei deferretur, & manus ei in locum Basilidis imponeretur.*] And so he goes on to shew that even the Bishop of *Romes* restoring of *Basilides*, was not valid to rescind the foresaid Ordination of *Sabinus*, which was thus made by the Bishops on the peoples suffrages. And yet our Diocesans

Eccl. l. 5. c. 18. out of *Apollonius* telleth us that *Alexander* a Montanist, being a thief, the Congregation of which he was Pastor (for that was his Diocess) would not admit him.
Cypr. Epist. 11. *Plebi* ———— *Secundum vestra Divina suffragia Conjurati & Scelerati de Ecclesia sponte se pellerent.*

have

---

* This is not the way of our Prelates Ordination. And this sheweth that the Churches in *Cyprians* days were not Diocesan, consisting of many particular Churches: else all the people could not have been present, beholders and consenters, at the Ordination of the Bishops.

† Still this shews, that the Churches of Bishops were then no greater then that all might be personally present, and fore-acquainted with his life.
Yea that it was the peoples duty not only to elect, but to reject, there's more then *Cyprian* affirm: *Eusebius Hist.*

have, alas, too commonly thrust on the people against their consent, such unworthy persons, as of whom we may say as *Cyprian* (*ibid.*) of these, [*Cumq; alia multa sint & gravia delicta quibus Basilides & Martialis implicati tenentur; frustra tales Episcopatum sibi usurpare conantur, cum manifestum sit ejusmodi homines nec Ecclesiæ Christi posse præesse, nec Deo sacrificia offerre debere.*] I have cited these words at large, because they are full and plain to shew us the practice of those times, and are the words of an *African* Syrod, and not of *Cyprian* alone, and shew that then the People had the chiefest hand in the Election or designation of the person, which is it that I have now to prove.

Sect. 86 *Pamelius* himself while he seeks to hide the shame of their Prelates Ordination, from the light of these passages of *Cyprian,* doth yet confess and say, [*Non negamus veterem Electionis Episcoporum ritum, quo plebe præsente, immo & suffragiis plebis eligi solent. Nam in* Africa *illum observatum constat ex electione Eradii Successoris D.* Augustini, *de quo extat Epistola ejus* 120. *In* Græcia *ætate* Chrysost. *ex lib.* 3. *de Sacer. In* Hispan.is *ex hoc* Cypriani *loco, &* Isidor. *lib. de Officiis. In* Galliis, *ex Epistel.* Celestin. *Pap.* 2. Romæ, *ex iis quæ supradiximus, Epist ad* Anton. Ubiq; *etiam alibi ex Epist.* Leonis 87, *Et perdurasse eam consuetudinem ad* Gregor. 1. *usq; ex ejus Epistolis: immo & ad tempora usq;* Caroli & Ludovici Imperatorum, *ex* 1. *lib.* Capitulorum *eorundem satis constat.*] This full confession from the mouth of an adversary, may save me the labour of many more allegations concerning the judgement and practice of the ancients.

Sect. 87. He that would see more may find enough in *Voetius de Desparata causa Papatus lib.* 2. *c.* 12. *Sect* 2. *& passim* And in *Blondel. de jure plebis: &* Goulartius *on the foresaid notes of* Pamelius *on* Cyprian, *p.* 205 Among others he there citeth those known Canons of the *Carthage* Councils, third and fourth out of *Gratian* [*Nullus ordinetur clericus nisi probatus, vel examine Episcoporum, vel populi testimonio*] Et [*Episcopus sine concilio clericorum suorum clericos non ordinet, ita ut civium conn ventiam & testimonium quærat*] (What and where is that Clergy without whose Council our Prelates Ordain not; and that people whose suffrages they require?) And saith *Goulartius,* [Observanda est Caroli us & Ludovici Constitutio [*Sacrorum Caninum*

Constantine in his Epistle to the people of *Antioch* tells them that [in the election of their Bishops all men should freely deliver their opinion, and the general suffrage of al should be equally considered; because Ecclesiastical Honours should be obtained and conferred without trouble and discord ———
Euseb.de vitâ Const. l 3. *c* 58.

noxum non ignari, ut Dei nomine sacrosancta Ecclesia suo liberius potiatur honore, assensum Ordini Ecclesiastico prabemus, ut Episcopi per Electionem Cleri & populi, secundum statua Canonum eligantur.] Its certain then that the people were sometime the sole choosers, and the Pastors the approvers ; and sometime the People and the Pastors joynt Electors ; and sometime the Pastors chose, but forced none on the people, against or without their Consent (as *Pamelius* confesseth) till Popular tumults, divisions, and other reasons occasioned the change of this ancient Custome. And therefore it is most certain, that an Election by the people may be a valid determination of the person.

Sect. 88. And the person being once sufficiently determined of, the power and obligation doth fall upon him immediately from God ; so that were it not that the Pastors Approbation is part of the Determination, there would be nothing left for Ordination, but the solemnizing of their entrance by Investiture, which is not essential to the Ministerial Office, but *ad bene esse,* makes to a compleat and orderly possession, where it may be had , and where it cannot, Election may suffice.

Sect. 89. *Voetius, de Desperata causa Papatus, lib.* 2. *sect.* 2. *cap.* 20. doth by seven Arguments prove against *Jansenius, Electionem tribuere Ministerium : & esse proprie ejus fundamentum.* The first Argument is from the Definition of Election : the second from the Canon Law, which giveth a Bishop his power before Consecration, and gives the Pope a power of governing the Church before he is inthroned or Consecrated. The third is *à similibus,* in *Oeconome* and *Policie* : the foundation of marriage-union is mutual Consent, and not Solemnization. Coronation (saith he) doth not make a King (he means, *not fundamentally,* but compleatively,) but hereditary Succession or Election. He may well be a King without Coronation, as (saith he) the custom is in *Castile, Portugal,* &c. The King of *France* dependeth not *pro jure regni* on the Archbishop of *Rhemes,* but saith *Barclay,* hath the right and honour of a King before his Coronation. An elect Emperour governeth before his Coronation. *Quoad potestatem administrandi regni (Gallici) unctio & Coronatio nihil addunt inquit Commentator sanctionis pragmat. fol.* 4. His fourth Argument is from the nature of all Relations. *cum posito fundamento & termino, in subjecto*

jecto dicuntur exiftere : atqui Solemnizatio, feu Confecratio, feu Ordinatio, feu Inveftitura (ἐχθρονισμὸν vocant patres Græci) illa externa quam nos confirmationem dicimus, neque eft fundamentum, neque terminus Minifterii, aut Miniftri; fed legitima electio & χειροτονία Ecclefia eft fundamentum Minifterii, & ifta vel illa particularis Ecclefia eft te minus, in quo eft correlatum Oves feu difcipuli, ad quod refertur relatum Doctoris feu Paftoris. (Though fome of this need explication and limitation, yet its worthy confideration.) His fifth Argument is from the Confeffions of the Adverfaries, citing *Sylveft. Prieras, Immanuel Sa, Onuphrius, Navarrus,* yea *Bellarmine* and Pope *Nicolas,* who maintain that [*In fummo Pontifice poft Electionem nulla alia requiritur confirmatio; quia ftatim ut electus eft fufcipit adminiftrationem.* And to this agreeth their Practice, who at the Council of *Trent* had many Bifhops *meerly Elect*, and *Elect Cardinals* are admitted to Elect a Pope. His fixth Argument is [*Quod Confecratio feu Inveftitura poteft abiffe aliquo in Cafu: Electio autem nunquam : ergo fundamentum Minifterii feu poteftatis Ecclefiaftica eft Electio & non Confecratio;* which he endeavours to confirm. My opinion of the *fundamentum poteftatis,* I have expreffed in my *Chriftian Concord* othrrwife : but yet I confent, as is there expreffed, to the Neceffity of the peoples Confent to our Office.

Sect. 90. Argument 20. If thofe in the Reformed Churches that are Ordained by Presbyters, have as good a call to the Minifterial Office, as the Princes of the Nations (yea any one of them) have to their Soveraignty or Power, then are they true Minifters of Chrift, and their adminiftrations valid to the Churches, and their Miniftry to be received. But the Antecedent is true : therefore fo is the Confequent. And I prove them both.

Sect. 91. The Secular power will be granted, as to the moft (at leaft) of Chriftian Princes and other Soveraigns : when the Holy Ghoft commandeth fubjection to the Higher Powers, even when they are Heathen, and come in as *Nero* did, *Rom.*13. we may well take it for granted that Chriftian Magiftrates, that have no better title then he, are fuch as we muft be fubject to : even thofe that have not fo lawful an entrance, as may juftifie their poffeff...

e

before God, may yet be such while they are in possession, as we must be subject to for Conscience sake and all their administrations are as valid to the innocent subjects, as if they had as good a title as the best. They that deny this, must overthrow almost all the Common-wealth's on Earth, and turn Subjection into Rebellion.

Sect. 92. The Consequence then is proved from the parity of Reason, in both cases. The title of such Princes is so far good, as that subjection is due to them, and their Government valid : our title to the Ministry is at least as good as theirs : therefore submission or obedience is due to us, and our administrations valid to the Church. And that our title is as good as theirs, will appear by a due comparison.

Sect. 93. 1. God is equally the Author of our Office, and of theirs. He that appointed the Magistrate to Rule by force, appointed the Ministry to Teach, and Guide, and Worship publikely before the Church. There is no Power but of God : even Magistrates could have none, unless it were given them from above. 2. Usurpation therefore is a sin in Magistrates as well as Ministers. And there is the same reason, why it should invalidate their actions, as ours, if we were guilty of it. 3. The Dissenters rule [*Nemo dat quod non habet*] concerneth the Magistrate as much as the Minister, and somewhat more. A man may do more in works of service to others without a special Office, then in Magisterial Government. Magistracy is a Relation that must have a foundation or efficient cause, as well as Ministry. If a *Giver* that himself hath the Power given, is necessary to make Ministers, then also to make Magistrate, (which yet is false in both, if you speak of humane Donation to the Soveraign) The effect can no more be without a cause in them then in us. 4. If the Election or Consent of the people be enough to make a Magistrate, or to be the foundation or donation (as they suppose of his authority, then much more may the election or consent of the people, with the approbation and investiture by Presbyters, and allowance of the Magistrate, prove those in question to be true Ministers. 5. No Prince on earth that ever I heard of, can prove any thing like an uninterrupted succession of legitimate Princes from a Predecessor immediatly authorized by God. If Hereditary Princes that are the Successors
fors

fors of Usurpers are not to be obeyed, it will be hard to find an Hereditary Prince that is to be obeyed : so that their case is worse then the case of Ministers.

Sect. 94. For, though 1. No Pastors ou Earth can prove an uninterrupted Succession of persons *lawfully* Ordained. 2. Nor is it necessary to prove a Local succession ; because God hath not tyed his Church to Towns or Countries , and a Church and Pastor that are banished into another Land, may there be the same Church and Pastor, though in and of another place : yet 1. We have a succession of possession in the Office itself. 2. And a succession of actual Ordination in great probability : no man can prove against us that we receive our Ministrie from any that were not actually Ordained. Yet this much is not Necessary to our Office.

Sect. 95. Object. *But Christ hath tyed the Office of the Ministry to a legitimate Ordination ; but he hath not tyed the Magistracy to a lawful Title.* Answ. Here are two falshoods barely affirmed, or implyed. One is that *a just Title* is less necessary to the Magistrate then the Minister ; when the Reason of both is the same. Title is the foundation of Right. Magistracie is a Right of Governing. No Relation can be without its Foundation. The other is, that God hath tyed the Office of the Ministrie to a *legitimate Ordination.* This is unproved, and I have proved the contrary before. It is *our Duty* to enter by *Legitimate Ordination* where it may be had ; and thus we do. But if any of our Predecessors (perhaps a thousand or five hundred years ago) did enter otherwise, that doth not invalidate our Ordination or Ministrie, nor is it any of our sin.

Sect. 96. As Ministers were at first Ordained by Imposition of hands, so Kings were chosen by God, and (in the Church) anointed by a Prophet, or special Officer of God ; and sometime by the people (that is, by their suffrages appointing it, or consenting to it) as appeareth, 1 *Sam.* 10.1. & 15.17. & 16. 13. & 24.6. 2 *Sam.* 2.4,7. & 5.3. & 12.7. & 19.10. 1 *King.* 1.45. & 5.1. 2 *King.* 11.12. & 23.30. 2 *Chron.* 22.7. so that there is as much in Scripture for this manner of their investiture, as there is for Ministers Ordination by imposition of hands ; yet may they be Kings that have no such Investiture ; much less all their predecessors. We then that *have* a due Investiture, may

prove

prove our Miniſtry, whatever our predeceſſors had.

Sect. 97. I come now to the Arguments of the adverſaries of our Miniſtrie, which I need not ſtand long on, becauſe they are few and ſcarce conſiderable, and ſufficiently anſwered in what is ſaid. And firſt its ſaid by a Learned man (*Diſſertat. de Epiſcop. contra* Blondel. *Præmonit. ad Lector. ſect.4.13.*) *[Nos illud in hac diſceptatione pro conceſſo poſitum cenſebimus, Neminem recte dare quod non habet : eumque aut eos qui hac poteſtate induti nunquam fuerint, ſine violatione aut ſacrilegio quodam ſibi arrogare aut aſſumere aut aliis æque à Deo non vocatis, aut miſſis communicare neutiquam poſſe. [Illud hic nobis unicum meminiſſe ſufficiet, unumquemque in Anglicana Eccleſia ab Epiſcopis ordinatum Presbyterum , nulla ordinandi alios facultate (aut per ſe, aut quà quolibet compariam catu munitum) præditum eſſe, nec igitur eam ſibi rectius arrogare poſſe, quam ſi Diaconorum, immo Laicorum unus, aut plures, tali poteſtate nullatenus induti, idem auſuri ſint.*] The ſumm is : *Presbyters have not this power . therefore they cannot give it.*

Sect. 98. Anſw. If the Argument run thus [*No man can give that which he hath not : Presbyters have not the Office of a Presbyter : therefore they cannot give it.*] I then deny the Minor : They are not *Presbyters*, if they have not the *Office* of a Presbyter : that therefore which *they have* (to ſpeak in the Diſſenters language) they *may give.*

Sect. 99. But if the Argument be this [*No man can give that which he hath not : Presbyters have not a power of Ordaining : therefore they cannot give a power of Ordaining*] I anſwer as followeth. 1. We receive not our Office by the Gift of man, whether Presbyters or Prelates. The Power is immediately from Chriſt, and men do but open us the door, or determine of the perſon that ſhall from Chriſt receive the power, and then put him ſolemnly into poſſeſſion. It is the firſt Error of the adverſaries, to hold that this power is given by men as firſt having it themſelves. In the Popes caſe *Bellarmine* himſelf will grant us this (*Reſponſ. ad 7 Theolog. Venet. p. 246.232.*) [*Sæpe (inquit) jam dictum eſt, Electionem Cardinalium non conferre poteſtatem, ſed deſignare tantummodo perſonam, cui Deus poteſtatem tribuit.*] And yet that [*In ſummo Pontifice poſt electionem nulla alia requiritur confirmatio, quia ſtatim ut electus eſt, ſuſcipit adminiſtrationem,*

strationem, *ut declarat* Nicol. *Papa* (*an. in nomine, dif. 23.*]
*pag.*175. And of the Power of Princes, the Diſſenters will grant
it (for we have it in their writings) that the *Power is from God
immediately*, though the people may e'ect the perſon. You will
thruſt out all Princes of the world by this Argument, and ſay,
[*No man giveth that which he hath not : the people have not a
Power of Government : therefore they cannot give it.*] I would
anſwer you as here : *God hath the Power*, and he giveth it : but
the people that have it not, may *deſign the perſon* that ſhall receive
it from God : as the Burgeſſes of a Corporation may chooſe a
Major or Bayliff to receive that power from the Soveraign (by
the Inſtrumentality of a Law or Charter) which they had not
themſelves to uſe or give. And ſo a Presbyterie (and ſometime
the people alone) may deſign the perſon that ſhall receive the
Office of the Miniſtrie from God, though they had it not themſelves to uſe or give.

Sect. 100. Reſp. 2. By this Argument and its ſuppoſition,
none are true Miniſters that are Ordained by *Prelates* : for they
have not the Power of the Miniſtrie to *Give*, but only to *Uſe* :
no Ordination is a Giving of the Power, ſave only by way of
Inveſtiture, which ſuppoſeth a Title and Right before, and is
not of abſolute neceſſity to the Poſſeſſion : for in ſeveral caſes it
may be without it.

Sect. 101. Reſponſ. 3. A man may *Inſtrumentally give* or
deliver both Right and Inveſtiture in that which he *hath not himſelf*, nor ever had. Your ſervant may by your appointment,
deliver a Leaſe, a Deed of Gift, a Key, or twig and turf, for
Poſſeſſion of houſe and lands, though he never had houſe or
lands or poſſeſſion himſelf. It is ſufficient that the Donor have
it, that ſends him.

Sect. 102. Reſp. 4. Presbyters have the Power of Presbyters, or the Miniſterial Office : and if they can *give that* (which
certainly they have,) then they can give a Power of *Ordaining*
other Presbyters. For to Ordain *others*, is no more then they do
themſelves in *giving the Power or Office which they have* : therefore if they may do it, thoſe that they give their Power to may
do it ; that is, may alſo give others that power which they
have.

Sect. 103. But as to our caſe in hand, it ſuffice h   we
H   _

prove, that Presbyters may give others the Office of Presbyters ; whether this Office contain a Power of Ordaining, is another Question, but soon difpatcht, if this be granted : becaufe (as is faid) to Ordain is nothing elfe but to inveft others with the Office or Power which we have our felves.

Sect. 104. Refp. 5. The Argument maketh more againft the Prelates Ordination, on another account ; becaufe that (as is proved already) that *Species* of Prelacie that was exercifed in *England* (the fole Governours of an hundred or two hundred Churches) is fo far contrary to the Word of God, that we may boldly conclude, that as fuch, they have no power to *ufe or give* : their very Office is humane, and deftructive of the true Paftoral Office : and therefore as fuch, they have lefs pretence of Divine Authoritie, then Presbyters, whofe Office is of God. Yet do I not make their Ordination Null, becaufe they were Presbyters as well as Prelates, and alfo were in Poffefsion of the place of Ordainers, and had the Magiftrates authority.

Sect. 105. Refp. 6. Presbyters have a Power of Ordaining : it is already proved. And to your confirmation (where you fay that the Bifhops gave them no fuch Power : therefore they have it not :) I anfwer : 1. I deny the Confequence. God gave it them : therefore they have it without the Bifhops gift. 2. If by [*Giving*] you mean but an accidental Caufation, or the action of a *Caufa fine qua non*, or a defignation of the Perfon that fhall receive it, then I deny the Antecedent. The Prelates (and Electors) defigned the perfon, and alfo invefted him folemnly in the Office, which containeth this Power of Ordination which you deny them.

Sect. 106. Obj. *The Prelates expreffed no fuch thing in their Ordination.* Anf. 1. It being not the Prelates but Chrift that makes the *Office*, we muft not go to the words of the Prelates, but of Chrift to know *what the Office is*, though we may go to the Prelates (while the work was in their hands) to know *who the perfon is.* If a Prelate Confecrate a Prelate, and yet mention not particularly the works that are pretended to belong to a Prelate, you will not think him thereby reftrained or difabled to thofe works. He that Crowneth a King, and they that choofe him, though they name not the works of his Office and Power, do thereby choofe him to all thofe works that belong to a King.

God

God hath set down in his Word, that the Husband shall be the Head or Governor of his Wife; if now the woman shall choose a certain person to be her Husband, and the Minister or Magistrate solemnize their Marriage, without any mention of such Governing Power, the Power doth neverthelesse belong to the man; because God hath specified by his Law the Power of that Relation, and the man is Lawfully put in the Relation that by the Law of God hath such a Power: so is it in the case in hand.

Sect. 107. But yet 2. I add, that the Prelates and the Laws of *England* gave to Presbyters a Power of Ordination. For in all their Ordinations, the Presbyters were to lay on hands with the Prelate (and did, in all Ordinations that I have seen.) And if they actually imposed hands and so Ordained, it was an actual profession to all that they were supposed to have the power of Ordination, which they exercised.

Sect. 108. Obj. *But they had no Power given them to do it without a Prelate.* Answ. 1. By Christ they had. 2. You may as well say, that Bishops have no Power to Ordain, because they were not (ordinarily at least) to do it without the Presbyters.

Sect. 109. Obj. Saith the foresaid Learned Author (*Dissert. Præmonit. sect.* 10. 11.) [*Unum illud lubens interrogarem, an Hieronymus, dum hic esset, & Presbyteratu secundario fungeretur partiaria tantum indutus potestate, præsente, sed spreto & insuper habito Episcopo, Diaconum aut Presbyterum ordinare (aut Presbytero uni aut alteri adjunctus) recte potuerit ? si affirmetur, dicatur sodes, qua demum ratione ab eo dictum sit, Episcopum sola ordinatione (& ergo ordinatione) à Presbytero disterminatum esse] sin negetur, quomodo igitur Presbytero Anglicano, cui nullam, quæ non Hieronymo potestatem, &c. ———*]
Answ. 1. This is none of our case in *England*: we Ordain not, *præsente sed spreto Episcopo*: but most Countreyes know of no Bishop that they have, but Presbyters. 2. *Hierom* might have Ordained with his fellow-presbyters, according to the Laws of Christ, but not according to the Ecclesiastical Canons, that then obtained, or bore sway. 3. *Hierom* plainly tells you, that it is by Ecclesiastical appointment for the prevention of schisme, that Bishops were set up so far as to have this power more then

Hh 3   Presbyters,

Presbyters, in the point of Ordination.   4. The English Presbyters are Parochial Bishops, and have an Office of Christs
making, and not of the Prelates; and are not under those Ecclesiastical Canons that restrained *Hierom* from the exercise of
this power.   And therefore whereas it is added by this Learned
Author [*Quid huic dilemmati reponi, aut opponi possit, fateor
equidem me non adeo Lynceum isse ut perspiciam*] he may see
that he could scarce have set us an easier task then to answer his
dilemma.

Sect. 110. The second and their principal objection is, that
*We have no precept or example in the Church for Presbyters Or-
daining without Prelates: therefore it is not to be done.* Answ. 1.
I told you before how Bishop *Usher* told me he answered this
Objection to King *Charls. viz.* from the example of the Church
of *Alexandria* where Presbyters made Bishops, which is more.

Sect. 111. But 2. I answer, you have no example in Scripture
or long after that ever Prelates of the English sort, did ordain, nor any precept for it, nor was such a Prelacy then
known, as is proved; and therefore their Ordination hath less
warrant then that by Presbyters.

Sect. 112. And 3. I have told you before of Scripture warrant for Ordination by a Presbyterie, and also by the Teachers
and other Officers of a single Church, as was the Church of *Antioch*. Prove that *there* was any Bishop.

Sect. 113. Lastly, it is confessed by the Dissenters that such
Presbyters or Bishops as are mentioned, *Act.* 20. *Phil.* 1. 1.
1 *Tim.*3. *Tit.*1,*&c.* had power of Ordination: But according
to the ~~the~~ judgement of most of the Fathers (that ever I saw or
heard of that interpret those texts) it is Presbyters that are
meant in all or some of those texts.   It is granted us also by the
Dissenters that the chief or sole Pastors of single Churches in
Scripture-times did ordain, and had the power of Ordination:
But the Presbyters of *England*, and other Protestant Churches are the chief or sole Pastors of single Churches; therefore, *&c.*

Sect. 114. Object. 3. *But the English Presbyters have broak
their Oaths of Canonical obedience, and therefore at least are schifmatical.* Answ. 1. Many never took any such oath, to my
knowledge: For my part I did not. 2. The particular persons
that

that are guilty muſt be accuſed : and neither muſt they be judged
before they ſpeak for themſelves , nor yet muſt others be condemned for their ſakes. In theſe parts, there is not one Presbyter I think of ten, who differs from the Prelates about Ordination , that ever took that oath.   And therefore it is few that can
be called Schiſmaticks on that account. Yea 3 And thoſe few that
did take that Oath, have few of them that I know of, done any
thing againſt the Prelates.

Sect. 115. Object. 4. *The Engliſh Presbyters have pull'd
down the Prelates, and rebelled againſt them, and therefore at leaſt
are guilty of Schiſm. Anſw.* 1. The guilty muſt be named and
heard: their caſe is nothing to the reſt. It is not one of ten I think,
perhaps of twenty, that can be proved guilty. 2. It was not
the Scripture Biſhops that they Covenanted againſt or oppoſed :
but only the irregular Engliſh Prelacy before deſcribed : And
the endeavour of reforming this corrupted Prelacy, and reducing
it to the Primitive frame, is in it ſelf no ſchiſm.

Sect. 116. Object. 5. *Ignatius commandeth them to obey
the Biſhops and do nothing without them. Anſw. 1. Ignatius alſo
commandeth them to obey the Presbyters as the Apoſtles of Chriſt,
and to do nothing without them.* 2. The Biſhops that *Ignatius*
mentioneth were ſuch as our Pariſh Biſhops or Presbyters are,
that have a Presbyterie to aſſiſt them : They were the chief Paſtors of a ſingle Church, as is before proved out of *Ignatius,* and
not the Paſtors of hundreds of Churches.

Sect. 117. I ſhall trouble the Reader with no more of their
objections, ſeeing by what is ſaid already, he may be furniſhed
to anſwer them all : but I ſhall now leave it to his impartial ſober
conſideration, whether I have not proved the truth of our Miniſtry and of the Reformed Churches , and the Validity of our adminiſtrations, and of our Ordination it ſelf ?

CHAP.

CHAP. VIII.

The greatneſs of their ſin that are now labouring to perſwade the People of the Nullity of our Miniſtry, Churches and adminiſtrations.

Sect. 1. Aving laid ſo fair a ground for my application, I think it my duty to take the freedom to tell thoſe Reverend perſons that oppoſe us in this point, the Reaſons why I dare not joyn with them, and the guilt that I am perſwaded they heap upon their own ſouls; Wherein I proteſt it is not mine intent to make them odious, or caſt diſgrace upon them (for I do with great reluctancy obey my Conſcience in the performance of this task:) but my intent is, if it be the will of God to give ſucceſs ſo far to theſe endeavours, 1. To humble them for their great and hainous ſin and ſave them from it; 2. And to ſave the Church from the diviſions and diſturbances that is already cauſed by them and their opinion; 3. However

Even thoſe Proteſtant Churches that have Superintendents are unchurched by them too, for want of a true Ordination: For their Superintendents were commonly ordained by meer Presbyters, or ſettled only by the Princes power. So in Denmark, when their

ſeven Biſhops were depoſed, ſeven Presbyters were Ordained Superintedents by *Johan. Bugenhagius Pomeranus* a Presbyter of *Wittenberge* in the Preſence of the King and Senate at the chief Church in *Haffnia*: See *Vit. Bugenhagii in Melch. Adam. vit. Germ. Theolog.* page 315.

to discharge my Conscience and tell them plainly, what frightneth me from their way.

Sect. 2. And 1. It seems to me (upon the grounds before expressed) that those men that would Nullifie all the Protestant Ministry, Churches and administrations, that have not Prelates, are guilty of schism, and are plain Separatists. They depart from truly Catholick principles. That man hath not the just Principles and Spirit of a Catholick, that can on such a pretence as this degrade or nullifie so many Learned, Godly Ministers, and unchurch so many excellent Churches of Christ ; they make a plain Schism, and separate from us on as weak grounds as the ancient Separatists did, whom yet they account an odious generation. And the writings of *Paget*, *Ball*, *Bradshaw*, *Hildersham*, *Bernard*, and the rest that defend our Ministry and Churches against the old Separatists, will serve in the main to defend them against these new ones, which therefore I refer the Reader to peruse. Many of the same Arguments are as forcible against this adversary.

Sect. 3. 2. And by this means they condemn themselves that have spoken so much against the Separatists, calling them Brownists, Schismaticks, and the like ; and now take up the cause (in the maine) that in them they so condemned. Will they turn Schismaticks that have spoken against Schismaticks so much ?

Sect. 4. 3. By this means also they exceedingly wrong the Lord Jesus Christ, by seeking to rob him of his inheritance : by telling him that his Churches are none of his Churches, and his Ministers are none of his Ministers, and his Ordinances are not his Ordinances indeed. Let them first prove that Christ hath renounced these Ministers, or unchurched or denied these Churches, or given them a bill of divorce : and then let them speak their pleasure. But till then they were best take heed what they do, lest they have not the thanks from Christ which they expect.

Sect. 5. 4. They go against the plain commands of Christ, and examples of his servants : Christ himself bid concerning such as cast out Devils in his name, but followed him not [*Forbid him not ; for there is no man that shall do a Miracle in my name that can lightly speak evil of me : for he that is not against us is on our part, Mark* 9. 37, 38, 39. He liked not their humour

Ii   that

that would have the *substance* of so good a work forbidden, for want of a due circumstance, mode, or accident. He commandeth us *to Pray the Lord of the Harvest to send Labourers into his Harvest, because the Harvest is great, and the Labourers are few :* And these men would have multitudes of Labourers thrust out, in the Necessity of the Churches. *Paul* rejoyced that *Christ was Preached,* even by them that did it *in strife and envy, thinking to add affliction to his bonds.* But these men would silence them that preach in sincere compassion of mens souls. *Moses* would not forbid *Eldad* and *Medad* prophecying, but wisht that all the Lords people were Prophets. While men do good and not harm, or more good then harm in the Church, I should see very good grounds, yea and Necessity for it, before I should silence them, or be guilty of silencing them.

Sect. 6. 5. They manifest a great deal of *selfishness* and *pride,* that dare thus consent to the injury of Christ, and the Church and souls of men , because they may not bear that Rule which is according to their principles and spirits. Self denial would do much to cure this.

Sect. 7. 6. And yet they do as self-seekers commonly do, even seek after misery and destruction to themselves. While they look (its like) at the honour, and forget the work, they plead for such a load and burden, as is enough to break the backs of many, even for the doing of a work that is so far beyond their strength , that its a meer impossiblity: How can one man do the works which Scripture layeth on a Bishop , for a hundred or two hundred Churches ? and for thousands that he never sees or hears of ?

Sect. 8. 7. And above all, I admire how the heart of a considerate Christian, can be guilty of so great cruelty to the souls of men, as these men would be, if they had their will, in the practice of their principles ? What if all the Churches that have no Prelates were unchurched ? the Ministers cast out as no true Ministers, or the people all prevailed with to forsake them, what would be done for the thousands of the poor ignorant careless souls that are among us ? when all that all of us can do is too little, what would be done if so many and such were laid aside ? How many thousands were like to be damned, for want of the

means,

means, that according to the ordinary way of God, might have procured their conversion and Salvation?

Sect. 9. If they say, that *others as good as they should possess the places*: I answer, they speak not to men of another world, but to their neighbours, that well know that there are few to be had of tolerable worth to possess one place of very many, if all that they oppose were cast out or forsaken. Do we not know who and what men they are that you have to supply the room with?

Sect. 10. If they say that *more obedient men would soon spring up, or many of these would change their mind, if they were forced to it*; I answer, 1. So many would be unchanged as would be a greater loss to the Church (if it were deprived of them) then ever Prelacy was like to repair. 2. And what should become of poor souls the while your young ones are a training up? 3. And in all ages after, the Church must lose all those that should dissent from your opinion.

Sect. 11. If you say that, *It is not your desire to silence all these Preachers that you disown*: I answer, How can that stand with your doctrine or your practice? Your Doctrine is, that they are Lay-men, and no true Ministers, nor to be heard and submitted to as Ministers, nor Sacraments to be received from them. And would you not have them then cast out? 2. Your practice is to disswade the people (especially the Gentry that are neer you)to separate and disown them accordingly; and it is done in many places. And would you not cast them out, whom you would have forsaken?

Sect. 12. If you say, *It is your desire that they should forsake their error and obey you, and so be continued and not cast out*: I answer, 1. But that is not in your power to accomplish, nor have you reason to expect it. They are willing to know the mind of God as well as you, and perhaps search as diligently, and pray as hard as you; and yet they think that its you that are in the wrong; you see that for many years the Reformed Churches have continued in this mind: And it appears that if they will not turn to your opinion, you would have them all cast out or forsaken. Christ shall have no servants, nor the Church any Pastors that will not be in this of your Opinion.

Sect. 13. 8. Hereby also you would run into the guilt of a

more

ımore grievous perfecution, when you have read fo much in
Scripture againſt perfecutors, and when you have heard of and
ſeen the judgements of God let out upon them. It is an eaſie
matter for any Perfecutor to call him that he would caſt out, a
Schiſmatick, or Heretick, but it is not ſo eaſie to anſwer him
that hath ſaid, *He that offendeth one of theſe little ones, it were*
better for him, &c. God will not take up with fair pretences or
falſe accuſations againſt his ſervants, to juſtifie your perfecution.

Sect. 14. 9. Yea you would involve the people of the Land,
and of other Nations, in the guilt of your perfecution; drawing them to joyn with you, in caſting out the faithful labourers
from the Vineyard of the Lord. This is the good you would
do the people, to involve their Souls into ſo deplorable a ſtate of
guilt.

Sect. 15. If you ſay, *It is you that are perfecuted,* as I read
ſome of you do : I anſwer. 1. If it be ſo, you are the more unexcuſable before God and man, that even under your perfecution,
will cheriſh, defend and propagate ſuch a doctrine of perfecution, as ſtrikes at no leſs then the necks of all the Reformed
Miniſters, and Churches that are not Prelatical, at one blow.
2. For my part, I have oft proteſted againſt any that ſhall hinder an able Godly Miniſter from the ſervice of Chriſt and the
Church, if he be but one that is likely to do more good then
harm. But I never took it to be perfecution to caſt out Drunkards, ſcandalous, negligent, inſufficient men, where better
may be had to ſupply the place: no more then it is perfecution
to ſuppreſs an abuſive Alehouſe, or reſtrain a thief from making
thievery his trade. 3. The preſent Governors do profeſs their
readineſs to approve and encourage in the Miniſtry any Godly,
able, diligent men that will but live peaceably towards the Commonwealth. And I am acquainted with none (as far as I remember) of this quality, that have not liberty to preach and
exerciſe the Miniſterial Office. 4. But if you think you are perſecuted, becauſe you may not Rule your Brethren, and perſe-
cute others, and take upon you the ſole Government of all the
Churches in a County, or more, we had rather bear your accuſations, then poor ſouls ſhould bear the pains of Hell, by your
neglect and perfecution : if you are perfecuted when your hands
are held from ſtriking; what are your Brethren, that cannot by
your

your good will have leave laboriously to serve God in a low estate, as the servants of all, and the Lords of none?

Sect. 16. 10. By this means also you shew your selves impenitent in regard of all the former persecutions that some of you and your predecessors have been guilty of. Abundance of most Learned Godly men have been silenced, suspended, and some of them persecuted to banishment, and some to death. The world hath had too few such men for exemplary abilities, diligence and holiness, as *Hildersham, Bradshaw, Bayn, Nicols, Brightman, Dod, Ball, Paget, Hering, Langley, Parker, Sandford, Cartwright, Bates, Ames, Rogers,* and abundance more, that some suffered unto death, and some were silenced, some imprisoned, *&c.* for not conforming to the Ceremonies: besides *Eliot, Hooker, Cotton, Norton, Cobbet, Davenport, Parker. Noyes,* and all the rest that were driven to *New England*; and besides *Ward* and all that were driven into *Holland*: and besides the thousands of private Christians that were driven away with them: And besides all the later more extensive persecution of such as were called Conformable Puritans, for not reading the Book for dauncing on the Lords day, and for not ceasing to preach Lectures, or on the Evening of the Lords day, and such like: All this I call to your mind, as the sin that should be lamented, and heavily lamented, and not be owned, and drawn or continued on your own heads by impenitencie; and how do you repent, that would do the like, and take your selves to be persecuted, if your hands are tyed that you may not do it? For my own part, I must profess, I had rather be a Gally-slave, or Chimney-sweeper, yea or the basest vermine, than be a Bishop with all this guilt upon my soul, (to continue,) how light soever many make of it, and how impenitently soever they justifie themselves.

Sect. 17. 11. Yea more, after all the warnings you have had, in the waies and ends of your predecessors, it seems that you would yet incomparably outstrip the most of them in persecution, if you had your way. For few of them did attempt, or make any motion, for degrading or denying most of the Protestant Ministers in *Europe*, or such a number as in *England* and *Scotland* are not Ordained by Prelates, and to unchurch all their Churches. This is far higher then these before you.

Sect

Sect. 18. 12. And take heed lest continuing in such a sin, after both prohibitions and judgements, you should be found *fighters against God.* If those that despise the Ministers of Christ, *despise Christ* himself, what shall we think of them that do it themselves, and *teach men so to do,* and *have pleasure in them that do it?* Its fearful to draw near that forlorn Condition of the Jews, 1 *Thes.*2.15,16. [—— *and have persecuted us: and they please not God, and are contrary to all men; forbidding us to speak to the Gentiles that they might be saved, to fill up their sins alway: for the wrath is come upon them to the uttermost.*]&c.

Sect. 19. 13. It is apparent that your doctrine and practice tendeth to let in the old ejected rabble of drunken, ignorant, ungodly persons into the Ministrie. (And what can be more odious to the most Holy. God !) For if once you cast out all those that have not Prelatical Ordination, or all that are against it, (especially after a former Ordination,) you must take in such as these, and with *Jeroboam,* make Priests of the vilest of the people, or else the places must be vacant : for we know that there are not able godly men to be had of your mind to supply the vacant places.

Sect. 20. 14. Your doctrine doth tend to harden malignant wicked men in their enmitie against a faithful Ministrie : and we see this unhappy success of it by experience. Our doctrine is so much against the inclination and interest of the flesh, and men are by corrupted nature at such an enmity to God, and all that is truly Spiritual and Holy, that we have as many enemies as hearers, till Grace do either restrain or change them. But when they have such an irritation and encouragement as this, and that from men that would be reputed as Godly as the best ; then no wonder if they are hardened in their malignity. When we would instruct them and mind them of their everlasting state, and help to prepare them for their latter end ; they are told by Learned men, that we are no Ministers but Lay-men and Schismaticks, and that it is their sin to own us, or receive the Ordinances of Christ from us as Ministers : and so the poor people turn their backs on us, and on the Assemblies and Ordinances of God ; and being taught by wise and learned men to disown us and despise us, they follow their drunkenness, and worldliness, and ungodlyness with greater security, and with less remorse: for

now

now they have a defensative against the galling doctrine of those precise Preachers, that would not let them alone in their sin : they were wont to be disturbed at least by Sermons, and sometime they purposed to return, and were in the way of Grace, and in some hope : but now they are taught by Learned Godly Divines to keep out of hearing, they can go on and sin in peace.

Sect. 21. 15. By this means also you rob God of his publike worship : People are taught to turn their backs on it : you teach them that it is better that God have no publike Ministerial worship at all, in Prayer, Praises, Sacraments, &c. then that he should have it from any but Prelatical Ministers ! O sacred doctrine ! And if you had your wills for the silencing or ejecting of all that are not Ordained by Prelates, how many hundred Church-doors must be shut up in the Christian world, or worse-l

Sect. 22. 16. By this means all Impiety would be cherished and let loose. When once the mouths of Ministers were stopped, the mouth of the swearer, and curser, and railer, and scorner at Godliness would be open : and so would be the mouth of the drunkard and glutton. If all that can be done, be so much too little, as experience tells us, what a case would the Nations be in, and how would iniquity abound, if Ministers were cast out ?

Sect. 23. 17. Yea it might endanger the Churches, by the introduction of Infidelity or Heathenism it self. For nothing is more natural as it were, to corrupted man : and if once the Ministry be taken down, and they have none, or those that are next to none, Infidelity and Atheism will soon spring up : And it will be a more dangerous sort of Infidelity, then is among many of the open Infidels, because it would be palliated with the name of Christianity, and leave men further from conviction, then some that never heard of Christ.

Sect. 24. 18. And it is a temptation to Infidelity and Contempt of the Church and Ministrie, when men shall see that one party of Christians doth thus unchurch another. They will think that they may boldly say that of us, which we say of one another ; one party unchurcheth all the Papists : these that we are now speaking to, do unchurch all the Protestant Churches

that

that are not Prelatical. The Papifts unchurch all but themfelves, and fo among them, they leave Chrift but a very fmall part of his inheritance.

Sect. 25. 19. Yea I fear that by Confequence (and too near and plain a Confequence) they diffolve the Catholike Church it felf. And if it be fo, let them judge whether their doctrine fubvert not Chriftianitie ? I ufe no violence for the inference. If want of Prelatical Ordination do Null the Proteftant Miniftrie and Churches, then it muft needs follow that far greater defects (and more againft the vitals of the Church) will do as much to unchurch the Romanifts, the Greeks, Armenians, Syrians, Ethiopians, Egyptians, &c. But alas, how eafie is it to prove that all thefe have far greater defects then the Prefbyterian Proteftant Churches ! and fo the whole muft fall together.

Sect. 26. 20. By all thefe means they joyn with the Quakers, and Seekers, and Drunkards in oppofing the fame Miniftrie that they oppofe. *You are no true Minifters of Jefus Chrift*, fay the Quakers, Seekers, and other Sects ; fo alfo fay thefe that now we are fpeaking of : and if they preach their doctrine, and fide with them againft the fervants of Chrift, let them be afraid left they partake of their Spirit and Reward.

Sect. 27. 21. Their doctrine and practice tendeth to grieve the hearts of the moft experienced gracious fouls. Should all the Minifters be caft out that are not Prelatical, and the places fupplyed, as they muft be in their ftead, with fuch as can be had, O what a day would it be to honeft humble fouls, that were wont to delight themfelves in the publike worfhip of God, and to find inftruction, and admonition, and confolation futable to their neceffities ! If now they fhould have all turned to what the Doctrine of thefe men portends, their fouls would be as in a Wildernefs, and famine would confume them, and they would lament as *David* in his banifhment, and the Jews in their captivity, to think of the daies that once they faw.

Sect. 28. 22. And doth it not imply a great deal of *unholinefs* and *enmitie to Reformation*, when men dare thus boldly unchurch the moft of the Reformed Churches, and pafs fuch defperate nullifying cenfures on the moft holy, able, painful Minifters of the Gofpel? O how many of them are ftudying, and watch-

watching and praying for their people day and night, and teaching them publickly and from houſe to houſe, and that ſometimes with tears, willing to ſpend and be ſpent ſo their Salvation, not ſeeking theirs but them ; and when they have done all, they are reproached as no Miniſters of Chriſt, and the people taught to diſown them and forſake them. Is this a ſign of a ſon of God, that is tender of his honour and intereſt? or of a Holy Gracious ſoul?

Sect. 29. 23. At leaſt by this means the hands of Miniſters are weakned in their work, and their difficulties increaſed, and their hearts grieved, becauſe of their peoples miſery. O if they could have but a free unprejudiced hearing with poor ſinners ſome good might be done! But they will not bear us, nor come neer us, or ſpeak to us : Eſpecially when they are taught to forſake us by ſuch men. I would not be the man that ſhould thus add burden and grief to the faithful Miniſters of Chriſt, upon ſuch an account, for all the Biſhopricks on earth.

Sect. 30. 24 They alſo diſtract the minds of Chriſtians, when they bear men thus degrading and unchurching one another ; ſo that weak perſons are perplexed, and know not what to think nor what Church or Religion to be of: yea it is well if many be not tempted hereby to be of no Religion at all : when they hear them condemning one another.

Sect. 31. 25. Theſe ſhew too much formality and Ceremoniouſneſs, when they ſo much prefer their own opinon, about a circumſtance, Ceremony or Mode, before the very being of the Churches and Miniſtry, and the ſubſtance of worſhip it ſelf, and the Salvation of men ſouls : As if it were better for Churches to be no Churches, then not Prelatical Churches : or for ſouls to be condemned, then to be ſaved by men that are not Prelatical. I ſpeak not theſe things to exaſperate them (though I can expect no better :) but in the grief of my ſoul for the ſad condition that they would bring men into.

Sect. 32. 26. They lay a very dangerous ſnare, to draw Miniſters to be guilty of caſting off the work of God. Fleſh and blood would be glad of a fair pretence for ſo much liberty and eaſe. O how fain would it be unyoakt, and leave this labourious, diſpleaſing kind of life! And when ſuch as theſe ſhall perſwade them that they are no Miniſters, they may do much to

K k   gratifie

gratifie the flesh. For some will say, *I am at a loss, between both wayes; I cannot see the lawfulness of Prelacy: and yet they speak so confidently of the nullity of all other callings, that I will forbear till I am better resolved* Another will say, *I find my self to be no Minister, and therefore free from the Obligation to Ministerial Offices; and I will take heed how I come under that yoak again, till I have fuller resolution.* Another will scruple being *twice Ordained,* and so will think it safer to surcease. At least they tempt men to such resolutions, that would discharge them from so hard a work.

Sect. 33. 27. By this means also they make the breaches that are among us to be uncurable, and proclaim themselves utterly unreconcileable to the most of the Protestant Churches. For if they will have no reconciliation or communion with them, till they shall confess themselves no Churches, and cast off all their Ministers, they may as well say flatly, they will have none at all. For no reasonable man can imagine or expect that ever the Churches should yield to these terms. When they are declared no Ministers or Churches, you cannot then have Communion with them as Ministers or Churches.

Sect. 34. 28. And it is easie to see how much they befriend and encourage the Papists in all this. Is it not enough that you have vindicated the Pope from being the Antichrist, but you must also openly proclaim that *Rome* is a true Church, their Priests true Priests, their Ordinances and Administrations Valid, but all the Protestant Churches that are not Prelatical are indeed no Churches, their Ministers no Ministers, &c: Who would not then be a Papist rather then a member of such a Protestant Church? How can you more plainly invite men to turn Papists, unless you would do it expresly and with open face? Or how could you gratifie Papists more?

Sect. 35. 29. And truly if all these evils were accomplished, the Ministers forsaken, iniquity let loose, the Ordinances prophaned by unworthy men, &c. we could expect nothing but that the judgements of God should be poured out upon us for our Apostacy: and that temporal plagues involuntary should accompany the spiritual plagues that we have chosen! and that God should even forsake our land, and make us a by word and an

hissing

hissing to the Nations : and that his judgements should write as upon our doors, *This is the people that wilfully cast out the Ministers and mercies of the Lord.*

Sect. 36. 30 And if all this were but accomplished , in the Corclusion I may be bold to ask, *what would the Devil himself have more , except our damnation it self ?* If he were to plead his own cause , and to speak for himself, would he not say the very same as these Learned, Reverend Disputers do ? would he not say to all our graceless people, *Hear not these Ministers : they are no true Ministers: Joyn not in Communion with their Churches, they are no true Churches ?* I doubt not but he would say many of the same words, if he had leave to speak. And should not a man of any fear be afraid, and a man of any piety be unwilling to plead the very cause of Satan, and say as he would have them say, by accusing so many famous Churches and Ministers , as being none indeed, and drawing the people so to censure them and forsake them ; This is no work for a Minister of Christ.

Sect. 37. Besides what is here said, I desire those whom it doth concern, that are afraid of plunging themselves into the depth of guilt and horror, that they will impartially read over my first sheet for the Ministry, which further shews the aggravations of their sin that are now the opposers and reproachers of them. Consider them, and take heed.

Sect. 38. But again I desire these Brethren to believe, that as it is none of the Prelatical Divines that I here speak of, but those that thus nullifie our Church & Ministry, while they own the Ministry and Church of *Rome*; so it is none of my desire to provoke even these, or injure them in the least degree : But I could not in this sad condition of the Church, but propound these hainous evils to their consideration, to provoke them to try, and to take heed lest they should incur so great a load of guilt, while they think they are pleading for Order in the Church. How can there be any charity to the Church, or to our brethren in us, if we can see them in such a gulf of sin as this, and yet say nothing to them, for fear of provoking them to displeasure ?

Sect. 39. And I think it necessary that all young men that are cast by their arguings into temptations of falling with them into the same transgressions, should have the case laid open to them, that they may see their danger ; and not by the accusations of

Schism

Schism be led into far greater real Schism, with so many other sins as these.

Sect. 40. Yet is it not my intent to justifie any disorders or miscarriages that any have been guilty of in opposition to the Prelacie. And if they can prove that I have been guilty of any such thing my self, I shall accept of their reproof, and condemn my sin as soon as I can discern it. Only I must crave that the usual way of presumption, affirmation, or bare names of crimes be not supposed sufficient for Conviction, without proof, and before the cause is heard. And also I do profess that for all that I have here said against the English Prelacy, and though I earnestly desire it may never be restored, yet were I to live under it again, I would live peaceably and submissively, being obedient, and perswading others to obedience, in all things lawfull.

CHAP. IX.

The sinfulness of despising or neglecting Ordination.

Sect. 1. IT is a thing so common and hardly avoided, for men in opposing one extream, to seem to countenance the other, and for men that are convinced of the evil of one, to run into the other as the only truth, that I think it necessary here to endeavour the prevention of this miscarriage : and having said so much against the Necessity of Prelatical Ordination, and in some cases of any, I shall next shew the greatness

of

of their sin that despise or neglect Ordination when it may be had.

Sect. 2. For the right understanding of what is to be said, I must again remember you, that though it be not at the Ordainers will to deprive the Church of Ministers, and it is none of the Question which they have to resolve, *Whether the Church shall have Ministers or none* (and therefore there may be Ministers without them, if they would hinder or refuse ;) And though it be not the Question which is put to their decision, *What kind of Ministers the Church shall have* (for that Christ hath determined of ;) nor yet *what Qualifications are necessary to them,* (for that also Christ hath already set down ;) yet is it a great and weighty case that is put to the decision of Ordainers, that is, *Whether this man be thus qualified as Christ hath described and required in Ministers ?* and *whether he be the fittest person* (or fit at least) *for the particular charge to which he is called ?* And the right determining of this question is a thing that the Churches welfare doth very much depend upon.

Sect. 3. And therefore it is the decision of this one Question, that Ministers, People and Magistrates themselves, must all contribute their powers and endeavours too in their several places. All that they have to do is but to see that the Churches have fit men, even such as are qualified as God requireth. The *People* must *choose* fit men : or consent to them when chosen for them : The *Pastors* must *try them, and Approve them, and only them* that are fit : The *Magistrate* must *encourage, assist* and *defend* fit men, and forbid such as are intolerably unfit, and not permit them to abuse the name and Ordinances of Christ, and wrong his Church.

Sect. 4. This treble guard at the door of the Church doth much tend to its security, and preservation from the great evils that intruders may introduce. And each party of the three hath a special interest which should make them carefull of the businesse. 1. The *people* have great reason to have a hand in it, and to be carefull : For it is *their Souls* for which their Overseers watch, and *their Salvation* that is concerned in it. And he that will not trust his Son with any Tutor without due choice, nor his state with every Lawyer, nor his body with every Physician, no nor his land, or cattle with every servant, but will choose the

best,

beſt, hath reaſon to know upon whoſe care he truſteth his ſoul.
For though it may be ſome excuſe, it will be no juſtification of
them that lie in ſin and miſery, to ſay, *Our Teachers did miſ-
lead us.* For if the blind lead the blind, it is both that fall into
the ditch: And as *Cyprian* ſaith (with the reſt of his Col-
legues,) *Epiſt.* 68. (*alias Li.* 1. *Ep.* 4.) [*Propter quod plena
diligentia, exploratione ſincerâ oportet eos ad Sacerdotium delegi,
quos à Deo conſtet audiri. Nec ſibi plebs blandiatur, quaſi im-
munis eſſe a contagio delicti poſſit cum Sacerdote peccatore commu-
nicans, & ad injuſtum atq; illicitum prapoſiti ſui Epiſcopatum
conſenſum ſuum commodans,* &c. ————] Beſides the work
of the Miniſtry is Teaching and Perſwaſive, and the ſucceſs is only
on the *Willing*: and ſeeing we can do nothing on them for their
good againſt their wills, or without their *own Conſent*, it is needfull therefore that ſome way or other their *Conſent* ſhould be
procured, unleſs we would fruſtrate all our labour, and miſs our
end. And alſo, a Church is a *Society Voluntarily conjoined for holy
Worſhip and Living:* and therefore it is contrary to the nature of
it, that they ſhould have Paſtors, or be members and not *Conſent.*

Sect. 5. And 2. For the *Magiſtrate*, there is great reaſon
that he have his part alſo in the work: For the honour of God
muſt be his End; the Law of God his chiefeſt Rule; the
Church of Chriſt his chiefeſt ſubjects; and the work of Chriſt,
his chifeſt care and buſineſs. And ſeeing he Ruleth *from* Chriſt, and
by Chriſt, and *for* Chriſt, it is neceſſary that he take care of the
quality, and enterance, and carriage of Miniſters, on whom Chriſts
work and honour doth ſo much depend.

Sect. 6. Yet is there here a ſpecial difference between the works
of theſe ſeveral parties in admitting men into the Miniſtry. The
proper or neceſſary work of the people, is but to diſcern and conſent: Whether they be the firſt Electors, is a matter of indifferency in it ſelf, & is ſometime fit, and ſometime unfit. The Magiſtrates
work is not to Ordain Miniſters; but carefully to Overſee the
Ordainers and the People, that they put in none but worthy men:
And if he find that they miſcarry, he is not (ordinarily at leaſt)
to take the work upon him, and Ordain fitter men himſelf: but
to correct them to whom the work belongs, for their male-ad-
miniſtration, and reſtrain them from miſdoing, and urge them
by due means to do it better, or cauſe them to be diſplaced that
are

are unreformable, that better may be chosen in their stead, that will be faithfull.

Sect. 7. And 3. The reason of the Ministers interest in the work, I shall more at large lay down anon. And though there be a possibility of frequent differences arising, through disagreement of these three several parties, yet Christ would rather use this treble guard for caution, then for the preventing of division, lay open his Church to the injury of intruders.

Sect. 8. And remember again, that it is not in the Power of Magistrates, Ordainers, People and all to make a Minister of Christ, of a man that wanteth the Essential Qualifications: *Ex quovis ligno non fit Mercurius.* He that is not qualified for the works Essential to a Minister, cannot by Ordination be made a Minister: No more then the bare stamp can make currant money of a piece of lead, when the Law makes the Mettal Essential to currant Coin: And no more then a license will make him a Schoolmaster that cannot read: or him a Pilot, that knows not how to Rule the ship: saith *Cyprian ubi sup.* [*Sed enim desiderio huic vestro, non tam nostra concilia, quam Divina præcepta respondent; quibus jampridem mandatur voce cælesti, & Dei lege præscribitur, quos & quales oporteat deservire altari, & Sacrificia Divina celebrare.* (Here he citeth Scripture) *Quæ cum prædicta & manifesta sint nobis, præceptis Divinis necesse est obsequia nostra deserviant: Nec personam in ejusmodi rebus accipere, aut aliquid cuiquam largiri potest humana indulgentia ubi intercedit, & legem tribuit Divina præscriptio.*] God gives not men authority to contradict his Law, or to Ordain a man uncapable of Ordination; nor introduce the form, where the matter is undisposed for it.

Sect. 9. Perhaps some will ask, *What should be done, in case that these three parties disagree: If the Magistrate would have one man, and the Ordainers another, and the people a third, or if two of them go one way, and the third another?* To which I answer, There are many things that must be taken into consideration for the right resolving of the case. Either the persons nominated are equal or unequal: Either they are all capable, or some of them uncapable: Either the welfare of that Church dependeth on the choice: or else it may be somewhat an indifferent case.
1. If there be but one Minister to be had, and the Dissenters
would

would have none, then it is paſt controverſie, that the Diſſenters are to be diſobeyed. 2. If one party would have a Godly, Able Miniſter, and the other would have an incapable, intolerable perſon, then it is paſt doubt, that the party that is for the worthy perſon ought to prevail, and it is his duty to inſiſt upon it, and the duty of the reſt to yield to him. 3. If any will make a controverſie in this caſe where there is none, and ſay, [*You ſay this man is fitteſt, and I ſay the other man* (that is uncapable) *is fitteſt, and who ſhall be judge ?*] The party that is in the right muſt hold to their duty, till they are perſecuted from it, and appeal to God, who will judge in equity. If a blind man ſay to a man that hath his eye-ſight [*You ſay that you ſee ; and I ſay that I ſee ; you ſay that it is day, and I ſay it is night ; who ſhall be believed?*] It is not ſuch words that will warrant a wiſe man to renounce his eye-ſight. God will judge him to be in the right that is ſo indeed. 4. But if really the ſeveral parties are for ſeveral Miniſters that are *all tolerable*, yet if there be any notable difference in their fitneſs, the parties that are for the leſs fit, ſhould yield to the party that is for the more fit. If you ſay, *They diſcern it not*, I anſwer, that is their ſin, which will not juſtifie them in a further ſin, or excuſe them from a duty. They *might* diſcern, if they were not culpable, in ſo great a difference, at leaſt whom they are bound to take for the moſt fit. 5. But if there be no great inequality, then theſe Rules ſhould be obſerved. 1. The *Magiſtrate* ſhould not deny the people their *Liberty* of choice, nor the *Miniſters* their *Liberty* in Approbation or diſſallowance : but only *Overſee* them all, that they faithfully do their ſeveral duties. 2. The *Miniſters* ſhould not hinder the people from their *Choice*, where both parties nominated are fit, but content themſelves with their proper work. 3. The *People* ſhould not *inſiſt* upon their *choice*, if the *Miniſters* to whom it belongeth, do diſallow the *perſon*, and take him to be unmeet, and refuſe to ordain him : becauſe obedience in ſuch caſes is their duty, and a duty that cannot tend to their loſs : at leaſt not to ſo much hurt to them as the contrary irregular courſe may prove to the Church. 4. If Magiſtrates or Miniſters would make the firſt *choice*, and urge the people to *conſent* if the perſon be fit, it is the ſafeſt way for the people to obey and conſent, though it were better for

the

the Rulers to give them more freedom in the choice. 5. If a people be generally ignorant (in too great a measure,) and addicted to unworthy men, or apt to divisions, &c. it is their safest way to desire the *Ministers* to choose for them. Or if they will not do so, it is the safest way for the Ministers to offer them a man: Yet so that Magistrates and Ministers should expect their *Consent*, and not set any man over them as their Pastor without consent some way procured. 6. But if they are *no Church*, but uncalled persons, and it be not a *Pastor of a Church*, but a *Preacher to Convert men*, and fit them for a Church-state, that is to be settled, then may the *Magistrate* settle such a man, and force the people to hear him preach. 7. If *Necessity* require not the contrary, the matter should be delayed, till Magistrate, Ministers and people do agree. 8. The chosen Pastors should decide the case themselves : They should *not accept* the place, and *Consent*, till all be agreed, unless there be a Necessity. And if there be, then the greatest necessity should most sway. If the Magistrate resist, he will forciby prohibite and hinder you from preaching. If the Ministers resist, they will deny you the right hand of fellowship. If the people resist, they will not hear nor join in worship nor obey. All these if possible should be avoided. The Peoples consent (to a Pastor of a Church) is of Necessity. We cannot do the work of Pastors without it. And therefore neither Magistrates or Ministers can drive us on where this is wanting (unless it be only to seek it, or only to do the work of Preachers to men without.) Unity and Communion with Neighbour-Churches is so much to be desired, that nothing but Necessity can warrant us to go on without it. And the Magistrates restraint is so great a hinderance, that nothing but Necessity can warrant us to cast our selves upon it. And therefore out of cases of Necessity, the Ministers nominated should not consent till all agree : But in cases of Necessity, the souls of men and the worship of God, must not be disregarded or neglected, though neighbour-Churches or Ministers disown us, or Magistrates persecute us.

Sect. 10. Remember these Distinctions for the understanding of what follows. 1. Its one thing to be Approved, and another thing to be solemnly Invested. Ordination consisteth of these two parts. 2. We must difference between Ordination, by one

L l
Pastor,

Pastor, and by many. 3. Between Ordination by Pastors of the same Church, or of many Churches. 4. Between Ordination by sufficient or insufficient Ministers. 5. And between Ordnation by Neighbour Ministers or Strangers. 6. And between Ordination by Divided Ministers, and Concordant. On these premised I propose as followeth.

Sect. 11. *Prop.* 1. Approbation by Ministers is ordinarily to be sought and received by all that will enter into the Ministry. I gave some Reasons before, *Chap.* 2. Which here I shall enlarge, by which the sinfulness of Neglecting this Approbation may appear.

Sect. 12. Reas. 1. It is the way that God hath appointed us in Holy Scripture, and therefore to be followed. They that Ordained Elders or Bishops in the Churches, did more then Approve them, but could do no less, 1 *Tim.* 4. 14. *Timothy* was ordained by the Imposition of the hands of the Presbyterie, 1 *Tim.* 3. 15. *Paul* giveth *Timothy* the description of Bishops and Deacons, that he may know how he ought to behave himself in the house of God, which is the Church, *&c.* That is, that he may know whom to Approve of or Ordain, *Tit.* 1. 5. *Titus* was to Ordain Elders in every City, *Acts* 13. 1, 2, 3. The Prophets and Teachers in the Church at *Antioch* did separate *Barnabas* and *Paul* to the work, with Fasting and Prayer, and imposition of hands. It was the Apostles that Ordained them Elders in every Church, *Acts* 14. 23. Suppose it must be read [by Suffrages] as many would have it, that proveth no more but that the People did consent : But still it is *Paul* and *Barnabas* that Ordained them Elders, though with the peoples suffrages, and it is they that are said to fast and pray in the next words. *Act.* 6. 3. Expresly shews that the People chose the Deacons, and the Apostles ordained them [Look ye out among your selves seven men of honest report, full of the Holy Ghost and wisdom, whom *we* may appoint over this business.] But I shall cut short this part of my task, because so much is said of it already by many that have written for Ordination, to whom I shall refer you.

Sect. 13. Reas. 2. If there be not a standing regular way for Trying and Approving such as enter into the Ministry, then men will be left to be their own judges, and if they can but get the

consent

confent of any Congregation, will prefenty be Paftors. But this courfe would tend to the ruine or confufion of the Church, as I fhall manifeft by evidence.

Sect. 14. 1. If all men may enter into the Miniftry that will, upon their own perfwafion that they are fit, the moft proud, felf-conceited, worthlefs men will be the readieft to go, and if t ey can get hearers, will moft abound in the Church; and the people will quickly have heaps of Teachers. For we all know that many of the Ignorant are leaft acquainted with their ignorance: and commonly the Proud have the higheft thoughts of them-felves, and think none fo fit to Teach and Rule as they. And what could be more to the fhame and hazzard of the Church, then to have it taught and guided by fuch ignorant unworthy men?

Sect. 15. 2. Moreover, Humble men are fo confcious of their weaknefs, and fenfible of the burden and greatnefs of the work, that they think themfelves unworthy, and therefore would draw back; and fo by their forbearance would give way to the forefaid proud intruders. And thus the Church would foon be darkened, defiled, and brought low, if all men were their own judges.

Sect. 16. 3. Moreover, it is the common difpofition of Er-roneous and Heretical perfons to be exceeding zealous for the propagating of their errors, and bringing as many as is pofsible to their mind. So that if all be left to themfelves, the moft He-retical will run firft, and carry their filth into the houfe of God, and feduce and undo men inftead of faving them.

Sect. 17. 4. By this means alfo the Covetous and fordid worldlings will crowd in: and men will do by Preaching, as they do by Ale-felling, even make it their laft Trade when others fail: and he that breaks in any other Trade, if he have but any volubility of fpeech, will prefently turn Prieft; till the Office and Ordinances of God feem vile, and be abhorred by the people. This muft be the Confequent if all be left to their own judgement.

Sect. 18. 5. And it is too known a cafe, that the people will bid fuch perfons welcome, and fo they will make a match. The erroneous and giddy party will have fuch as are futable to them. And the Covetous party will have him that will do their work beft cheap: if they will preach for nothing or for little, he

shall

ſhall be a man for them, though he would lead them to perdition. If it be poyſon, they'l take it, if it coſt them nothing. And
many there be that will have their own kindred or friends to
make Prieſts of; and all that they have intereſt in muſt joyn
with them on the account of friendſhip. And the childiſh injudicious ſort of Chriſtians will follow them that have the
ſmootheſt tongues, or beſt opportunities and advantages to prevail with them. And ſo they will *be toſſed up and down, and carryed to and fro with every wind of doctrine, according to the cunning
ſleight and ſubtilty of men, by which they lie in wait to deceive.*]
Eph. 4. 14. *And they will be carried about with divers and
ſtrange doctrines,* Heb. 13. 9.

Sect. 19. Reaſ. 3. And when the *Miniſtrie* is thus corrupted (by making every man judge of his own fitneſs) the
Church will be corrupted, and degenerate into a common ſtate,
and ceaſe to be a Church (if Reformation do not ſtop the gan-
grene.) For it commonly goeth with the Church according to
the quality of the Miniſtrie. An ignorant Miniſtrie, and an ignorant people; an erroneous Miniſtrie, and an erring people;
a ſcandalous Miniſtrie, and a ſcandalous people commonly go
together. Like Prieſt, like people is the common caſe.

Sect. 20. Reaſ. 4. And by this means Chriſtianity it ſelf
will be diſhonoured, and ſeem to be but a common religion, and ſo
but a deceit, to the great diſhonour of Jeſus Chriſt; for the
world will judge of him and his cauſe, by the lives of them that
teach it and profeſs it.

Sect. 21. Reaſ. 5. And by this means God will be provoked to depart from us, and be avenged on us for our diſhonour-
ing him. If he would ſpew out of his mouth lukewarm *Laodicea,* what would he do to ſuch degenerate ſocieties? If moſt of
the ſeven Churches, *Rev.* 2 & 3. had their warnings or threatnings for ſmaller faults, what would ſuch corruptions bring us
to, but even to be plagued or forſaken by the Lord?

Sect. 22. Reaſ. 6. If you ſhould be men of ability and
fitneſs for the work your ſelves, that enter without Approbation
and Ordination, yet others might be encouraged by your example that are unfit: and if you once thus ſet open the door, you
know not how to keep out woolves and ſwine: all the perſons
before deſcribed will take the opportunity, and ſay, *Why may*

not

not we enter unordained, as well as such and such?

Sect. 23. Reas. 7. By this means also you will leave many sober godly persons unsatisfied in your Ministry, as not knowing whether they may own you as Ministers or not; & how much you should do to avoid such offence, me thinks you might perceive.

Sect. 24. Reas. 8. By this course also you will walk contrary to the Catholike Church of Christ, and that in a cause where you cannot reasonably pretend any necessity of so doing. Ever since Christ had a Ministry on earth, the constant (ordinary) way of their admittance hath been by Ministerial Ordination. If any man despise this, and be contentious, we have no such Custome, nor the Churches of God. Is it a design beseeming an humble man, a Christian, a sober man, to find out a new way of making Ministers now in the end of the world? as if all the Ministers from the Apostles dayes till now, had come in at a wrong door, and wanted a true Calling? This is too near the making a New Ministry: and that's too near the Making of a new Church: and that's too near the feigning of a new Christ. The Church hath many promises, that the gates of Hell shall not prevail against it; that Christ will be with her Ministers to the end of the world, they being given by him for the perfecting of the Saints, and edifying of the Body of Christ, till we all come in the unity of the faith, and knowledge of the Son of God, to a perfect man, &c. Eph. 4. 12, 13. And therefore we must not easily believe, that the Ministry of the universal Church have been falsly called or admitted untill now, and you have found out a better way at last.

Sect. 25. Reas. 9. You would bring that irrational confusion into the Church of the living God, which is not to be introduced into the basest Commonwealth or society in the world. You have more wit then to let all men play the Physitians: but will first have them tryed by men of their own Profession: or else the lives of many may pay for your Licentiousness. You will have Schoolmasters approved by them that have Learning, before you will commit your children to their trust. And shall every man be a Teacher and Ruler that will in the Church of Christ, as if it were the only confused contemptible Society in the world? God is not the God of Confusion, but of Peace, as in all the Churches, faith the Apostle, 1 Cor. 14. 33.

Sect.

Sect. 26. Reas. 10. Do but consider how high, and holy, and honourable a Calling it is to be a Minister of the Gospel: and then it will appear, that it is horrible Profanation of Holy things, to suffer all that will, to invade it. They are to be the Embassadors of Christ, and speak as in his Name, and to be Stewards of his Mysteries and Houshold, and to stand near him, as at his altar, and to dispense his treasure, to magnifie and praise his Name, and to administer his holy Sacraments, &c. And should all that will, be taught to usurp or invade such an holy Calling?

Sect. 27. Reas. 11. Consider also, how great a *Trust* it is that is committed to all that are Ministers of the Gospel. The souls of men are committed to them : the Mysteries of God, the precious promises and glad tidings of Salvation are committed to them : the order and affairs of the house of God are committed to them : those that are Christs Sheep, his Jewels, his Friends, his Brethren, his Spouse, his Members, and as the apple of his eye, are committed to them. And is it sutable to so great a Trust, that men untryed, unapproved, that do but think well of themselves, and their own doings, shall at their pleasure take so great a charge? What man of honour and wit among you, will give every man leave to be your Steward, that hath but folly and pride enough to think himself fit for it? and will not rather choose your Stewards your selves?

Sect. 28. Reas. 12. And is it not evidently notorious Cruelty to the souls of men, to cast them upon every unworthy fellow that will but be impudent enough to undertake the charge? Do you set so light by mens everlasting Joy or Torment? You would not so contemptuously cast away mens lives : and will you so contemptuously cast away their souls? And what a contempt is it of the blood of Christ, that the purchase made by it should be thus neglected? You will lock up your money, and look to your goods, and take care of every groat of your estates : and shall the souls of men, and the blood and the inheritance of Christ be no more regarded? This is unjust.

Sect. 29. Reas. 13. Yea and it is a way of Cruelty to the men themselves, if every man that is sick of self-conceit, or Pride, shall have leave to exercise it, and run themselves into unspeakable guilt, by undertaking such works as they are no way able for : Alas, have not these poor sinners transgressions

enough

enough of their own already, but you must encourage them to draw the blood of souls, and the sins of so many others upon their heads? O what a burden do they take upon them! and what a dreadful danger do they run into? Had you faith and any pitty of souls, you would rather study to do your best, to prevent mens destroying of themselves and others, and falling altogether into the ditch. I know you'l say, that you are guilty of no such thing : it is the saving, and not the destroying of souls that you intend by being Ministers unordained : but your intentions will not justifie your cruel and destructive practices. Its plain that you teach men by your doctrine and example to be their own judges of their fitness for the Ministry, or to neglect the judgement of the Pastors of the Church : and what better can this course produce?

Sect. 30. Reas. 14. Either you are fit for the Ministry, or unfit : if fit ; why should you be afraid of tryal? He that doth evil comes not to the light : it is a sign of an ill cause that cannot endure a just tryal. But if you are unfit, is it not better to forbear?

Sect. 31. Reas. 15. Your very refusing of a tryal doth give the people sufficient reason to question your call and fitness for the work, or your humility at least : for humble men think meanlyer of themselves, then to judge themselves meet for such great employments, when they have not the encouragement of men that are more fit to judge : the good men of old were wont to run away from a Bishoprick, or Pastoral dignity in the sense of their unfitness : so that the Bishops were fain to seek and send after them : and *Gregory* of *Neocesarea* was Ordained by *Phedimus* when he was three daies journey from him, even against his will ; and then charged by him in the name of Christ to yield unto the Call. And what then shall we think of that sort of men, that think themselves so good and worthy, as to run on their own heads, without due approbation?

Sect. 32. Reas. 16. It is natural for man to be *Partial* in his own Cause : insomuch as no law or equity will allow men to be witnesses or judges for themselves in the smallest civil controversie : and shall they be judges of themselves in so great a cause? Are not others more impartial?

Sect. 33. Reas. 17. You cast away your own encouragement

ment and support, and create vexation to your own Consciences. There are so many difficulties to be conquered in this work,
and so many sufferings to be endured, that if a man be not clear
that his Call was good, he is like to be left to great discomforts.
We have exceeding great labours to undergo : we have abundance of enemies and impediments to strive with : we have
many a scorn and unthankful return, and perhaps imprisonment
or death to undergo: we are our selves, alas, too weak and insufficient, and must depend on God for daily helps. And with what
confidence can you expect his help, if you Call your selves, and
enter not by his Approbation ? And how will you ever go
through all this, and suffer so much with Christian comfort, when
you cannot say that you are sent of God, and have nothing
but your own overweening conceits of it ? Could you but say,
[I entered by the way that God appointed, and was not my
own Judge] you might have some more boldness and confidence
of Gods assistance.

Sect. 34. Reas. 18. The most that plead against Ordination,
that are worthy the name of sober Christians, do plead but
against the *Necessity* of it, and cannot deny it to be *lawful* : and
should not all the reasons before mentioned prevail with you to
submit to a *lawful* thing ?

Sect. 35. Reas. 19. And if it be thus undenyable, that men
must not be their *own* Judges, it will soon appear that *Ministers*
are the standing Judges of mens fitness for this work, because
no other Judges are appointed to it, or capable of it. It must be
an ordinary stated way of Approbation, that can give us satisfaction : for if God had left the case at large, for men to go to
whom they will, it would be all one as to go to none at all, but
to be Judges themselves. And if a standing way of Approbation must be acknowledged, let us enquire where it is to be found :
and look which way you will, and you shall find no other, but
this which is by men of the same Calling with them that are to
be Ordained.

Sect. 36. For 1. Magistrates it cannot be : none that I know
pretend to that. Magistrates in most of the world are Infidels :
and therefore cannot there be Ordainers : and none of them
hath the work committed to them by Christ, nor do any that I
know, assume it to themselves.

Sect.

Sect. 37. And 2. The people it cannot be : For 1. No man can shew a word of precept or example for it ; nor prove that ever God did give them such a power : Consent or Election is all that can be pretended to by them. 2. It is a work that they are commonly unable for : the Schollars may as well Try and Approve of their Schoolmaster. We confess the People must by a judgement of discretion, endeavour to find out the best they can : but if they had not helps, and if they were also called to a judgement of direction and decision, what work would they make ? Do the Major vote, (or the Minor either) in most or almost any Congregations, understand whether a man know the meaning of the Scripture, or be able to defend the truth, or whether he be Heretical or sound in the faith, &c. ? God would not set men on a work that is thus beyond the line of their Capacity. It is a thing not to be imagined, that they that call us to be their Teachers, should already be commonly able to Judge whether we are sound or unsound, and able to teach them or not : for this importeth that they know already as much as we (for wherein they are ignorant, they cannot judge of us.) And if they know as much already, what need have they of our Teaching ? 3. And it is contrary to the subjection and inferiority of their Relation : they that are commanded to learn and obey us as their Guides, may yet consent or choose their Teachers, when Approved, or to be Approved by abler men ; but they cannot be imagined to be appointed by God to Ordain their own Overseers : this is a most ungrounded fiction.

Sect. 38. Reas. 20. On the other side, it is the Pastors of the Church, and only they that are fitted to be the standing Approvers or Ordainers, as will appear in these particulars. 1. It is they that are justly supposed to be of competent abilities to try a Minister. If here and there a Gentleman or other person be able, that is a rarity, and therefore no standing way for the Church in Ordaining Ministers can be gathered thence. 2. Ministers are doubly devoted to God and to his Church : and therefore should have, and ordinarily have, the tenderest care of the Church. 3. It is justly supposed that Ministers are ordinarily the most pious and conscionable men that are to be had (or els they are too blame that choose them to be Ministers) And therefore they may be expected to be most faithful in the work. 4. And

Mm

they

they are fewer, and have leſſer perverting intereſts, and therefore are like to be leſs divided in ſuch determinations, then the people that are ſo many, and of ſo many intereſts and minds, that if it were not for the Moderation of Magiſtrates and Miniſters, they would almoſt everywhere be all to pieces, one being for one man, and another for another ; ſome for one of this mind and way, and ſome for one of another ; ſome for the Orthodox, and ſome for the Heretical. 5. Laſtly, it is Miniſters, whoſe Office God hath tyed Ordination to, and who have time to wait upon it as their duty : ſo that lay all this together, and I think the firſt Propoſition is proved, for the Neceſſity (ordinarily) of the Paſtors Approbation, and the ſinfulneſs of neglecting it.

Sect. 39. Prop. 2. It is not only the Paſtors of one particular Church, but alſo the Paſtors of Neighbour churches that hold Communion with that Church, that ſhould regularly Approve or Ordain Miniſters : though I deny not but he may be a Miniſter that hath no Ordination but by the Paſtors of a particular Church, yet I conceive that this is not a regular courſe.

Sect. 40. My reaſons are theſe. 1. Becauſe if it be ordinarily tyed to the Paſtors of the ſame Church only to Ordain, then it will be done ordinarily without any Paſtors at all. For moſt particular Churches in the world have but one Paſtor : and when he is dead, there is none left to Ordain ; and therefore others, or none muſt do it in ſuch caſes.

Sect. 41. And 2. If there be one left, and all the power be left in him, the welfare of the Church would run too great an hazzard : if every man ſhall be Ordained a Miniſter that can procure the Approbation of a ſingle Paſtor, the Church will be ſubjected to moſt of the lamentable miſeries before mentioned, ſuppoſing that men were judges for themſelves.

Sect. 42. And 3. We find in Scripture, that it was not the way appointed by the Holy Ghoſt, for ſingle Paſtors to Ordain. The forecited Texts and examples are a ſufficient proof.

Sect. 43. If any ſay, that the Ruling Elders may concur, I anſwer. Though I make no great matter of it, nor would not raiſe a contention about it, yet I muſt ſay, that I never yet ſaw any ſatisfactory proof, that ever God did inſtitute ſuch Elders

as

as this Objection meaneth, in the Church: that is, 1. Such as are not Ordained, but come in by meer Election. 2. And such as have the Power of Discipline and Oversight without Authority to preach or administer the Sacraments. I think these are but humane creatures; though I doubt not but there may be such as *Actually* shall *forbear* preaching and administration of the Sacraments, when some of their colleagus are fitter for it.

Sect. 44. But 2. If such an Office *can* be proved, I despair of seeing it proved from Scripture, that they have authority to *Ordain*. 3. And how can they have *Authority*, when most of them have not *Ability?* And I think it is supposed that they have not *Ability to Preach*, in them that deny them *Authority:* and if they want *Ability to Preach*, its two to one but they want Ability to *Try and Approve of Preachers*. 4. And how come they to have Power to Ordain others, that are not Ordained themselves, but are admitted upon bare Election? 5. And this course would prostitute the Churches to unworthy men, as aforesaid.

Sect. 45. And 4. It is not a contemptible Consideration, that the chief Pastor of every particular Church, hath ever since the second Century at least, been Ordained by the Pastors of other Churches. And how it was before, we have but very defective Evidence, except so much as is left us in the Holy Scriptures, of which we have spoke before.

Sect. 46. And 5. The Church of Christ is a Chain of many links: a Society united in Christ the Head, consisting as a Republike of many Corporations, or as an Acedemy of many Colledges: and a greater Union and Communion is requisite among them, then among the parts of any other Society in the world. And therefore seeing it is the duty of Neighbour Pastors and Churches, according to their Capacity to hold Communion with that particular Church and its Pastors, it seems reasonable, that they have some antecedent Cognisance and Approbation of the persons that they are to hold Communion with.

Sect. 47. And 6. It is considerable also, that whoever is according to Christs institution Ordained a Minister of a particular Church, is withall (if not before) Ordained a *Minister simply*; that is, one that may as a separated Messenger of Christ, both preach for the Conversion of those without, and gather Churches where there are none, and *pro tempore* do the Office

of

of a Minifter, to any part of the Catholike Church, where he cometh and hath a Call. And therefore as he is fimply a Minifter, and the Unconverted world, or the Univerfal Church are the Objects of his Miniftry, the Paftors or Members of that particular Church where he is fettled, have no more to do in Ordaining him then any other. As a Corporation may choofe their own Phyfitian, Schoolmafter, &c. but cannot do any more then other men, in Licenfing a man to be in general a Phyfitian, Schoolmafter, &c. So may a Church choofe who fhall be *their Teacher*, but not who fhall be fimply *a Teacher* or Minifter of Chrift, any more then an other Church may do, that's further from him.

Sect. 48. And 7. It is alfo confiderable, that it is the fafeft and moft fatisfactory way to the Church and to the Minifter himfelf, to have the *Approbation of many*. And it may leave more fcruple concerning our Call, when one or two or a particular Church only do Approve us.

Sect. 49. And 8. It is granted in their writings by thofe that are for Ordination by a particular Church only, that the Concurrence of more is *Lawful*: and if Lawful, I leave it to Confideration, whether all the forementioned accidents make it not fo far convenient, as to be ordinarily a plain duty, and to be preferred where it may be had.

Sect. 50. Yet do I not plead for Ordination by Neighbour Paftors, as from a Governing Authority over that particular Church: but as from an intereft in the Church Univerfal, and all its Officers within their reach, and from an intereft of Communion with Neighbour Churches.

Sect. 51. And it is obfervable in Scripture, that the Itinerant Minifters, that were fixed and appropriated to no particular Church, for continuance, (fuch as the Apoftles and Evangelifts were, and *Titus*, *Timothy*, and fuch others) had a Principal hand in the work of Ordination whereever they came. It was they that Ordained Elders in every City, in every Church.

Sect. 52. *Prop.* 3. If any fhall cull out two or three or more of the weakeft injudicious, facile Minifters, and procure them to Ordain him; his courfe is irregular, and his call unfatisfactory, though the formal part be obtained to the full. For it is not for meer formality, but to fatsfie the perfon called, and the
Church,

Church, and to secure the Ministry and sacred works and souls of men, from injury by Usurpers, that God hath appointed the way of Ordination: And therefore it is fraud, and not obedience, for any man so to use it, as to cheat himsef and the Church with a formality, and frustrate the Ordinance, and miss its ends.

Sect. 53. *Prop.* 4. If any man, avoiding the Orthodox and Unanimous Ministry, shall apply himself for Ordination to some divided schismatical or heretical persons, that will Approve him, and Ordain him, when the others would reject him, this also, as the former, is fraud and self-deceit, and not obedience; upon the last mentioned grounds. It is the basest treacherous kind of sinning, to turn Gods Ordinances against himself, and to sin under the shelter and pretence of an institution. By using the means in opposition to its end, they make it no means, and use it not as a means at all. Though Pastors must Ordain, yet is it not all kind of Pastors Ordination that should satisfie an honest meaning man; but that which hath the qualifications suited to the Rule and end.

Sect. 54. In such cases of unjust entrance, if the People sinfully comply, and the man have possession, it may be the duty of some particular persons, that cannot help it, (having done their own parts in disowning it) to submit, and not therefore to separate from the Church, except in desperate extraordinary cases (not now to be enumerated:) And all the administrations of such a man shall be not only Valid to the innocent, but without any scruple of conscience may be used and received, with expectation of a promised blessing.

Sect. 55. But yet *quoad debitum* it is the Churches duty (except in Cases of Necessity,) to disown such intruders, and to suspect and suspend obedience, to those that indirectly enter, (by a few ignorant, or schismatical Ordainers, refusing the tryal of the unanimous abler Orthodox Ministry) till they have either perswaded the man to procure their Approbation, or have themselves sought the Judgement of the said United Ministers concerning him. And seeing all the Churches of Christ should be linkt and jointed together, and hold communion and correspondency, according to their capacities, the Members of a particular Church are bound in reason, and to

those

those ends, to advise in such suspicious cases with neighbour Churches, and not to receive a Pastor that comes in by way of Discord, or that neglecteth or refuseth the concordant way. For he that entreth in a divisive way, is like to govern them accordingly, and still to shun the Communion of the Brethren.

Sect. 56. This *Cyprian* fully shews in the fore-mentioned *Ep.* 68. p. 201. perswading the people to shun the unworthy though they were Ordained by Bishops, adding [*Ordinari nonnunquam indignos, non secundum Dei voluntatem, sed secundum humanam præsumptionem; & hæc Deo displicere, quæ non veniant ex legitima & justa Ordinatione, Deus ipse manifestat, &c.* ─────] Necessity may justifie some things that otherwise would be irregularities : but when [*Per urbes singulas* (that is, in every Church) *Ordinati sint Episcopi, in ætate antiqui, in fide integri, in pressura probati, in persecutione proscripti, ille super eos creare alios pseudo-Episcopos audeat*] this is a fact that the poeple should disown. And [*Qui neq; unitatem spiritus nec conjunctionem pacis observat, & se ab Ecclesiæ vinculo, atq; à Sacerdotum collegio separat, Episcopi nec potestatem potest habere, nec honorem, qui Episcopatus nec unitatem voluit tenere, nec pacem. Cyprian Epist. 52. ad Antonian.*

Sect. 57. *Prop.* 5. Solemn Investiture is the last part of Ordination, by which the man that by consent of the people and himself, and by the Pastors Approbation, had received from Christ a Right to the Power, and Honour, and Priviledges, and an Obligation to the Duties of the Office, is solemnly introduced and put in Possession of the place.

Sect. 58. Though in some cases a man may exercise the Ministry upon the foresaid Approbation and Election (which are most necessary) without this solemn investiture, yet is it ordinarily a duty, and not to be neglected : And the people should require the performance of it : I need not stand upon the Proof : for it is proved before by what was said for Approbation, seeing they have ever gone together. Though fundamentally he be a Christian that hath entered Covenant with Christ : yet before the Church he is Visibly no Christian that hath not been Baptized, or at least made open Profession of that Covenant. Though *fundamentally* they are Husband and Wife that are contracted, or knit together by private Consent ; yet *in foro Civili,* in Law sense, fence, and before men, they muſt be ſolemnly married, or elſe they are judged fornicators. And ſhould any fantaſtical perſons ſeek to caſt by this publick inveſtiture or ſolemn Marriage, as unneceſſary, he would but let in common Whoredoms : The ſolemnity or publication in ſuch Caſes is of great Neceſſity. And its much conducible to the greater obligation of Paſtor and people to be ſolemnly engaged together: and to have ſolemn Prayer for Gods bleſſing, tendeth to their proſperity.

Sect. 59. When men are Ordained only to the Miniſtry in General, it may be done in one place as well as another, (that is otherwiſe convenient.) But if they are alſo Ordained to be Paſtors of a Particular Church, it is the fitteſt way by far, that they be Ordained in the face of the Church, that the people and they may be mutually engaged, &c. Though yet this be not abſolutely neceſſary.

Sect. 60. And thus I have diſpacht, with the brevity intended, this weighty point, concluding with theſe two requeſts to my Brethren that ſhall peruſe it : 1. That before they let out their diſpleaſure againſt me for contradicting any of their conceits, they would humbly, impartially, and with modeſt ſelf-ſuſpicion, both ſtudy and pray over what they read, and not temerariouſly ruſh into the battell as pre-engaged men. 2. That they will alway keep the faith and charity, and ſelf-denyal and tenderneſs of Chriſtians upon their hearts, and the great Ends and Intereſt of Chriſt and Chriſtianity before their eyes; and take heed how they venture upon any controverted points or practice, as a Means that certainly contradicteth *the Spirit of Chriſtianity*, and the *great Ends* (the Churches Unity, Peace and Holineſs, &c.] which all true means are appointed, and muſt be uſed to attain. And *whereunto we have already attained, let us walk by the ſame Rule, and mind the ſame things*, Phil. 3. 16. *Remembring that in Chriſt Jeſus neither circumciſion availeth, nor uncircumciſion, but a new creature. And as many as walk according to this Rule, Peace be on them and Mercy, and on the Iſrael of God*, Gal. 6. 15, 16.

Finitur, May 19. 1658.

The Third
DISPUTATION:
FOR

Such sorts of Episcopacy, or
Disparity in Exercise of the Ministry, as is Desirable or Conducible to the Peace and Reformation of the Churches.

By *Richard Baxter.*

LONDON,

Printed by *Robert White,* for *Nevill Simmons,* Bookseller in *Kederminster, Anno Dom.* 1658.

AN

Epiſcopacy Deſirable for the Reformation, Preſervation, and Peace of the Churches.

CHAP. I.

Of General unfixed Biſhops or Miniſters.

§. 1. T is but deluſory dealing of them that make the world believe that the queſtion between the Prelatical Divines and the reſt of the Reformed Churches, is, *Whether the Church ſhould be Governed by Biſhops?* This is a thing that is commonly granted : But the controverſie is about the *Species of Epiſcopacy :* Not whether Biſhops,

but

but *what sort* of Bishops should be the ordinary Governours of the Church of Christ?

§. 2. And therefore it is also very immethodical and unsatisfactory of most that ever I read for Episcopacy, that plead only for *Episcopacy in General,* but never once *define* that sort of Episcopacy which they plead for, but go away with it as smoothly when the question is unstated, as if they understood themselves, and others were capable of understanding them; and so they lose their Learned labours.

§. 3. I have already in the first Disputation told you among ten several sorts of Episcopacy, which they be that I think desirable, and which I judge tolerable, and which intolerable. And I have there already given you the Reasons why I judge such a general unfixed Bishop to be of standing use to the Church and world, as here we are speaking of: and therefore I shall forbear here the repeating of what is said already.

§. 4. That the world and Church should still have such a *General Itinerant unfixed Ministry,* as that was of the *Apostles, Evangelists* and others, having there already proved, I have nothing to do more but to shew the use of it, and to answer the objections that some very learned Reverend Divines have used against it.

§. 5. The principal use of a general Ministry, is for the converting of the unconverted world, and Baptizing them when converted, and Congregating their Converts into Church order, and setling them under a fixed Government. And the next use of them is, to have a Care, according to the extent of their capacity and opportunities, of the Churches which they have thus Congregated and setled, and which are setled by other Ministers.

§. 6. Let it be remembred that we are not now disputing of the *Name;* but of the *Thing* : It is not whether such an Officer of Christ be to be called *an Apostle* or an *Evangelist,* or a *Prophet,* or a *Bishop,* or a *Presbyter:* But whether unfixed general Ministers, to gather Churches and settle them, and take the care of many, without a special Pastoral charge of any one above the rest, were appointed by Christ for continuance in his Church: This is it that I affirm, and have already proved.

§. 7. Nor yet is it any of our Question, *Whether the difference between these general unfixed Ministers and ordinary fixed Pres-*

byters, *be in point of* Authority *or of* exercise *only*. Whether they are two distinct *Species* of the Ministry, or but one & the & same *Office in Specie*, variously exercised : I have given in my thoughts of this before, so far as I can yet reach : But if it be granted that some should *ordinarily exercise* their office generally and ambulatorily over many Churches, as others ordinarily must exercise it fixedly in one particular Church, I shall not contend whether they are to be called *One Office* or *two* : nor yet whether the fixed Minister may not extraordinarily upon a special reason, do the same work as the itinerant Minister in the same way. But Ministers there must be for both these works.

§. 8. And that some should make the general work before mentioned their ordinary business, and not take the pastoral Charge of any particular Church, I conceive (besides the former proofs) is further manifest, 1. In that the work of Converting Unbelievers, and bringing them into a fitness for Church Communion, is the work that is to go first, and is the greatest work: Its the greatest in weight(præcisively considered, and as to the *terminus à quo* of the change that it effects:) and it is the greatest in regard of opposing difficulties: the winning of a soul, which rejoyceth Angels, and rejoyceth Jesus Christ himself, will have so much of Satans malice to oppose it, and hath so much resistance in the heart of the sinner, that it requireth the whole work (in ordinary) of those Ministers that are specially called hereunto.

§. 9. And 2. Withall it commonly falls out, that there are far *greater numbers* to be converted, then to be Governed after Conversion: If it be not so in some Countries (where the face of God hath shined most effectually) yet in others, and in most it is: even in the far greatest part of the world. O how many millions of souls are there that perish for lack of knowledge, and know not for want of teaching; and never heard of Jesus Christ in any likely manner to prevail, in all their lives ? Surely such multitudes of Miserable souls, yea Nations, require Ministers wholly set upon this work.

§. 10. And 3. It ordinarily falls out too, that the unconverted unbelieving part of the world do live at a great distance from the Churches of Christ: and therefore the same man that is

Pastor

Paſtor of a Church hath not opportunity to ſpeak to them. Or if they live in the ſame Country, they ſeldom meet in greateſt numbers in the ſame Aſſemblies: And therefore when the Paſtor is upon his own work, it is requiſite that there be ſome to ſpeak to the reſt.

§. 11. And yet I doubt not but as there are hypocrites in moſt Churches, and among us many that by their ignorance, or impiety we have cauſe to judge to be yet no Chriſtians, are our Ordinary hearers, ſo the Paſtors of the Churches may and muſt endeavour their converſion, and much ſuit their preaching to the condition of ſuch ſouls. But yet thoſe millions that in other parts of the world (and perhaps in *Ireland*, *Wales* and the Highlands of *Scotland*, too many ſuch may be found) that neither know what Chriſtianity is, nor are the Ordinary hearers of a fixed Miniſtry, and live not within the reach of ſuch, ſhould have a Converting Itinerant Miniſtry for themſelves.

§. 12. Moreover, 4. The Paſtoral work is it ſelf ſo great, and the charge that we take of particular Churches, and our obligation to them ſo ſtrict, that it will uſually it ſelf take up the whole man, and will not allow a Paſtor time for the other work on thoſe at a diſtance yet uncalled, without neglecting the ſouls that he hath undertaken to overſee.

§. 13. And 5. For want of ſuch general Miniſters, the ſtate of perſons is in ſome places confounded, and the world and the Church are thruſt together, as if there were no difference to be made. Becauſe there are no Miniſters known but Paſtors, therefore there are no People known but as Chriſtians, where yet the very knowledge of Chriſtianity is too rare. Whereas if (where numbers and diſtance make it neceſſary) the preparing Miniſtry had firſt done their part, it would have prevented much dangerous confuſion, and ſelf-deceit that followeth hereupon in many places.

§. 14. And 6. By the miſtaken ſuppoſition, that ſuch generall or unfixed Miniſters are ceaſed, men have been drawn to ſet Lay-men upon the greateſt and nobleſt work of the Miniſtry: and a conceit is hence riſen among ſome, that becauſe this is not proper to the Paſtors of a Church, therefore it is not a Miniſterial work, but the work of gifted Brethren: And hereupon uncalled men are tempted to exerciſe it: and by laying

aſide

aside the officers appointed hereunto by Christ, the burden is cast on the weakest men.

§. 15. Yea 7. By this means many Ministers themselves understanding not the Nature and extent of their own Office, when they do but preach to any that are not of the Church that they have charge of, imagine that they preach but as meer Laymen; and if they preach for the Conversion of unbelievers, they profess it to be no act of their office: which is an act that hath more inconveniences then I shall now express.

§. 16. And 8. Which is worst of all, by supposing that no Ministers are now to be appointed for the Conversion of Infidels, and gathering and planting Churches, it is come to pass that the most necessary work in all the world is neglected, cast off, and almost quite unknown in the world: except Mr. *Eliots* and a few with him in *New England*, and some of the Jesuites and Fryars in the *East-Indies* and *America*, who have been sent, or have adventured themselves for the Converting of the Nations. Were it but known and considered, how much of the Will of Jesus Christ is to be fulfilled by this most blessed work, Princes would have studied it, and contributed their assistance; and many would have been ready to have offered themselves to God for the work, when now it is looked on as no part of our duty, not only because that sluggishness and cowardize calleth it impossible, and the adventure unreasonable; but also because we think it was a work that was proper to Apostles and Evangelists; and Ministers are now tyed to their proper flock. And thus the poor unbelieving world is left in their sin.

§. 17. And 9. I doubt by this mistake and neglect we forfeit the benefit of that special promise, in too great a measure. *Mat.* 28. 20. and miss of that eminent assistance and presence of Christ with our Ministry, that otherwise we might expect. If we did go into the world, and preach the Gospel to the Nations (having used our industry first to learn their languages,) we might expect that Christ would alwayes be with us to the end of the world, in a way of assistance and owning of our Labours, answerable to our engagements for him, and service to him. Were we deeplier engaged for Christ, and did with *Peter* cast our selves into the Sea, or walk on the Waters at his

Call,

Call, we should find Christ acting as if he were answerably engaged for our indemnity, or at least for our eminent encouragement and reward. If ever we might expect Miracles again, it would be upon our engagement in the antient work; though I know that even for this they are now no more necessary, nor I think, promised.

§. 18. And 10. We do hereby seem to accuse Christ unjustly of Mutability, supposing that he had setled one sort of Ministry and Government in his Church for one Age only, and then changed it for another, that is ever after to continue alone. I know the extraordinary work of that age (to plant Churches by new doctrine and Miracles, and reveal the new Articles of Faith and Practice in Scripture to the world) did require such enablements thereto, which ordinary works do not require : and therefore the Apostles, as immediatly sent, and as inditing Scriptures, and working Miracles, and Prophetically bringing new Revelations have no Successors. But the Apostles as preaching to the Nations, and as planting Churches, and as setling them, and taking care of their prosperity after they had planted them, and as exercising their Ministry itinerantly, as not fixed to a special charge, thus they have Successors, the work being ordinary, and such as should be done now as well as then; and must continue while the necessity of it doth continue.

§. 19. There needeth no other proof of this, then by observing that it was not Apostles only, but *all* the Ministry at first, that was thus unfixed and itinerant ; and that the Apostles assumed such to their assistance, and employed them all their dayes in this work.

§. 20. The seventy Disciples as well as the Apostles were at first by Christ sent forth in this Itinerant way, for the Conversion of the inhabitants of *Judea*. And thus *John* the Baptist had preached before them. And after Christs Resurrection and Ascension, it was not only the Apostles, but it was they that were scattered abroad, that went everywhere preaching the Word, *Act.8.4.* And who were these ? [*Act.8.1. They were all scattered abroad throughout the regions of* Judæa *and* Samaria, *except the Apostles.*] And the Evangelists of those times are confessed to have exercised this Itinerant Ministry : so did *Barnabas, Silas, Mark, Epaphroditus, Tychicus, Trophimus, Timothy,*

Timothy, Titus, Luke, and others ordinarily. It was the first and most ordinary way then of exercising the Ministry.

§. 21. And if we lived our selves in Heathen or Infidel Countreys, we should be soon taught by experience, that this must be still an ordinary work. For what else is to be done till persons be converted and brought into the Church? They must be made Disciples before they can be used as Disciples, and taught to observe all things that Christ hath commanded.

§. 22. But against this it is objected, 1. That *the Apostles were extraordinary Officers, and therefore have no Successors.* To which I answer, 1. That I have before shewed in what they were extraordinary, and in what not : in what they have no Successors, and in what they have. As Apostles sent immediatly by Christ to Reveal a new doctrine, and confirm it by Miracles, they have no Successors : but as general Ministers of Christ to convert souls, plant Churches, and take a care of many, they have Successors ; call them by what name you please. 2. And what if the Apostles have no Successors? Had the seventy Disciples none? Had *Apollo, Titus, Timothy, Silas, Barnabas,* &c. none? Had all the itinerant converting Ministers of those times none, that were not affixed as Pastors to a particular Church?

§. 23. Obj. 2. *But at least in the extent of their charge the Apostles were extraordinary, in that they were to preach the Gospel to all Nations.* I answer ; in point of exercise, being furnished with tongues and Miracles for the work, they were obliged to go further, or to more Nations then most particular Ministers are now obliged to go : but that is not because we want Authority, if we had ability and opportunity, but because we want ability and opportunity to exercise our Office. The Apostles were not bound to go into every Nation of the world, inclusively ; but to avoid none, but go to all, that is, to as many as they could. Otherwise they had sinned in not going to *Mexico, Peru, Brasile,* the *Philippine* or *Molucco Islands,* to *Japon, China,* &c. And it is *our* duty to extend our Ministry for the Conversion of as many as we have Ability and opportunity to do. That which was common to the *planting and watering Ministry* in the Apostles dayes, was not proper to the Apostles : but to go up and down the world to Convert, and Baptize, and plant, and water

Churches,

Churches was then common to such (as *Apollo, Silas,* &c.) therefore, &c.

§. 24. Obj. 3. *But* (say others) *the Apostles were not at last such unfixed Ministers as you imagine, but fixed Diocesan Bishops.* Peter *was Bishop of* Antioch *first, and of* Rome *after :* Paul *was Bishop of* Rome : James *of* Jerusalem, &c. ——— Ans. That any Apostle was a fixed Bishop, taking on him *durante vita* the special Pastoral charge of one particular Church or Diocess, as his peculiar, is 1. Barely affirmed, and therefore not to be believed. 2. And is contrary both to the tenor of their Commission, and the History of their Ministrations. And 3. Is also contrary to Charity it self, and therefore is not worthy of any credit. The Apostles were not so lazy or uncharitable, as to affix themselves to Parishes or Diocesses, and leave the Nations of the world in their unbelief ; and to cease the work that they were first sent out upon, before the necessity of it ceased. *Peter* and *Paul* were Bishops of *Rome,* as they were of other Churches which they planted and watered, and no more : even as *Paul* was Bishop of *Ephesus, Philippi, Corinth,* &c. And *James* was either no Bishop of *Jerusalem,* or no Apostle (but as many think, another *James.*) Indeed *pro tempore* not only an Apostle, but other Itinerant Ministers were Bishops of the places where they came ; that is, were Officers of Christ, that might exercise any act of their Office (Teaching, Governing, administring Sacraments, &c.) to any people that gave them a Call, or so far as opportunity and need required. And so I doubt not but every Minister now may do in any Church on earth. If he be invited to stay a day, or week, or month among them, and do the work of a Minister, yea or if he be invited but to preach a Sermon to them, he may do it, not as a private man, but as a Minister in general, and as their Teacher or Pastor *pro tempore,* & *ad hoc,* that give him the invitation. For though the first Call to the Ministry, separating us to the Gospel of God, do give us our Authority in general to perform any Ministerial act ; yet I have before shewed that a further Call is neeedfull for the particular exercise of this power : and this is usually by the people : who may sometime call a man to be their stated Pastor, and sometime but to exercise some one Pastoral act, or else to exercise all but *pro tempore,* as there is need.

§. 25.

§. 25. And by this means it came to pass that the line of Succession in many Churches is drawn down from the Apostles, by *Eusebius, Hierom,* and other antient writers. Not because the Apostles were the stated fixed Bishops of those Churches, as the Successors were ; but because they first planted and Governed them, and were their Bishops *pro tempore* till they had settled Bishops over them ; and then went and did the like by other places : so that one Apostle, or Evangelist, or unfixed Minister, might be the root of Succession to many Churches, even as many as they first planted : but their Successors had but one Church.

§. 26. Object. 4. *But what use is there among us for such Ministers as these, when all the Nations are Converted from Infidelity already ?* Answ. 1. If there were no use of such with us, we must not forget the lamentable necessity of them abroad in the world. 2. As I before said, experience of the ignorance and unbelief of many about us in the best Parishes, doth cause me easily to believe that in *Ireland,* and part of *Scotland,* and *Wales,* and other places where settled Ministers are few, such an Itinerant Ministry is of necessary use among us. 3. But yet where there are settled Teachers enough, they may be spared : for if we had Parishes that had not the knowledge of Christ, it is a greater work of mercy to such a Parish, to settle a converting Teacher among them to fit them for a Church-state, that so they may have frequent Teaching, then to send them but now and then a Sermon. But where Ministers are not so plentiful, it were a great sin for an able man to confine himself to one Town or Parish, and neglect the Countrey round about. 4. And also there is use for Itinerants to water and take care of the Churches which are planted, as the Apostles and others formerly did.

§. 27. Concerning these unfixed Ministers, I add these following Propositions. 1. That such Ministers may not deprive the fixed Pastors of any of their Power : they may not disable them from Governing their own Churches as fully as if there were no Itinerant Ministers. If they are admitted *pro tempore* to assist the Churches where they come, that will not enable them to hinder them, or assume a Lordship or a Rule over the Pastors of the Churches.

§. 28. 2. These Itinerant unfixed Ministers, are not so obliged to perpetual motion, but that they may reside for a considerable

derable

derable time in a place, either for the following on the work of
Conversion, where they find a plenteous harvest, or for setling
Churches, or surpresing heresies or disorders, or because of
their own disability to travail. And thus *Paul* staid at and about
Ephesus in *Asia* three years, *Act.* 20. 31. Their stay must be
prudentially apportioned to their work and opportunities.

: §. 29. 3. No Itinerant Minister can (of himself) exclude
another from his Province, and appropriate it to himself, and say,
Here I will work alone, or here I have greater Authority then you :
nay it was usual for these Ministers to go by companies, or more
then one (as *Paul* and *Barnabas*, *Paul* and *Silas*, *Paul* and
Timothy, Titus, &c.) so that it was no mans Province or Diocess where they came. For they that Convert Souls to Christ
and not to themselves, and Baptize into his name and not in their
own, do know the greatness of the work and burden, and therefore are glad of all the assistance they can get : when those that
do nothing, are the men that thrust others out of the Vineyard,
and say, *This is my Diocess or Province, you have nothing to do
to labour here.*]

§. 30. 4. Yet may there lawfully and fitly be a Prudential
distribution or division of their Provinces among such unfixed
Converting Ministers : for to be all together and go one way,
must needs be a neglecting of most of the world; and so not a
wise or faithful performance of the work of Christ. And therefore some should go one way, and some another, as may most
promote the work.

§. 31. And ordinarily it is most convenient, that there go
more then one to the same people, (and therefore they will not
be like a fixed Diocesan Bishop) for they have many wayes
need of mutual assistance : one would be oppressed with so great
a work, and have many disadvantages in the performances. *Paul*
used not to go alone.

§. 32. The persons to be exercised in this ambulatory Ministration, may be determined of, and their Provinces distributed
any of these three wayes, or all together. 1. By the Judgement
and Consent of Pastors. If many shall choose out one, or two,
or more, as fit for such a work, the persons chosen have reason to
obey, unless they can prove, or know the Pastors to be mistaken,
and so to have been misguided in their choice. The Prophets and

Teachers,

Teachers of the Church at *Antioch* muſt ſend or ſeparate *Saul* and *Barnabas*, for the ſpecial work in which the Holy Ghoſt would imploy them, *Act.*13.1,2. which ſeems to me, to be but a ſecondary Call to ſome ſpecial exerciſe of their former Office, one way rather then another. Thus alſo by mutual agreement their Provinces may be allotted and divided.

§. 33. 2. By the Magiſtrates appointment and command alſo, may this be done. Though he make not Miniſters, yet may he do much in aſſigning them their Provinces, Seats, and Stations: and it is our duty to obey his Commands in ſuch caſes, if they be not plainly deſtructive to the Church: much more if they are beneficial to it.

§. 34. 3. Alſo by a Miniſters own diſcerning of a fit opportunity to do good, either by the Magiſtrates bare permiſſion, the peoples invitation, or their willingneſs, or not oppoſing; or though they do oppoſe, yet ſome other advantages for the work may be diſcerned, or Hopes at leaſt. Now though the *Call of Ordination* muſt be from the Paſtors of the Church, and neither Magiſtrates nor people can make us Miniſters, yet the *Call* of *Opportunity* may be from the people and Magiſtrate, more commonly then any. And he that is already a Miniſter, needs not alwayes another Call for the exerciſing of his Miniſtry, ſave only this *Call* by *Opportunity*. He had his *Authority* by that Call that placed him in the Office; which was done at firſt, and muſt be done but once. But he hath his *Opportunity and ſtation* for the *exerciſe* of that Authority by the people and Magiſtrates, and perhaps may receive it over and over many times.

§. 35. 5. This way of exerciſing the Miniſtry is not alike neceſſary in all times and places; but with great variety; it is exceeding neceſſary in ſome Countreys, and not in others, but uſeful in ſome degree in moſt as I conceive.

§. 36. If the Queſtion be, whether ſuch a Miniſtry be uſeful in theſe Dominions, or not? I have anſwered before, that in ſome darker and neceſſitous parts, where ignorance doth reign, and Miniſters (or able ones at leaſt) are ſcarce, there ſuch an exerciſe of the Miniſtry is neceſſary: but in other parts it is not of ſuch neceſſity: yet much work there may be for ſuch, or for thoſe in the next Chapter mentioned, in moſt Countreys: of them therefore I ſhall next ſpeak.

Qo CHAT

CHAP. II.

Of fixed Pastors that also participate in the work of the unfixed.

§. 1. IT is not only the *unfixed* Ministers that may lawfully do the fore-described work, but the *fixed* Pastors of particular Churches may take their part of it ; and ordinarily should do somewhat toward it : though not so much as they that are wholly in it.

§. 2. I shall here shew you, 1. What such may do. 2. On what terms. 3. And then I shall prove it. And 1. They may as Ministers of Christ, go abroad to preach where there are many ignorant or ungodly people in order to their Conversion. 2. They may help to Congregate Believers into holy Societies, where it is not already done. 3. They may Ordain them Elders in such Churches as they Congregate. 4. They may oft enquire after the welfare of the Neighbour Churches, and go among them, and visit them, and strengthen them, and admonish the Pastors to do their duties. 5. They may instruct and teach the Pastors in publike exercises. 6. They may exercise any acts of Worship or Discipline upon the people of any particular Church, which giveth them a due invitation thereto. 7. They may publikely declare that they will avoid Communion with an impious or heretical Church or Pastor.

§. 3. But 2. As to the mode or terms, it should be thus performed. 1. No Pastor of a single Church must leave his flock a day or hour without such necessary business as may prove his Call to do so. We must not feign a Call when we have none ;

or pretend neceſſities. He that knows his obligations to his particular charge, and the work that is there to be done, methinks ſhould not dare to be ſtepping aſide, unleſs he be ſure it is to a greater work.

§. 4. And 2. No Paſtor of a Church ſhould be buſie to play the Biſhop in another mans Dioceſs, nor ſuſpect or diſparage the parts or labours of the proper Paſtor of that Church, till the ſufferings or dangers of the Church do evidently warrant him, and call him to aſſiſt them.

§. 5. 3. No Miniſter of Chriſt ſhould be ſo proud as to overvalue his own parts, and thereupon obtrude himſelf where there is no need of him (though there might be need of others) upon a conceit that he is fitter then other men to afford aſſiſtance to his Brethren. When the caſe is really ſo, he may judge it ſo: eſpecially when his Colleagues or fellow Miniſters judge ſo too, and deſire him to the work: but Pride muſt not ſend out Miniſters.

§. 6. 4. A Miniſter that hath divers fellow Presbyters at home, to teach and guide that Church in his abſence, may better go out on aſſiſting works then other men. And ſo may he that hath help that while from Neighbour Presbyters, or that hath ſuch a charge as may bear his abſence for that time, without any great or conſiderable loſs.

§. 7. 5. And a man that is commanded out by the Magiſtrate, who may make him a Viſiter of the Churches near him, may lawfully obey, when it would not have been fit to have done it without ſuch a command, or ſome equivalent motive.

§. 8. 6. A man that is earneſtly invited by Neighbour-Miniſters or Churches, that call out to him, *Come and help us*, may have comfort in his undertaking, if he ſee a probability of doing greater good then if he denyed them, and if they give him ſatisfactory reaſons of their Call.

§. 9. 7. Men of extraordinary abilities, ſhould make them as communicative and uſeful to all as poſsibly they can: and may not ſo eaſily keep their retirements, as the Weak may do.

§. 10. 8. And laſtly: No man ſhould upon any of theſe pretences uſurp a Lordſhip over his Brethren, nor take on him to be the ſtated Paſtor of Paſtors, or of many Churches as his ſpecial

cial Charge. It is one thing to do the common work of Ministers abroad, by seeking mens Conversion, and the planting of
Churches, or else to afford assistance to many Churches for their
preservation, establishment or increase : and its another thing to
take charge of these Pastors and Churches, as the proper Bishop
or Overseer of them. The former may be done; but I know no
warrant for the later.

§. 11. That fixed Ministers may do all these forementioned
works, with the aforesaid Cautions, I shall briefly prove. 1. By
some general Reasons, speaking to the whole ; and 2. By going over the particulars distinctly, and giving some reason for
each part.

§. 12. And 1. It is certain that a Minister doth not cease to
be a Minister in general, nor to be an Officer authorized to seek
the Discipling of them without, and Congregating them, by his
becoming the Pastor of a particular Church : therefore he may
still do the common works of the Ministry where he hath a Call,
as well as his Pastoral special work to them that he hath taken
special care of. As the Physitian of an Hospital or City may
take care also of other persons, and cure them, so he neglect not
his charge.

§. 13. 2. A Minister doth not lay by his Relation or Obligations to the unconverted world, nor to the Catholike Church,
when he affixeth himself to a special charge. And therefore he
may do the work of his Relations and Obligations, as aforesaid.
Yea those works in some respects should be preferred, because
there is more of Christs interest in the Universal Church, or in
many Churches then in one ; and that work in which the most of
our ultimate End is attained, is the greatest work : that in which
God is most honoured, the Church most edified, and most honour
and advantage brought to the Gospel and cause of Christ, should
be preferred : But ordinarily these are more promoted by the
Communication of our help to many (as aforesaid) then by
confining it to one particular Church. The commonest good is
the best.

§. 14. 3. Oft-times the Necessity of such Communicative
labours is so apparently great, that it would be unmercifulness
to the Churches or souls of men to neglect them. As in case of
Reforming and setling Churches (upon which *Luther* , *Me-*
lanchthon,

lanchthon, *Chytraus, Bugenhagius, Pomeranus, Calvin,* and others were so oft imployed.) As also in case of resisting some destructive heresies : In which case one able Disputant and prudent adviser, and person that hath interest in the people, may do good to thousands , even to many Countries, and more then multitudes of others could do. And God doth not set up such lights to put under a bushell, nor warrant any man to hide his talents ; nor doth he bestow extraordinary gifts for ordinary sevice only, but would have them used to the utmost advantage of his cause, and for the greatest good of souls.

§. 15. 4. And it is not the taking up of another calling or *Species* of Ministerial Office : For the Ministry is one office (distinct from that inferiour sort of Ministry of Deacons) and containeth the power and obligation of doing all th.s, when we have particular Cals : It is but the exercise of the same office which we had before. We do but lay out our selves more in some parts or acts of that office, then more retired Pastors do.

§. 16. And 5. It belongeth to the Magistrates to take care of the Church and the right exercise of the gifts of their subject Ministers : and therefore if they command one man more labour then another, even the Planting, or Visiting of Churches, it is our Duty to obey them.

§. 17. More particu'arly : 1. That *a fixed Pastor may preach abroad among the unconverted,* I hope none will deny. It was the ancient custom of the fixed Bishops, besides the feeding of their flocks, to labour the Conversion of all the Countries about them that were unconverted : The example of *Gregory* of *Neocesarea* may suffice, who found but seventeen Christians in the City, but converted not only all that City. (except seventeen) but also most of the Countries about , and planted Churches, and ordained them Bishops. And so have abundance others done, to the increase of the Church.

§. 18. And 2. That fixed Bishops may *congregate new Churches where there are none,* of such as they or others do convert, is in the foresaid constant practice of the Pastors of the ancient Churches, put past doubt. But so, as that they ought not to Congregate those Churches to themselves, and make themselves the Bishops or Archbishops of them when they have a special charge already ; but only settle them under Bishops of their own. And

this

this is but by directing them in their duties, and trying the person, and investing him that is to be their Pastor. Whether one or more must do this work, I have spoken already in the former Disputation.

§. 19. 3. And *that such as thus convert a people, or Congregate them, may* (according to the fore-mentioned Rules) *Ordain them Pastors, by the peoples suffrages or Consent,* is also sufficiently proved in that foregoing disputation: and therefore may be here past by.

§. 20. 4. And *that such may take care of all the Churches within their reach, so far as to do them what good they can,* is plain in the Law of Nature that requireth it; and in the general commands of the Gospel seconding the Law of Nature; while we have time we must do good to all men; Especially to the houshold of faith. And its plain in the Nature of the Catholick Church and of its members, and in the nature of the work of Grace upon the soul. We are taught of God to love one another: and the End of the Catholick Society is, (as of all Societies) the common good, and the Glory of God: and the Nature of true members is to have the *same care one for another,* that so there may be no schism in the body, and that they all suffer and rejoice with one another, in their hurts, and in their welfare, 1 *Cor.* 12.25, 26. It is therefore lawfull for Pastors to improve their talents upon these common grounds.

§. 21. 5. That *such setled Pastors may Teach or Preach to one another,* is a thing not doubted of among us. For we commonly practice it at Lectures and other meetings of Ministers, as formerly was usual at visitations, and Convocations. And if it be lawful to teach Ministers, then also to do those lesser things before and after mentioned. Yet do we not preach to one another as Rulers over our Brethren, but as Ministers of Christ, and Helpers of them in the work of grace. As when one Physitian healeth another, he doth it as a Physitian, helping and advising a Brother in necessity: but when he cureth one of his Hospital, he doth it as a Physitian performing his trust to one of his charge. So when a Pastor preacheth to Pastors, he doth it not as a private man, but as a Pastor obliged to help his Brethren: But when he preacheth to his People, he doth it as

one

one that hath the charge of their souls, and is their guide to life everlasting.

§. 22. 6. *And that Pastors may exercise acts of Discipline and administer the Sacraments to other Congregations, upon a sufficient Call,* is evident from what is said already. If they may Preach to the Pastors themselves, they may help to Rule the flock: For, as is said, they cease not their Relation to the Church of Christ in general, by being engaged to one Church in particular. If general Ministers, such as Apostles, Evangelists, *&c.* might administer the Sacraments where they came in Churches that were not any of their special charge above others, then may other Ministers of Christ do it upon a sufficient Invitation, though the Congregation be none of their special charge: And in so doing, they act not as private men, nor yet as the stated Pastors of that flock, but as Pastors, Assistant to the stated Pastors, and Ruling *pro tempore* the people under them in that Assisting way: Even as a Physitian helpeth another in his Hospital, when he is desired, and that neither as a Private Ordinary man, nor as Superiour to the Physitian of the Hospital, nor as the *stated* Physitian of it himself, but as the *temporary assistant Physitian* of it. Or as a Schoolmaster helpeth another in his School for a few dayes in Necessity, as his *temporary assistant.*

§. 23. 7. And upon the same grounds it will follow that *one Church or Pastor on just occasion may avoid Communion with another, and declare that they so resolve to do*; and this without usurping any Jurisdiction over them, it being not the casting out or Excommunicating of a member of our charge, as the Rulers of that Church, but the obeying of a plain command of the Holy Ghost, which requireth us to Avoid such, and have no company or Communion with them, and with such no not to eat: And therefore it is a fond Argumentation of the Papists, that would conclude their Pope to be Head and Governour, as far as they find he ever did excommunicate.

§. 24. He that doubteth of any of this, must not first enquire, Whether a Minister have so much *Power,* but first *Whether* he may be *obliged* to so *much work* and *suffering* as his *duty.* And then he shall find that if there were no special examples or commands, yet the general commands, which require us to do good

while

while we have time to all; to be the servants of all, and seek their salvation, &c. do as certainly oblige us to particular duties, as if they were named.

§. 25. Object. *That cannot be: For, a General command of doing good to all, obligeth not a Minister any more then another man: But it obligeth not another man to Preach, administer Sacraments, &c. therefore it obligeth not a Minister.* Answ. To the Major I answer, that 1. It may oblige *to more*, where it obligeth not *more*, as to the Essence of the obligation. 2. The General command obligeth several men to several acts according to their several Abilities, opportunities and capacities. If all be required to improve their Masters stock or, talents, yet all are not required to improve the same talents, because they have not the same: But one hath *Riches* to improve, and the general command obligeth him to improve that talent: And another hath *strength*, another *interest* and *friends*, another *wit*, and another *learning*, and every man is bound to improve *what he hath*, and not *what he hath not*. The command of Doing good to all doth oblige a *Physitian* to help to *cure* men, and a *Magistrate* to benefit them by *Government*, and a *Lawyer* by *Counsell* for their estates, and a *Minister* by the works of a Minister, for their salvation. If you should say that [*this General command doth bind a Magistrate, or a Physitian no more then another man: but it bindeth not another man to do good by Ruling or by Physick, therefore neither doth it bind them;*] would not the fallacy be obvious? So is it here.

§. 26. It being proved that such *Assistant Ministerial* works may be performed by a *fixed Pastor* to *those about him*, and within his reach, it will clearly follow that convenient means may be used to bring this to performance, and help the Churches to the actual benefit of such Assistance. And by the three forementioned wayes it may be done. As 1. If the Pastor and People of any Neighbour Church, or the people alone, where there is no Church, do invite such men to come and help them.

§. 27. And 2. The Neighbour Pastors may agree together for the perswading of the fittest men among them to undertake such Assistances: as is usual in the setling of Lectures; and as in this County we have successfully for above these two years used the help of four Itinerant Lecturers, that have taken their

several

several circuits, one Lords day in four, (which was every Lords day among them all) to help their neighbours.

§. 28. And if the Invitation of a People, or the Agreement of Paſtors may do this, no doubt then but the prudent Government of a Magiſtrate may do it. And he may appoint Certain Paſtors their bounds and Circuits, and appoint them to afford convenient aſſiſtance to the Paſtors and people within thoſe bounds. And *thus* he may make them *Viſitors of the Churches and Country about them*, in which viſitation, they may Teach, and do other Miniſterial offices by Conſent; and may by the Magiſtrates command, take notice whether the Churches be duly Conſtituted and Governed, and may acquaint the Magiſtrate how things are; and may fraternally Reprove the Negligent Paſtors and people where they come; And alſo may provoke them to Reformation, both of Church conſtitution and Church-adminiſtrations; And theſe viſitors may give notice to the neighbour Churches, of ſuch Paſtors as they find unfit for the Miniſtry, that by conſent they may be diſowned by the reſt.

§. 29 And though one Paſtor have not of himſelf (as a Paſtor) ſo much Power over any of his Brethren, as to require him to come to him to give him an account of his wayes, yet 1. The Aſſociated Paſtors may deſire him to appear among them to give them ſatisfaction, when there is matter of offence : (For one may better travail to many, then many to one.) And 2. The Magiſtrate may lawfully command Miniſters to appear before ſuch Paſtors as he hath appointed to be Viſitors; and then it will be their duty in obedience to the Magiſtrates command.

§. 30. Yet Magiſtrates muſt take heed that they put not the *ſword* into the hands of Miniſters, nor enable them with coercive power, by touching mens bodies or eſtates : We do not only forbear to claim ſuch a power, but we *diſclaim* it, yea and humbly and earneſtly beſeech the Princes and Senates of Chriſtian Common-wealths, that they would keep the ſword in their own hands, and not put it into the hands of any Miniſters, and then we could better bear the claims and uſurpations, not only of Exorbitant or tranſcendent Prelates, but of the Pope himſelf. Let them come unarmed, and have no weapon but ſpiritual the word of God, and then we ſhall leſs fear them. The Diviſions and tyranny, & bloodshed through the Churches hath been by trusting coercive Magisterial power in the hands of Ministers of the Gospel. Though I confess I think it not a thing unlawfull in it self for a Minister to be a Magistrate also, yet I think that nothing but necessity can warrant it ; and so much as hindereth him from the work of his calling (which requireth a whole man) without this Necessity, is utterly unlawfull. Were there a Country that had no other persons tolerably fit, I doubt not but the same man that is a Minister or Pastor, might be a Justice of Peace, Parliament man, or a Prince : But while there are others that are capable of bearing these burdens, he is not worthy to be a Minister of the Gospel, that would wish the least of them upon his shoulders. Either Magistracy or Ministry is enough for one. Had the English Prelates been armed with none but spiritual weapons, they had never appeared so terrible or so odious.

§. 31. It seemeth a course that suiteth with the state of the present Churches among us, to have in every County, three or four such able, faithfull Pastors to be by the Magistrate made Visitors of the rest, not giving them any power of medling with mens bodies or estates, but joining with them a Magistrate as a Justice or Commissioner, that *one* may *perswade*, and the *other constrain*, as far as the Soveraign Power shall think fit. This is not to set up any *New office* or the least part of an office in the Church. As it is meerly accidental to the Being of a Physitian, whether he be tyed to a City, or to an Hospital, or to a County, or to no place, but practice as he findeth opportunity ; these being but the various modes of using the same * Office and works ; so may we truly say of the Ministry.

§. 32. Yet is there no such *Necessity* of this appointment of Visitors or Superintendents, or Assistants by the Magistrate, or by agreement of Ministers, or any such course, as if the *Being*, or the welfare of the Church were laid upon it.   For without any such Elections or Appointments, the Graces and Gifts of the Spirit of Christ will shew themselves, and be communicative for the Edification of the Churches. We see by common experience, that where no one man is commanded or commended by the Magistrate to the care of many Churches, above his brethren, yet some men are as diligent and faithfull in doing good to all within their reach, as if they had been chosen and nominated to

the

* The Jesuits and Fryars do not take the Generals or Governors of their Orders to be men of another Order, though they have a Power of Ruling, and that Tyrannically.

the work. Many able painfull Minifters of Chrift , that thirft for mens falvation, do go up and down among the ignorant, or weak, and preach in feafon and out of feafon , notwithstanding the burden of their particular flocks , which they faithfully bear.

§. 3 3. And the parts and graces of thefe men do win them audi-ence and refpect where they come, without any Humane Authority to awe men. In almoft all parts of our Countrey we have either fettled or movable Lectures : and when do we fee a thin Congregation before a lively rowfing Minifter , or any man of great ability in the work ? No, but we fee the Temples crowded ; and find that the people reverence and hearken to fuch men as thefe, in whom the Spirit of God appears.

§. 3.4. Yea and the Minifters themfelves will *confult* with the *Wife*, and *Love* the *good*, and *learn* of thofe that are *ableft* to *teach* them : and imitate the ableft preachers as neer as they can. So that I may truly fay, that there is a certain kind of Natural, or rather, fpiritual Epifcopacy every where exercifed in the Church. A great light that burneth and fhineth above others, will draw the eyes of many to it : and if it be fet on a hill it will hardly be hid. *Calvin* was no Prelate ; and yet his Gifts procured him that Intereft, by which he prevailed more then Prelates for the conformity of the minds of many to his own. There is fcarce a Country but hath fome able judicious Minifter, who hath the *Intereft* of a Bifhop with the reft ; though he have no higher an office then themfelves. Gods Graces deferve and will procure refpect. Even in Civil Councils, Courts, Committees, we fee that fome one of leading parts, is the Head of the reft though their authority be equal.

§. 35. And indeed the conveniences and inconveniences are fuch on both fides, that it is not an eafie matter to determine, *Whether appointed Vifitors or Superintendents, be more defirable then thefe Arbitrary Vifitors that have the Natural Epifcopacy of Intereft procured by their meer abilities.* On the one fide, if Magi-ftrates appoint fuch Vifitors, the people, yea and many Minifters will the more eafily fubmit, and bear, and obey, and more unani-moufly concur, then if we offer our affiftance without any fuch appointment : Thats the convenience : But then heres the in-convenience: The Magiftrate may choofe an unworthy man, and

then

then he may be *feared*, but not *honoured* nor loved; but greater lights will be greater still, let the Magiftrate fet the leffer on never fo high a Candleftick : And then the Minifters and people will meafure their efteem of the man according to his worth, and that will irritate his difpleafure ; For when he is lifted up he either looks to be valued by his *Height*, and not his *Light* or *Worth*, or elfe that his *Light* fhould be judged of by his *Height*. And as this will turn to heart-burnings and divifions, fo the efteem that is procured by humane Conftitution, will be more humane, and ordinarily lefs Divine then the calling and work of a Divine requireth. On the other fide, if none be appointed by the Magiftrate, but every man go forth in the ftrength of his zeal and Abilities ; we are like to be caft on many difadvantages with carnal temporizing men, and to have lefs unity among our felves: But then that unity, and peace, and refpect, and fuccefs that we have will be more voluntary and pure.

§. 36. The beft way then, if we could hit it, feems to be the joining of both thefe together. To have fuch Magiftrates as will appoint only the moft judicious, able, faithfull Minifters to be Vifitors of the Churches, that fhall go forth both in the ftrength of the Spirit of Chrift, with eminency of gifts, and alfo in the ftrength of the Magiftrates Commiffion. But if this cannot be attained, I fhall not long for conftituted Vifitors or Superintendents ; but fhall be content with the Holy Ghofts appointment.

§. 37. It is therefore the moft Chriftian courfe to lay no greater ftrefs on thefe modes and forms of Miniftration then they will bear ; and therefore to live obediently and peaceably under either of them ; obeying fuch Vifitors as are appointed by the Magiftrate, and honouring the graces of the Spirit, where there is no fuch appointment ; and not to think the Church undone when our conceits about fuch things are croft.

CHAP.

CHAP. III.

It is Lawfull for the several Associations of Pastors to choose one man to be their President, durante vita, *if he continue fit.*

§ 1.  Come next to speak of a third sort of Ministry, which hath a greater resemblance to the ancient Episcopacy, then any of the rest : Yea indeed is the same that was exercised about the second or third Century after Christ. And that is, the fixed Presidents of the Presbyters of many Churches associated. In the first settlement of Churches, there was either a single Pastor to a single Church ; or many Pastors, in equality, at least of Office : And whether from the beginning or afterward only, one of them became the stated President, is very uncertain : of which anon. But when the Churches encreased in magnitude, and many Congregations were gathered under one Presbyterie, then that Presbyterie also had a stated President, as the Congregational Presbyteries perhaps had before. And thus he was an Archbishop under the name of a Bishop, that awhile before was either unknown, or else must needs be esteemed an Archbishop.

§ 2. That these men should take the *Pastoral charge of many Churches,* c

q

the Presbyters, upon pretence of a Presidency, or superiority, is I think, a matter not warrantable by the word of God.

§. 3. But that such *Associations* of the Pastors of many Churches should ordinarily be, for the sake of Union and Communion; as also that it is lawfull for these Associated Ministers to choose one among them to be their *President,* is granted by all.

§. 4. But all the question is, *Whether these Presidents should be only pro tempore,* or *durante vita,* supposing that they forfeit not the trust? I shall not say much of the point of *convenience*; but I affirm, that of it self it is *lawful* to choose a President that shall be fixed *durante vita, si tam diu bene se gesserit.* Yea it is *lawfull now in England,* as things stand.

§. 5. And 1. It may suffice for the proof of this, that it is nowhere forbidden in Nature or in Scripture; directly or by consequence: and therefore it is lawfull: Where there is no law, there is no transgression: They that say that it is a thing forbidden, must prove it from some word of God; which I think, they cannot do.

§. 6. 2. If it be lawfull to choose a fixed President for half a year, or a year, or seven year, then is it lawfull to choose and fix such a President for life (on supposition still of a continued fitness) But it is lawful to choose such a one for a year, or seven year: therefore also for life.

§. 7. The Antecedent is granted by the Presbyterian, Congregational and Erastian party, (which are all that I have now to do with:) For all these consented that D. *Twiss* should be President of the Synod at *Westminster,* which was till his death: or else was like to have been till the end; And so another after him. And ordinarily the Provinces and Presbyteries choose a President till the next Assembly. And I remember not that ever I heard any man speak against this course.

§. 8. And then the Consequence is clear, from the parity of Reasons: For 1. Seven years in contracts is valued equal with the duration of a mans life. 2. And no man can give a Reason to prove it Lawfull to have a President seven years, or a quarter of a year, that will not prove it Lawfull in it self to have a President during life. And Accidents must be weighed on both sides, before you can prove it *Accidentally* evil: And if it be

but

but fo, it may be one time good, if by accident it be another time bad. The weightieft accident muft preponderate.

§. 9. 3. Order is a thing lawful in Church Affemblies and Affairs : the ftated Prefidency of one, is a ftated Order in Church Affemblies : therefore it is lawful that all things be done in Order, is commanded, 1 *Cor.*14.40. And therefore in general Order is a *duty*, which is more then to be *Lawful*. And though the *particular wayes of Order* may yet be comparatively indifferent, yet are *they Lawful*, as the *Genus* is *neceffary*.

§. 10. And that this Prefidency is a point of Church Order, is apparent in the nature and ufe of the thing : and alfo in that it is commonly acknowledged a matter of Order in all other focieties or Affemblies, though but for the low and common affairs of the world : in a Jury you will confefs, that Order requireth that there be a Foreman : and in a Colledge that there be a Mafter : and that an Hofpital a School, and all Societies, have fo much Order at leaft as this, if not much more. And why is not that to be accounted-Order in the Church, that is fo in all other focieties ?

§. 11. 4. That which maketh to the Unity of the Churches or Paftors (and is not forbidden by Chrift) is both lawful and defirable : But fuch is a ftated Prefidency : therefore, &c. The Major is grounded 1. On nature it felf, that tells us how much of the ftrength, and beauty, and fafety of the Church, and of all focieties doth confift in Unity. The Minor is apparent in the Nature of the thing : 1. That Prefidency makes for Unity, is confeft by all the Churches that ufe it to that end. 2. And the continuance of the fame makes fomewhat more for Unity then a change would do : there being fome danger of divifion in the new elections : befides other and greater inconveniences.

§. 12. 5. The perfon that is moft fit (*Confideratis Confiderandis*) fhould be chofen Prefident : But one and the fame perfon ordinarily is moft fit *durante vita* : therefore one and the fame perfon fhould be continued Prefident. God doth not ufe to change his gifts at every monethly or quarterly Seffions of a Claffis or Provincial Synod. Either the Prefident chofen was the fitteft at the time of his choice, or not : if he were not, he was ill chofen : if he were fo then, its like he is fo ftill, at leaft for a long time. And a mans ability is fo great and confiderable a qualification

cation

eation for every imployment, that it muſt be a very great accident on the other ſide that muſt allow us to chooſe a man that is
leſs able. A change cannot be made in moſt places, without the
injury of the Aſſembly and of their work. The worthieſt perſon therefore may lawfully be continued for the work ſake.

§. 13. 6. That way is lawful that conduceth to the Reconciliation of diſſenting and contending Brethren (ſuppoſing it not
forbidden by God.) But ſuch is the way of a ſtated Preſidency,
durante vitâ : therefore, *&c.* Though the Major be paſt doubt,
yet to make it more clear, conſider, that it is 1. A Learned party (as to many of them) with whom this Reconciliation is deſired : and therefore the more deſirable. 2. That it is a numerous party : even the moſt of the Catholike Church by far. All
the *Greek* Church, the *Armenian, Syrian, Abaſſine*, and all others
that I hear of, except the Reformed, are for Prelacy : and among
the Reformed, *England* and *Ireland* had a Prelacy, and *Denmark, Sweden*, part of *Germany, Tranſilvania*, have a ſuperin-
tendency as high as I am pleading for at leaſt. And certainly a
Reconciliation, and as near a Union as well may be had, with
ſo great a part of the Church of Chriſt, is a thing not to be deſpiſed ; nor will not be by conſiderate moderate men.

§. 14. And it is very conſiderable with me, that it is the future and not only the preſent Peace of the Churches that we
ſhall thus procure. For it is eaſie to ſee that Epiſcopacy is neither ſuch an upſtart thing, nor defended by ſuch contemptible
reaſons, as that the Controverſie is like to die with this age : undoubtedly there will be a Learned and Godly party for it, while
the world endureth ; unleſs God make by Illumination or Revelation ſome wonderful change on the Sons of men, that I think,
few men do expect. And certainly we ſhould do the beſt we can
to prevent a perpetual diſſention in the Church. Were there not
one Prelatical man now alive, it were eaſie to foreſee there would
ſoon be more.

§. 15. Yet do I not move, that any thing forbidden by God
ſhould be uſed, as a means for Peace or Reconciliation with men.
It is not to ſet up any Tyranny in the Church, nor to introduce
any new Office that Chriſt hath not planted : it is but the orderly diſpoſal of the Officers and affairs of Chriſt, which is pleaded for.

§. 16.

§. 16. Object. *But (some will say) your Minor yet is to be denyed; for this is not a way to Reconciliation. A stated Presidency will not please the Prelates that have been used to the sole Jurisdiction of a whole County, and to sole Ordination.* Answ. 1. We know that the moderate will consent. 2. And some further accommodation shall be offered anon; which may satisfie all that will shew themselves the Sons of Peace. 3. If we do our duty, the guilt will no longer lie on us, but on the refusers of Peace: but till then, its as well on us as on them.

§. 17. 7. That which is lawfully practised already by a Concurrence of judgements, may lawfully be agreed on: But the Presidency (or more) of one man in the Assemblies of Ministers, is in most places practised (and that lawfully) already: therefore, &c. There is few Associations, but some one man is so far esteemed of by all, that they give him an actual or virtual Presidency, or more: why then may they not agree expresly so to do?

§. 18. 8. Lastly, The so common and so antient practice of the Churches, should move us to an inclination to reverence and imitation, as far as God doth not forbid us, and we have no sufficient reason to deter us: of which more anon.

§. 19. Yet are not they to be justified that raise contentions for such a Presidency, and lay the Churches Peace upon it. I see not yet but that it is a thing in it self indifferent, whether a man be President a moneth, a year, or for his life: and therefore I plead only for condescending in a case indifferent, for the Churches peace: though accidentally order may make it more desirable in one place: and jealousies, and prejudice, or danger of usurpation, may make it less desirable in another place. But none should judge it necessary or sinful of it self.

§. 20. If you ask, *What Power shall these stated Presidents have?* I answer, 1. None can deny, but that it is fit that in every Association of Churches, there should be a certain way of Communication agreed on. And therefore that some one should be chosen to receive such Letters or other matters that are to be Communicated, and to send them, or notice of them unto all. This is a *service*, and the *power* of doing such a *service* cannot be questional ... eth ... u q

§. 21. . It is me ... d ... equa at the ... rest

reft, as with *bufinefs*, fo with *times* and *places* of meeting : the nomination of fuch times and places, or the acquainting others with them when agreed on, is a fervice that none can juftly que-ftion : and therefore the lawfulnefs of the power to do it, may not be queftioned.

§. 22. Object. *But what's this to Government ? this is to make them Servants, and not Governors.* An'w. It is the more agree-able to the will of Chrift, that will have that kind of greatnefs fought among his Minifters, by being the fervants of all.

§. 23. But 3. He may alfo be the ftated Moderator of their Difputations and Debates : this much I think will eafily be grant-ed them ; and I am fure with fome (as I fhall fhew anon) this much would feem fatisfactory. The Principal Prefident or Ma-fter of a Colledge is thought to have a convenient precedency or fuperiority, though he have not a Negative voice. And why the Prefident in an Affociation of Paftors fhould have a greater Power, I fee as yet neither neceffity nor reafon.

§. 24. But 4. If Peace cannot otherwife be obtained, the matter may be thus accommodated, without violation of the Principles or Confciences of the Epifcopal, Presbyterian, or Con-gregational party. 1. Let it be agreed or confented to, that no man be put to profefs, that it is his judgement, that Bifhops fhould have as *jure divino* a Negative voice in Ordination. This was never an Article of Faith : it is not neceffary to be put among our *Credenda*. It is only the *Practice* that is pretended to be neceffary, and a *fubmiffion* to it. Seeing therefore it is not to be numbred with the *Credenda*, but the *agenda*, let Action without profeffed Belief fuffice. 2. Yea on the fame reafons, if any man be of a *Contrary* judgement, and think himfelf bound to declare it modeftly, moderately, and peaceably, let him have liberty to declare it, fo his practice be peaceable. 3. This being premifed, *Let the Prefident never Ordain, except in cafe of necef-fity, but with the prefence or confent of the Affembly of the Affo-ciated Paftors.* 4. And *let the Paftors never Ordain any, except in cafes of Neceffity, but when the Prefident is there prefent, nor with-out his Confent.* And in Cafes of *Neceffity* (as if he would de-prive the Churches of good Minifters, or the like) the Epifcopal men will yield it may be done.

§. 25. If fome think the Prefident *Muft* be one, and others
only

only think he *May* be one ; it is reasonable, if we will have peace, that our *May be* yield to their *Muſt be*. For ſo *we* yield but to what we confeſs lawful : but if *they* ſhould yield, it muſt be to what they judge to be ſinful. If it be not lawful to hold their *Muſt*, that is, that a Biſhop hath a Negative voice, yet is it lawful to forbear *de faſto* to Ordain till he be one, except it be in caſe of Neceſſity.

§. 26 If in an Aſſociation there be a company of young or weak Miniſters, and one only man that is able to try him that is offered to the Miniſtry, as to his skill in the Greek and Hebrew tongues, and his Philoſophy, *&c.* is it not lawful here for all the reſt to conſent that they will not Ordain any, except in caſes of Neceſſity, but when the foreſaid able man is one ? Who can doubt of this ? And if it be lawful in this caſe, it is much more lawful, when both the ability of the ſaid perſon, and the Peace of the Churches doth require it : or if it be but the laſt alone, I think it may well be yielded to.

§. 27. *But* (the Epiſcopal men will object,) *if every man ſhall have leave to Believe and Profeſs a Parity of Miniſters, the Preſident will but be deſpiſed, and this will be no way to Peace, but to Contention. Anſw.* You have but two remedies for this, and tell us which of them you would uſe. The firſt is, to force men by Club-law to ſubſcribe to your Negative voice, or not to hold the contrary : The ſecond is, to caſt them all out of the Communion of the Churches, that are not in judgement for your Negative voice, though they be Moderate, Peaceable, Godly men. And he that would have the firſt way taken, is a Tyrant, and would be a Cruel Perſecutor of his Brethren as good as himſelf. And he that would take the ſecond way, is both Tyrannous, and Schiſmatical, and far from a Catholike peaceable diſpoſition ; and if all muſt be caſt out or avoided by him, that are not in ſuch things of his opinion, he makes it impoſsible for the Churches to have peace with him.

§. 28. But they will further object : *If in Neceſſity they ſhall Ordain without the Preſident, this Neceſſity will be ordinarily pretended ; and ſo all your offers will be in vain. Anſw.* Prevent that and other ſuch inconveniences, by producing your weightieſt reaſons, and perſwading them ; or by any lawful means : but we muſt not have real Neceſſities neglected, and the Churches ruined,

ruined, for fear of mens unjuſt pretences of a Neceſſity: that's but a ſad Cure.

§. 29. But on the other ſide it will be objected, *This is but patching up a peace. If I think that one man hath no more right then another to a Negative voice, why ſhould I ſeem to grant it him by my practice?* Anſw. As when we come to Heaven, and not till then, we ſhall have *perfect Holineſs* ; ſo when we come to Heaven, and not till then, we ſhall have *perfect Unity and Peace.* But till then, I ſhall take that which you call *Patching*, as my Duty, and our great Benefit. If you think one man have not a Negative voice, we neither urge you to ſay that he hath, nor ſo much as to ſeem to own his claim. You ſhall have leave in the publike Regiſter of the Aſſociation, to put it under your hand, that [*Not as owning the claim of the Preſidents Negative voice, but as yielding in a Lawful thing for Peace, you do Conſent to forbear Ordaining any without him, except in Caſes of Neceſſity.*] This you may do, without any ſhew of contradicting your Principles, and this is all that is deſired.

§. 30 Queſt. *And may we not for peace ſake, grant them as much in point of Juriſdiction, as of Ordination, and Conſent to do nothing without Neceſſity, but when the Preſident is one, and doth Conſent?* Anſw. Either by *Juriſdiction* you mean *Law making*, or *Executive Government*. The firſt belongs to none but Chriſt, in the ſubſtance of his Worſhip ; and the Circumſtances no man may *Univerſally* and *Unchangeably* determine of. but *pro re nata*, according to emergent occaſions, the *Magiſtrate* may make Laws for them, and the *Paſtors* may make *Agreements* for *Concord* about them : but none ſhould determine of them without need: and therefore here is no work for *Legiſlators* (the Uſurpers that have grievouſly wronged the Church.) And for *Executive Government*, either it is over the *People*, or over the *Paſtors*. To give a Negative voice to the Preſident of an Aſſociation of the Paſtors of many Churches, in Governing the *People of a ſingle Church*, is to ſet up a new Office (a fixed Paſtor of many Churches) and to overthrow Government, and introduce the noxious ſort of Prelacy, which for my part, I intend not to be guilty of. And for proper Government of the *Paſtors*, I know none but God and Magiſtrates that have that Power. Every Biſhop, ſaith *Cyprian*, and the Council of *Carthage*, hath Power

of

of his own will, and is responsible for his Actions to God, and none of us are *Episcopi Episcoporum*, Bishops of Bishops. But there is a *Communion* among Pastors and Churches to be exercised, and so an avoiding or rejecting from Communion: and this some call (improperly) a Government. And in this, for my part, I should consent, where peace doth require it, that *we will not agree upon the rejecting of any Pastor of our Association* (no more then to the Accepting or Ordaining of them) *without the President, but in cases of Necessity*: and that just on the terms exprest about Ordination.

§. 31. As for instance, in a *particular Church*, there is a *Communion* to be held among all the *members*, though none of them but the *Officers* are *Governors* of the Church. And in many cases where the Peoples Consent is needful, its common to stand to a Major vote: and so great a stress is laid on this, that by many of the Congregational way the Government of the Church is said to be in the Major vote of the people: and yet 1. This is indeed *no Government* that belongs to them; but *Consent to Communion or Exclusion*; and 2. No Scripture doth require a Minor part to stand in all cases to the decision of a Major vote, nor give a Major vote any *Rule* over the Consciences of the Minor part (shew us this voting power in Scripture) And yet 3. All agree, that upon natural Reasons and General Rules of Scripture, the Churches are allowed, yea obliged, in lawful things, for maintaining *Unity and Peace*, to stand to the judgement of a *Major vote*, (in Cases that belong to them to vote in) though there be no particular word for it in the Scripture: Even so *Associate Pastors* have not a *proper Government* of one another, neither by *Presidents* or *Major votes*, (though over the people they have,) but are all under the Government of *God* and the *Magistrate* only. And yet they may in acts of *Consent* about Communion or Non-communion with one another, prudentially agree, to take the *Consent* of the *President*, or of the *Major vote of Pastors*, or of both, where Peace, or Order, or Edification requireth it: except in cases of Necessity.

§. 32. Quest. *But what will you take for a Case of Necessity? which you will except? Answ.* 1. If the President be dead. 2. Or sick, or absent and cannot come 3. Or if he be malignant, and wilfully refuse to Consent that the Church be well provided for or Governed. 4. And withall supposing that without the great hurt or hazzard of the Churches, we cannot delay the business, till he be one, or do Consent. 5. Especially if he be set in enmity against the welfare of the Church : and by pretence of a suspending vote would destroy the Church, and bring in unworthy hurtful persons or things. In all such Cases of *Necessity*, its time to lay by our humane Rules for peace and Order.

§. 33. Object. *But who shall be judge of this Necessity ?* Answ. The *Magistrate* only shall be the *Compelling Judge.* The people shall be the *Discerning Judges* : the *Pastors* shall at least have as much power as the *People* : each of them shall *Discern,* so far as they must *obey and execute.* And *God* only shall be the *final Judge.*

§. 34. Object. *But this will but cause Divisions and Confusions ; while the President thinks one thing Necessary, and the Pastors another, and the People another.* Answ. I answered this before. Reason must not be cast by, and the Churches ruined, and poyson and destruction taken in, on pretence of such inconveniences. If such a Case of difference fall out, each man will execute as he discerneth or judgeth, (being to answer for his own actions, and having none that can undertake to answer for him) And when we all come to the Bar of God for final Judgement, he that was in the right shall be justified, and he that falsly pretended Necessity against duty shall bear the blame.

§. 35. Object. *But in the mean time, the Churches will be divided.* Answ. 1. I told you there is no more hope of a *perfect Unity* on earth, then of *perfect Holiness.* 2. When two evils are before us, (though neither must be *chosen*; for *Evil* is not an Object of *choice,* unless as seeming good, yet) the *Greater* Evil must be first and most studiously repelled. And the deformity and destruction of the Churches, and the casting out of the Gospel and Worship of God, is a greater Evil then disorder about good actions, and differences about some Circumstances of Necessary works.

§. 36. All this that I have said about the Negative (*de facto*, though not *de jure*) that I would have Consented to for peace, I intend not to extend to those Cases and Countries where peace requireth it not, but rather the contrary : much less to encourage any to think such a Negative Necessary in it self. Some things

things may be Lawfully granted that are unlawfully and upon miſtake deſired,

§. 37. Laſtly underſtand alſo, that when I ſpeak of yielding to this Negative voice in Ordination, to the Preſident of ſuch an Aſſociation, I intend not to exclude the Presbyterie of a particular Church (where it is ſufficient) from the ſaid Power and exerciſe of Ordination: of which I am to ſpeak, in the following Chapter, which is *of the Preſident of ſuch a Presbyterie.*

CHAP. IV.

It is Lawful for the Presbyters of a particular Church, to have a fixed Preſident, during life.

---

§. 1.  Come now to the moſt Ancient fixed Biſhop that the Church was acquainted with, except the meer *Epiſcopus Gregis,* the Overſeer of the flock; and that is, *A Preſident of many Elders in one particular Church.* The Dioceſan B.ſhop was long after this: The firſt Biſhops (if you will call them ſo) in the Church were the firſt mentioned Itinerant Biſhops that were ſent abroad to convert ſouls and gather Churches, and afterward took care to water and confirm them. The next ſort of Biſhops (and the firſt ſo called) were the fixed Paſtors of particular Churches, that cannot be proved to have any ſuperiority over Presbyters. The th.rd

ſort

fort of Bishops (in time , and the first fixed Bishops that were superiours to other Pastors) were these Presidents of the Presbyteries of particular Churches. And these are they that now we have to speak of. And I shall prove that it is not unlawful to have such.

§. 2. But first I must tell you what I mean; and shew you that such may be had among us. I have in one of the former Disputations, defined a *particular Church*. It should ordinarily consist of no more then may hold *personal Communion together in Gods publick Worship*. But yet take notice, 1. That it tendeth to the strength and honour of it, that it be not too small; but consisting of as many as are well capable of the Ends. 2. And it is lawfull for these to have some other meeting places for part of the Church, besides the principal place which is for the whole. Chappels of ease may lawfully be made use of, for the benefit of the weak, and lame, and aged, that cannot alwayes or often come to the common Assembly. And where such Chappels are not, it is lawfull to make use of convenient houses. Yea if there were no Place to be had, sufficiently capacious of a full Assembly, or else if persecution forbad them to meet, it might still be but one Church, though the members met in several houses ordinarily : as five hundred in one, and three hundred in another , or one hundred only in several places, every one going to which house he pleased, and having several Pastors that in Society and by Consent did guide them all. But though somewhat disorderly may be born with in cases of Necessity; yet 1. As it is Necessary to the Ends, and so to the Being of a particular Church that they be a Society capable of personal Communion; and the personal Teaching, Guidance and Oversight of the same Pastors, So 2. It is desirable, as much tending to Order and Edification, that all of them that are able do frequently meet in one Assembly , for the Worshipping of God with one heart and mouth. And this is the Church I speak of.

§ 3. It is not of *Necessity to the Being* of such a particular Church that it have more Pastors then one : And when one only is the Pastor or Governour, that one alone may do all the works of a Pastor or Governour (For what else is his Office, but the state or Relation of a man obliged and authorized to do such works?)

.The

The Learned Dr. *H. H.* thinketh that the Apostles planted r one in Scripture times but single Pastors or Bishops (called also Presbyters) in every Church, with Deacons under them, without any other Presbyters (subject or assistant) over that Church. This I conceive cannot be proved, nor so much as the probability of it ; nay I think, at least a probability, if not a certainty of the contrary may be proved, of some Churches. But yet it is most likely that it was so with *many* Churches. And reason tells us, that the thing being in it self indifferent, was suted by the Apostles to the state of the particular Churches that they planted. A *small* Church might well have a *single* Pastor, when a *large* Church, especially in times of persecution, when they must assemble in several houses at once, required more. Some places might have many persons fit for the Office , and some but one : Which cases must needs have some Variety.

§. 4. Where there are *more* Pastors in such a Church, then one, I know of *no Necessity* that one should have any superiority over another: nor can I prove that it was so from the beginning. Some Divines of the Prelatical Judgement think that this was an Ordinance of the Apostles, at the first planting of such Churches ; Others of them think that it was of their *appointment*, but not actually *existent* till after Scripture times. Others of them think, that as *Hierom* saith, it began when factions rose in the Church, not by Divine Ordination, but Ecclesiastical agreement, for the preventing or cure of schism.

§. 5. The first Church that we find it in, in History, is that of *Alexandria.* And *Alexandria* was a place exceedingly given to sedition, tumults, and divisions : the contentions between *Cyril* and *Orestes*, the murder of *Hypatia* by *Peter* and his company, the assault made upon *Orestes* by *Ammonius* & the other *Nitrian* Monks, and many such feats in the dayes of *Theophilus, Dionysius*, and up to the beginning, do shew what they were. And *Socrates* saith of them expresly, *li. 7. cap. 13.* that [*The people of* Alexandria *above all other men, are given to Schism and contention ; for if any quarrel arise at any time among them, presently hainous and horrible offences use to follow, and the tumult is never appeased without great blood-shed.*] such were the *Alexandrians.*

§. 6. But yet it is certain that the Original of this custom, of setting up one as President or chief-Presbyter in a particular Church, cannot be found out, so as to say, by whom and when it was first brought in. But if it began upon the death of *Mark* at *Alexandria*, it must needs be long before the death of *John* the Apostle, (in that Church, what ever other Churces did.) But it seems that there was then a difference and indifferency in this point, and that other Churces did not presently imitate the Churches of *Alexandria* and *Rome* herein. He that reads *Clemens Epistle* to the *Corinthians* without partiality, I think will be of *Grotius* mind (before cited, *Epist. ad Gal. ad Bignon.*) that *Clemens* knew not any such Prelacy among the *Corinthians*, when he wrote that Epistle : And so we may say of some other Witnesses and Churches in those times, and afterwards in many places.

§. 7. It is not another *Order* of Ministers, or *Office*, that was in such Churches distinct from the Presbyters that assisted them. Their Presidents or Eminent Bishops were not made then *Episcopi Episcoporum, vel Pastores Pastorum*, as having an *Office* of Teaching and Governing the *other Pastors* , as *Pastors* have of teaching and Governing the *flock*. But they were only the *chief Presbyters*, or chief Bishops or Pastors of that Church, as an *Archdeacon* is to the *Deacons* when he is made such by their choice, as *Hieroms* comparison is (*ad Evagr.*)

§. 8. Nor is it lawfull now, even in the smallest Parish, for any *One* to assume such a superiority over any Presbyters (though such as have their maintenance from him, and are chosen by him, and are called, his *Curates*) as if he were of a Superiour *Order* or *Office*, and so the Governour of the other as his inferiours.

§. 9. But yet that a *Primacy of degree*, or *Presidency*, or *stated Moderatorship* of one in such a Church and Presbyterie, is lawfull, I think with small labour may be evinced. And 1.All the Arguments before used, for the *Presidency* of one in an *Association*, will prove this *Parochial Presidency* with advantage.

§. 10. 2. It is a thing that is constantly or very ordinarily practised among us already , with common approbation , or without contradiction, as far as I have heard. Many places have one Minister only that is presented by the Patron ; and this one Pastor hath divers with him (or as the common saying is, *Under him :*)

him :) If it be a great Congregation, many have a **Curate** or af-fiftant in the Town with them, and other Curates at Chappels that depend on that Town. Though there be but one Chap-pel in this Parifh where I live, yet this Church hath three or four Prefbyters, and three or four Deacons. And the Law of the Land doth give one Minifter only the *Maintenance* (called the Benefice) and the Power of the Temple, and the calling of Affemblies, and the choice of Curates, whom he is to maintain. And they that are chofen and maintained by him, muft and will be ruled by him; at leaft in all *circumftantial* things. It belongs not to them to Rule even the *People contrary* to Gods word; nor in *fubftantials* to inftitute new Ordinances of Worfhip : But in *circumftantials* which are left to humane determina-tion (as time, place, particulars of order, decency, *&c.*) no doubt but the chief Paftors in each Parifh, do exercife actually a Negative Vote, and the Curates do nothing without their con-fent. So that this fort of *Prefidency* being common among us, without contradiction I may take it for granted that it hath the common confent. And if any allow not of fo much as is *com-monly ufed*, yet a *Prefidency* is a *far lower thing*.

§. 11. 3. This fort of P.efidency, (yea with fuch a Nega-tive voice as in the foregoing Chapter is granted) is ufually grounded on *Nature* and the *General Rules* of Scripture, and warranted by them. *Nature* teacheth us, that the younger and more ignorant and unlearned, fhould (proportionably) fub-mit to the Elder and Wifer, and in a fort be Ruled by them. And *Scripture* faith the fame, 1 *Pet.* 5. 5. [*Ye younger fubmit your felves unto the Elder.*] Even the *aged Woemen* (that were no Officers) *muft teach the younger, Tit.* 2 4. Now it common-ly falls out that in every Parifh that hath many Minifter, there is but one that is aged, or grave, and that one common-ly is more Learned and judicious then the reft, who are ufually fome young unexercifed men. Now in fuch cafes. (which is common) no man can deny that authority to age or Wifdom that is naturally due to it, nor exempt the younger ignoranter men from that fubmiffion which naturally they are bound to. Equality of Office may ftand with inequality of gifts and age, and confequently of duty

§. 12. 4. ae good of the Curch requireth it that the diproportion of Minifters gifts in one and the fame Congregation fhould be the ordinary cafe (And rules muft be fitted to ordinary cafes, rather then to extraordinary.) For God doth not (as we fee by long and fad experience) beftow his excellent gifts fo commonly, as that one Church (ordinarily) fhould have many Learned able men: There are but few that are of eminency for judgement and other Minifterial abilities : Not one for many Parifhes : If therefore many of thefe fhould be placed together in one Church, it would be againft the common good, and an unjuft ingroffment, and injurious unto others. Providence therefore by the rarity of eminent parts, doth teach us to make it the ordinary courfe, that in every Congregation where there are many Paftors, fome one of chiefeft parts be chofen to be ftanding Moderator of the reft.

§. 13. 5. That which is lawfull for *Private men* to do towards one another, is lawfull Prudentially for *Paftors* that are confcious of their own imperfection, to do towards one that they think more able then themfelves. But it is lawful for Private men to *be fubject one to another in humility* : therefore it is lawfull for fuch Paftors, 1 *Pet.* 5. 5. [*Yea all of you be fubject one to another, and be cloathed with humility*] A voluntary fubjection to another, in lawfull actions, is nowhere forbidden, but here commanded ; and is a great part of Chriftian felf denyal : and therefore lawful.

§. 14. 6 And it is a thing that dependeth fo much on the Wifdom and will of Presbyters, that no man *can hinder* it. I can make another Minifter a Bifhop to me, whether other men will or not. *Honor eft in honorante.* I can 1. In judgement efteem him more able, yea or more authorized, then other men. 2. And I can have recourfe to him for advice. 3. And I can give him a Negative vote in all my Minifterial Actions, fo far as they are left to humane determination : I can refolve to do nothing in fuch matters, but by his confent. And if I find reafon for this in his abilities, and my difabilities, it is Lawful. The thing therefore being Lawfull, and fuch as none can hinder me from, I fee not why it may not be made the matter of Confent, when the Churches Peace requireth it.

§. 15. 7. Moreover, as Divifions juftly provoked the Churches at firft to think of fuch lawful means, for the cure ; fo our

Divifions

'Divisions, or danger of them, do make it as Neceſſary, or convenient, now as then.   We ſee to our ſhame, that in moſt or many Congregations, Miniſters that are *equal* or neer to an equality in parts and place, can hardly agree and live in Peace : but
they are jealous of one another, and envying each others eſteem
and intereſt (Though I confeſs this is ſo odious a vice, that its
an abominable ſhamefull thing, that any Miniſter of Chriſt ſhould
be tainted with it: but ſo it is; we cannot hide it.) And therefore it
is our ordinary courſe to have ſuch a diſparity of age, and parts,
and intereſts, that one may have the preheminence, and ſome rule,
and the reſt be ruled by him.

§. 16. 8. Laſtly, the Antiquity and ſpeedy Univerſality of
this courſe, is a ſtrong argument to make men moderate in the
point. For 1. It ſeemeth a moſt improbable thing that *all* the
Churches, or *ſo many*, ſhould ſo *ſuddenly* take up this *Preſidency,*
Prelacy, or *Diſparity* without ſcruple or reſiſtance, if it had been
againſt the Apoſtles minds.   For it cannot be imagined that all
theſe Churches that were planted by the Apoſtles, or Apoſtolical
men, and had ſeen them and converſed with them, ſhould be
either utterly ignorant of their minds, in ſuch a matter of pub-
lique practice, or elſe ſhould be all ſo careleſs of obeying their
new received doctrine, as preſently and unanimouſly to *conſent*
to a change, or *endure* it without reſiſtance.   Would *no Church*
or *no perſons* in the world, contend for the retention of the Apoſtolical inſtitutions?   Would *no Church* hold their own, and
bear witneſs againſt the corruption and innovations of the reſt?
would *no perſons* ſay, [*you go about to alter the frame of Govern-*
ment newly planted among us by the Holy Ghoſt ; *It was not thus*
in the dayes of Peter, *or* Paul, *or* John; *and therefore we will have no*
change.]   This ſeems to me a thing incredible, that the whole
Church ſhould all at once almoſt ſo ſuddenly and ſilently yield to
ſuch a change of Government. And I do not think that any man
can bring one teſtimony from all the volumes of Antiquity to
prove that ever Church or perſon reſiſted or diſclaimed ſuch a
change, in the times when it muſt be made, if ever it was made,
that is, in the firſt or ſecond ages.

§. 17. Yea 2. It is plain by the teſtimony of *Hierom* before mentioned and other teſtimonies of antiquity, that in *Alexandria,* at
leaſt, this practice was uſed in the dayes of the *Apoſtles* them-

S ſ   ſelves.

felves. For they teftifie that from the dayes of *Mark the Evangelift* till the days of Heroclas *and* Dionyfius, *the Presbyters chofe one from among them, and called him their Bifhop.* Now it is fuppofed by the beft Chronologers that *Mark* was flain about the fixty third year of our Lord, and the tenth of *Nero*; and that *Peter* and *Paul* were put to death about the fixty fixth of our Lord, and thirteenth of *Nero*, and that *John* the Apoftle died about the ninety eighth year of our Lord, and the firft of *Trajan*, which was about thirty five years after the death of *Mark*. Now I would leave it to any mans impartial confideration, whether it be credible that the holy Apoftles, and all the Evangelifts or Affiftants of them, then alive, would have fuffered this innovation and corruption in the Church without a plain difowning it and reproving it : Would they filently fee their newly eftablifhed Order violated in their own dayes, and not fo much as tell the Churches of the fin and danger? Or if they had indeed done this, would none regard it, nor remember it, fo much as to refift the fin? Thefe things are incredible.

§. 18. And I am confident if the *judicious godly people had their choice*, from the experience of what is for their good, they would commonly choofe a fixed Prefident or chief Paftor in every Church. Yea I fee, that they will not ordinarily endure that it fhould be otherwife. For when they find that God doth ufually qualifie one above the reft of their Teachers, they will hardly confent that the reft have an equal power over them. I have feen even a fober unanimous Godly people, refufe fo much as to give their hands to an affiftant Presbyter whom yet they loved, honoured and obeyed, though they were urged hard by him that they preferred, and all from a loathnefs that there fhould be a parity. I know not one Congregation to my remembrance, that hath many Minifters, but would have one be chief.

§. 19. Object. *But,* (the Prelatical men will fay) *our Parifhes are not capable of this, becaufe they have commonly but one Paftor, nor have maintainance for more.* Anfw. 1. Though the greater number have but one yet it is an ordinary cafe to have two, or three, or more, where there are Chappels in the Parifh, and the Congregations great, as in Market Towns. And if ever we have Peace and a fetled faithfull Magiftrate that will do his part

for

for the house of God, we shall certainly have many Ministers in great Congregations : Or else they are like to be left desolate ; For Ministers will over-run them , for fear of undertaking far more work then with their utmost pains they are able to perform.

§. 20. And 2. There are few Congregations, I hope, of Godly people , but have some private men in them that are fit to be Ordained Assistant Presbyters,though not to govern a Church alone (without necessity) yet to assist a Learned, judicious man, such as understand the body of Divinity, (as to the great and necessary points) and are able to pray and discourse as well as many or most Ministers, and to exhort publickly in a case of need. He that would imitate the example of the Primitive Church (at least in the second Century) should Ordain such as these to be some of them *Assistant Elders*, and some of them *Deacons* in every Church (that hath such ;) and let them not teach publickly, when a more learned, able Pastor is at hand to do it ; but let them assist him in what they are fittest to perform ; Yet let them not be *Lay Elders* : but authorized to all Pastoral administrations,and of one and the same office with the Pastor, though dividing the exercise and execution according to their abilities and opportunities ; and not comming in without Ordination, nor yet taking up the Office only *pro tempore*. And thus every Parish, where are able Godly-men, may have a Presbyterie and President.

§. 21. Till then 3. It is granted by the Learned Dr. *H. H.* that it is not necessary to the being of a Bishop that he have fellow Presbyters with him in that Church : If he have but *Deacons* it may suffice. And this is easie to be had.

§. 22. And indeed 1. The parts of many very able Christians, are too much buried and lost as to the Church, for want of being drawn into more publick use. 2. And it is it that tempteth them to run of themselves into the Ministry, or to preach without Ordination. 3. And yet few of these are fit to be trusted with the Preaching of the word, or guiding of a Church alone, no nor in equality with others ; for they would either corrupt the doctrine, or divide the Church. But under the inspection and direction of a more Learned judicious man, as his assistants, doing nothing against his mind, they might be very serviceable

to

to some Churches. And such a Bishop with such a Presbyterie and Deacons (neither Lay, nor usually very Learned) were the ancient fixed Governours of the Churches, if I can understand antiquity.

CHAP. V.

Objections against the Presidency forementioned, answered.

§. 1. **B**UT it is not likely but all these motions will have Dissenters on both sides; It were strange if in a divided age and place, and among a people engaged in so many several parties, and that so deeply as now men are, there should any healing remedy be propounded, that should not have abundance of opposers: Most men are prejudiced and affected at their Education, or opportunities, or parties, or several interest sway them. And therefore I expect that most should reject all that I say, and some of them with much reproach and scorn. Our disease were not so great and dangerous, if it could but endure the remedy. But let us consider some of their Objections.

§. 2. Object. 1. The *unpeaceable* men of the Prelatical way will say [*This is but to turn a Bishop into a Parish-Priest; and to make him the Ruler of a Parish and a Curate or two, and in many places, of no Ministers at all: A fair Promotion. It seems you would leave them but a name and shadow, and make them to be contemptible.*

§. 3. *Answ.* 1. Remember that I grant you also the *Presiden-*

cy

cy of *Associations*, &c. which you may call an *Archbisboprick*
if you please. 2. Is it *honour* that you contend for , or *labour*
and *service* to the Church ? If honour, you must get it by being
the *servants* of others, and not by being Lords of the Clergy
or heritage of God. If you are seeking honour of men, and
founding offices in the Church, by such directors as ambition,
you are not the men that we can hope for Peace or Holiness from,
and therefore can have little treaty with you , but to lay by
your wickedness. But if it be *service* that you contend for, in order to the Churches good, try first whether a *Parish* will not find
you work enough. I have tried it, and find that if I were ten men,
I could find as much as I am able to do, in this one Parish. Though
I do as much as I am well able night and day, and have so many
helpers, yet it is so great a trouble to me, that my work and
charge is quite too great for me, that I have been often tempted
to desert it, and go to a smaller place : And nothing stayes me
but this consideration , that God requireth no more then I can
do, and that its better do what I can then nothing : and that if
I leave them , the next is like to do no more. Could I but speak
with each man in my Parish by personal Instruction, once a
moneth, or once a quarter, or half year, it would put me into
high expectations of making a very great change among them,
by this means : But when I am not able to speak to them past
once a year, or two years, I must needs fear lest the force of former
words will be lost before I come again. And yet must you
needs have *more work and service,* and *more souls* to answer for ?
To deal plainly and faithfully with you, Brethren, impartial
standers by conceive that its time for you rather to be more diligent in a smaller charge, and to lament your negligence in your
Parishes, and publickly to bewail that you have by your idleness
betrayed so many souls: letting them alone in their ignorance and
ungodliness, and commonly doing little in your charges, but what
you do at Church in publick. ~~Overseers~~ think that most of you
are fitter for smaller charges rather then for greater. I doubt
this will offend many. But you were better use it to your Repentance and Reformation, then your offence.

§.4. And 3. I pray you consider how your Passion and partiality maketh you contradict your selves. Do you not use to reproach the *Presbyters*, that they would all be Bishops, and they
would

Marginal note: Its more then Dr. *H. H.* speaks of the Primitive Bishops, that had no Presbyters under them but one or more Deacons.

would have a Bishop in every Parish, and so are against Bishops, that they may be Bishops themselves? And what! is a Parish Bishoprick so great a prize for *our* Ambition, and yet is it so contemptible to *yours*? Are *we proud* for seeking to be *Parish Bishops*, and do *you* take it as an empty name or shadow? At least then confess hereafter, that *your Pride* is so much greater then ours, that the Mark of our Ambition is taken by you to be a low dishonourable state.

§. 5. And 4. I would intreat you impartially to try, whether the Primitive Apostolick Episcopacy fixed in particular Churches were not a *Parochial Episcopacy*? Try whether I have not proved it before? And if it were, will you pretend to antiquity, and Apostolick institution, and yet despise the primitive simplicity, and that which you confess was settled by the Apostles? Let the Eldest carry it without any more ado.

§. 6. And 5. At least say no more that you are for *Episcopacy*, and we against it: when we are for *Episcopacy* as well as you. It is only your *transcendent*, or *exorbitant* sort of Episcopacy that we are against. Say not still that we have no Power of Ordination, because we are not Bishops; but because we are only *Bishops of one Church*. Put the controversie trúly as it is, *Whether it be lawful for the Bishop of one Church with his Prebytery to Ordain?* Yea or whether many such Associated may Ordain? Or rather, whether it be tyed to the Bishop of many Churches (as you would have it :) that is, *Whether Ordination belong to Archbishops only?* Is not this the controversie?

§. 7. And then 6. Why do you in your *Definitions* of Episcopacy (which you very seldom and sparingly give us) require no more then a *Parochial* Episcopacy, and yet now despise it as if it were no Episcopacy at all? Tell us plainly what you mean by a Bishop? I thought you meant a *Primus Presbyterorum*, or at least, a Ruler of People and Presbyters? And is not this to be found in a Parish Bishop, as well as in a Bishop of many Parishes, or Churches? Change your *Definition* from this day forward, if you must have a change of the thing defined, as it seems you must.

§. 8. And I wou'd know whether you can prove that it is *Essential* to a Bishop to have more Churches or Parishes then one? I'ove it if you are able. Was not great *Gregory* of *Naocesarea* a Bishop

Bishop with his *seventeen souls* ? And was not *Alexander* (the Colliar) whom he Ordained at *Comana*, a Bishop, though but of a small Assembly ? Do not some of you confess, that Bishops in Scripture-times had no subject Presbyters, and consequently had but a single Congregation ? If then a Parish or Congregational Bishop were a true Bishop, why may he not be so still ?

§. 9. *Object.* 2. *But the Church under Christian Princes should not be conformed to the model of the Church under persecution : Shall Bishops have no more power and honour now then they had then ? We see in* Constantines *dayes a change was made. Must they be tyed to a Parish now, because they were Bishops only of a Parish in Scripture-times ?*

§. 10. *Answ.* 1. We would not have them persecuted now, as they were then, nor yet to want any due encouragement or assistance that a Christian Magistrate can afford them. But yet we would have Gods Word to be our Rule, and Bishops to be the same things now as then, and we would not have men make the prosperity of the Church a pretence for altering the Ordinances or Institutions of Christ, and making such changes as their conceits or ambitious minds incline them to. We shall never have a Rule nor fixed certainty, if we may change things our selves on such pretences. Pretend not then to Antiquity, as you do.

§. 11. And 2. I have in the former Disputation proved by many Reasons, that it was not the mind of the Apostles themselves, that the Parochial or Congregational Churches which they planted, should be changed into another sort of Churches. Nor is there any reason for it, but against it, in the prosperity of the Church, and piety of Magistrates. For 1. Pious Magistrates should help to keep, and not to break Apostolical institutions. 2. And pious Magistrates should further the good of the Church, and not hurt it to advance ambitious men.

§. 12. For 3. Ministers are for the Churches, and therefore no change must be made on such pretences that is against the good of the Churches. If every Parish or Congregation then, were meet to have a Bishop and Presbyterie of their own, why shall the Church be now so abused, as that a whole County shall have but one Bishop and his Presbyterie ? If every Hospital or Town had a Physitian with his Apothecaries and Mates, in your Fathers dayes, would you be there benefactors, by ... that

all

all the County shall have but one Physitian with his Apothe-caries ? Or if every School had a Schoolmaster in your Fore-fathers dayes, will you say, there shall be but one in your dayes, in a whole County ? Do you thus think to honour Physitians and Schoolmasters, to the ruine of the people and the Schools ? So do you in your advancement of Bishops. Upon my certain ex-perience I dare affirm it, that every Parish of four or five thousand souls, yea of a thousand souls, hath need of such a Presbyterie for their Oversight. And is not he that hath a Coun-ty on his hands, like to do less for this Town or Parish, then if he had no more then this ? If your Bees swarm, you will not keep them all still in an hive, nor think of enlarging the hive to that end : but you will help the swarm to an hive of their own. If your Children marry, you will rather settle them in Families of their own, then retain all them and all their Children in the Family with your selves. So if a Bishop of one Church should Convert all the Countrey, he should rather settle them in seve-ral Churches, proportionable to their numbers and distances, then to call them all *his own Church.*

§. 13. Object. 3. *But by this means the Church would be pestered with Bishops. What a number of Bishops would you have, if every Parish-Priest were a Bishop? We read not of such numbers as this would procure, in the antient times.*

§. 14. *Answ.* 1. I find where Christ commandeth us to pray the Lord of the harvest to send forth Labourers (that is, more Labourers) into the harvest, because of the greatness of the harvest. But I find not where he once requireth us to pray or wish that there may not be too many, for fear of pestering the Church, or diminishing the honour of the Clergy. Mens purses, I warrant you, will hinder the over-abounding of them; and Gods providence doth not enrich too many with abilities and willingness for the work. Do *you* undertake that they shall not be too *bad*; and I dare undertake they will not be *too many.*

§. 15. And 2. Is it not the felicity and glory of the Church which you object as an inconvenience or reproach ? O blessed time and place that hath but *enow* that are able and faithfull ! But I never knew, nor heard, nor read of the age that had too many that were good and faithfull in the work. Would you not have a chief Schoolmaster in every School, or Town, for

fear

fear the Land should be pestered or overwhelmed with School-masters? Why how can there be too many, when people will imploy no more then they need? O miserable Church that hath such Bishops, that are afraid Gods vineyard should be furnished with labourers, lest their greatness and honour should be diminished! Do you not see how many thousand souls lie still in ignorance, presumption and security for all the number of labourers that we have? And see you not that six parts of the world are Infidels, and much for want of Teachers to instruct them? And yet are you afraid that there will be too many? What could the enemy of the Church say worse?

§. 16. *Object. We do not mean too many Teachers, but too many Bishops; that is, too many Governours of the Church. Answ.* I. God knoweth no Governours Ministeriall but teachers: It seems you would have somewhat that you call *Government* and leave the *labour of Teaching* to others: As if you knew not that it is they that are *especially worthy of the double honour that labour in the word and doctrine,* 1 *Tim.* 5. 17. Or as if you knew not that even the Government of Pastors is mostly by teaching. 2. Government and Teaching go together, and are both necessary to the Church; And the diminishing the number of Governours and of Teachers is all one: As a Physitian doth Govern all his Patients in order to their cure, and a Schoolmaster all his schollars in order to their learning; so doth a Pastor all his flock, in order to their sanctification and salvation. And for the Government of the *Ministers themselves,* the number shall be increased as little as may be. Parish Bishops will Govern but a few; and therefore they can wrong but few, by their mis-government.

§. 17. *Object.* 4. *But by this means we shall have unworthy, raw, and ignorant men made Bishops: What kind of Bishops shall we have, if every Parish Priest must be a Bishop? Some of them are boyes, and some of them empty, silly souls to make Bishops of.*

§. 18. *Answ.* I shall lay open the nakedness of this Objection also, so that it shall be no shelter to domineering in the Church. 1. Awake the sparks of humility that are in you, and tell us openly, whether you think your selves more able worthy men to Govern a County, or a hundred Parishes, then such as we are to Govern one? Though I have been many and many a time tempted with *Jonas* to run away from the charge that is cast

T t   upon

upon me, as a burden too heavy for me to bear, and I know my self to be lamentably insufficient for it: yet I must profess, that I am so proud as to think my self as able to be the Pastor or Bishop of this Parish, as most Bishops in *England*, yea or any one of them, to be the Pastor and Governour of a County, or an hundred or two hundred Parishes. Were you humble, or did you dwell at home, or take an account of your own abilities, when you reproach others as unable to be the Bishops of a Parish, and think your selves able to be the Bishops of a Diocess and contend for it so eagerly?

§.19. And 2. I further answer you: We will leave you not a rag of this Objection to cover your nakedness. For if any Pastors or Parish Bishops be more ignorant then others, and unfit to Teach and Rule their flocks without the assistance, teaching or direction of more able men, we all agree that its the duty of such men to *Learn* while they are *Teachers*, and to be *Ruled* while they are *Rulers*, by them that are *wiser*. For as is said, a *Parity* in regard of *office*, doth not deny a *disparity* of *gifts* and *parts*: And we constantly hold, that of men that are equal in regard of office, the younger and more ignorant should learn of the aged that are more able and wise, and be *Ruled* by their advice, as far as their insufficiency makes it necessary. And will not this suffice?

§. 20. And 3. If this suffice not, consider that Associated Pastors are linked together, and do nothing in any weighty matters of common concernment (or of private, wherein they need advice) without the help and directions of the rest. And a young man may govern a Parish by the advice of a Presbyterie and also of Associated able Pastors, as well as such Bishops as we have had, have governed a Diocess.

§. 21. And yet 4. If all this suffice not, be it known to you that we endeavour to have the best that can be got for every Parish: and Novices we will have none, except in case of meer necessity: And we have an act for rejecting all the insufficient, as well as the scandalous and negligent: and any of you may be heard that will charge any among us with insufficiency. Sure I am we are cleansing the Church of the insufficient and scandalous that the Prelates brought in, as fast a we can: if any prove like them, that since are introduced, we desire that they may

speed

speed no better. What side soever they be on, we desire able faithfull men, and desire the ejection of the insufficient and unfaithfull. And youth doth not alway prove insufficiency. Witness *Timothy*, whose youth was not to be despised. At what age *Origen* and many more of old began, is commonly known. *Vigelius* was Bishop at twenty years of age (the *Tridentine* Bishop) We will promise you that we will have none so young to be Parish Presbyters, as *Rome* hath had some Popes and Cardinals and Archbishops and Bishops. Nor shall any such ignorant insufficient men, I hope, be admitted, as were commonly admitted by the Prelates.

§. 22. Object. 5. *But the Apostles and Evangelists had a larger circuit then a Parish, and therefore so should their Successors have?* *Answ.* I grant you that they had a larger circuit, and that herein, and in their ordinary work they have successors : And we consent that you shall be their Successors. Gird up your loins, and travail about as far as you please, and preach the Gospel to as many as will receive you (and sure the Apostles forced none) and convert as many souls as you can, and direct them when you have done in the way of Church-communion, and do all the good that you can in the world, and try whether we will hinder you. Have you not liberty to do as the Apostles did ? Be ye servants of all, and seek to save all, and take on you thus the care of all the Churches, and see who will forbid such an Episcopacy as this ?

§. 23. Object. 6. *But it seems you would have none compelled to obey the Bishops, but they only that are willing should do it : and so men shall have liberty of conscience, and anarchy and parity and confusion will be brought into the Church.* *Answ.* 1. I would have none have liberty for any certain impiety or sin : And yet I would have no sin punished beyond the measure of its deserts. And I would not have preachers made no Preachers (unless the Church may spare them) because their judgements are against Diocesan Bishops : and therefore I would have none silenced or suspended for this. 2. And what is it that you would have thats better ? Would you have men forced to acknowledge and submit to your Episcopacy ? And how ? Small penalties will not change mens judgements, nor consciences. Silencing or death would deprive the Church of their labours · and so we must

lose

lofe our Teachers left they difobey the Bifhops. If this be your cure, it difgraceth your caufe. We defire not Prelacy at fo dear a rate. Its a fad order that deftroyes the duty ordered.

§. 24. Object. *But this is to take down all Church-Government, if all fhall have what Government they lift.* Anfw. 1. Was there no Church-Government before the dayes of *Conftantine* the Emperour? 2. Do you pretend to antiquity, and fly from the Antient Government as none? You fhall have the fame means as all the Bifhops of the Church had for above three hundred years to bring men to your obedience: and is that nothing with you? Why is it commonly maintained by us all, that the Primitive ftate was that pureft ftate, which after times fhould ftrive to imitate, if yet it was fo defective as you imagine? 3. And why have you ftill pretended to fuch a power and excellent ufefulnefs in the Prelatical Government, if now you confefs that it is but anarchy, and as bad as nothing, without the inforcement of the Magiftrate? What Magiftrate forceth men to obey the Presbyteries now in *England*, *Scotland*, or many other places? 4. Yet it is our defire, that the Magiftrate will do his duty, and maintain order in the Church, and hinder diforders, and all known fin: but fo, as not to put his fword into the hand or ufe it at the pleafure of every party that would be lifted up. Let him prudently countenance that way of Government, that tendeth moft to the good of the Churches under his care; but not fo as to perfecute, filence, or caft out, all fuch as are for a different form, in cafe where difference is tolerable. 5. And in good fadnefs, is it not more prudent for the Magiftrate to keep the fword in his own hands if really it be the fword that muft do the work? If Epifcopal Government can do fo little without the compulfion of the Magiftrate, fo that all the honour of the good effects belongeth to the fword, truly I think it prudence in him to do his part himfelf, and leave Bifhops to their part, that fo he may have the honour that, it feems, belongs unto his office, and the Bifhop may not go away with it, nor the Presbyterie neither. Let the fecular Bifhop have the honour of all that Order and unity that arifeth from compulfion: and good reafon, when he muft have the labour, and run the hazzard if he do it amifs: and let the Ecclefiaftical Bifhops have the honour of all that order and unity that arifeth from their management

of

of the spiritual sword and Keyes. 6. And lastly I answer, that this is not the subject that you and we have to dispute of. It is Ecclesiastical Government by Ministers, and not secular by Magistrates that is our controversie. It is of the Power left by Christ to Pastors and not to Princes

§. 25. Object. *But at least those should be excommunicated that deny obedience to their Bishops : that is a Power that is left in the Bishops themselves, whether the Magistrate consent or not.* Answ. 1. Excommunication is a sentence that should fall on none but for such gross and hainous sin, if not also obstinacy and impenitency in them, as is mentioned in Scripture: Using it in cases of controversie and tolerable differences, is but a tearing and dividing the Church. 2. We take it not for our duty to excommunicate you, because you are for Diocesan Prelacy : therefore you should not take it for yours to excommunicate others because they are against it. For 3 If your *species* of Episcopacy be such as I have proved it, you have more need to repent and amend, and ask forgiveness of God and men, then to excommunicate them that are not of your opinion, and for your sin. 4. But if you take this to be your duty, who hath hindered you from it these twelve years? You had liberty, for ought I know, to have discharged your consciences, and to have excommunicated us all. 5. But you might so easily see what was like to come of it, that it is no wonder that you forbore. If such a Ministry and such a people as are now your adherents (whose description I forbear) should execute your sentence, and cast us and our adherents out of their communion, what contempt would it bring upon you in *England?* The Ale-houses would be shut up for the most part, against us : But that and the rest, would be easily born : I think this is not your way.

§. 26. Object. 7 *But what need you form us a new sort of Episcopacy? were we not well enough before? Why did you pull down that which was well planted, and now pretend to commend a better to us? We were well if you had let us alone.*

§. 27. Answ. 1. But We were not well, because *you would not let us alone.* The Ministers that were silenced, and imprisoned, and banished, and the thousands of people that were fain to follow them, and all those that were undone by your prosecutions in *England,* were not well. But this is a small matter : The ig-

Tt 3   norant

norant Congregations that had ignorant and drunken guides, where Piety was ſcorned as Puritaniſm, and impiety made a thing of nothing , and where Satan was ſo commonly ſerved ; the many hundred Congregations in *England* that never knew what true Diſcipline meant, nor never ſaw in all their lives, a drunkard, oppreſſor, railer, blaſphemer, either caſt out, or penitently confeſs his ſin, before the Church , all theſe were not well,though you were well. 2. Whether we were well before, I have ſhewed in my firſt Diſputation, and thither I refer you. 3. And whether we have *brought in a new Epiſcopacy*,or only *caſt out a new one* , and deſire to bring in the *Old*, we are content to put it to an equal tryall. We all concurr in offering you this motion. *Let the oldeſt ſtand, and the neweſt be caſt out.*

§. 28. Objeƈt. 8. *Judge now by the effeƈts : The Epiſcopacy which you blame , did keep up Order and Unity in the Church: It kept under thoſe weeds of hereſie and error that ſince ſprung up : We had then no Quakers , nor Seekers, nor ſuch other Seƈts as now abound : This ſwarm of Errors ſhews which Government is beſt.*

§. 29. *Anſw.* This is a groſs fallacy, *à non cauſa pro cauſa:* to which I return you my anſwer in theſe ſeven conſiderations. 1.You tell us of the good that you think you did: but you tell us not of the hurt. I hope I love Diviſions or Hereſies as little as ever a Biſhop in *England* : and yet I muſt profeſs that I had rather an hundred times, have things continue as they are with all our ſwarms of hereſies,then to be reſtored to their ancient paſs. Our loſs is as great as *Joſephs* in being removed from the Priſon to *Pharaohs* ungodly family : I mean in ſpirituals (of ſeculars anon.) I know not of an Anabaptiſt,Separatiſt, Quaker or any other Seƈtary in the Town that I live in,for all this noiſe ; unleſs you will take a few Infidels for Seƈtaries, or a few ignorant Papiſts, or thoſe of your own way. But on the other ſide, I hope there are many hundreds that truly fear God , that formerly were drowned in ignorance and ungodlineſs. The families that were wont to curſe and ſwear and rail at Godlineſs,do now worſhip God,and ſet up holy inſtruƈtions,and caſt out ſin : and this is *our* change: And in ſome meaſure,I have reaſon to believe that it is ſo in other places alſo.

§. 30. 2. The Errors of the times are many of them *your own*, and therefore you exclaim againſt *your ſelves.* It is *of your own ſelves*

selves that men arise, that write against *Original sin*, and for *Liberty of Prophecying*, (which is more then Liberty of Belie-ving) and for a kind of *Limbus Patrum* and *Infantum*, and for humane *Satisfactions* for sin to God, and for the *Primacy of* the Pope, and that all our Protestant Churches are no Churches, or Ministers no Ministers, that have not Prelatical Ordination, yea and a Succession of it ; with many the like (to say nothing of other *Pelagian* weeds.) It doth not therefore become you to reproach us with our swarms of Errors while you introduce them.

§. 31. 3. There were Heresies and Sects even in the dayes of Prelacy. Had you not then the Familists, the Grundletoni-ans, (such as *Hacket*, and *Coppinger*, and *Arthington*) and the Anabaptists, and Separatists, and Antinomians, and Papists, and such like ? besides the contentions between the Arminians and Antiarminians, and the contentions raised by Episcopacy it self, and the Ceremonies that it upheld ? Who were they that rose up against the Bishops, and pulled them down, if there were Unity under them, as you pretend ?

§. 32. 4. The truth is, it was the Magistrate and not Epis-copacy that kept that Unity and Peace among us which we had ; and that kept under Heresies so much as they were kept under. Take not therefore the Magistrates honour to your selves. Who would have attended your Courts, or submitted to your censures, had it not been for fear of the Secular power ? I think but few. You know the Hereticks themselves obeyed you not for Consci-ence sake. Nor would they have regarded your Excommuni-cation, if the Magistrate would have let them alone. If it was the spiritual sword in your hands that kept out Heresies, why did you not keep them out since, as well as then ? You have the same power from Christ now as ever you had. And I hope the fears of persecution will not hinder you from your duty : espe-cially when you can name so few that have suffered for exerci-sing Church-discipline by Episcopal power ! at least this was no hinderance a few years ago. For my part, I heartily wish you free from persecution, if you are not. But again I tell you, that which I suppose you know ; that as free a Toleration of Prelacy in *England* as there is of Presbyterie, were the likelyest way to bring you into perpetual contempt. For we cannot but know, that besides a few Civil engaged Gentlemen, Ministers, and others, your main body would consist of those that for their notorious impiety, scandal or ignorance, are thought unmeet for Church-communion by others: and that when you came to exercise Discipline on them, they would hate you and fly from you as much as ever they did from Puritans: and if you did indulge them, and not reform them or cast them out, your Church would be the Contempt of the sober part of the world, and your own sober members would quickly relinquish it for shame. For [the Church of *England*] if you would needs be so called, would be taken for the *sink* of all the other Churches in *England*. This is a clear and certain truth that is easily discerned, without a Prophetick spirit : and the dishonour of all this would reflect upon your Prelacy.

§. 33. 5. And further, I answer your Objection ; that it is not the insufficiency of other Church-government in comparison of Prelacy, that was the inlet of our Heresies and Divisions; but it was the Licentiousness of a time of war, when all evil spirits are turned loose, and the subtilty of the Papists that have taken advantage to spawn among us the Quakers, and Levellers, and Behemists, and other Paracelsians, and the Seekers to confound and dishonour us if they could, and to promote their cause. And in times of war, especially when such changes in the Civil state ensue, and so many adversaries are watching to sow tares, such things are common.

§. 34. 6. And you cannot say, that it comes from the insufficiency of other Government in comparison of yours, because you see no other Government setled instead of yours, so far as to be seconded by the sword or secular power ; no nor so far as to have a word of command or perswasion to the people to obey it, (except an Ordinance that in most places was hindered from execution :) nor is there any one Government so much as owned alone by the Magistrate. Besides, that the Civil power it self restraineth not those that you speak of, as to the most of them.

§. 35. 7. Lastly, if you would compare your Prelacy with other Government, compare them where the case is equal. Hath not Presbyterie in *Scotland*, and in *France* (with much less help and countenance from the Magistrate) kept out Heresies and

divisions,

divisions, as much at least, as ever Prelacy did? It is certain that it hath.

§. 36. And yet I must add, that the multitude of Sects and Heresies that sprung up in the first, and second, and third Ages, was no such dishonour to the form of Government then used in the Church, as should encourage any man to dislike or change it. If it was Prelacy that was used, then swarms of Sects and Heresies may come in notwithstanding Prelacy (even in better hands then yours.) But if it were not Prelacy that was then the Government, Heresies are no more a shame to that Government now.

§. 37. I know many Readers will think, that this writing that purposely comes for Peace, should not be guilty of repeating and remembring the faults of others, nor speak to them so plainly as is liker to exasperate then pacifie. But to these I say, 1. Their Objections which they insist on, cannot be answered but by this opening of the truth. And 2. The truth is, those men that own all the abuses and persecutions of the late Prelates, and are impenitent as to their guilt, and wish and would have the same again, are no fit materials for a concordant frame. If their business be destroying, they will never well joyn with us in building and in healing. Repentance is the best Ingredient in our Salve. We consent to the same conditions that we propose, and will thank them if they will help us to Repentance; especially of such sins as are destructive to the Churches peace.

§. 38. And the Godly Moderate Episcopal men do concur with us in the blaming of the abuses of their party. Saith that good and peaceable Bishop *Hall* in his modest offer to the Assembly, *pag.* 3. [*I should be a flatterer of the times past, if I should take upon me to justifie or approve of all the carriages of some, that have been entrusted with the Keyes of Ecclesiastical Government: or to blanch over the corruptions of Consistorial Officers: in both these there was fault enough to ground both a Complaint and Reformation: and may that man never prosper, that desires not an happy reformation of whatsoever hath been, or is amiss in the Church of God.*]

§. 39. Object. 9. *But it is not only the abuses of Episcopacy, but the thing it self that hath been Covenanted against in* England, *and opposed: nor is it only the* English *Prelacy, but all Episcopacy:*

Uu   and

and therefore your motion for another species is like to find but small acceptance.

§. 40. *Answ.* It is not true that all Episcopacy hath been Covenanted against or taken down in *England.* Nor is it true of any of the sorts of Episcopacy which I have here mentioned. It was only that which was then existent that was taken down, and only the English frame of Arch-bishops, Bishops, Deans, and the rest, as here they Governed, that was Covenanted against. Of which I shall speak more anon in answer to the Objections of others.

§. 41. *Object.* 10. *You have covetously seized on the Revenues of the Bishops, and made your selves fat with their Possessions, and this was the prize that you aimed at in taking them down.* *Answ.* The world seeth the falshood of this slander, in the open light; and therefore for your credit sake, you were best recant it. *England* knoweth that the Bishops lands were sold, and given to the Souldiers, and not to the Presbyters. It maintained the Army, and not the Ministry. And that the Dean and Chapters lands is gone the same way, or the like, to pay the debts of the State. And that Presbyters have none of them all, save that here and there one that had about ten, or twenty, or thirty pound a year, have somewhat in Augmentation, that the Churches may not be left to Readers, and blind Guides, as they were in the Prelates dayes. I that have a fuller maintenance then most in all the Country where I live, do receive but about eighty pound and sometimes ninety pound *per annum:* and did I need to pull down Prelacy for this?

----

§. 42. I Come now to the Objections of the other side, who will be offended with me for consenting for peace, to so much as I here do? And 1. Some will say, that *we are engaged against all Prelacy by Covenant, and therefore cannot yield to so much as you do; without the guilt of perjury.*

§. 43. *Answ.* That this is utterly untrue, I thus demonstrate. 1. When the Covenant was presented to the Assembly, with the bare name of [*Prelacy*] joyned to Popery, many Grave and Reverend Divines desired that the word [*Prelacy*] might be explained, because it was not all Episcopacy that they were against.

againſt. And thereupon the following Concatenation in the parentheſis was given by way of explication : in theſe words, [*that is, Church-government by Arch-biſhops, Biſhops, their Chancellors and Commiſſaries, Deans, Deans and Chapters, Arch-deacons, and all other Eccleſiaſtical Officers, depending on that Hierarchy.*] By which it appeareth that it was only the Engliſh Hierarchy or frame, that was Covenanted againſt : and that which was then exiſtent, that was taken down.

§. 44. 2. When the houſe of Lords took the Covenant, Mr. *Thomas Coleman* that gave it them, did ſo explain it and profeſs, that it was not their intent to Covenant againſt all Epiſcopacy : and upon this explication it was taken : and certainly the Parliament were moſt capable of giving us the due ſenſe of it ; becauſe it was they that did impoſe it.

§. 45. 3. And it could not be all Epiſcopacy that was excluded, becauſe a Parochial Epiſcopacy was at the ſame time uſed and approved commonly here in *England*.

§. 46. 4. And in *Scotland* they had uſed the help of Viſitors for the Reformation of their Churches, committing the care of a County or large Circuit to ſome one man, which was as high a ſort of Epiſcopacy at leaſt, as any I am pleading for. Beſides that they had Moderators in all their Synods, which were temporary Biſhops.

§. 47. 5. Alſo the chief Divines of the late Aſſembly at *Weſtminſter*, that recommended the Covenant to the Nations, have profeſſed their own judgements for ſuch a Moderate Epiſcopacy as I am here defending : and therefore they never intended *the excluſion of this by the Covenant*.

§. 48. Object. 2. *By this we ſhall ſeem mutable, while we take down Epiſcopacy one year, and ſet it up again the next.* Anſw. We deſire not the ſetting up of that which we have taken down; and therefore it is no mutability.

§. 49. Object. 3. *But this will prepare for the reſtauration of the old Epiſcopacy. By ſuch degrees it invaded the Church at firſt : and if we let in the preparatory degree, the reſt in time is like to follow ; all that we can do is little enough to keep it out.*

§. 50. Anſw. 1. If we had no other work to do, we would do this as violently as you deſire : but we have the contrary extream to take heed of and avoid; and the Church it

may be, to procure. 2. As we muft not take down the Miniftry, left it prepare men for Epifcopacy, fo neither muft we be againft any profitable exercife of the Miniftry, or defirable Order among them, for fear of introducing Prelacy. 3. Nor is there any fuch danger of it, as is pretended : as long as the Magiftrate puts not the fword into their hands, and no man can be fubjected to them, but by his own Confent, what need we fear their encroachments on our liberties. 4. It is not in your power to hinder the *Species* of Epifcopacy that is pleaded for, from being introduced : but only to with-hold your own confent, and hinder peace and unity. For any Minifter that will, can efteem another his fuperiour, and be ruled by him, and do nothing without his confent : Thefe are the actions of his own free-will. 5. As long as you are free from violence, if you find an evil or danger, you may draw back

§. 51. Object. 4. *Have we not fmarted by them late enough already ? fhall we fo foon be turning back to Ægypt ? Anfw.* That which you have fmarted by, we defire you not to turn back to ; but that which is Apoftolical, pure, and profitable to the Church, and thats not *Ægypt.*

§. 52. Object. 5. *You do all this for Peace with Epifcopal Divines : and where is there any of them that is worthy fo ftudious a Pacification ? Do they not commonly own their former impieties and perfecutions ? Are they not meer formalifts and enemies to practical Godlinefs ? Would they not ruine the Church, and do as they have done, if they had power ? Hath God brought them down for their own wickednefs, and fhall we fet them up again ?*

§. 53. *Anfw.* 1. All are not fuch as you defcribe : Many of them are godly able men, that defire and endeavour the good of the Church. 2. If there were none in this age worthy of our communion, yet, if we will have a lafting peace, we muft extend the terms of it fo far as to comprehend all that are fit for Communion. And fuch we may eafily know, there will be of this opinion throughout all ages. 3. And moft of the Churches in the world being already for a higher Prelacy then this, we fhould agree with them as far as well we may.

§. 54. Object. 6. *But the Parliament have enacted in the fettlement of the Civil Government, that Popery and Prelacy fhall not be tolerated. Anfw.* That is, the Englifh Prelacy excluded by the Covenant,

venant, and that, as it would be exercifed by violence, and forced upon diffenters. Its known what Prelacy was in *England*; and they cannot rationally be interpreted to fpeak againft any but what was among us, and taken notice of under that name. You *fee* the fame Power allow a *Parochial Epifcopacy*, and alfo *Approvers* of all that are admitted to publick preaching; and you fee they allow an *Itinerant Miniftry* in *Wales*: and they join *Magiftrates and Minifters* for the ejecting of the infufficient Minifter: and they never forbad or hindered a *ftated Prefidency*, or any thing that I have pleaded for: yea they continued a *Moderator* of the Affembly at *Weftminfter* for many years, even to his death. And what fuller evidence would you have that it is not any fuch Epifcopacy whofe liberty they exclude, under the name of Prelacy? Only they would not have the *Hierarchy by Lay-Chancellors* to govern the Church, and that by force of the fecular power annexed unto theirs: and fo they deny them Liberty to deprive all other men of their liberty. But this is nothing to the matter in hand.

§. 55. To conclude, let it be noted, in anfwer to all other objections, that the Prefidency, or preheminence pleaded for, doth enable no man to do harm; but only give themfelves advantage to do good. They can hinder no man from preaching, or praying or holy living, or improving his abilities to the good of the Church: Nor can they Govern any man further then they have his own Confent. All which being well confidered, I may conclude that this much may be granted in order to the healing and Reforming of the Churches.

CHAP.

CHAP. VI.

The sum of the foregoing Propositions, and the Consistency of them with the Principles of each party, and so their aptitude to Reconcile.

§. 1. HE summ of all that I have propounded is, that though we cannot, we may not embrace the Government by Prelacy, as lately exercised here in *England* (how confidently soever some appropriate the title of the Church of *England* to the adherents of that frame,) yet would we not have the Church ungoverned, nor worse governed, nor will we refuse for peace such a kind of Episcopacy as is tolerable in the Church. And there are *four* sorts of *Exercise* of the Ministry, which if you please, you may call *Episcopacy*, which we shall not refuse when it may conduce to Peace.

1. Parochial Bishops.

§. 2. I. We shall consent that the *Ancient Parochial Episcopacy* be restored : that is, that in every Parish that hath a particular Church, there may be a Pastor or Bishop setled to govern it, according to the word of God : And that he may be the chief among the Presbyters of that Church, if there be any : And may assume fit men to be assisting Presbyters to him, if there be such to be had. If not, he may be content with Deacons. And these Parochial Bishops are most antient, and have the Power of Ordination.

§. 3.

§. 3. Yet do we not so tye a Church to a Parish, but that in places where the ignorance, infidelity, or impiety of the people, or the smalnes of the Parishes is such, as that there are not fit persons enough in a Parish to make a convenient particular Church, it may be fit for two, or three, or four (in necessity) Neighbour Parishes to joyn together, and to be formed into one particular Church. The several Ministers keeping their stations, for the teaching of the rest as *Catechumens*, but joyning as one Presbyterie, for Governing of that one particular Church, that is Congregate among them. And having one President, without whom nothing should be done in matters left to humane determination. Yet so, that the Presbyters be not forced to this, but do it freely.

§. 4. II. We shall consent that these Parish *Churches be Associate*, and that in every Market Town (or such convenient places as shall be agreed on) there may be frequent meetings of the Pastors, for Communion and Correspondency ; and that one among them be their *standing Moderator durante vita*, or their *President* (for so I would call him rather then Bishop, though we would leave men to use what name they please) And to him should be committed the Communicating of times and places of meeting, and other businesses and Correspondencies. And the Moderating of the debates and disputations.

2 The stated Presidents of Associated Pastors.

§. 5. And for my part I would consent for peace that *de facto* no Ordination be made in either of the foresaid Presbyteries, without the President, but in cases of Necessity : so be it 1. That none be *compelled* to own any other *Principle* of this Practice, then a *Love of Peace* ; and none be compelled to profess that he holdeth the President to have *de jure* a Negative voice : yea that all have liberty to write down on what other Principles they thus yeild, that the *Practice* only may suffice for Peace.

§. 6. III. We shall consent also, that one in a Deanry or Hundred, or other convenient space, may by the Magistrate be chosen a *Visitor of the Churches and Countrey* about him ; having Power only to take notice of the state of things, and gravely to admonish the Pastors where they are negligent, and exhort the people, and provoke them to Holines, Reformation and Unity, only by perswasions from the Word of God   more then any Minister may do that hath opportunity :   we desire
the

3 A Visiter of the neighbour Churches, and Countrey.

the Magiſtrate to deſign a particular perſon to do it (requiring Miniſters and people to give him the meeting,) becauſe that which is every mans work is not ſo well done, as that which is ſpecially committed to ſome. And we deſire that he may acquaint the Magiſtrate how things are.

§. 7. And to avoid the inconveniences of dividing theſe works, we are deſirous that theſe two laſt may meet in one man : and ſo he that is choſen by the Paſtors, the Preſident of their Aſſociation, may be choſen his Viſitor by the Magiſtrate, and do both ; which may be done by one in every Market-town (which is truly a City in the antient ſenſe) and the circumjacent Villages. Yet this we cannot make a ſtanding Rule (that one man do both) becauſe the *Paſtors* muſt chooſe their *Preſident*, and the *Magiſtrate* his *Viſitor*; and its poſſible they may not alwayes concur. But if the Magiſtrate will not chooſe ſuch a Viſitor, the Paſtors may. But then they can *compel* none to *meet him or hear him*.

§. 8. IV. Beſides theſe three (or two, whether you will) before mentioned, we ſhall conſent that there be a general ſort of Miniſters, ſuch as the Apoſtles, Evangeliſts, and others in thoſe times were, that ſhall have no ſpecial charge, but go up and down to preach the Goſpel, and gather Churches where there are none, and contribute the beſt aſſiſtance of their Abilities, Intereſt and Authority for the reforming, confirming, and right ordering of Churches. And if by the Magiſtrates Command, or Miniſters conſent there be one of theſe aſſigned to each County, and ſo their Provinces prudentially diſtinguiſhed and limited, we ſhall not diſſent. Yet we would have ſuch but where there is need.

§. 9. V. Beſides theſe four ſorts of Biſhops, we are all agreed on two ſorts more; 1. The *Epiſcopi gregis*, or Paſtors of every Congregation, whether they have any aſſiſtant Presbyters or no, or being themſelves but ſuch aſſiſtant Presbyters. 2. The Magiſtrate, who is * a ſecular Biſhop, or a Governor of the Church by force. And we deſire the Magiſtrate to be a nurſing

Marginal notes:

Theſe two to be in one man.

4. General unfixed Miniſters.

* So *Conſtantine* calls himſelf a Biſhop. *Euſeb. vit. Conſt. l* 4. *c* 24.

And he made his Court a Church, and aſſembling the people, did uſe to take, the holy Scriture, and deliver Divine contemplations out of it, or elſe he would read the Common-Prayers to the whole Congregation, *cap.* 17. And it is plain that it was *Conſtantine* that kept the Churches in Unity and Peace, when the Biſhops elſe would have broken them to peices. And the Emperours frequently took down and ſet up Biſhops at their pleaſure, eſpecially in the Patriarchial Seats as *Rome*, *Conſtantinople*, *Antioch*, *Alexandria*.   Father

Father to the Church, and do his duty, and to keep the sword in his own hand; and for forcible deposing Ministers, or any punishment on body or estate, we desire no Bishops nor other Ministers may be authorized thereto: But if Pastors exclude an unworthy Pastor from their Communion, let the *Magistrate only* deprive him *forcibly* of his place and maintenance, if he see cause. When the Council of *Antioch* had deposed *Paulus Samosatenus*, he would not go out of the house: And all the Bishops in the Council could not force him out, but were fain to procure the Heathen Emperor *Aurelian* to do it. It lyeth as a blot on *Cyril* of *Alexandria* that he was the first man that arrogated and exercised there a secular Coercive Power, under the name of a Bishop of the Church.

§. 10. There is enough in this much to satisfie any moderate honest men for Church-government, and for the healing of our Divisions thereabout: And there is nothing in this that is inconsistent with the Principles of the moderate of any Party.

§. 11. 1. That *a Church organized*, called by some *Ecclesia prima*, *should be no greater* then I have mentioned, is not contradictory to the Principles of the Episcopall, Presbyterians, Congregationall or Erastian. Indeed the two first say, that *it may be bigger:* but none of them say, *It must be bigger*. The Presbyterians instances of the Church of *Jerusalem* (which scrued to the highest, cannot be proved neer half so great as some of our Parishes) and such other Churches, are but for the *may be*, and not for the *must be*. And therefore if they be peaceable, this will make no breach.

§. 12. 2. That *Parochial Churches and Associations have fixed Presidents*, is nothing contrary to any of their Principles, as far as I am able to discern them.

§. 13. 3. That *Pastors may be lawfully appointed to visit and help the Country and the neighbour Churches*, and exhort them to their duty, and give the Magistrate information of their state, is a thing that none can justly blame, any more then preaching a Lecture among them. Nor do I know any party that is against it, (of these four.)

§. 14. And 4. *That there may be more General Ministers to gather, and take care of many Churches*, I think none of them will deny. Sure the Itinerant Ministers in *Wales* will not: Nor

Xx   yet

yet that these may have their Provinces diſtinguiſhed. If I could imagine which of all theſe ſorts would be denied, I would more fully prove it, yea and prove it conſiſtent with the Principles of each party; but till then its vain.

§. 15. The only point that I remember, like to be queſtioned, is, the *conſenting to forbear Ordination in ſeveral Presbyteries, till the Preſident be one, except in caſe of Neceſſity*: And nothing is here queſtionable, that I obſerve, but only *Whether it be conſiſtent with the Principles of the Congregational party*, ſeing they would have all Ordination to be by the Elders of their own Church, and where there are none, that it be done by the people without Elders. To which I anſwer, 1. That we here grant them that a Congregational Presbyterie with their Preſident may ordain an Elder for that Congregation. 2. The Moderate Congregational men do grant us that the Elders or Paſtors of other Churches may lawfully be called to aſſiſt them in Ordination, though they think it be not neceſſary. It is not therefore againſt their Principles, to do ſo. For ſure they may do a Lawful thing, eſpecially when the Churches Peace doth lie ſo much upon it as here it doth.

§. 16. I conclude therefore that here are healing Principles brought to your hands, if you have but healing inclinations to receive them. Here is a ſufficient remedy for our Diviſions, upon the account of Church-government, if you have but hearts to entertain them, and apply them. But if ſome on one ſide will adhere to all their former exceſſes and abuſes, and continue impenitent, unchurching the beſt of the Proteſtant Churches, that are not Prelatical (while they unchurch not the Church of *Rome:*) And if others on the other ſide will ſtifly refuſe to yield in things that cannot be denied to be lawfull, yea and convenient for the Churches, and ſet more by all their own conceits then by the Peace of Brethren, and conſequently the proſperity of the Church, we muſt leave the care of all to God, and content our ſelves that we have done our duty.

CHAP.

CHAP. VII.

Some inftances to prove that moderate men will agree upon the foregoing terms.

§. 1. LEST any think that it is a hopeleſs work that I have motioned, and the parties will not agree upon theſe terms, I ~~ſhall~~ ſhall next prove to you that the godly and moderate of each party, are agreed already (at leaſt the Epiſcopal and Presbyterians, and I think the reſt:) and that its in Practice more then Principles that we diſagree.

§. 2. I. I will begin with the *Epiſcopal Divines,* of whom there ate two parties, differing much more from one another, then the one of them doth from the Presbyterians. The ancient Biſhops and the moderate of late, did maintain the Validity of Ordination by Presbyters, and own the Reformed Churches that had other, ſuppoſing their Epiſcopacy uſefull to the perfection or well being of a Church, but not neceſſary to the being of it. And this ſort of men (who alſo agree with us in doctrine) we could quickly be reconciled with. But of late years there are many Epiſcopal Divines ſprung up, that embracing the Doctrine called Arminianiſm, do withal deny the Being of the Miniſtry and Churches that want Prelatical ordination: and with theſe there is no hope of concord, becauſe they will have it on no other terms then renouncing our Churches and Miniſtry, and being *again ordained by them,* and thus coming wholly over to them. Theſe ſeparate from us, and pretend that our Churches have no true Worſhip (wonderous audacity,)and our Miniſters are no true Miniſters, and call the Church into private houſes (as D. *Hide* expreſſly in his [Chriſt and his Church] in the beginning of the Preface; and many others.) Of whom I ſpoke before.

§. 3. That the ancient Engliſh Biſhops that hold to the doctrine of the Church of *England,* and are peaceable men, are eaſily agreed with us, I first prove from the example of Reverend Bishop *Hall.* In his *Peace-maker* he hath these words, [*Pag.* 46, 47, 48, 49. *The Divisions of the Church are either General betwixt our Church and the other Reformed; or special with those within the bosome of our own Church; both which require several considerations. For the former, blessed be God, there is no difference in any essential matter betwixt the Church of* England *and her Sisters of the Reformation: We accord in every point of Christian Doctrine without least the variation.* (N B.) *Their publike Confessions and ours, are sufficient convictions to the world, of our full and absolute agreement. the only difference is in the form of outward administration: Wherein also we are so far agreed, as that we all profess this form not to be essential to the being of a Church* (N. B.) *though much importing the well or better being of it, according to our several apprehensions thereof; and that we do all retain a reverent and loving opinion of each other in our own several-wayes: not seeing any reason why so poor a diversity should work any alienation of affection in us, one towards another: But withall, nothing hinders but that we may come yet closer to one another, if both may resolve to meet in that* Primitive Government (*whereby it is meet we should both be regulated*) *universally agreed on by all antiquity; wherein all things were ordered and transacted by the Consent of the Presbyterie, moderated by one constant President thereof: the Primacy and perpetual practice whereof no man can doubt of that hath but seen the writings of* Clemens *and* Ignatius, *and hath gone along with the History of those primitive times* —— *We may well rest in the judgement of* Mr. John Camero, *the Learnedst Divine, be it spoke without envy, that the Church of* Scotland *hath afforded in this last age:* [Nullus est dubitandi, locus, *&c. There is no doubt at all, saith he, but that* Timothy *was chosen by the Colledge of the Presbyters, to be the President of them, and that not without some authority over the rest, but yet such as have the due bounds and limits*]. *And that this was a leading case, and common to other Churches, was never denyed by any author. Words may not break square, where the things are agreed. If the name of a Bishop displease, let them call this man a Moderator, a President, a Superintendent, an Overseer; Only for the fixedness or change of this person, let the ancient and universall practice of Gods Church be thought worthy to oversway. And if in this one point* (N. B.) (*wherein the distance is so narrow, we could condescend to each*

other,

other, all other circumstances and appendances of varying practices
or opinions, might without any difficulty be accorded. But if there
must be a difference of judgement in these matters of outward Policy, why should not our hearts be still one? why should such a diversity be of Power to endanger the dissolving of the bond of brother-
hood? May we have the grace but to follow the truth in Love, we
shall in these several tracts overtake her happily in the end, and
find her embracing of Peace, and crowning us with blessedness]
So far Bishop *Hall*; so that you see that only the fixing of
the Moderator or President will satisfie such as he: and
so with him and such as he, for my part I am fully agreed already.

§. 4. And here by the way, because there are so many Episcopal separatists of late, that hazzard the souls of their partial followers, and because the right habituating of the mind with Peace
is an excellent help to a sound understanding, and the escaping
the errors and hainous sins that Faction engageth too many in, I
therefore make it my request to all that read these lines, but soberly to read over that *one Book of Bishop *Halls*, called the *Peace-*
maker, once or twice: which if I could procure, I think I should
do much to the Peace of these Churches, and to the good of
many endangered souls, that by passionate and factious leaders
are misguided.

§. 5. The same Reverend man in his Humble Remonstrance
hath these words, Pag. 29, 30, 31. [*The second is intended to*
raise envy against us, as the uncharitable censurers and condemners
of those Reformed Churches abroad, which differ from our Govern-
ment: wherein we do justly complain of a slanderous aspersion cast
upon us: We love and honour those Sister Churches, as the dear
spouse of Christ; we bless God for them; and we do heartily wish
unto them that happiness in the Partnership of our administration,
which I doubt not but they do no less heartily wish unto themselves,
Good words you will perhaps say; but what is all this fair comple-
ment, if our act condemn them? For if Episcopacy stand by Di-
vine right, what becomes of these Churches that want it? Malice
and ignorance are met together in this unjust aggravation:
1. *Our position is only affirmative, implying the justifiableness and*
holiness of an Episcopal calling, without any further imp   n:
Next, when we speak of Divine right, we mean not an   e. Law.

of God requiring it upon the absolute Necessity of the Being of a Church (what hinderances soever may interpose) but a Divine institution warranting it where it is, and requiring it where it may be had.   Every Church therefore which is capable of this form of Government, both may and ought to affect it ——— but those particular Churches to whom this power and faculty is denyed, lose nothing of the true essence of a Church, though they miss some thing of their glory and perfection —— And page 32. [Our form of Government ——— differs little from their own, save in the perpetuity of their (προεστῶτος) Moderatorship, and the exclusion of that Lay-Presbyterie which never till this age had footing in the Christian Church.] ———— And Page 41, 42. [Alas my Brethren, while we do fully agree in all these, and all other Doctrinal and Practical points of Religion, why will you be so uncharitable, as by these frivolous and causeless Divisions to rend the seamless coat of Christ? It it a Title, or a Retinue, or a Ceremony, a Garment, or a Colour, or an Organ Pipe, that can make us a different Church, whiles we preach and profess the same saving truth, whiles we desire (as you profess to do) to walk conscionably with our God according to that one Rule of the Royall Law of our Maker, whiles we oppose one and the same common enemy, whiles we unfeignedly endeavour to hold the unity of the Spirit in the bonds of Peace? —— For us, we make no difference at all (in the right and interest of the Church) betwixt Clergy and Laity, betwixt the Clergy and Laity of one part and of another: we are all your true Brethren; we are one with you, both in heart and brain, and hope to meet you in the same heaven: but if ye will needs be otherwise minded, we can but bewail the Churches misery and your sin. ——] You hear how this good Bishop was far from a separation.

§. 6. How contrary to this, is the foresaid writing of Dr. Hide (which I instance in, because it is come new to my hand) who stigmatizeth the front of his book with the brand of separation, and that of one of the most rigid and unreasonable kinds. Thus he begins, [" When Conscientious Ministers cannot associate in " the Church, and Conscientious Christians cannot go to Church, and " Customary Christians go thither, either to little purpose, because " to no true worship, or to great shame, because to no true Mini- " sters, tis fit the Church should come to private houses]——

Doth

Doth he not begin very wifely and charitably? What could the moſt Schiſmatical Papiſt ſay more? What! *no true worſhip! no true Miniſters!* and *but Cuſtomary Chriſtians* that come thither? Yes, and that's not all: he purſues it with an exprobration, that we are *faln from our Religion,* (p. 4.) and yet that's not all: he adds, [" *Here ſeems yet to be a very bad certainty of their Re-* " *ligion; and how can there be a better Certainty of their ſalva-* " *tion? unleſs (that we may gratifie their ſingularity more then* " *our own veracity) we will ſay, There may be a company of* " *good Chriſtians out of the Communion of Saints, or a Commu-* " *nion of Saints out of Chriſts Cath.like Church.*] Should we laugh or weep at ſuch a man as this? What! *no communion of Saints,* but with the ſeparating party of the Prelates? Unhappy we that live in *England,* and can meet with ſo ſmall a number of theſe Saints. Is the *Catholike* Church confined to *this party?* and *Salvation* to *this Church?* Tranſcendent Papal arrogancy! Its well that theſe Prelates are not the only Key-keepers of heaven! for we ſee how we ſhould then be uſed. I muſt tell this Dr. and all of-his mind, that it is an eaſier way to Heaven, then we dare hope to come thither by, to joyn our ſelves to their ſeparating Communion of Saints, and live as the moſt that we are acquainted with, that are of that Saint-like Communion. He had been better have talked at theſe rates to men of another Age or Nation, then to us that ſee the lives of their adherents. We never changed our Religion nor our Church. What if he *read* his prayers, and I ſay mine without book ; or what if he pray in *white,* and I in *black?* or what if he *kneel* in receiving the Euchariſt, and I *ſit* or *ſtand?* or what if he uſe the *Croſs in baptiſme,* and I baptize no better then the Apoſtles did without it ; do theſe or ſuch like make us to be of two *Religions?* Do I change my *Religion,* if I read with a pair of ſpectacles, or if I look towards the South or Weſt, rather then the Eaſt *&c.?* We ſee what theſe men would make the *Chriſtian Religion* to be. Were the Apoſtles no Chriſtians, becauſe they had no kneeling at the Euchariſt, nor Croſs in Baptiſm, nor Surplice, nor (at leaſt our) Common Prayer-book, *&c?* Dare you ſay they were no Chriſtians? or yet that Chriſtian Religion was one thing then, and another thing now? And for our Churches, we do not only meet in the *ſame places,* but we have the *ſame doctrine,* the *same worship* (in every part, though he talk of our no true worship; as if Praying, Praising God, *&c.* were no true worship :) the things changed were by the imposers and defenders (see Dr. *Burgess* Rejoynder) professed to be no parts at all of worship, but meer accidents ; we have the *same people*, save here and there a few that separate by yours and others seducement, and some vile ones that we cast out ; we have abundance of the *same Ministers* that we had. And yet must we have *no worship, Ministry, Communion of Saints, or Salvation*, because we have only a Parochial and not a Diocesan Episcopacy ? Forsooth we have lost our Religion, and are all lost men, because our Bishops have but single Parish churches to oversee (which they find a load as heavy as they can bear,) and we have not one Bishop to take the Government of an hundred or two hundred Churches. At *Rome* he is a damned man that believeth not in the Pope : and is out of the Catholike Church, because he is out of the subjection of the Pope : and with these men, we are lost men, if we never so much believe in *Christ*, because we believe not in an Archbishop, and are out of the Catholike Church and Communion of Saints, because we will not be ruled by such Rulers as these. And what's all this, to such Counties as this where I live, and most else in *England* that I hear of, that know of no Bishop they have (and they rejected none,) nor doth any come and command them any Obedience ? Must we be unchristened, unchurcht and damned, for not obeying, when we have none to obey, or none that calls for our obedience ? But I shall let these men pass, and leave them in their *separation*, desiring that they had Catholike spirits and principles. This much I have said to let men see, that there is no possibility of our union with this sort that are resolved on a *separation*; and that it is not these Novelists and Dividers, but the antient Episcopal party of *England* that we can easily agree with.

§. 7. The next that I shall instance in, that was agreed with these Principles of ours, is the late Reverend and Learned Bish p *Usher*, of whose Concord with us, I have two proofs. The one was his own profession to my self. The other is his own writings, especially his Propositions given in to King *Charls*, now printed, called [*The Reduction of Episcopacy to the form of Synodical Government, received in the ancient Church*] which
consisteth

consisteth of four Propositions (having first proved that all Presbyters have the power of Discipline and Church-government :) the first alloweth the single Rector of the Parish to take notice of the scandalous, reprove, admonish, and debar them from the Lords Table. The second is, that in every Rurall Deanry, all the Pastors within the Precinct, may by the Chorepiscopus or Suffragan, be every month Assembled in a Synod, and according to the Major part of their voices, he conclude all matters that shall be brought into debate before them, as Excommunication &c. The third is, for a Diocesan Synod once or Twice a year, where by the consent of the Major part of the Rectors, all things might be concluded by the Bishop or Superintendent, call him whether you will, or in his absence, by one of the suffragans, whom he deputes to be Moderator. The fourth is for Provincial and National Synods in like sort.

§. 8. And when I had perused these papers (in *M. S.*) I told him that yet one thing was left out, that the Episcopal party would many of them stick at more then he, and that is, a Negative voice in Ordination in the President, to which and the rest I proposed this for accommodation in brief [1. *Let every particular or Parish Church have a Bishop and Presbyters to assist him, where possibly they can be had. 2. Let all these Associate and their several Associations have a stated President. 3. Let all men be at liberty for the name, whether they will call him a Bishop, President, Moderator, Superintendent, or the like. 4. And for the Negative voice in Ordination, let all Ministers of the Association agree that de facto they will not Ordain without him, but in Cases of Necessity; but let every man be left free to his own Principles on which he shall ground this practice, and not be bound to consent, that de jure a Negative vote is due to the President.*] These terms did I propose to the Bishop for Accommodation, and intreated him to tell me plainly his judgement, whether they are satisfactory and sufficient for the Episcopal party to yield to for Peace and Communion ? and his answer was this [*They are sufficient, and moderate men will accept them, but others will not, as I have tryed : for many of them are offended with me for propounding such terms.*] And thus this Reverend Bishop and I were agreed for Peace in a quarter of an hour ; (the truth of which, I solemnly profess :) and so would all the Ministers and Christians

Yy

in

in *England*, if they were not either wiser or foolisher, honester or dishonester then he and I. And this I leave on Record to Posterity, as a testimony against the dividers and contenders of this age, [*That it was not long of men of the temper and principles of this Reverend Archbishop and my self, that the Episcopal party and their dissenting Brethren in* England, *were not speedily and heartily agreed: for we actually did it.*] To no honour of mine, but to the honour of this peaceable man, and the shame of the unpeaceable hinderers or refusers of our Reconciliation, let this testimony live, that Posterity may know whom to blame for our Calamities; they all extoll Peace when they reject it and destroy it.

§. 9 For a third witness of the Reconcileableness of the Moderate Episcopal party on these terms, I may well produce Dr. *Holdsworth*; who subscribed these same Propositions of Bishop *Usher* to the King: and therefore was a Consenter to the same way of Accommodation.

§. 10. A fourth witness is Dr. *Forbs* of *Scotland*, who having written purposely a Book called his *Irenicon*, for Accommodation on such terms, I need to say no more of him, but refer you to the Book. I shall name no more of the Episcopal party. These four are enow to my purpose.

§. 11. That the *Presbyterians* (of *England* specially) are willing to close upon these terms of a fixed Moderator, I prove; 1. By the profest Consent of that Reverend Learned servant of Christ Mr. *Thomas Gataker*, a Member of the late Assembly at *Westminster*, who hath professed his judgement of this matter in a Book against *Lilly*. I refer you to his own words, for brevity sake.

§. 12. My next witness, and for brevity, many in one, shall be Mr. *Geree*, and the Province of *London*, citing him in their *Jus Divinum Ministerii, pag. Append.* 122. the words are these | *That the Ancient Fathers in the point of Episcopacy, differ more from the high Prelatist then from the Presbyterian: for the Presbyterians alwayes have a President to guide their actions, which they acknowledge may be perpetual* durante vita modo se bene gesserit; *or temporary to avoid inconvenience, which Bilson takes hold of as advantagious, because so little discrepant, (as he saith) from what he maintaineth.*] See the rest there.

§. 13.

Dr. *Holdsworth*.

Dr. *Forbs*.

Gataker.

The *London Province*.

§. 13. 3. *Beza* (the Leader against Prelacy) saith, *de grad.* *Beza.* *Minist. Evang. Instituti Divini est, ut in omni cœtu Presbyterorum unus sit qui ordine præeat & præsit reliquis. It is of Divine Institution that in every Assembly of Presbyters, there be one that go before and be above the rest.* | And dividing Bishops into Divine, Humane, and Diabolical , he makes the Humane tolerable Prelacy to be the fixed President.

§. 14. 4. *Calvin* (who is accused for ejecting Episcopacy) *Calvin.* See also *Dan. Colonius* in his *Disputat. ex Institut. Calv. l. 4. Disp. 2. §. 18. 24.* besides what he writes of it to *Card Sadolet,* saith in his *Institut. lib. 4. cap. 4. §. 1.* [*Ea cautione totam suam Oeconomiam composuerunt (Ecclesiæ veteris Episcopi) ad unicam illam Dei verbi normam, ut facile videas nihil fere hac parte habuisse à verbo Dei alienum.*] §. 2. [*Quibus ergo docendi munus injunctum erat, eos omnes nominabant Presbyteros. Illi ex suo numero in singulis civitatibus unum eligebant, cui specialiter dabant titulum Episcopi : ne ex æqualitate, ut fieri solet, dissidia nascerentur. Neque tamen sic honore & dignitate superior erat Episcopus, ut Dominium in Collegas haberet : sed quas partes habet Consul in Senatu, ut referat de negotiis, sententias roget, consulendo, monendo, hortando, aliis præeat, authoritate sua totam actionem regat ; & quod decretum Communi Consilio fuerit, exequatur : id munus sustinebat Episcopus in Presbyterorum cœtu*] & §. 4. fine [*Gubernationem sic constituti nonnulli Hierarchiam vocarunt, nomine (ut mihi videtur) improprio, certe scripturis inusitato : Cavere enim voluit spiritus sanctus, nequis principatum aut dominationem somniaret, quum de Ecclesiæ gubernatione agitur. Verum si rem, omisso vocabulo, intueamur* (N. B.) *reperiemus veteres Episcopos non aliam regendæ Ecclesiæ formam voluisse fingere ab ea quam Deus verbo suo præscripsit*] This he writes after the mention of Archbishops and Patriarcks, as well as of Bishops governing in Synods.

§. 15. Where by the way let me give you this observation, that Bishops Governing but in Synods can have no other power of Goverment, then the Synods themselves have : But *Synods themselves as such* are not directly for *Government* , but for *Concord* and *Communion* of Churches, and so *consequently* for well-governing the several *flocks* : Nor hath a Synod any Governing Power over a particular Pastor, as being his superiour appointed to that end : but only a Power of Consent or Agree-

ment

ment : to which for unity, and communion fake, he is confe-
quentially obliged ; not by Virtue of Gods Command, that requireth us to obey the Higher Power (for three Paſtors are
not made ſo the Rulers of one) but by virtue of Gods commands that require us to do all things in Unity, and to maintain the Peace and Concord of the Churches, and to avoid Diviſions and diſcord.

§. 16. If any think that this doth too much favour the Congregational way, I muſt tell him that it is ſo true and clear,
that the Epiſcopal men that are moderate acknowledge it. For
inſtance : the Reverend Biſhop *Uſher* did, without asking, of
himſelf profeſs to me that it was his judgement [*that certainly
Councils or Synods are not for Government but for Unity, and that
a Biſhop out of Council hath the ſame Governing Power as all the
Council, though their vote may bind him for Unity to conſent.*

§. 17. This being ſo, it muſt needs follow that an Archbiſhop,
or the Preſident of a National, Provincial, Dioceſan, or Claſ-
ſicall Aſſembly, or of any Aſſociation of the Paſtors of many
Churches, hath no ſuperiour Governing power over the Parochial or Congregational Biſhop of one Church ; but only in
concurrence with the Synod, a Power of Determining by way
of *Agreement*, ſuch points as he ſhall be obliged for Unity and
Communion to conſent to and perform, if they be not contrary
to the word of God. This evidently follows from this Reverend
Archbiſhops doctrine, and the truth.

§. 18. And if any ſhall think that the *Presbyterians* will not
yield that a *particular* Church do ordinarily conſiſt but of *one
full Congregation*, I confute them by producing their own Con-
ceſſions : in the *London* Miniſters *Jus Divinum Miniſterii. Ap-
pend. pag.* 123. they plainly ſay, that [*The later* (Biſhops)
were Dioceſan, the former (that is the Biſhops of the firſt or ancient times) *were Biſhops only of one Congregation*] And pag. 82.
they ſay [*Theſe Angels were Congregational, not Dioceſan: In
the beginning of Chriſtianity, the number of Believers, even in the
greateſt Cities were ſo few, as that they might well meet,* ἐπὶ τὸ αὐτὸ
*in one and the ſame place. And theſe were called, the Church of
the City, and therefore to ordain Elders* καὶ ἐκκλησίαν, and κατὰ
πόλιν, *are all one in Scripture*] Thus far they yield to the Congregational men.

§. 19.

§. 19. 5. One other witnefs of the Presbyterians readinefs to accommodate on thefe terms, I fhall give, and no more, and that is Mr. *Richard Vines*, a man that was moft eminent for his management of the Presbyterian caufe in the Affembly, and at *Uxbridge* Treaty, and in the Ifle of *Wight* ; the Papers there prefented to the King are to be feen in Print. When we did fet up our Affociation in this County, I purpofing to do nothing without advife, and defigning a hearty clofure of all fober Godly men, Epifcopal, Presbyterian, Congregational and *Eraftian* : did confult firft about it by Letters with Mr. *Vines*, and in his anfwer to mine, he approved of the defign, and thought our diftance very fmall, and yielded to a fixed Prefidency, though not to a Negative voice : (which I would have none forced to.) Becaufe they are too long to put into this fection, I will adjoyn that part of his Letter that concerns this fubject, prefixing one that went next before it, againft the felling of the Church lands, that the Bifhops may fee how little fuch men, as he confented to it or liked it ; and may take heed of charging them with Sacriledge.

§. 20. Laftly the *Eraftians* are known to be for Epifcopacy it felf, fo be it, it come in by the power of the Magiftrate. And that nothing propofed croffeth the Principles of the *Congregationall* men, I have fhewed before : But whether really we fhall have their confent to a Peace upon thefe propofed terms, I know not ; becaufe their writings that I have feen, do not meddle with the point, fave only one Congregational man, Mr. *Giles Firmin*, hath newly written for this very thing, in his *Treatife of Schifm againft* Dr. Owen, *page* 66, 67, 68. I defire you to read the words to fave me the labour of tranfcribing them. In which he giveth us to underftand, that fome of the Moderate Congregational Party, will joyn with us in a Reconciliation on thefe terms : Whether many or all will do fo, I know not. Let their practife fhew whether they will be the firft or the laft in the Healing of our Divifions. But if they refufe, we will not for that refufe to Love them as Brethren, and ftudy to perform our duty towards them : as knowing that we fuffer much more when we come fhort of our duty and love to others, then when they come fhort of their duty and love to us.

Mr. *Richard*

Mr. *Richard Vines* his Letters before mentioned as a Testimony that the Presbyterian Ministers are not against a fixed President, or that Episcopacy which Bishop *Hall, &c.* would have been satisfied with.

Reverend Friend,

I *Received your two last; and as for a Schoolmaster I shall do the best I can to propound one to you, &c. As for your Question about Sacriledge, I am very near you in present opinion. The point was never stated nor debated in the Isle of* Wight. *I did for my part decline the dispute: for I could not maintain the cause as on the Parliaments side: and because both I and others were unwilling, it was never brought to any open debate: The Commissioners did argue it with the King: but they went upon grounds of Law and Policy; and it was only about Bishops Lands: for they then averred the continuance of D. and Chapiters Lands to the use of the Church. Some deny that there is any sin of Sacriledge under the Gospel: and if there be any, they agree not in the definition: Some hold an alienation of Church goods in case of Necessity; and then make the Necessity what and as extensive as they please. The most are of opinion that whiles the Church lies so unprovided for, the donations are not alienable sine Sacrilegio. If there were a surplusage above the competent maintenance, it were another matter. Its cleer enough that the Donors wills are frustrated, and that their General intention and the General use,* viz. *the maintenance of Gods worship and Ministers, should stand, though the particular use might be superstitious. I cited in my last Sermon before the Parliament (unprinted) a place touching Sacriledge out of* Mr. *Hildersham on* Psal. 51. *It did not please. You may find the words in his book by the Index. If his description of it be true, then you will still be of your own mind. I dare encourage no purchasers; but do desire to have some more of your thoughts about it, and I shall return you mine: as I do my thanks for your excellent and worthily esteemed Treatise which you vouchsafed to prefix my name before: Sir, I have no more time or paper but to subscribe my self*

Your truly loving Friend

London, July 20.   R. Vines.

Sir

THough I should have desired to have understood your thoughts about the point of Sacriledge, that so I might have formed up my thoughts into some better order and cleerer issue then I did in my last: yet to shew unto you how much I value this correspondence with you, I am willing to make some return to your last. And first touching the Schoolmaster intended, &c. ——— The Accomodation you speak of is a great and a good work for the gaining into the work such useful parts and interests as might very much heal the discord, and unite the strength of men to oppose destructive ways, and in my opinion more feasible with those men then any other, if they be moderate and godly: for we differ with them rather about some pinacles of the Temple, then the foundation or abbuttresses thereof. I would not have much time spent in a formula of doctrine, or worship: for we are not much distant in them and happily no more then with one another: But I would have the agreement attempted in that very thing which chiefly made the division, and, that is Government; heal that breach and heal all: there begin and therein labour all you can. What influence this may have upon others I know not in this exulceration of mens minds: but the work speaks it self good, and your reasons for the attempting of it are very considerable. For the Assembly, you know, they can meddle with just nothing but what is sent unto them by Parliament or one house thereof (as the order saith) and for that reason never took upon them to intermeddle therein. What they do in such a thing, must be done as private persons, and not as in the capacity of Assembly men, except it come to them recommended by the Parliament. The great business is to find a temperament in ordination and government, in both which the exclusion or admittance of Presbyters (dicis causa) for a shadow, was not regular: and no doubt the Presbyters ought and may both teach and govern, as men that must give account of souls. For that you say of every particular Church having many Presbyters, it hath been considered in our Assembly, and the Scripture speaks fair for it, but then the Church and City was of one extent: no Parishes or bounds assigned out to particular men (as now) but the Ministers preacht in circuit, in common and stood in relation to the Churches as to one Church in b meeting haply in divers houses or places (as is still the manner of some Cities in the Low Countries.) If you will follow this model, you must lay the City all into one Chuch particular, and the Villages half a dozen of them into a Church: which is a business here in England of vast design and consequence. And as for that you say of a Bishop over many Presbyters, not over many Churches; I believe no such Bishops will please our men: but the notion as you conceive it, hath been and is the opinion of learned men. Grotius in his commentary on the Acts in divers places and particularly Cap. 17. saith, that as in every particular Synagogue (many of which was in some one City) there was ἀρχισυνάγωγ; such was the Primitive Bishop: and doubtless the first Bishops were over the community of Presbyters as Presbyters in joint relation to one Church or Region; which Region being upon the increase of believers, divided into more Churches, and in after times those Churches assigned to particular men: yet he the Bishop continued Bishop over them still. For that you say, he had a Negative voice, thats more then ever I saw proved, or ever shall, I believe for the first two hundred years; and yet I have laboured to enquire into it. That makes him Angelus princeps, not Angelus præses as Dr. Reignolds saith Calvin denies that, & makes him Consul in Senatu. or as the Speaker in the house of Parliament, which as I have heard that D. B. did say, was but to make him fore-man of the Jury. Take heed of yeilding a Negative voice. As touching the Introduction of ruling Elders, such as are modelled out by Parliament, my judgement is sufficiently known: I am of your judgement in the point. There should be such Elders as have power to preach as well as rule: I say power; but how that will be effected here I know not, except we could or would return to the Primitive nature and constitution of particular Churches: and therefore it must be helped by the combination of more Churches together into one as to the matter of Government, and let them be still distinct as to Word and Sacraments. That is the easiest way of accommodation that yet occurs to my thoughts. Sir I fear I trouble you too long, but it is to shew how much I value you and your Letters to me: for which I thank you, and rest

Yours in the best bonds

R. Vines.

Septemb. 7.

Though

THough Mr. *Vines* here yield not the Negative Voice to have been *de facto* in the first or second age, nor to be *de jure*, yet he without any question yielded to the stating of a President, *durante vita*, if he prove not unworthy, (which was one chief point that I propounded to him.) And I make no doubt but he would have yielded to a voluntary Consent of Presbyters *de facto* not to ordain without the President, but in case of Necessity: But that I did not propound to him. And the difficulties that are before us *de facto* in setting up a Parochiall Episcopacy which he mentioneth, I have cleared up already in these papers, shewing partly that the thing is already existent, and partly how more fully to accomplish it. All would be easie, if Holy, Self-denying, Charitable hearts were ready to entertain and put in execution the honest, healing Principles that are before us, and obvious to an ordinary understanding : Or (if still the Pastors will be contentious) if Holy, Peaceable Magistrates would seriously take the work in hand, and drive on the sloathful and quarrelsome Ministers to the performance of their duty.

The Episcopacy of the Protestant Churches in *Poland*.

ADrian. Regenvolscius Histor. Ecclesiast. Sclavonicar. Provinc. lib. 3. page 424.

N. B. *Quoniam à prima Ecclesiarum in minoris Poloniæ Provincia, Reformatione, usu & consuetudine receptum est, ut è senioribus hisce omnium Districtuum, quorum nomina 36. recensuimus, unus Primarius, sive in ordine Primus, qui vulgo Superintendens Ecclesiarum minoris Poloniæ vocatur, Synodisque Provincialibus præsidet ; totius Synodi Provincialis authoritate, consensu ac suffragiis eligatur, ac, non quidem per impositionem manuum, (propter evitandam Primatus alicujus suspicionem, aut juris ac potestatis alicujus in cæteros seniores speciem,) benedictione tantum, fraterna apprecatione, Officiorum quæ hocce concernunt munus prælectione, piisq; totius Synodi precibus, Regiminis duntaxat & Ordinis boni in Ecclesia Dei causa, inauguratur ad declaratur; No-*

Z z   *mina*

mina Primariorum horum Seniorum, five Minor. Polon. Ecclesiarum superintendium.]————

The Churches of the *Bohemian* Confess. called *Unitatis Fratrum,* have among the Pastors of the Churches, their Conseniors, and Seniors, and one President over all. *Id. Regen. Volf. p 315.* [*Seniores five superattendentes Ecclesiarum Bohemicarum & Moravicarum,* &c. ——— *plerumq; è Censenioribus eliguntur, ac per impositionem Manuum publicamq; inaugurationem, in munus Senioratus ordinantur ac consecrantur. Et longa consuetudine in Ecclesiis trium harum provinciarum receptum est, ut è senioribus unus Primarius (five in ordine Primus) quem vulgo illi Præsidem vocant, non eligatur quidem, nec pecularariter Ordinetur, sed post decessum aliorum, ipso Ordinationis tempore prior succedat*]

FINIS.

The Fourth
DISPUTATION:
Of a Form of
LITURGY:

How far it is Necessary, Desirable, or Warrantable; In order to a Peace between the Parties that differ herein, and too uncharitably prosecute their difference.

By *Richard Baxter.*

LONDON,

Printed by *Robert White,* for *Nevil Simmons,* Bookseller in *Kederminster, Anno Dom.* 1658.

Qu. *Whether a stinted Liturgy, or form of Worship, be a desirable means for the Peace of these Churches?*

Nneceffary prolixity is not fo acceptable to the Reader that loves both Truth and time, but that I may take it for granted that you defire me to leave out fuperfluities in this Difpute. 1. The Etymologifts fhall be better agreed among themfelves of the derivation of λειτυργὸς and λειτυργία, before I will trouble you with their judge-ments. But we are commonly agreed that λειτυργία is oft ufed for *any Miniftration*, but more ftrict-ly, and ufually for a *publick Miniftration*, or *any work of publick office*; and yet more ftrictly from the Septu-agint, Ecclefiaftick writers have almoft confined it to *Holy Miniftration*, or *publick fervice* or Worfhip of God. The feveral ufes of the word in Scripture, and prophane and Ecclefiaftick Writers, you may find in fo many Lexicons at plea-fure, that I fhall pafs by the reft. *Bellarmine* doth too grofly pretend that when its applied abfolutely to holy things, the word is taken alwayes in the New Teftament, for a Miniftration in

facri

sacrificing. A little obfervation may confute that miftake.
Nor is it agreeable either to Scripture or the ufe of the Antient
Church, to call only *Forms* of publick worfhip that are *written*,
by the name of a *Liturgy*. Whether it were *Form*, or no *Form*,
Written or *not written*, *Premeditated* or *extemporate*, *Words* or
Actions, all the *Publick holy Miniftration*, or *fervice* of God, was
of old called *The Churches Liturgy*: And fo men may be for *a
Liturgy* that are not for *a Prayer Book*. But latter times have
moft ufed the word for thofe *ftinted forms*, that fome call *Offices*
containing both the *Rubrick* or *Directory*, and *the Form of words*
prefcribed as the matter of the fervice. And feeing that thofe that
now we fpeak to, underftand it in *this* fenfe, we muft fpeak as
they do, while we are fpeaking to them.

2. Note that it is not any *one* part of Publick Worfhip that we
fpeak of *alone*, either Prayer, Praife, or other part, but we fpeak
of the *whole frame*, and therefore of a *Liturgy*, or *Prefcribed words*
in *General*, becaufe that is the controverfie that the times call us
to decide.

That which I take to be the Truth, and ufefull to our
Healing, I fhall lay down in thefe ten Propofitions following.

Prop. 1. *A ftinted Liturgy is in it felf Lawfull.*

2. *A ftinted Liturgy in fome parts of publick holy fervice is ordinarily neceffary.*

3. *In the Parts where it is not of Neceffity, it may not only be
fubmitted to, but defired when the Peace of the Church requireth it.*

4. *There is fo great difference between Minifters, and People,
and Times, that it may be convenient and eligible to fome, at fome
times, and unfit and not eligible to others, and at other times.*

5. *The Minifters and Churches that earneftly defire it, fhould
not by the Magiftrate be generally or abfolutely forbidden the ufe of
a convenient prefcribed Liturgy.*

6. *To prefcribe a frame of ftinted fervice, or Prayer, &c. and
lay a Neceffity, or the Peace of the Church upon it, and to punifh,
filence, fufpend, excommunicate, or reproach the able, peaceable,
godly Minifters, or people that (juftly or unjuftly) fcruple the
ufing of it, is fo great a fin, that no confcionable Minifters*
fhould

should attempt it, or desire it, nor any godly Magistrate suffer it.

7. *The safest way of composing such a Publike Form, is to take it all, for matter and words, out of the Holy Scriptures.*

8. *Yet is not this of such Necessity, but that we may join in it, or use it, if the form of words be not from Scripture.*

9. *The matter of a common Liturgy, in which we expect any General Concord, should not be any unnecessary things, much less things doubtfull, or forbidden.*

10. *Forms of Publick Prayer should not be constantly used by Ministers that are able to pray without them: and none else should be admitted ordinarily to the Ministry, but such as are able competently to pray without such Forms; unless in great Necessities of the Church.*

These ten Propositions are the summ of all that I shall trouble you with, which I shall now review, and prove in order.

Prop. 1. **A** *Stinted Liturgy is in it self lawful.*
This is thus proved:

Argument 1. *That which is not directly or consequentially forbidden by God, remaineth lawfull: A stinted Liturgy is not directly or consequentially forbidden by God: therefore it remaineth lawfull.*

The Major is undoubted, because nothing but a Prohibition can make a thing unlawfull. *Sin is a transgression of a Law: Where there is no Law, there is no transgression:* And yet I have heard very Reverend men answer this, *that it is enough that it is not commanded, though not forbidden.* Which is plainly to deny both Scripture and Civil Principles. Precept makes Duty, or a Necessity *ex præcepto*: Prohibitions make an action sinfull, which is prohibited, as Precepts prove an Omission sinfull of the Duty commanded. But *Licitum* which is between Duty and sin, is that which is neither commanded nor forbidden. And such an act is not *Actus Moralis*, being neither good nor evill.

Here note these two things. 1. That though we say that a Liturgy is in it self lawfull, and that all things not forbidden are lawfull;

Lawfull; yet in the actuall exercise *hic & nunc*, it will be hard to find one actuall use of it, which is not a duty, or a sin. For though I am not of their mind that think every act both simply and respectively considered is a duty, or a sin (For 1. then every act must be *Actus Moralis*, and so deliberate and chosen, which is not true; as for instance, the winking of the eye, &c. 2. Then nothing were indifferent. 3. Then every act must have a Reason for it. 4. And the Consciences of Christians must be perpetually tormented: as *e.g.* to give a reason when I walk, why I set the right foot forward before the left; or when two eggs of a bigness are before me, why I take one rather then the other: these are not moral acts.) Yet I must needs think that in the worship of God, its hard to imagine such a case, in which the using of a Liturgy will do neither good nor harm: Or in which a man cannot discern, whether it be like to do more good or harm: and so make it the matter of election or refusal. And therefore as *Paul* makes *Marriage indifferent* in *it self*, when its hard to find a case, in which it shall not be a duty or a sin to particular persons, so say I of the point in question: and yet possibly sometime such cases there may be. A man sometimes in Prudence may find that constantly to use a form would be to him a sin, by reason of the ill consequents, and so it wonld be constantly to disuse it: And therefore may find himself bound (by accident) sometimes to use, and sometimes to disuse it: And yet may see no reason at all, as to the particular day and hour, why he should use or disuse it this day rather then another, or in the the Morning rather then the Evening.

2. Note also that God being the supream Lawgiver of the Church, having by *Moses* given a Law to *Israel*, did in general command, *Deut.* 12.32. that they should *add nothing thereto, nor take ought therefrom*: And consequently, we may conclude it *prohibited* under the Gospel; Nay indeed the very prohibition of self-idolizing makes it a sin for any man to arrogate that Legislation which is the Prerogative of God. For that were to deifie himself. And so this General prohibition doth make all unwarrantable Additions to be sinfull, that is, all Additions which God hath not authorized men to make. But then, such *additions* are not *sinfull formally*, because *not commanded*, but because *forbidden* by the General prohibition of [*not adding.*]

Now

Now for the Minor, *that a stinted Liturgy is not forbidden*, we need no other proof then that no Prohibition can be produced. If it be prohibited, it is either by some *special Prohibition*, or by the *General* prohibition of *not adding*: But it is by neither of these, therefore not at all. *Speciall prohibition* I never yet saw any produced. God hath nowhere fo bidden a form of Prayer. And the General prohibition of *not adding*, extends not to it. For 1. It is the *Worship* of God which is the matter that we are there forbidden to add: But the Praying with a *form, or without a form, as such*, are neither of them any part of the worship of God; nor so intended (as we now suppose) by them that use it: It is but an indifferent *Mode or Circumstance* of Worship, and not any *part* of Worship. 2. If Prayer with a form be an Addition to Gods Worship, then so is praying *without a form* (for God only Commands Prayer, but neither commands a *form*, nor that we *forbear a form*) But the Consequent is false, as the Opponents will confess; therefore so is the Antecedent. 3. Undetermined mutable Modes and Circumstances are none of the prohibited Additions, but left to humane determination. But such is the form in question. God hath bid us *Preach*, but not told us whether we shall study a *form of express* words alwayes before hand, but left that to prudence: more instances will be added under the next Argument; and therefore I shall now forbear them.

   Argum. 2. *The Prudential Determination of such Modes and Circumstances of worship as God hath left to humane Determination, is Lawfull. A stinted form or Liturgy may be such a Determination; therefore a stinted form or Liturgy may be (or is in it self) lawfull.*

Argum. 2.

   The Major is past doubt, if the Hypothesis be first proved, that some modes and circumstances of worship are left to humane Prudential Determination. And thats easily proved thus.

   Those Modes or Circumstances of worship which are Necessary *in Genere*, but left undetermined of God *in specie*, are left by God to humane Prudential Determination: (else an Impossibility should be necessary.) But many such there are that are Necessary *in Genere*, but left undetermined of God

in

in specie, therefore many such are left to humane Prudential Determination.

The Minor is sufficiently proved by instances. God hath made it our Duty to Assemble for his Publick Worship: But he hath not told us in what *place*; nor in *what seats* each person shall sit. Yet some *place* is necessary: and therefore it is left to mans Determination: Nor hath he tied us for weekly Lectures to any one day; nor on the Lords day, to begin at any *one* certain *hour*: and yet *some day and hour* is necessary; which therefore man must determine of. So God hath commanded us to read the Scriptures: But hath not told us whether they shall be *printed or written*; whether we shall read *with Spectacles* or *without*; what *Chapter* we shall read on such or such a day; nor how much at a time; Ministers must *preach* in season and out of season: But whether they must *stand* or *sit*, or *what text* they shall preach on, or how long, and whether in a *prepared form* of words or not, whether they shall *use notes*, or *not*, or use the *Bible*, or recite texts by memory, *&c.* none of these things are determined by God; and therefore are left to humane prudential determination. Abundance of such undetermined circumstances may be enumerated about Singing, Praying, Sacraments and all duties.

Now that the form of Liturgy is of this nature is manifest; God hath bid us Pray; but whether in fore-conceived words, or not, or whether in words of other mens first conceiving or our own, or whether oft in the same words or various, and whether with a Book or without, these are no parts of Prayer at all, but only such undetermined Circumstances or Modes as God hath left to our prudential Determination: And the forementioned Instances, about Reading, Preaching Singing, *&c.* are as pertinent to our question as this of Prayer, they being all parts of the Liturgy, or publick service, as well as this.

Argum. 3. *There are many express Examples in Scripture for forms of Gods service: therefore they are unquestionably lawful.* The *Psalms* of *David* were of common use in the Synagogues and Temple-worship, and also in Private; and indited to such ends. *Hezekiah* commanded the Levites to *sing Praise unto the Lord, with the words of* David *and of* Asaph *the seer*, 2 Chron. 29.30. The 92. *Psalm* is entitled [*A Psalm or song for the*
Sabbath

Sabbath day] Pfal. 102 is entitled, *A Prayer of the afflicted when he is overwhelmed, and poureth out his complaint before the Lord.*] The reft were of ordinary publike ufe. *Pfalms* are Prayers and Praifes to God for the moft part : and both as Prayers, and Praifes, and as *Pfalms*, they are part of the Liturgy. 1 Chron. 16.7. [*On that day David delivered firft this* Pfalm, *to thank the Lord, into the hands of* Afaph *and his brethren.*] The fong of *Mofes* is delivered in form, *Exod.* 15. And the Saints in the *Revelations* 15.3. are faid to *fing the fong of* Mofes, Numb.10.35,36. there is an oft-repeated form of *Mofes* prayer. There is a form for the people, *Deut.*21.7,8. *Judg.*5. there is *Deborahs Song* in form. There is a form of Prayer, *Joel* 2.17. Abundance more may be mentioned but for tedioufnefs. I fhall now only add, 1. That the *Lords Prayer* is a form directed to God as in the third perfon, and not to man only as a Directory for prayer in the fecond perfon : it is not [*Pray to God your Father in Heaven that his Name may be hallowed, his Kingdom come,* &c.] But [*Our Father which art in Heaven, Hallowed be thy Name,* &c.] And it feems by the Difciples words that thus *John* taught his Difciples to pray, *Luk.* 11.1. So that we have in the Scripture the mention of many fet forms of fervice to God, which therefore we may well ufe.

Argum. 4. *It is lawful to pray to God in the fet Words that we find in Scripture : but fo to pray (in the fet words of Scripture) is a form; therefore a form is Lawful.*

I do not here plead example, as in the laft Argument, but the Lawfulnefs of praying in *Scripture words.* They that deny this, muft be fo fingular and unreafonable, as that there is no need of my confutation for the manifefting of their error. And that it is to us a fet form if we take it out of Scripture, as well as if we compofe it, or take it out of another Book, is paft all queftion. A multitude of the prayers of holy men are left on record in the Scripture, befide thofe that were the prefcribed forms of thofe times : He that will but turn to his *Concordance* to the word [*O Lord*] and then to all the cited Texts, fhall find many fcore, if not hundred Texts that recite the prayers of the Saints; which when we ufe, we ufe a form, which we there find written.

Argum. 5. *That Jefus his Approbation of forms*

therefore we may use them.

His Approbation is proved, 1. By his owning and citing *Davids Psalms, Luk.*20.42. & 24.44. &c. 2. By his using a *Hymn* with his Disciples at the Passover or Eucharist, which we have great reason to think was a form that had been of use among the Jews. But however, if Christ had newly then composed it, yet was it a form to his Disciples. 3. By his thrice repeating the same words in his own prayer. 4. By his teaching his Disciples a form, as *John* taught his. 5. By his never expressing the least dislike of the old Jewish custom of using forms: nor doth Scripture anywhere repeal it, or forbid it. 6. The Apostles command the use of *Psalms* and *Hymns*, which cannot be ordinary in the Church without forms. All this proveth Christs approbation.

Argum. 6.   Argum. 6. *If it be lawful for the people to use a stinted form of words in publike prayer, then is it in it self lawful for the Pastors : but it is lawful for the people :* for the Pastors prayer (which they must pray over with him, and not only hear it) is a stinted form to them, even as much as if he had learnt it out of a Book. They are to follow him in his method and words, as if it were a Book prayer.

Argum. 7.   Argum. 7. *It is lawful to use a form in Preaching : therefore a stinted Liturgy is lawful.* 1. Because preaching is a part of that Liturgy. 2. Because the reason is the same for prayer, as for that in the main. Now that studyed formed Sermons are lawful, is so commonly granted, that it shall save me the labour of proving it (which were easie.)

Argum. 8.   Argum. 8. *That which hath been the practice of the Church in Scripture times, and down to this day, and is yet the practice of almost all the Churches of Christ on earth, is not like to be unlawful : but such is the use of some stinted forms of publick service : therefore,* &c. That it was so in the Jews Church, and approved by Christ, I have shewed. That it hath been of antient use in the Church since Christ, and is at this day in use in *Africk,* *Asia,* *Europe,* even among the Reformed Churches in *France, Holland, Geneva,* &c. is so well known, that I think I need not stand to prove it : yea those few that seem to disuse it, do yet use it, in *Psalms,* and other parts of worship, of which more anon.

Prop.

Prop. 2. *A Stinted Liturgy in some parts of publick holy ser-* Prop.
vice is ordinarily necessary.

This Proposition is to be proved by instances, and the proof of
the parts. The parts where a set form is usually necessary, I
shall enumerate: desiring you by the way to understand, 1. That
I speak not of an *Absolute Necessity ad finem*, as if no other
could be accepted; but a *Necessity of Duty*. it ought to be done,
as the best way. 2. That I say but [*ordinarily*] as excepting
some unusual cases.

1. The Communication or revealation of the will of God to
the Church by Reading of the Holy Scriptures, is part of the
publick service of God. As *Moses* and the Prophets were read
every Sabbath day, so by parity of reason should the Gospel;
and *Paul* required the publick reading of his Epist'es, *Act.*13.
27. & 15.21. 2 *Cor.*3.15. *Luk.*16.29 *Col.*4.16. 1 *Thes.* 5. 27.
*Rev.*1.3. But this Reading of the Scriptures is the using of a
set form in publike service. For they are the same words that
we read from day to day, and usually Must read.

2. The Publick Praysing of God by singing of *Palms*, is a
part of publick worship: and a most excellent part, not usually
to be omitted. But this part of worship is ordinarily to be used
in a stinted form: because the gift of composing *Psalms ex tempore* without a prepared form, is not usual in the Church: and
if it were so to one, it is not to the rest that must use this worship. Had we not stinted forms of *Psalms*, we should have ill-
favoured work in the Church.

3. Baptisme is usually to be administred in a form of words:
for Christ hath prescribed us a form, *Matth.* 28. 19. [*Baptizing them in the Name of the Father, and of the Son, and of the
Holy Ghost*] I think few sober men will think it ordinarily. meet
to disuse this form.

4. The use of a form in the *Consecration and Administration*
of the Lords Supper (though not through the whole action)
is ordinarily most fit: for Christ hath left us a form of words,
Take ye, Eat ye, &c.] which are most exact, and safe, and none
can mend. And *Paul* reciteth his form, 1 *Cor.*11. And small
alterations in the very words of Baptisme, or Delivering the

Lords

Lords Supper, may eafily corrupt the Ordinance in time.

5. The very Sacramental *Elements and Actions* are ftinted forms of Adminiftration, which none may alter. As the wafhing with water, the breaking of bread, and powring out of wine, and giving them, and taking them, and eating and drinking. *&c.* Thefe are *real* forms, not to be changed, at leaft without Neceffity, if at all.

6. The Bleffing of the people in the Name of the Lord, was done by a prefcribed form of old, *Num.*6.23. and is ufually to be done in a form ftill. For in all thefe forementioned parts of worfhip, fhould we ftill ufe new expreffions, when fo few and pertinent muft be ufed, we fhould be put to difufe the fitteft, and ufe fuch as are lefs fit.

7. In our ordinary Preaching a form (not impofed, unlefs in cafes of great Necefsity and unfitnefs, but) of our own premeditating, is ufually fitteft : I think few men are fo weak as to prefer (with moft preachers) unprepared Sermons, before thofe that have more of their care and ftudy. And then at leaft, the Text, Method, and fomewhat of the words muft be premeditated, if not all.

8. Ordinarily there fhould be fomewhat of a form in Publick Confeffions of the Churches faith. For how elfe fhall all concur ? And it is a tender point to admit of great or frequent mutations in : fo that in Baptifme, and at other feafons when the Chriftian faith is to be openly profeffed by one, or more, or all, a form that is exact, is ufually meet to be retained ; though in many perfonal Cafes, explicatory enlargements may do well.

9. If there be not a frequent ufe of many of the fame words, and fo fomewhat of a form, in Marriage, Confirmation, Abfolution, Excommunication, the danger will be more, then the benefit by mutation will be.

10. And with fome Minifters (of whom anon) even in Prayer, efpecially about the Sacraments, where there muft be great exactnefs, and the matter ordinarily, if not alwayes the fame, the ordinary ufe of a form may be the beft and fitteft way.

In the moft of thefe Cafes 1. The Nature of the thing fufficiently proves the ordinary fitnefs of a form. 2. The conftant Practice of almoft all Churches (if not all) is for it : even

they

they that scruple forms of Prayer, use constantly forms of Praise, of Reading, of Sacraments, &c. 3. The rest are proved fittest as aforesaid by the Apostles generall Rules, 1 *Cor.* 14. 26, 40. *Let all things be done to Edifying:* and *Let all things be done decently and in order.* Now in the cases before mentioned, the Edification of the Church (to say nothing of Order) requireth the ordinary use of forms.

Prop. 3. *I*N *those parts of publick worship where a form is not of ordinary necessity, but only Lawfull; yet may it not only be submitted to, but desired, when the Peace of the Church doth accidentally require it.*

This Proposition needs no proof, but only explication. For he is far from the temper of a Christian that sets so light by the Peace of the Church, that he would not use a Lawfull means for the procurement of it , when *Paul* would become all things to all men to save some, and would eat no flesh while he lived rather then offend his weak brother.

But here you must take these cautions, lest you misunderstand this Proposition.

1. The Peace of the *whole Church* must be in our eye, before the peace of a part ; and of a great and more considerable part, rather then of a smaller, *caeteris paribus.*

2. It is supposed that (besides the simple lawfulness of the thing) there be also no other accidental inconveniencies on the other side (that will follow the use of a form) that is of sufficient moment to weigh down the argument from the Churches Peace. For when a thing is only good or evil, (I mean, necessary or sinfull,) by Accident, and not in it self, we must consider which side hath the most weighty accidents, and accordingly must choose or refuse it.

3. It is not the fullfilling of the humours of every unreasonable expectant, or every proud Magisterial usurper that is the *Peace of the Church,* that now we speak of : If a few proud men will hold no Peace with us, unless we will serve God in their unnecessary forms, as if none had wit enough but they, to know in what words the Churches should serve God : and all must speak but

Nota.

what

what they teach them, it is not the humoring of these Proud usurpers that is the *Peace* thus to be bought.

4. We must look to the *future* as well as the *present* Peace of the Churches : And therefore if any will hold no Peace with us now, unless we will own some formal Engine that is like to make hereafter more division then unity in the Churches, (by laying the Unity or Peace of the Church on things that will not bear it, and making things necessary , that are not necessary, nor to be made so) in such cases , it is not our duty to betray the geneneral or future Peace of the Church for our private or present Peace.

5. The desireableness of this Peace of the Church which we must seek, must be much judged of by its tendency to the promoting of holiness , the saving of mens souls, the furthering of the Gospel , and prosperity of the Church in spiritual respects : For a Peace that undermineth and betrayeth these, is not desireable. The means is to be valued by its tendency to the attainment of the End.

6. There is need therefore of very great prudence, to compare things with things, for a man to know how to carry himself in such cases. For imprudent oversights, or laying greatest stress on smallest things, and slighting greater, will make men live in constant sin by abusing things indifferent.

But still the Proposition holds good with these cautions, that forms and such like indifferent things are to be used or disused much with respect to the Churches Peace.

Note.

Prop. 4.

Prop. 4. *S*O *great is the difference between men and men, times and times , that forms may be a duty to some men, and at some times , and a sin to other men, and at other times.*

As to private men in their families , it may be one mans duty to use a form, or book, and another mans sin, so is it with Ministers also in the Assemblies. Three distinctions (among others) are obvious, in which this is manifest.

1. Some Ministers are better able to perform Gods publick worship (except in the fore-excepted cases) without a form : and some are better able to do it by a form.

2. Some

2. Some Ministers have a *People* that are scrupulous of using forms, and some have people that scruple the disusing them, and some have both sorts mixt.

3. Some Churches live under Magistrates that command a form, or with Churches that unanimously agree on a form ; and others live in times and places where there is no such commands or Agreements. And according to these differences it may be one mans duty, and anothers sin to use some forms.

1. Gods work shou'd be done in the most edifying manner. Where Ministers are able to perform the publick prayers of the Church in the most profitable manner without a form, there it is their duty to disuse a form, unless some other greater accident preponderate. Still remember that for Psalms and other fore-excepted parts, I take it for granted that ordinarily a form is necessary. But our main question now is of Praying and Preaching, and that especially with respect to one standing form that is not usually varied in Prayer, and an imposed form, or composed by others, in Preaching. It should be the ordinary case of the Church that Ministers should be able to do these without a constant form of words ; to the peoples greater edification. But yet it is not alway so. And where it is not, it is better for Ministers to use a form, then to do worse, and dishonour the work of God, and wrong the Church by their erroneous or over-rude defective management. I know the great objection will be, that such men are not fit to be Ministers, and that its better to have none. But this is sooner said then proved. I am far from desiring any man to undervalue the precious mercy of an able Ministry, and from wishing for formalities and reading Pastors instead of the learned able guides that we here enjoy. I hope I should do or suffer as much as another to prevent so great a Calamity as an ignorant, unable, or negligent Ministry. But yet I am fully satisfied of it, that its better for the Church to have Readers then none.

1. Consider that there have been some very Learned able Divines (Doctors of Divinity) that by age, or other decay of Memory, or natural impediments disabling them from extemporate performances, cannot do any thing in the worship of God without the help of Notes or books ; or at least without prepa-

ration for expreſſions ; when yet upon preparation, and by convenient helps, they excell many extemporate men.

2. The Neceſſities of the Church may require an allowance or toleration of ſuch as have not ability to compoſe extemporate Prayers, or Sermons , no nor to prepare ſuch upon deliberation neither, but meerly read the Sermons and Prayers compoſed by others. I know ſome will not believe that ſuch ſhould be Miniſters; But they would have them only read as private men, rather then the people ſhould have nothing : For they think that a man that cannot preach or pray is no more capable of being a Miniſter , then a man that cannot command an Army is capable of being a Commander, &c.

But 1. Let ſuch brethren conſider that there may be all abilities *eſſentially* requiſite to a Paſtor, without the ability of praying or preaching without a form (Though ſtill I pray God to ſave us from a *Neceſſity* of ſuch.) A man that can Teach men the ſubſtance of the Chriſtian Religion , and adminiſter the Sacraments, and Overſee and Govern the flock, hath as much ability as is neceſſary to the *Being* of a Paſtor. But thoſe may have all this that cannot fitly preach or Pray without a form. They may be godly men, able in conference to inſtruct the people in the ſubſtance of Religion, and to read the Scriptures, and the Holy writings of godly men, and to adminiſter Sacraments, and prudently and diligently guide the people. And by the ſame rule as you will conclude it better that (e g.) *Wales*, *Ireland*, &c. have private men to read good books, rather then none, leſt they turn heathens ; I may alſo conclude that it is better for them to have Churches and Paſtors of this weaker ſort, then to have none, and leave their children unbaptized, and live without the Sacraments, and Church-Communion, and Government.

2. Conſider I beſeech you (which moves me more then any thing elſe) the ſtate of the Chriſtian world. In *Æthiopia*, *Syria*, *Armenia*, *Ruſſia*, *Grecia*, and abundance of other Churches of Chriſt there are very few Preachers, but meer Readers: And can any man think that it is beſt for all theſe Churches to be without Miniſters, and Sacraments, rather then to have ſuch ? O that God would give them better ! But till then I ſhall pray that

he

he will continue thefe among them, rather then leave them de-
ftitute. I know many godly judicious men, of able parts for
conference, that yet are unable to compofe a Sermon .(though
if they could, it were a form) that yet I am confident by
Reading fuch Practical Books as are now extant, and by prudent
overfight, might be tolerable Paftors for many a Congregation
in *Wales*, that now have none.

2. In a time and place where no obligation by Magiftrates
Commands, or Churches Agreements is laid upon us for the
ufe of forms, I am fully perfwaded we fhould make no more ufe
of them, then Neceffity compelleth us to do : But the thing being lawfull, the Command of a Magiftrate, or the agreement
of the Churches may go far in moving us ; And indeed muft prevail with us, unlefs in cafes where there are weightier Accidents
to weigh down on the other fide. For obedience and Agreement
or Concord in Lawfull things is our duty, where we have
not fome greater reafon to forbid it. There is much difference
between men that are left at liberty, and men that are bound
by lawfull Governours. Yea though they do not well in commanding, yet may we be bound to obey, when the matter is fuch as belongeth to their jurifdiction, and not forbidden
by God.

3. A man is alfo much to regard the minds of his people : not
out of man-pleafing difpofition, but in order to their good.
Prudence will tell us which way is likeft to attain our Ends.
Food is to be fitted to mens tempers and ftomacks, and Phyfick,
to their difeafes. If a Church be fo weak that they cannot bear
the difufe of forms, and others fo weak that they cannot bear
the ufe of them, the Paftor muft fit his practice to their Edification, till he can bring them to a wifer judgement, that fo they
may receive that which indeed is moft fit to edifie them. Prudence muft guide us in the circumftantials of worfhip, which
are left to our Determination ; that we may vary them as
the condition of our flock requireth, to their good, (of which
more anon :)

Prop. 5. **Prop. 5.** THE *Miniſters and Churches that earneſtly deſire it, ſhould not by the Magiſtrate abſolutely, and generally prohibited the uſe of a convenient ſtinted Liturgy.*

Note here that I ſpeak not of the deſires of any inconſiderable perſons, contrary to the deſires of that whole Church. If a few ignorant or wilfull people ſhould be eager for a form, when the Paſtor is able and willing to manage the work of God without it, and the Congregation profeſſeth that it hindereth their Edification (by what accident ſoever, I am not now queſtioning,) it is fit that thoſe unreaſonable perſons ſhould be denyed their deſires (in that Church) rather then the whole Congregation. Alſo if the Magiſtrate ſhould perceive that a whole Congregation, or many, or the Paſtors themſelves are eager for ſome one particular form, out of a corrupt humour, and in any ill deſign to the diſturbance of the Churches Peace, or that they will needs have an unlawfull Form, that for matter is erroneous, or for manner abſurd, or apt to breed unreverence, or hinder Edification, the Magiſtrate ſhould prohibite this : Yet ſo, that Prudence and Moderation meaſure out his penalties in ſuch a ſort, as that the Churches Edification be not hindered by his over-rigorous correcting mens diſtempers.

But out of theſe and ſuch like Caſes, when it is meer weakneſs that cauſeth Paſtors or people to be ſet upon a (lawfull) form, The Magiſtrate ought not to prohibite them by ſuch reſtraints, as ſhall deprive them of the liberty of worſhipping God, or hinder their Edification.

The Reaſons of this Propoſition are theſe. 1. Becauſe the thing being Lawfull, no Power ſhould cauſeleſly reſtrain men from the uſe of Lawfull things. God having left men to their Liberty, none ſhould without great reaſon deprive them of it.

2. The Magiſtrate ſhould not hinder the Peoples Edification in the manner of Gods worſhip : But in many places a ſtinted Liturgy is moſt for the peoples Edification. Therefore, &c. Whether it be the Miniſters weakneſs, or the peoples, that makes it moſt uſefull to them, yet when the Magiſtrate cannot cure

that

that weakneſs, he muſt bear with them.   It was the weakneſs of *Nicodemus* that made him he could not bear the day-light, in coming to Chriſt; yea and ſuch a weakneſs, as ſhewed, or was joyned with an unregenerate ſtate, and yet Chriſt would rather teach him privately then not at all.

3. Where Conſciences are ſcrupulous, and think it a ſin to worſhip publikely without a form, (though it be their error yet) the Governors are not to drive them away from it; becauſe then they will not publikely Worſhip God at all: And *no worſhip is worſe* then a *lawful form* of worſhip.

4. A Miniſter that is for the Neceſſity of a form (though erroneouſly) may be in other reſpects ſo uſefull to the Church, that he ſhould not be laid by and loſt to the Church for ſuch a thing as this.

5. The uſe of ſome forms (as aforeſaid) being neceſſary, and of other forms, not only lawfull, but of almoſt common reception through all the Churches on earth, Governors ſhould be very cautelous in denying men liberty in that which almoſt all the Churches have Liberty in, and more; even that which is their conſtant uſe.

Prop. 6. *TO preſcribe a Form of Prayer, Preaching (or other ſervice where is no Neceſſity of it) and to lay a Neceſſity on it, as to the thing it ſelf, or the Churches Peace, &c. and to puniſh, ſilence, ſuſpend, excommunicate, or reproach as Schiſmaticks, the able, godly, peaceable Miniſters or People, that (juſtly or unjuſtly) dare not uſe it, is ſo great a ſin, that no Godly Miniſters ſhould deſire or attempt it, nor any godly Magiſtrate ſuffer it.*

This was the great ſin of the late Magiſtrates and Prelates in *England*; and it is the main difference between their party and others at this day.   The Magiſtrate doth not forbid men uſing a form or Liturgy (though they forbid one particular Liturgy more ſtrictly then I could wiſh:) But there is a very few of theſe men that I know of, that can be contented with a Liberty of uſing it themſelves, if they may not have all others compelled to do as they do, and go to God with the words that they have formed for them, or that are held in their eſteem they muſt be all Schiſmaticks that will not uſe their form, and the Churches Peace muſt be laid upon it, and no man muſt be thought meet to preach or pray that will not be of their opinion, but the ableſt Paſtors of the Church muſt be ſilenced and caſt by, if they will not uſe the Common-Prayer. The ſinfulneſs of this practice ſhall be manifeſted in the next diſpute more fully, to which I reſerve the moſt of my reaſons againſt it : In the mean time let theſe few be well conſidered.

1. *It is a certain way to the Diviſion of the Church* : when men will lay its Unity or Peace on that which will not bear it, they are the moſt deſperate diſturbers and dividers of it. If one form of Prayer or Preaching had been neceſſary to the Churches Unity or Peace, Chriſt or his Apoſtles might as eaſily have compoſed it, as they did other neceſſaries. Nay experience tells us, that it is not held neceſſary by men themſelves : For the Romaniſts uſe one or more forms : and the *Grecians* another, and the *Ethiopians* another, and ſo of other Churches. In the *Bibliotheca Patrum* how many Liturgies have they given us ? And if no one of all theſe is neceſſary to all Churches, then not to any one Church, further then accidents, and mens impoſitions make it neceſſary. And no man ſhould make that neceſſary, that is not ſome way neceſſary before. It is eaſie to know that either the Form as ſuch, or ſomewhat in the Form, is like to be ſcrupled by ſome, even godly, able men : and ſo it will prove an engine of diviſion. The Church hath been brought to that torn divided condition that it is in, by this arrogancy of domineering impoſers, that muſt lay its Peace on their unneceſſary devices : and will not let us have unity in Chriſt and his Inſtitutions and peace upon his terms.

2. *By this means the people will be involved in the guilt of bitter contending, and hating all that conform not to their way, and uncharitably reproaching them as ſchiſmaticks,* and conſequently of diſliking the very doctrine that they preach, or hold, and the way they take ; and thus if uncharitableneſs, and all this ſin, the off-ſpring of it, be the way to Hell, then you may ſee what a notable ſervice they do to Satan, and how they enſnare and undo mens ſouls, that make ſuch forms of common Neceſſity to the Unity or Peace of the Church.

3. *By this means they will involve themſelves and the Magiſtrate*
in

in the guilt of perfecution : For no better will it prove, even in many cafes where the refufers fcruples are unjuft.

4. *By this means they will hinder the Edification of the Church.* What if a Minifter have a Congregation that (fuppofe upon miftakes) do fcruple thefe forms, and by prejudice or weaknefs are hindered from ferving God with cheerfullnefs and profit, where they are ufed ; muft we be bound to deny them that mode of worfhip which their weaknefs doth require ? and to force them to that which will not down with them ? Muft a Phyfitian be bound to give all his Patients one kind of dyet ? What if it be wholefome ? Will you fay, *If that will not down with him, he fhall have none : let him die ?* This is contrary to the end of our office : we are commanded to do all to Edification, which this doth contradict.

5. *It is contrary to the Office, Power and Truft of the particular Paftors of the Church, to be thus compelled in variable things.* As it is the office of a Phyfitian to judge what dyet and phyfick to prefcribe his Patients, and to vary it as perfons do vary in their tempers and difeafes, and to vary it with the fame perfons, as their condition changeth and requireth it : and as it would be foolifh Tyranny againft the very office of the Phyfitian to reftrain him from this exercife of his prudence by a Law, and to tye him to give one kind of food or phyfick to all ; fo is it in our prefent cafe. What is a Paftor, but the guide of a Congregation in the worfhip of God ? *&c.* And if Magiftrates and Bifhops take this work out of their hands by their unneceffary prefcriptions, they fo far prohibite him to do the work of a Paftor. What a grief is it to a Minifter (that being in the place, and knowing the people, is the moft competent Judge what is fit for them) to be conftrained by men that know not the ftate of his flock, to crofs their Edification, and to be forbidden to ufe his prudence and due power for their fpiritual good ?

6. *And what a finful arrogant ufurpation is this, for any man to be guilty of ?* It is Chrift that hath given his Minifters their Power, and that for Edification : and who is he that may prefume to take it from them ? If they are unworthy to be Minifters, let them not be Ordained, or let them be degraded or depofed. But if they muft be Minifters, let them do the work

of Minifters; left as he that defpifeth them, defpifeth Chrift, fo he that reftraineth them from their duty, and depriveth them of the exercife of their power unjuftly, be found one that would arrogate an authority over Chrift.

7. *And what intolerable Pride is this, for a few Bifhops to think fo highly of themfelves, and fo bafely of their more judicious Brethren, as if no man muft fpeak to God but in their words?* Thefe forms of Prayer are conceived and invented by fome body. And why fhould the Conceiver think fo highly of his own underftanding, as if he were fit to teach a whole Nation what they muft daily fay to God? and why fhould he think fo unworthily of all others in comparifon of himfelf, as if none but he (and his Companions in this ufurpation) knew how to pray or utter their minds, but by his dictates or prefcriptions? Is this Humility?

8. Moreover *this Impofition of forms (as before defcribed) doth difcover too much Cruelty to the Church:* when they had rather Minifters were caft afide, and the people left in darknefs, then Minifters fhould teach them, and worfhip God with them, that will not tye themfelves to the very words that they devife for them. What abundance of ignorant, drunken Readers and other Minifters were fuffered in *England,* while the learned, godly, painful Minifters were caft out, and filenced, or perfecuted, becaufe they would not conform to all the forms and ceremonies impofed by the Bifhops? And fo how many thoufand fouls may we think are gone to Hell, through the ignorance or ungodlinefs of their Guides, as if their damnation were more defirable, then their falvation by the teaching of Minifters that dare not ufe the Common Prayer Book and Ceremonies? I know they will fay, that fuch Schifmatical Preachers do more hurt by breaking the Churches peace, then they do good by converting fouls. But who was it that laid thefe fnares in their way? Who laid the Churches peace upon your inventions? Had not the Church a fure Rule, and an happy order, and unity, and peace, before your Common prayer Book or Ceremonies were born? Why muft the Church have no peace but upon fuch terms? Who made this Neceffity, that all men muft be taken for intolerable fchifmaticks that dare not ftint themfelves in the publick worfhip by your impofitions? Will you not be confounded

ed before God, when thefe Queftions muft be anfwered? The Church might have kept both Peace and her Paftors, if you had let all alone as the Apoftles left it, and had not turned the forms of your Devotions to be a fnare for others.

9. *And it is great unmercifulnefs to the Souls of particular men,* when you will drive them into fuch fnares, and compell them to go againft their confciences in indifferent things: whatever is not of faith is fin. And whether they believe it good or bad, you will compell them to practife all that you impofe. Have you not Confciences your felves? Do you not know what it is for a man to be driven againft his Confcience? If not, you are no Chriftians: and then no wonder if you want the Charity and compaffion of Chriftians, and fo eafily for nothing, abufe and injure the Chriftian caufe.

10. *And in thus doing, you deal unjuftly, and do not as you would be done by.* You would have *Liberty your felves* now to ufe a Liturgy: And why fhould not others have Liberty to difufe it? Either you take it for a thing Neceffary in it felf, or for Indifferent. If as Neceffary, then you are fo much the more arrogant and injurious to the Churches, and your ufurpation is the more intolerable, and you do much to Juftifie them that deprive you of your own liberty: For I know no Liberty that you fhould have to make univerfal Laws for the Church: or to make new duties by your own meer wills, or turn Indifferent things into Neceffary, and fo to multiply our work, and burden, and danger; and to filence, fufpend or excommunicate all that dare not fubmit to your ufurped Dominion. But if you take it for a thing in it felf Indifferent, whether we pray in a Form of prefcribed words, or not, then as we are content that you have your Liberty on one part, you have as juft caufe to allow us our liberty on the other, and to do as you would be done by.

11. And by thefe Impofitions, *you fet up a New Office or Power in the Church, Confifting of a New Legiflation, and a Government of the Church* by fuch new humane Laws. We know no Lawgiver but 1. Chrift as to univerfal Laws of ftanding neceffity to the Churches, in the matters of Salvation. And 2. Magiftrates to make by-laws under Chrift for a juft determination of thofe mutable circumftances that ought to be determined by humane *Prudence*; a

es to direct and guide the people as there is cause. As for Bishops or Councils, we know of no Legiflative Power that they have over their Brethren, though Agreements they may make, which may be obligatory, 1. by confent, as other contracts, 2. and in order to unity, where the cafe requireth fuch Agreements. But to fet up a New fort of Jurifdiction in the Church, by Legiflation to make Forms and Ceremonies obligatory, and by Executions to punifh Paftors that will not practife them, is a dangerous device.

12. Laftly by this means you *will harden the Papifts, that by their Inventions and Impofitions have divided the Church, and been guilty of fo much ufurpation and tyrannie*; For how can we condemn that in them that is practifed by our felves? And though in number of Inventions and Impofitions they exceed, yet it is not well to concur with them in the *kind* of unneceffary Impofitions, and fo far to Juftifie them in their injury to the Church.

If none of thefe or other Reafons will alloy the Imperious diftemper of the Proud, but they muft needs by a ufurped Legiflation be making Indifferent things become neceffary to others, and domineer over mens Confciences, and the Church of God, we muft leave them to him, that being the Lord and Lawgiver of the Church, is Jealous of his Prerogative, and abhorreth Idols, and will not give his glory to another, and that delighteth to pull down the Proud, and humble them that exalt themfeves.

But yet how far an Agreement or voluntary Confent of the Churches is defirable as to a Liturgy, I fhall fhew more anon.

---

7. Prop. 7. *THE fafeft way of compofing a ftinted Liturgie, is to take it all, or as much as may be, for words as well as matter, out of the Holy Scriptures.*

Reaf. 1. This way is leaft lyable to fcruple, becaufe all are fatisfied of the infallible Truth of Scripture, and the fitnefs of its expreffions, that are not like to be fatisfied with mans. And it is a laudable difpofition in the Creature to prefer the words of God before all other, and therefore not to be difcouraged in any.

Reaf. 2. This way tends moft to the peace of the Church. All will unite in the words of God, that will not unite in the
forms

forms and words of men. If they underſtand not a word of God, yet knowing it to be true, they will not quarrel with it, but ſubmit : But if they underſtand not the words of men, they will be ready to ſuſpect them, and ſo to quarrel with them, and ſo the Churches peace will be broken. Beſides, the judgements of men being fallible, many will ſuſpect that its poſſible there may be ſome error in their forms, though we ſee them not, and God ſhould be worſhiped in the ſureſt way.

Reaſ. 3. There is no other words that may be preferred before the words of God, or ſtand in Competition with them : and therefore me thinks this ſhould eaſily be decided.

Object. But the Scripture hath not forms enough for all the Churches uſes. *Anſw.* It hath matter and words for ſuch Forms. Without any additions, ſave only terms of Connection, the ſentences of holy Scripture may ſuffice the Church for all its uſes, as to forms.

Object. But men may ſpeak untruths in Scripture words if they will, and by miſplacing and miſapplying them, may make them ſpeak what was never meant in them. *Anſw.* But 1. When they uſe no expoſitory terms of their own, but meerly recite the words of Scripture, the perverting them will not be ſo eaſie or common : And 2. When they have placed them how they pleaſe, the people are left at liberty to interpret them according to the ſence they have in the Scripture, and not according to what mens miſplacing may ſeem to put upon them : when we profeſſedly make our forms out of Gods word, we do as it were tell the people that they muſt give each ſentence its proper interpretation as its meant in Scripture, becauſe we pretend not to change it, but to uſe it. But when its our own words that we compoſe our own impoſed forms in, the people are left more uncertain of the ſoundneſs. For the maker is the Interpreter.

Object. But the Church hath antient venerable forms already ; and who may preſume to alter them ?

Anſw. 1. Hath it any that are more Ancient or more venerable then the Scripture ? undoubtedly it hath not ; nor any but muſt ſtoop to Scripture. 2. All that is in the words of Scripture, we are contented be continued (at leaſt. 3. If it were lawful for the firſt deviſers or compilers of theſe Forms, to

Ccc 2   make

make a new Liturgy, when the Church had so many before, then is it lawful for others to do the like. And if the compilers of the first of those Liturgies, might make a new one in their own words, why may not others make a new one in the Scripture words, that will be new only as to the connexion of Sentences ? 4. The Church of Rome that is most for their forms, have yet so often innovated, that they have no reason to condemn it in others.

---

8. Prop. 8. *Though it be safest and most venerable in Scripture words, yet is not this of so great necessity, but that we may lawfully use a Liturgy that is not thus taken out of Scripture.*

As long as the matter is agreeable to Scripture, it is more for Conveniency, then necessity, that the words be thence, as is easily proved.

1. In our Preaching we judge it lawfull to speak words that are not in the Scripture : therefore by parity of reason, we may do so in Prayer.

2. In our *extemporate* Prayers we judge it lawfull to use our own words that are not taken out of Scripture : therefore we may do so in a Liturgy.

3. Some persons may be so strange to Scripture language, that for a time more familiar Phrases may be more edifying to them.

4. Words are but to express our minds : If therefore our words are congruous expressions of sound and well ordered conceptions, they are not only lawful, but convenient. And therefore it is not warrantable for any man to quarrel with expressions because they are not Scriptural, nor to scruple the use of Liturgies, because the forms are not in the words of Scripture.

---

9. Prop. 9. *The matter of a common Liturgy in which we expect any general Concord, should not be any doubtfull or unnecessary things.*

1. It should impose no doubtfull or unnecessary ceremonies,

(of which I shall speak by it self in the next Disputation.)
2. It should not restrain men needlesly in things indifferent, by
determining of mutable circumstances, as time, place, gesture,
vestures, words, &c. (Of which also in the next.) 3. It should
not make those things to be of general indispensable immutable
necessity, that are but sometimes necessary, or meet; but Pastors should have their Liberty to vary them as there is occasion.
4. Much less should any thing Materially dubious and uncertain
be put in.

For God will be worshipped in knowledge and faith. And,
as is said before, the Church will be divided, and the Consciences of men ensnared, by laying so much on unnecessary
things. And therefore though such imposers pretend to a perfecter Unity and Concord, then in a few Generals or Necessaries
can be had, yet they will find they miss their mark.

Prop. 10. *HUmane Forms of publick prayer, or other wor-*
ship (excepting the fore-excepted Necessary
cases, as Psalms, &c.) should not be constantly used by Mi-
nisters, that have their liberty, and are able to pray without them:
Nor should any be ordinarily admitted into the Ministry (except
in the great necessities of the Church) that are not able to pray with-
out such forms.

Prop. 10:

In this Proposition are these considerable points implyed, and
expressed. 1. That it is not unfit to have forms by the common
Agreement of the Pastors, to be used when its meet (as is before and after expressed.) There are few Nations in the world,
so well provided for with able Ministers, but that some places
must be supplied with men that have need of forms of Prayer,
if not of Preaching, composed by others. And therefore it is
fittest that such should have Forms that are Agreed on by all.
And therefore I doubt not but when we came newly out of Popery, and had not a full supply of preachers, it was a wise and
lawfull course to compose a common form of Prayer. For,
1. It will be the surest way to keep out unsoundness and abusive
passages, when nothing is allowed as a publick form but what
hath obtained the common consent. 2. It will be the way of fullest
concord: whilst there is more of Concord
in

in it, to have one (that is approved found) then to have as many as men please. 3   The Churches may the better know whom
to hold communion with in Prayer, (though the Pastors may be
unable to pray without forms) when they know the substance
of their Prayers.   4. The Magistrate may the better do his duty
and be responsible for the service that is offered to God, even by
the weakest Pastors, and see that Gods name be not abused.   It
is therefore desirable that a Common Liturgy be extant.

2. And for the *use of it*, let these Rules contained in the Proposition be observed.

1. Let no man be ordained a Minister that is not able to Pray
without a Form, in such a manner as is not dishonourable to
the worship of God, unless the Necessity of the Churches shall
require it.   All friends of the Church will agree to this, that
the Church have the ablest Pastors that can be got.

2. But because it is not to be hoped for that all the Churches
can be thus supplied (at least in haste,) if the Ordainers or
Approvers shall appoint any to the work in *Wales* or other ne-
cessitous places, that are not able competently to administer Sacraments, *&c.* without a Form of Prayer, let them tye such to
use the Form Agreed on.

3. If they approve only of such as are able to do it without
a form, but yet so weakly (some of them) as is less to the Churches Edification , then the form would be, let such be advised,
sometimes to use the Form, and sometime to forbear it, till they
are more able.

4. And that it may be no dishonour to the publick Form, that
it is used only by the weak, let the Ablest Ministers sometime use
it , but with these cautions : 1. Let them not be compelled to it
against their judgements, but perswaded.   2. Let not the ablest
use it so frequently as the weak, (unless their own judgement require it.) Let the weaker use it ofter, and the Abler
more seldom.

5. Let neither of them (that can competently worship God
without it) use it *Constantly* ; but sometime use it, and sometime forbear it.   And this is the main point that I intend in
this Proposition , and therefore shall now briefly give my Reasons for.

Reas. 1. *The constant use of forms (and so of Ceremonies and*
any

any Indifferent things) doth potently tend to perswade the people that they are matters of *Necessity,* and not indifferent. All the words that you can use will not satisfie them that it is indifferent, if you use it not Indifferently. We see by experience the power of custome with the vulgar.

But you will say, *What if they do overvalue it as necessary, what danger is in that?* I answer very much. 1. They will offer God a blind kind of service, while they place his worship in that which is no part of worship (as forms are not, as such) but an indifferent circumstance. 2. They will be hereby induced to uncharitable censures of other Churches or persons that think otherwise, or disuse those customs. 3. They will be strongly induced to rebell against their Magistrates and Pastors, if they shall judge it meet to change those customs. 4. They will turn that stream of their zeal for these indifferent things, that should be laid out on the matters of Necessity: and perhaps in vain will they worship God, by an outside hypocriticall worship, while they thus take up with mens Traditions. 5. They will forsake Gods own Ordinances, when they cannot have them cloathed with their desired mode. All this we see in our dayes at home. The most ignorant and ungodly do by hundreds and thousands, reject Church discipline, and Sacraments, and many of them the Prayers and Assemblies themselves, because they have not the Common Prayer, or because the Churches kneel not at the Lords Supper in the act of Receiving, and such like. So that it is a grievous plague to our peoples souls to be led into these mistakes, and to think that Circumstances and things indifferent, are matters of Necessity.

And yet on the other side, lest the *constant disuse* of all convenient forms, should lead the people into the contrary extream, to think them all unlawfull (and so to be guilty of the like uncharitable censures and evils as aforesaid) I think it safest, that the ablest men should sometime use them. And this Indifferent use of them, will lead the people to indifferent thoughts of them, and so they will not provoke God by blind worship, nor be so ready to fly in the faces of their Ministers when they cross them here
what a stir have we if men

if the dead (in cafe of Minifters abfence, or other hinderance)
have not fomewhat faid over them at the grave ; and in fome
places, if Minifters go not in proceffion in Rogation week, and
many fuch like cuftoms. If thefe were fometime ufed (in a good
and lawfull way) it would keep men from miftaking them to
be unlawfull ; and if they were fometime difufed , people would
not take them as things neceffary , nor fo hate and reproach
both Minifters and brethren that neglect them, or do not alwayes
humour them herein , yea or that were againft them, nor would
men feparate on thefe accounts.

Reaf. 2. *The conftant ufe of Forms of Prayer depriveth people of
their Minifters gifts, and potently tendeth to work the people into a
dull formality, and to a meer outfide heartlefs kind of fervice,* Which
is as great an enemy to ferious Devotion, and confequently to
mens falvation, as almoft any thing thats to be found among profeffed Chriftians in the Church. How dangeroufly and obftinately do fuch delude themfelves, and think that they are as upright-
ly religious as the beft? and fo refufe all the humbling convincing light that fhould bring them to a change, and blindly
mifapply the promifes to themfelves , and go on in meer prefum-
ption to the laft : and all becaufe they thus draw neer to God
with their lips , and fay over a form of words , when their
hearts are far from him, and they know not, or obferve not what
they fay.

And that conftancy in Forms doth potently tend to this
dead formality, we need no other proof then experience. How
hard doth the beft man find it to keep up life and ferioufnefs in
the conftant hearing or fpeaking of the fame words ? If you
fay that it is our fault ; I grant it : but it is an uncurable fault
while we are in the flefh : or at leaft its few that ever are
very much cured of it , and non wholly. Theres much alfo in
nature it felf to caufe this. ʼA man that delighteth in Mufick is
weary of it , if he have conftantly the fame inftrument and
tune : or at leaft cannot poffibly have that delight that Variety would afford him.   So is it in recreations , and oft in dyet ;
and other things. Novelty affecteth : Variety pleafeth : Com-
monnefs dulleth us.   And though we muft not therefore have
a New God, or a New Chrift, or a New Gofpel (the fulnefs
of thefe affordeth the foul a daily variety : and alfo their perfect

fect goodnef is such as leaves no need of a variety in kind, yet is it meet that Ministers should have a gratefull variety of *Manner*, to keep up delight and desire in their people. A sick stomack cannot take still the same Physick, nor the same dish. I know that an ancient prudent man, especially the Learned Pastor himself, that better comprehendeth what a form of words contains, can make a much better use of forms, then younger Christians can do. But I think with all, I am sure with the generality, (to whom we must have respect) a constant form is a certain way to bring the Soul to a cold insensible formal worship.

And on the other side, if a form be *Constantly disused*, and people have not sometimes a recitall of the same, again and again, it may tend to breed a childish levity, and giddyness in Religion; as if it were not the matter, but meer Novelty and variety that did please; And so it may also easily make Hypocrites, who shall delude themselves with conceits that they delight in God and in his word, when it is but in these novelties, and varieties of expression, that they are tickled and delighted; and their itching ears being pleased, they think it proves a work of saving grace on the heart. And therefore to fix Christians and make them sound, that they grow not wanton in Religion, and be not as children carryed up and down with variety of doctrines or of modes, I think it would be useful to have a moderate seasonable use of some forms as to the manner, as well as often to inculcate the same matter; Avoiding still that constancy that tends to dull their appetites, and make them weary or formal in the work.

Reas. 3. *The constant use of a stinted Liturgy, or form of Prayer, doth much tend to the remisness and negligence of the Ministry.* When they know that the duty requireth no exercise of their invention, and that before the Church they may as well perform it with an unprepared as with a prepared mind, it will strongly tempt them (and prevail too commonly) to neglect the stirring up of their gifts, and the preparing of their minds. When they know that before men they may (in Reading a Prayer) come off as well without any regard to their hearts, as with the greatest seriousness of devotion, we must expect that most should do accordingly: For we see that Ministers are men, and too many

are

are carryed as well as others, with the stream of temptation. But those Prayers and other duties that depend upon their parts, require preparation, or at least some present care and diligence for the awakening of their hearts, and excitation of their faculties.

Reas. 4. But the *principal danger* of *a constant use of prescribed forms, is left it should let in an unworthy Ministry into the Church.* For though I had rather have as weak Ministers as I before described, then none; yet it will be very dangerous when such are tolerated because of Necessity, left the negligence of Ordainers and Approvers will take advantage of this, and pretend necessity where there is none, or hearken to them that come with such pretences, and so undo the Church by an ignorant insufficient Ministry; so hard is it for men to avoid one extream without running into another. Now the utter prohibition of stinted forms will prevent this, but not without an evil on the other side. And therefore to avoid the evils on both sides, me thinks it would be best to let such forms be used, but unconstantly, unless by men that will lie under the dishonour of being able to do no better. And that dishonor will hinder men from resting in them, and the frequent exercise of other mens gifts, will awaken them to their duty, and the necessity of it will as well keep out insufficient men as if there were no form at all. For an insufficient man can no more perform the work once a day, without a form, then twice a day. I shall add no more Reasons, because they that write against forms of Prayer, though they run too far, have said enough of the inconveniences. The motion that I make being for a voluntary and an unconstant use of them, I must expect to meet with objections on both sides, which I shall briefly answer.

Q. 1, Object. 1. Those that are utterly against forms, will say that I am *opening under pretence of Peace and Liberty a way to let in an unlawfull worship and a lazy insufficient Ministry.* To which I answ. 1. For them that take all forms to be unlawfull, I think them fitter for compassion then disputes, and judge their reason to be as low as the Quakers that cry down the use of hourglasses, and sermon-notes, and preaching on a Text of Scripture. 2. And for the rest of the objection, its answered before. The use of a Liturgy in the way described, will not more Countenance

tenance a lazy infufficient miniftry, nor hurt the Church, then if there were none.

Object. 2. *But what need is there of it? Are we not well without* Object it? *why would you difturb our peace, to pleafe the adverfaries?* Anfw. 1. We are *not without* a Liturgy, as fhall be further fhewed, and therefore you cannot fay we are *well with-out it.* 2. Some yong weak Minifters (we muft fpeak the truth) do wrong both Baptifm and the Lords Supper by many mifcarriages, for want of further helps. 3. *Wales* and many parts of *England* muft be fupplyed with Forms, or be without, which is worfe. 4. The Confciences of many of thofe that you call adverfaries (and I call Brethren) muft be indulged with the *liberty* of a convenient form, or elfe we fhall not walk charitably.

On the otherfide it will be objected, by them that would Object. have all men forced to the conftant ufe of forms, 1. that *If we have not forms, men may vent what they pleafe in prayer: fome rail in prayer, and fome vent error, and fome rebellion, &c. Anfw.* 1. This Argument makes againft all Prayer of Minifters, but what is prefcribed. For if you force them to a form, and yet give them leave with their Sermons to ufe alfo either extemporate or formed Prayers of their own, they may as well vent rebellion, herefie or malice in them, as if they had no Liturgy at all. And if you would have Minifters ufe no prayer but what they read out of the impofed books, for fear of thefe inconveniences, you will fhew your felves enemies to the Church, and cure an inconvenience with a mifchief. 2. And if men were forbidden all prayer but by the Book, yet it is more eafie to vent error or malice in a Sermon. So that unlefs you tie them alfo to forbear preaching fave out of an impofed book, you are never the better. And if you would do fo, you are forry helpers of the Church. 3. You have a better remedy then thefe at hand. Put no fuch Jnfufficient men, or Hereticks into the Miniftry, that will fo abufe prayer: or if they be crept in, put them out again, and put better in their places, that will not abufe it. If fome Phyfitians kill men by ignorance or malice, will you tie them all to go by a Book and give but one medicine, or will you not rather caft out the unworthy, and licence only abler men?

Object.

Object. 2.　　*Object.* 2. *But how can I Joyn with a Minister in prayer, If I know not before hand what he will say, when for ought I know he may pray blasphemy or heresie?*

Answ. 1. By this objection, you take it to be unlawful to joyn with any prayers at all, whether publick or private, but what you know before: And so it seems you think all prayer but whats by the book, unfit for any but a solitary person. And if this be your mind, that your Book-Prayers must needs shut out all others, blame not men so much to shut out your Book, when you so far provoke them. 2. According to this Objection you must not send for the Minister to pray with you when you are sick, or in trouble, unless he tye himself to your Book. And why then may not another do it as well as he; or at least, the sillyest man that can read as well as the most able? 3. It is the work of the Minister, to be the peoples mouth in prayer to God, and therefore if he fail in the manner of his own work, it is his sin, and not yours, and you may no more refuse for that to joyn with him, then subjects may refuse to obey the soveraign power because of some miscarriages, yea or to fight for them, and defend them. 4. Your presence signifieth not your consent to all that you hear from a Minister: And your Heart is not to follow him in evil, but in good: and therefore seeing you are at liberty, what cause of scruple have you? 5. It is supposed that no man is ordinarily admitted, or tolerated in the Ministry, that will so abuse prayer that men may not lawfully joyn with them. If they are such, cast them out: If you cannot cast them out, if they are Hereticks or Blasphemers, come not neer them. But if they are men fit for to be tolerated in the Ministry, you have reason to trust them so far in their office, as not to expect Heresies or Blasphemies from them, till you hear them: And if you hear them guilty of such, after a First and Second admonition avoid them. But let not wicked uncharitable censures be an argument against the worship of God. You know not but a Physitian may poison you, and yet you will choose the best you can, and then trust your lives with him. You may much more do so by a Minister, because you proceed not by so implicite a faith in the matters of your Salvation. You may refuse any evil that the Minister offereth.

Object. 3.　　*Object.* 3. *But many of them speak nonsense and unreverent*
Words,

words, and abuse Gods worship. Answ. Get better in their stead, that are able to do Gods work in a more suitable manner. But see that your quarrelsome capricious wits, do not odiously aggravate imperfections, or make faults where there are none. And remember that you have not Angels, but men to be your Pastors; and therefore imperfections must be expected: But a blessing may accompany imperfect administrations. But if People, Patron, and Ordainer will choose weak men, when they may have better, they may thank themselves. A Common Prayer book will make but an imperfect supply, instead of an able Minister: Though in some cases I am for it, as aforesaid.

Object. 4. But prayer is a speaking to God: and therefore Object. 4. *men should say nothing but what is exactly weighed before hand.*

Answ. 1. We grant all this. But men may weigh before hand the matter of their requests, without preparing a form of words: or a man may fore-consider of his words, without a Prayer-book. 2. *Preaching is a speaking in Gods name, as though God speak by us, and as Christs embassadors in his stead.* 2 Cor. 5. 19, 20. And to speak as in Christs stead, and Gods name, requireth as great preparation, as to speak to God in the peoples name. It seems more, as it were to represent Christ in speaking, then to speak to Christ while we represent but the people And therefore by this argument you should let no man preach neither, but by a book prescribed, 3. God is not as man, that looks most at oratory and fine words. It is an humble, contrite, faithfull, honest heart that he looks at: And where he sees this, with earnest desires, and that the matter of Prayer is agreeable to his will, he will bear with many a homely word. One Cold request, or the least formality and dulness of affection, and carelesness and disesteem of the mercy, is more odious with God, then a thousand Barbarisms, andSolæcisms, and unhandsome words. Yet the tongue also should carefully be lookt to: but men should not mistake themselves, and think that God judgeth by the outward appearance, and as man judgeth. 4. Still I say, get Ministers that are able to do better if you have insufficient ones. A man on a common prayer-book is likelier to provoke God, by a careless, heartless, customary service, and meer lip labour, let the the words be never so exact, then another (that fears God) is like to provoke him by disorderly or unhandsome words: Though both should be avoided.

Object

Object. 5.   *Object. 5. Our minds are not able to go along with a Minister on the sudden, unless we knew what he will say before hand.*

Answ. A diligent soul that marketh what is said, may with holy affections go along with a Minister without knowing what he will say before hand. The experience of Christians confuteth this objection. 2 And this would not only plead for a form, but shut out all other prayer : which is sufficient to disgrace it with any understanding man.

Object. 6.   *Object. 6. The publick Prayers of the Church are they that we must own by our concurrence : His own conceived Prayers are but the Private Prayers of the Minister.   Answ.* The Minister is a publick person , and his prayers publickly made for and in the Church, are as much the Publick prayers of that Church as if they were read out of an imposed Book : But indeed when many Churches Agree in a form, that form may so far be called the Common Prayers of all those Churches : but its no more the Publick Prayers of any one Church then sudden conceived prayer is. And when there is no form, yet the *matter* may be the Common Prayer of all Churches.

Object. 7.   *Object. 7. But what confusion will it make in the Church if one Congregation shall have a Form, and another none, and every man shall be left to do what he list in Prayer ?*

Answ This is the voice of that Ignorance, Pride, and Dividing usurpation that hath caused all the Schisms and troubles of the Church. Must the Churches have no Peace but on your imposed terms ? Must none be endured, but all cast out of the Church of God that dare not say your forms of prayer, though they are as wise and pious and peaceable as you ? Nothing but Proud arrogancy and uncharitable cruelty will say so. 2.But if we must needs all Agree in the manner of our Prayers, we must shut out all forms, and agree all to be without them (which yet I consent not to.) For there is no one Form that you can expect that all should agree in , thats of humane invention : Not but that we *may* well do it : but it *will not be.* 3. How had the Church Unity before any of your forms were known ? 4. If it be no blemish for several Nations to have several Forms , and manners , it is tolerable for several Congregations, 5. How did the Ancient Churches maintain their Unity, when Liturgies were in use, and the variety was

so

so great as is commonly known ? Many Churches had no singing of Psalms (*Vid. Pamel. in Cyprian. de Orat. Dom. Not.* 6.) Others used it by the whole Assemblies (see *Ball's* Friendly Tryal, *page* 60. citing the Authors that attest it) Other Churches did use to sing by course, or two at a time. (See it proved by *Ball ibid.* out of many witnesses.) This variety and much more consisted then with Unity, and may do now, when forced uniformity will not. 6. We are all now at Liberty what Gesture we will use in singing Psalms, *&c.* and is here any discord hence arising ? But men were forced to kneeling only in Receiving the Lords Supper, and there came in discord. Mens fancies makes that seem confusion that is no such thing. No more then that all that hear or pray, have not the same coloured cloaths, complections, *&c.*

Object. 8. *But should not men obey Authority in forms and matters of indifferency?* Answ. They should, if they be indeed indifferent. But should Authority therefore ensnare the Church with needless Impositions ? All men will not be satisfied of the Indifferency. I have heard many say that they would preach in a fools Cap and Coat if authority command them. But is it therefore fit that Authority should command it ? All men will not judge it lawfull to obey them in such cases, and so there will be needless snares laid to intrap and divide men.

Object 9. *But antiquity is for set forms, and therefore Novelty, must not be permitted to exclude them.*

Answ. 1. Let Scripture be the Rule for deciding this, which is the chief witness of Antiquity : and let the oldest way prevail. 2. Forms were at first introduced in Variety, and not as necessary for the Churches Unity to Agree in one : And they were left to the Pastors Liberty, and none were forced to any forms of other mens composing When *Basil* set up his New forms of Psalmodie and other Worship, which the Church of *Neocasarea* were so offended at, he did not for all that impose it on them, but was content to use it in his Church at *Cæsarea.*

Object. 10. *No man can now say what is the worship of God among us, because there is no Liturgy, but its mutable as every person pleases.*

Answ. We have a Liturgy, and are agreed in all the parts of worship. To have forms or no forms is no part of it, but a circumstance or mode. *T H E*

The ſumm.   THE ſumm is this ; 1. We have already a ſtinted Liturgy. 1. A form of Doctrine in Scripture, 2. Real forms in Sacraments 3. A verbal form in Baptizing, 4. A form in delivering the Lords Supper. 5. A Creed (uſed at Baptiſm) as a form of confeſſion. 6. We Read the Pſalms as Liturgical forms of praiſe and prayer. 7. We have forms of ſinging Pſalms. 8. We have a form of bleſſing the people in the End. 9. And of Excommunication (ſee the Government of the Church, &c.) 10. And of Abſolution. 11. And of Marriage. 12. And Miniſters preparation makes much of their Sermons a form. 13. And they are at liberty to pray in a form if they Pleaſe.

Beſides forms of Catechiſms.

2. No more is neceſſary (of it ſelf) unleſs (accidentally) Authority or Peace, &c. require it.

3. If Peace, &c. require a form, let it be one, by common Agreement as neer as may be, taken out of Scripture, even in words, and as much of the old as is conſiſtent with this Rule retained.

4. Let it not contain any doubtfull or unneceſſary things, but be as much certain and neceſſary for the matter as may be.

5. Let none be forced to uſe it, but ſuch as by Ordainers or Approvers, are judged inſufficient to worſhip God without it, and yet are allowed or Tolerated in the Miniſtry.

6. Let no Tolerated Miniſters be Abſolutely forbidden to uſe it.

7. Let none be ſuffered to lay the Unity and Peace of the Church on it, and ſuſpend, excommunicate or reproach all that diſſent from them in uſing or not uſing it.

8. In times of Liberty, let none uſe it conſtantly (but the unab'e before excepted.) But let the weaker uſe it oftner, and the abler ſeldomer, yet ſometimes (voluntarily, and cæteris paribus, ſtill looking to the ſtate of their flocks, and fitting all to their Edification.)

9. When Magiſtrates command it, or the Agreement of Paſtors and Peace of the Churches (though accidentally by mens infirmity) require it, let none refuſe the frequent uſe of lawfull forms.

10. But let none deſire or endeavour the introducing of any ſuch Neceſſity of this or any indifferent thing, that is not firſt Neceſſary by ſome conſiderable antecedent occaſion to the Edification of the Church.

This much wil pleaſe the moderate, but not the ſelf conceited.

FINIS.

The Fifth
DISPUTATION:
Of Humane
CEREMONIES:
Whether they are neceſſary, or profitable to the Church, and how
far they may be impoſed or obſerved?

By *Richard Baxter.*

LONDON,
Printed by *Robert White,* for *Nevil Simmons,* Book-
ſeller in *Kederminſter, Anno Dom.* 165⁵.

Qu. Whether Humane Ceremonies be Necessary or Profitable to the Church?

CHAP. I.

Distinctions and Propositions in order to the Decision.

§. 1.  THE discussion of the Controversie about the Etymologie of the word [*Ceremony*] is unnecessary to our ends; and would be more troublesome then usefull Whether it be derived *ab oppido Cære,* or *à carendo,* or *à Caritate,* or *Cerere,* as several mens conjectures run, or rather as *Scaliger* and *Martinius* think, from *Cerus,* which *in veteri lingua erat sanctus,* it sufficeth us that it signifieth a *sacred rite. Servius* saith that all sacred things among the Greeks were called ὄργια, and among the Latines *Ceremoniæ.* But by *Ceremonies* we mean only the *[Rites or Order]* about the worship of God.

as are deviſed and appointed to be uſed, by men, without any ſpecial Revelation from God, or any extraordinary inſpiration of
his Spirit, by which the inſtitution might have been juſtly aſcri-
bed to God as the certain principal cauſe.

§. 2. There is ſo much ambiguity partly in the terms, and
partly in the ſuppoſed or implyed paſſages that will riſe before us
in the diſpute, that I judge it neceſſary to make the way to the
true deciſion of the controverſie, and your right underſtanding of
it by theſe diſtinctions following, and then to lay down the truth
in certain Propoſitions.

§. 3. *Diſt.* 1. We muſt diſtinguiſh between ſuch Ceremonies
as God hath left to humane determination in his worſhip,
and ſuch as he hath not ſo left; but hath either 1. *Expreſly* forbidden them in particular. 2. Or in a *General* prohibition forbidden them, or 3. Hath given no man authority to inſtitute
them. So great difference is there between things that commonly go under the name of Ceremonies, that they are not in this
Controverſie to be confounded, if we would not loſe the truth.

§. 4. *Diſt.* 2. We muſt diſtinguiſh between *Ceremonies* commanded by *man as in Gods name*, and by pretence of a *Commiſſion
from him*; and ſuch as are only commanded in *mens own names*,
or at leaſt on pretence of nothing but a *General Power*.

§. 5. *Diſt.* 3. We muſt diſtinguiſh between *Ceremonies* commanded by men *as neceſſary duties or means of worſhip*, and ſuch
as are only commanded as *indifferent things*.

§. 6. *Diſt.* 4. We muſt diſtinguiſh between *Ceremonies* impoſed by a *Lawfull Magiſtrate*, or *Church-Governours*, and ſuch
as are impoſed by *uſurpers*, or men without authority.

§. 7. *Diſt.* 5. We muſt diſtinguiſh between *Ceremonies* impoſed as *Univerſally* to be *practiſed* by all ages, or all people, in
the Church at leaſt, and ſuch as are impoſed only on ſome *one
Congregation or Nation* by their proper Governours, and that as
things mutable, that upon ſpecial occaſion were taken up, and
may ſo be laid aſide again.

§. 8. *Diſt.* 6. We muſt diſtinguiſh between *Ceremonies* commanded as things *neceſſary to the being* of the Church or Worſhip,
or only *neceſſary to the Order* and convenient adminiſtration,
and *better being* of them (in the judgement of the impoſers.)

§. 9. *Diſt* 7. We muſt diſtinguiſh between the abſolute command

mand of Governors imposing such ceremonies, upon grievous penalties, or without tolerations; and the simple recommending them, or requiring them to be used with (expressed or implyed) exceptions.

§. 10. *Dist.* 8. We must very much difference the *several Countreys* where such things are imposed, and the several *sorts of People* on whom, and the *several seasons* in which they are imposed, and thence foresee the effects or consequents that are like to follow.

§. 11. *Dist.* 9. We must distinguish between the *Commanding* of such *Ceremonies*, and the *Obeying of such Commands*. Its one thing to ask whether it be necessary, profitable, or lawfull to Impose them? and another whether it be necessary or lawfull to use them when commanded?

§. 12. *Dist.* 10. We must distinguish between that which is Necessary or Profitable to the order or Peace of *one Church or Nation* : and that which is necessary or profitable to the order, peace or unity of *many Churches or Nations*, among themselves : or supposed to be so.

§. 13. These Distinctions premised to remove ambiguity; I lay down that which I conceive to be the truth in these Propositions following; which having mentioned, I shall re-assume and confirm such of them as seem of neerest concernment to the Question.

§. 14. Prop. 1. *Such Ceremonies as God hath wholly exempted from humane power to determine of, or institute, or hath given man no power to institute, are not necessary, or profitable to the Church, nor may they lawfully be instituted by man.*

§. 15. Prop. 2. *In such unlawfull Impositions, it is a great aggravation of the sin, if men pretend that they are the Institutions of God, or that they have a Commission from God to institute or impose them, when it is no such matter ; and so pretend them to be D.vine.*

§. 16. Prop. 3. *If things unlawfull (either forbidden, or that want authority) are commanded as indifferent, it is a sinfull command, but if commanded as parts of Gods Worship or necessary to the Being or well being of the Church, it is an aggravation of the sin.*

§. 17. Prop. 4. *Things indifferent, lawfull and convenient, are sinfully Commanded if . . . are pretended to be more necessary then they a . . .*

3.

§. 18. Prop. 5. *A thing convenient and profitable, is sinfully commanded, when it is commanded on a greater penalty, then the nature and use of it doth require, and the common good will bear.*

§. 19. Prop. 6. *It is not lawfull to make any thing the subjects Duty by a command, that is meerly Indifferent, antecedently both in it self, and as cloathed with all accidents.*

§. 20. Prop. 7. *Some things may be lawfully and profitably commanded at one time and place, and to one sort of People, that may not be lawfully commanded at another time, or to another people : no nor obeyed, if so commanded.*

§. 21. Prop. 8. *Those Orders may be Profitable for the Peace of the Churches in one Nation, or under the Government of one Prince, that are not necessary or profitable in order to the unity or Peace of the Churches under divers Princes.*

§. 22. Prop. 9. *There is no meer humane Universal Soveraign Civil, or Ecclesiastical over the Catholick Church, and therefore there is no power given to any from God, to make Laws that shall universally bind the Catholick Church.*

§. 23. Prop. 10. *If it be not our own Lawfull Governors Civil or Ecclesiastical, but Usurpers that command us, we are not therefore bound to obey them, though the things be lawfull.*

§. 24. Prop. 11. *The Commands of lawfull Governors about lawful Ceremonies are ordinarily to be understood with exceptions, though there be none exprest, as that in certain cases it is not their will that such commands should bind us.*

§. 25. Prop. 12. *It may be very sinful to command some Ceremonies, which may lawfully, yea must in duty be used by the subject when they are commanded.*

§. 26. Prop. 13. *Though they are not Commanded, nor called Necessary, but professed to be indifferent, yet constantly to use Indifferent things, doth breed that custome which maketh them to be taken as necessary by the people, and usually doth very much hurt.*

§. 27. Prop. 14. *Yet certain things that are commonly called Ceremonies may lawfully be used in the Church upon humane imposition, and when it is not against the Law of God, no person should disobey the commands of their lawfull Governors, in such things.*

§. 28. Having laid together these Propositions, I shall review them, in a very short explication and confirmation, and insist more largely on those of chief concernment.

CHAP.

CHAP. II.

*Such Ceremonies as God hath forbidden,
or given man no Power to institute,
are not to be imposed on the Church, as
profitable or lawfull.*

§. 1. THAT some Ceremonies (things commonly so called) may Lawfully be commanded, and some not, me thinks should easily be yielded. I meet with none that are against all indeed, though some think the name [*Ceremony*] unfitly applyed to those Circumstances which they consent to : And that any should think that the wit and will of Ceremonie-makers hath no bounds imposed by God, is most unreasonable. All the business therefore is to know what God hath authorized Governors to institute, and what not?

§. 2. And here they that claim a Power of introducing new Institutions, must produce their Commission, and Prove their power if they expect obedience. For we are not bound to obey every man that will tell us he hath such Power.

§. 3. For the right understanding of this, it must be supposed, as a Truth that all Protestants are agreed in, that the written word of God is his law for the government of the universal Church to the end of the world; and consequently that it is sufficient in its kind, and to its use, and consequently that nothing is to be introduced, that shall accuse that law of imperfection, or which did belong to God himself to have imposed

by

by his law. If we once forsake the Scripture sufficiency (what ever the Papists or Infidels vainly say against it,) we have nothing left in which we may agree.

§. 4. God hath already in his written Laws, instituted his publick worship-ordinances: and therefore he hath done it perfectly: and therefore he hath not left it unto man to come after him and mend his work, by making other ordinances of worship, as to the substance of them. He hath given us one faith, and no man may preach another, and *one Baptism*, and no man may institute another: and so of the like. If any one bring another Gospel, though an Angel, he is to be accursed, *Gal.* 1. 7, 8.

§. 5. Yet is it in the Power of man to determine of such Modes and Circumstances as are necessary to the prrformance of that worship which God hath instituted in his word: And therefore lawfull Governors may in such cases bind us by their commands.

§. 6. The things that are committed to humane determination, are such as are commanded in general by God himself (either in Scripture or nature,) but are left undetermined *in specie, vel individuo*: so that it is not a thing indifferent, whether a choice or determination be made or not, but only whether it be *this* or *the other* that is chosen by the determination. But where the thing it self *in genere* is not necessary, or no humane election or determination necessary, because God himself hath determined of it already, there men are not to meddle, as having no authority from God.

§. 7. I shall first give some instances of the former sort (the Lawfull Ceremonies) and then name the latter (that are unlawfull,) which I shall afterward give my reasons against. And 1. It is left to humane determination what *place* the Publick assemblies shall be held in. God having commanded us to frequent such assemblies, and not forsake them, doth oblige us to some place in general, and to a fit place. He that bids us preach, and hear, and pray, and assemble to these ends, doth plainly bid us, do this *some where*. It is impossible to meet, and not in a *Place*. And in that he hath not determined of any place himself, he hath left it to our reasons to determine of as occasion shall require. God hath not commanded to build a

Temple

Temple in such a place rather then another : or to go thither to worship rather then another place (but by consequence and generall directions :) nor hath he determined what *place* the Minister shall stand to preach in, or where all the people shall have their seats. All these are but the circumstances of a holy action, which are left to humane prudence.

§. 8. 2. It is left to man to determine of the *Time* of holy duties, except only where God hath determined of it already. As that the Lords day shall be the Day for publick holy Assemblies, is a thing that God himself hath determined ; and here we have nothing to do but to discern his determinations and obey them. But withall he hath in Generall commanded us to *preach in season and out of season*, and to Assemble frequently, on severall great occasions : And here he hath not determined of the *Time*, but left it to humane prudence upon emergent occasions, and according to their several cases, to determine of what hour on the Lords day we shall begin ; how long the Sermon shall be ; what hour the Assembly shall be dismist : what daies the Lords supper shall be administred, and how oft : when any shall be Baptized : what day the Lecture shall be on, or any more private meetings for edification : what hour, or just how oft men must pray in secret, or with their families : these with the like are undetermined by God (and good reason, as I shall shew anon,) and left to our selves and to our Governors: *Some Time* or other we are commanded by God himself to choose.

§. 9. 3. It is left to the determination of humane Prudence, what *Utensils* to imploy about the publick worship of God. For these in Generall are commanded by God, and so made necessary ; as also in the nature of the thing. He that commanded us to do the work, that is not to be done without convenient *Utensils*, doth thereby command us virtually the use of instruments fit for the work. What form and proportion the Temple where we meet shall have, is left to men: whether we shall preach in a Pulpit ? and what shall be its shape ? where we shall read ? whether we shall Baptize in a River, or Pond, or Spring, or Font, or Bason, and what materials, whether stone or Silver, or Pewter, *&c.* they be made of ? whether we shall

receive

receive the Lords supper at a Table, or in our seats, and whether the Table shall be of wood or stone? whether it shall be round, or long, or square? whether it shall stand in the East or West end of the Temple, or the middle? whether it shall have rails, or no rails? whether the Bread be of wheat or other convenient grain? what vessel the Bread shall be put in? and what grape the wine shall be made of? and what vessel it shall stand in? and be delivered in? whether a cup, or other like vessel? whether of silver, wood, or pewter, &c? All these are left to humane prudence. In general, it is necessary that some such utensils in each case there be: but the special sort is left indifferent to our choice So also the Bibles themselves, whether they be Printed, or Written, and in what hand, or colour? Whether bound, or in a Role? are things indifferent in themselves, and left to humane reason to determine. The like may be said of other utensils of worship, necessary *in genere*.

§. 10. 4. God hath not determined *in what language* the Scripture shall be read or preacht to such or such a congregation (though by the generall Rule, that all be done to edification, and that we speak to the understanding, there is sufficient direction for it) But he that commandeth us to preach, implyeth that we translate the Scripture, and preach and read in a language fittest for the peoples edification. And if (as in many places of *Wales*) there be two languages equally understood, we may indifferently choose that which we think most agreeable to the generall rules.

§. 11. 5. The Scripture hath commanded us in generall to sing Psalms: but it hath not told us whether they shall be in Rithme, or Meeter, or in what tune we shall sing them. These *modes* are left to humane Prudence to determine of.

§. 12. 6. When there are *divers Translations* of the Scripture in the same language, or divers versions of the Psalms in the same language (as in *England*, here are the old version, the *New-England* version, Mr. *Rous*'s first, and his second (or the Scots,) Mr. *White*'s, Bishop *Kings*, *Sands*'s, Mr. *Bartons*, &c.) God hath not told us which of all these we shall use, but given us generall directions, according to which our own Reason, or our Governors should make choice.

§. 13. 7. God hath commanded us to *Read the holy Scriptures*, and to expound them to the people, that they may understand

and

and practise them: But he hath not told us *what Book of Scripture*, or *what Chapter* we shall read at such a day, or on such or such occasions; nor yet what order we shall observe in Reading; whether we shall begin the Scripture, and go on to the end; or whether we shall read more frequently some subjects of greatest use, and which? These therefore are left to humane prudence to determine of by generall rules.

§. 14. 8. Though God hath commanded us to Read the Scripture, and to sing Psalms, &c. yet hath he not told us just *how much we shall read at a time*, or sing at a time : and therefore this also is a matter left to humane Determination.

§. 15. 9. Though God hath commanded us to Preach the Gospell, and told us what to preach, and given us generall Rules for our direction, yet hath he not told us *what text*, or *subject* we shall preach on such or such a day : nor yet what *Method* we shall follow, there being various methods, sutable to severall Texts and people : It is left therefore to humane prudence to choose both Subject, Text and Method.

§. 16. 10. God that hath commanded us to pray, and praise him, and preach, &c. hath not told us just *what words we shall use* in any of these holy exercises. He hath indeed given us the *Lords Prayer*, which is our Rule for matter, and Method, and a lawfull form for words : but he hath not tyed us to this only, nor told us what words we shall use besides this: whether we shall use words long before premeditated (call'd a form) or only such as are immediately or neer before our speaking premeditated, or in speaking, adapted to the matter in hand ? whether our premeditated prayers shall be expressed in our *own* words, or such as are prescribed us by *others* ? whether such forms shall be expressed in *Scripture words*, or not ? whether we shall sing the *Psalms of David*, or compose any Evangelical Hymns our selves ? whether many Churches shall use one and the same form of words, or various ? whether our Sermons, and Catechisms, and Confessions of faith, shall be a studied or prescribed form of *words*, or the *matter and method* only studied ? &c. These, with many other such like, are left by God, as things undetermined, that men may determine of them prudentially as occasions require, according to his directions.

§. 17. 11. He that hath commanded us to express our min'

in severall cases about his worship, (as in Confession of our sins, in Profession of our faith, in choosing of our Pastors, in Consenting to the casting out, or taking in, or restoring of members, in renewing promises of obedience, and the like) hath hereby made a *Profession* necessary in *general*, and so hath made it our duty to signifie our Consent in all these cases, by *some convenient sign* : For mans mind is not known to others, but by signs. But he hath not tied us absolutely *to any particular sign*. If a Confession of faith be read, and we are called to signifie our Consent, or if we are called to signifie our Consent to be Church members, or to be guided by our Pastors, or submit to Discipline ; God hath not tyed us in such Cases, whether we shall signifie this Consent by *speaking*, or by *subscribing our names* (Isa. 44 3, 4, 5.) or by *lifting up the hand*, or by *laying it on a Book* , (as in swearing) or by *standing up*, or such like. A *sufficient signification* or *Profession* of our minds is necessary ; but the *special sign* is left to our own, or our Governors determination. Of which I shall speak more anon.

§. 18. To this end, and on these terms was *the sign of the Cross* used *heretofore* by Christians, and to this end they used *standing in publick worship every Lords day* (forbidding *kneeling*,) and afterward *standing up at the Creed*: as also *adoring with their faces towards the east, &c.* They used these only as significations of their own minds, instead of words ; As the Prophets of old were wont by other signs, as well as words to prophesie to the people. And as *Eusebius* tells us how *Constantine* measured the length and bredth of a man on the earth with his spear, to tell the Covetous how little must serve them (only a grave place) after death. And I dare not condemn the Cautelous use of such Professing signs as these : Though the tongue be the chief instrument, yet not the only instrument to express the mind ; and though words be the *ordinary* sign, yet not the only sign. *Dumb* men *must* speak by other signs : And usually more silent signs are fitter for Assemblies, to avoid disturbance : And sometimes more *Permanent* signs (as *subscription*, or a *stone* or *pillar* of Remembrance, as *Josh.* 24, *&c.*) are more desirable. And this is left to humane prudence.

§. 19. And therefore I durst not have reproved any of the ancient Christians, that used the *sign of the Cross, meerly as a* *Professing*

Professing signal action, to shew to the Heathen and Jews about them, that they believed in a Crucified Christ, and were not ashamed of his Cross. The *occasionall, indifferent* use of this, when it is *meerly* to this end, I durst not have condemned. Nor will I now condemn a man, that living among the enemies of a Crucified Christ, shall wear a Cross in his hat, or on his breast, or set it on his doors, or other convenient place, meerly as a professing sign of his mind, to be but instead of so many words, q. d. [*I thus profess my self the servant of a Crucified Christ, of whom I am not ashamed.*] Whether these things be *fit or unfit,* the time, place, occasion, and other circumstances must shew : but the *Lawfulness* I dare not deny.

§. 20. 12. He that hath commanded us to celebrate the publick worship, and to preach, pray, praise God, *&c.* doth imply in this command that we must do it in *some Gesture* or other : For it is impossible otherwise to do it. But he hath not tied us to any one : In prayer we may kneel or stand : In singing Praises (and Petitions) to God, we may kneel, stand, or sit : At the Lords Table, though we have an exmaple of *sitting* at the celebrating and receiving that Sacrament, yet no express command, nor a certain obligation. It is therefore left to humane prudence, to order our gestures by the general Rules, of Order, Decency, Edification, *&c.* in Preaching, Praying, Hearing, Singing, Receiving, *&c.* For God hath not tied us himself to any one particular gesture.

§. 21. 13. God that hath required us to celebrate his worship, doth imply that we must do it in a *decent Habit :* Nakedness is a shame : Cloathing we must wear : but he hath not told us what it must be : Whether Linnen or Woollen : whether black or white : or of what shape and fashion ; This therefore is left to humane Prudence:

§. 22. 14. God that hath commanded us to celebrate his Praise and other publick worship, hath left it to our Liberty and Prudence to make use of such *Helps of Nature, or of Art,* as may most conduce to further our obedience, and stand in a due subserviency to his institutions. As for instance : he that hath commanded us to study his word and works, hath not prescribed me a *certain Method* for my studies, nor told me what Languages or *Sciences* I shall learn, or *first* learn : nor what Authors

I shall read in Logick, Physicks, Metaphysicks, &c. It is implyed that in all I use the best helps, and in the best order that I can. So he that bids me read the Scripture, hath not tyed me to read only a *Printed*, or only a *Written* Bible ; nor to read with spectacles or without. He that hath commanded me to Preach, hath not told me whether I must *write* my Sermon before or not : or use *Notes* for the help of my memory, or not ; but hath left these to be determined as general Rules, and emergent accasions and circumstances shall direct us. And he that hath commanded us to preach and pray, hath not told us whether we shall use the help of a *Book*, or not : nor whether we shall use an *hour-glass* or a *clock* to measure our time by. He that hath commanded us cheerfully and joyfully to sing his Praises, hath not told us whether we shall use the meeter, or any melodious tune to help us : or whether we shall use or not use a Musical Instrument : or the help of more Artificial singers, or choristers? These are left to our reason to determine of, by general rules which nature and Scripture have laid down.

§. 23. 15. In *Civil* actions, that are *Religious only finally*, and by Participation, and not any acts of special worship, it is lawfull to use *Symbolical Rites*, that are in *their kind* neer of kin to *Sacraments in their kind*, and may be called, *Civil Sacraments* : such is the sealing and delivery of Indentures, or other Covenant writings : and the delivery of Possession of a *house* by a Key, and of the *Temple* by a *Book* and *Bel-rope*, and of *Land* by a *twig and turf* ; and of *Civil Government* by a *Crown*, or *Scepter*, or *Sword*, &c. And such is the use of a *Ring in Marriage*.

§. 24. 16. Though God hath commanded that certain persons thus and thus qualified shall be *elected and ordained Ministers* of Christ, and separated to the Gospel of God ; yet hath he not nominated the *individual persons*, but left it to man to choose them, according to the directions that he hath given them : Prudence therefore is here the judge.

§. 25. In all these cases, it is no usurpation, nor addition to the word or institution of God, for man to determine : It is but an obeying of Gods commands : All these are Necessary in their *Genus*, and commanded us of God, and the *Species* (or individuals in the last case) no where by the word of God determined of :

so

so that if we muſt not determine of them our ſelves, the Scripture ſhould contradict it ſelf, or oblige us to natural impoſsibilities. Had God ſaid, [Thou ſhalt Pray, at ſome Time, Place, in ſome Habit, Geſture, &c. but neither I, nor thou ſhall determine what,] this had been no better.

§. 26. Moſt of theſe forementioned particulars, are but abuſively or improperly called *Ceremonies*, they being only the determination of Circumſtances and Modes, and ſubſervient common helps, which are Religious only Relatively and by Application, being in themſelves but ſuch common modifications as are neceſſary in Civil and Common moral actions. Yet becauſe the word [*Ceremonie*] is an equivocal, let them be ſo called.

§. 27. Though all theſe things are left to humane Determination, and ſo are Indifferent in themſelves, before; yet may they become *Accidentally Neceſſary* or unlawfull. And though man muſt Determine of them, yet not *as he liſt*, without a Rule: but by thoſe ſufficient General directions which God hath given in Scripture, and the End and Nature of the work. And to croſs theſe directions is a ſin in him that doth determine.

§. 28. Though all theſe are left to humane Prudence, yet not alwaies to the Governors to be paſſed into *Laws*, and *forced* on the ſubjects. Moſt of the points forementioned, ought not to be ſtatedly determined by Law, but left to him that is upon the place to determine of, according to variation of occaſions (of which anon.)

§. 29. Yet if juſt Authority ſhall (injuriouſly) determine of them, it may be the ſubjects duty to obey; except in ſome caſes to be after mentioned; Becauſe they are not matters aliene to their Power, and without their line: but only its an imprudent over-doing in a work that is belonging to them, in its manner and ſeaſon to be done.

§. 30. Having ſhewed you what man *May* determine of, in worſhip: I ſhall next ſhew you what he *may not* determine of: or what is exempted from his power. And 1. Some things as to the *Subſtance*. 2. Other things only as to the *Manner*, are out of mans power.

§. 31. 1. No man may bring a New Revelation, which he received not from God, (whether it be about greater or ſmaller
points.)

points,) and say to another, or himself, *This you or I are bound to believe, by a Divine faith:* For nothing but a Divine Revelation can be the material object of a Divine faith.

§. 32. 2. And as far is it from the power of this man, to say [*I received not this from God, but yet you are bound to believe it as from me, with a faith as certain and confident, as a faith Divine.*] For this were to equall man with God.

§. 33. 3. And far is it from the power of man to obtrude at all upon another any supernatural matters, and Command him to believe them, though but with a *humane faith,* when he cannot prove that the things are committed to him, nor give men an Evidence of their Credibility. He may not say [*Though God revealed not these supernatural matters to me, yet hath he given me Authority to command you to believe them, or made it your duty to believe them, when I speak them, though without Evidence of Credibility.*] So that here are three sorts of things about matters of Belief that man may not do. The first is, that he may not *Counterfeit a Divine Revelation :* and the 2. is, he may not *command* men to believe *his lawfull humane testimony, with a faith equall to Divine :* and 3. he may not *command* so much as a *humane faith* to supernatural assertions which he had *no authority* to utter. I speak this about mens power in matters of faith, as preparatory to that about worship.

§. 34. In like sort, 1. Man may not say [*This God hath commanded you in or about his worship*] when it is not so: For this were to *belie* God, and to add to his Law, as if it said that which it doth not say. Here none I hope will gainsay me.

§. 35. And 2. No man may of his own head Command any thing in or belonging to the worship of God : but he must have either a Special or General warrant and command from God himself to do it. Gods Law must either make the thing Necessary *in specie,* and so leave man nothing about it but to second it by his Law, and see it executed: or else Gods Law must make the thing Necessary *in genere,* and so leave man to determine of the *species* (as is oft said.) But where neither of these are done by God, man hath no Power for the imposing of that thing.

§. 36. More particularly, 1. God hath not left it to the
Power

Power of man to add to the *ten commandments* any universal precept for obedience. 2. Nor to add to the *Lords Prayer* and other holy Scripture, any general article of request to God. 3. Nor to add any *officers* to his Church, that are strictly Divine, or for Divine uses. 4. Nor to add any *substantial ordinance of worship.* 5. Nor to add any *substantial* part of holy *Discipline.* 6. Nor to institute any *new Sacrament* in the Church, or any thing that hath the *Nature* of a Sacrament, though it have not the *name.*

§. 37. It seemeth to me that *Mystical signs* stated by man in Gods publick worship, directly to work grace on his soul from God, and that as instituted, and also to oblige man to God again, are unlawfully brought into the Church.

§. 38. By what hath been said, you may see which of the late English Controverted Ceremonies, I take to have been Lawful, and which unlawfull. Too many years did I spend long agoe about these controversies; and the judgement that then I arrived at, I could never find reason since to change, notwithstanding all the changes of the times, and the helps I that have since had; And it was and is as followeth.

§. 39. 1. About Episcopacy (which was the principal point, concomitant with the Ceremonial Controversie) I have given you my thoughts before. 2. The ceremonies controverted among us, were especially, *The surplice, the gesture of Kneeling in Receiving the Lords supper,* the *ring in Marriage, Laying the hand on the Book in taking an Oath, the Organs and Church musick, Holy daies, Altars, Rails,* and the *Cross in Baptism.* (To say nothing of the matter or form of the Prayers.)

§. 40. And 1. If the *surplice* be Imposed by the Magistrate (as it was) who is a lawfull Governor, and that directly but as a *Decent Habit* for a Minister in Gods service, I think he needlesly strained his Power, and sinfully made an engine to divide the Church, by making such a *needless law,* and laying the Peace of the Church upon it; But yet he medled with nothing but was within the reach of his Power in the general. *Some Decent Habit* is Necessary; Either the Magistrate or the Minister himself, or the Associated Pastors must determine what. I think neither Magistrate nor Synod should do any more then hinder undecency: But yet if they *do* more, and tye all to *one Habit,* (and suppose

Ggg it

it were an undecent Habit) yet this is but an *imprudent use of Power*. It is a thing within the Magistrates reach ; He doth not an *aliene* work, but his *own* work amiss: and therefore the thing *in it self* being *lawfull, I would obey him,* and use that garment, if I could not be dispensed with. Yea though *Secondarily the whiteness* be to signifie Purity, and so it be made a teaching sign, yet would I obey: For *secondarily,* we may lawfully and piously make Teaching signs of our food and rayment, and every thing we see. But if the Magistrate had said that the *Primary* reason or use of the *Surplice* was to be an *instituted sacramental sign,* to work grace on my soul, and engage me to God, then I durst not have used it, though *secondarily* it had been commanded as a *decent garment. New Sacraments* I durst not use, though a *secondary* use were lawfull.

§. 41. 2. And for *Kneeling at the Sacrament,* I doubt not at all, but the imposing it, and that on such rigorous terms, tying all to it, and casting all out of the communion of the Church, or from the participation of the Sacrament that durst not use it, was a very grievous sin, and tended to persecution, injustice, and Church-dividing. It is certainly in a doubtful case the safest way to do as Christ and his Apostles, and the universal Church did for many hundred years. That none should Kneel in publick worship on the Lords day, no not in Prayer, much less in receiving the Eucharist, was a Custome so ancient and Universal in the Church, that it was every where observed before general Councils were made use of; and in the first general Council of *Nice,* it was made the last Canon ; and other general Councils afterward renewed it; so that I know not how any Ceremony can possibly pretend to greater Ecclesiastical Authority then this had. And to cast out all from Church Communion in Sacraments that dare not go against the examples of Christ and his Apostles, and all the Primitive Church, (who long received the Eucharist in another gesture) and against the Canons of the first and most famous, and other succeeding general Councils, this is a most inhumane part. Either the gesture is *indifferent in it self* or not : If it be, how dare they thus divide the Church by it, and cast out Christians that scruple it, when they have these and many other reasons of their scruples (which for brevity I omit.) If they say that *Kneeling* is of *it self Necessary,* and *not Indifferent,* because it is *Reverent* &c. then 1. They make Christ an Imperfect Lawgiver :

giver: 2. They make himself, or his Apostles, or both to have been sinners. 3. They condemn the Catholick Church of sin. 4. They condemn the Canons of the Chief general Councils. 5. And then if the Bishops themselves in Council should change the gesture, it were unlawfull to obey them. All which are consequents that I suppose they will disown. What a perverse preposterous Reverence is this? when they have leave to lie in the dust before and after the very act of receiving, through all their confessions and prayers, yet they will at other times stand, and many of them sit at prayer, and sit at singing Psalms of Prayer and Praise to God, and yet when Christ doth invite them to a feast, they dare not imitate his Apostles and universal Church in their gesture, lest they should be sinfully unreverent.

§. 42. But yet, as sinfully as this Gesture was imposed, for my part I did obey the imposers, and would do, if it were to do again, rather then disturb the Peace of the Church, or be deprived of its Communion. For God having made *some Gesture* necessary, and confined me to none, but left it to humane Determination, I shall submit to Magistrates in their proper work, even when they miss it in the manner. I am not sure that Christ intended the example of himself and his Apostles as obligatory to us that shall succeed. I am sure it proves *sitting lawful*: but I am not sure that it proves it *necessary*: (though *very convenient*) But I am *sure* he hath *commanded me obedience and peace.*

§. 43. 3. And for the *Ring in Marriage*, I see no reason to scruple the lawfulness of it : For though the Papists make a *Sacrament* of *Marriage*, yet we have no reason to take it for any ordinance of Divine worship : any more then the solemnizing of a contract between a Prince and People. All things are sanctified and pure to the Pure: but that doth not confound the two Tables, nor make all things to be parts of Worship that are sanctified. The Coronation of a King is sanctified as well as Marriage, and is as much a *Sacrament* as Marriage, and the *Ceremonies* of it might as well be scrupled : especially when God doth seem to go before them by the example of *Anointing*, as if he would confine them to that Ceremonie ; which yet was none of his intent, nor is it much scrupled.

§. 44. 4. And though the *taking of an Oath* be a sort of worship,

worſhip, yet not the *natural* worſhip of the *firſt* Commandment, nor the *Inſtituted* of the *ſecond*, but the *Reverent uſe of his name* in the *third* ; ſo that it is not *primarily* an act of worſhip, but *Reductively*, and *Conſequentially* : It being the principal uſe of an Oath to *Confirm the Truth*, and *End ſtrife*, by appealing to God, which appellation is indeed an acknowledgment of his Government and Juſtice. And the *laying the hand upon the Book*, or *Kiſſing it*, is but a Profeſſing ſign of my own Intentions, ſuch as my words themſelves are : and therefore is left to humane choice, and a lawfull thing. And I have met but with very few, among all our Ceremonies, that queſtioned this.

§. 45. 5. And for *Organs* or other *inſtruments of Muſick* in Gods worſhip, they being a Help partly *natural*, and partly *artificial*, to the exhilarating of the ſpirits, for the praiſe of God, I know no argument to prove them *ſimply unlawfull*, but what would prove a *cup of wine* unlawful, or the *tune* and *meeter*, and *melodie* of ſinging unlawful. But yet if any would abuſe it, by turning Gods worſhip into carnal Pomp, and levity, eſpecially by ſuch non-intelligible ſinging, or bleating as ſome of our Choriſters uſed, the Common people would have very great reaſon to be weary of it, as *accidentally* evil.

§. 46. 6. And as for *Holy daies*, there is great difference between them : Thoſe are lyable to *moſt queſtion* that are obtruded on the Church with the *greateſt confidence*. As for ſuch daies as are appointed upon ſome *emergent occaſions*, that aroſe ſince Scripture was indited, and are not common to all times and places of the Church, there is no more queſtion whether the Magiſtrate may command them, or the Paſtors agree upon them, then whether a *Lecture-day*, or *faſt-day*, or *thanſgiving-day* may be commanded, or agreed on : *ſome time* for Gods worſhip, beſides the Lords Day muſt be appointed : And God having not told us *which*, the Magiſtrate *may*, on fit occaſions. And this is no derogation from the ſufficiency of Scripture : For the *occaſion* of the day was *not exiſtent*, when the Scripture was written : ſuch occaſions are various according to the various ſtate of the Church in ſeveral ages and Countries. And therefore to keep an Anniverſary day of Thankſgiving, ſuch as we keep on the *fifth of November* for our deliverance from the *Papiſts powder plot*, is no more queſtionable then to keep a Lecture. Nor for

my

my part do I make any scruple * to Keep a Day in Remembrance * In point of Lawfulness ; of any eminent servant of Christ, or Martyr, to praise God for For Conveniency is according to several accidents. their doctrine or example, and honour their Memorial. But the hardest part of the Question is, *whether it be lawfull to keep daies, as holy, in celebrating the memorial of Christs Nativity, Circumcision, Fasting, Transfiguration, Ascention, and such like ?* And the great reasons of the doubt are, 1. Because the *occasions* of these holy daies was *existent* in the Apostles daies : and therefore if God would have had such daies observed, he could as easily and fitly have done it by his Apostles in the Scripture, as he did other the like things. 2. And this is a business that if it were *Necessary*, would be *Equally necessary to all Ages and Parts* of the Catholick Church. And therefore it cannot be *necessary*, but it must be the *Matter of an universal Law*. And God hath made no such Law in Scripture : And so Scripture sufficiency, as the Catholick Rule of faith and universal Divine obedience, is utterly overthrown : which if we grant, and turn Papists to day ; we shall have as strong temptations to make us turn Infidels to morrow, so poor is their evidence for the supplemental Traditional Law of God. 3. And God himself hath already appointed a day for the same purposes as these are pretended for. For the *Lords Day* is to commemorate the *Resurrection*, as the great Triumphant act of the Redeemer, *implying all the rest* of his works : so that though it be *principally* for the *Resurrection*, above any single work of Christ, yet also for *all the work of Redemption* : And the *whole* is on that day to be commemorated with holy Joy and Praise. Now when God himself hath set apart one day in every week to commemorate the whole work of Redemption, it seems an accusing of his Institutions of insufficiency, to come after him to mend them, and say *we must have an anniversary day for this or that part of the Work*. 4. The *fourth Commandment* being one of the Decalogue, seems to be of so high a nature, that man is not to presume to make the like. Else why may we not turn the ten commandments into twenty or a hundred ? But it seems a doing the same or of like nature to what God hath done in the fourth commandment, if any will make a necessary stated holy day to the universal Church. 5. And it seems also that these Holy daies (excepting *Easter and Whitsontide* and other *Lords daies*) are but of later introduction. Many passages of Antiquity,

quity feem to intimate, that *Chriftmas Day it felf* was not of many hundred years after Chrift. I remember not any before *Gregory Nazianzene* that *feem* to fpeak of it. The allegations out of fpurious authors, and that of later date, fuch as the counterfeit *Clement, Dionyfius, Cyprian, &c.* are brought to deceive and not to convince. 6. Yea more, *the time was a matter of* controverfie among the Churches of the Eaft and Weft, for many hundred years after Chrift. *Epiphanius*, and the Churches of *Iudæa* and all thofe Eaftern parts, took the *fixth* of *January* to be the day (fee *Cafaubones Exercitat.* on this, and *Cloppenburgius* more fully in *Thef.*) *Chryfoftome* faith, it was but ten years before he wrote that *Homilie* that the Church at *Conftantinople* was perfwaded by them at *Rome* to change their account of the day : And is it poffible that, when for about four hundred years or more the Churches were utterly difagreed of the day, that it was then *Commonly kept as an Holy day* ? The *keeping* of it would fure have kept a common knowledge of the day : Or at leaft, the difference of obfervation would have raifed contention, as the difference about Eafter did : can any believe that the famous Council of *Nice*, and the vigilant Emperour, that were fo exceeding impatient of a diverfity of obfervations of Eafter, would have let a diverfe obfervation of Chriftmas alone, without once thinking or fpeaking of it, when they were gathered about the like work, if the Church had commonly obferved it then as a Holy day ? Or was the Church of *Iudæa* where Chrift arofe, in any likelyhood to have loft the true account of the day, if it had been obferved by Apoftolical Tradition from the beginning ? 7. And it feems that God did *purpofely* deny us the obfervation of this Day, in that he hath *certainly kept the time unknown to the world.* The confidence of fome bewrayes but their ignorance. Chronologers are never like to be agreed of the *year*, much lefs of the *moneth or day* ; fome think we are *four* years too late, fome *two* years, *&c.* Many think that Chrift was born about *October* (as *Scaliger, Broughton, Beroaldus, &c.*) and many ftill hold to the old Eaftern opinion, for the Epiphany being the Nativity, on *Jan.* 6. and others are for other times ; but none are certain of the time. 8. Sure we are, *where there is no Law, there is no Transgreffion* : but here is no Law of God commanding Chriftmas day or the other Holy daies ; therefore there is no tranfgreffion gression in *not keeping* them. And then 9. it *is not so sure that* there is no transgression *in keeping them*: therefore the surer side is to be taken. 10. And it seems strange that we find not so much as any ancient * general Council making any mention of Christmas or such daies (though of the Martyrs daies some do.) All these reasons (which I run over hastily) and many more (which for brevity I pretermit) do seem to make it a very hard question, whether the keeping of this sort of Holy daies be lawfull.

§. 47. And it is not to be much stuck at, that a Day to Christ doth seem more necessary and pious, then a Day in commemoration of a Martyr, or a particular Mercy: For in the highest parts of Gods worship, God hath left man least to do, as to Legislation and Decisions: and usurpations here are far most dangerous. A *weekly Day* is somewhat more then an *Anniversary*: And yet I think there is few of the contrary minded, but would doubt whether man might impose on the Church the observation of another *weekly Holy day*, in commemoration of *Christs Nativity*. The *worship of God* is a more excellent and necessary thing, then the veneration due to a worthy person; And yet we have not so much liberty to make new waies of worshiping God, as of veneration to men. So is it here, though even the Daies that are for the memorial of the Saints, are ultimately for the honour of God; yet those that are set apart directly and immediately to commemorate the work of Redemption, are Relatively much higher, and therefore seem to be more exempted from the Determination of humane laws.

§. 48. By this and much more, I am fully satisfied, 1. That the keeping of these daies is a thing of it self *unnecessary*: 2. And that there being none on earth that can justly pretend to a power of universal Government over the whole Catholick Church, it is certain that none on earth can bind the Catholick Church to such observances; (The Canons of Pastors are *Authoritative Directions to their own flocks* that are bound to obey them, so it be in lawful things; but to *other Churches*, or to their *fellow Pastors* they are but *Agreements*, and how far they bind, I shall shew anon.) 3. And even in a single Church, or a Province, or Nation, I am satisfied that it is a great sin for Magistrates or Pastors to *force* all that scruple it, to the observation

* The Provincial *Consil Agath. Can.* 14. is the first that I remember mentioning them.

tion of thefe daies, and to lay the *unity or Peace* of their Churches on it, and to caft out, cenfure, reproach, or punifh them that dare not obey fuch impofitions for fear of fining againft God. And it is a moft dfingenuous thing to infinuate and put into the minds of men accufations of the *Impiety* of the diffenters; and to perfwade the world that it is irreligioufnefs, or humorous fingularity, when it is fo known a thing to all that know them, that the perfons that fcruple or difown thefe daies, do ordinarily walk in uprightnefs and the fear of God in other matters, and profefs that it is only a fear of breaking the Laws of God that keeps them from conformity to the will of others : and that they are reproached by the multitude of the obfervers of thefe daies, for their fpending the Lords Day in Holy exercifes, which the reproachers fpend too much in idlenefs, fenfuality or prophanefs ; and it is not long fince many of them were caft out of the Minifterial fervice or fufpended, for not reading a Book authorizing Dancing and other recreations on the Lords day. In a word, to reproach them as Precifians and Puritans, for the ftrictnefs of their lives, and yet at the fame time to per-fwade men that they are ungodly for not keeping Holy daies, or not kneeling at the Sacrament, is not ingenuous dealing, and draws too neer the Manners of the Pagans, who called the Chriftians *ungodly*, becaufe they durft not offer their facrifices, and when they dragd them to the judgement-feats, they cryd *Tollite impios*, as it themfelves were the *Godly men*: I compare not the matter of the caufes here, but only the temper of the perfons, and manner and juftice of proceedings.

§. 49. And yet for all this I am refolved, if I live where fuch Holy daies as thefe are obferved, to cenfure no man for obferving them, nor would I deny them liberty to follow their judgements, if I had the power of their Liberties ; provided they ufe not reproach and violence to others, and feek not to deprive them of their Liberties. *Paul* hath fo long agoe decided thefe cafes, *Rom.* 14. & 15. that if men would be Ruled by the word of God, the controverfie were, as to the troublefome part of it, at an end. They that through weaknefs obferve a Day to the Lord, that is not commanded them of God, fhould not judge their brethren that obferve it not : and they that obferve it not, fhould not defpife or fet at naught their weaker (though cenforious)

rious) brethren that observe it ; but every one should be fully perswaded in his own mind. The Holy Ghost hath decided the case, that we should here bear with one another.

§. 50. Yea more, I would not only give men their Liberty in this, but if I lived under a Government that peremptorily commanded it, I would observe the outward rest of such a Holy day, and I would preach on it, and joyn with the Assemblies in Gods worship on it. Yea I would thus observe the Day, rather then offend a weak brother, or hinder any mans salvation, much more rather then I would make any division in the Church. I think in as great matters as this did *Paul* condescend when he circumcised *Timothy*, and resolved to eat no flesh while he lived rather then offend his brother, and to become all things to all men for their good. Where a thing is evil but by accident, the greatest Accidents must weigh down the less. I may lawfully obey and use the day, when another doth unlawfully command it : And I think this is the true case.

§. 51. 7. And for the next ceremony, the *Name and form of an Altar*, no doubt it is a thing indifferent, whether the Table stand this way or that way : and the Primitive Churches used commonly the names of *Sacrifice*, and *Altar*, and *Priest*, and I think, lawfully: for my part, I will not be he that shall condemn them. But they used them but *metaphorically*, as Scripture it self doth, *Heb.* 13. 10, 15, 16. *Rom.* 12. 1. *Ephes.* 5. 2. *Phil.* 2. 17. & 4. 18. All believers are called *Priests*, and their service, *Sacrifices*, 1 *Pet.* 2. 5, 9. *Rev.* 1. 6. & 5. 10. &. 20. 6. I conceive that the dislike of these things in *England* (the form and name of an Altar, and the Rails about it) was not as if they were simply evil : But 1. because they were illegal innovations, forced on the Churches without Law, or any just authority. And 2. because the way of those times did cause men to suspect, that somewhat worse was intended to be brought in by such preparatives ; especially when the Ministers were cast out.

§. 52. 8. But of all our Ceremonies, there is none that I have more suspected to be *simply unlawfull then the Cross in Baptism.* The rest, as I have said, I should have submitted to rather then hinder the Service or Peace of the Church, (had I been put to it : For living in those daies in a Priviledged place, I had my liberty in all save *Daies* and *the Gesture.*) But this I durst

Hhh   never

never meddle with. And yet I know that many think it as reasonable, and more venerable then any of the rest. Yet dare I not *peremptorily say that it is unlawfull* : nor will I *condemn either Antients or Moderns that use it* : nor will I *make any disturbance in the Church about it*, more then my own forbearance will make : only my own practice I was forced to suspend, and must do if it were again imposed on me, till I were better satisfied. The Reasons that most move me, I shall give you in the end, but some of them take at the present.

§. 53. 1. This is not the meer *circumstance* of a Duty, but a *substantial humane ordinance of worship* : nor is it necessary *in genere* that man ordain any such *symbolical Mystical signs* for Gods worship : And therefore it is a matter totally exempt from humane Power. There *must* be *some Time, some place, some gesture, some vesture, some utensils*, &c. But you cannot say that, *There must be some teaching symbols*, or mystical *signs, stated* by humane institution in Gods worship : There is no command to man in Scripture *de genere* to institute any such thing. And therefore in the case of *Circumstantials* I shall usually (of which more anon) obey the Magistrate, even where he doth mistake, because it is his own work, though he misdoe it : But *here* his action is like that of a judge *in alieno foro*, in another court, where he hath no power, and therefore his judgement is null. It is not an act of Authority to make and state new mystical signs (that are such in their primary use,) in Gods worship : For there is no Power but of God : And God hath given no such power : They that say, *he hath*, let them prove it if they can. *Natural and Artificial* helps we disallow not : But *Instituted signs*, that have what they have by *Institution*, and that as *a solemn stated ordinance*, I know not that ever God required or accepted from the invention of man. I doubt this will prove a meer usurpation, and nullity, and worse.

§. 54. 2. Yea I suspect it will prove *a humane Sacrament* : either *fully a Sacrament*, or so *neer a kin to Sacraments*, as that man hath nothing to do to institute it. The common prayer saith, that [*a Sacrament is an outward visible sign of an inward spiritual grace, given to us, ordained by Christ himself, as a means whereby we receive the same, and a pledge to assure us thereof*] (in the

the Catech.) Let us try by this definition whether the *Cross in Baptism* as used in *England*, be a Sacrament.

§. 55. And 1. I may take it for granted that the want of the *Name*, makes it not to be no Sacrament. And 2. whereas in the definition, it is said that it is [*ordained by Christ himself*] that belongs to a *Divine* Sacrament only, and not to a *humane* Sacrament devised by usurpers. Otherwise you must say, that there is no such thing possible as a *humane Sacrament* imposed by usurpers on the Church: what if all the essentials of a Sacrament, such as are found in Baptism and the Lords supper, be invented by man, and forced on the Church, is it therefore *no Sacrament?* or only, *no Divine Sacrament?* However, let us not differ about bare names and words: It is the *same thing* that you call *a Sacrament*, when *God* is the ordainer: and sure it will not prove it lawfull because *man* is the ordainer; that's it that makes it *unlawfull*, because he wants authority, and acts as an usurper. The Papists affirm that man hath not power to make new Sacraments; no not the Pope himself. Let not us go further.

§. 56. And 1. the *outward visible sign* here is the *Cross* made in the fore-head: 2. *The inward and Spiritual grace* is, a holy *Resolution to fight manfully under the banner of Christ, and to persevere therein.* The *Cross* signifieth the Instrument of the sufferings of Christ, and that we do own this Crucified Saviour, and are not ashamed of him, and will manfully fight under him. So that here is 1. *a signification of Grace to be wrought on the Soul, and given us by* God. 2. an *engagement to perform the duties of the Covenant our selves.* On Gods part, we are to receive by this sign, both *Qualitative* or *actual* Grace, and *Relative* Grace. 1. The Cross is to teach our understandings, and help our memories, and quicken up our dull affections, by minding us of a Crucified Christ and the benefits of his Cross.

§. 57. That it is ordained for this use, appeareth from the words (anon to be recited) in the use of it, and by those words prefixed before the Common prayer-book, [*of Ceremonies; why some are abolished, and some retained*]- where they say that they [*be not darke and dumb Ceremonies, but are so set forth that every man may understand what they do mean, and to what use they do*] and [*that they are such as are apt to stir up the dull mind of man, to the remembrance of his duty to God, by some notable and special signification, whereby he might be edified.* So that this and such other (if there be more such) are appointed by their signification to teach the Understanding, and stir up the dull mind of man to the remembrance of his duty to God : Which are good works, but to be *done only* by good means.

§. 58. And that *this is a way of working Grace in the same kind as Gods word and Sacraments do,* is undeniable. For the word and Sacraments do work Grace but *Morally,* by propounding the object, and so objectively *Teaching, Remembring,* and *Exciting,* and thus working on the Understanding, Memory, and Will, and Affections. However the spirit may work within, its certain that the *ordinances* work no otherwise. And not only Protestants are agreed on this, but one would think that the Jesuits and all of their mind should be most of all for it. For faculties, they that will not confess any Physical determination of the will but make all operations both of Word, Sacraments, and Spirit it self, to be but suasory or Moral, one would think should hold more tenaciously then others, that Sacraments work Grace but Morally. And if no Sacraments do more then objectively Teach and excite ; and the *Cross* is appointed to do as much in this, then there is no difference between them to be found.

§. 59. And then for *Relative Grace,* it is plain, that by the sign of the Cross as well as by Baptism, we are entred into a *state of Christianity* ; and so it is an *Investing Sacramental sign* ; It lifteth us *under the banner of Christ Crucified :* And that is the very essential nature of the Sacrament of Baptism it self. As *Listing* investeth the soldier in his Relation, and consequently in his Priviledges, so doth Baptism by Gods appointment ; and Crossing is supposed by mans appointment, to invest men in the Relation of the soldiers of Jesus Christ.

§. 60. Yea (more then is expressed in the Definition of a Sacrament in the Common prayer-book) if you judge it essential to a Sacrament to be an *engaging Covenanting sign,* the *Cross* is instituted to this end. Yea more then that ; if you judge it *essential* to a *Sacrament,* to be an *engaging sign in the very Covenant of Grace it self,* and not only in some particular promise, this also is the end of its appointment. It is to engage our selves to a Crucified Christ as our Captain and Saviour by his Cross, and to bind.

bind our selves to the Duty of Soldiers or Christians to our lives end : aad consequently to teach us to expect the priviledges of faithfull servants and Soldiers from a Crucified Christ.

§. 61. All this is expressed in the very words of Ministerial application, in the common Prayer-book : which are these [*we receive this Child into the Congregation of Christs flock, and do sign him with the sign of the cross, in token that hereafter he shall not be ashamed to confess the faith of Christ crucified, and manfully to fight under his banner, against sin, the world, and the Devil, and to continue Christs faithfull soldier and servant unto his lives end, Amen.*] So that you see here it is used as a listing, investing, Covenant sign, engaging us to be Christs soldiers, and not to be ashamed of his Cross, or to confess his faith, and manfully to fight, *&c.* and to persevere.   What's wanting here to make a Sacrament ?

§. 62. Yet had it been but *a bare Professing sign*, like *writing or lifting up the hand*, to signifie *consent*, instead of *words*, I durst not have concluded so hardly of it : And thus it seems in ancient times it began to be brought into use : and the *voluntary* use of the *cross* on several occasions, in many countries at this day, doth seem to be no other.   But, for my own part, I dare not be guilty by consent, of making a *humane Sacrament*, or *stating* such an *engaging Sacramental sign*, to all these uses, in the publick worship of God.   I had rather suffer or leave my Ministry, then venture on this, while I see so much to make me fear that it is a sin.   But again I say, as I reverence the ancients that used the cross (I think amiss, and yet more warrantably then we,) so I presume not to censure them that judge it lawfull ; but only give the reasons that make me doubt, and rather think it to be unlawfull, though still with a suspicion of my own understanding, and a love and honour to dissenters.

§. 63. As for the *Common prayer* it self, I never rejected it because it was a form, nor thought it simply unlawfull, because it was *such a form*, but have made use of it, and would do again in the like case.   But I must needs say, 1. That the shreding it into such abundance of small parcels seemeth to me very inconvenient.   It seems too light and ludicrous to toss sentences so formally between the Priest and Clerk, and to make such a multitude of Prayers confifting but of a fentence, or two at moft: And it feemeth to be tautologie and vain repetition to repeat over the fame word fo oft: and a taking of Gods name in vain, or too unreverently, to begin with his *Titles and Attributes*, and end with his *name* again, and the *merits or fake of Chrift*, and this at almoft every fentence: as if we had done with him, and were taking our leave, and had forgot fomewhat that called us to begin again: and thus we begin and end, and begin and end again, it may be twenty times together. 2. But the *enforcing impofition* of thefe Prayers, is moft to be condemned; of which I have fpoken in the former Difputation. But for my part, I cenfure none that ufe them, nor take them to be therefore men of *another Religion or worfhip*: It is but a modal difference in the fame worfhip.

§. 64. The Emperor *Conftantine* was very much for Liberty for Diffenters, and againft perfecution of them, upon tolerable differences: yet he himfelf was wont to write Prayers and Orations or Sermons of his own making *(Eufeb. in vita Conftant. l. 4. c. 55. & 32. & 29.)* and readeth fome common prayers himfelf to the Congregation in his houfe, c. 17. (For he made his houfe a Church, and preached in it ordinarily himfelf, though he was both a Lay-man, and unbaptized; His fermon about Chriftianity to the Clergie is publifhed by *Eufebius*: and he preached a funeral Oration about the Immortality of the foul in his ordinary preaching place, a little before his death: *Eufeb. ib. c. 55. & c. 29. & c. 17.*) He giveth his foldiers a form of Prayer, *ib. c. 20.* commanding them that were Chriftians to obferve the Lords Day, and fpend it in holy exercifes, and not to labour on that day, *(ib. c. 18. 19. 23.)* and alfo to honour the Holy daies confecrated to the Martyrs, *(c. 23.)* that is, to their memorial. And commanding the very Heathen foldiers to pray as they conld, though not in the Church but in the fields together. And in none of this dare I condemn him.

§. 65. The fumm of all that I have faid, is this; *that Man may determine of modes and circumftances of worfhip, Neceffary and Commanded in genere, but not determined by God in fpecie. But to make new worfhip-ordinances, or inftitute Sacraments, or Sacramental figns, or any thing elfe, for which in genere he hath no commiffion, this is fimply unlawfull.*

§. 66

§. 66. But this is not all : There is a *second* thing *unlawfull* also ; and that is the *misdetermining of those same modes and circumstances*, which he is authorized to determine. For he is (as is said) to do it by Gods General Rule. Here therefore we must thus conclude. 1, that every misordering of such great affairs, is the sin of them that do it. 2. But yet that the subject is not exempted from obedience by every such mistake of the Governor : but by some, he is.

§. 67. If the mischoosing of such circumstances by Church-governors, be but an inconvenience, and do not destroy the ordinance it self, or frustrate the ends of it, we are to obey : 1. For he is the judge in his own work, and not we : 2. the thing is not sinfull, though inconvenient. 3. Obedience is commanded to our lawfull Governors. Of this we shall say more in the last Chap.

§. 68. But if a Governor so misdetermine but a mode or circumstance, as will overthrow the *substance and ends of the worship*, I would not obey, except some greater evil were like to follow my not obeying at that particular season, then the frustrating of the duty it self would come to : As for example ; If a Governour make a new Sacrament, I will not obey, because his command is null, and the thing simply evil. If he miscommand a Circumstance of *Time, or Place, or Gesture*, I will consider the *consequents*. If he command the solemn Assemblies to be held *a mile or two or three* from the people, I will obey him, if it be but as far as I can go without frustrating the work it self. But if he command us all to go *ten miles or twenty miles* to worship, I would obey for some time to avoid a greater evil ; but ordinarily I would no more obey, then if if he forbad all Christian assemblies ; for it comes all to one. So if he command the Assemblies to be at *break of day*, or after *sun setting*, I would obey. But if he command that we Assemble only at *midnight*, what should I do then ? The thing is not simply unlawfull : He doth but misdo his own work. And therefore for some times I would obey, if it were necessary, to avoid a greater evil. But if he make it the *ordinary case*, I would not obey : because it destroyeth the worship it self in a manner, as if he simply forbad it, and this he hath no power to do. An *inconvenient gesture* I would use in obedience, and to avoid a greater evil : But I

would

would not obey him that would command me *to stand on my head* alwaies in hearing.   An *unhansome vesture* I would use in obedience to a lawfull Governour, and to avoid a greater evil : But not so ridiculous a vesture as would set all the people on laughing so as to frustrate the work that we assemble for.

§. 69. In all such cases where Governors act not as *usurpers* in a matter that they have no authority in, but only *misdo their own work*, it much concerneth the subjects to foresee whats like to be the Consequents of their obeying or disobeying, and accordingly to do that which tendeth most to the Ends of the work : still holding to this Rule, *that we must obey in all things lawfull.*

§. 70. And when we do obey in a case of miscommanding, it is not a doing evil, that good may come of it, as some do misconceive : But it is only a submitting to that which is ill commanded, but not evil in him that doth submit. It is the determiner that is the cause of the inconvenience, and not the obeyer.   Nor is it inconvenient for me to obey, though it be worse perhaps to him that commandeth.   While he sinneth in commanding, he may make it my Duty to obey.

CHAP.

CHAP. III.

Prop. 2. *In such unlawfull impositions. (as aforementioned) it is an aggravation of the sin, if Governors pretend that their Ceremonies are Divine.*

§. 1. I shall be brief in the rest, having been so long on the former. The reason of this Proposition is clear : because 1. As is aforesaid, such pretenders do falsly accuse the Lord, and corrupt his word, and add to it their own inventions: contrary to those severe prohibitions, *Deut.* 12. 32. *Rev.* 22. 18.

§. 2. 2. Because it shews that man to be a false Prophet, or false teacher, that will say, *Thus saith the Lord*, when God hath not spoken it : and that will take the name of God in vain, affixing it to a lye. And as many judgements are threatned to such, so people are commanded not to hear them.

§. 3. 3. It tendeth to the destruction of all Divine faith and obedience : while the fixions of men are pretended to be doctrines or Laws of God, it tendeth to confound things *Divine* and *Humane* ; and so to bring the people to a loss, that they shall not know what is the will of God, and what the will of men.

§. 4. Let men therefore take heed how they affirm their Ceremonies to be Divine : as the Papists do, that feign them to be of Apostolical Tradition. Some presume to tell the world, that it is God by Apostolical Tradition that hath instituted Christmas day, or other such Holy daies, (besides the Lords-day,) or that hath instituted the Cross in Baptism, or the fast of Lent, yea and some of their common prayers ; abundance of humane inventions are thus audaciously fathered on God, which is enough to make people the more cautelous in receiving them : and I am sure makes it a more hainous sin in the imposers. We justly take it to be an odious thing of Hereticks and Papists, to affix the names of *Clemens, Dionysius, Ambrose, Austin,* and other holy ancient writers, to their forgeries, and corrupt writings : And how much greater is their sin, that dare affix the name of God himself to their Ceremonious inventions or traditions ?

§. 5. Such persons forsake the doctrine of the common prayer-book, where the Ceremonies are confessed to be *humane inventions.* The foresaid Preface [*of Ceremonies, &c.*] begins thus : [*Of such Ceremonies as be used in the Church, and have had their beginning by the Institution of man ; some at the first were of Godly intent and purpose devised, and yet at length turned to vanity and superstition : some entred into the Church by indiscreet devotion, and such a Zeal as was without knowledge : and because they were winked at in the beginning, they grew daily to more and more abuses; which not only for their unprofitableness, but also because they have much blinded the people, and obscured the Glory of God, are worthy to be cut away, and clean rejected. Other there be, which although they have been devised by man, yet it is thought good to reserve them still* ——] so that you see here is no pretence to a Divine institution, or Apostolical Tradition, but all is the devices of man.

§. 6. And after it is there said [*that the Ceremonies which remain are retained for a Discipline and order, which upon just causes may be altered and changed, and therefore are not to be esteemed equal with Gods Laws.*] And I hope the justness of the cause by this time is apparent.

CHAP.

CHAP. IV.

Prop. 3. & 4. *If things unlawfull are commanded as indifferent, or things indifferent as Necessary, they are sinfully imposed, and the more, because of such pretenses.*

§. 1. THE calling things *Indifferent*, that are unlawfull, will not make them Indifferent. If men will invent and introduce new Sacraments, and when they have done, say [we intend them not for Sacraments or necessary things, but as indifferent accidents of other Duties,] this will not make them things indifferent: For it is not the altering of a name that maketh it another thing.

§. 2. If things *Indifferent* be imposed as *Necessary*, they become a sin to the Imposer, and oft-times to the Practiser. For 1. It is a falsification, when the thing is pretended to be Necessary that is not: And untruths in Laws, are far from being commendable. 2. It tends to deceive mens understandings, to esteem things Necessary that are not. 3. It tends to draw men to vain endeavours : while they use those things as Necessary (*Duties* or *Means*) that indeed are none, they lose their labour by the mistake. 4. It tendeth to corrupt mens Affections, by breeding in them a false kind of zeal for the things that they mistake to be so necessary.

§. 3. Yea we said it tends to engage men in parties and

devifions, and perfecutions againft diffenters : or at leaft, to deftroy their charity, and make them have contemptuous thoughts of their brethren, and perhaps cenforious bitter words; when all is falfe, and founded in their miftakes. For who will not think hardlier of him that differeth from him, or oppofeth him in a *Neceffary* point (or that he takes for fuch) then in a thing Indifferent ? the greater the matter, the greater will be your diftafte.

§. 4. Yea more, it will make men Impenitent in fuch fins? For if once they think their ceremonies to be Neceffary, they will think it no fin, but a fervice of God, to vilifie them that are againft them, as fchifmaticks, and fingular, and proud, and humorous, and what not ?

§. 5. As therefore it is a haynous fin of the Papifts, to impofe their ceremonies, on pain of damnation (if they were the judges, wo to others,) fo is it no fmall aggravation of their fin, that pretend a Neceffity (of *Duty* or *Means*) of any their Ceremonies, when there is none fuch. Multitudes take the keeping of Chriftmas day, and fuch other, the Kneeling in receiving the Lords Supper, &c. to be things of themfelves neceffary, fo that a Governour fhould fin that fhould alter or difpence with them, or the perfons fin that do not ufe them. *What, fay they, fhall we not keep a Day for Chrifts Nativity ? fhall we be fo unreverent as not to kneel when we receive, &c ?* And thus they alter the things to themfelves, by feigning them to be in themfelves Neceffary, which are not fo.

§. 6. Yet doth not every fuch miftake of another, no not of the impofers, make that a fin to me which was indifferent. Otherwife all my Liberty were in the power of another mans conceits : and he might make all my meat, drink, cloaths, time, place, gefture, &c. *in fpecie*, to be unlawfull, by commanding them as neceffary, or under fome unfound notion : But this is not fo.

§. 7. But in fuch cafes, though they cannot fo deftroy our liberties, yet may they make it our duties fometime to forbear that which elfe we need not to forbear, left our practice make others take it as a Neceffary thing ; and fometime though we muft obey or do the action, yet may it become our duty, to fignifie (in a convenient way) that we difclaim the conceit of Neceffity.

CHAP.

CHAP. V.

Prop. 5. *A lawfull and convenient thing is sinfully commanded, when it is commanded on a greater penalty then the nature and use of it doth require, or then the common good will bear.*

---

§. 1. When the penalty exceedeth the crime, it is injustice. There may be injustice as well in punishing an offender too much, as in punishing him that is no offender, with a smaller punishment. But if the *penalty* be destructive to the Church or common good, it is an aggravated injustice.

§. 2. When Magistrates therefore are disposed to punish men for crossing their wills in the matters of God, it neerly concerns them to look about them, and take heed first what they punish them for, and then, with what kind of punishment they do it. If it be Good and not Evil that men are punished for, it is persecution. If it be really evil, either its great or small, publick or private, &c. If it be an evil that endangereth the Commonwealth, or Church, or the souls of men, let them punish men in such a way as best tends to the security of the society or souls of men that are endangered. But if the person in his calling or station be usefull to the Church, or Commonwealth, let him not be so punished as to be made useless. If the Bishops had punished Non-conformists w

punished, with paying twelve pence a day &c. I should, comparatively, scarce have blamed them : For it had been but to make Ministers fare harder, or live poorlier, or work for their livings, or to pay their penalties, and the Church might still have had their labours : but to silence and suspend them, and that when there were no better to supply the room (then such as were put in,) this was to punish the Church of Christ, and the souls of men (and that with everlasting punishment) for the (real or supposed) faults of the particular ministers : which was not just.

§. 3. *Object.* But (saith the Preface to the common prayer-book) *though the keeping or omitting of a Ceremony in it self considered, be but a small thing ; yet the wilfull and contemptuous transgression and breaking of a common order and discipline, is no small offence before God.*

§ 4. *Answ.* 1. You should therefore put no such snares on men by your commands, as to impose upon them needless things, when you think the penalty of disobeying you will be damnation. 2. But how came you to see into the hearts of men, that their non-conformity is wilfull and contemptuous? when they themselves profess that they would obey you if they durst. They think they stand at the brink of Hell, and should wilfully sin against God if they did obey you: and you come behind them, with silencing and imprisonment, and drive them on, while they cry out to you for compassion, and protest that they are ready to obey as far as they can see the lawfulness of the thing : and yet you say, its wilfulness and contempt. 3. And why doth not your Law except from punishment all those that conformed not, that were not *wilfull* or *contemptuous* ? The Act for conformity makes the penalty to be Imprisonment half a year for the first fault : a year for the second, and during life for the third, beside deprivation : and Imprisonment during life for the second offence, if the person have no Benefice : and this is besides the Ecclesiastical censure. 4. If the work of Church Governors be to make small matters great, and make that damnable that before was lawfull, and this without any necessity at all, it will tempt the people to think such Governors to be the plagues of the earth.

§. 5. I confess it is lawfull for me to wear a Helmet on my head

head in preaching: but it were not well if you would institute the wearing of a Helmet to signifie our Spiritual *militia*, and then resolve that all shall be silenced and imprisoned during life that will not wear it. It is lawfull for me to use spectacles, or to go on crutches: But will you therefore ordain that all men shall read with spectacles, to signifie our want of spiritual sight: and that no man shall go to Church but on crutches, to signifie our disability to come to God of our selves? So in circumstantials, it is lawful for me to wear a feather in my hat, and a hay-rope for a girdle, and a haircloth for a cloak. But if you should ordain that if any man serve God in any other habit, he shall be banished, or perpetually imprisoned or hanged, in my opinion you did not well: especially if you add, that he that disobeyeth you must also incur everlasting damnation. It is in it self lawfull to kneel when we hear the Scriptures read, or when we sing Psalms: but yet it is not lawfull to drive all from hearing and singing, and lay them in prison if do it not kneeling. And why men should have no communion in the Lords Supper that receive it not kneeling (or in any one commanded gesture,) and why men should be forbidden to preach the Gospel, that wear not a linnen surplice, I cannot imagine any such reason as will hold weight at the bar of God.

§. 6. If you say, *why should we not be obeyed in indifferent things? and why should men trouble the peace of the Church?* I answer. 1. Subjects must obey in all things lawfull. 2. But your first question should be, why you should *command*, and. *thus* command unprofitable things? will you command all men to wear horns on their head in token of pushing away their spirituall enemies; and will you resolve that God shall have no service, nor men any Sacraments or Church communion; no nor the liberty of the common air, nor salvation neither, unless they will obey you? And then will you condemn them, and justifie your selves by saying [why should not the Church be obeyed?] 3. You govern not *perfect but imperfect* men; and therefore you must rule them as they are, and fit your laws about things indifferent to their state, and not expect perfection of understanding and obedience from them, when God himself expecteth it not: suppose therefore they manifest their imperfection in not discerning the Lawfulness of your command, pr...

are ready to obey them, if they durſt ; the queſtion that neerlyer concerneth your own conſciences (that are the impoſers) to diſcuſs, is, what reaſon you have to drive all men from Gods Church and ſervice, that (ſuppoſe through their imperfection) dare not conform themſelves in worſhip to your pleaſure ? Where hath God ſet you on ſuch a work, or given you any ſuch commiſſion ? 4. And where you ſay, *They ſhould not diſturb the Church* ; I anſwer, Are you ſo blind that you ſee not that it is you that diſturb the Church ? If you will make ſuch laws without neceſſity, which common wit and reaſon may tell you, all men are never like to be ſatisfied in and obey, and then caſt out all that will not obey them, as the diſturbers of the Church, this is but an aggravated ſelf-condemning.   If they be guilty, you are ſo much more : If they ſin and diſturb the Church by diſobedience, you diſturb it much more ſinfully, by laying ſuch ſnares as ſhall unavoidably procure it, and then taking occaſion by it, to make a greater diſturbance by your cruel execution.   If the Fly offend and deſerve death by incau- telous falling into the Spiders web, what doth the Spider deſerve, that out of her own bowels ſpred ths net in the way, and kils the Fly that's taken in it ? (yet draw no venom from the ſimilitude, for it runs not on all four, nor is it my meaning to apply the venom to you.)   Your own actions moſt concern your ſelves. Try whether you do well in commanding and puniſhing, as well as whether others offend in diſobeying. I ſhall provoke all to obe- dience in things lawful : But if they ſhould obey you (more perfectly then God,) you may yet be condemned for your wick- ed cruel Laws.

CHAP.

CHAP. VI.

Prop.6. It is not lawfull to make any thing the subjects duty by a command, that is meerly indifferent antecedently, both in it self, and as cloathed with its accidents.

§. 1.  THE reason is evident: because Nothing but Good can be the just matter or object of the Governours desire: and therefore nothing but Good can be the just matter of his Laws. By[Good] I mean, Moral, or Civil Good, or Relative Physical Good: the Good of Profit, or Honesty: And by[Indifferent] I mean not [that which is neither a flat sin, nor a flat absolute duty.] For so an *Indifferent* thing may be sometime commanded. Nor do I mean any Middle thing between *Bonum Metaphysicum* and *non bonum:* for there is none such. But I mean by *indifferent*, that which is not antecedently *Appetible*, a *Desirable Good*, though it be not it self an evill to be avoided, or a hurtfull thing. *Bonum publicum*, the common good is the End of Government, and therefore it must be somewhat conducing to the *Common good*, (or at least to the good of some particular person) that is the just object of the Governours desire, and matter of his law. For nothing but Good, doth conduce to Good, of it self. Nay it is therefore *Good, bonitate*

K k k

medii, as a Means, becaufe it conduceth to that which is Good, *bonitate finis*, as an End; or that is defirable for it felf. Defire hath no object but *quid appetibile*, a Defirable Good. And a Governour fhould make no Laws but for fomewhat that is defirable to himfelf as Governour.

§. 2. And 2. Nothing fhould be made the matter of a Law but what is Defirable to the Common wealth, as well as to the Governour. For men muft be Governed as men. Punifhments indeed are not defirable for themfelves: but yet by accident they are defirable to the Common good: and the matter of Precepts fhould be much more defirable then Punifhment.

§. 3. And 3. If unprofitable things be made the matter of Laws, it will tend to the contempt of Laws and Government: and people will think it a burden and not a benefit, and will defire to be freed from it; and this will tend to the diffolution of Societies.

§. 4. And 4. All Government is *from* God, and *for* God, and fhould be by him: God is the Beginning and *End*, the firft efficient and ultimate final caufe of all juft Government: And therefore all the parts of it muft favour of the Goodnefs of the firft Efficient, and be levelled at God as the ultimate end, which nothing but Good is a means to. Of him, and by him, and for him are all things, *Rom.* 11. 36.

§. 5. Moreover 5. If idle words and idle thoughts be fins that muft be accounted for, then idle Laws much more. And idle they muft be if they be about unprofitable things. And they are not only idle themfelves, but occafion idle words and actions in others.

§. 6. Moreover 6. It is the judgement of the Impofers that difobedience to their Laws is a fin againft God, which deferveth condemnation; (For Proteftants know no venial fins, and Papifts take fins againft the Popes and Councils Decrees to be Mortal.) But it is a cruelty next to Diabolical, to lay before men an occafion of their Damnation *for Nothing*. When they firft make their Laws, they know (or elfe they are unworthy to be Governours) that fome will obey them, and fome will not. If therefore they think that fome (and many) will incur the

guilt

guilt of sin unto damnation by their disobedience, they must have somewhat of greater worth then the souls of those men to encourage them to make those Laws. For had there been no such Laws, there would have been none of that transgression, and consequently no damnation for it.

§. 7. Yea 7. It is sufficient to prove that nothing but some Good may be the *Matter* of a Law, in that they inflict penalties, and so great penalties upon the breakers of them. There must be a proportion between the Precept and the Sanction. The Commination or penal part of the Sanction, depriveth men of some Good: and therefore it should command, as great a good at least as it depriveth men of: Especially when the penalty is to be cast out of the Church and service of God, this is not to be done for nothing.

§. 8. Quest. *But is it not the Law that is the Rule of Moral Good? and consequently nothing Good or Evill, but as Conform or Disconform to the Law? And if so, then nothing but things indifferent must be commanded. For all things are Morally indifferent, till the Law take away the Indifferency, by its precepts or prohibitions.*

§. 9. Answ. You must distinguish between Divine and Humane Laws, and Primary and subservient Laws, and between the several sorts of Good before mentioned. And so I answer, 1. The Law is not the Rule of Natural Good, though it be of Moral. And therefore that which is commanded, is supposed to have some Natural Good or aptitude to be a Means of Good, that so it may be the fit matter of a command. 2. Gods Laws are the Primary Laws, which are the first Rule of Moral Good. Mens Laws are but subservient, to procure the due execution of Gods Laws. And therefore in the greatest cases the Indifferency is taken off before by the Law of God: and mens laws are to second Gods Laws, and rather to drive men on to that which already is their duty, then to make them new duties: Though New duties also they may make in subserviency to, and for the performance of the Old. But there must be a *Physical Goodness*, which is the *Aptitude* of the *matter* to attain the End as a *means*, before that matter can justly receive the impress of a command, and be made a Duty. Gods own Law of Nature is Antecedent to his Positive Laws: and in supernatural

Pos-

Positives, there is a supernatural adapting of the Matter before it receive the supernatural stamp of a Duty.

§. 10. *Object. But if a Magistrate may not make Laws about Indifferent things, then may he not make any Laws at all: For Evill may not be commanded: And that Good which God hath commanded already, having a higher stamp then mans authority, needs no such Law.*

§. 11. *Answ.* I have heard this Argument insisted on in the reign of the Ceremonies, above any other: but it deserveth not such high esteem. For 1. The work of the Magistrate, at least about the worship of God (and so of the Pastors) is not *directly* to make new duties: but to procure Obedience to the Laws of God. And therefore they are to command the same things again that God hath commanded, and to forbid the same that he hath forbidden. If a Magistrate make a Law, and see it disregarded, he may make another to quicken men to obedience and execution of the former. 2. And this is not vain, though it have the stamp of a higher authority before (unless you will say that humane Government is vain;) For Magistrates are seen when God is *unseen*; Corporal penalties are *felt*, when Hell fire is *unseen*, *unfelt*, *and too little believed*. *Present* things have an advantage for operation. 3. And we grant that some things neither *commanded* nor *forbidden* before, may be commanded or forbidden by a Magistrate, so they be not Indifferent as to their *Usefulness* and *Aptitude*, to be a means for the obtaining of that which is the end of the command.

§. 12. It is charged on Mr. *Jacob* by Dr. *John Burgess* and others, as an error, that he thought *nothing indifferent at all*: and Dr. *Burgess* confuteth him by instancing *in various gestures in hearing, where it is indifferent which we use; and if I have two Eggs of a quality and quantity equal, before me, it is indifferent which I eat:* therefore, &c. ———

§. 13. To this I say, 1. Many things simply considered are Indifferent (as to marry or not marry, which *Paul* disputeth of,) which yet being cloathed with accidents, or Circumstances, shall *ordinarily* be a *Duty*, or *a sin in the Use* to a particular person. 2. Nothing is *Indifferent* between *Lawfull* and *Unlawfull*; but many things are *Indifferent* between a *Duty* and a *Sin*. 3. I conceive that where any thing is *Indifferent*

between

between *Duty* and *sin*, in the *Use*, as Circumstantiated, it is not *actus humanus*, a proper morall act. But as *Permission* is vainly numbred with proper acts of Law, it being but a *Non impedire*, a Negation of an act; so *Indifferency* is as vainly annumerated to the products of a Law. For there needs no act of Law to make a thing *Indifferent*, that is *Neither commanded nor forbidden*. For instance, it is Indifferent for me to *wink* with my eyes ordinarily, because it is not a Moral act that a man is to use his reason about, to bring every twink of the eye to an Election, or Refusal; but we may leave it to Natural instinct. So in Dr. *Burgesses* instances, *Whether I sit or stand at Sermon*, (if I be equally disposed, *& cateris paribus*) is not a humane Moral act: *Whether I eat this Egg or that when they are equal*, is not a Moral act: Nor do I properly *Choose*, but *take* indifferently without choice. And where there is no use of *choice*, the act is not *Moral*, except in the Intention of the end, or in deliberating accesses.) Yet I grant that Moral acts may be exercised about these objects: A scrupulous mind may be put to consider, whether this *Gesture or that*, *this Egg or that* is to be *chosen*: but it must conclude, that *neither is to be chosen*, but *either to be taken Indifferently* Which is but to say, that *the Deliberation was a Moral act*; but *the choosing was not*, for it was but a *Taking*, and not a Choosing: And the *Deliberation* stopt before it came to a *choice*, yea and *purposely avoided it*, concluding that the object was not *a Matter of choice*, and the act was not *to be a Moral act*: Morality hath but two *Species*, *Good* and *Evil*: and *Indifferency* is no third *Species*, but a *Negation of Morality*: viz. of *Good* or *Evil*.

§. 14. Yet may *one Accident* take off the *Indifferency*, and make the action *Good or Evil*. And though the Governours themselves should well weigh Accidents, and prefer the chief, and lay no more upon them then they deserve: yet because the Accidents are oft distant, and unseen, and the Ruler is the Judge of them, therefore the people should ordinarily obey, when they see them not themselves.

§. 15. Object. *But in case the Genus is commanded by God, and the Species are equal, may not the Governr tie us to one of the two? Especially in case the people* ....

them, or else will do nothing, because they cannot resolve which way to do it. For instance: if sitting, standing and kneeling be equally convenient at the singing of Gods Praises, if the people be in a doubt which to use, or at least if they fall into contention about it, may not the Governours interpose, and limit them to one? If you be the conductor of Travailers or Souldiers, and they come to a place where the way divideth, though both wayes are equally good and neer, yet you must command them one way, and choose for them, because else they will go no way at all.

§. 16. *Answ.* 1. In this case you are not to choose one *Ge-sture* or one *Way* rather then another, unless they make it necessary by Accident. But tell them of the Indifferency and Equality, and drive them on to Action. And so you only choose and cause them to choose *Action* before *Cessation*, but not *this way* before *that.* 2. If this will not serve, but they will *do nothing*, unless you determine of their *Gesture* or *Way*, you must then command one rather then another, because they can use but one, and some one they must use. But in thus doing, your comparing, taking *This* rather then the *other*, is not to be done by *Election*, nor be a humane act, there being no more Reason (thats supposed) for one then for the other. But though you name them one *Way* or *Gesture* only (when they necessitate it,) you do it but as *choosing* their *Action* before their cessation; this therefore is all that is Moral in your Act: and that you Determine them to Action by Naming *This way* and not *the other*, is good (for the Determination for Duty sake was eligible:) but that it was *rather to This* then *the other*, was *Indifferent*, and not Moral: For of that you had *no Reason*: and where there is *no Reason*, there is no Morality.

§. 17. All this considered, I leave it to the consideration of common Reason, and of men that have any pitty for the Church or their own souls, whether it be a Prudent or Christian course to make Laws for the Church about things *Indifferent*, that have nothing in the Nature of them to induce them hereunto: and then to cast out Ministers and other Christians for not obeying them, and deprive men of the greatest blessings, on the account of things indifferent.

§. 18.

§. 18. If God have left us at Liberty by not commanding or forbidding, then man should not take that Liberty from us without great cause, and without some Accidental good that is like to come by depriving us of that liberty, and the Good must be greater then the Accidental evill. Why should any man on earth deprive the Church of Liberty in that thing where God thought not meet to deprive him of it, unless he can prove that time, or place, or some special accident hath altered the case? In any case which standeth with us just as it did in Scripture times, we must no more be deprived of our freedom by man, then we are by God: Had it been best for us, God would have done it.

CHAP. VII.

Prop. 7. *Some things may be lawfully and profitably commanded at one Time and Place, and to one sort of people, that may not at or to another; no nor obeyed, if commanded.*

§. 1. HE case is so plain in point of *Commanding*, that it is past all doubt. Many Accidents may make that destructive at one Time and place, that would be profitable at another. *Pauls* precepts and practice in becoming all things to all men, do manifest this.

§. 2.

§. 2. * The Papiſts themſelves are convinced of this : and therefore ſometime granted the *Bohemians* the uſe of the cup for the Laity in the Lords Supper : and profeſs that it is in the Power of the Pope and Council to do the ſame by other places. Yea when they burn men for the Proteſtant Religion in one Countrey, they tolerate it in another, for fear of a greater evil. And when they torment men in one age and place for uſing a Bible in the vulgar tongue, in another place or time, they themſelves tranſlate it.

§. 3. It is therefore a very great ſin in Governours, unneceſſarily to make ſuch things the *matter* of a common ſtanding Law which is ſo variable, yea and muſt be varied according to diverſity of times and places : Theſe things ſhould be left to the Prudence of the Governours that are on the place. No wiſe General will take a Commiſſion for the Command of an Army, if he muſt be tied up before hand, when to march, and when to ſtand ſtill, and which way to go, and how to fight in all the variable Circumſtances. Shall Governours pretend to be ſo much wiſer then God, as to make a ſtanding Law for that which God thought beſt to leave at liberty, to be varied as occaſions vary ?

§. 4. The Engliſh Church Laws do tie the Miniſters to a particular habit, and to the particular Chapters of Scripture that we muſt read : and if the Law givers had pleaſed, they might as well have tied us to that particular Text which they will have us preach on, and forbid us to chooſe a Text as a Chapter : And they might have as well tyed us to particular Pſalms in ſinging, as in Reading. But all this is againſt the nature of our office, and the good of the Church : And therefore it is not fit matter for a Law. If I know my hearers to be moſt addicted to Drunkenneſs, muſt I be tyed up from Reading or Preaching againſt that ſin, and tyed to Read and Preach only againſt Covetouſneſs or the like, becauſe it ſeemeth meet to Governours to tye me to a conſtant courſe ? If I have a tractable people, it may do them no harm to limit them to this or that geſture, veſture, &c. But what if they be prejudiced againſt a thing that in it ſelf is lawfull, and take it to be a ſin, and reſolve that they will rather forbear Gods Ordinances then uſe a thing that their Conſciences are againſt ? muſt I needs exerciſe or

preſs

* The Pope bound *Henry* the fourth King of *France* that no Magiſtrates tolerate Hereſie, except in that which cannot be done without tumult or war.] *Dolula* p. 1362. ad. 1595. So that when he feareth loſing by it himſelf, the good man makes conſcience of murdering them that he will call hereticks : but at another time 30000. to be murdered in *France* in a few daies (*Dolula* ſaith 40000.) was a bleſſed work !

press a Gesture, vesture or such Ceremonie, when I see it tendeth to the destruction of my flock? Must I needs deny the Lords Supper to all my flock, if they dare not receive it in this or that gesture (let it be sitting or kneeling,) and all because I am commanded to do so?

§. 5. Suppose it here granted that the thing being lawfull, it is the peoples sinful weakness that causeth them to refuse it; and that the power commanding me no otherwise to deliver it, is such as in things lawful I am bound to obey; yet is it not a thing lawfull to punish the peoples infirmity in a circumstance so severely as with an excommunication, or a denying them the communion of the Church in the Lords supper. In such a case my first duty is, to tell the Magistrate that such a Law is sinfully cruel and destructive to the Churches peace. If that will not prevail with him to repeal or suspend such an unrighteous law, my next duty is, yet to perswade the people to obey him: (for we suppose the gesture or ceremony commanded now to be lawful:) But if I can neither prevail with the Magistrate to forbear his imposition, nor with the people to obey him; my next duty is to forbear the execution of his unrighteous penalty: I dare not be his executioner, in excluding all Christs servants from his house or holy Communion, that dare not do every circumstantial action that is imposed on them: For the penalty is flat contrary to the Commands of Christ. Yet would I not resist the Magistrate, but lay down my office, if the Churches necessity did not forbid me to lay it down: but if it did, I would do my office, and suffer what the Magistrate should inflict upon me.

§. 6. And indeed, I might else be obliged by a Magistrate to excommunicate or deny Communion to all Christians within my reach: For all Christians are imperfect; and there is not one but is liable to error in a greater matter then a gesture or circumstance, such as we have now before us: no nor one but doth actually err in as great a matter: and therefore one as well as another, on this account may be cast out: But Christ would not have this dealing in his Church.

§. 7. How tender are his own expressions, his practise and his laws towards those that are infirm! He came to preach the Gospel to the poor, and heal the broken-hearted, and lay upon them an easier yoak and lighter burden. He will not break the

And therefore when I said before that in case of Necessity I would rather Kneel, then not communicate, yet I now add that I would for all that rather be imprisoned or otherwise persecuted, then cast out of the Churches Communion all that dare not kneel or conform in such a circumstance: And yet this were Ministers then commanded on great penalties to do.

L ll   bruised

Luke 4. 18.
Matth.11 28.
Matth.12.20.
Isa. 42.2,3. &
40.11. Mat.
18. 6. Luke
17 2.
Rom. 14.1 &
15.1,2. & 14
13,15, 20,21,
23.

bruifed Reed; nor quench the fmoaking flix : he carryeth the
Lambs in his arms, and gently driveth thofe with young : The
little ones that believe in him muft not be offended : It were
better for him that offendeth one of them (by injurious
perfecution) that a miltone were hanged about his neck, and
that he were caft into the fea : Him that is weak (even) in
in the Faith, we muft receive (and therefore muft not caft him
out that doubteth of a ceremony.) And they that are ftrong
muft bear with the infirmities of the weak, and not to pleafe
our felves, but every one to pleafe his neighbour for his good to
edification. No man fhould put a ftumbling block, or occafion
to fall in his brothers way. If we grieve our brother by our
meats (or other indifferent things) we walk uncharitably :
we muft not for fuch things deftroy them that are the work of
God, and for whom Chrift died. It is good neither to eat flefh,
nor to drink wine, or any thing whereby he ftumbleth or is offended, or is made weak. He that doubteth is condemned if he eat,
becaufe he eateth not of faith. And we muft not be too forward in
damning men for a morfel of bread, or a garment, or a gefture.

§. 8. Moreover, the Miniftry hath a certain end, to which
all our adminiftrations are Means : even the faving of our flock,
and the Pleafing of God thereby : And if Magiftrates will
command us to order but a lawful Circumftance fo as fhall not
only crofs, but deftroy thefe *ends*, we muft as foon leave our
Miniftry as obey him: Our Power is *given us to Edification and not
to Deftruction* : Not only thofe things that of themfelves deftroy,
but thofe that are like to be the occafions of fuch an event,
through the infirmity of the people, muft be by us avoided. To
command us a way of Miniftration that fhall (though but
accidentally) damn men, and that unneceffarily, is to deftroy
our office, by deftroying the end, which is mens falvation. If men
will deftroy themfelves by the only means of falvation(Chrift and
the Gofpel) this will not excufe us from preaching that Gofpel:
but if men will deftroy themfelves by a Ceremony, or unneceffary circumftance, I will take it out of their way if I can.
It is a Lawfull thing for all fick people in *England* to eat of one
particular difh of meat, as well as on others : But if the Law-
givers command that all Phyficians fhall give no man Phyfick
that.

that will not be tyed only to such or such a dish, I would not be a Physician, if I must obey that command; what if my Patient have a weak stomack and cannot eat of that dish, or be peevish, and will not? must I therefore be guilty of his death by denying him my necessary help, because the Magistrate forbiddeth me? He may as well forbid us all to visit the sick, or relieve the poor, or cloath the naked, if he can but find the least infirmity that they are guilty of. And I think that Christ will not take it for an excuse in judgement if any man say [Lord, I would have relieved them, cloathed them, healed them, but that the Magistrate forbad me; and I thought it the part of a seditious rebell not to obey my governors.] Yet I should much less desire to be in that Ministers case (whose labours are necessary to the Church) that had no better an excuse for his denying to preach the Gospel, or to admit the servants of Christ to holy Communion, then that the Magistrate forbade him: Our Ministration is a work of Charity, to be exercised upon voluntary receivers: And if a Magistrate have power to forbid us to preach or grant the Sacraments and Communion of the Church to any that wear not black or blew, or white or red, or that kneel not at the Sacrament, or such like, then may be as well or much better forbid us to give alms to any that wear not a horn on their backs, and an iron ring about their arms as Bedlams do: No Magistrate can dispence with Charity, especially in so great a case as mens salvation: no more then the Pope can dispence with Oaths and Covenants.

§. 9. We have therefore the use of our Reason left us to weigh the tendency of a Magistrates commands, even where the act commanded is in it self indifferent: For the Magistrates Power, and the Ministers, are from one Fountain, and are but Means to one and the same end: And neither of them hath any power to destroy that end: And therefore if by accident, through the weakness of my flock, the observation of a trivial circumstance would undo them, I would not use it, no not in obedience to the Magistrate: but would resolve with *Paul* never to eat flesh while I live rather then to offend or destroy my brother. But if I find by the weighing of all accidents, that my obedience will do no such hurt to the Church and Souls of men, but as much good as my not obeying, then (in such indifferent cases) I would

readily

readily obey : But otherwise I would appeal to God, and bear the Magistrates persecution. No means can be justly pleaded against the end (and least of all, a bare ceremony.) For it is no Means when it destroyeth the end.

§. 10. On this account it is that it hath alwaies by wise men been reckoned a tyrannical unreasonable thing, to impose all the same ceremonies and circumstances upon all places as upon some ; and it hath been judged necessary that every Church have their liberty to differ in such indifferent things, and that it hath been taken for a wise mans duty, to conform his practice in such indifferent circumstances, to the several Churches with which he shall have communion, as *Ambrose* professeth he would do, and would have others do the same.

§. 11. If any think (as too many do) that such a diversity of circumstances is a disorder and confusion, and not to be endured, I shall further tell these men anon, that their opinion for an hypocritical unity and uniformity, is the true bane of Christian unity and uniformity, and that which hath brought the confusion and bloody wars into the Christian world, and that our eyes have seen, and our ears have heard of : And it were as wise an objection for them, if they should charge us in *Britanie* with Confusion, and drive us to a separation or division, because the *Scots* wear blew caps, and the *English* hats : or because some *English* wear white hats and some black ; and so of other circumstances.

§. 12. Did I live in *France* or other Popish Countries, or had lived in *England* at the abolition of Popery, I should have thought it my duty in many indifferent circumstances to accommodate my self to the good of those with whom I did converse ; which yet in another Countrey, or at another time, when those things were as offensive as then they were esteemed, I durst not have so done. And therefore our Common Prayer-Book it self with its Ceremonies might be then, commendable, in many particulars, which now are reformable. And so in *Ethiopia, Greece,* or *Spain,* those things would be very laudable, that are now in *England* deservedly vituperable. And several Ceremonies in the primitive times had such occasions and concomitants, that made them tolerable that now seem less tolerable : The case is not the same, though the Materials be the same.

CHAP.

CHAP. VIII.

Prop. 8. *Those orders may be profitable for the Peace of the Churches in one Nation, that are not necessary to the Peace of the Churches in many Nations.*

§. 1. Mention this 1. Because the Romanists are so peremptory for the Necessity of their ceremonies through all the world : as if the unity, peace, or well being of the Church, at least, did hang on these. And yet sometimes they could dispence with the different rites of the Greeks, if they could but have got them under their power by it.

§. 2. Also 2. Because the Protestants called Lutherans, stick so rigidly on their ceremonies (as Private Confession, Exorcism, Images, Vestments, &c.) as if these had been necessary to the unity of the Churches. And the Pacifiers find a difficulty in reconciling the Churches of several nations, because these expect an uniformity in ceremonies.

§. 3. And so necessary doth it seem in the judgement of some deluded souls, that all Churches be one in a visible Policy, and uniformity of Rites, that upon this very account they forsake the Protestant Churches and turn Papists. As if Christ were not a sufficient Head and Center for Catholick union, and his Laws and waies sufficient for our terms of uniformity, unless we are

all

all of a mind and practice in every custome or variable circumstance that God hath left indifferent.

§. 4. I need no other Instance then 1. what *Grotius* hath
given of himself * (in his *Discuss. Apologet. Rivet.*) who professeth that he turned off upon that account, because the Protestants had no such unity : And 2. What he said before of
others (by whom he took no warning, but did imitate them)
in his Epist. to Mr. *Dury* (cited by Mr. *Barksdale* in his Memo-
rials of *Grotius* life) where he saith [*Many do every day forsake
the Protestants, and joyn with the Romanists, for no other Reason
but because they are not one Body, but distracted parties, separated
Congregations, having every one a peculiar Communion and
rites* ——] And they that will turn Papists on such an inducement, deserve to take what they get by their folly.

* See my wri-
ting of *Gro-
us* Religion.

§. 5. Did not these men know that the Church hath alwaies
allowed diversity of Rites ? Did not the Churches differ till the
Nicene Council about Easter day, and one half went one way,
and another half the other way ? and yet *Polycarp* and the
Bishop of *Rome* held communion for all their differences? and
Irenaeus pleads this against *Victors* temerity in excommunicating the *Asian* Churches ? Did they not know that the Greek,
and Armenian, and Romane Churches differ in many Rites, that
yet may be parts of the Catholick Church notwithstanding such
differences ? Yea the Romanists themselves would have allowed
the Greeks, and Abassines, and other Churches a difference of
ceremonies and customes, so they could but have subjugated them
to the Pope.

§. 6. Yea more, the several orders of Fryars and other Religious men among the Papists themselves are allowed their differences in Rites and Ceremonies ; and the exercise of this allowed
Difference doth make no great breach among them, because
they have the liberty for this variety from one Pope in whom
they are all united. What abundance of observations do the
Jesuites, Franciscans, Dominicans, Benedictines, Carthusians, and
others differ in ? And must men needs turn Papists because of
the different Rites of Protestants, when they must find more variety among them that they turn to ? The matter's well amended with them, when among us, one countrey use three or
four Ceremonies which others do disuse : and among the
Papists,

Papists, one order of Fryars useth twice as many different from the rest; yea in habit, and diet, and other observances they many waies differ. What hypocrisie is this, to judge this tolerable, yea laudable in them, and much less so intolerable in us, as that it must remove them from our Communion?

§. 7. And how sad a case is it that the Reconciliation between the Lutherans and other Protestants should in any measure stick at such Ceremonies? what if one courtrey will have Images to adorn their Temples, and will have exorcism, and other Ceremonies, which others do disallow and desire to be freed from? may we not yet give each other the right hand of fellowship? and take each other for the Churches of Christ? and maintain brotherly Charity, and such a correspondency, as may conduce to our mutual preservation and edification?

§. 8. Yea in the same Nation, why may not several congregations have the liberty of differing in a few indifferent ceremonies? If one part think them lawfull, and the other think that God forbids them, must we be forced to go against our Consciences, for a thing of no necessity? If we profess our Resolution to live peaceably with them that use them, and only desire a toleration our selves, because we dare not wilfully sin against our light, will charity deny us this? If men forbear a thing (suppose) indifferent for fear of Gods displeasure and damnation, and profess that were it not for this they would conform to the wills of others, are those Christians or men that will come behind them and drive them into hell without compassion, and that for things indifferent?

CHAP.

CHAP. IX.

Prop. 9. *There is no meer Humane Universal Soveraign, Civil or Ecclesiastical, over the whole Church, and therefore none to make Laws Obligatory to the whole.*

§. 1.]  ADD this, becauſe of the ſpecious pretences of ſome, that ſay we are bound to an uniformity in Ceremonies by the Church: and call all *Schiſmaticks*, and ſuch as ſeparate from the *Catholick Church*, that diſown and diſuſe ſuch Ceremonies as on theſe pretences they obtrude. And by the *Church* that thus obligeth us, they mean, either ſome Univerſal Soveraign Power: or elſe an univerſal Conſent of the Church eſſential (as they call it.) And that Soveraign muſt be the Pope or a General Council.

§. 2. If it be Univerſal Conſent of all Believers, that they ſuppoſe to be the obliging power, I ſhall anſwer them, 1. That Believers are not Governours and Law-givers to the Univerſal Church, no nor to a particular Church. If that point of the Separatiſts be ſo odious that aſſerteth the multitude of Believers to be the Governours of a particular Church, and to have the power of the Keyes: what then ſhall we think of them that give them, (even to ſuch as they call the Laity themſelves)
the

the Government, yea in the higheſt point even Legiſlation, over the Univerſal Church it ſelf.

§. 3. And 2. I add, that the Diſſent of thoſe Churches that refuſe your Ceremonies, doth prove that there is no Univerſal conſent: If all muſt conſent, we muſt conſent our ſelves before we be obliged. We are as free as others, we gave none power to oblige us by their conſent. If we had, it had been Null: becauſe we had no authority ſo to do, and could not have obliged our ſelves, by a univerſal Law, or perpetual contract. Or if we had, we had alſo power, on juſt occaſion to reverſe a ſelf-obligation. But no ſuch thing *de facto* can be pretended againſt us.

§. 4. And if ſuch an obligation by conſent ſhou'd be pretended, 3. I would know whether it was by *this* or by ſome *former* generation? Not by *this* as is certain. Nor by any *former*: For former ages had no power to bind all their ſucceſſors in Ceremonies about the worſhip of God. Shew whence they had ſuch a power, and prove it, if you can: we are born as free men, as our anceſtors were in this.

§. 5. And 4. I would be ſatisfied, whether every mans conſent in the world be neceſſary to the *Univerſality*, or not? If *it be*; then there are no Diſſenters: or no obligation becauſe no Univerſal conſent. If *not*; then how many muſt conſent before we are obliged? you have nothing to ſay, but [*a Major part*] where you can, with any ſhew of reaſon, reſt: And 1. How ſhall we know in every Pariſh in *England*, what mind the Major part of the Chriſtians through the world are of, in point of ſuch or ſuch a Ceremony? 2. Yea by this rule, we have reaſon to think that both Papiſts and Proteſtants muſt change their Ceremonies, becauſe the greater part of Chriſtians (in Eaſt and South, and ſome in the Weſt) are againſt very many of them.

§. 6. But if it be the Authority of a Soveraign Head that is pleaded as obliging the univerſal Church to an uniformity in Rites and Ceremonies, we muſt know who that Soveraign is. None that we know, pretend to it but the Pope and a General Council. And for the Pope we have by many volumes proved him an Uſurper, and no authorized Head of the Church Univer-

Mm m ſal:

fai: The pretended Vice-Chrift, is a falfe Chrift. The firft ufurpers pretended but to a Soveraignty in the Roman world, but had never any fhew of Government over the Churches in *Ethiopia, India*, and the many Churches that were without the verge of the Roman Emp're.

§. 7. And as for General Councils, 1. They are no more the Vifible Head and Soveraign of the Church then the Pope is. This I have proved in another Difputation by it felf. 2. There neither is nor can be any Council truly univerfal, as I have there alfo fhewed. Its but a delufory name. 3. There never was any fuch in the world, fince the Church (which before was confined to a narrow room) was fpread over the world. Even at *Nice*, there was no proper reprefentative of almoft any but the Churches under the Roman Emperours power : Few out of the Welt, even in the Empire: and none out of almoft any of the Churches without the Empire: (For whats one Bifhop of *Perfia*, or fuch another of another Countrey, and perhaps thofe prove the Roman fubjects too, that are fo called?) If there was but one from *Spain*, and only two Presbyters of *Rome* from *Italy*, and one from *France* (if any) and none from many another Countrey in the Empire, no wonder if there was none from *England, Scotland*, or *Ireland, &c.* And therefore there can be no univerfal obligation on this account.

§. 8. Councils are for Concord by Confultation and confent, and not a Soveraign or fuperiour fort of Governing power. And therefore we that confented not are not obliged : and if we had confented, we might on weighty reafons have withdrawn our confent.

§. 9. The Orders eftablifhed by General Councils have been laid afide by almoft all, and that without the repeal of a Council : Yea fuch Orders are feemed to prefuppofe the cuftom of the Univerfal Church, if not Apoftolical Tradition, to have been their ground.

§. 10. Among many others, let us inftance only in the laft Canon of the Nicene Council, that forbidding Kneeling, commandeth all to pray only ftanding on the Lords Dayes, *&c.* And this was the common ufe of the Church before, as *Tertullian* and others fhew, and was afterwards confirmed again in a General Council : And yet even the Church of *Rome* hath caft

it

it off; much more the Proteſtant Churches. No General Council hath been of more authority then this of *Nice* : No Ceremony of more common uſe then this ſtanding in prayer on the Lords dayes : So that it might as much as any, be called the conſtitution and cuſtom of the Catholick Church. And yet we ſuppoſe not theſe now to bind us to it : but have caſt it off without the repeal of any other General Council And why are we more bound then by the ſame authority to other Ceremonies then to this? And if to *any*, then to *which*, and to *how many*, and where ſhall our conſciences find reſt?

§. 11. Even the Jeſuites themſelves ſay that the General diſuſe of a practice eſtabliſhed by Pope and Council, is equall to an abrogation, without any other repeal, ſo it be not by the ſaid powers contradicted. And certainly all ſuch diſuſe began with a few, and proceeded further : we are allowed then to diſuſe ſuch things.

§. 12. It would grieve a man that loves the Church to hear the name of the Church abuſed by many dark, though confident diſputers, when they are pleading for their Ceremonies, and Holy dayes, and laying about them with the names of Schiſmaticks againſt all that will not do as they do [O (ſay they,) *Theſe men will ſeparate from the Catholick Church, and how then can they be the Children of the Church?*] And 1. Which is it that is called by them the Catholick Church ? Little do I know, nor am able to conjecture. Did the Catholick Church make the Engliſh Common-Prayer Book ? what! were the then Biſhops in *England* that conſented in that work, the whole Church of Chriſt on earth ? God forbid. Or did ever any General Council authorize it ? I think not. And if they would tell us what General Council commanded *Chriſtmas Day*, or Kneeling at the Sacrament, &c. they would do us a pleaſure : but I think they will not.

§. 13. And 2. What if theſe things had all been commanded by a General Council ? May not a man diſuſe them without ſeparating from the Church ? I think, as good as you are, you do ſome things your ſelves that God himſelf hath forbidden you to do ; and yet will be loth to be therefore taken for men that ſeparate either from the Church or God. And when you read the Books of Heathen Philoſophers ; when you adore not toward the East, or when you pray & receive the Sacrament, Kneeling on the Lords Dayes, would you be taken to separate from the Catholick Church, for crossing its ancient customs, or Canons? But these perverse and factious reasonings we must hear to the dishonour of Christianity and Reason it self, and that from men that scorn the supposed meanness of others ; yea and se: poor souls seduced into separation by such empty words? And this is one of the present judgements on this land.

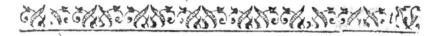

CHAP. X.

Prop. 10. *If it be not our Lawfull Governours that command us, but usurpers, we are not formally bound to obey them, though the things be lawfull which they command.*

§. 1. WE may be bound by some other Obligation perhaps, to do the thing which they command us, but we are not formally (though sometime Materially) bound to obey them : For it is not *formally* obedience unless it be done *eo nomine* because commanded, or for the Authority of the Commander. If the Pope or any usurper should command me to pray or to give alms, I will do it, but not because he commandeth me, but because God commandeth me : and therefore I will not obey him but God : But if a Parent or Magistrate or Pastor command it me, I will do it both because it is commanded me, by God and them,

and:

and so I will obey both God and them. If an usurper command me to do a thing in it self indifferent, I will not do it because he commandeth it : but yet if accidentally it become my duty, by conducing to anothers good, or avoiding their offence or hurt, or any other accident, I will use it for these ends, though not for his command.

§. 2. The Pope 1. As the Vice-christ or universall Head, is an usurper, and therefore hath no authority to command me or any man (in that relation) the smallest Ceremony. 2. The Pope as Patriarch of the West, is an humane creature, and not of Divine institution, and was indeed a sinfull institution from the first of his creation ; but if it had been otherwise, yet since is that Patriarchship become unwarrantable, since he hath forfeited it, and the world hath found the mischiefs of it. So that no man is therefore bound to use one lawfull Ceremony because the Pope as Patriarch of the West commandeth it. 3. If this were not so, yet *Brittain* and *Ireland* were from the beginning none of his Patriarchate, nor did at *Nice* consent to it : and therefore have the less appearance of any obligation.

§. 3. The Authority of General Councils cannot be pretended as obliging men in Conscience to the English Ceremonies. 1. Because indeed General Councils are not a superiour Power for proper Government of the Church having authority to command particular Bishops, or Synods, as their subjects ; but they are only necessary for Union and Communion of Churches and mutual assistance thereby : and so their Canons bind but by virtue of the General commands that require us to maintain the Unity and Communion of the Churches.

§. 4. And 2. If it were otherwise, there is few, if any of these Ceremonies that are commanded by any true General Council. They that can prove any such thing, let them do it : but till we see it, we will not be forward to believe it. Yea 3. Some of them, General Councils have made Canons against ; as I before shewed in the Case of Kneeling at the Sacrament on the Lords dayes. And therefore the neglecters of our Ceremonies sin not against a General Council.

§. 5. The Common plea is, that we are bound to use these Ceremonies in obedience to the Church of *England* : and that we are not true sons of the Church if we refuse it. But is

Mmm

it that is called by them [*The Church of England*] In a Political sense, I know no such thing as a Church of *England*, or of any Nation on earth ; that is, There is no one Society united in any one Ecclesiastical Soveraign, that can truly be called [*the Church of England*], or of any other Nation. The whole Catholick Church is One, as united in Christ the Head: And every particular Church, associated for personal Communion in Gods Worship, is one ; being a part of the Catholick Church, and united in, and individuated by their relation to their several Pastors. But a National Church under one chief Ecclesiastick Government, I find no mention of in Scripture ; but contrarily, [*the Churches of* Judæa, Galatia, *&c.*] or any other Countrey where there were many, are alway mentioned in the Plural number ; and never called *one Church*.

§. 6. Yet will we quarrel with no men about meer names or words. If by [*a National Church*] be meant any of these following, we acknowledge that there is such a thing. 1. If all the particular Churches in a Nation do Associate, for Communion and mutuall assistance, and so use to meet by their officers in one National Assembly ; I confess the Association usefull, if not necessary, and the Assemblies to be maintained, and for unity sake obeyed in things lawfull : And though *Scripture* call not such National Associations by the name of [*a Church*] in the singular number, yet we shall leave men to their Liberty in such names. If all the Schoolmasters in *England* should hold General Assemblies, to agree what Books to read in their Schools, *&c.* if any man would therefore call all the Schools in *England* in the singular number, by the name of [*the School of* England,] I would not differ with him for a word. 2. Or if the Churches are all called *One* that are under one Christian Magistrate, I will confess the thing to be true that is pretended to be the reason of the name: All the Churches do owe obedience to the Magistrate. But he is no Essential part or Ecclesiastical Head of the Church : and therefore it is very improperly denominated from him ; or called [*One*] on that account : No more then all the Schools are *one* because he is their Soveraign. It is the Common-wealth that is specified and individuated by the Magistrate as the Soveraign Power ; and not the Churches.

ches. But yet it is but an *improper word*, to call all the Churches one Church on that account, which we contend not about.

§. 7. But it is the *Thing* that we stick more at then the name. A *General Head* doth properly specifie and individuate the *Body*. Prove either, 1. That the Archbishop of *Canterbury* or any other. 2. Or an Assembly of Bishops or Presbyters, is properly an Ecclesiastical Head, having Authority from Jesus Christ to be the chief Ruler of all the Churches in the Land and then I will confess that we have properly and strictly *a National Church*. But no such thing can be proved.

§. 8 As for an *Assembly*, I have already shewed (which Bishop *Usher* asserted to me) that they are not superior Governors, nor instituted *gratia Regiminis*, but *gratia unitatis* ; having no more Rule over particular Bishops, then a Convention of Schoolmasters over a particular Schoolmaster. If they say that Kings and Parliaments give Power to Convocations, I answer, that can be but such as they have themselves : which we shall speak of anon, and is nothing to this place.

§. 9. And as for a Primate or Archbishop (of *Canterbury*, e. g.) 1. It will be a hard task to prove Archbishops, as such, to be of Divine Institution. 2. And it will be harder, even Impossible, to prove Archbishops of the English *species*, as such, to be of Divine institution. 3. And certainly Christ hath nowhere told us, that every Nation shall have such a Head, nor every Province, nor every County : nor told us whether there shall be one over ten Nations, or ten over one : Their limits are not to be found in Scripture (supposing there were such an office there known.) 4. Nor is it anywhere determined, that such a City shall have the preheminence, and *Canterbury*, *v. g.* be Ruler of all the rest. All these are of meer humane institution : And therefore that which the imposers of Ceremonies call [*the Church of England*] is a meer humane thing, which therefore can bind us no further then the Magistrate can authorize them to do.

§. 10. But the stronger pretence will be, that the particular Bishops of *England* were severally officers of Christ, authorized to Govern their several flocks, and therefore a Convocation of these Bishops *binds us in conscience gratia unitatis* The People they oblige as their Rulers : and the several Presbyters also

also as their Rulers, and the several Bishops, *gratia unitatis*, for avoiding of schism.

§. 11. *Answ.* This also is an insufficient evidence to prove our Consciences obliged to their Ceremonies, *eo nomine*, because of their Canons or commands. For though we acknowledge *a sort* of Episcopacy to be warrantable, yet that *this* sort that made the Canons in question, is not warrantable, I have proved at large in the former Disputation on that question. Such Pastors of a Dioces as our Bishops were, have no word of God to shew for their office (further then as they are Presbyters,) but we have shewed already, that their office is unlawful. And therefore though their actions as Presbyters may be valid, yet their actions are Null which were done by pretence of this unlawfull sort of office, (they being no other way enabled thereto.) On this ground therefore we are not bound.

§. 12. If it could be pretended that at least as Presbyters the Convocation represented the Presbyters of *England*, and therefore thus their Canons binds us to the use of ceremonies, Common prayer, *&c.* I should answer, that 1. Even Synods of Presbyters or the Lawfullest sort of Bishops, oblige but *gratia unitatis*. 2. That the late Synod at *Westminster* was as truly a Representative of the Presbyters of *England*, as the Convcaotion ; where such consent, if any were given, was retracted. 3. By actuall dislike signified by disuse, the Presbyters of *England*, for the most part, have retracted their Consent. 4. Yea most that are now Ministers never gave such Consent. 5. Even all particular Pastors and Churches are free, and may on just reason deny consent to such impositions.

§. 13. There remains nothing then, that with any shew of strength can be pretended, as continuing our obligation to Ceremonies, from Authority, but that of the Civil Power that commanded them. But to that I say, 1. So much as was lawfull, we confess that we were bound to use, while we had the command of the Civil power : But nothing unlawfull could be made our duty by them. 2. the Civil Power hath repealed those laws that bound us to these ceremonies. The Parliament repealed them : the late King consented, at least, for the ease of tender Consciences (as he spoke) that men should have liberty to forbear them. And the present Rulers are against them, whom we see even the ceremonious obey in other matters.

§. 14. Let

§. 14. Let thofe then that would fubjugate our Confciences to their ceremonies, make good their foundation, even the Authority by which they fuppofe us to be obliged, or they do nothing: If all their impofitions were proved things indifferent and lawfull, thats nothing to prove that we muft ufe them, till they prove that lawfull authority commandeth them. The Civil Powers do not command them : And the Ecclefiafticks that command them, prove not their authority over us. In the matters of God, we will yield to any man that bids us do that which God hath bidden us do already: But if they will exercife their power by commanding us more then God commands us, and that unneceffarily, we muft crave a fight of their commiffion.

§. 15. And if men that have no Authority over us, shall pretend Authority from God, and go about to exercife it by Ceremonious impofitions, we have the more reafon to fcruple obeying them, even in things indifferent, left we be guilty of eftablifhing their ufurpation, and pretended office in the Church, and fo draw on more evils then we forefee, or can remove.

CHAP. XI.

Prop. 11. *The Commands of Lawfull Governors about Lawfull Ceremonies, must be understood and obeyed with such exceptions as do secure the End; and not to the subverting of it.*

---

§. 1. THE proof of this is obvious. These humane Ceremonies are appointed but as means to a further end. But that which would cross and overthrow the end, doth cease to be a Means; and cannot be used *sub ratione medii.*

§. 2. Order, and Decency are the pretended ends of the Imposed Ceremonies; and the right worshiping of God, and the good of mens souls are said to be the greater and remoter ends, and the glory of God the ultimate end. If then I have good assurance that I cannot use such or such a ceremony but it will prove the subversion of Order, or Edification, (though it should be by accident, through the infirmity of men,) I know no reason I have to use them, when such a mischief would follow, unless they can shew me some greater good that also will follow, which may recompence it.

§. 3. Therefore the commanding of unnecessary ceremonies, on such Penalty, as was done in *England,* and *Scotland,* to
the

the silencing of the Preachers, and dissipating of the flocks, and casting out that worship, or hindring that Edification that was pretended to be their end, was preposterous both in the commanders and obeyers; and proved not convenient means to the ends pretended.

§. 4. If I be enjoyned by the Magistrates (whom I mention as of more undoubted authority then our Bishops,) to read such and such chapters, and preach on such and such texts through the year; I am in reason to interpret their commands with this exception [*when it doth not apparently cross the main end.*] So that if in my course I should be commanded to read and preach of an alienc subject, when my hearers are running into schism, sedition, heresie, &c. I will suppose that if the Magistrate were present, he would allow me to read or preach according to the matter of present necessity. And if I were commanded to read the Common prayer in a Surplice and other formalities, I hope if the Church were all in an uproar, and the stools flying about my ears, as the women at *Edinburgh* used the Bishop, I might think it would not tend in that Congregation to order or Edification, to use such Ceremonies: Were they things of Gods institution, they would not edifie the people till they were prepared to receive them ; and therefore that preparation should go first.

§. 5. Indeed it is the Pastors office to be the guide of his flock in the worship of God, and therefore to judge *pro re nata,* what subject to speak on to them, and what circumstances to choose, that may be most suitable to time, and place, and persons, to promote his ends, even the good of souls: And therefore no Magistrates should take the work or power of Pastors from them ; though they may oversee them in the use of it.

CHAP.

CHAP. XII.

Prop. 12. *It may be very sinfull to command some ceremonies, when yet it may be the subjects Duty to use them when they are commanded.*

---

§. 1. I Add this Proposition as necessary both for Rulers and for Subjects : For Rulers ; that they may not think that all may be lawfully Commanded which may be lawfully done when it is commanded. And for subjects ; lest they think that all things are unlawfull to be done, which are sinfully commanded.

§. 2. Some Governors think, that the Sermons and Arguments that charge the people with sin for disobeying them, do all justifie them for making the Laws, which others should obey : And all the words that are spent in aggravating the sin of the disobedient, they think are spoken in justification of their commands. And on the contrary, many people think that all that is said against the laws or penalties, is said in justification of their disobedience. And they are so lamentably weak that they cannot discern, how that can lawfully be obeyed, that is sinfully commanded : when yet the case is very plain.

§. 3. If a thing be simply unlawfull, as being forbidden by God himself, there no command of man can make it lawfull. But if it be but inconvenient or evil only by some accident or circumstance, it is possible for the commands of Governors to take off the accidental evil, and make it become a duty. For example,

It

It is not lawfull for me to travail one mile in vain: nor is it lawfull for a Prince to *command* me to travail a mile in vain: And yet if he send me such a *command*, to appear before him at such a place, (yea though it be many miles) it may become my duty to obey him. Otherwise subjects should not be bound to appear before any judicature, till they were satisfied of the cause, which is absurd. If a Prince command his officers to execute some unjust sentences, if they know it not, at least, it may be no sin of theirs, (in many cases) though it be his. Every war that is unlawfully undertaken by the Prince, is not unlawfull in all his Souldiers: Some of them that have not opportunity to know the evil of his undertaking, may be bound to obey (the case of others I determine not.)

§. 4. So if a *Pastor* call the Assembly at an inconvenient hour, or to an inconvenient place, though it be his sin to do so, yet is it their Duty to obey. If in the manner of Prayer he (tolerably) miscarry, they may not therefore refuse to join with him. If of two Translations of Scripture, or two versions of the Psalms, he use the worser, (so it be tolerable) they must obey.

§. 5. Yet if the miscarriage be so great in the ordering even of these circumstances, or in the Manner of Duties, as shall overthrow the Duty it self, and be inconsistent with the ends, or bring greater evils upon the Church, then our refusing to obey the Pastors (in those cases) can do; then (as I have before shewed) we are not bound to follow him in such a case: But otherwise we are.

§. 6. The Reasons of this are obvious and clear. Even because it is the *office of* the Governours to determine of such Circumstances: It is the *Pastors office* to guide and oversee the flock. And so the determining of Time and Place of worship, (that's undetermined) belongeth to his office: and the choice of the subject on which he shall preach, the leading them in prayer, and praise, and choice of versions, translations, and other ordinary helps in his work. And therefore when he determineth these, he is but in his *own way*; and doth but his *own work* and therefore he is therein the judge; if the case be controvertible. If none shall obey a Magistrate or Pastor in the works of their own office, as long as they think he did them not

the

the best way, all Government then would be presently over-thrown, and obedience denyed. We are sure that God hath commanded us to obey them that are over us in the Lord, (1 *Thes.* 5. 12. *Heb.* 13. 7, 17, &c.) And therefore a Certain duty may not be so born upon uncertain conjectures, or upon every miscarriage in them, that we owe it to. This would unchurch all Churches (as they are Political Societies) For if Pastors be taken down, and the work of Pastors, the Church is taken down : And if Government and obedience be taken down, then Pastors and their work is taken down ; Which will be the fruit of this disorder.

§. 7. And the things in which the Pastor is now supposed to err, are not of themselves unlawfull ; but only by such an accident, as being over-weighed by another accident, shall cease to make them unlawfull. For instance: If the Pastor appoint a more imperfect version of the Psalms to be sung in the Church (as is commonly done in *England,*) the obeying of him in the use of this, will not bring so much hurt to the Church as the disobeying on that account would do : For besides the sin of disobedience it self, the Church would be in a confusion, if they forsake his conduct that preserves the union ; and some will be for this, and some for that, and so the worship it self will be overthrown. But if the Pastor would command a version so corrupt as would overthrow the duty it self, or be as bad as non-performance, the Church is then to seek redress, and not obey him. So if he command a Time inconvenient, but tolerable (as to meet at sun rising or sun setting) it were better obey then dissolve the Church (if we cannot be otherwise relieved) But if he appoint a Time thats intolerably unfit (as at midnight) I would not obey (except in such necessity, as leaves to that time or none) the same I spoke before of other circumstances.

§. 8. On the other side, if Magistrates or Pastors shall think their Imposition lawfull, because the people may lawfully obey them, they are as much mistaken. Even many of those Divines that wrote for conformity to the late Ceremonies, did take it to be the sin of those that imposed them, as they were imposed, and would have written as much against the Imposition, if they had but had liberty : I mean such writers as Mr. *Sprint*,

Mr.

Mr. *Paybody*, Dr. *John Burgess* (who told the King of *Pollio's* glasses that were broken by *Cæsar*, that no more anger and danger of mens lives should follow ; and would have had him so to have used our Ceremonies.) So *Zanchy* that judged the Ceremonies such as might lawfully be used, did write to the Queen to take them down, and not leave them as snares to cast out the Ministers, and at the same time he wrote to the Ministers to use them, in case the Queen would not be perswaded to forbear the imposing and urging of them.

§. 9. If I be bound to obey a Governour if he set me to pick straws, or to hunt a feather, it followeth not that he may lawfully command it. I have heard many pleading for Ceremonies say, that if the Magistrate commanded them, and would not otherwise permit them to preach the Gospel, they would preach in a fools Coat, and a fools Cap with a feather, rather then forbear. But I do not think that any of them would justifie that Ruler that would make such a Law, that no man should preach or celebrate the Sacraments, but in a fools Coat and Cap : such might expect to be judged by Christ, as the scorners of him and his Ordinances.

CHAP.

CHAP. XIII.

Prop. 13. The Constant use of things indifferent should not be (ordinarily) commanded ; but they should be sometimes used, and sometimes disused.

§. 1. WILL say but little of this, because I have opened it before in the Disputation about Liturgies. The Reasons of it are plain. 1. Indifferent things should be used as indifferent things, and therefore with some indifferency.

§. 2. And 2. The people else will be brought to think them Neceſſary, if they be conſtantly uſed, and cuſtome will grow to a Law: And no contradicting this by doctrine will ſerve turn to rectifie the miſtake: For we cannot be alway nor oft preaching on ſuch things: And if we were, yet practice is much more obſerved by them then doctrine; which commonly they underſtand not, or forget.

§. 3. And 3. Hereupon their minds will receive a falſe impreſſion about the nature of their Religion, and they will be brought to worſhip they know not how, and to ſet a high value on that which is not to be valued ; and conſequently it will kindle a falſe zeal in their affections, and corrupt all their devotions.

§. 4. And 4. It will make them diſobedient againſt Magiſtrates or Paſtors that would take them off from their falſe apprehenſions, and miſguided practices : and if they live in a place
where

where the Governours are against their cuftoms, they will diſo-
bey them on pretence of duty to God, and think that they do him
ſervice in it.

§. 5. Yea 5. They will be uncharitably cenforious againſt
their Brethren that are not of their mind, and look on them as
men that are ſelf-conceited or irreligious, as the Papiſts do by
all that do nō entertain every opinion which they annumerate
with the Artic'es of their faith, and every practice which they
place their Religion in.

§. 6. We ſee all this by ſad experience among our ſelves.
The impoſers of our Ceremonies and the maintainers of them,
did ſtill profeſs that they were no parts, but Accidents of
worſhip; and they pleaded for them but as things indifferent.
And yet now the Magiſtrate, and their lawfull acknowledged
Paſtors, would bring the people in ſome of theſe Ceremonies
to change their cuſtoms; they will not do it, in many places, but
make conſcience (as they profeſs) of Geſtures, and forms and
Dayes, and ſuch like, as if they had been of Divine Inſtitution.
If they be things Indifferent, why may not they diſuſe an Holy
day one year as they uſe it another or diſuſe a form of Prayer
one day, as they uſe it another, or recieve the Lords Supper one
time ſitting, as they do another time kneeling? But this they
will not endure to yield to: ſo that you ſee that conſtant uninterrupted uſe, hath made cuſtome a Law with them, and given
the Lie to the Doctrine of the Biſhops themſelves, that call'd
them but indifferent things; and cauſed the people to place Gods
worſhip in them.

§. 7. And on the other ſide a conſtant purpoſed diſuſe of
convenient Modes and Circumſtances of worſhip, may draw
people to think them things unlawfull, and to riſe up againſt
them as innovations, and ſtrange things, when they are impoſed.

§. 8. Yet here we muſt diſtinguiſh of indifferent things.
Some are ſo convenient, that we cannot frequently vary, but
with great inconveniency and wrong to the Church (as a due
hour for Aſſembling, and a convenient place, and the beſt Tran-
ſlations, and verſions of the Pſalms, the fitteſt Utenſils for
worſhip, &c.) In all theſe caſes it were giddineſs to vary frequently and without need; and yet worſe to tie men up from

varving

varying when they find need. Other things are of ordinary inconvenience, which therefore ordinarily should be difused: though in some cases of necessity they must be allowed. Other things depend upon the will of men, and there is no great difference in point of convenience between the using and difusing them, but what the will of man doth cause: (as in our vestures, our gestures in some of the Ordinances, as in hearing, singing Psalms, and in abundance of Ceremonies or Circumstances, this is the case.) These are they that I say should be used, but unconstantly.

§. 9. As for them that cry out of Confusion and Sacriledge, and irreligiousness, and I know not what, if Ceremonies be not constantly used, and all forced to them, but be used with an indifferency; the distempers of their own souls contracted by such Customs, is a sufficient argument to move a sober considerate man, to desire that the Church may be delivered from such endangering customs. They do but tell us that custom hath made ceremonies become their very Religion! And what a kind of Religion is that?

CHAP.

CHAP. XIV.

Reasons against the Imposing of our late Controverted Mysticall Ceremonies, as Crossing, Surplice, &c.

§. 1. OW far Ceremonies are lawfull or unlawfull to the users, I have shewed sufficiently already: and therefore may omit the fourteenth Proposition as discussed before : But so eager are the minds of men to be exalting themselves over the whole world, and puting yoaks on their Brethrens necks, even in the matters of God, and setting up their own wills to be the Idols and Law-givers to all others, that I take it for the principal part of my task, to give in my Reasons against this distemper, and to try if it be possible to take men off from Imposing or desiring, the Imposition of unnecessary things. I durst not desire the Imposing of our Mysticall Ceremonies, but had rather they were abolished, or left indifferent, for these followings Reasons.

§. 2. *Reas.* 1. To impose new symbolical Rites upon the Church which Christ hath not imposed, doth seem to me to be an usurpation of his Soveraign power. It belongeth to him to be the Law giver of his Church. No man hath Power to make him a new worship. Officers are but to see his Laws executed : and to determine only of such circumstances, as are needfull for the well executing them. To make new Symbols or instituted

signs

figns to teach and excite Devotion, is to make new humane Ordinances: whereas it belongs to us only to use well such as he hath made: and to make no Laws but such as are thus need-full for the executing of his Laws. But of all this I have more largely spoken already.

§. 3. *Reas.* 2. The imposing of these Mystical Rites doth seem to accuse Christ of ignorance or negligence, in that he hath not himself imposed them, when he hath taken upon him that Royall office to which such Legislation doth belong. If Christ would have such Rites imposed on the Churches, he could bet-ter have done it himself, then have left it to man. For 1. These being not mutable circumstances, but the matter of standing Laws, are equally necessary or unnecessary to this age of the Church as to that in which Christ lived upon earth, and to those Countreys in which he conversed as to these. If Images, Crossing, significant garments, &c. be needfull to be imposed in *England*, why not in *Judæa, Galatia, Cappadocia, Asia, &c.* And if they are needfull now, why not then? No man can give a rational cause of difference, as to this necessity. If therefore Christ did neither by himself nor by his Apostles, (who formed the first Churches, and delivered us his mind by the Spirit) institute and impose these Rites, then either the imposing of them is needless, and consequently noxious: or else you must say that Christ hath omitted a needfull part of his Law and worship, which implies that he was either ignorant what to do, or careless and neglective of his own affairs, which are not to be imagined. *Moses* left nothing out of the Law that he delivered, that was to be the standing matter of the Law: nor omitted he any thing that God required in the instituting of the Legal worship. But Christ was faithfull to him that appointed him as *Moses* was in all his house, *Heb.* 3. 2, 3. therefore certainly Christ hath omit-ted nothing that was to be a standing Gospel Law and Worship nor done his work imperfectly.

§. 4. *Reas.* 3. And as this Imposition of Mystical Rites doth imply an accusation of Christ, so doth it imply an accusation of his Laws, and of the holy Scriptures, as if they were insuf-ficient. For if it belong to Scripture sufficiency to be the full revelation of the will of God concerning Ordinances of worship and duties of universal or stated Necessity, then must we not
imagine

imagine that any such are left out. If Scripture be Gods Law, it is a perfect law: And if it belong to it as a Law to impose one stated Symbol, Ordinance, or matter of worship, then so it doth to impose the rest of the same nature that are fit to be imposed. If we will do more of the same that Scripture was given for to do, we accuse it, while we seem to amend it.

§. 5. *Reaf.* 4. And by this means we shall be brought to a loss for the Rule of our Religion. For if once we leave the holy Scriptures, we shall not know where to fix. If God have not instituted all the Ordinances of Worship (such as Sacramental, or Mystical Rites, &c.) that are meet to be statedly Imposed on the Churches, then we are uncertain who is to be the institutor of them. The Pope will claim it: and General Councils will claim it: and Provincial Councils, and particular Bishops will claim it: and Princes will claim it: and we shall be at a loss for our Religion.

§. 6. *Reaf.* 5. But whoever it be that will be the master of our Religion they will certainly be men, and so it will become a humane thing. Whereas Divine worship supposeth a Divine institution : and it is an act of obedience to God, and therefore supposeth a Law of God : For without a Divine Law there cannot be obedience to God.

§. 7. *Reaf.* 6. These impositions seem to be plain violations of those prohibitions of God, in which we are forbidden to add to his worship, or diminish from it. As *Deut.* 12.32. [What thing soever I command you, observe to do it : thou shalt not add thereto, nor diminish from it.] Object. *But we add nothing to the Word of God, though we impose such Mystical Rites as he imposeth not. Answ.* The text doth not say *Thou shalt not add to my Command*] but [*Thou shalt not add to the thing that I command thee.*] It is the Work, Worship, or Ordinances that you are forbidden to *add to, or diminish from,* and not the Word or Law it self only.

§. 8. *Reaf.* 7. It seemeth to be a very great height of *Pride* that is manifested in these impositions. 1. When men dare think themselves wise enough to amend the work of Christ and his Apostles, and wise enough to amend the holy Scrip ure   r this exceeding Pride? How can man more   n can i t himself, then by pretending himself to be wiser then his Maker and Redeemer? Is it not bad enough to equalize your selves with him, unless you exalt your selves above him? If you do not so, what mean you by coming after him to correct his Laws, or mend his work, and make better laws and ordinances for his Church then he himself hath done? 2. And I think it is no better then Pride for men so far to exalt themselves above the *Church of God*, as to institute new signs and ordinances, and say, [*I command you all to worship God according to these my institutions and inventions: and he that will not thus worship him, shall not have liberty to worship him at all, nor to live in the Communion of Christians.*] What's Pride and arrogancy, if this be not?

§. 9. *Reas.* 8. None knoweth the mind of God concerning his worship, but by his own Revelation: If therefore he have not Revealed it to man, that he would be served by such mystical Rites, and Ceremonies, then no man can know that it will please him. And if it Please him not, it will be lost labour and worse: and we may expect to hear [*who requireth this at your hands?*] How do you know that it pleaseth him to be served by Images, Exorcisms, Crossings, and many pompous Ceremonies? He hath nowhere told you so. And your will is no proof of the will of God.

§. 10. *Reas.* 9. God would not have taken down the Legal Ceremonies, and delivered us from them as a burden, and commanded us to stand fast in the Liberty with which Christ hath made us free, and not again to be entangled with the yoak of bondage *Gal. 5. 1.* if he would have given men leave to have imposed the like burdensome observances at their pleasure. If you say that these present Ceremonies are not burdensome; I aske, why then were those of Gods institution burdensome? That yoak was streight and burden heavy; and Christ hath called us to take upon us his yoak that is easy, and his burden that is light. *Matth. 11. 28.* It was not only the threatnings conjunct against the disobedient, that made the Jewish Ceremonies to be a burden, which they were not able to bear, *Act. 15.* nor yet because they were but Types (for to be Types of Christ, was their highest honour:) But also because they were numerous, and required labour and time, and were unnecessary (when Christ was come) and so against the liberty of the Church, as

Cc

Col. 2. 16 &c. And is it a likely thing that God would take down his own inſtitutions when they became unneceſſary, and at the ſame time gıve commiſſion to the Paſtors of the Church to ſet up unneceſſary Ceemonies of their own ? Yea or give them leave to do it, without his commiſſion ? If it be ſuch a mercy to be delivered from Divine Ceremonies, when they grew needleſs, and a liberty which we are commanded to ſtand faſt in, I know not why men ſhould impoſe on us unneceſſary Ceremonies of their own, and rob us of our Mercies.

§. 11. *Reaſ.* 10. The impoſition of unneceſſary Ceremonies, is a certain means for the Dıviſion of Chriſtians, and therefore is but an engine of the Devill, the great divider. As the Papiſts ſet up a Vicechriſt and falſe Center of union, under pretence of the unity of Chriſtians, when nothing is ſo great a cauſe of their diviſion, ſo uſually the Impoſers of Ceremonies pretend the Unity and Peace of Chriſtians to be their end, when they are moſt effectually dividing them. They are preſerving the houſe by caſting fire into the thatch. There is no more effectual means of Diviſion, then to ſet up impoſſible terms of unity, and tell men, that they muſt Agree upon theſe or none. All Chriſtians will unite in Chriſt, and Agree in all the eſſentials of Chriſtianity, and all that is the known word of God : But no wiſe man will expect that all Chriſtians ſhould ever Unite and Agree about the Myſtical ſigns and Ceremonies of mans invention and impoſition. Come to a Congregation that walke in unity and holy order in the ſimplicity of faith and Scripture ordinances, and make Laws to this Church, that no man ſhall joyne in the worſhip of God that will not Croſs bimſelf, and be ſprinkled with holy water, and bow toward the Altar, and wear a ſword and helmet, to ſignifie the ſpiritual warfare, and ſuch like, and try whether this courſe will not divide the Congregation ; Men are liker to agree in few things then in *many* ; in *Certain* truths, then in uncertain *Controverſies* ; in *Divine ordinances*, then in *Humane inventions.* Undoubtedly if you impoſe ſuch Ceremonies, multitudes of honeſt Chriſtians will diſſent. And if they diſſent, what will you do with them ? If you leave them to their liberty, then your Ceremonies are not impoſed. If you do not ; you will drive them to a ſeparation, and break all in pieces by your violence, and exasperation of mens minds.

§. 12. *Reas.* 11. And by this means you will be led, and also lead others into the haynous guilt of persecuting the members of Christ. For when you have made Laws for your Ceremonies, you will expect obedience, and take all for schismaticks or disobedient that refuse them; and its like your laws will be backt with penalties; you will not be content to have the liberty of using these Ceremonies themselves, and to leave all other to their liberties. We hear (and formerly heard it more) how impatient almost all of this way are of diversity in Circumstances and Ceremonies. They take it to be intolerable confusion to have diversity in these things: what say they? shall one use one gesture, and another use another? what confusion will this be? or if a few of the wiser sort have more wit, yet custome will bring the multitude to this pass. We see now, they will not endure to joyn with those that sit at the Lords Supper, though they may kneel themselves. If they see but two or three shops in a Town open on Christmas day, they throw stones at them and break their windows, where they dare, and are ready to rise up against such as enemies in war. Besides you will take it as a contempt of your Laws, if men do not conform to them: And if you use the Ceremonies, and others disuse them, you will think they censure your practice by their forbearance. And its like they will be forced to give some *reasons* of their forbearance: And those Reasons must needs be against your way, and consequently seem to disparage you, so that I may take it for granted, that those that would have Ceremonies, would have them forced on the Church, and so would raise a persecution to maintain them.

§. 13. And then this persecution when its once begun, its never like to stay till it reach to the height of Cruelty. For 1. When you have begun, you will think that you are engaged in honour to carry it on, and not to suffer every poor man or woman to disoby you, and disparage your wisdom. 2. And if you lay but a gentle penalty on dissenters, it will do no good on them (but perhaps excite them to the more opposition.) When Conscience is engaged against you, it is not small mulcts nor imprisonment neither that will alter the judgements or the waies of such. And therefore you must either proceed to

blood

blood or banishment, or you miss your ends, and will but be opposed with greater animosity.

§. 14. *Reas.* 12. And then this will raise an *odium* upon your Government, and make men look upon you as tyrants : For naturally men pitty the suffering party, especially when it is for the cause of God, or Profession of more then ordinary exactness in the obeying of Gods commands : And then mens minds will by this be tempted to disloyal jealousies, and censures, if not to the opposition of the Rulers.

§. 15. *Reas.* 13. And it were an evil which your Ceremonies will never countervail, if it were but the *uncharitableness* that will certainly be raised by them. When you will persecute men, and force them against their Consciences in such indifferent things (as you call them) you will occasion them to judge you persecutors, and cruel, and then they will censure you as ungodly, yea as enemies to the Church : And then you will censure them for schismatical, and self-conceited, and refractory disobedient people. And so Christian love, and the offices of love will be extinguished, and you will be mutually engaged in a daily course of hainous sin.

§. 16. *Reas.* 14. And it will be the worse, in that your persecution will oft fall on the most consciencious persons. Hypocrites and temporizers dare do any thing ; and therefore will follow the stronger side, and obey him for their worldly ends. But the upright Christian dare not do that which is displeasing to God, for a world : He is the man that will be imprisoned, or banished, or rackt, or slain, rather then he will go against his Conscience. And is it not a horrid thing to make such Laws, that the most conscionable are likest to fall under, and to perish by ? May it not make you tremble, to read that God himself doth call such his Jewels (*Mal.* 3. 16, 17.) and faith, he that toucheth them, toucheth the apple of his eye, and that it were better for him be cast into the depth of the sea with a Milstone about his neck, that offendeth one of these little ones ? Away with the Ceremonies that are unnecessary, and yet have such effects, and bring you into such danger.

§. 17. *Reas.* 15. And then a more grievous evil will follow : the Ceremony will devour the substance, and shut out the preachers, and consequently the w. . . . . world. . . . . rd.

For you will never give men Liberty to forbear them. And when godly Ministers will not be conformable to your will, you must silence them, left they draw the people from you. And so the ignorant must be left in their ignorance, and the prophane in their prophaness, and the godly in their sorrows for want of their faithful Teachers, and the ordinances of grace.

§. 18. *Reas.* 16. And then it will follow, that ignorant, idle, ungodly Ministers must be taken in to supply their rooms : For if the best disobey you, you will think your selves necessitated to take such as will obey you. And so God shall be dishonoured, his word and work abused, his people grieved, his enemies encouraged, the wicked hardened, and the unworthy Ministers themselves undone and destroyed ; and all for a few unnecessary ceremonies of your vain invention.

§. 19. *Reas.* 17. And now it were more unexcusable then ever before, to Impose such unnecessary burdens on the Churches, when we have so lately seen and felt the sad and miserable effects of such impositions. We are scarce out of the fire, that this straw and rubbish kindled in this land. We are the men that have seen the Churches divided by them, and the preachers cast out for them, and persecution occasioned by them, and the Nation hereupon corrupted with uncharitableness, the Bishops against the people, and the people against the Bishops ; and war and misery hence arising. And yet shall we return to the occasion of our misery, and that while we confess it to be a needless thing ?

§. 20. *Reas.* 18. Yea this course is like to kindle and maintain *Divisions between the Churches of several Nations*, as well as among those that are under the same government. For either you will have all the Christian world to join with you in your Mystical and unnecessary Ceremonies, or not : All cannot be expected to join with you : For 1. The world will never agree in such humane unnecessary things. 2. There is no universal governor to Impose one Law of Ceremonies on all the Churches. Christ only is the universal King and Head : and he hath done his part already. If you will have more universal Laws, you must first have another universal King or Head. And there is none such. Only the Pope and a General Council

pretend

pretend to it ; and they are both deceived (in this) and would deceive us. They are none of our Lords, as I have elsewhere proved. But if you expect not universal Concord in your Mystical signs and Ceremonies; then 1. Why should you cast out your Preachers and brethren, for those things which other Nations may be so well without : and hold communion with forreigners that avoid them, and deny Communion to neighbors as good, that are of the same mind? And 2. This will make forreign Churches and you to grudge at one another, and the diversity will cause disaffection : especially when you persecute your members for the cause thats theirs. We find now by experience, that the Images, Exorcism, Crossing, &c. of the *Lutherans* doth exceedingly hinder their Peace with other Churches, while others censure them as superstitious ; and they by custome are grown so highly to value their own Ceremonies, as to censure and disdain those that are not of their mind.

§. 21. *Reas.* 19. It easily breedeth and cherisheth *ignorance and formality* in the people. You cannot keep them from placing their Religion in these Ceremonies : and so from deceiving their souls by such a Pharisaical Religiousness, in washings and observances : And so in vain will they worship God, while their worship is but a Conformity to the doctrines, traditions, and inventions of men. *Mat.* 15.

§. 22. *Reas.* 20. To prevent these evils (and yet in vain) your Rites and Signs must bring New doctrines, and new labours into the Church, which will exceedingly hinder the doctrine and work of Christ. The Ministers must teach the people the meaning and use of all these Ceremonies (or else they will be dumb signs, contrary to your intent, and the use of them will be vain) And if we must spend our time in opening to our people the meaning of every ceremony that you will impose : 1. It will be but an unsavoury kind of preaching. 2. It will divert them and us from greater and more needful things. Yea we must teach them, with what *Cautions,* in what *manner,* to what *ends,* &c. to use all these Ceremonies : or else they will turn them all to sin ; if not to Popish, yea to heathenish formalities. And alas, how much ado have we to get our people to understand the Creed, and the kernel of the Gospel, the essentials of Christianity, and the two Sacraments of Christ, yea

tion, and some short Catechism that containeth these? And when we have done our best in publick and in private, we leave many of them ignorant what these two Sacraments are, yea or who Christ himself is. And must we put them to so much more labour, as to learn a *Rationale* or exposition of all the Ceremonies, holy dayes, &c? We shall but overwhelm them, or divert them from the Essentials.

And here you may see the unhappy issue of humane wisdom and false means. It is to be teachers of the ignorant that men pretend these Signs, Images and Ceremonies to be usefull. And yet they are the causes of ignorance, and keep men from necessary knowledge. If you doubt of this, do but open your eyes, and make use of experience : See whether among the common people the most Ceremonious are not commonly the most ignorant ? yea and the most ungodly too ? It is a truth so notorious, that it cannot be denyed. Who more ignorant of the Sacraments, then they that rail at them that sit in the act of receiving? Who more ignorant of the doctrine of the Gospel ? who more obstinate enemies of a holy life, more worldly, self-conceited, licentious, prophane, despisers of their faithfull Teachers, then the most zealous persons for all these Ceremonies?

§. 23. *Reas.* 21. Moreover these new Laws and services introduce also a new office into the Church. There must be some of pretended Power to impose all these Ceremonies, and see them executed : or else all is vain. And no such office hath Christ appointed. Because men thought it necessary that all the Christian world should have but one way and Order in the Ceremonious worship which was commonly approved, therefore they thought there was a Necessity of one Head to maintain this unity of order : and so came up the Pope, (as to one cause.) And so in a Nation, we must have some one or more Masters of Ceremonies, when Ceremonies are kept a foot. And so whereas Christ hath placed officers in his Church to teach and guide them, and administer his own Ordinances, we must have another sort of officers, to make Laws for Mystical signs and Ceremonies, and see them executed, and punish the neglecters, and teach the people the meaning and the use of them. The Primitive Bishops had other kind of work ; we find directions,

ons to the Paſtors of the Church containing the works of their office (as to *Timothy, Titus, &c.*) But we no where find that this is made any part of their work, to make new Teaching ſigns and Ceremonies, and impoſe them on the Church, nor have they any directions for ſuch a work : which ſurely they much needed, if it had been their work indeed.

§. 24. *Reaſ.* 22. When we once begin to let in humane Myſtical Rites, we ſhall *never know where to ſtop,* or make an end. On the ſame ground that one Age inventeth three or four, the next think they may add as many , and ſo it will grow to be a point of devotion , to add a new Ceremony (as at *Rome* it hath done) till we have more then we well know what to do with.

§. 25. *Reaſ.* 23. And the miſerable plight that the Chriſtian world hath lain in many ages by Ceremonies, may warn us to be wiſe. *Auguſtine* complaineth that in his time the Church was burdened with them, and made like the Jewiſh Synagogue. The moſt of the Churches in *Aſia* and *Africa* are drowned too deeply in Ceremonious formality, turning Religion into ignorant ſhews. The Church of *Rome* is worſe then they ; having made God a worſhip of hiſtrionical actions, and ſhews and ſigns and Ceremonies: ſo that millions of the poor blind people worſhip they know not *whom* nor *how.* And if we abate only of the *number,* and keep up ſome of the ſame *kind,* (even Symbolicall Rites of mans inſtitution, to teach us, and excite our devotion) we ſhall harden them in their way, and be diſabled from confuting them. For a Papiſt will challenge you to prove juſt how many ſuch ſigns are lawfull: And why he may not uſe threeſcore as well as you uſe three, when he ſaith he is edified by his number, as you ſay you are with yours?

§. 26. *Reaſ.* 24. It is not inconſiderable that God hath purpoſely eſtabliſhed a ſpiritual kind of worſhip in the Goſpel , telling us that God is a Spirit, and will be worſhipped in ſpirit and in truth : Such worſhippers doth God require and accept : Bodily exerciſe profiteth little. The kingdom of God is not in meats or in drinks, but in Righteouſneſs, and Peace, and Joy in the Holy Ghoſt : Neither Circumciſion availeth any thing in Chriſt Jeſus, nor uncircumciſion, but a new creature, and faith that worketh by love, God will ne h called men off from Ceremoniousness to spirituality, if he had delighted in Ceremony.

§. 27. *Reas.* 25. The Worship of God without his blessing is to little purpose. No man can have encouragement to use any thing as a Means to teach him and help his devotion, which he hath no ground to believe that God will bless. But there is no ground (that I know of) to believe that God will bless these Instituted Teaching *signs* of mans inventions to the Edifying of our souls. For God hath no where bid us devise or use such signs. 2. Nor no where promised us a blessing on them (that ever I could find) And therefore we have no encouragement to use them. If we will make them, and impose them our selves, we must undertake to bless them our selves.

§. 28. *Reas.* 26. As vain thoughts and words are forbidden us in Scripture, so no doubt but *vain actions* are forbidden: but especially in the worship of God: and yet more especially when they are Imposed on the Church by Laws with penalties. But these Mystical Rites of humane institution are vain. You call them your selves but [*Things indifferent:*] And they are vain as to the use for which they are pretended, that is, to *Teach and Edifie, &c.* having no promise of a blessing, and being needless imitations of the Sacraments of Christ. Vanity therefore is not to be imposed on the Church. My last Reason will fullier shew them to be vain.

§. 29. *Reas.* 27. We are sure the way in which *Peter*, and *Paul*, and the Churches of their times did worship God, was allowable and safe: and that Princes and Prelates are wise and righteous overmuch, if they will not only be more wise and righteous then the Apostles in the matters of Gods worship, but also deny their subjects liberty to worship God, and go to heaven in the same way as the Apostles did. If *Peter* and *Paul* went to heaven without the use of Images, Surplice, the Cross in Baptism, kneeling in receiving the Lords Supper, and many such Ceremonies, why should not we have leave to live in the Communion of the Church without them? would you have denied the Apostles their liberty herein? Or will you be partiall? Must they have one way, and we another? They command us to imitate them: give us leave then to imitate them, at least in all things that your selves confess to be lawfull for us.

§. 30.

§. 30. *Reaf.* 28. Hath not God purpofely already in the Scripture determined the Controverfie, fuppofing your Ceremonies (which is their beft) to be indifferent. He hath interpofed alfo for the decifion of fuch doubts. He hath commanded, *Rom.* 14. 1, 3. that we [*Receive him that is weak in the faith, but not to doubtfull difputations*] (much lefs to imprifonment or banifhment) [*Let not him that eateth, defpife him that eateth not ; and let not him that eateth not, judge him that eateth, for God hath received him*] Nay we muft not fo much as offend or grieve our brother, by indifferent things. *Verfe* 13. 15. 21. *to the end.* And fo *Chap.* 15. 1. *We that are ftrong ought to bear the infirmities of the weak, and not to pleafe our felves.*] So that the cafe is decided by the Spirit of God expreffly, that he would have weak Chriftians have liberty in fuch things as thefe ; and would not have Chriftians fo much as cenfure or defpife one another upon fuch accounts. And therefore Prelates may not filence Minifters, nor excommunicate Chriftians on this account ; nor Magiftrates punifh them, efpecially to the injury of the Church.

§. 31. *Object.* But this is *fpoken only to private Chriftians, and not to Magiftrates or Prelates.* *Anfw.* 1. If there had been any Prelate then at *Rome,* we might have judged it fpoken to them with the people. And no doubt but it was fpoken to fuch Paftors as they then had. For it was written to all the Church, of whom the Paftors were a part. And if the Paftors muft bear with diffenters in things indifferent, then moft certainly the Magiftrates muft do fo. 2. If Magiftrates are Chriftians, then this command extendeth alfo unto them. God hath fufficiently told us here that he would have us bear with one another in things of fuch indifferency as thefe. If God tell private men this truth, that he would have men born with in fuch cafes, it concerns the Magiftrate to take notice of it. Either the error is *tolerable,* or intolerable. If *intolerable,* private men muft not bear with it. If *tolerable,* Magiftrates and Paftors muft bear with it. It is as much the duty of Private Chriftians to reprove an erroneous perfon, and avoid him, if intolerable and impenitent, as it is the duty of a Magiftrate to punifh him by the fword, or the Paftor by Church-cenfures. If therefore it be the duty of Chriftians fo to ...

by a forbearnce of their rebukes and Censures ; then is it the duty of Magiftrates to tolerate them, by a forbearance of penalties; and of Paftors to tolerate them by a forbearance of excommunication. Who can believe that God would leave fo full a determination for tolerating fuch perfons, and yet defire that Prelates fhould excommunicate them, or Princes imprifon, banifh or deftroy them. Some Englifh Expofitors therefore do but unreafonably abufe this text, when they tell us that Magiftrates and Prelates may thus punifh thefe men, whom the reft of the Church is fo ftraitly commanded to bear with and not offend.

§. 32. So *Col.* 2. 16. to the end [*Let no man judge you in Meat or Drink, or in refpect of an holy day, or of the new Moon, or of the Sabbaths, &c.*] ver. 20. [*Wherefore if ye be dead with Chrift from the rudiments of the world, why as though living in the world are ye fubject to Ordinances? (Touch not, tafte not, handle not, which all are to perifh with the ufing,) after the commandments and doctrines of men : which things have indeed a fhew of wifdom in will-worfhip and humility, and neglecting of the body, not in any honour to the fatisfying of the flefh.*] Here alfo God fheweth that it is his will that fuch Matters fhould not be made Laws to the Church, nor be impofed on his fervants; but their freedom fhould be preferved. Many other texts exprefs the fame, which I need not cite, the cafe being fo plain.

§. 33. *Reaf.* 29. Moreover, me thinks every Chriftian fhould be fenfible, how infufficient we are to perform the great and many duties that God hath impofed upon us already. And therefore they fhould have little mind to be making more work to the Churches and themfelves, till they can better difcharge that which is already impofed on them by God. Have not your felves and your flocks enough to do to obferve all the precepts of the Decalogue, and underftand all the doctrines of the Gofpel, and believe and obey the Gofpel of Chrift, but you muft be making your felves and others more work? Have you not fin enough already in breaking the Laws already made, but you muft make more Laws and duties, that fo you may make more fin? If you fay, that your precepts are not guilty of this charge, you fpeak againft reafon : The more duty, the more neglect we fhall be guilty of. See how the Lord *Fall-land* urgeth this Objection on the Papifts. And it is confiderable

fiderable, that by this means you make your felves unexcufable for all your negle&s, and omiffions toward God. Cannot
you live up to the height of Evangelical San&ity ? Why then
do you make your felves more work ? Sure if you can do more,
it may be expe&ed that you firft do this that was enjoyned
you. If you will needs be Righteous (materially) overmuch,
you are unexcufable for your unrighteoufnefs.

§. 34. *Reaf.* 30. Laftly, confider alfo, that all your Myftical
Teaching Signs, are needlefs things, and come too late, becaufe
the *work is done that they pretend to*: God hath already given you
fo perfe& a dire&ory for his worfhip, that there is nothing
more that you can reafonablydefire. Let us perufe the particulars.
1. What want you in order to the Teaching of our underftand-
ings ? Hath not God in his word and his works, and his Sacraments, provided fufficient means for our inftru&ion, unlefs you
add your Myftical figns? Will your Ceremonies come after and
teach us better then all thefe Means of God will do ? We fee by
the Difciples of Ceremonies, what a Mafter they have. 2. What
want you for the exciting of dull affe&ions, that God hath not
provided you already ? Have you Ceremonies that can give
life, and are more powerfull remedies againft Corruptions, and
more effe&uall means of Grace then all the inftitutions of God ?
Or hath God left any imperfe&ion in his inftitutions for your
Ceremonies to fupply ? Wou'd you have plain Teaching in feafon and out of feafon? This God hath appointed already : and
fetled the Miniftry to that end. Would you have men taught
by a Form of words ? Why you have a copious Form : The
whole Scripture is a form of words, for mens inftru&ion. And
yet we deny not but out of this Form you may gather more
contra&ed forms for the inftru&ion of your flocks. Catechizing
and publick and private teaching are Gods own Ordinances.
Would you have a Dire&ory for Prayer, Confeffion and
Thankfgiving? Scripture is a Dire&ory ; and out of it we fhall
be glad of any dire&ion that you will gather for us. Would
you have forms of Words for Prayer and Praife ? Scripture
hath given you many : the Lords Prayer, the Pfalms, and many
more. And if you think you can do better, you have liberty
to do it your felves. And is not that enough ? God hath left
it indifferent to us whether we ufe a fet form or not. If

you be not wiſer then God, do you leave it indifferent alſo.
Would you have a ſtated day for Goſpel-worſhip in Commemoration of the work of our Redemption? Chriſt and his Apoſtles
have taught you to obſerve one, even the Lords day to theſe
Ends. Would you have exciting myſtical inſtituted ſigns? Chriſt
hath appointed you Baptiſm and the Lords Supper, which ſignifie the very ſubſtance of the Goſpel: Can your ſigns do more?
Or is a greater number more deſirable? Why may not a few
of Chriſts inſtitution, full and clear, that have a promiſe of his
bleſſing, ſerve turn without the additions of mens froathy wits?
Uſe the Lords Supper ofter, and with more preparation, and
you will need no Sacramental Rites of your own. If Chriſts
ſigns will not do it, in vain do you hope for it from the deviſes
of men. Gods Ordinances have no blemiſhes and wants that
need your patches. Do that which Scripture hath cut out for
you, and I warrant you, you'l find no want of ſuch additions.
The making of the Law and Rule of Worſhip is Gods work, the
obeying it is yours. Its a courſe moſt perverſe when you fail
and deal falſly in your own work, to fall upon Gods work, and
take on you to mend that. Do your own well, in obeying, and
judge not the Law, and trouble not the Church with your additions.

§. 35. Yet ſtill remember, that we allow both Magiſtrates and
Paſtors to ſee to the execution of Gods laws, and to determine of
Circumſtances in order thereto that are neceſſary *in genere*. But
it is only 1. Such Myſtical ſigns as *in genere* are not commanded
us, and left to mans determination, that I ſpeak of. 2. And alſo
the needleſs determination of circumſtances, and making Laws
for ſuch things as ſhould be left to the prudence of every Paſtor,
to be varyed as occaſion requireth.

CHAP.

CHAP. XV.

Reasons for Obedience in Lawfull things.

§. 1. LEST men that are apt to run from one extream into another, should make an ill use of that which I have before written, I shall here annex some Reasons to perswade men to just obedience, and preserve them from any sinfull nonconformity to the commands of their Governours, and the evill effects that are like to follow thereupon.

§. 2. But first I will lay together some Propositions for decision of the Controversie ; How far we are bound to obey mens precepts about Religion ? Especially in case we doubt of the lawfulness of obeying them ? and so cannot obey them in faith ?

§. 3. Briefly : 1. We must obey both Magistrates and Pastors in all things lawfull which belong to their offices to command. 2. It belongs not to their office to make God a new worship ; But to command the Mode and Circumstances of worship belongeth to their office : for guiding them wherein God hath given them generall rules. 3. We must not take the Lawfull commands of our Governours to be unlawfull. 4. If we do through weakness or perversness take Lawfull things to be unlawfull , that will not excuse us in our disobedience. Our error is our sin, and one sin will not excuse another sin. Even as on the other side, if we judge things unlawfull to be lawfull, that will not excuse us for our disobedience to God in obeying men. 5. As I have before shewed, many things that are miscommanded, must be obeyed. 6. As an erroneous judgement will not excuse us from Obedience to our Governours, so much less will a *doubtfulness* excuse us. 7. As such a doubting, erring judgement cannot obey in (plenary) faith, so much less can he disobey in faith. For it is a known Command of God, that *we obey them that have the Rule over us :* but they have no word of God against the act of obedience now in question. It is their own erring judgement that intangleth them in a necessity of sinning (till it be changed.) 7. In doubtfull cases, it is our duty to use Gods means for our information : and one means is to consult with our Teachers, and hear their words with teachableness and meekness. 8. If upon advising with them we remain in doubt about the lawfulness of some Circumstance of order, if it be such as may be dispensed with, they should dispense with us : if it may not be dispensed with without a greater injury to the Church or cause of God, then our dispensation will countervail, then is it our duty to obey our Teachers, notwithstanding such doubts : For it being their office to Teach us, it must be our duty to believe them with a humane faith, in cases where we have no Evidences to the contrary : And the Duty of Obeying them being certain, and the sinfulness of the thing commanded being uncertain and unknown, and only suspected, we must go on the surer side. 9. Yet must we in great and doubtfull cases, not take up with the suspected judgement of a single Pastor, but apply our selves to the unanimous Pastors of other Churches. 10. Christians should not be over-busie in prying into the work of their Governours, nor too forward to suspect their determinations: But when they know that it is their Rulers work to guide them by determining of due Circumstances of worship, they should without causeless scruples readily obey, till they see just reason to stop them in their obedience ; They must not go out of their own places

to

to search into the Actions of another mans office, to trouble themselves without any cause.

§. 4. And now I intreat all humble Christians readily to obey both Magistrates and Pastors in all Lawfull things ; and to consider, to that end, of these Reasons following. *Reas.* 1. If you will not obey in Lawfull things, you deny authority, or overthow Government it self, which is a great ordinance of God, established in the fifth commandment with promise: And as that commandment respecting societies and common good, is greater then the following commands, as they respect the private good of our neighbours, or are but particular Means to that Publick good, whose foundation is laid in the fifth commandment, so accordingly the sin against this fifth commandment must be greater then that against the rest.

§. 5. *Reas.* 2. In disobeying the lawfull commands of our superiors, we disobey Christ, who ruleth by them as his officers. Even as the disobeying a Justice of Peace or Judge is a disobeying of the soveraign Power ; yea in some cases when their sentence is unjust. Some of the ancient Doctors thought that the fifth commandment was the last of the first Table of the Decalogue; and that the Honouring of Governors is part of our Honour to God, they being mentioned there as his officers, with whom he himself is honoured or dishonoured, obeyed or disobeyed : For it is Gods Authority that the Magistrate, Parent, and Pastor is endued with, and empowred by to rule those that are put under them..

§. 6. *Reas.* 3. What confusion will be brought into the Church if Pastors be not obeyed in things lawfull? For instance : If the Pastors appoint the Congregation to Assemble at one hour, and the people will scruple the time, and say, it is unlawfull, and so will choose some of them one time, and some another, what disorder will here be ? and worse, if the Pastors appoint a Place of worship, and any of the people scruple obeying them, and will come to another place, what confusion will here be ? People are many, and the Pastors are few : and therefore there may be some unity if the people be Ruled by the Pastors; but there can be none, if the Pastors must be ruled by the people, for the people will not agree among themselves : and therefore if we obey one part of them, we must disobey and displeafe the reft. And their ignorance makes them unfit to rule.

§. 7. *Reaf.* 4. Moreover, difobedience in matters of *Circum-ftance*, will exclude and overthrow the *fubftance* of the worfhip it felf. God commandeth us to pray: If one part of the Church will not joyn with a ftinted form of Prayer, and the other part will not joyn without it, both parties cannot be pleafed, and fo one part muft caft off Prayer it felf, or feparate from the reft. God commandeth the reading, and preaching, and hearing of the Scripture, and the finging of Pfalms : but he hath left it to man to make or choofe the beft Tranflation of Scripture, or verfion of the Pfalms. Now if the Paftor appoint one verfion, and Tranflation, and the Church joyn in the ufe of it, if any members will fcruple joyning in this Tranflation or verfion, they muft needs forbear the whole duty of Hearing the Scripture, and finging Pfalms in that Congregation. If they pretend a fcruple againft the appointed time or Place of worfhip, they will thereby caft off the worfhip it felf. For if they avoid our *Time* or *Place*, they cannot meet with us, nor worfhip with us.

§. 8. *Reaf.* 5. And when they are thus carryed to feparate from the Congregation, upon fuch grounds as thefe, they will be no where fixt, but may be ftill fubdividing, and feparating from one another, till they are refolved into individuals, and have left no fuch thing as a Church among them. For they can have no affurance or probability, that fome of themfelves will not diffent from the reft in one Circumftance or other, as they did from their Paftors and the Church that they were of before.

§. 9. *Reaf.* 6. By this means the wicked that are difobedient to their Teachers, and rejeﬅ the worfhip of God it felf, will be hardened in their fin, and taught by profeffors to defend their ungodlinefs : For the very fame courfe that you take will ferve their turns. They need not deny any Duty in the fubftance, but deny the circumftance, and fo put off the fubftance of the Duty. If a wicked man will not hear the word preached, he may fay [*I am not againft preaching ; but I am un-fatisfied of the lawfulnefs of your Time or Place, I am in judge-*

ment

ment *against coming to your Steeple-house, or against the Lords Day.*] And so he shall never hear, though he say he is for hearing. If a wicked man will not be personally instructed, or admonished, or be accountable to the Church or Pastors for any scandals of his life, nor submit to any discipline, he may say [*I am for discipline, I know it is my duty to be instructed: but I am not satisfied that I am bound to come to you when you send for me, or to appear at such a place as you appoint : the word of God nameth no time or place, and you shall not deprive me of my liberty.*] If a wicked man would not hear or read the Scripture, or sing Psalms, he may say that he is for the duty, but he is only against this and that Translation and version : And so while every version is excepted against, the duty is as much evaded as if it were denied it self. By this device it is that the Rebellion of unruly people is defended : They run to the *circumstances* of the duty, and ask, [Where are they bound to come to a Minister ? or to be examined by him in order to a baptism or Lords supper ? or to speak their consent to be Church members, or to subscribe to a Profession, or to read an English Bible, or to hear in a Steeple-house, with many such like.] Thus also it is that they put off family prayer, and ask, [*Where are they bound to pray in their family Morning and Evening ?*] and so keep no constancy in family prayer at all, under pretence of denying only the circumstances.

§. 10. *Reas.* 7. By this disobedience in things lawfull, the members of the Church will be involved in contentions, and so engaged in bitter uncharitableness, and censures, and persecutions, and reproaches of one another : which scandalous courses will nourish vice, dishonour God, rejoyce the enemies, grieve the Godly that are peaceable and judicious, and wound the consciences of the contenders. We see the beginning of such fires are small, but whither they tend, and what will be the end of them, we see not.

§. 11. *Reas.* 8. By these means also Magistrates will be provoked to take men of tender consciences for factious, unruly, and unreasonable men, and to turn their enemies, and use violence against them, to the great injury of the Church : when they see them so self-conceited and refusing obedience in lawfull circum nces

§. 12. *Reaf.* 9. By this means alfo the converfion and eftablifhment of fouls will be much hindred, and people poffeffed with prejudice againft the Church and ordinances, when they take us to be but humerous people, and fee us in fuch contentions among our felves. To my knowledge, our late difference about fome fuch leffer things, hath turned off, or hindered abundance of people from liking the holy doctrine and life which we profefs.

§. 13. *Reaf.* 10. It will feem to the wifeft, to favour of no fmall meafure of *Pride*, when people on the account of lawfull circumftances, dare fet themfelves againft their Govenors and Teachers, and quarrel with the ordinances of God, and with the Churches: Humble men would fooner fufpect themfelves, and quarrel with their own diftempers, and fubmit to thofe that are wifer then themfelves, and that are fet over them for their guidance by the Lord. There may more dangerous *Pride* be manifefted in thefe matters, then in Apparel, and fuch lower trifles.

§. 14. *Reaf.* 11. Confider alfo what yielding in things lawfull the Scripture recommendeth to us? How far yielded *Paul* when he circumcifed *Timothy?* Act. 16. 3. And when he [*took the men, and purified himfelf with them in the Temple, to fignifie the accomplifhment of the daies of purification, untill that an offering fhould be offered for every one of them*] and this for almoft feven dayes, *Acts* 21. 26, 27. with the foregoing verfes.

§. 15. So 1 Cor. 9. 19, 20. [*For though I be free from all men, yet have I made my felf fervant unto all, that I might gain the more: And unto the Jews I became as a Jew, that I might gain the Jews; to them that are under the Law, as under the Law, that I might gain them that are under the Law: To them that are without Law, as without Law (being not without Law to God, but under the Law to Chrift) that I might gain them that are without Law. To the weak I became as weak, that I might gain the weak: I am made all things to all men, that I might, by all means fave fome, and this I do for the Gofpels fake, &c.*] Study this example.

§. 16.

§. 16. Read also *Rom.* 14. *and* 15. Chapters, how much condescension the Apostle requireth even among equals, about meats and dayes. And *1 Cor.* 8. 13. the Apostle would tie up himself from eating any flesh while the world standeth, rather then make a weak brother to offend. Many other passages of Scripture require a condescension in things of this indifferent nature, and shew that the Kingdom of God doth not consist in them.

§. 17. And *Matthew* 12. 1, 2, to 9. you find that hunger justified the Disciples of Christ for plucking and rubbing the ears of Corn on the Sabbath dayes. And hunger justified *David* and those that were with him, for entring into the house of God, and eating the Shew-bread, which was not lawfull for him to eat, nor for them which were with him, but only for the Priests. And the Priests in the Temple were blameless for prophaning the Sabbath day.] Now if things before accidentally evil, may by this much Necessity become lawful and a duty, then may the commands of Magistrates or Pastors, and the Unity of the Church, and the avoiding of contention, and offence, and other evils, be also sufficient to warrant us in obeying, even in inconvenient Circumstantials of the worship of God, that otherwise could not be justified.

§. 18. *Reas.* 12. Lastly consider, how much God hath expressed himself in his word to be pleased in the *Obedience* of believers. Not only in their Obedience to Christ immediately, but also to him in his officers, *1 Sam.* 15. 22. [*Behold, to obey is better then Sacrifice,* &c.] Col. 3. 20, 22. [*Children obey your Parents in all things (that is, all lawfull things) for this is well-pleasing to the Lord*] [*Servants Obey in all things your Masters according to the flesh, &c.*] And Obedience to Pastors is as much commanded. *1 Thes.* 5. 12, 13. [*We beseech you brethren to know them which labour among you, and are over you in the Lord, and admonish you, and esteem them very highly,* &c.) Heb. 13. 17. [*Obey them that have the rule over you, and submit your selves, for they watch for your souls as they that must give account,* &c.] So *Verse* 7. & 24. *1 Tim.* 5. 17, &c.

§. 19. As the General Commission to a Parent, or Master, or

Rrr   Magistrate

Magistrate to Govern their inferiour relations, doth authorize them to many particular acts belonging to their office, that were never named in their commission: so your general command to obey them, obligeth you to obey them in the said particulars. And so it is also betwixt the Pastors and the flock in matters belonging to the Office of a Pastor.

§. 20. If a Child shall ask a Parent, [*Where doth Gods word allow you to command me to Learn this Catechism, or read this Divine writings, or repeat this Sermon, or write it? &c.*] doth not the question deserve to be answered with the rod? The General Commission for parents to Govern their children is sufficient; so if a Schoolmaster command his Schollers to come to such a place to School, and to take their places in such an Order, and to learn such books, and do such exercises, &c. the General Commission that he hath to teach and Govern them, will allow him to do all this. (Though it will not allow him to set his Schollers to any Artifice or Manual Operation alien to his profession.) So if a Minister determine of the variable Circumstances of worship, as what place the people shall come to, and at what time, to be Catechized, examined, instructed, &c. what Translation or Version of Psalms to use, what Utensils to make use of about Gods service, or such like, he is warranted for this by his *General* Commission. And if he miss it in the manner, by choosing inconvenient circumstances, or by unnecessary determination of points that should rather be left undetermined to liberty, though this be his own sin, it will not excuse the people from obedience; unless the error of his directions be so great as would frustrate the Ordinance it self, or do more harm then our disobedience would do; which in Circumstantials is rarely found.

§. 21. And thus I have finished this discourse of Ceremonies; a Subject that may seem unseasonable at such a time when we are disburdened of Ceremonies. But the offence and vehement accusations of the Ceremonious, hath made it seem necessary to me, while they accuse Dissenters of

schism

schism and obstinacy, and reproach them as Puritans, and seem ready to act their second part in casting out those *very prophyt* that be not of their mind, if it were in their power: when yet they call the Ceremonies but *things indifferent*; and Preachers and Gods Ordinances are not *Indifferent* things to us.

FINITUR. July 9. 1658.

Satisfaction to certain CALUMNIATORS.

I Am informed from *London*, and several parts of the Land, that some of my Books having lately been sold at excessive rates by the Booksellers, it is commonly reported that it is caused by my excessive gain, which say they, is at least three or four hundred pounds a year. I think the Lord that doth not only employ me in his service, but also vouchsafe me the honor and benefit of being evil-spoken of for doing him the best service that I can, *Mat.*5.11,12. I *Pet.*4.13,14,15,16. Blessed *Augustine* was put to vindicate himself by an oath, from the infamy of a covetous design, which was raised by one godly woman, upon a disorderly action of other men, and to that end he wrote his 225. Epistle. I find no call to use his oath; but yet I judge it my duty to imitate him in patience, and in rescuing the slanderers from their sin, that they abuse not their souls by uncharitable surmises, nor their tongues by false reports. To which end I give them this true information: The two first Books I printed, I left to the Booksellers Will; for all the rest, I agreed with them for the fifteenth Book, to give to some few of my friends, hearing that some others agreed for the tenth. Sometime my fifteenth Book coming not to an hundred, and sometime but to few more, when of Practical Books I needed sometime 800. to give away. Because I was scarce rich enough to buy so many, I agreed with the Bookseller, (my Neighbour,) to allow 18. d. a Ream (which is not a penny a quire,) out of his own gain towards the buying of Bibles, and some of the practical Books which he printed, for the poor: Covenanting with him, that he should sell my Controversal Writings as cheap, and my Practical Writings somewhat cheaper then books are ordinarily sold. To this hour I never received for my self one penny of mony from them for any of my Writings, to the best of my remembrance: but if it fell out that my part came to more than I give my friends, I exchanged them for other Books: My accounts and memory tell me not of 5.li that ever was returned for me on these accounts, which was on literary occasions: so that my many hundreds a year is come to never a penny in all, but as abovesaid, in some exchange of Books. And the price I set on my Books which I exchanged for theirs at the dearest rates, is as followeth, ∫ Treat. of Conversion, 2.s. Treat. of Crucifying the World, 2.s. Disput. of Justificat. 2.s. 4.d. The Call to the Unconverted, 8.d. Disput. of saving Faith, 5.d. Of the Grotian Religion, 6.d. Directions for found Conversion, 8.d. Disput. of Right to Sacraments, &c.

These are all my bargains and my gains. And I chose the honesteſt Book-ſellers that I could meet with, according to my ſmall meaſure of wit and ac-quaintance; who told me, they ſtill made good their Promiſes. And now cenſorious Slanderer, tell me, what thou wouldſt have had me to have done more? If I had got Food and Rayment out of my own hard labors, had it been unlawful or diſhonourable, when Bookſellers get ſo many hundred pounds by one Book, that never ſtudied nor ſpent their time and coſt for it, as I have done? And yet doſt thou reproach me that receive not a groat? But becauſe I will not oblige my ſelf to the ſame courſe for the future, and that thou mayſt know at what rates I ſerve thee, let me tell thee, that in theſe labors early and late my body is waſted, my precious time laid out, and ſomewhat of my Eſtate, and ſomewhat of the labor of my friends. I can-not have twenty quire of my writing well tranſcribed, under fifty pounds. And who ſhall pay for this, or maintain me in thy ſervice? I have troubled a Neighbour-Miniſter in the tedious work of tranſcribing my Characters (for ſome books,) for which, neither lit nor I had ever one penny. Theſe perſonal matters are unſavory to me, and I take it for a great injury that thou putteſt upon me a neceſſity of mentioning them. But I have yielded this once to thy unrighteous importunity, that thou mayeſt hereafter learn what to believe and utter, and make more conſcience of thy cenſures and reports. And that thou mayſt have the utmoſt relief that I can, procure thee for the time to come, I ſhall agree with my Bookſellers, to ſell all that I publiſh at three farthings a ſheet, and to print the price of every book at the bottom of the Title page.

Farewell.

October 11.

1658.

Richard Baxter.

Lightning Source UK Ltd.
Milton Keynes UK
UKHW031301101022
410237UK00010B/1646